DICTION

GERMAN SYNONYMS

Donald R. Richards
7. 4. 69

PF 3591
.F37
1968

DICTIONARY
OF
GERMAN SYNONYMS

BY

R. B. FARRELL

Professor of German in the University of Sydney, Australia

CAMBRIDGE
AT THE UNIVERSITY PRESS
1968

PUBLISHED BY
THE SYNDICS OF THE CAMBRIDGE UNIVERSITY PRESS
Bentley House, 200 Euston Road, London, N.W. 1
American Branch: 32 East 57th Street, New York, N.Y. 10022

First Edition 1953
Reprinted with corrections 1955
1961
1962
1963
1966
1968

INDIANA
PURDUE
LIBRARY
SEP 1976
FORT WAYNE

WITHDRAWN

Reprinted in the United States of America

CONTENTS

PREFACE	*page* vii
DICTIONARY OF GERMAN SYNONYMS	1
LIST OF WORDS TREATED	404
GERMAN WORD LIST	410

PREFACE

This work has grown out of my experience of university teaching. As the inability of students to use words correctly impressed itself upon me more and more, I came to see that this was due in the first place to the immense difficulties inherent in the study of words, and in the second to the complete lack of adequate dictionaries, whether English-German or entirely German, and of other reference-works such as Fowler's *Modern English Usage*. Dictionaries such as Eberhard's *Synonymisches Wörterbuch*, incidentally out of print for many years, have their uses, but are insufficient for the needs of the English-speaking learner in that their explanations, naturally enough, do not take into account his special difficulties. The present work represents a new departure in taking as the starting point of each article the difficult English word or group of words and in proceeding on this basis to explain the German terms. With its help a systematic study of words and, ultimately, a more sensitive feeling for their values should be possible both at school and at university level.

Only common difficult words, and within this restricted scope rarely the names of concrete objects, have been treated, i.e. principally those English terms which in each of their senses require to be translated by a number of German terms. The fact that German lacks terms of such wide application as 'take', 'way', 'leave', 'keep', 'power' (to mention only a few of the more notorious), and must therefore use specific terms, perhaps to a greater extent than even French, is an indication of what is here attempted. The English word is taken singly or in a group. In a few cases, where the magnitude of the difficulty seemed to call for it, a further explanation has been attached in brackets to the examples. Footnotes which extend the group or refer to related terms liable to be confused have also been added in order to inculcate in the student the habit of examining words in groups. Such notes are in the form of hints designed to open up fresh avenues of investigation; they are not exhaustive explanations. In the arrangement of any group of English words the most general term is usually placed first. The meanings and shades of meaning of the English word become clear through the explanation of the German term. Only in a few cases was it thought necessary to give a special explanation of the former. Sometimes the divisions are made on the basis of the meanings of the English word or words (occasionally taken from the Oxford dictionaries), so that the same German term may appear more than once in the same article. In other cases the German words themselves form the divisions, and so explain by implication the various meanings of the English. The explanations, which differ in their degree of fulness, concentrate on normal prose usage of to-day, but point out usage in poetry and elevated prose diction as well as obsolete uses (e.g. with *Gemüt* and *Sinn*). They also draw attention to a few errors made by Germans (e.g. *scheinbar* for *anscheinend*). Grammatical constructions have been treated only in rare cases where their understanding is indispensable for the correct use of a word. References are given to such works as the *Shorter Oxford Dictionary*, the *Pocket Oxford Dictionary* (referred to as *S.O.D.* and *P.O.D.* respectively), to Webster's *Dictionary of Synonyms* and Fowler's *Modern English Usage*, where they seem necessary or particularly helpful.

The work is addressed primarily to students and teachers, but I venture to think that parts of it will not be without interest to lexicographers. My warmest thanks are due to the following for their generous help, not only in discussing the examples, but in criticizing the explanations: the late Dr V. Stadler (former lecturer in German in the University of Sydney), Dr K. von Stutterheim (his successor), and Mr A. Scheidt.

R. B. FARRELL

ACCEPT 1. **Annehmen:** to accept what is offered to one, the receiver being free to accept or reject. The object may be a thing, or a belief, point of view,[1] excuse, and the like.

Er nahm das Geschenk, den Vorschlag, die Herausforderung an.
Die Bedingungen wurden von dem geschlagenen Feinde angenommen.
Er nahm den christlichen Glauben an.
Meine Entschuldigung wurde nicht angenommen.

2. **Hinnehmen:** to accept passively something inflicted on one.[2]

Unter den Umständen mußten wir die Niederlage, die Beleidigung, unser Schicksal, die Tatsache, hinnehmen.
Er hat es hingenommen, daß sie wegging.

3. **Übernehmen, auf sich nehmen:** to assume, to shoulder a responsibility, duty, task, and the like.

Er will die Verantwortung dafür nicht übernehmen, auf sich nehmen.

4. **Aufnehmen:** to take, to admit, to receive into a society, organization, and the like.[3] A phrase involving *in* with the accusative must follow.

Er wurde in den inneren Kreis nicht aufgenommen.

5. **Akzeptieren** may, but never need, be used for *annehmen* in the sense of 'accept'. It is also used for *gelten lassen* in the sense of accepting anything of a mental order (reasons, excuses, and the like) that are offered one.

The only sense in which, for lack of a German equivalent, it must be used is that of accepting a person as a friend or as a suitable member of an organization. It can be used absolutely or followed by a phrase expressing 'by whom' or 'where'. It cannot be followed by *in* with the accusative, i.e. it is not an equivalent of *aufnehmen*.

Ich habe ihn als Freund akzeptiert.
Er war im (vom) inneren Kreis akzeptiert.[4]
Wenn er Sie mal akzeptiert hat, dann kann Sie nichts in seinen Augen heruntersetzen.

[1] *Annehmen* also means 'to adopt' a suggestion, a belief, a child; 'take on' workers, a facial expression; 'assume', 'suppose'.

[2] *Sich mit etwas abfinden*: to resign oneself to a thing (e.g. *sich mit der Lage, seinem Schicksal, einer Tatsache, a.*).

[3] See also under 'take' in the sense of 'take an attitude'.

[4] *Empfangen* (received) could be used in this sense; *als gleichberechtigte.*

6. **Gelten lassen:** to accept as valid (reasons, excuses, and the like).

Ich lasse diese Erklärung, diese Einwendung, nicht gelten.
Seine Erfahrungen im Ausland hat man hier gelten lassen.
Tatsachen muß man gelten lassen.

7. The past participle (accepted) used adjectivally. In the sense of 'generally recognized' *angenommen* cannot be used alone.

Im allgemeingültigen Sinne des Worts.
Entgegen der allgemeinen Meinung.
Der allgemein angenommene Brauch in internationalen Beziehungen.

ACCIDENT, DISASTER 1. In the sense of 'mishap' **Unfall** is of lesser proportions than **Unglück**. The former involves one or at most a few, the latter many, people. Both may be fatal, the latter almost always. *Unglück* is not normally pluralized. It corresponds to 'disaster' and to 'accident' when this is extensive.[1]

Ihm ist mit seinem Fahrrad ein Unfall passiert.
Er ist in einem Autounfall umgekommen.
Wir sind gegen Unfälle versichert.
Hunderte von Menschen wurden in dem Eisenbahnunglück getötet (accident or disaster).
Das Unglück, das Deutschland getroffen hat, ist unermeßlich (disaster).

2. In the sense of 'chance' **Zufall** must be used.

Ich traf ihn durch Zufall.
Es ist ein Zufall, daß ich gewählt wurde.

ACCUSE, SUE 1. Neither **beschuldigen** nor **anschuldigen** are legal terms. *Beschuldigen*[2] suggests a precise accusation, while *anschuldigen*, in accordance with one of the meanings of *an*, suggests the hurling of accusations at someone, wildly and therefore less precisely.

Man beschuldigte ihn des Mordes an seinem Bruder.
Wir können nicht umhin, Sie zu beschuldigen.
Man beschuldigte ihn ungerechterweise.
Man hat mich in wüster Weise angeschuldigt.
Jahrelang war er den wildesten Anschuldigungen ausgesetzt.

2. **Anklagen** and **verklagen** are both legal terms. *Anklagen* is used in criminal cases, *verklagen* in petty offences, accidents (e.g. manslaughter)

[1] *Unheil* is a reversal of our fortunes, well-being, caused by persons, or things thought of as persons, particularly when the action is wanton. It thus corresponds to 'trouble' thus used, rather than to 'disaster'. *Er hat viel Unheil angerichtet. Unglück* can also mean 'misfortune' and 'unhappiness'. See 'unfortunate'.

[2] *Bezichtigen* is an elevated and less usual term for *beschuldigen. Gerichtlich belangen*: to take to court. *Auf Schadenersatz klagen*: sue for damages.

and civil suits, therefore 'to sue'. Both may be used in elevated diction and poetry without strictly legal implication.

Sie sind des Mordes angeklagt.
Er wurde wegen Hochverrats angeklagt.
Er wurde wegen einer Schuld verklagt.

'Hör'an, was ich dir sag'!
Dein Schätzlein ich verklag';
Derweil ich dieses singen tu',
Herzt er ein Lieb in guter Ruh,
Ein Stündlein wohl vor Tag.'

(Mörike, *Ein Stündlein wohl vor Tag.*)

ACT, ACTION, DEED The chief distinction between 'act' and 'action' is that the former is brief, single, while the latter is extended in time and may comprise a series of acts. Again, with 'act' one thinks of the result, the whole, while with 'action' the process is designated. In the plural, 'acts' does not differ so sharply from 'actions' for the very reason that it ceases to be single. In the moral sense of 'conduct' they are practically identical. 'Deed', too, draws attention to the result and often conveys the idea of achievement (in a good sense) or of something that is outstanding by virtue of its proportions (e.g. an evil deed).

None of the terms discussed can be applied to trivial things. Thus while one can speak of *ein Akt der internationalen Höflichkeit*, the only translation for 'as an act of courtesy he placed his car at my disposal' would be: *als höfliche Geste stellte er mir seinen Wagen zur Verfügung.*

'Act' and 'action' followed by 'in' and the gerund present difficulties in translation (e.g. the action of the Government in confiscating an issue of a certain newspaper caused its fall). In this case a more specific term such as *Schritt* is required.

German has no general term for 'action' in the sense of 'doing something to deal with a matter', and consequently no general term for 'to take action'. It is, therefore, difficult to translate such phrases as: to refrain from action (in the matter), to recommend action, to clamour for action; they considered the report but decided against action. In these phrases 'action' means 'the taking of action'. In most cases of 'action' used in this sense German requires a specific term.

'Action' in the legal and military senses is not discussed in this article.

Fowler's *Modern English Usage*, which has been drawn on for this article, should be consulted under 'act', 'action'.

1. **Handlung** is a conscious expression of the will. It is only possible in statements which describe, judge or by implication draw attention

to the motives of 'acts' or 'actions'. This reference to the motive means that the action may be a purely inner impulse which does not find external expression and that what is termed *Handlung* (and 'action' in English) may in reality be an abstention from action (contrast the other words discussed, particularly *Tat*).

Handlung translates both 'act' and 'action' when they imply this reference. It is not necessarily an action extended in time, but because of its concern with motives, it does not, unlike 'act', evoke the impression of a single, clearly visualized exertion of power.

Examples of verbs which can govern *Handlung* are, e.g., *begehen, vornehmen*, which in themselves draw attention to motives.

Sind unsere Handlungen frei oder nicht frei?
Nur aus seinen Handlungen kann man auf seine Gesinnung schließen.
Seine Handlungen waren schwer zu durchblicken.
Jetzt habe ich meine Handlungsfreiheit wiedererlangt.
Uneigennützige Handlungen kommen wohl vor, aber selten.
Nach langem Zögern hat er die notwendige Handlung endlich vorgenommen.
Ich habe seine Handlungen eine ganze Weile beobachtet.
Daß er dem Krankenhause sein Vermögen zur Verfügung stellte, war eine anständige Handlung.
Eine edle Handlung muß man anerkennen.
Wir dürfen seine Handlungen nicht kritisieren.
Da hat der Mann endlich einmal eine anständige Handlung begangen.
Er hat eine sträfliche, unzüchtige, höchst zweifelhafte, Handlung begangen.

'*Du wirst mir zugeben, sagte Albert, dass gewisse Handlungen lasterhaft bleiben, sie mögen geschehen, aus welchem Beweggrunde sie wollen.*' (Goethe, *Werther*.)

'*. . . du überspannst alles, und hast wenigstens hier gewiß Unrecht, daß du den Selbstmord, wovon jetzt die Rede ist, mit großen Handlungen vergleichst: da man es doch für nichts anderes als eine Schwäche halten kann.*' (Goethe, *Werther*.)

'*Ein gewisser Mangel an Fühlbarkeit, ein Mangel — nimm's, wie Du willst; daß sein Herz nicht sympathetisch schlägt bei — oh! — bei der Stelle eines lieben Buchs, wo mein Herz und Lottens in einem zusammen treffen; in hundert anderen Vorfällen, wenn's kommt, daß unsere Empfindungen über eine Handlung eines dritten laut werden.*' (Goethe, *Werther*.)

'*Was bleibt uns übrig als. . . das kleinste aufgefundene Blättchen nicht gering zu achten; zumal da es so schwer ist, die eigensten, wahren Triebfedern auch nur einer einzelnen Handlung zu entdecken, wenn sie unter Menschen vorgeht, die nicht gemeiner Art sind.*' (Goethe, *Werther*.)

2. **Tat** has as its closest English equivalent 'deed' (i.e. feat, exploit, achievement). In stylistic effect it also resembles 'deed', although its flavour is not quite so old-fashioned. It refers to the completed act or action, the result, which is seen plastically and as a whole. Whether it is brief or lengthy, morally good or bad, is irrelevant. Its outstanding characteristic is that it is vivid, dramatic, refers to something of imposing proportions, and is personal in that one thinks of the doer as an individual (contrast *Akt*).

It is therefore the only rendering for 'deed', 'feat'.

It must be used to translate 'act' (sometimes 'action') in the sense of 'an act characteristic of' (the following noun denoting the type of person).

It also means 'instant of doing' (e.g. *auf frischer Tat ertappt werden*).

When it is accompanied by a word or phrase describing its nature, one thinks of the doer (contrast *Akt*). For this reason the description is generally given by a preceding adjective or a noun which forms a compound with *Tat*. A following descriptive genitive is not impossible, but is less common (again, contrast *Akt*).

Like 'deed', *Tat* means 'act' and 'action' in antithesis to 'word', 'plan', 'thought'. The effect of this use, which is limited to literary diction, is emotional or slightly antiquated. For a prosaic equivalent see *handeln* (both as verb and noun). *Ausführung* can also be used in an antithesis.

Tat can be followed by a dependent infinitive which describes the act or action only if it is qualified by an adjective. 'Act' or 'action' followed by 'in' and the gerund requires no such adjective. Thus: *seine mutige Tat, den Knaben aus von Haifischen verseuchten Gewässern gerettet zu haben, verdient öffentliche Anerkennung* (his act, action, in rescuing...).

Die Rettung der Schiffbrüchigen war eine heroische Tat (act, action, deed).

Der Abschluß des Handelsvertrages war des Ministers letzte Tat.

Die Abschaffung der Folter war eine Tat, auf die Friedrich der Große stolz sein konnte.

Die Ermordung dieses Gefangenen war eine grauenhafte Tat.

Er hat eine gute Tat getan.

Gleich nach der Tat wurde er verhaftet.

Es war eine verbrecherische Tat, aber eine, die die Einbildungskraft fesselt.

Moskau behauptet, die Ermordung des Brigadiers Mallaby sei nicht die Tat javanischer Nationalisten, sondern der Japaner.

Das war eine barmherzige Tat, daß Sie ihm zu diesem Posten verholfen haben.

Es war eine Tat, die er bitter bereuen sollte (e.g. falsely denouncing a friend; contrast example with *Handlung*).

England kann es sich als eine gerechte Tat anrechnen, daß es die Anerkennung der Souveränität der kleinen Staaten durchsetzte.

Das Anzünden des Dorfes war eine Verzweiflungstat.

Ein Mann der Tat (in conversation one more frequently hears *aktiver Mann*).

Nach so vielem Zögern müssen wir endlich mal zur Tat schreiten (with emotional emphasis).

Auf den Entschluß muß die Tat folgen.

Es ist nicht immer leicht, einen Gedanken in die Tat umzusetzen.

Wir verlangen Taten, nicht Worte.

'*Aber auch im gemeinen Leben ist's unerträglich, fast einem jeden bei halbweg einer freien, edlen unerwarteten Tat nachrufen zu hören: der Mensch ist trunken, der ist närrisch! Schämt euch, ihr Nüchternen! Schämt euch, ihr Weisen!*' (Goethe, *Werther*.) (The stress is on the concrete reality, seen as complete, not on the motives involved.)

'*. . . doch hatte er sich gesagt, es solle keine übereilte, keine rasche Tat* (i.e. suicide) *sein, er wolle mit der besten Überzeugung . . . diesen Schritt tun.*' (Goethe, *Werther*.)

'*Aus dem Blut auf der Lehne des Sessels konnte man schließen, er habe sitzend vor dem Schreibtische die Tat* (i.e. suicide) *vollbracht.*' (Goethe, *Werther*.)

3. **Akt** is not the equivalent of *Tat*, though in certain uses it occurs in deceptively similar phrases. One of its characteristic senses is that of something staged (hence *Akt* in a drama), often a ceremonial or symbolical act. It tends to acquire this sense when not accompanied by a descriptive phrase (e.g. a following genitive describing its nature, but not an adjective such as *erst*, *letzt*).

When it is followed by a descriptive genitive meaning 'of the nature of', it is impersonal, a judgment which assigns the act to a class denoted by the noun in the genitive case. The sentence *das ist ein Akt der Barmherzigkeit, daß Sie ihm zu diesem Posten verhelfen wollen* is sober, impersonal in tone. This characteristic means that *Akt* often refers to an act of the state or to acts of groups, masses of people, since in such cases attention is not concentrated on an individual doer. Again, unlike *Tat*, since *Akt* has nothing of the meaning of 'deed', 'achievement', it need not refer, either, to anything striking or of impressive proportions (e.g. *Gewalttat* suggests something such as the murder of an important personage, *Gewaltakt* the plundering of a store). For this reason *Akt* cannot be combined with *Greuel* (but: *Greueltat*, an atrocity).

The above example (*Akt der Barmherzigkeit*) reveals another characteristic of *Akt* which distinguishes it from *Tat*. It makes one think less of the completed whole than of the fact that something is going on, i.e. a process.

The phrase which assigns *Akt* to a class is normally a following genitive, not a preceding adjective (cf. French: *une bonne action*; but: *un acte de bonté*). It forms, however, a limited number of compound nouns (see examples below). In the sense of an act staged it may be preceded by an adjective.

Die Übergabe des Schwertes war ein feierlicher Akt.
Das Erscheinen des Generals zu diesem Zeitpunkt war ein symbolischer Akt.
Der Aufruf an das Volk war unter den Umständen ein Akt der Verzweiflung.
Das Töten der Schwerkranken wurde als Akt der Barmherzigkeit bezeichnet.
Die Rehabilitierung von Dreyfus war ein Akt der Gerechtigkeit.
Sein letzter Akt war, die weiße Fahne zu hissen.
Die Abschaffung der Folter war einer der ersten Regierungsakte Friedrichs des Großen.
Gewaltakte, Terrorakte, wurden in jedem Teil des Landes begangen.
Die Ermordung der Gefangenen war ein Racheakt.
Es war von seiten Hitlers ein Akt des Wahnsinns, Rußland anzugreifen.
Sabotageakte kommen jetzt selten vor.
Es war ein Akt der Gerechtigkeit, daß die Souveränität der Kleinstaaten wiederhergestellt wurde.

4. **Tun** (noun) is used in the sense of the general conduct, actions, or doings of an individual. It is vaguer than the other terms, but always refers to serious acts or actions. It occurs in the common phrases: *sein Tun und Treiben, sein Tun und Lassen.*

Er ist für sein Tun verantwortlich (acts or actions).
Sein Tun und Treiben scheint mir höchst verdächtig (goings-on).
Von seinem Tun und Treiben an diesem Abend wissen wir garnichts.
Das Tun eines Narren ist nicht vorauszusehen.
Sein übles Tun hat ihn in Verruf gebracht.

5. **Aktion** denotes an elaborate operation, planned and carried out in stages. It normally refers only to such actions when undertaken by the State. It is not a legal term and cannot be applied to legal action taken by the State, unless this be police action. Furthermore, it does not form fixed phrases (such as 'to take action'). In the singular it is always preceded by the definite or indefinite article, or *jede, manche*, etc.

Die Millionen von Menschen, die durch den Krieg heimatlos geworden sind, wieder anzusiedeln, ist eine riesenhafte Aktion.
Die Aktion, durch die die Inflation verhindert werden sollte, ist gescheitert.

Umfangreiche Aktionen wurden unternommen, um in allen Ländern die Erzeugung von Nahrungsmitteln zu steigern.

In seinen Aktionen zieht gewöhnlich der Staat nur den Machtfaktor in Betracht (*Handlungen* would be correct, but would draw attention away from the action itself to the motive).

Eine Säuberungsaktion wurde durchgeführt.

6. **Handeln** (noun): 'action' as opposed to inactivity, thought, words. It is a more prosaic and less dramatic term for *Tat* used in this sense. Since it is really the equivalent of the gerund, 'acting', it can only be used in combinations where this would be possible. Thus, it could not be used in the genitive to translate 'a man of action', but would be appropriate in rendering 'a man born for action' (*zum Handeln geboren*). It is most common as the subject of a sentence or preceded by *in, von, zu.*

In conversation *handeln* used as a verb is more common.

Jetzt ist Handeln nötig. (In conversation: *jetzt muß gehandelt werden.*)

Ihm gefällt die Betrachtung, nicht das Handeln.

Handeln ist nicht seine Stärke.

Handeln kommt unter diesen Umständen nicht in Betracht.

Von Handeln kann im Augenblick nicht die Rede sein.

Im Handeln versagt er immer.

Wenn es zum Handeln kommt, ist er immer brauchbar.

7. 'Action' in the sense of 'taking action in a matter'.

(a) **Vorgehen:** 'action taken' in the sense of a 'step or series of steps taken' to deal with a specific matter. Similarly, the verb *vorgehen* can mean 'to proceed' in a matter. It is commonly used of the taking of official action. If it means 'to proceed against' someone (police action) it must be accompanied by some intensifying adverb such as *energisch.* It cannot be used as a noun to form fixed phrases (e.g. to take action). In translating 'action' followed by 'in' and the gerund ('his action in closing the banks'), *Vorgehen* cannot take a dependent verbal infinitive after it, but either a clause (e.g. with *als*) or *im, beim* with the substantival infinitive.

It should only be used in a judgment, expressed or clearly implied.

Das Vorgehen des Premierministers, als er die Banken schloß, führte zum Sturz der Regierung.

Sein Vorgehen gegen die Presse ließ den Verdacht aufkommen, daß er sie gern unterdrückt hätte.

Sein Vorgehen in dieser Angelegenheit war höchst zweifelhaft.

Die drei Mächte sind entschlossen, ihr gemeinsames Vorgehen aufrechtzuerhalten.

Gegen Unbefugte wird scharf vorgegangen.

(b) **Einschreiten** (as verb): to take official action against someone, in the sense of 'intervene'. *Gegen* or an equivalent must follow. It is stronger and more circumscribed than *vorgehen.*

Die Polizei schritt gegen die Schieber ein.

(c) **Schritt:** step, *démarche*, as in English.

Wir müssen Schritte unternehmen, um diesen Machenschaften zu steuern.
Der Schritt, mit dem die Türkei ihre diplomatischen Beziehungen zu Deutschland abbrach, sollte mit Genugtuung angesehen werden.

(d) **Maßnahme:** measure. It is wider than *Schritt. Treffen* and *ergreifen* are used with it in the sense of 'take'.

Der Senat hat sich mit dem Bericht eingehend befaßt und daraufhin Maßnahmen getroffen, um das Lehrpersonal der medizinischen Fakultät zu vergrößern.
'*Ich bin überzeugt, die Griechen werden sowohl unsere militärischen als auch unsere politischen Maßnahmen begrüßen.*' (Churchill.)

(e) **Unternehmen** can be used with *etwas* or *nichts*, as the case may be, in a general way to translate 'take action', i.e. in dealing with a matter (to do something about it). It is less precise, less official than *Schritt, Maßnahme, Vorgehen*, etc. The sphere of action needs to be stated unless it is clearly implied.

Wir müssen etwas unternehmen, um ihn zur Vernunft zu bringen.
Es wird von den Frontkämpferverbänden verlangt, daß in der Wohnungsfrage etwas unternommen wird (action in...is demanded).

(f) **Ausführung** may be used in the sense of 'put into action' or 'the taking of action' in antithesis to 'word', 'thought', etc.

Das Unternehmen war vielversprechend als Planung, enttäuschend aber in der Ausführung (in action).

8. 'Act', 'action' used in reference to trivial matters.

The foregoing terms apply only to 'acts' and 'actions' of considerable proportions. They cannot be used for petty doings. The following are examples:

Es war eine Dummheit, mit so wenig Benzin so weit fahren zu wollen (an act of stupidity).
Als Beweis seines guten Willens fuhr er uns zwei Stationen entgegen (as an act of goodwill).
Er hat uns zahllose Beweise seines Wohlwollens gegeben, geliefert (shown us countless little acts of kindness).
Seine zahllosen Freundschaftsbeweise sind nicht unbemerkt geblieben.

Sein Ausreißen setzte ihn dem Verdacht aus (his action in clearing out).
Das letzte, was sie tat, bevor sie zu Bett ging, war, daß sie die Milchkanne herausstellte (her last act).
Sie wußten erst später, wie großzügig sie gehandelt hatte (...knew of her generous act, action).

ADD[1] 1. Mathematical calculation ('add up'). **Addieren:** to add up figures. **Zusammenrechnen:** to add up in order to arrive at an estimate. *Er rechnete die Kosten zusammen.*

2. Verbs compounded with *hinzu*. The idea of addition is given by *hinzu*, while the verb (often one of the 'put' group) specifies the manner. *Hinzu* indicates addition to the end, not to the body of a thing.

(a) **Hinzufügen** and **hinzusetzen** are the commonest and are used of adding remarks (points, items, etc.) to something already said or written. The latter is also used of signs (punctuation). While *hinzufügen* suggests that the added part is integrated into the whole, *hinzusetzen* indicates a less organic addition. The former is used of important, the second of trivial matters. Neither can be said of objects in the sense of joining them together.

Der Redner fügte ein paar Bemerkungen zu dem hinzu, was er schon gesagt hatte.
'Wir stehen vor einem schweren Entschluß', fügte der Minister hinzu.
Er fügte seinem Brief noch ein paar Zeilen hinzu.
Dem Programm wurde noch eine Nummer hinzugefügt.
Um den 'Eulenspiegel' aufzuführen, wurden dem Orchester noch ein paar Instrumente hinzugefügt.
'Ihr seid alle verrückt', setzte er hinzu.

(b) Other verbs compounded with *hinzu*.

(i) **Hinzutun** (see 'put').

Er tat noch einige Steine zu dem Haufen hinzu.
Noch zwei Koffer wurden zu seinem schon schweren Gepäck hinzugetan.

(ii) **Hinzulegen** (see 'put') is used particularly of money.

Ich lege noch etwas hinzu, und dann können Sie das Haus kaufen.
Er legte noch einige Papiere hinzu.

(iii) **Hinzunehmen:** to include at the end as an afterthought.

Wir können ihn für das Kommittee hinzunehmen (not when forming it, but as an extra, an afterthought).
Nehmen wir diese paar Tatsachen hinzu, und der Fall wird klar.

[1] 'To add to' (intransitive use) must be translated by 'to increase'.

(iv) **Hinzukommen:** to be added, of intangibles.

Zu seinen Geschäftssorgen kam noch der Tod seiner Frau hinzu.

(v) Further:

Er trug noch ein paar Steine (zu dem Haufen) hinzu.
Schreiben Sie seinen Namen hinzu (to a list).
Es wurde beschlossen, die deutschen Militärs zu den Kriegsverbrechern hinzuzuzählen.
Gießen Sie noch ein paar Tropfen hinzu.

3. Often the simple verb without *hinzu* is used, particularly if the thing to which the addition is made is stated. *Noch* is added, if necessary.

Noch 50 Mark wurden auf die Rechnung geschlagen.
Tun Sie noch ein Stück Zucker in den Tee.

4. Verbs compounded with *ein*, sometimes *hinein*, express the idea of insertion into the body of a thing. Examples are:

Sie könnten hier ein einsilbiges Wort einfügen.
Eine neue Szene ist zwischen diesen beiden eingeschoben worden.
Ich möchte noch ein Fach in den Bücherschrank einbauen, einsetzen.
Das können Sie noch hineinschreiben.

5. Examples of other specific terms are:

Dem Haus wurde ein neuer Flügel angebaut.
'*Die angefügte Robinsonade...verbindet das Motiv der Weltflucht mit dem des kuriosen Erlebnishungers*' (inorganically) (J. Petersen, *Die Wissenschaft von der Dichtung*).
Dem Lehrpersonal wurde ein neues Mitglied zugewiesen.
Er häufte Sieg auf Sieg, Schmähung auf Schmähung.

AFFECT To affect 'always presupposes a stimulus powerful enough to evoke a response or elicit a reaction' (Webster's *Dictionary of Synonyms*). It thus means 'to produce an effect' of various kinds (physical, material, emotional, intellectual) on a person or thing. The effect may or may not be a change, a modification. When 'affect' implies an unfavourable effect, German generally must make this clear by a specific verb or the addition of an adverb bearing this sense.

'Affect' is also a synonym of 'concern', which is listed by Fowler (*Modern English Usage*) as one meaning and assailed as wrong usage by Webster (see *berühren* and *betreffen*).

Both Fowler and Webster, who should be consulted on this word, point out the confusion between 'affect' and 'effect' (verbs) and at the same time distinguish between them. 'Effect' as a noun corresponds to both 'affect' and 'effect' (affect: have an effect on).

1. Berühren

(a) To make an impact on the mind. This impact includes feeling, but not emotion in the fuller sense (i.e. not 'to move', which is *rühren*[1]). It must be accompanied by an adverb. Two uses occur:

(i) To affect one's sensibilities, either pleasantly or unpleasantly. As the contact suggested by *berühren* is never strong,[2] it cannot be combined with such adverbs as *gräßlich, schauderhaft, tragisch.*

Ihre Stimme berührt mich angenehm, unangenehm.
Diese Landschaft hat mich wohltuend berührt.
Dieses Gedicht berührt mich wie Kitsch.

(ii) Negatively or with a virtual negative with adverbs such as *sichtlich, sonderlich, wenig,* i.e. indicating extent.

Er war von ihrer Not nicht sichtlich berührt.
Ihre Not hat ihn nicht sonderlich berührt.
'*Sogar der Wechsel der Jahreszeiten berührt den Stadtbewohner wenig*' (A. Huxley, quoted in Webster's *Dictionary of Synonyms* under 'affect').

(b) To have a bearing on a matter, particularly on one's interests. An adverb is not necessary. Unless otherwise stated, the effect is unfavourable. 'Touch' is also possible in this sense.

Berührt das Ihre Chancen?
Dieser Vorfall berührt die englisch-russischen Beziehungen.
Diese Maßnahmen berühren die Großgrundbesitzer.
Der Krieg hat unsere Lebensweise nicht empfindlich berührt.

2. Betreffen means 'to be aimed, directed at', 'to hit', in a vague way. It differs from the simple verb *treffen* in that the sense is not literal and that it does not denote one clear, forceful act.[3] It rather suggests indirect

[1] See 'move' and 'touch' for an explanation of *rühren.*

[2] See 'touch' for an explanation of *berühren.*

[3] *Treffen* means 'to hit the mark', literally with a missile, or figuratively (see 'catch'). It suggests an act that has the swiftness of an arrow. When an evil is the subject, the object is normally a person. If it is a thing, the effect is that of personification (e.g. *der Preissturz hat mein Geschäft schwer getroffen*). With evils there are two uses. (*a*) To hit, to strike home, without further qualification. In this case the subject must be something sharp and sudden (e.g. *der Blitz, der Schlag, hat ihn getroffen*). (*b*) The severe effects are emphasized by some adverb such as *schwer, hart.* In this case the subject may be something broader (e.g. *das Unglück hat ihn schwer getroffen*). *Treffen* is also used in a number of fixed phrases in the sense of 'to fall on', 'to find the mark'. *Ihn trifft die Schuld* means no more than that a crime has been committed and the evidence points to him as the guilty party. Similarly, it carries no further implications in the phrases: *die Verantwortung, der Vorwurf, trifft mich.*

effects and the diffusion of these over a wide area, and frequently carries the implication that the object is just one of a number of things affected. The subject may be: (*a*) a law, regulation or the like, the sense being 'to concern',[1] and the question of whether the effect is favourable or otherwise being left open; (*b*) an evil. In the latter case it is often something broad and diffuse.[2,3] Except in the sense of 'concern', *betreffen* cannot be used actively in the simple tenses.[4]

Diese Maßnahmen betreffen die Großgrundbesitzer.
Sie sind von den neuen Bestimmungen mit betroffen.
Ganz Europa ist von der Grippe, von einer Hungersnot, betroffen worden.
Nicht weniger als 5 Dörfer wurden von der Überschwemmung betroffen.
Der Preissturz hat mein Geschäft auch betroffen.
Das Unglück hat ihn betroffen (the disaster has affected him, i.e. amongst others; not 'has befallen him').

3. **Wirken** and compounds.

If 'affect' implies an unfavourable effect, *ungünstig* or some equivalent must be added.

(a) **Wirken:** to produce an effect on, a reaction from a person in the sense of engaging the powers of his mind (thoughts, feelings, and the like), or acting on parts of the body. It does not indicate any change or modification of the person or thing affected. Its use in the passive voice is not possible.

Dieses Gedicht wirkt auf mich wie Kitsch.
Die Landschaft wirkt sehr wohltuend auf mich.
'*Auf das Trommelfell wirken höchstens acht Oktaven aus der unendlichen Lautskala*' (Jeans, quoted in Webster's *Dictionary of Synonyms* under 'affect') (our ear-drums are affected by...).
Gewitter wirken sehr ungünstig auf Geisteskranke.

[1] *Betreffen* translates 'to concern' when a thing is the subject (e.g. *was mich betrifft*: as far as I am concerned). It differs from *angehen* in suggesting a higher degree of concern and often a need for action. *Das betrifft uns alle* (we must do something about it). *Das geht uns alle an* (we must not ignore it). Being weaker, *angehen* is generally more appropriate in negative statements (e.g. *das geht mich nicht an*). *Anlangen* and *anbelangen* are still weaker. The form *anbetreffen* is not in common use.

[2] But circumscribed subjects are possible in the sense not of 'affect', but to find the correct mark. *Der Vorwurf betrifft mich* (i.e. applies to me). *Treffen* with such words (e.g. *Spott, Beschimpfung*) is much stronger.

[3] Other senses of *betreffen* are: *er war ganz betroffen* (past participle can mean 'taken aback'); *die betreffenden Minister* (the present participle can mean 'concerned', i.e. following the noun).

[4] *Das Unglück, das die Stadt betroffen hat* (but: *traf*). *Treffen* must be used actively in the simple tenses, generally with the addition of some adverb such as *hart* or *schwer* (see p. 12, n. 3(*b*)). It can also be used, like *betreffen*, actively in the compound tenses and passively. *Die ganze Stadt wurde durch das Unglück hart getroffen* (or: *betroffen*).

(b) **Einwirken:** to produce a change or modification.

Schopenhauer, Wagner und Nietzsche haben auf Thomas Manns Entwicklung tief eingewirkt.

Die Dürre hat auf die Ernährungslage gradezu katastrophal eingewirkt.

(c) **Sich auswirken** means that the effects spread to and embrace a large number of persons, things, etc. It is implied that the process is slow, i.e. that an interval of time elapses between the cause and effect; also that the effect is important or extensive.

Was in Europa geschieht, wirkt sich auf die ganze Welt aus.

Die Rationierung, der Krieg, hat sich auf unser ganzes Leben ausgewirkt.

4. **Ändern an** with *was* (as a question), *nichts* (in the negative) as object is used in the sense of making an alteration to a part, not the whole.[1] It can only be used positively if accompanied by *viel* or an equivalent. The interrogative and negative forms are much commoner. It can be combined only with nouns denoting things (not persons or substances) capable of modification in the sense of undergoing a different development.

Das ändert nichts an meiner Einstellung Ihnen gegenüber, an der Frage, an dem Ausgang des Krieges.

Ändert das was an Ihren Chancen?

Das ändert sehr viel an unseren Plänen.

5. **In Mitleidenschaft ziehen** denotes the spreading of states, conditions, and the like from one person or thing to another. It is much used of ailments spreading from one part of the body to another, but may also be applied to other things than evils.

Das ganze Bein ist jetzt durch das Gift in Mitleidenschaft gezogen.

Was in Europa geschieht, zieht die ganze Welt in Mitleidenschaft.

6. **Angreifen,** as an equivalent of 'affect', means 'to have an injurious effect on' a thing or a person. The subject must be a thing, the object a person or a thing. The thing may be (*a*) an evil (such as a disease) which operates adversely, either temporarily or permanently, on a person or a part of the body; (*b*) anything which eats away, corrodes, makes inroads on something else.

(a) *Die Überanstrengung, die Hitze, hat sein Herz angegriffen.*

Seine Augen, Nerven, Leber, Gesundheit, sind stark angegriffen.

Der Krebs hat nun auch seine Lunge angegriffen.

Meine Erkältung hat meine Stimme angegriffen.

[1] See 'change'.

(b) *Feuchtigkeit greift den Stahl an.*
Die Ferien haben meine Kasse gewaltig angegriffen.

7. **Schaden** (to damage; see 'damage') and **beeinträchtigen** (to impose a disadvantage on, to encroach on, to prejudice) and similar verbs must sometimes be used when 'affect' denotes an adverse effect.

Das lange Herumstehen im kalten Wasser hat ihm nicht geschadet.
Die tropische Hitze hat den Nahrungsmitteln geschadet.
Der Hunger hat seine Widerstandskraft beeinträchtigt.

8. **Nahe gehen:** to upset emotionally, cause grief to, because of misfortune.

Der Tod seiner Frau ist ihm sehr nahe gegangen.

9. **Bewegen:** to affect strongly in an emotional sense. It is applicable when 'affect' suggests powerful emotion. See 'move'.

Sie war sehr stark bewegt.

AGAIN 1. **Wieder** in the sense of 'again'[1] denotes no more than a repetition, a recurrence, a return to the same, without there being any necessary connection between the two occasions. In referring to future intentions it is therefore unemphatic and leaves the point of time vague.[2]

Ich habe ihn wieder gewarnt.
Ich habe ihn wieder daran erinnert.
Wir müssen uns hierüber wieder unterhalten.
Der Mann ist wieder da.
Ich tue es nicht wieder.

2. **Nochmals** suggests a repetition in a chain, generally with the suggestion that the original occasion was insufficient.[3] It is most often used with reference to something written or said.

Ich habe ihn nochmals gewarnt.
Ich habe ihn nochmals daran erinnert.
Ich habe ihm das nochmals eingeschärft.
Nochmals: die deutsche Romantik enthielt allerlei Gefahren.
Wir müssen ihn nochmals fragen.

[1] In the sense of a recurrence *wieder* often means 'back'. *Ich komme gleich wieder.* Sometimes in the sense of retaliation, e.g. *wiedervergelten.*

[2] *Wiederum* expresses the idea of recurrence with emotional emphasis, but only to indicate that the recurrence is an adversative to something else. '*Mussolini war dabei suggeriert worden, eine internationale Konferenz zur Entspannung der Lage vorzuschlagen. Aber wiederum ließ man sich in Rom durch anderslautende Nachrichten beruhigen und glaubte, Attolico übertreibe.*' (Erich Kordt, *Wahn und Wirklichkeit.*)

[3] *Abermals* has the same meaning as *nochmals*, but is now obsolete except in elevated diction.

3. **Nochmal** suggests that the occasion is the last one. Unlike *nochmals* it does not imply a chain of repetitions. It is an abbreviation of *noch einmal*, but does not express the idea as sharply.

Ich habe ihn nochmal, noch einmal, gewarnt.
Versuchen Sie es nochmal!
Sehe ich Sie nochmal, bevor Sie reisen?

4. **Noch** alone can be used when the context makes the meaning of 'again' clear by the presence of some term such as 'before'.

Sehe ich Sie noch vor Ihrer Abreise?

AGREE, BE AGREED 1. To share a person's opinion, to be in agreement.

(a) **Übereinstimmen, die Ansicht (Meinung) teilen, der Ansicht sein.**

All these phrases mean 'to share a person's opinion', without further implications. As *übereinstimmen* is a long word, it tends to be more literary than conversational. It must be followed by *mit*.

Ich teile Ihre Ansicht, daß die Lage ernst ist.
Ich bin derselben Meinung (I agree).
Ich stimme mit Ihnen, Ihrer Auslegung, überein.
Ich stimme damit überein, daß eine größere Anstrengung nötig ist.

(b) **Einverstanden sein** means that no objections are raised. It can also be used without *mit*.

Ich bin mit Ihrer Auslegung einverstanden.
Ich bin jetzt einverstanden, daß eine größere Anstrengung nötig ist.

(c) **Einig sein** is stronger than *übereinstimmen* in suggesting such identity of view as to constitute only one mind, not two minds that are alike. The reflexive dative of the pronoun may, but need not, be added. It cannot be used absolutely.[1]

Die Sachverständigen waren (sich) über den Fall nicht einig.
Ich bin mit meinem Partner darüber einig, daß wir jetzt ausverkaufen müssen.

(d) **Recht geben,** followed by the dative, is conversational in tone. It is particularly useful to translate 'agree' used absolutely.

Ich gebe Ihnen recht. (I agree!)

2. To reach an agreement after discussion or thought, to come to the same opinion.

[1] *Er ist einig mit sich selbst*: he is at harmony with himself.

(a) **Einig werden** implies the precedence of the agreement by debate or discussion of some length. It is used mainly in reference to formal deliberations (e.g. of a committee).

Das Kommittee wurde darüber einig, daß gewisse Änderungen wünschenswert seien.
Sie wurden endlich handelseinig.

(b) **Sich einigen** can imply immediate or quicker agreement than *einig werden.*

Sie müssen sich mit ihm über die Bücher einigen, die zu bestellen sind.
Sie haben sich über die nötigen Schritte sehr schnell geeinigt.

(c) **Verabreden:** to agree upon, often in the sense of an appointment. It is a loose, sometimes casual, arrangement,[1] and suggests a virtual absence of initial differences. Being casual, it is out of place between people who are conscious of their class inequality.

Sie haben die nötigen Schritte verabredet.
Sie verabredeten den Ort der Zusammenkunft.
Wir haben uns verabredet, daß wir uns um 3 Uhr treffen (more commonly: *wir haben uns auf 3 Uhr verabredet*).

(d) **Vereinbaren:** to agree upon something which contains not inconsiderable initial differences and requires effort to settle. The agreement is more binding than in the case of *verabreden.*

Sie haben die nötigen Schritte vereinbart.
Wir haben vereinbart, daß wir uns immer um 5, nicht um 3 Uhr treffen (the difference denoted by the change of arrangements makes the use of *verabreden* impossible).

3. To tally, to coincide, of things: **übereinstimmen**[2] (in general and of grammatical concord).

Sein Bericht stimmt nicht mit Ihrem überein.

4. To consent with a view to action.

(a) **Einwilligen** is used in reference to important matters.

Er willigte darin ein, daß die Maßnahmen verschärft werden sollten.
Die Bank willigte ein, der Firma größere Kredite zu gewähren.

(b) **Einverstanden sein:** to be in agreement, satisfied. *Einverstanden!* is used like 'agreed!' to denote definite or hearty acceptance.

Ich bin einverstanden, daß Sie dieses Zimmer benutzen.
Sind Sie damit einverstanden, den Brief abzuliefern?

[1] One sense of 'arrangement' is a loose agreement. See 'arrange'.
[2] More colloquially: *stimmen zu. Das stimmt nicht zu dem, was Sie früher sagten.*

(c) **Bereit sein (sich erklären):** to be (declare oneself) prepared. *Sich erklären* can have a formal effect. *Bereit sein* may indicate mere unexpressed willingness as well as an explicit agreement. See 'prepare'.

Sind Sie bereit zu schweigen?
Ich war bereit, ihm unter gewissen Bedingungen zu helfen.
Haben Sie sich bereit erklärt, diese Verpflichtungen zu übernehmen?
Die Universität erklärte sich bereit, den jungen Mann zum Studium zuzulassen.

(d) **Sich verständigen:** to come with someone to an understanding, which may be implicit as well as explicit, and emotional as well as intellectual.

Sie haben sich darüber verständigt, sein Versteck nicht zu verraten.

(e) **Recht sein** is conversational in tone, and, unless the context indicates the contrary, refers to an attitude of mind, not an expressed agreement.

Ist es dir recht, daß er heute früher weggeht? (Are you agreeable...?)

5. **Sich vertragen.** See 'bear'.

(a) To be compatible, to get on amicably.[1]

(b) Of food.[2]

Sie vertragen sich schlecht.
Ich vertrage kein Fleisch (meat does not agree with me).

ALL, WHOLE A. With singular nouns.

1. Applied to things.

All is normally used only with nouns which are collective, i.e. plural in sense. It is declined and the definite article omitted. The possessive adjective may, however, follow without declension of *all*. The effect suggests emotion, not calculation.[3] In other cases *ganz*, which implies a more calculating attitude, must be used.

Mit allem Metall der Welt kann Deutschland den Krieg nicht gewinnen.
Alles Gold in der Welt wird dir das Glück nicht geben.
Alles Fleisch, das ich hier gekauft habe, ist zart gewesen.
All mein Geld ist hin.
All mein Hab und Gut ist verloren.

[1] Similarly: *auskommen. Sie kommen gut miteinander aus.*
[2] Similarly: *bekommen. Fleisch bekommt mir nicht.*
[3] 'Whole' also suggests calculation, but 'all' is used freely to refer to an impression. E.g.: 'all the city was decked with flags'.

In aller Welt werden Sie das nicht finden (romantic in style).
Der Bankier hat sein ganzes Geld verloren.
Die ganze Stadt ist mit Fahnen geschmückt.
Der ganze obere Teil der Mauer wurde zerstört.
Die ganze Klasse stand auf.
Das ganze Innere des Apfels war schlecht.
Ganz Deutschland leidet an Unterernährung.

2. With nouns which do not denote things *all* is used freely. Where *ganz* could also be used, it is more emotional than the latter, and it is less specific than *jeder* in cases where both are possible. It remains undeclined when followed by the definite article, the demonstrative or possessive adjective.

Alle Mühe war vergebens.
Alles Unglück kommt von seiner Unentschlossenheit (*das ganze U.* would be a more prosaic statement).
'*Denn alle Schuld rächt sich auf Erden*' (Goethe).
Ich bin die ganze Zeit hier gewesen.
Seine Aufrichtigkeit ist über allen, jeden, Zweifel erhaben.
Sie müssen alle, jede, Aufregung vermeiden.

B. With plural nouns.

'All' and 'all the' are normally translated by *alle*, i.e. with omission of the definite article. This individualizes, unlike *all die*, which has the same meaning, but is often elevated or emotional in style. *Alle die* means 'all those', and is normally followed by a relative clause. *Die* is here accented, i.e. *diejenigen*.

Alle Häuser in der Straße wurden zerstört.
Alle Vorbereitungen sind schon getroffen.
All die Dichter, die jemals gelebt haben, könnten ein solches Gefühl nicht ausdrücken.
Alle die Studenten, die mitkommen wollen, sollen sich melden.

ANGRY, ANNOYED[1] **1.** German has no term which corresponds exactly to 'annoy' in the sense of to irritate a person, to cause him to lose his equanimity or patience, to jar his nerves. *Verdrießen*[2] comes close to this meaning and to 'vex' (though not as 'perplex'), but is now as little

[1] *Zorn* and *zornig* suggest passion and correspond most closely to 'wrath' and 'wrathful'.

[2] *Verdrießlich:* peevish (applied to a person), irritating, vexing (applied to the cause of annoyance). This term and *Verdruß bereiten* (*machen*, etc.) are used more extensively than the verb.

used as the latter verb. *Auf die Nerven gehen*, a much used expression, can suggest annoyance as the result of a continuous, but not a momentary, irritant.

2. *Böse*, as applied to persons, is, except with *auf*, possible only where there are ties of affection, friendship and the like. It then does not denote a high degree of anger, but rather displeasure[1] which can be shown by silence or a look. It is commonly used of parents who desire to give their children a sign of their displeasure. The simple dative or *mit* with the dative may follow, the former meaning 'to have something against' a person, the latter that one is 'not on speaking terms with' a person. It is used regularly in the imperative as a request not to take a thing amiss.

Further, it is the normal term for 'angry' when applied to animals, and in this case indicates an aggressive attitude.

Ich bin ihm böse (I have something against him).
Ich bin mit ihm böse (I do not speak to him).
Ich bin auf ihn böse (I am furious with him).
Sei mir mal nicht (colloquially: *nich'*) *böse.*
Der Hund, der Stier, ist böse.

3. **Sich ärgern** has a range of application which includes both 'annoyed' and 'angry', but not the weakest use of the former nor the strongest use of the latter. It is the commonest term to indicate in everyday life irritation, annoyance, anger. **Ärgerlich**, which is less frequent, is also weaker and corresponds to the weaker uses of 'irritated', 'annoyed'. It is applied both to the person and to the cause of his irritation. In the former case it sometimes suggests a disposition to nervous irritability. Both terms indicate an impulse to inflict punishment on the cause of annoyance or anger.[2,3]

Ich habe mich über dich geärgert.
Ich habe mich furchtbar geärgert, er ließ mich eine Stunde lang warten.
Seine dumme Ausrede hat mich geärgert.
Ihn ärgern schon die Fliegen an der Wand.
Es macht mich manchmal ärgerlich, wenn er dauernd dreinredet.

[1] *Ungehalten* also suggests displeasure or disapproval, which can express itself by a rebuke.

[2] *Verärgern* suggests an attitude or at least something more than a momentary outburst. A thing or a person who eventually disappoints us or makes us lose patience owing to his conduct can be the cause of the state indicated by this word. It does not necessarily imply outward demonstration of feeling. *Seine Ausflüchte, seine Vorschläge, haben mich verärgert. Du hast ihn verärgert* (alienated his goodwill).

[3] *Reizen*: to irritate, to anger by provocation. *Reiz' den Hund nicht. Aufgebracht*: incensed. *Unwillig*: mildly indignant. *Empört*: indignant at something considered to be an outrage.

ANNOUNCE, PROCLAIM, REPORT 1. **Bekannt machen (geben)** are the most general terms for 'announce' whether in reference to trivial or to important matters. *Geben* is more official (e.g. of the Government) than *machen*. With a personal object *bekannt machen* can only mean 'to introduce'. Neither expression is used of the Press in the sense of 'report'.[1,2]

Die Regierung gibt bekannt, daß sie die Möglichkeit einer Herabsetzung der Steuern prüfen werde.
Die totalen Kriegsverluste werden nicht mehr bekannt gegeben.
Der Besuch des Königs wurde bekannt gegeben.
Der Vorsteher gab es der Schule bekannt, daß die Prüfungen früher stattfinden würden.
Er machte seine Absicht bekannt, ins Ausland zu gehen.

2. **Ankündigen:** to announce with regard to the future, i.e. to something which is to take place. A wide public as audience is generally implied.[3]

Verschärfte Maßnahmen wurden angekündigt.
Der Besuch des Königs wurde für den März angekündigt.
Die Schriftleitung kündigte an, daß die Zeitung nach Ende des Monats nicht mehr erscheinen würde.

3. **Verkünden:**[4] to proclaim, to promulgate far and wide, to all and sundry, ceremoniously and with reference to matters of importance.

Der Sieg wurde überall verkündet.
Ein neues Gesetz wurde verkündet.
Das Evangelium verkünden.

4. **Melden**[5] denotes a general report or announcement that is brief and refers to: (*a*) announcements made by the Press; (*b*) the announcing to an authority or superior of some fact (e.g. an arrival, a theft); (*c*) the denunciation of a person. Unlike *ankündigen*, *melden* does not necessarily refer to the future. It is not used in an informal or friendly announcement.[6]

[1] *Kund tun, machen, geben* are used only in elevated diction.
[2] *Bekanntmachung*: a public notice or proclamation.
[3] *Kündigen*: to give notice that one intends to leave one's employment or one's lodgings. Also: to terminate friendship.
[4] The form *verkünden* is more common than *verkündigen*, while *ankündigen* is much more used than *ankünden*.
[5] *Anmelden*: to enter one's name on a list in order to receive attention or consideration in some matter. *Seine Ansprüche, ein Telephongespräch, anmelden. Vermelden* is used only in fixed, conventional phrases. *Mit Respekt zu vermelden.*
[6] *Sich melden* is said jocularly to a friend in order to announce one's presence; e.g. over the telephone (*ich wollte mich nur melden*). Other uses include it as a military expression: *er legte das Gewehr beiseite und meldete sich.*

ANNOUNCE

Die Zeitungen melden den Besuch des Königs.
Zwanzig Grad Kälte wurden gemeldet.
Es wird aus Berlin gemeldet, daß die Russen durchgebrochen sind.
Er meldete seinen Vorgesetzten den Fall.
Der Diener hat mich, meine Ankunft, gemeldet.
Sie müssen sich, den Diebstahl, bei der Polizei melden.
Er meldete ihn beim Lehrer (reported, denounced him to...).

5. **Berichten:** to report in detail, to give an account, either officially or informally. The reference to detail excludes the sense of 'announce'.

Die Zeitungen berichten über die Gerichtsverhandlungen fast lückenlos.
Der Botschafter berichtete über die Einstellung der Regierung, bei der er beglaubigt war.
Berichten Sie uns ein bißchen von Ihrer Reise.

6. **Anzeigen:** to report or to announce something to authorities as a duty; to denounce, whether as a duty or wrongfully.

Er hat seine Verlobung angezeigt.
Er hat den Verkauf seines Hauses angezeigt.
Er hat ihn bei der Polizei angezeigt (denounced).

ANSWER, REPLY, REJOIN, RETORT Sense: to say something in return.

1. **Antworten** only can translate the intransitive use of 'answer' and 'reply'. When followed by *auf* in order to render the transitive use, it differs from *beantworten* in suggesting nothing more than that the question has elicited a response, i.e. without reference to any specific type of content. **Beantworten**, on the other hand, means 'to deal with the question' with some measure of fullness.

Er hat noch nicht auf meinen Brief geantwortet.
Er antwortete auf meine Frage nur mit 'Ja'.
Er beantwortete meinen Brief, meine Frage, sehr ausführlich.

2. **Erwidern** means primarily 'to return something given' in the same or the opposite kind (e.g. *Liebe mit Liebe, Haß, erwidern*). As a synonym of *antworten*, it suggests an opposing statement, and approaches very closely to **entgegnen** (to counter with an objection).

Auf meine Behauptung erwiderte er, daß er das Gegenteil für wahr halte.
Er entgegnete, daß mein Argument sich auf falsche Prämissen stütze.

3. **Versetzen** suggests a lively answer in conversation.

Auf meine Frage versetzte er, daß ich die Frage falsch gestellt hätte.

ANXIOUS, EAGER, ZEALOUS 1. Sense: desirous. As there are no exact German equivalents except for 'zealous', only approximations are possible, the following being the commonest.

(a) **Eifrig** means 'zealous' rather than 'eager', and should only be used when these two terms are practically interchangeable, i.e. when 'eager' suggests zeal in doing a thing. Like 'zealous', *eifrig* cannot be followed by the infinitive, which is, however, possible after *großen Eifer zeigen.*

Er ist sehr eifrig in der Schule.
Er ist ein eifriger Parteianhänger.
Er lernt sehr eifrig.
Er hat meinen Vorschlag eifrig befürwortet.
Er zeigt großen Eifer zu lernen.

(b) **Begierig:** desirous of getting possession of something which satisfies an appetite or insistent desire, for oneself, not for others. It rarely refers to the desires of the higher self,[1] although an intellectual interest may be involved. *Er ist begierig, sie kennen zu lernen* can easily suggest sexual interest. It can be followed by an infinitive.

Er ist begierig nach Ruhm.
Er ist begierig, schnell reich zu werden.
Er ist begierig zu prüfen, ob die Ähnlichkeit sie täuschen wird.
Ich bin begierig, die Geschichte zu hören.

(c) **Neugierig** (curious), **gespannt** (literally: tense) are used in the sense of 'to desire to make acquaintance with, to experience', something hitherto unknown. *Gespannt* suggests that the outcome is anxiously awaited.

Ich bin neugierig, ihn kennen zu lernen.
Ich bin gespannt, was daraus wird (anxious to know, to see).
Ich bin gespannt, Furtwängler dirigieren zu hören.

[1] *Gierig* emphasizes still more strongly the desire for possession, often in an animal way, and approximates to 'avid'. It cannot be followed by the infinitive (e.g. *er trinkt gierig*). *Begierde* refers only to strongly emotional desires and is thus more restricted in application than 'desire'. *Begierde* concentrates attention on the subject, *Begier* on the desire itself. *Das erweckte in ihm die Begier nach Ruhm. Da erwachte in ihm die Begierde nach Ruhm.* On the other hand, only *Begierde* admits a plural. The same distinction applies to *Zier* and *Zierde. Gier* suggests a covetous desire of the lower order, often avidity, the state of desire. When 'desire' means no more than wish it must be translated by *Wunsch* (e.g. *sein Wunsch, ein Abkommen zu treffen*). Similarly *wünschen. Begehren* is to desire strongly, emotionally to crave (e.g. *den Tod begehren*). *Verlangen*, which can also mean 'to require', 'to ask' (see 'ask') suggests a need which is accompanied by a state of restlessness owing to its non-fulfilment. It is often followed by *nach* to express the remoteness of fulfilment. *Lust*, like English 'lust', originally meant 'desire', the meaning of pleasurable sensation being a later development. The original meaning is preserved in many phrases (e.g. *Lust haben*) and in the plural (*Lüste* = carnal desires).

(d) **Möchte (gern)**, 'should, would like', must often be used in reference to simple matters. The addition of *gern* suggests a slight fear of difficulties.[1]

Ich möchte gern nach Hause kommen, bevor der Sturm losbricht.
Er möchte immer gefallen.

(e) **Es liegt einem an**...means 'to attach importance to the realization of' a thing. It does not render the implication of fear conveyed by 'anxious', and instead of suggesting the emotion of desire it presents the aim as something understood and calculated as well as wanted. It should be used only of things that have a measure of importance, and not in impulsive statements.

Es liegt mir sehr daran, ihn kennen zu lernen.
Es liegt mir daran, nach Hause zu kommen, bevor der Sturm losbricht.

(f) **Darauf brennen** should only be used when 'to burn to...' is possible in English.

Er brennt darauf, mitzuhelfen.

(g) **Bemüht sein** can mean 'to be anxious' only when the context implies that the subject is already active, endeavouring to carry out a purpose.[2] It is often combined with *eifrig*.

Er war bemüht, einen guten Eindruck zu machen.
Er ist eifrig bemüht, der Erste zu sein.

(h) **Bedacht sein auf** can be used in the sense of 'intent upon', 'concerned with', i.e. in reference to some absorbing purpose.

Er ist darauf bedacht, nichts falsch zu machen.

[1] The commonest meaning of *mögen* is now 'to like'. Except after the form *möchte* a following infinitive is more common in the negative than in the positive (compare English 'care'). Otherwise *gern* and an appropriate verb is used. It is commonest with noun objects which refer to (*a*) people, (*b*) food and drink, again more in the negative than the positive, although it is also found with other types of object. In the latter case, however, *gern haben* is more usual. *Gern leiden mögen* is common with a personal object (*ich mag ihn gern leiden*). Examples: *Ich möchte (nicht) ins Theater gehen. Ich mag solche Sachen nicht hören. Sie mögen sich. Ich mochte ihn ganz gern. Ich mag Kartoffeln nicht. Ich habe diese Farbenmischung gern. Gern* with the appropriate verb is common to render 'like' followed by the gerund. *Ich gehe gern ins Theater.*

[2] *Sich bemühen:* to endeavour. It stresses the consciousness of purpose, whereas *sich mühen* emphasizes the toil itself involved in doing a thing, and means 'to toil', 'to labour'. The latter verb is rarely followed by the infinitive. Exceptions: '...*daß ich mich ernstlich mühen mußte, von allerlei Vermutungen ergriffen, wenigstens unbefangen zu scheinen*' (E. T. A. Hoffmann, *Die Elixiere des Teufels*).

'*Du trägst seit alten Tagen*
Ein seltsam Märchen mit dir um,
Und mühst dich es zu sagen.' (Mörike, *Mein Fluß*.)

(i) **Gespannt sein** is in conversation the commonest phrase with the sense of 'to be anxious to know'.

Ich bin sehr gespannt, wie er darauf reagiert.
Ich bin gespannt, was er dazu sagen wird.

2. Sense: worried, worrying.[1]

Er ist besorgt um seine Gesundheit.
Sie ist eine besorgte Mutter.
Es war ein besorgniserregender Augenblick.
Sie wartete voller Besorgnis.

APPARENTLY

Scheinbar differs from **anscheinend**[2] in the same way as *Schein* from *Anschein* (see 'appearance'). The distinction between *scheinbar* and *anscheinend* is being obliterated more and more, even with careful writers.

Er hat nur scheinbar seinen Standpunkt verändert (ostensibly).
Sie haben es anscheinend sehr eilig.

APPEAR, SEEM This article deals with these verbs when followed by an adjective with or without 'to be'. As with 'to be', the insertion or omission of *zu sein* after *scheinen* is determined not by the sense but solely by the formal requirements of the phrase. *Scheinen* followed by the infinitive is extremely rare in compound tenses.

1. **Scheinen:** a subjective judgment based on feeling, approximating to the meaning of 'consider'. If the judgment is not that of the speaker but of some other person (indicated by the second or third person in the dative case), it is implied that the speaker definitely knows that the judgment is that of this other person. In cases where the speaker cannot know of the judgment as a fact (e.g. with the future tense or in combinations with modal verbs[3]) *scheinen* is not used. These cases arise with the first person (the speaker) no less than with the second and third persons.

Die Bedingungen scheinen mir hart (*zu sein*) (or *Ihnen, ihm*, etc., to which could be added some such phrase as *wie ich höre* to complete the sense).

[1] *Ängstlich* means 'timid', 'fearful', in a nervous way, i.e. it stresses the fear, not the desire to see a positive result.

[2] *Scheinbar*, but not *anscheinend* is used adjectively.

[3] *Scheinen* is found in combination with modal verbs in poetic or dignified and elevated diction.

'Heimlich muß ich immer weinen,
Aber freundlich kann ich scheinen
Und sogar gesund und rot.' (Goethe, *An Mignon.*)

Thomas Mann in *Briefe an einen Schweizer* published in *Schweizer Annalen* (Nr. 9/10, 1945) writes: '*Auch steht man nicht so allein, wie es einem selbst und Außenstehenden in den trübsten Augenblicken scheinen mag.*' *Mögen* used optatively is for the same reason followed by *scheinen* not *erscheinen* (e.g. *möge es scheinen*...).

APPEAR

Es schien mir, Ihnen, ihm, unmöglich, daß jemand so schlecht sein könne.
Seine Handlungsweise scheint mir (Ihnen, ihr), gesinnungslos zu sein.
Es schien den die Gefangenen in Freiheit setzenden Truppen unmöglich, daß der Mensch solche Greuel begehen könnte (the addition of *zu sein* after *unmöglich* would be cumbersome).
Sie scheinen zufrieden (zu sein) (mir is implied).
Scheint Ihnen der Gedanke so lächerlich?

2. **Erscheinen**[1] implies less a judgment than an impression, often, but not necessarily, visual. With *mir, uns* it expresses the impression of the speaker(s). With the dative of the second or third person it refers to an impression received by this person, which the speaker reports not as a fact known to him, but as an impression gained by him. Since the speaker may very well have an impression about his own or other people's reactions in cases where these cannot be definitely known, *erscheinen* can be used with the future tense and with modal verbs. When the recipient of the impression is not mentioned, the sense is that anyone or everyone receives it. Since we tend to state our own reactions as judgments, *scheinen* is more common with the first, *erscheinen* with the second and third persons.

Die Bedingungen werden (müssen) Ihnen wohl hart erscheinen.
Es erschien mir unmöglich, daß jemand so schlecht sein könne.
Seine Handlungsweise kann ihr nicht anders als gesinnungslos erscheinen.
Es erschien den Truppen, die die noch überlebenden Gefangenen befreiten, unmöglich, daß der Mensch solche Greuel begehen könnte.
Lassen Sie es so erscheinen, als ob der Vorschlag von ihm kommt.
Er kann nach Belieben heiter oder traurig erscheinen.
Erscheint Ihnen der Gedanke so lächerlich?

APPEARANCE A. Outward appearance in relation to reality. The German words also translate 'semblance'.

1. **Schein:**[2] outward appearance(s) as opposed to reality. It can be used only when the purpose of the statement in which it occurs is to make this opposition clear.

Der Schein trügt.
Dem Schein nach ist er zu Zugeständnissen bereit.
Er spricht mit dem Schein der Überzeugung.
Die Entscheidung hat den Schein der Billigkeit an sich (ist aber tatsächlich unbillig could be added).

[1] *Erscheinen* cannot be followed by an infinitive.
[2] *Schein* is used to form many compounds (e.g. *Scheinblüte, ein Scheinheiliger*) and may be rendered into English by such adjectives as 'sham', 'mock', 'illusory'.

Unter dem Schein der Legalität setzten sie ihre Maßnahmen durch.
Der Schein ist gegen ihn.
Sie denken nur daran, den Schein zu wahren.

2. **Anschein:** outward appearance(s) which seem(s) to the judge, who may, but need not, be the speaker, probably to correspond to reality, though it may not.

Allem Anschein nach ist er zu Zugeständnissen bereit.
Er spricht mit dem Anschein, als ob er selbst davon überzeugt sei.
Die Entschuldigung hat den Anschein von Billigkeit an sich (to which could be added: *und ist es tatsächlich auch,* an addition impossible in the example involving *Schein*).
Um ihre Maßnahmen durchzusetzen, hatten sie den Anschein der Legalität nötig.
Das Bild hat den Anschein der Lebenswahrheit.
Der Starrkrampf erweckt den Anschein des Todes.

B. Look, aspect, air of a person or thing.

1. **Äußeres** refers to the general appearance of a person, particularly face and clothes in so far as care is bestowed on them.

Sie achtet sehr auf, vernachlässigt, ihr Äußeres.
Von ihrem Äußeren halte ich nicht viel.
Ich habe ihr Äußeres überhaupt nicht in Betracht gezogen, als ich sie engagierte.
Lassen Sie sich nicht von ihrem Äußeren irreleiten.
Weiße Haare betonten noch mehr die Vornehmheit seines Äußeren.

2. **Äußere Erscheinung** refers also to the general appearance, but can only be applied to a high personage or to a person of some years.[1]

Es ist nur seine äußere Erscheinung, die etwas taugt.

3. **Aussehen**[2] refers to the general impression of a person or thing, to the natural look, not to clothes.

Sie hat ein frisches Aussehen.
Sie hat das Aussehen eines Bauernmädchens.
Das Aussehen des Parks gereicht der Stadt zur Ehre.

[1] *Erscheinung* can only be used to refer to the personality and to bearing behind externals. It is used with *sein*, not *haben*, and corresponds to apparition rather than appearance. *Sie ist eine anmutige Erscheinung.*

[2] *Ansehen* is now obsolete in this sense. '*Sie scheinen keine Schelmen, und haben doch auch nicht das Ansehen von ehrlichen Leuten*' (Goethe, *Werther*). '*Aber er hatte ein düstres, störrisches Ansehen*' (E. T. A. Hoffmann, *Die Elixiere des Teufels*).

C. **Erscheinen** must be used in the sense of 'act of appearance'.[1]

Sein Erscheinen zu diesem Zeitpunkt war ganz unerwartet.

APPOINT, NOMINATE, ENGAGE Sense: to declare a person as one's choice for a position or task.

'Appoint' is used in the following combinations: (1) to appoint someone; (2) to appoint someone (as) (e.g. manager); (3) to appoint someone to a position; (4) to appoint someone to do something.

1. **Ernennen** is used in two ways. (*a*) To appoint, i.e. by an individual or a body possessing power of appointment without submission to the vote of an electorate. (*b*) To nominate, when this is done by an executive officer whose prerogative it is to make a selection which has then to be submitted to confirmation by the body in which power resides. Sometimes 'appoint' is used in this sense of 'nominate', particularly in reference to nomination by an executive officer after this has received confirmation. It does not mean 'nominate' in the sense of the proposal of a candidate by a member of the electorate.[2]

Ernennen, like 'appoint', is not used of humble work. Further, it can be followed by the title of the person, but not by that of the office.

Der Senat der Universität hat ihn zum Professor ernannt.
Er wurde zum Kriegsminister ernannt.
Sie werden hiermit zum Mitglied des Prüfungsausschusses ernannt.
Die Firma ernannte ihn zu ihrem Schiedsrichter.
Ich habe ihn zu meinem Agenten ernannt.
Der Präsident der Vereinigten Staaten ernennt seine Staatssekretäre (nominates, appoints).

2. **Bestellen** implies that the appointment is made from above, e.g. by a controlling body. Further, it is most commonly used of appointment to a special task. In reference to a permanent position it is only possible if the appointment is made by an exalted personage such as a king, or in old-fashioned language. It can be followed by the title of the person, but not by that of the position.[3]

Er wurde zum Vormund, Vertreter, bestellt.
Er wurde zum Prüfungsassistenten bestellt.

[1] *Erscheinung* would mean apparition in the sense of 'ghost'.

[2] 'Nominate' in this sense is: *vorschlagen*; *jdn. als Kandidaten aufstellen.*

[3] A closely related meaning of *bestellen* is: to request or command a person to call on one or to go to a specified place. *Ich habe ihn für 4 Uhr bestellt*, i.e. have made an appointment for him to call on me at 4 o'clock. *Er ist nach Berlin bestellt worden*, requested or commanded to go to Berlin. This meaning is now more common than that of 'appoint to a position'. Ambiguity can arise unless the context removes it. Examples: *Als junger Mann wurde J. S. Bach zum Domorganisten bestellt. Als Domorganist wurde J. S. Bach nach Leipzig bestellt* (either appointed to, or requested to come to L.).

Die Regierung hat ihn zum Richter, hat einen Richter, bestellt, um die Vergangenheit der Internierten zu prüfen.
Ehemalige Soldaten werden als Hilfspolizei bestellt.
Er wurde als Hilfslehrer an diese Schule bestellt (not *als Lehrer* which refers to a permanent position).
Ein Ausschuß wurde bestellt, um die Zustände im Kriegsgefangenenlager zu untersuchen.
Der König bestellte ihn zu seinem Leibarzt.
Goethe bestellte Dr. Riemer zu seinem Sekretär (old-fashioned; today the meaning would be 'asked him to go to his secretary').

3. **Anstellen** is applied to permanent work of a middle or lower order, and within this framework means 'to appoint', 'to engage'.[1]

Er wurde als Dozent, als Lehrer für Geschichte, als Sekretär, als Arbeiter, angestellt.

4. **Einsetzen** most commonly suggests a specific purpose, often when a matter is urgent or when energy is required. It is used more frequently than any other term in reference to the appointment of a committee, but is rarely applied to a permanent appointment. It may be followed by a prepositional phrase denoting the office.

Während des Krieges wurden in Deutschland politische Offiziere eingesetzt, um die Haltung der Truppen zu überwachen.
Er wurde als zeitweiliger Lehrer eingesetzt.
Er wurde ins Polizeipräsidentenamt eingesetzt.
Ein Ausschuß wurde eingesetzt, um dem Minister Empfehlungen über Emigrantenfragen zu machen.

5. The following terms are commonly used in the sense of (*a*) to appoint to a position; (*b*) to appoint to the place where a position is held:

Übertragen, to transfer an office to someone; **zuweisen,** to assign.[2]

Der Lehrstuhl, das Amt, wurde ihm übertragen.
Er wurde diesem Schiff als Arzt zugewiesen.

[1] *Anstellen* cannot be used for casual work of a humble kind (use *dingen*, to hire for remuneration), nor for any permanent exalted position or temporary work demanding outstanding gifts (e.g. to engage an artist). *Ein Angestellter:* an employee (e.g. *ein Bankangestellter*). *Beschäftigen* corresponds to 'employ' only in the sense 'to keep busy', and, by implication, to provide enough work to absorb a specified number of hands. *Diese Fabrik beschäftigt* 1000 *Arbeiter.* It does not mean 'to take on' (see *anstellen*), and is not used in the passive voice in the sense of 'to be in the employ' of a specified person, firm, or the like. In this sense *angestellt sein in, bei* or the various equivalents of 'to have a position, job' (see 'position') must be used. *Er ist in einer Bank, bei Wertheim, angestellt.*

[2] *Zuweisung* is often used for 'appointment', particularly to a minor administrative position. *Der Referendar erhielt eine Zuweisung nach Hildesheim.*

APPOINT

Berufen can be used of appointment to a place in the case of an important position. See 'call'. Similarly: *einen Ruf erhalten nach; einem Ruf folgen nach.*

Er ist ins Reichsinnenministerium berufen worden.
Er hat einen Ruf nach Berlin erhalten.

APPRECIATE 1. **Würdigen** suggests a due awareness, recognition or understanding of the quality, worth of, or of the reason for a thing, and a willingness to pay tribute to these.[1] It must be distinguished from **schätzen**, which merely indicates a liking, and states that a person or thing makes a personal appeal to one.[2]

Er ist ein Mann, dessen wahrer Wert nie recht gewürdigt worden ist.
Ich würdige deine Ansicht, obwohl ich nicht damit übereinstimme.
Nur wenige Menschen sind tolerant genug, die Motive ihrer Gegner zu würdigen.
Hast du es recht gewürdigt, daß er dieses Opfer für dich brachte?
Er würdigt moderne Musik nicht.
Ich würdige deine Haltung, wenn ich sie auch nicht schätze.
Er schätzt moderne Musik nicht.
Dieses Lied wird allgemein geschätzt.
Nichts schätze ich gegen Abend so sehr wie ein Glas Sherry.
Er schätzt diesen kleinen Ort, die friedliche Schönheit der Landschaft.

2. When *würdigen* and *schätzen* are used in combination with **wissen** (i.e. *zu würdigen, schätzen, wissen*), the sense is 'to have the capacity to appreciate'. German requires the insertion of *wissen* when the idea of capacity is stressed, even though in English it is expressed merely as an implication of 'appreciate'. In the positive form *zu würdigen, schätzen, wissen* frequently registers a formal or polite expression of appreciation or gives an assurance in case of doubt and the like that one is not insensitive to a thing. The negative indicates a deficiency in the subject.

Ich weiß die mir erwiesene Ehre wohl zu würdigen.
Ich weiß Ihre Schwierigkeiten zu würdigen.
Einen Besuch in der Gemäldegalerie weiß er doch nicht zu würdigen.
Ich weiß Ihre Bemühungen zu schätzen.
Er weiß die Architektur dieser Stadt nicht zu schätzen.
Viele wissen die Schönheit des eigenen Landes nicht zu schätzen.

[1] *Würdigen* has a number of other meanings. Note particularly that of 'to think worthy of', 'to condescend to give' (e.g. *ich würdigte ihn meines Vertrauens, keines Blickes*).
[2] *Schätzen* also means 'to estimate'. See article.

3. The following can also be used as approximations to 'appreciate'. They have other, and more frequent, renderings into English than 'appreciate'.

(a) **Verständnis haben für** can refer to emotional as well as intellectual understanding. It suggests that agreement is more unreserved than is the case with *würdigen*. See 'understanding'.

Ich habe Verständnis für Ihre Schwierigkeiten, Ihre Situation.
Er hat kein Verständnis für Kunst.

(b) **Sinn haben für:** to have a sense, a specially developed faculty of the mind, for a thing. See 'sense'.

Er hat keinen Sinn für Musik, für historische Werte.

(c) **Ein Verhältnis haben, finden, zu etwas:** to have, to find, an inner kinship, bond of sympathy, between oneself and a thing. See 'relation'.

Er hat ein inniges Verhältnis zur Kunst des Mittelalters.
Ich finde kein Verhältnis zur modernen Musik.

APPROACH 1. Literal sense. In space or in time.
(a) **Sich nähern** expresses in general the idea of approach in space without specifying the manner. It tends to suggest approach from some distance. With reference to time it can only be applied to an activity, i.e. not pure time, such as 'spring', 'midnight'. It must be followed by an object in the dative case.

Er näherte sich mir, dem Haus.
Der Zug näherte sich dem Bahnhof.
Das Schiff nähert sich dem Hafen.
Die Armee nähert sich der Stadt.
Wir nähern uns der Mitte der Oper.
Der Krieg nähert sich seinem Ende.

(b) **Näher kommen,** with the same sense as *sich nähern*, translates 'approach' used intransitively. It is also the normal prose term as applied to time.

Er, der Zug, der Frühling, Mitternacht, kommt näher.

(c) **Nahen** suggests a manner of approach in space which grips the beholder by being dignified, imposing, momentous, and the like. It suggests, moreover, that the approaching person or thing is close at hand. It is used of time in literary, mainly elevated, contexts. It occurs both transitively (governing the dative case) and intransitively. In transitive use it is normally reflexive when referring to space. Without *sich*, in reference to things, the impression of majesty is still further heightened.

APPROACH

Der König naht.
Er naht sich dem König, dem Thron.
Das Schiff naht (sich) langsam dem Hafen.
Der Krieg naht seinem Ende (not reflexive in reference to time).
Der Frühling, Mitternacht, naht.

2. To approach with a request or about a matter.

(a) **Angehen um:** to ask for.

Er ging mich um 1000 *Mark an.*

(b) **Herantreten an** suggests a ceremonious, diplomatic, or at least careful, approach.

England tritt an Rußland mit Vorschlägen heran.

3. To approach a subject of study: **(heran) gehen an.**

Voll Vertrauen ging er an seine Arbeit (heran).
Wir müssen vorsichtig an dieses Problem (heran) gehen.

4. To approach in value: **sich nähern** (material values), **heranreichen an** (immaterial values).

Der Wert dieses Besitzes nähert sich einer Million.
Keiner der anderen romantischen Dichter reicht an Mörike heran, was Gedankentiefe und Formvollendung betrifft.

5. To approximate to, to be practically the equivalent of: **nahe kommen.**

Was Sie jetzt sagen, kommt einer Verneinung Ihrer früheren Behauptung nahe.

ARRANGE[1] 1. To put objects, words, thoughts or matters in a certain order, to dispose.

(a) **Ordnen:** to dispose in an orderly, often practical way, according to some principle. It does not suggest the arranging of visible things in an aesthetic pattern, but may be applied to literature and music (e.g. words, scenes, movements).[2]

Er ordnete die Bücher in seiner Bibliothek nach Schriftstellern.
Er ordnete die Papiere auf seinem Pult.
Er hat seine Angelegenheiten noch nicht geordnet.
Das Ganze ist unübersichtlich geordnet (a piece of writing).

[1] Arrangement. The phrase 'make arrangements' is explained in this article. *Plan* is widely used (*was sind die Pläne für heute abend?*—i.e. with regard to entertainment). *Arrangement* is mostly an arrangement of flowers and the like.

[2] *Anordnen* means 'to put, arrange', in a series; also 'to order' as a synonym of 'command'. See 'order'.

(b) **Einrichten:** to arrange the furniture in a room, each item in relation to the whole.

Das Zimmer ist geschmackvoll eingerichtet.

(c) **Zurecht machen:**[1] to adjust small things so as to bring them into the right or desired order or pattern.

Machen Sie Ihre Haare zurecht.
Sie machte die Kissen auf dem Bett zurecht.
Er machte die Möbel im Salon für die Gesellschaft zurecht.

2. Plan details beforehand.

(a) **Veranstalten** suggests elaborate arrangements with regard to something big, often a function or ceremony.

Die Beamten haben einen Besuch zum Flughafen veranstaltet.
Ein Ball, ein Konzert, ein Siegesfest wurde veranstaltet.

(b) **Vorkehrungen treffen** implies the doing of a considerable number of things, which may be the manipulating of objects, speaking, writing, and the like. It can suggest, further, that the measures are designed to eliminate the possibility of adverse developments.

Das Hotel hat Vorkehrungen getroffen, um 150 *Gäste aufzunehmen* (furnished rooms, ordered food, engaged and instructed staff, etc.).
Das Touristenbüro hat alle nötigen Vorkehrungen für meine Reise getroffen (booked train-tickets, rooms in hotels, etc.).
Alle Vorkehrungen sind für die Wahlen getroffen worden.

(c) **Planen** is used of both large- and small-scale organizing.[2,3]

Wir haben einen kleinen Ausflug für Sonntag geplant.

(d) **Vermitteln:** to arrange a thing by negotiations, as a mediator between people. The object is normally the result of the negotiations.

Eine Heirat, den Hausverkauf, vermitteln.

(e) **Sich (es) so einrichten, dass**. This phrase translates 'arrange' when the latter is followed by the infinitive, in the sense of 'to arrange (matters) with regard to oneself'. Used with *es* the meaning can be 'with regard to someone else'. The sense of *einrichten* is 'to manipulate' matters,

[1] Specific terms compounded with *zurecht* also translate 'arrange'; e.g. *zurechtlegen, zurechtrücken. Sie rückte die Kissen zurecht, um bequemer zu liegen.*

[2] *Arrangieren* is possible in this sense.

[3] Specific terms meaning 'to attend to (details)' are: *besorgen* (to attend to); *ins Reine bringen* (to finalize, to give final form to). *Der Sekretär hat alle Einzelheiten für die Besprechung ins Reine gebracht.*

important or trivial, for the realization of a purpose. In this use its object can only be *sich, es* or a word meaning 'matters' (*Dinge, Sachen*, etc.).

Können Sie sich (es) so einrichten, daß Sie spätestens um 5 Uhr hier sind?
Ich richte mich (es) so ein, daß ich den Nachmittag frei habe.
Ich habe es so eingerichtet, daß er morgen meine Arbeit übernimmt.

(f) **Anstalten treffen:** to make elaborate, often ceremonious, arrangements. A following infinitive is possible.

Er hat Anstalten getroffen, den Minister zu empfangen.

3. To come to an agreement[1] with a person.

(a) **Ausmachen** implies the working out of a practical question, an examination of it from a number of sides. It is common in conversation.

Wir haben ausgemacht, wieviel wir dafür bezahlen wollen.
Ich machte den Ort mit ihm aus, wo wir ihn treffen wollten.
Ich habe mit ihm ausgemacht, mein Auto gegen sein Motorboot einzutauschen.
Sie machten einen Plan aus, der die Finanzen wieder in Ordnung bringen würde.

(b) **Abmachen** stresses the finalizing of a definite agreement.

Es ist abgemacht, daß wir morgen fahren (settled).
Ich kaufe Ihr Auto, das ist abgemacht.

4. To arrange a musical composition: **bearbeiten, einrichten.**

ASK 1. **Bitten** must be used in the sense of 'request'[2] and implies that the asker is a suppliant, **verlangen** that both parties consider themselves on an equal footing. *Verlangen* has also the sense of 'require' when the subject is a thing.[3]

Er bat um Hilfe, eine Unterredung.
An der Grenze wurde verlangt, daß wir unsere Pässe zeigen sollten.
Ich bat ihn, mir seinen Paß zu zeigen.
Die Schullehrer haben eine Gehaltserhöhung verlangt.
Diese Arbeit verlangt eine eingehende Prüfung aller Dokumente.

[1] See also *verabreden* under 'agreement'.

[2] (*Sich*) *etwas erbitten* (often reflexive) means 'to request something' with success or with the certainty of success. *Den beiliegenden Katalog erbitte ich mir nach Durchsicht zurück. 'Die Gabe des zweiten Gesichts sei über ihn verhängt, er . . . würde sie nie von Gott erbeten haben'* (R. Huch, *Weiße Nächte*). *Ersuchen* is strong and direct. It is often used in formal or official statements and notices. *Die Botschafter ersuchten Stalin um eine Unterredung. Es wird dringend ersucht, nicht in den Wagen zu spucken. Um etwas nachsuchen* is less strong and less direct. It cannot govern a direct object. *Die Botschafter suchten bei Stalin um eine Unterredung nach. Er hat um eine Stellung nachgesucht.*

[3] See also footnote to 'anxious' (p. 23, n. 1) for a further explanation of *verlangen.*

2. **Fragen** must be used in the sense of 'to ask a question'.[1,2]

Er fragte, was für Absichten sie hätten.

ATTITUDE 1. **Haltung:** a manner of being, feeling, thinking in the sphere of moral deportment. It is a constant, unchanging manner, as far as the matter to which it is directed is concerned. It excludes on the one hand action, and, on the other, the taking up of a purely intellectual stand or point of view. In this sense it also translates the synonymous term 'bearing'.[3] 'To take' is *einnehmen* when combined with *Haltung*.

Er nahm eine scharfe, herausfordernde, abweisende, passive, Haltung ein.
Die realistische Geisteshaltung.
Eine Haltung von leben und leben lassen.
Er hat eine höchst gesunde Haltung in Bezug auf Sexualfragen.

2. **Verhalten** is less static than *Haltung*, but can denote a more or less passive attitude of watching and waiting. It is characteristically qualified by such words as *passiv, ruhig, geschickt, klug*, and cannot be combined with adjectives which express a high degree of activity (e.g. *aktiv, energisch*). The relationship[4] between subject and object it can imply is a reaction[5] to and adjustment to a changing situation. It is not used with verbs which imply a static attitude (e.g. *haben, einnehmen*).

Sein Verhalten in der Angelegenheit war sehr lobenswert.
Sein Verhalten in religiösen Fragen ist nicht ganz eindeutig.

3. **Einstellung**[6] refers predominantly to an intellectual attitude, i.e. a fixed point of view with regard to a problem. 'Take' in this connection is translated by *einnehmen*, 'to' by *zu* or *gegenüber*.

Seine Einstellung dem Leben gegenüber.
Meine Einstellung ist, daß der Streik gerechtfertigt war.
Er nahm den Kritikern gegenüber eine höchst feindliche Einstellung ein.
Er hat eine höchst gesunde Einstellung Sexualfragen gegenüber.
Ich bin mir über meine Einstellung nicht ganz klar.

[1] *Befragen* is 'to question fully or insistently'. *Anfragen* (*bei jemandem*) is 'to enquire' about matters which receive only a short reply, mostly officially. *Sie könnten bei dem betreffenden Minister anfragen. Ausfragen*: to question fully, to interrogate.

[2] *Fragen* is used passively in commercial contexts in the sense of 'to be in demand'. *Dieser Artikel wird sehr gefragt.* Compare the noun: *Nachfrage.*

[3] *Haltung* also means 'carriage', i.e. of the body.

[4] *Verhalten* denotes a relationship of the type explained. 'Relationship', however, is *Verhältnis*, which does not mean 'attitude'. See 'relation'.

[5] *Verhalten* is also applied to a chemical reaction.

[6] The verbs related to *Einstellung, Stellung* and *Verhalten* are widely used. Note: *eingestellt sein* (only with *sein*); *sich stellen zu etwas* (only in reflexive use); *sich verhalten* (only in reflexive use). What is your attitude to...? (in a casual question) *Wie stellen Sie ich zu...? Was ist Ihre Einstellung...?* expects a more detailed answer.

4. **Stellungnahme** refers only to an attitude towards big questions or important matters. It can also denote an attitude taken in an official capacity in the sense of official comment. Since it contains *nahme*, it cannot be combined with *einnehmen*.

Seine Stellungnahme in der Alkoholfrage.
Die Regierung behält sich ihre Stellungnahme vor.
Die Berichte wurden ohne Stellungnahme weitergeleitet.

5. **Stellung:** one's inner disposition to a person or a thing. Since it is natural, spontaneous, it is unaffected by reflection. In this sense it is followed by *zu*. The phrase *Stellung nehmen* refers to an official attitude, comment.

Seine Stellung zum Tode.
Der Minister hat schon Stellung dazu genommen.

ATTRACT 1. **Anziehen** is used in the following ways: (*a*) of a force of nature; (*b*) to stir pleasurable feelings of anticipation;[1] (*c*) to cause to follow as a disciple. To be attracted by a person or thing: *von jdm., etwas, angezogen sein.* To be attracted to a person or thing: *zu jdm., etwas,* **hingezogen** *sein.*

Der Magnet zieht das Eisen an.
Salz zieht Feuchtigkeit an.
Sie zieht ihn stark an.
Das Bergsteigen zieht ihn nicht an.
Dieser Beruf zieht mich nicht an.
Der Kommunismus zieht viele Menschen an.
Er fühlt sich von ihr stark angezogen.
Er fühlt sich zu ihr stark hingezogen.

2. The sense of 'draw to oneself' in any way other than those treated in the above section, e.g. deliberately, is often rendered by **auf sich ziehen**. This may be used to translate 'attract attention', particularly when a deliberate effort is implied, i.e. by a person. When a thing is the subject **erregen** (see 'excite') is more common. In conversation, shorter phrases such as *aufmerksam werden,*[2] *auffallen* (to strike, to catch one's attention) are preferred.

Ich versuchte, seine Aufmerksamkeit auf mich zu ziehen.
Wir zogen feindliches Feuer auf uns.
Das Bild erregte meine Aufmerksamkeit.

[1] Synonyms are: *zusagen, reizen* (see 'charm'). *Der Posten reizt mich nicht.*
[2] To draw one's attention to: *jdn. auf etwas aufmerksam machen.*

Sein Gesichtsausdruck fiel mir auf, ließ mich aufmerken.
Als ich vorbeiging, wurde ich plötzlich auf seinen Gesichtsausdruck aufmerksam.

AVOID 1. Clearly distinguished uses of *meiden* and *vermeiden.*

(a) **Meiden** is normally used in the sense of avoiding (i) persons,[1] (ii) places, (iii) a concrete situation which has the effect of a person or place. Its meaning is: to give a wide berth to a person or place.

Ich habe ihn immer gemieden.
Er meidet seine alten Freunde.
Er meidet den Ort, wo er überfallen wurde.
Er hat den Krieg gemieden (only in the sense of the theatre of war, i.e. a place).
Ich habe die Gefahr, die mit diesem Weg verbunden ist, gemieden (I kept away from the place where the danger was).

(b) **Vermeiden** is normally used in the sense of refraining or escaping from doing a thing, the latter being represented by a noun or an infinitive phrase.

Er hat den Fehler diesmal vermieden.
Sie müssen jede Anstrengung, alle Aufregungen, vermeiden, solange Ihr Herz geschwächt ist.
Wir müssen jede Anspielung auf dieses Thema vermeiden.
Dieser Ausdruck wird besser vermieden.
Schweden hat den Krieg vermieden.
Ich vermied es, ihm meine wahre Meinung zu sagen.
Ich habe die Gefahr vermieden, zu viel zu sagen.

2. Cases in which the distinction between *meiden* and *vermeiden* is subtle. The tendency is always to use *vermeiden* in such cases, while even careful speakers prefer it in conversation, since *meiden* is apt to sound precious.

The distinction is that *meiden* stresses the intention, whereas *vermeiden* merely draws attention to the result or indicates an intention without stressing it. *Meiden* therefore suggests more vividly the state of mind of the subject. It is appropriate when emphasizing the urgent need for avoiding a thing or the scruples with which it is avoided. Its intensity sometimes approximates it to 'shun'. A dictionary would say: *dieser Ausdruck wird in guter Sprache gemieden.* When Thomas Mann in *Tristan* uses *meiden* with a verbal noun as object instead of the normal *vermeiden,* the effect is to illuminate the peculiar mind of the subject (Herr Spinell): '*Von da an mied er das Zusammentreffen mit Anton Klöterjahn so weit als*

[1] In conversation *jdm. aus dem Weg gehen* is more common.

tunlich.' This use, i.e. with a verbal noun (or infinitive) as object, should be left to accomplished writers.

Vermeiden can thus be regarded as the normal term for all cases not falling under 1 (*a*) when no particular emphasis is required. Thus: *wir haben dieses Thema vermieden*; but: *wir müssen ein so heikles Thema um jeden Preis meiden.* The use of *vermeiden* with a personal object occurs, but is slovenly. Thus: '*Ich wäre so gern einmal mit ihm grob geworden, aber man konnte nicht dazu kommen. So vermied ich ihn lieber, obwohl er mich zu suchen schien*' (*Theater*, Hermann Bahr).[1] In the following sentence from *Die Brüder Lautensack* by Feuchtwanger *meiden* would have been more vivid, since the author is obviously describing the intention and attitude of mind of the subject. '*Proell, nachdenklich, mühte sich, den Blick des anderen zu vermeiden, versuchte, skeptisch zu lächeln.*' Further examples are:

Meiden Sie unter allen Umständen dieses Thema.
Wenn Sie es machen können, vermeiden Sie dieses Thema.
Ich meide diese Verpflichtung.
Ich vermeide alle Verpflichtungen.
Meiden Sie Alkohol.
Der Arzt sagte mir, soweit ich kann, soll ich Alkohol vermeiden.
'*...und es schien, als ob er nicht nur die undelikaten Äußerungen tiefer und feierlicher Gefühle, sondern auch die Gefühle selbst fürchtete und mied .*' (Thomas Mann, *Buddenbrooks.*)

BAD, EVIL, WICKED

The adverb 'badly' presents difficulties of translation since some of the German terms are not used adverbially in all senses corresponding to their adjectival use.

1. **Schlecht:** lacking positive quality, failing to conform to a standard deemed proper or desirable, without value, therefore actually, not potentially, bad (see *schlimm*). The deficiency may manifest itself in any sphere: moral, intellectual, aesthetic, material, physical, practical. The judgment made is purely objective (contrast the other terms).

It also translates 'poor' with reference to quality. The distinction between 'bad' and 'poor' used in this sense can be rendered in German only by a circumlocution (e.g. a poor, a bad, performance). Applied to food and drink it means poor in quality unless the particular food or

[1] Examples of *vermeiden* with a personal object do occur, particularly in older German. '*Er schien...sie* (=her) *absichtlich zu vermeiden.*' '*Er vermied mich mit sichtlicher Angst und Beklemmung*' (both examples from E. T. A. Hoffmann's *Die Elixiere des Teufels*). '*Ich vermied meine Freundin und begrüßte sie kaum*' (Mörike, *Lucie Gelmeroth*).

drink excludes this meaning (*ein schlechtes Ei* = a bad, rotten egg). 'Bad' in this case can only be translated by *schlecht werden* (to be, go bad) or some specific term (e.g. *das Fleisch ist ein bißchen angegangen*).

'Bad for' in the sense of 'harmful for' can be translated by *schlecht für*.

Applied to persons it means bad in character, corrupt, depraved. It does not mean 'naughty'.

It is used in impersonal phrases with reference to health, economic circumstances, general conditions.

It can be used adverbially in all senses corresponding to its adjectival use. A special adverbial use is the sense of 'hardly', 'not very well' (e.g. *ich kann heute schlecht kommen*).

Ein schlechter Mensch (*Mann* means 'husband'), *ein schlechter Kerl, ein schlechtes Kind* (in all three examples: bad in character), *ein schlechter Lehrer* (inefficient), *ein schlechter Präsident* (lacking the qualities necessary in a president), *ein schlechtes Buch* (worthless as a piece of writing, but not corrupting), *ein schlechtes Gedicht, ein schlechter Geruch, schlechter Geschmack, eine schlechte Gewohnheit* (not necessarily injurious), *eine schlechte Zensur, ein schlechter Einfluß* (only injurious by implication, i.e. because of the attraction of *Einfluß*), *ein schlechter Ruf, schlechte Absichten, ein schlechter Scherz, ein schlechtes Ergebnis* (indicating a poor performance), *ein schlechtes Gewissen, schlechte Aussichten, schlechte Nachrichten, eine schlechte Lage, schlechte Zeiten, eine schlechte Laune, schlechte Wege, ein schlechtes Deutsch, ein schlechter Lügner* (not clever), *eine schlechte Gesichtsfarbe, schlechtes Wetter, ein schlechtes Gewitter* (only in the sense of a poor representation of a storm on the stage), *schlechtes Fleisch* (poor), *schlechter Stoff* (poor), *schlechte Qualität.*

Das Fleisch ist schlecht geworden.

Es war schlecht von Ihnen, mich hinters Licht zu führen.

Zu viel Rauchen ist schlecht für Sie.

Es ist schlecht für sie, allein zu leben.

Er spricht schlecht, er arbeitet schlecht, er hat schlecht geschlafen, er hat sie schlecht behandelt, er denkt schlecht von ihnen.

Es geht ihm gesundheitlich, geschäftlich, schlecht; es steht schlecht mit seinen Plänen; mir wurde schlecht bei dem Gedanken.

2. **Schlimm** differs from *schlecht* in being less definite in its reference to the objective fact, person or thing, and in expressing subjective feeling about a fact. In its objective reference it means 'bad in effects', i.e. not that a person or thing is bad in himself or itself, lacks quality. Its indefiniteness is that it fluctuates between actually and potentially bad effects. *Eine schlechte Lage* is one that is definitely and actually bad as

it is and suggests no possibility of change. *Eine schlimme Lage*, while not excluding actual badness, expresses a feeling that the situation has not yet finally crystallized and may develop, in the sense of becoming either worse or better. In its suggestion of a possible development *schlimm* approximates closely to 'serious' (e.g. *eine schlimme Verwundung*).

It is used mainly with words which either mean or imply effects.

The emotional participation of the speaker expressed by *schlimm* manifests itself in various ways, e.g. as emphasis or familiarity. When applied to nouns which can also be qualified by *schlecht*, this characteristic of *schlimm* becomes strikingly clear in that the whole phrase betrays subjective feeling. In the following examples the tone of each is different, that of the first objective, detached, that of the second revealing the emotional impression made by the object: (*a*) *Wegen seines schlechten Rufes ist er nicht gewählt worden.* (*b*) *Halten Sie sich lieber fern von ihr, sie hat ja einen ganz schlimmen Ruf. Schlecht* would be possible in the last example, though with a change of tone. *Schlimm*, however, would be out of place in the first.

Another consequence of the subjective character of *schlimm* is that it is not necessarily as objectively serious as *schlecht*, though it is more so than *arg* and *übel*, and hence does not indicate as high a degree of objective badness. *Sein Einfluß ist schlecht gewesen* is a more definite statement than *sein Einfluß ist schlimm gewesen*, which may mean no more than that his influence has led to a few follies.

It follows, furthermore, from the emotional connotation of *schlimm* that it cannot qualify nouns denoting a person unless these themselves also possess this character. Thus, while it cannot be combined with *Mensch*, it is possible to say: *du bist mir aber ein ganz schlimmes Bürschchen, ein schlimmer Patron.*

On the other hand the subjective colouring is present to a less extent when it qualifies nouns which do not admit the idea of quality, but merely point to an actual or possible result or development (*schlimme Folgen, ein schlimmes Zeichen, ein schlimmer Unfall*).

Schlimm can be applied attributively but not predicatively, to an affected part of the body in the sense of 'sore' (see also *böse*).

As an adverb *schlimm* is practically restricted to a few fixed phrases: *die Sache steht schlimm; schlimm dran sein* (*schlimm* being in both cases as much adjectival as adverbial); *er ist schlimm zugerichtet; ihm ist schlimm mitgespielt worden.*

Schlimm occurs regionally in expressions which are not standard German. Thus: *es geht mir schlimm, ich habe ihn schlimm ausgezankt, schlimm krank.*

The following examples are divided into two classes: (*a*) those in which *schlimm*, not *schlecht* must be used; (*b*) those in which the noun could also be qualified by *schlecht*, if other necessary changes of tone are also made.

(*a*) *Wir haben eine schlimme Niederlage erlitten.*
Der Schaden ist schlimm.
Er hat einen schlimmen Anfall von Rheumatismus gehabt.
Das war ein schlimmer Fehler.
Das ist ein schlimmer Biß.
Er hat einen schlimmen Verstoß gegen das Anstandsgefühl begangen.
Wir haben ein sehr schlimmes Gewitter gehabt (can suggest damage).
Seine Schmerzen sind heute ganz schlimm.
Das Schlimmste ist, daß er sich seiner Taktlosigkeit garnicht bewußt ist.
Ich befürchte das Schlimmste.
Es wird schlimm für Sie sein, wenn Sie dabei ertappt werden.
Ich habe einen schlimmen Finger.

(*b*) *Das sind ja schlimme Aussichten.*
Die Nachrichten werden immer schlimmer.
Wir haben schlimme Zeiten durchgemacht.
Er ist in einer ganz schlimmen Lage.
Ich weiß nicht, was die Kerle wollen, aber sie kommen ja sicher mit schlimmen Absichten.
Ach, eine schlimme Gewohnheit ist das!
Ich habe schlimme Erfahrungen mit ihm gemacht.

3. **Arg** suggests that the object to which it is applied strikes the eye because its 'badness' is great in extent, amount. It conveys no precise knowledge of the objective fact, but merely this impression of extent. *Der Schaden war sehr arg* is a statement which clearly illustrates this point. At the same time *arg* expresses the emotional participation of the speaker in the fact. This is not very strong, and despite the extent of the 'badness' does not view this as seriously as *schlimm* does. It can, e.g., suggest a show of sympathy, which may or may not be sincere, or a reproach which is friendly in tone. It differs, therefore, from *schlimm* (i) by telling still less about the objective fact, (ii) by expressing weaker feeling about the fact.

While certain uses of *arg* are common throughout Germany, others are regional (particularly in southern Germany and Austria). Some of these regional uses were once more widespread, but are now old-fashioned, often biblical. In general, *arg* may be used freely when applied to evils, less so, it is true, as an adverb than an adjective (see paragraph below) and less with persons, their thoughts, feelings, and the like than with nouns denoting purely objective evils. Thus *Der Arge* (the devil), *ein arger Schelm*, *arge Gedanken* have an old-fashioned flavour, though *ein arger Lügner* (arrant, outrageous), *ein arger Spötter, ein arger Opiumraucher* are still said in all parts of the country. The person designated by this type of noun is an agent, the meaning of *arg* being that he indulges in the activity to an enormous extent. Examples of objective evils are: *eine arge Niederlage, ein arges Mißverständnis.*

As an adverb *arg* is still more restricted to dialect and old-fashioned diction. This is exclusively so when it modifies an adjective. *Arg hungrig, arg schön,* even *arg saudumm* belong to everyday speech in the southwest. With verbs the position is so complicated that it is impossible to draw a clear line of demarcation between standard and dialectal use. The following explanation describes nothing more than a tendency. The most prevalent standard use of *arg* is to refer to a state or the effects of an action. In other words, it is found less where great activity or a clear act on the part of a person is suggested. Thus, it is avoided with transitive verbs in the active voice, if these denote one clear act performed by a person, since they draw attention from the result to the act and the subject. For example: *er wurde arg verwundet, beschädigt; der Schuss* (i.e. a non-personal subject) *hat ihn arg verwundet* (but not in translating 'I wounded him badly'). On the other hand the active voice is used with verbs which do not imply one clear act (e.g. *ich habe ihn arg zugerichtet*). With intransitive verbs: *er lügt sehr arg, er hat arg gelitten* (a state).

Since *arg* suggests something large, it is more used as an adverb with such verbs as *verwundet, beschädigt,* than with, e.g., *gebissen.*

In dialect *arg* is used in any combination: *der Hund hat mich arg gebissen, er singt sehr arg.*[1]

The following are examples of the use of *arg* in standard German:

Er hat arge Kopfschmerzen.
Die Schmerzen sind heute sehr arg.
Es besteht ein arger Mangel an Nahrungsmitteln.
Sie haben sehr arge Fehler gemacht.
Das war ein arges Mißverständnis.
Die Niederlage war arg.
Das ist doch zu arg (that's the limit).
Er hat mit seinen Planungsversuchen arge Verwirrung angerichtet.
Die Kälte, die Hitze, ist heute sehr arg.
Er ist ein arger Säufer (*schwer* is, however, more common).
Er wurde arg geprügelt.
Das Buch ist arg zerlesen.
Man hat ihm arg mitgespielt.
Man hat ihn arg zugerichtet.

[1] The following use of *arg* in Goethe's *Werthers Leiden* is old-fashioned: *das ist die Sünde, die ich ärger hasse am Menschen als alle andere.*

Das hat uns arg durcheinandergebracht.
Wir haben uns arg in ihm getäuscht.
Der Sturm hat das Haus arg beschädigt.

4. **Übel** expresses an emotional dislike; particularly with reference to what is offensive to the senses, but mostly points to no objective characteristic on the person or thing that is rejected. In a few cases it does, however, vaguely suggest unsavouriness in a criminal sense (e.g. *ein übler Patron, Geselle*). 'Nasty'[1] is often a more appropriate English equivalent than 'bad'.

Since it makes no objective statement, its range of application is almost unlimited (both adjectivally and adverbially).

Nicht übel is used like 'not bad' in the sense of 'pretty good'.

Übel corresponds to 'evil' only in the colloquial use of the latter, i.e. in the normal sense of *übel* as described above. Its range of application in an objective sense was greater in earlier German.

Ein übler Bursche, ein übles Buch, ein übler Geschmack, üble Nachrichten.
Das Ergebnis war ganz übel.
Der Film war garnicht übel.
Er ist übel daran.
Mir wurde übel dabei.
Ich gönne ihm Übles.

5. **Böse** translates both 'wicked' and 'evil' in a moral sense. It is also used of ills that afflict one. When applied (attributively) to a sore part of the body it is stronger than *schlimm* and suggests inflammation. Of illness it means 'malignant' (cf. *bösartig*). In all uses it is highly active in its literal sense of 'doing harm', or at least 'willing harm', and in some transferred senses (e.g. menacing).

Ein böser Mensch, Charakter.
Der Böse (the devil).
Eine böse Zunge, eine böse Tat, ein böser Lügner, böse Gedanken, ein böser Einfluß, böse Absichten, ein böses Gewissen, eine böse Krankheit, böse Nachrichten, böse Tage, böse Zeiten, ein böser Finger, ein böses Auge.

6. The adverb.

Owing to the restricted adverbial use of *schlimm* and *arg* other terms must be used. Recourse must often be had to the much used word *schwer* (grievously, gravely, seriously, severely), which, however, is somewhat stronger and more precise than 'badly' (e.g. *er ist schwer operiert worden* = he has had a bad operation; *er ist schwer gestürzt* = he fell badly).

Garstig, nasty, is applied only to what is offensive to the senses.

BAD

Some of the terms in common use are somewhat colloquial. *Tüchtig* so used verges on the conversational. Examples: *Der Wind hat mich tüchtig zerzaust.* See footnote to 'severe' (p. 315, n. 4(*b*)). Another term: *er ist in seinem Examen restlos durchgefallen.*

BEAR Sense: to sustain, endure.

1. **Tragen** is 'to bear' in a general way anything conceived as a burden, to accept it. A strain on the feelings is not necessarily implied. The object generally denotes in itself a burden. *Tragen* is therefore inapplicable in a sentence such as: I cannot bear his voice. In older German it was sometimes used in the sense of *ertragen.*

Sie müssen die Verantwortung dafür tragen.
Die Transportkosten müssen von Ihnen getragen werden.
Sie trug ihr Schicksal ohne zu klagen.
Er hat den Verlust zu tragen (financially).
'*Er trug ihre Unarten mit Geduld*' (Goethe, *Das Märchen*) (only *ertragen* is possible in ordinary present-day prose).

2. **Ertragen** stresses the patience and perseverance with which particularly trying evils are borne. Its object need not in itself denote a burden.

Er ertrug seine Leiden, seinen Verlust, sein Schicksal, sehr tapfer.
Ich konnte seine Stimme, die Hitze, nicht länger ertragen.

3. **Vertragen** means 'to be able to bear', to take, a thing, because it is compatible with our physical, mental or emotional constitution. It suggests less ability to bear a thing at any particular moment than as a general characteristic of our make-up.[1]

Er verträgt keine Kritik.
Nicht alle Wahrheiten vertragen eine objektive Analyse.
Er verträgt keinen Spass.

BEAT, THRASH **Prügeln** means in the first place 'to administer corporal punishment' with a stick or a cane, then with one's hands, fists, and the like. Reflexively, it means 'to fight', particularly of boys. **Verprügeln** draws attention to the result, i.e. the damage.

Der Vater prügelte seinen Sohn.
Er verprügelte ihn nach Strich und Faden.
Sie haben sich geprügelt.
Sie haben sich schrecklich verprügelt.

[1] *Vertragen* often needs to be translated by other English terms. See article on 'take'. *Mein Magen verträgt keine Pfannengerichte* (fried foods do not agree with me). See 'agree'. *Sich mit jemandem vertragen*: to get on with a person.

BEFORE (conjunctive) **Bevor** is the general term. **Ehe** should only be used to express emotional participation, often with a sense of urgency which suggests that the moment for action is fast passing, or as a warning.[1]

Bevor wir landeten, wurde unser Gepäck von einem Zollbeamten durchsucht.
Ehe er es verhindern konnte, war er gefangen.

BEHAVE, BEHAVIOUR, CONDUCT[2] None of the German terms has as wide a range of application as 'behave' and 'behaviour', which can be used of persons, animals, and things. In reference to persons it can, e.g., be conscious or unconscious, instinctive or volitional or the result of training. It is used of persons and animals as a psychological, of substances as a scientific, term.

1. **Benehmen** and the verb *sich benehmen* refer to the behaviour of individuals considered as free human beings in society. In so far as a standard is implied, it is that of common human decency or of good manners in society. (*Er hat kein Benehmen* = he has no manners.) Since the reference to the individual human being is so strong, these terms are not applied to large units (e.g. a country) or to official behaviour.

Sein Benehmen ist gut, schlecht, höflich, haarsträubend.
Sein Benehmen läßt viel zu wünschen übrig.
Er hat sich mir gegenüber sehr freundlich benommen.
Der Kerl benimmt sich sehr komisch.

2. **Betragen** and the verb *sich betragen* refer to special codes, rules, and prescriptions in much the same way as 'conduct'. Like the latter they carry a strong implication of moral responsibility and therefore of consciousness of one's acts. They can therefore only be applied to human beings.

Der Junge hat sich in der Schule schlecht betragen.

3. **Sich aufführen,** accompanied by an adverb of manner, refers to the impression one makes, the figure one cuts, in doing a thing. It suggests something unusual and has a subjective connotation. It requires some more expressive adverb than *gut*.

Er hat sich blödsinnig, tadellos, aufgeführt.
Die Soldaten haben sich schlecht aufgeführt.

[1] In conversation both *bevor* and *ehe* are often avoided and replaced by other suitable conjunctions, e.g. *als*, followed by *schon* in the next clause. *Als sie heraufkam, hatte sie schon sauber gemacht.*

[2] Deportment, bearing, i.e. as a result of discipline, is *Haltung*. See further under 'attitude'.

4. **Verhalten** and the verb *sich verhalten* can denote conscious or unconscious behaviour under given conditions. It is therefore used as a psychological term in reference to individuals or animals, a scientific term when applied to substances (i.e. in the sense of 'reaction'). It is also the appropriate term when the element stressed in behaviour is the taking of an attitude[1] (e.g. in relation to a country, a government).

Unter diesen Bedingungen verhält sich der Mensch ganz passiv.
Rußlands Verhalten in der Angelegenheit war unverständlich.

BELIEF 1. Both **Glaube** and 'belief' can refer to (*a*) trust in a person, in God, in a thing; (*b*) mental, and partly emotional acceptance of a thing as true; (*c*) the thing believed, i.e. the content of the action or state of belief. 'Belief' is, however, a wider term than *Glaube*. The latter implies more complete acceptance and a greater absence of evidence based on the senses and on reason than 'belief' necessarily does. This becomes particularly clear when it is followed by a *daß* clause (particularly in the expression *im Glauben, daß . . .*). A higher degree of credulity is implied than is always implied by 'belief'. *Glaube* thus approaches the absoluteness of faith. Like 'faith' it admits no plural.[2,3]

Mein Glaube an ihn, an Gott, an die Güte der menschlichen Natur, ist unerschütterlich, ist erschüttert.
Sein Glaube, daß Gott ihm helfen würde, hat ihn nie verlassen.
Sein Glaube, daß alle gegen ihn sind, ist typisch für seinen jetzigen Geisteszustand.
Er handelte im Glauben, daß er mir damit helfen würde.
Das ist mein Glaube.
Er ist bereit, für seinen Glauben zu kämpfen.

2. When 'belief' is a close synonym of 'opinion', 'conviction', 'supposition', and the like, i.e. when it implies limited credence or does not exclude recourse to evidence, it must be translated by terms such as *Meinung, Überzeugung, Annahme.* Similarly, it must be rendered by *Vertrauen* in the sense of 'trust in a person' when some consideration by the mind, particularly in the form of doubts, is implied. See article on 'trust'.

Ich neige zu der Ansicht, daß die Aufgabe unsere Kräfte übersteigt.
Es ist meine Überzeugung, daß ein dritter Weltkrieg nicht unvermeidlich ist.

[1] For a fuller explanation of *Verhalten* see 'attitude'.
[2] *Glauben* as a verb does not exclude the examination of evidence. See article on 'think'.
[3] In the English equivalents of phrases such as *im guten Glauben, auf Treu und Glauben,* 'faith' is also used.

Seine Annahme, daß die verschärften Maßnahmen ruhig hingenommen würden, erwies sich als falsch.
So viel ich weiß, hat er das Angebot angenommen.

BELONG 1. **Gehören** (plus dative) denotes possession.

Das Buch gehört der Staatsbibliothek.
Der Hut gehört mir.
Neu-Kaledonien gehört Frankreich.

2. **Angehören:** to be a member of society or to be a unit in a group.

Er gehört einem Musikverein an.
Welchem Jahrhundert gehört Klopstock an?
Dieses Buch gehört meiner Bibliothek an.
Er gehört dem Jahrgang 1920 *an.*

3. **Gehören** (plus *zu*) approximates to *angehören* in the sense of 'to be a part of', but means a necessary, integral part of a whole.[1]

Der Teil (des Buches) gehört zum Ganzen.
Dieses Glas gehört zu meiner Uhr.
Die Worte gehören zu diesem Lied.
Elsaß gehört jetzt zu Frankreich.
Die baltischen Staaten gehören zur russischen Interessensphäre (also *angehören* in the sense of being a member).

4. **Gehören** (plus *in*) is used to indicate the place where a person or a thing belongs, its proper place, and, in extended use, the category in which he or it is to be classified. It may be followed in the same way by other prepositions (e.g. *auf*, *unter*, *vor*).

Dieses Buch gehört in die Staatsbibliothek.
Er gehört in diese Menschenklasse.

BEND, BOW, STOOP, INCLINE 1. **Biegen:** to bend an object in any direction. Intransitively, it is applied to an object that changes its direction (e.g. a road). It draws attention to the curve or angle.

Er bog den Draht, das Eisen.
Der Nagel ist gebogen.
Der Mast, der Zweig, biegt sich im Winde.
Mein Arm ist so steif, daß ich ihn nicht biegen kann.
Er saß mit gebogenem Rücken da.
Die Straße biegt hier nach rechts (ab).

[1] *Gehören zu* is also used in the sense of 'to be one of'. *Er gehört zu den Besten in der Klasse.* It is also used in the sense of 'to be required for'. *Es gehört Mut dazu.*

2. **Bücken** is the general term for 'to stoop' or 'to bend down or over'. It is mostly reflexive and conveys implications such as stooping to pick something up or to pass through a low opening. The past participle is also used in the sense of 'stooped', both literally and figuratively (i.e. by age, cares, or the like).

Er bückte sich, um einen Bleistift aufzuheben, um in den Wagen einzusteigen, um vom feindlichen Feuer nicht getroffen zu werden.

Er ist vom Alter, Kummer, gebückt (bent, stooped).

3. **Beugen** means 'to bend downwards', generally through the effect of something weighty (literally and figuratively). Reverence or submission may be implied. It thus translates 'to bow' or 'to bend' some part of the body as an expression of an emotional attitude. Reflexively, it means 'to bow' in the sense of 'to submit' to some greater power, but not as a salutation.

Der Zweig war unter der Last der Früchte gebeugt (bent downwards; *gebogen* would merely emphasize that it was not straight, and would not necessarily suggest weight).

Er beugte das Haupt, als er die traurige Nachricht vernahm.

Er ist vom Kummer tief gebeugt.

Er muß sich vor dem Schicksal beugen.

4. **Verbeugen** is only used reflexively and is the general term for 'to bow' as a salutation.[1]

Er verbeugte sich, als er vorgestellt wurde.

5. **Neigen** suggests, applied to persons, liking or favour or a sign of understanding; applied to things, a weight, which is, however, less heavy than in the case of *beugen*, i.e. 'to incline'.[2]

Sich verneigen means 'to bow' as a salutation, but is a less general term than *sich verbeugen*, and suggests ceremony. *Sich neigen* in the sense of a salutation does not suggest a deep bow.

Sie neigte das Haupt, um ihm ihre Huld zu bezeigen.

Die Bäume neigten ihre Äste.

Er neigte sich vor dem Fremden.

Er verneigte sich auf galante Art.

BLAME,[3] CENSURE 1. To judge a person or thing as deserving condemnation. This sense implies that the question of who or what is

[1] *Knicksen*: to curtsy.

[2] *Neigen* is used in general of anything that inclines or declines gradually. *Die Strasse neigt sich hier zur Stadt* (slopes).

[3] *Blamieren*, a much used term in conversation, mainly reflexive, does not mean 'to blame', but 'to put in the wrong', often in such a way that one feels small or foolish before others. *Er hat sich gewaltig blamiert. Er möchte sich nicht blamieren.* Similarly the noun: *das war eine furchtbare Blamage.*

responsible for an act or state of affairs is already settled, and that the only issue is whether this deserves condemnation.

(a) **Tadeln** means 'to censure', i.e. 'to pronounce an adverse judgment on' (*S.O.D.*). It can only translate 'blame' in contexts which do not imply the actual utterance of such a judgment, i.e. in those which are concerned with the question of whether one should pronounce a judgment of censure (e.g. in combination with *nicht können*). In all its uses *tadeln* is sharper than 'blame'.

Ich tadelte ihn wegen seines Leichtsinns.
Ich kann ihn nicht wegen des Unfalls tadeln (the accident was caused by him, but the circumstances were not such as to justify my speaking words of censure; i.e. I cannot blame him for...).
Er ist wegen des Fiaskos nicht zu tadeln.

(b) **Jemandem einen Vorwurf machen aus**. This expression is the closest equivalent to the sense of 'blame' defined in **1**. It occurs mainly in negative use. *Vorwurf* in this combination does not necessarily imply a spoken reproach.

Ich kann ihm aus dem Unfall keinen Vorwurf machen.
Ich machte ihm keinen Vorwurf aus dem, was er tat.
Ich habe mir nichts vorzuwerfen (I have nothing to blame myself for).

(c) **Übelnehmen, verübeln, verargen.** These terms used with *nicht können* suggest a measure of understanding for what has been done.

Man kann es ihr nicht verübeln, daß sie ihn verließ.

2. To fix the responsibility for something done, to put the blame on the proper shoulders. Here it is a question of determining who or what has caused something of which one disapproves.

(a) **Verantwortlich machen für.** This phrase often tends to suggest an interest in compensation.

Ich kann ihn für den Unfall nicht verantwortlich machen (someone or something else caused it).
Sie müssen das Wetter, nicht mich dafür verantwortlich machen.

(b) **Schuld sein an:** to be to blame for. In accusing directly (i.e. in the second person) the person judged responsible this expression is often preferable to *verantwortlich machen*, since the latter emphasizes too much the position of the accuser.

Sie sind schuld an dem Unfall (you are to blame...; I blame you...).

BLIND, DAZZLE **1. Blind machen** is generally used in the figurative sense of robbing a person of control over his emotions, thoughts, actions, but not in the senses described under *blenden* and *verblenden*. Its use in the literal sense, which is rare, and somewhat slovenly can only denote a process, i.e. not a sudden action.

Die Leidenschaft hat ihn blind gemacht.
Seine Interessen machten ihn den Tatsachen gegenüber blind.

2. **Blenden:** to dazzle through the eye, both literally and figuratively. 'Blind' used as an equivalent of 'dazzle' is similarly translated. Further, it means 'to blind deliberately' in the literal sense.

Die Sonne blendet mich.
Von dem Aufwand des Festes geblendet, gab er dem Geschäftsinhaber weiteren Kredit.
Die Gestapoagenten blendeten ihre Opfer.

3. **Verblenden:** to blind or dazzle by putting into a trance-like state approaching madness. Romantic characters are often portrayed as being in the grip of such states.

Von den Gewinnaussichten verblendet, stürzte er sich in ein Geschäft, das nie und nimmer gut gehen konnte.
Verblendet folgte er seinem Schicksal bis ans Ende.

4. **Erblinden** is an intransitive verb which means 'to go blind'. Sentences, in which 'blind' is used transitively, are best turned by this verb or *blind werden* (see *blind machen* under 1).

Er ist als Folge der Explosion erblindet, blind geworden.

BLOCK This article deals with 'block' only in so far as it is translated by *sperren* and *versperren*.

1. **Sperren** is 'to block', literally and figuratively, by official action. It is often rendered into English by 'shut'[1] or 'stop'.

Die Straße ist gesperrt (by a chain, rope, or the like).
Mein Bankkonto ist gesperrt.

2. **Versperren:** to block the passage of a person by standing or placing an obstacle in front of him or by an obstacle placed there without human agency; also to block a view.

Ich stand vor ihm und versperrte ihm auf diese Weise den Durchgang.
Die Straße ist durch Felsblöcke versperrt.
Die Bäume versperren uns die Aussicht.

[1] *Sperren* can also mean 'to close' or 'to shut' a building or the like, officially or unofficially and 'to lock' a person or thing in a place. To lock up, i.e. imprison: *einsperren*.

BODY Körper: 'body' as opposed to 'mind'. It therefore refers to matter and is applied as an anatomical term to the body of living beings, also to any thing considered as an entity (e.g. a planet). In further use it suggests a visible surface and shape. Therefore: *Körperpflege*; *körperliche Züchtigung*; *ein schöner, verwachsener, Körper*. It excludes any implication of human feelings, sentiments and life in its non-physical aspects. It is **Leib** which conveys this suggestion and is conceived as the vessel of the soul. Being informed with the latter, it is used in the expression *der Leib des Herrn*. Further, in such compounds as *Leibarzt, Leibgarde, Leibstandarte*, which stress life in its human rather than its physiological aspect. *Leib*, however, is sometimes used vaguely in a physiological sense, particularly in the phrase *am ganzen Leibe* (=all over).[1] *Er zitterte, schwitzte, am ganzen Leibe*. Where, on the other hand, the reference is to something visible on the surface, *Körper* is the correct term. *Er hat rote Flecken am ganzen Körper. Er ist wund am ganzen Körper.*

A 'dead body' must be translated by *Leiche* (see 'corpse').

BOTHER, TROUBLE, CONCERN ONESELF ABOUT, LOOK AFTER, SEE TO These terms are treated only as far as they are translated by the two German words discussed in this article.

Kümmern is in present-day German used almost exclusively as a reflexive verb, and means 'to do something' for a person or about a thing. **Bekümmern** is not limited to reflexive use. When used reflexively, it implies activity like *kümmern*, but suggests more feeling and is therefore stronger. In non-reflexive use it means 'to trouble', 'to distress', 'to concern'.

Sie müssen sich ein bißchen um ihn kümmern.
Er hat sich in rührender Weise um seinen jüngeren Bruder gekümmert.
Kümmere dich darum, daß die beiden Briefe morgen auf die Post kommen.
Sie gingen nach Hause, ohne daß sich jemand um das Boot kümmerte.
Sein Schicksal bekümmert mich.
'*Seit er in Dresden in den Gemälden der Galerie schwelgte, beneidet er jeden Künstler, den kein Zweifel um das Wahre, das sich nirgends findet, bekümmere, sondern der im Glauben an die Idealwelt des Schönen lebe*' (J. Petersen on Kleist, *Aus der Goethezeit*).

BOY[2] The German terms rarely refer to a male adult.

1. **Knabe** is applied to a boy up to the age of puberty. In poetry it can

[1] Similarly in phrases not translated by 'body': *eine Wut im Leibe haben*; *etwas am eigenen Leibe spüren*. *Leib* forms numerous fixed phrases.

[2] *Bube* is a 'lad' in so far as he is inclined to mischievous tricks. In the southern dialects *Bub*' is often used simply for *Knabe*. *Bursche* excludes childhood, and suggests vigour and an enterprising spirit.

denote a youth (normally *Jüngling*). It is an objective, not a familiar term. It is occasionally used somewhat ironically to refer to an adult, generally by a still older man. Used otherwise it has a suggestion of the poetical.

Sie haben zwei Knaben und drei Mädchen.
Er ist kaum den Knabenjahren entwachsen.
Eine Knabenschule.
Ist der Knabe Schmidt wieder hier gewesen? (ironically).
'*...jetzt kam Tell mit seinem Knaben über den Platz gegangen*' (G. Keller, *Der Grüne Heinrich*).

2. **Junge** may be used up to the age of seventeen or eighteen. It is a more familiar term than *Knabe* and may also mean 'son'. In the plural (the form without '*s*') it can mean 'sons' up to the age of twenty-two or twenty-three. *Die blauen Jungs*[1] refers to sailors. In compounds it denotes a boy who performs menial tasks.

Er ist ein netter Junge.
Mein Junge, du mußt fleißiger arbeiten!
Seine beiden Jungen sind im Kriege gefallen.

BRAIN **Gehirn** is a more dignified expression than **Hirn** and is the usual term in the sense of 'mind'. The latter is used particularly of animals, in compounds, and with a derogatory connotation. Many idiomatic expressions formed with 'brain' are translated by other terms.

Das Gehirn des Menschen wiegt so und so viel.
Sein Gehirn arbeitete sehr schnell.
Wir haben Schafhirn gegessen.
Er ist hirnverbrannt.

BREAK **A.** Literal.

1. *Brechen* and its compounds are used only of solid objects.[2]

(a) **Brechen,** transitive and intransitive, is applied to clean breaks, division into parts, fractures of parts of the body.

Er hat sich das Bein, den Arm, den Hals, gebrochen.
Die Mutter brach die Schokolade in drei Stücke und gab den Kindern je eines.
Er brach das Eis.
Er brach das Siegel.
Der Wind hat den Ast gebrochen.
Das Brett, der Zweig, brach, als zu viele Menschen sich darauf setzten.
Der Wind war so stark, daß der Mast brach.

[1] In parts of northern Germany (e.g. in the Hanseatic towns) *die Jungs* has the meaning of 'the kids'. [2] *Eine Blume brechen*: to pluck a flower.

(b) **Zerbrechen,** transitive and intransitive, means 'to break into two or more pieces' (i.e. smash into fragments) in such a way that the object becomes useless. Similarly **zerschlagen** (only transitive).

Ich habe das Glas zerbrochen, als ich die Uhr abnahm.
Ich ließ das Bild fallen und dabei zerbrach das Glas.
Er hat die Fensterscheibe zerschlagen.

(c) **Abbrechen** should be used when the breaking off of a tip of a thing is implied.[1] The object may be the thing broken, not merely the part broken off.

Ich habe meinen Bleistift, mir den Zahn, den Schlüssel, den Rand des Tellers, abgebrochen.

2. *Reißen* and its compounds are applied to non-solid objects which can tear.

Reißen: (intransitive and passive with *sein*) 'have a tear', implies tension, to snap, therefore not with paper unless there is pressure from inside. **Zerreißen:** (transitive and intransitive) to tear, to snap, into two or more pieces.

Das Papier, in das die Schuhe gewickelt sind, ist zerrissen.
Der Schnürriemen zerriß, riß, ist zerrissen, gerissen.
Der Film riß, zerriß, dauernd.
Das Seil ist gerissen, zerrissen.
Das Seil riß, zerriß. (The latter implies great force.)

3. **Umknicken:** to break anything pliable such as a plant.

Sie haben diese Pflanze umgeknickt, als Sie dagegen stießen.

4. **Platzen:** to burst from within.[2]

Ich habe so viel in die Tüte gesteckt, daß sie geplatzt ist.
Das Wasserrohr, der Asphalt, ist geplatzt.

5. Specific terms are: **aufschlagen:** to break an egg in order to fry it, etc.; **springen:** to break (of a spring), e.g. *die Feder ist gesprungen.*[3]

[1] Other compounds of *brechen* are: *aufbrechen, erbrechen* (to break open); *einbrechen in* (to break, force one's way into a place); *durchbrechen* (inseparable: to penetrate a line; separable: to break a thing into two parts); *herausbrechen* (to knock a piece out; e.g. *ein Stück ist aus dem Glas herausgebrochen*); *losbrechen* (of a storm); *unterbrechen* (to interrupt; e.g. *die ununterbrochenen Ebenen Norddeutschlands*).

[2] *Platzen* is 'to explode from within', often with a detonation. *Bersten* is used mainly of large natural objects and is mostly poetical (e.g. *die geborstene Erde*).

[3] *Gesprungen* often means 'cracked' (of a glass, etc.).

6. **Kaputt,** used mostly predicatively, means 'broken' in the vague, colloquial sense of the term, specially of machines and gadgets.

Der Federhalter, die Tür, ist kaputt.
Das Auto, Radio, Feuerzeug, ist kaputt.
Das Kind hat die Spielsachen kaputt gemacht.

B. Figurative. **Brechen** is used in the following ways:

(a) To violate one's plighted word.
Sein Versprechen, Wort, brechen.

(b) To vanquish, subdue opposition.
Jemandes Willen, Widerstand, brechen.

(c) To crush by misfortune.
Er ist ein gebrochener Mann.

(d) Of the heart.
Es hat sein Herz gebrochen.

(e) To end.
Das Schweigen, einen Zauber, brechen.

(f) To emerge (often with *hervor*).
Der Mond brach aus den Wolken hervor.

(g) To change.
Die Stimme bricht (from boyhood to adolescence).

BROAD, WIDE (literal sense) The subtle distinctions which certain uses of the English words possess (though often obliterated in common speech) are not present in *breit* and *weit*, which are easily distinguishable from each other. See Fowler's explanation of 'broad' and 'wide' in *Modern English Usage.*

1. **Breit** is applied to the horizontal extent of a surface with regard to its length, whether (*a*) the exact measurement is stated, or (*b*) simply a large extent is meant. It translates in this sense both 'broad' and 'wide'. Its opposite is *schmal* (narrow).[1]

Die Gasse ist nur 5 Meter breit (broad or wide).
Eine breite Straße, ein breiter Fluß ('wide' draws attention to the limits, 'broad' concentrates attention on the surface itself and also makes an appeal to the eye).
Ein breites Gesicht, breite Schultern.

[1] In figurative use *breit* means 'diffuse'.

2. **Weit** corresponds to 'wide' in the sense of 'spacious', 'expansive', i.e. in all directions. As in the case of 'wide' one thinks of the remote limits more than of what lies between. Its opposite is *eng*, i.e. narrow in the sense of cramped, constricted on all sides, whereas *schmal* is narrow between two straight lines.[1]

Ein weiter Raum, eine weite Fläche, die weite Welt, ein weiter Abstand, eine weite Öffnung, ein weites Loch, weite Schuhe, Hosen, Ärmel, ein weit offenes Fenster.

BURN A. Brennen.

1. Intransitive.

(a) To be on fire, whether due to accident or design.

Das Haus, die Scheune, das Bettzeug, brennt.

(b) Of the means of heating and lighting.

Die Sonne, das Feuer, die Lampe, das Gas brennt.

2. Transitive.

(a) To use for fuel or to keep a lighting apparatus burning, i.e. with reference to the type, but not the quantity, of fuel used.

Wir brennen nur Holz in unserem Ofen.
Sie brennt die ganze Nacht eine Kerze.

(b) To treat, to process, certain substances with fire (not to burn them up).

Kohlen, Lehm, Holz, Ziegel brennen.

(c) When an adverb or a prefix is used to indicate the result *brennen* must be used.

Das Haus wurde niedergebrannt (*leergebrannt*).

(d) Similarly to bring about by burning:

Ein Loch in das Brett, ein Zeichen in das Holz brennen.

B. Verbrennen.

1. To burn up, consume, destroy, incinerate.

(a) Of persons and things.

Im Mittelalter wurden Hexen verbrannt.
Die Abfälle müssen verbrannt werden.
Das Haus wurde vom Feinde verbrannt.

[1] *Weit* also means 'far' in a relative sense (e.g. *wie weit ist die Stadt noch von hier?*). *Fern* is 'far' in an absolute sense. In a few phrases 'wide' means 'far' (e.g. *weitgefehlt*: wide of, far from, the mark).

(b) In stating the amount, but not the type, of fuel, etc. burnt.

Wir verbrennen jede Woche 5 Säcke Holz.

2. To burn on the surface, an external agency as subject (contrast *brennen* 1 (b)).

Die Sonne, der heiße Teller, hat mich arg verbrannt.

3. To burn and injure a part of the body.

Ich habe mir den Finger verbrannt.
Ich bin gegen den Ofen gestolpert und habe mich verbrannt.

C. With reference to the spoiling of food **anbrennen** (to begin to burn, to catch fire; i.e. inceptive force) is much used, either intransitively or in the passive voice. The transitive use of 'burn' in this sense is translated by *anbrennen lassen*, or by otherwise turning the phrase so as to use *anbrennen* intransitively.

Die Suppe brennt an.
Die Suppe ist angebrannt.
Die Köchin ließ die Suppe anbrennen.
Passen Sie auf, daß die Suppe nicht anbrennt (be careful not to burn...).

BURY 1. **Beerdigen** is the normal term for burying a person in the earth with proper funeral rites.

Er wurde am 15. Mai auf dem protestantischen Friedhof beerdigt.

2. **Bestatten** stresses the ceremonial of burial. It can be burial in any form, e.g. cremation, not necessarily consignment to the earth.

Er wurde in einem Mausoleum bestattet.

3. **Beisetzen:** to bury in a vault by the side of one's family or ancestor. Also: to bury at sea.

Er wurde in der Familiengruft beigesetzt.
Auf hoher See beigesetzt.

4. **Begraben:** to bury in a pit, sometimes without ceremony, and therefore of animals and objects as well as persons. With reference to objects it may mean 'to bury' under anything, often with a suggestion of disorderliness. Used figuratively it means 'to renounce'.

Er wurde bei lebendigem Leibe, lebendig, begraben.
Der Hund wurde im Garten begraben.
Ich fand das Buch unter einem Haufen alter Zeitungen begraben.
Wir haben das Kriegsbeil begraben.
Wir mußten unsere Hoffnungen begraben.

5. **Vergraben** is in present-day German often used in the figurative sense of hiding, withdrawing from view, often with the suggestion of immersing oneself in an occupation.

Sie vergrub ihr Gesicht in den Händen.
Nach dem Skandal mußte er sich für zwei Jahre auf dem Lande vergraben.
Für 14 Tage vergrub er sich in seinem Arbeitszimmer.

6. **Einscharren:** to cover slightly or carelessly.

Der Hund scharrte den Knochen ein.

BUSY 1. **Beschäftigt sein,**[1] **zu tun haben.** *Beschäftigt* is more intense and more specific than *zu tun haben* which is mostly used in reference to small matters which make it impossible for one to devote one's attention to other things. *Beschäftigt* can only be used predicatively after the verb *sein* and in reference to a person. *Vielbeschäftigt* may be used attributively before a noun standing for a person.

Ich kann Sie heute nicht sehen, ich habe zu tun.
Ich habe so viel zu tun, daß ich nicht ausgehen kann.
Der Kanzler ist mit Finanzfragen beschäftigt.
Er ist ein vielbeschäftigter Mann.

2. 'To keep busy' may be translated by the following phrases: *Zeit in Anspruch nehmen* (time element stressed); *zu schaffen machen* (cause trouble); *eine ziemliche Lauferei verursachen* (colloquial in the sense of 'to keep on the move').

Die vielen Sitzungen nehmen meine Zeit sehr stark in Anspruch. (*In Anspruch nehmen* with a personal object suggests: to take toll of.)
Die Beschaffung einer Einreiseerlaubnis nach Deutschland hat ihm viel zu schaffen gemacht.
Die Reisevorbereitungen haben mir eine ziemliche Lauferei verursacht.

3. In reference to places and periods of time specific terms must be used. *Belebt* is frequently applied to places.

Sie wohnen in einer sehr belebten Straße.
Ich habe einen gehetzten Tag hinter mir.
Am Donnerstag gibt es immer eine schreckliche Hetze (colloquial: Thursday is always a frightfully busy day).

[1] *Geschäftig* is strictly speaking not 'busy', but suggests the fussiness of small folk. *Er hat eine außerordentlich geschäftige Art.* The verb *schaffen* (weak form) is used with indefinite pronoun objects such as *viel, nichts* in the sense of 'to get through' work. *Ich habe heute nichts, nicht sehr viel, geschafft.*

CALCULATE, RECKON Sense: to compute.

1. **Rechnen** means 'to perform a mathematical computation', and often states the result in numerical terms, this being the only possible type of object. The manner of calculation is not suggested.[1]

Er rechnet schnell.
Genau gerechnet, schulden Sie ihm 98 *Mark.*
Ich rechne 10 *Mark für die Reisekosten.*

2. **Ausrechnen** suggests a simple calculation on the basis of concrete material which one has before one.[2]

Ich habe noch nicht ausgerechnet, wieviel ich ihm schulde.
Ich habe mir schon ausgerechnet, wie viel ich verdienen würde, wenn ich meine Möbel verkaufe.
Ich rechne mir aus, daß wir noch 5 *Kilometer gehen müssen.* (On the basis of given facts, therefore, the sentence tends to express exactness of conclusion, whereas: *Ich rechne, daß wir noch...* expresses more a guess.)

3. **Errechnen** can suggest a new discovery by calculation, often by a stroke of genius. It sometimes implies that the method of arriving at the result is puzzling or mysterious. Again, it can present the result as a mere possibility.

Einstein hat errechnet, daß das Licht keiner graden Linie folgt.
Wie ist diese Zahl errechnet worden?
Er errechnete die Kurve der Rakete.

4. **Berechnen** differs from *rechnen* in having as its object the thing whose measurements or the like are to be calculated. In this it resembles *ausrechnen* and *errechnen*. It can be used in place of these, but without their special implications. It is the appropriate term whenever purpose or the adaptation of means to ends is stressed. In transferred use it is therefore applied to a person who is calculating by temperament.[3]

Ich werde den Umfang des Dreiecks berechnen.
Er berechnete die Kurve der Rakete.
Der Astronom berechnete den Abstand der Planeten voneinander.

[1] Other senses of *rechnen* translated by 'calculate', 'reckon' and also 'count' are: (*a*) to expect, be prepared for (e.g. *wir rechnen mit einer Niederlage*); (*b*) to rely on (e.g *ich rechne darauf, daß du bald zu uns kommst*). *Rechnen zu:* to reckon among, as one of.

[2] The past participle *ausgerechnet* is used idiomatically to denote surprise or good-humoured resignation. *Er mußte ausgerechnet Dienstag kommen* (Tuesday of all days). *Ausgerechnet er hat es gesagt* (he of all people).

[3] *Berechnen* is also used for 'reckon' in the sense of 'charge'. *Der Lieferant berechnet extra für die Transportkosten.*

Haben Sie auch berechnet, daß Sie neben den Anschaffungskosten noch erhebliche Extraausgaben haben werden?
In der Kalkulationsabteilung werden die Herstellungskosten berechnet.
Er ist sehr berechnend.

CALL,[1] SUMMON, NAME 1. **Rufen** in all literal uses means 'to produce a sound' loudly enough for it to carry some distance. It may be used of persons or things, most frequently with the implication of conveying a message, an order or a summons.[2] These suggestions are present in all figurative uses (e.g. *die Pflicht ruft*; *Gott rief ihn zu sich*). 'To call to a person' can only be **zurufen.**

Wer ruft da?
Der Wächter, der Kuckuck ruft.
Die Glocke ruft zum Unterricht.
Die Mutter rief die Kinder zu sich, zum Essen.
Er rief mich ins Nebenzimmer.
Er rief um Hilfe.
Er rief nach einem Glase Bier.
Die Heimat ruft.
Er rief mir die Zeit zu.
Er rief mir zu, ich solle nicht weitergehen.

2. **Berufen** means (*a*) to call to an exalted position[3] (see 'appoint'); (*b*) to summon a person to a place, i.e. an order given by a superior to an inferior.

Er wurde auf den Thron, ins Außenministerium, berufen.
Der Minister berief seinen Sekretär in sein Arbeitszimmer (summoned; does not imply use of the voice).

3. Other compounds of *rufen.*[4]

(a) When 'call' is an abbreviation for 'call in', 'call to one', 'summon', for use, consultation and the like, **herbeirufen** must be used.

Er rief das Taxi, den Arzt, herbei.

[1] For the senses 'to visit', 'to stop', see the dictionaries.
[2] Thus in the sense of 'to wake' in the morning only *wecken* can be used, since raising of the voice is not implied.
[3] *Berufen*, used adjectivally, means 'inwardly qualified'. *Er war der berufene Mann für den Posten.*
[4] *Anrufen* must be used in the sense of 'to telephone'. It also means 'to call upon', 'to invoke', 'to appeal to', particularly in reference to an authority. *Aufrufen* in the sense of 'to call upon' refers to an exhortation to action and is followed by *zu*. *Er rief den Schutz des Gesetzes an. Er rief das Volk zu größeren Anstrengungen auf.*

(b) **Einberufen:** (1) to call, convene, a meeting;[1] (2) to call up for military service, i.e. as an administrative act, *rufen* in phrases such as *zu den Fahnen rufen* being emotional.

Der Reichstag, eine Sitzung, wurde einberufen.
Alle wehrfähigen jungen Männer wurden zum Heer einberufen.

4. In the sense of (*a*) 'to name so-and-so'; (*b*) 'to describe or characterize as' (*P.O.D.*), **nennen** is the general term. **Benennen** means 'to give a thing a distinguishing name' which establishes its character, particularly, though not exclusively, one based on a principle of classification. Thus it can only mean 'to name for the first time', but not 'to name' in the sense of 'to mention'.[2] **Heißen**, used transitively in the sense of 'call', always implies emotional participation in the statement made, and is therefore most common in exclamations. It also means 'to be called' in reference to the name of a person or thing.

Er nennt sich einen Philosophen.
Ich nannte ihn einen Lügner (or *hieß*, with emotional emphasis).
Das nenne ich eine Gemeinheit.
Das heiß' ich aber fest schlafen!
Er wurde nach seinem Vater genannt.
Der Botaniker wußte nicht, wie er die neue Pflanze benennen sollte.
Wenn wir den Geist der Sturm-und-Drang-Bewegung benennen wollen, so halten wir uns am besten an Goethes Wort: 'Gefühl ist alles.'

CARE, CAREFUL, CAUTIOUS **A**. The words treated in this section cannot be used to translate 'take care' and 'be careful' followed by an infinitive or a 'that' clause.

1. **Sorgfältig:** painstaking in doing a thing in order to do it well. It lacks the negative sense of 'cautious' which 'careful' also has. Since it refers to the doing of a thing, it occurs chiefly as an adverb, or as an adjective applied to a thing done, a piece of work. It is not common with nouns which denote persons, being attached in this case mainly to those which denote workers of some kind (often ending in *er*), and to the word *Mensch*. *Sorgfältig* cannot be used to translate 'to be careful with'.

Ein sorgfältiger Mensch, Arbeiter, Lehrer.
Er ist nicht sehr sorgfältig bei der Wahl seiner Worte.
Das ist eine sorgfältige Übersetzung, Abschrift.
Sie müssen die Sache einer sorgfältigen Prüfung unterziehen.

[1] *Zusammenberufen*: to call together, either in reference to a committee or the like, or its members. *Ich werde sie im geeigneten Augenblick zusammenberufen.*
[2] To change a name can only be *umbenennen*. *Die Straße ist umbenannt worden.*

Der Plan ist sehr sorgfältig ausgedacht.
Er hat es sehr sorgfältig nachgezeichnet.
Er schreibt sehr sorgfältig.
Er kleidet sich sehr sorgfältig.

2. **Sorgsam:** solicitous, i.e. in reference to a state of mind, and particularly a permanent attitude which prompts action.

Eine sorgsame Mutter.

3. With nouns (but not verbs) which refer to the arts and imply an aesthetic effect *sorgfältig* is not used. The idea must be expressed variously in German.

Ein um Präzision im Ausdruck bemühter (ein auf...bedachter) Schriftsteller.
Ein gepflegter Stil.

4. **Vorsichtig:** cautious; i.e. careful in its negative sense of refraining from doing certain things because one foresees the danger with which they are attended.

Ein vorsichtiger Mensch.
Er ist immer vorsichtig in seinen Meinungsäußerungen.
Seien Sie vorsichtig, Sie können leicht rutschen.
Seien Sie vorsichtig mit dem Gewehr.
Das war eine vorsichtige Antwort.
Er ging sehr vorsichtig zu Werke.

5. **Behutsam** means 'cautious', but refers exclusively to action, never to the thought behind it. It cannot therefore be applied adjectivally to persons.

Er trat behutsam ins Zimmer.

B. To be careful, to take care; followed by an infinitive or clause.

1. **Aufpassen** is the most general term and is appropriate in all but elevated or very serious contexts.

Ich passe immer auf, den Termin nicht zu versäumen.
Sie paßt immer auf, daß es genug im Hause zu essen gibt.
Sie müssen aufpassen, daß Sie mich rechtzeitig benachrichtigen.
Er paßt nicht immer auf, was für eine Wirkung seine Worte haben.
Ich passe immer auf, das, was er sagt, aufzuschreiben.

2. **Achten auf** suggests a higher degree of attention than *aufpassen*, but is by no means strong. It is used particularly in the imperative to impress instructions on a person.

Achten Sie darauf, daß die Kinder gute Manieren haben.
Achten Sie darauf, daß Sie das Paket heute noch abschicken.
Ich achte darauf, mich regelmäßig bei der Polizei zu melden.

3. **Acht geben auf** is stronger than *achten*, and implies a warning, i.e. watch, lest something untoward should happen.

Sie müssen acht geben, daß man Sie nicht übervorteilt.
Geben Sie acht darauf, daß die Kinder sich nicht anstecken.
Er gibt acht darauf, daß er nicht in schlechte Gesellschaft gerät.

4. **Sich in acht nehmen** is used when the following infinitive or clause contains a negative (i.e. to take care not to...). *Nicht* is more correctly omitted, but sometimes inserted. It suggests a warning of a danger.

Nehmen Sie sich in acht, daß Sie ihm nichts Wichtiges mitteilen.
Nimm dich in acht vor ihm. (The phrase need not be split.)

5. Other expressions which can be used in this sense are: *sich hüten* (to beware; with omission of the negative before the following infinitive); *dafür sorgen* (to make arrangements, provision); *zusehen* (to see to it that...); *Sorge tragen* (emphatic, final, apt to be biblical in tone).

Ich werde mich schön hüten, mich da sehen zu lassen (I'll take good care not to...).
Er sorgt immer dafür, daß Wein im Hause ist.
Sehen Sie nur zu, daß Sie die Gelegenheit nicht versäumen.
Sie müssen dafür Sorge tragen, daß er den Eid leistet.

C. The words treated in **B** and also *vorsichtig* may be followed freely by prepositional phrases.

Seien Sie vorsichtig mit den Gläsern, Sie können sie leicht zerbrechen.
Geben Sie acht auf Ihre Gesundheit, Temperatur, Verdauung.
Nehmen Sie sich mit Ihrer Gesundheit in acht.
Nehmen Sie sich vor dem Hund in acht.

CATCH 'Catch' has both the active sense of 'pursue and seize' and the passive of 'receive' or 'be subjected to' something.

1. **Fangen:** to get into one's power, either by a trap,[1] which may be a net and the like, or by laying hold of a thing by the hand, the mouth, etc. These images are present in all figurative uses.

Unsere Katze ist zu alt, um noch Mäuse zu fangen.
Wir haben viele Fische mit dem Netz, aber keine mit der Angelschnur gefangen.

Fangen also translates 'to trap'.

Viertausend Mann wurden vom Feind gefangen genommen.
Der Hund fing das ihm zugeworfene Fleisch mit dem Maul.
Er hat den Ball gefangen.
Dieser Verbrecher hat sich in seinen eigenen Schlingen gefangen.

2. **Auffangen:** to intercept a thing in the air, mostly something falling from above, in order to prevent it falling further or hitting something else.

Er stürzte die Treppe herunter, und im letzten Augenblick habe ich ihn aufgefangen.
Er fing den Koffer auf, der eben zum Fenster herausgefallen war.
Ich fing das Buch auf, das er mir zuwarf.
Er stellte eine Tonne heraus, um den Regen aufzufangen.

3. **Erwischen:** to catch in the nick of time, i.e. someone or something that is about to elude one. This element is always stressed.

Die Polizei hat den Verbrecher am Bahnhof erwischt.
Ich habe den Briefträger gerade noch erwischt, als ich von zuhause wegging.

4. For 'catch' in the sense of 'seize and retain one's grip on' a thing (e.g. I caught him by the scruff of the neck) see 'seize'.

5. **Einholen:** to catch up, overtake.

Können Sie das andere Auto noch einholen?

6. **Erreichen:** to reach in time (of means of transport), when it is a question of whether one will arrive in time.[1]

Ich habe den Zug nicht erreicht.

7. **Überraschen:** to surprise, descend upon, envelop, of an evil. (See footnote to 'wonder', p. 402, n. 2.)

Sie wurden vom Regen, von der Flut, von einem Luftangriff überrascht.

8. **Ertappen:** to come unawares upon a person who is in the act of doing something, in the sense of 'catch out', 'detect'. The construction used is: *dabei, wie...* (*auf* also with noun).[2]

Er hat ihn auf frischer Tat ertappt.
Ich habe ihn dabei ertappt, wie er das Geld nahm.

9. To become entangled, stuck. The commonest German terms are **hängen bleiben** (*in, an, auf, etwas*), the literal sense of 'hanging' being

[1] When the intention of catching a certain train (boat, etc.) is emphasized, but not the question of whether one will be in time for it or not, *fahren mit* must be used. *Ich möchte mit dem 6 Uhr Zug fahren.*

[2] *Betreffen bei* is used in the same sense, but is less common.

preserved, and **stecken bleiben** (*in etwas*), i.e. to get stuck.[1] English says either 'her dress caught in the barbed wire' (i.e. intransitively) or 'she caught her dress in the barbed wire', with practically identical meaning. In German only the intransitive form is possible, and where it is a question of a person, a part of him or of his clothing, the person is made the subject of the sentence, the part caught being expressed by a phrase with *mit*. To make the part the subject would suggest that the part is separated from the whole person.

Sie blieb mit ihrem Kleid am Stacheldraht, an einem Nagel, hängen.
Er stürzte vom Dach, blieb jedoch in den Ästen eines Baumes hängen.
Das Auto blieb im Schlamm stecken.
Das Boot blieb auf dem Grund stecken.
Ich bin mit der Hand in der Flasche stecken geblieben.[2]
Die Gräte blieb ihm im Hals stecken.

10. **Zu spüren bekommen:** to be subjected to, to suffer with reference to something violent. See 'feel'.

Das Schiff bekam die ganze Wut des Sturms zu spüren.
Du wirst seinen Zorn zu spüren bekommen.

11. **Treffen:** to hit. For *treffen* see also **13**.

Die Kanonenkugel traf das Flugzeug in der Mitte.
Er traf ihn auf die Schläfe.

12. **Sich holen** is said of a contagious sickness (see 'get').

Er hat sich die Masern geholt.

13. **Treffen:** to catch atmosphere, tone and the like, in reference to art.

In diesem Gedicht hat er den echt lyrischen Ton getroffen.
Shakespeare hat die Atmosphäre einer Sommernacht wunderbar getroffen.
Die Ähnlichkeit ist sehr gut getroffen.

14. **Einfangen** is only correctly used in reference to art in the sense of catching a number of scattered, elusive impressions and unifying them.[3]

Er hat alles eingefangen, was in der Luft lag, und es dann im Gedicht in wunderbarer Weise wiedergegeben.

[1] Where the idea of remaining is not stressed, these expressions are inapplicable (e.g. *er ist zwischen zwei Züge geraten*).

[2] None of these expressions are appropriate in the first person, present indicative, to tell others that one is caught. In this case verbs with *fest* are common. *Meine Hand ist zwischen zwei Stühlen festgeklemmt.*

[3] *Einfangen* also means 'to corner and catch' an animal, bird, etc.

15. **Heraushören:** to be receptive to a tone and the like, in reference to art, i.e. from the point of view of the listener, beholder, not of the creator.

Sie haben den Ton der impressionistischen Lyrik ganz richtig herausgehört.

16. **Verstehen:** to catch the meaning of something said. It also translates 'hear' used to state that one has not caught a remark. In this sense *hören* is not used alone, but coupled with some adverb such as *richtig*.

Ich habe Ihre Bemerkung nicht ganz verstanden (nicht richtig gehört).

17. **Verfangen** is used in several ways.

(a) Intransitively in the sense of 'prove effective', 'catch on', 'interest'.

Diese Tricks verfangen nicht mehr bei uns.
Ihre Tränen verfangen nicht mehr bei ihm.

(b) Reflexively in the sense of being caught in an enclosed space, of wind and the like (French: *s'engouffrer*).

Der Wind hat sich im Schornstein verfangen.

18. **Einschnappen:** of locks, bolts, etc.

19. Catch and make one's own, in reference to someone else's habits, style, mannerisms, etc. This sense can often be rendered by verbs with the prefix *ab* (*ablernen, abgucken, abhören, ablauschen*).

Er hat Heine diesen Ton abgelauscht (caught from).

CHANGE, EXCHANGE, ALTER, TRANSFORM Only *umändern* and *wandeln* and its compounds can normally be followed by *in* (to change into, turn into).

1. **Ändern** is the most general term. It must be used in the sense of 'to change a part' of a whole, 'to make a small change', i.e. 'to alter', and is frequently used in the sense of 'to change a whole', 'to make radical changes'. It is the most usual term in reference to a deliberate or a sudden change, but can also, chiefly in reflexive use, be applied to unconscious changes of nature, particularly in so far as they are sudden (see *verändern*). It is used of external acts, inner movements of feeling and thought, changes of external nature.

Ändern Sie dieses Wort in Ihrem Aufsatz.
Die Tatsache ist nicht mehr zu ändern.
Sie hat ihr Kleid geändert (either made alterations to details or changed it as a whole).

Sie haben ihre Pläne, die Gesetze, ihre Meinungen geändert.
Er hat sich in letzter Zeit geändert (in his conscious self, i.e. his views, conduct, rather than in physical appearance).
Der Volkscharakter hat sich geändert.
Das Wetter hat sich geändert.

2. **Verändern** is mostly used to denote the result of an unconscious process of change in human or external nature. In this sense it occurs mainly as a reflexive or in the passive voice. Used otherwise, it mostly means 'to change' more or less involuntarily something about one's person. It is also, though less frequently, used in reference to the changing of things external to the self, particularly something broad, e.g. the appearance of a whole town. *Sich ändern* = change character or attitude; *sich verändern*: in appearance.

Er sieht verändert aus.
Als ich nach 20 Jahren zurückkehrte, fand ich die Stadt vollkommen verändert.
Der Nationalcharakter hat sich in den letzten 100 Jahren langsam verändert.
Nach dem Krieg haben sich die Machtverhältnisse in Europa stark verändert.
Er verändert den Ton, die Stellung, den Gesichtsausdruck.
Sie haben ihre Wohnung von Grund auf verändert.
Umstände verändern die Sache.
'*...den Fluß der Zeit, welcher vieles...fortwährend verändert*' (Th. Mann, *Dr. Faustus*).

3. **Abändern:** to change the inner structure of a thing, particularly with reference to the text of a document (not isolated words), and to a system.

Wir müssen die Bestimmungen abändern.
Das Prüfungssystem ist abgeändert worden.
Der Plan muß abgeändert werden.

4. **Umändern:** to rearrange the parts so that something new is formed. It may be followed by *in*.

Er hat das Haus in eine kleine Fabrik umgeändert.

5. **Wechseln:** to give, substitute one thing for another of the same kind, whether tangible or intangible, and for the same purpose, often discarding the old. It can translate 'exchange' in a few cases. It is used particularly of money and means 'to substitute' the same value in smaller coins, but not, in correct use, in another currency.

Ich habe mein Geld gewechselt.
Ich muß meine Kleider wechseln.
Er wechselte die Pferde.
Er wechselte sein Zimmer.
Er wechselte seine Pläne.
Er wechselte seine Ansichten.
Er wechselte den Text des Liedes.
Er wechselte seine Diät.
Sie wechselten Blicke.
Sie wechselten Plätze, Ringe, Briefe.

6. **Tauschen:** to exchange one thing for another, which need not be of the same kind or for the same purpose. It therefore translates 'barter' in a commercial sense. While *wechseln* involves two things but not necessarily two persons, *tauschen* emphasizes the latter and the equality of the exchange. It is used where intimate feelings are implied. The sense of discarding the old is excluded. It is impossible, therefore, with a word such as *Ansichten.*

Sie tauschten Münzen.
Er tauschte ein Pferd gegen drei Schweine.
Sie tauschten die Pferde.
Ich muß meine Kleider tauschen.
Sie tauschten ihre Rollen.
Sie tauschten Plätze (exchanged, whereas *wechselten* could mean simply that they went to other seats, not necessarily an interchange).
Sie tauschten Ringe, Blicke, Küsse (*wechseln* impossible with *Küsse*).

7 **Austauschen** emphasizes the equality of the exchange, a mutual give and take. It is therefore the correct term in reference to free association such as social or diplomatic intercourse. The object may be persons, things or ideas.

Die beiden Länder haben ihre Minderheiten ausgetauscht.
Die Universitäten tauschen Professoren aus.
Sie tauschen Briefmarken aus (more on a friendly than on a strictly commercial basis).
Sie saßen stundenlang da und tauschten Erfahrungen, Ansichten aus.

8. **Auswechseln** means (*a*) in technical things, to take out an old and put in a new part; (*b*) to change people from one sphere to another. It is not a dignified term, and so cannot be used in reference to ideas.

Der Fahrer wechselte den Reifen aus.
Die Gefangenen wurden ausgewechselt.

9. **Umtauschen:** to return goods one has bought to the seller and receive others of the same kind, the original purchase not being what is desired; and more generally, to exchange a thing for another thing one wants more.

Ich muß das Buch, die Schuhe, mein Geld, umtauschen.
Ich habe mein altes Radio gegen ein neues umgetauscht.

10. **Eintauschen:** to trade in one thing for another, which can but need not be of the same kind. (*Der Bauer hat seine Pferde gegen einen Traktor eingetauscht.*) **Einwechseln:** to change money of one currency for that of another. (*Belgische Franken in englische Pfunde einwechseln.*)

11. **Wandeln,**[1] mostly reflexive, denotes an inner change of nature, a transformation (compare *verändern*). It can be followed by *in*. In itself it does not indicate the extent of the change.

In den letzten 10 Jahren hat sich sehr viel gewandelt.
Seine Anschauungen haben sich gewandelt.
Seine Liebe hat sich in Haß gewandelt.

12. **Verwandeln**[2] indicates a complete and, generally, a quick change (not necessarily a change of nature). It can therefore suggest magic, or, in reference to the real world, that the result is unrecognizable. It can be followed by *in*.

Der Krieg hat die Landschaft in eine Wüste verwandelt.
Ich erkenne ihn nicht mehr, er ist wie verwandelt.
Sie wurde in eine Hexe verwandelt.
Seine schauspielerische Begabung ist so groß, daß er sich in fast jeden Menschentyp verwandeln kann.

13. **Umwandeln:**[3] to transform one thing into another. It is used only of things of considerable size, and almost exclusively of deliberate actions (i.e. not of changes of nature). It is followed by *in*.

Ich habe den Blumengarten in einen Gemüsegarten umgewandelt.
Das Haus wurde in eine kleine Fabrik umgewandelt (stresses the completeness of the change, while *umändern* suggests a rearrangement of parts).

CHARM, APPEAL 1. In the sense of a spell which radiates from a person and produces a harmonious and soothing effect, the only German

[1] The noun *Wandel* refers to change as a general phenomenon of life. (*Überall sieht man Wandel. In den letzten Jahren ist ein grundlegender Wandel im politischen Leben der Völker eingetreten.*)

[2] *Vertauschen* and *verwechseln* mean 'to mistake for', 'to confuse' one thing with another. *Vertauschen* is actually 'to take the wrong' thing (e.g. *sie haben ihre Hüte vertauscht*), *verwechseln* 'to confuse mentally' (e.g. *ich habe die beiden Brüder verwechselt; ich verwechselte die beiden Geldsorten*).

[3] To change, turn one thing into another in reference to small things: *machen aus* (e.g. *aus den Fleischresten machte ich eine Pastete*). 'Turn into', with reference to big things, also must be translated in the same way as 'change into'.

equivalent is **Scharm**. When a thing produces charm of this kind, **Zauber** may be used. **Reiz** suggests a strong stimulation of the senses, accompanied not by a feeling of harmony, but by desire. It corresponds more closely to 'appeal'.[1]

Er, sie, hat Scharm.
Die Musik, die Landschaft, übt einen sanften Zauber auf mich aus.
Sie hat einen unwiderstehlichen Reiz für ihn.

2. The verb *reizen* means 'to appeal to', 'to attract' or 'to tempt' by rousing desire, rather than 'to charm'.[2] To charm painful feelings: *lindern* (=assuage). In other uses of 'charm', synonyms must be used: e.g. *bezaubern* (=enchant).[3]

Ihre Figur reizt ihn sehr.
Der Posten reizt mich.
Die Schönheit der Landschaft, die ihn umgab, linderte seinen Kummer.
Die Landschaft hat mich bezaubert.

3. The adjective 'charming' can be rendered by *scharmant* in the sense defined in section 1. *Reizend* is, however, used more widely and loosely than *Reiz*, and does not suggest desire as strongly as the latter. It does not exclude the feeling of harmony, though it does not emphasize it. It is mostly applied to small, graceful things.

Sie ist reizend, eine reizende Frau.
Das Buch, die Musik, die Landschaft, ist reizend.

CHEEK **Wange** differs from **Backe** (sometimes *der Backen*) in two ways. (1) It refers only to the part of the face immediately beneath the eyes and extending downwards as far as the nose reaches. Further, it denotes only the visible external side of the flesh. *Backe* extends to the ears and downwards to the jaw (*Kinnbacken*=jaw) besides referring to the inside of the mouth. (2) *Backe* is the term in ordinary use, *Wange* being a more elevated and poetical term, though both are applied to young children. In technology, e.g. the cheek of a vice, *Backe* is always used.

Er hat rote Backen, blühende Wangen.
Ich gab ihm einen Backenstreich.

[1] *Anmut* and *anmutig* refer to 'grace' of form or manner, particularly in reference to movement. Thus *ein anmutiges Gedicht* suggests its formal qualities as harmonious movement. *Ein anmutiges Bild* is one which reveals this quality in its lines.

[2] *Reizen* also means 'to provoke', 'to irritate' (see 'angry'), particularly with a personal subject. *Sie reizt ihn ständig.*

[3] *Zaubern* means 'to practise magic, work charms'. *Bezaubern* is 'to enchant' in the sense of 'charm, delight', but not so as to rob of all will-power. *Verzaubern* denotes an absolute state, to cast over a person a spell which robs him of his consciousness of everything else. It suggests a trance. The distinction between *behexen* and *verhexen* is similar, i.e. to bewitch.

CHEEK

Er hat dem Mädchen die Wangen gestreichelt.
Er hat dem Kinde die Wangen (die Backen) gestreichelt.
Der alte Herr hat rote Bäckchen.

CHOICE, SELECTION **Wahl** is the act of choosing, while **Auswahl** refers to the things or persons chosen.

Die Wahl eines Berufs ist manchmal schwer.
Eine Auswahl der besten lyrischen Gedichte.

CHOOSE, SELECT[1] 1. **Wählen** stresses the decision involved in the act of choosing. With a personal object it can only mean 'to elect'.

Ich habe gewählt.
Wählen Sie!
Ich habe dieses Sofa, dieses Haus gewählt.
Wir haben dieses Muster gewählt.

2. **Auswählen:** to choose from a considerable number of persons or things. This reference to number must always be clearly implied. With things there is a suggestion that the thing or things selected are taken into the hand or separated from the others for examination. From this it follows that *auswählen* is generally applicable only with such things as can be carried by hand (e.g. a chair, but not a sofa or a house). With persons the implication is that of a careful selection. Intransitive use is, in the light of this explanation, not possible.

Ich habe diese Bücher für die Bibliothek ausgewählt.
Wählen Sie sich eins aus!
Der Präsident hat seine Minister sorgsam ausgewählt.
Hundert Mann wurden für den Angriff ausgewählt.
Ich habe ein schönes Pferd ausgewählt.[2,3]

3. **Sich aussuchen** is used more familiarly without reference to the type of object and without implying a decision which requires discrimination.

Haben Sie sich schon ausgesucht, was Sie essen wollen?
Er hat sich ein paar Leute für die Arbeit ausgesucht.

4. Choose, followed by the infinitive.

(a) If the personal, at times arbitrary, element in 'choose' is strong (to follow one's fancy, to do as one pleases), **belieben** (personal or impersonal)

[1] *Kiesen* and *küren* are now used only in verse or very elevated diction.

[2] The prefix *er*, added to any of the words discussed (and to *lesen*), suggest the value of what is chosen (e.g. *erlesene Pracht*). They are used mainly in the past participle as adjectives.

[3] When *aus* is prefixed to *er*, the sense is 'chosen out of many'. These verbs, too, are mainly used in the past participle (e.g. *das auserwählte Volk*).

may be used as a polite formula, ironically or to indicate an inclination not based on serious reasons.

Nehmen Sie, was Ihnen beliebt.
Ach, Sie belieben zu kommen.
Wenn es Ihnen beliebt, heute zu Hause zu bleiben, so tun Sie das ruhig.

(b) When the act of choosing is preceded by serious consideration **vorziehen** may sometimes be used.[1]

Er zog es vor, von seinem Amte zurückzutreten, als (rather than) *nachzugeben.*

CLAIM When followed by an infinitive or a clause 'claim' can be rendered by **in Anspruch nehmen** only in the sense of 'to assert' something good about oneself. **Für sich** is generally added. In the sense of 'to assert' something about someone else or about a misadventure that has befallen oneself **behaupten** must be used.

Rußland nimmt als einziges europäisches Land für sich in Anspruch, dieses Jahr eine gute Ernte gehabt zu haben; aufrichtig für den Frieden arbeiten zu wollen.
Rußland behauptet, daß Amerika und England einen neuen Krieg vorbereiten.
Er behauptet, sein Leben sei gefährdet.

CLEVER, SKILFUL, SHREWD[2] 1. **Geschickt** refers to dexterity in doing things, particularly with the hands or in handling people. In the latter case a clever manœuvre, a capacity for making quick adjustments, slipping out of difficulties, is suggested. In neither application is it a term of superlative praise. It does not refer to intellectual ability or brilliance.

Er ist geschickt mit seinen Händen.
Er ist geschickt im Zeichnen.
Er ist ein geschickter Arzt, Handwerker.
Der Arzt hat die Operation geschickt ausgeführt.
Das war ein geschicktes Manöver.
Er hat die Verhandlungen sehr geschickt geführt.

[1] *Gewählt* as an adjective means 'choice' and is applied to the use of language (e.g. *ein gewähltes Deutsch*).

[2] The terms discussed in this article must also be used on occasion to translate 'adroit', 'dexterous', 'smart' and the like. None of the English corresponds closely to any of the German terms. *Fix* and *patent* are used colloquially for 'quick', 'bright', 'smart', 'slick', and the like (e.g. *ein fixer Junge, eine fixe Antwort*). *Patent* is applied only to persons.

2. **Gewandt** implies a talent which manifests itself in a form that is neat, elegant and the like. It suggests an impression of artistic skill, particularly in movement. It is a term of higher praise than *geschickt*.

Er ist ein gewandter Redner, Diplomat, Tänzer.
Das war eine gewandte Abwehr.

3. **Klug** suggests clear- and far-sightedness, wisdom, and prudence in action. It is a quality which a diplomat must possess, but may also be ascribed to a child or a dog in the sense of not acting blindly or wildly. It does not refer to pure intellect, but contains something of 'shrewd' (i.e. quick and clear-sighted enough to guess) and 'astute' (wideawake).[1]

Er ist ein kluger Diplomat, Vater.
Er hat klug und besonnen gehandelt.
Es war nicht sehr klug von dir, ihm so viel zu sagen.
Das war eine kluge Antwort.

4. **Gescheit** approaches the meaning of *klug*, but in fine discrimination implies rather shrewdness, a capacity not to allow oneself to be deceived, than skill in action; common sense, solidity of judgment, rather than brilliance. It is a much used term in conversation, and often has a colloquial ring.

Er ist ein gescheiter Kerl, er täuscht sich nie.
Er hat einen gescheiten Bericht über die Lage geschrieben.
Er hat sehr gescheit gehandelt, geantwortet.

5. **Geistreich** refers to brilliance of mind which expresses itself in clever, often witty, sayings or remarks. See footnote to 'mind' (p. 224, n. 4).

Eine geistreiche Komödie, Bemerkung.

6. In the sense of 'talented' none of the above terms can translate 'clever', particularly in the phrase 'to be clever at...'. **Begabt**, gifted, is the most general term. The following examples include other approximations.

Er ist für Mathematik, Sprachen, sehr begabt (clever at).
Er hat eine rasche Auffassungsgabe für Sprachen.
Er ist ein begabter, aufgeweckter, (more colloquially) *heller Junge.*

CLIMB 1. **Klettern** means to climb vertically (upwards or downwards) and suggests difficulty. *(Er)steigen* is simply 'to go up'.

[1] 'Shrewd' and 'astute' lead to the group 'crafty', 'sly', etc., which imply secretiveness. *Schlau* refers particularly to cunning in the execution of designs; *listig* draws attention to the secrecy with which a thing is done; *hinterlistig* suggests mendacity and trickery.

Er kletterte den Baum hinauf, auf den Baum (*den Baum hinauf* suggesting slower progress than *auf den Baum*).
Er kletterte über den Zaun.
Er ist die Leiter heruntergeklettert.

2. **Erklimmen** means 'to scale' great heights.
Sie haben den Gipfel erklommen.

3. **Sich ranken:** to climb along, of plants.
Die Rosen ranken sich am Spalier entlang.

COMFORTABLE, COSY 1. **Bequem** is applied to things and persons. It means 'comfortable' of such things into or on to which the body or part of it fits comfortably. Contact between the thing and the body is implied. It can thus be used of a motor-car, but not of a house.[1]

It is not applied to persons except adverbially in combination with such verbs, as *liegen, sitzen,* which clearly imply the type of object which provides the comfort. 'I am, feel, comfortable' in this sense must therefore be translated by *ich liege, sitze, bequem,* as the case may be. After *sein* with a personal subject *bequem* is impossible in this sense.[2] To make oneself comfortable = *es sich bequem machen.*

It is applied to uncritical mental activity which takes a rosy view of things.

Bequem translates the adverb 'comfortably' in the sense of 'without effort'.

Diese Schuhe, dieser Anzug, dieser Lehnstuhl, der Wagen ist sehr bequem.
Ich liege, sitze, hier sehr bequem.
Machen Sie es sich da bequem.
Eine bequeme Ansicht.
Wir können den Bahnhof bequem in einer halben Stunde erreichen.
Das Haus ist, liegt, bequem.

2. **Behaglich** is applied in the first place to feelings which are compounded of the sensation of mental and physical relaxation and ease and

[1] *Bequem* also translates 'convenient', 'handy' when applied to objects as close synonyms of 'comfortable', i.e. well adapted to the posture or movements of the body or part of it, easy to handle (e.g. *Der Apparat ist sehr bequem zu handhaben. Dieser Koffer ist sehr bequem zu tragen*). In an extended sense it is applied in the expression *bequem liegen* to places in the sense of 'to be conveniently situated, easy to reach'. *Der Ort, das Hotel, liegt sehr bequem.* Also: *eine bequeme Verbindung.* In the above senses *bequem* may be followed by the infinitive. *Es ist sehr bequem, einen solchen Apparat zu besitzen, hier zu wohnen. Unbequem* is much used in the sense of giving bother.

[2] Applied to a person *bequem* does not mean 'comfortable', i.e. easy to get on with, but 'easy-going', i.e. averse to effort (e.g. *ein bequemer Mensch*). In some uses 'comfortable' and 'easy-going' are close synonyms (e.g. *ein bequemes Leben*).

of sensuous well-being (e.g. *ein behagliches Gefühl, ich fühle mich behaglich*). It is then used of such an atmosphere (clearly shown in the impersonal phrase: *es ist behaglich in...*). People who habitually feel in this way and show it in their actions are termed *behaglich*. Finally, it is applied to a few objects of the external world that prompt such sensations and have such an atmosphere about them (e.g. a small room rather than a big house).[1]

Er fühlt sich behaglich: he is, feels, comfortable.

Ein behaglicher Zustand.
Ich fühle mich hier sehr behaglich.
Er führt ein sehr behagliches Leben.
Ich fühle mich sehr behaglich in diesem kleinen Zimmer.
Mein Zimmer ist klein, aber ganz behaglich.
An einem Winterabend sitzt man sehr behaglich am Ofen.

3. **Gemütlich** is applied to feelings not so much of ease and harmony with the world, but rather of friendly intimacy, with a touch of sentiment and at times of imagination. It is a much used term and carries a large number of implications, which cannot all be rendered by any single English word. When applied to things and places it remains untranslatable, but approximates more to 'cosy' than 'comfortable'.

Ein gemütliches Zimmer.
Ein gemütlicher Abend (carries human implications beyond 'cosy').

4. **Angenehm,** pleasant, must often be used for lack of a more precise term. It is wide enough to imply physical comfort, though much more vaguely than 'comfortable' does.

Das Hotel war ganz angenehm.
Das war eine angenehme Reise.

5. **Komfortabel** is only a commercial term used in advertising houses (*ein komfortables Haus*). A similar phrase is *mit allem Komfort der Neuzeit.*

6. **Gut** is used (*a*) of financial circumstances; (*b*) of physical condition in relation to sickness.

Er lebt in guten Verhältnissen.
Er ist gut situiert.
Nach dieser Medizin fühle ich mich viel besser.
Der Patient hat eine gute Nacht gehabt.

[1] *Unbehaglich* has a wider range of application (e.g. *ein unbehagliches Haus*).

7. Other approximately equivalent terms sometimes used are: **glatt** (in the sense of being able to do a thing with a comfortable margin to spare); **leicht** (easy).

Er hat das Examen glatt bestanden.
Sechs Personen gehen glatt in diesen Wagen hinein.
Dieser Wagen kann leicht sechs Personen fassen.

COMMON, GENERAL 1. **Gemein**[1] meant, originally, 'opposed to particular', i.e. common to many, but admitting exceptions. In this sense it is no longer freely used. Numerous fixed expressions, in which it occurs, have, however, survived in common use. These refer mostly to public life, state institutions and the like. It is also commonly applied to words which in themselves denote an evil (e.g. *ein gemeiner Verbrecher*). Its freest use is to denote lack of quality, refinement, but it is in this sense stronger than 'common', approximating more closely to 'vile', 'mean of spirit'.[2]

Fixed phrases are given in dictionaries (e.g. *das gemeine Wohl, Recht*). A sentence such as '*die Lüge ist gemein* (prevalent) *bei ungezogenen Leuten*' (Sanders-Wülfing, *Handwörterbuch der deutschen Sprache*) is no longer normal German. Similarly '*das gemeine Volk*', and '*der gemeine Mann*' have been discarded in favour of '*das einfache Volk*', '*der einfache Mann*'. The form *gemeinhin*, not *gemein*, is used adverbially (e.g. *es wird gemeinhin angenommen*...).

2. **Allgemein** means in the first place 'universal, admitting no exception'. It has, however, come to mean also 'common to most, if not all'. In the emphatic predicative position it only has the former sense. Even in attributive use it should only be used when 'general' could be substituted for 'common', i.e. when the exceptions are negligible, not in the sense of 'widespread'. It is used freely as an adverb.

Das ist die allgemeine Meinung, die allgemeine Erfahrung.
Es ist allgemeines Gerede.
Es ist allgemein bekannt (common knowledge).
Es wird allgemein angenommen, daß der König bald abdanken wird.

3. In the sense of 'prevalent, widespread', but not 'general, almost universal', terms such as the following must be used: **gebräuchlich** (=customary), **üblich** (=usual), **häufig, weit verbreitet, alltäglich**. See footnotes to 'habit' (pp. 156–7).

[1] Only *gemein* amongst the German words forms fixed phrases.
[2] Examples: *eine gemeine Gesinnung*; *gemeine Redensarten*; *eine gemeine Sorte Zigaretten*; *ein gemeiner Kerl*; *das war gemein von Ihnen.*

Es ist eine gebräuchliche Redensart.
Seine Klagen werden allzu häufig.
Solche Leute sind so häufig wie Blaubeeren.
Diese Ansicht ist weit verbreitet.
Es ist eine alltägliche Erfahrung.

4. **Gemeinsam:** shared by two or more, joint, concerted. This term does not express frequency, but the idea of community.

Der gemeinsame Feind.
Unser gemeinsamer Besitz.
Wir haben gemeinsame Interessen.
Es ist ihr gemeinsamer Garten.
Wir müssen gemeinsame Schritte unternehmen.
Sie verfolgen ein gemeinsames Ziel.

5. **Gewöhnlich** and **ordinär** must be used in the sense of 'lacking quality' and 'vulgar'[1] respectively. *Ordinär* is stronger than 'ordinary',[2] which approximates more closely to *gewöhnlich*. *Gemein* is stronger than either term.

Sie ist sehr gewöhnlich, ordinär, in ihrer Sprache.
Es ist eine ganz gewöhnliche Sorte Wein.

COMPLAIN **Sich beschweren:** to make a statement about an offence done to one to the relevant authority. **Sich beklagen:** to give vent to one's feelings of having been wronged, of annoyance, grievance and the like in words spoken to a third party. **Klagen:**[3] to give expression to a grievance, to talk of a bodily ailment, an untoward fate that has overtaken one, but without necessarily implying a reproach to anyone.[4] The complaint may be expressed in wails and lamentations.

Ich habe mich bei der Polizei beschwert.
Er rief den Kellner zu sich und beschwerte sich über das schlechte Essen.
Er hat sich über Sie beschwert.
Er beschwerte sich über den Arzt, daß er nicht kam.
Er hat sich über Sie beklagt.
Der Schüler beklagte sich über die Strafe, die ihm auferlegt wurde.
Er beklagte sich über die schlechte Ernährung.
Er klagt über Kopfschmerzen, die schlechte Ernährung.

[1] *Vulgär* is very little used.
[2] *Alltäglich* also means 'ordinary, undistinguished', but does not mean 'vulgar'. *Ein ganz alltäglicher Mensch.*
[3] *Auf etwas* (e.g. *Schadenersatz*) *klagen*: to sue for damages. See 'accuse'.
[4] With a direct object of the thing accompanying dative of the person *klagen* suggests the 'pouring out' of one's sorrow to a listener (*jdm. sein Leid klagen*).

COMPLETE,[1] PERFECT, ENTIRE The distinctions between *vollkommen, vollständig* and *völlig* are less perceptible in their adverbial than in their adjectival use. This means that while in some contexts it is possible to use two or more as adverbs without radically changing the sense, only one is possible as an adjective. In the sentence given by Duden: *du kannst mit der völligen Wiederherstellung deiner Gesundheit rechnen*, it would be incorrect to use *vollkommen*. Both terms, however, are possible as adverbs. *Deine Gesundheit ist völlig* (or *vollkommen*) *wieder hergestellt.*

In adjectival use the meaning of *vollkommen* and *vollständig* is much more clearly defined in the predicative position, which possesses greater objectivity than the attributive use. *Völlig* is not used predicatively.

1. **Vollkommen** denotes quality and thus corresponds to 'perfect',[2] which tends to be its only meaning in the predicative position, except in cases where 'complete' and 'perfect' are practically interchangeable. In the attributive position the sense of 'perfect' is commonest with nouns which denote objects.

Both in the sense of 'complete' and 'perfect', *vollkommen* indicates an absolute state which the speaker regards as final and which he looks upon with detachment. In other words, it is objective in the attitude it expresses and static in its reference to the objective fact (contrast *völlig*). It concentrates, furthermore, attention on the whole, not on the parts and their individuality (contrast *vollständig*).

Duden in his introduction to the *Stilwörterbuch* censures the widespread use of *vollkommen* where the idea of value is absent, and gives as an example of this undesirable practice: *Das ist vollkommen unnötig.* This use is, however, felt to be less objectionable than the English 'perfect' in the sense of 'complete'.

Er ist ein vollkommener Narr.

Das ist vollkommener Unsinn.

Sein Glück ist vollkommen (perfect or complete; *vollständig* and *völlig* impossible).

Seine vollkommene Unschuld ist klar erwiesen (*vollständig* and *völlig* impossible).

Sie haben im Rahmen der Gesetze vollkommene Freiheit, zu tun, was Sie wollen.

Es war eine vollkommene Niederlage für den Feind.

[1] Study together with 'quite' (see article).

[2] *Vollendet* (=consummate) is a close synonym. *Perfekt* is not used in the full sense of 'perfect', but is applied with some exaggeration to skills, achievements (e.g. *eine Sprache perfekt sprechen*). *Tadellos* is much used in conversation as a term of praise (e.g. *er hat die Rolle tadellos gespielt*).

Seine vollkommene Gleichgültigkeit seinen Verpflichtungen gegenüber ist bekannt.
Ihre vollkommene Unkenntnis der Lage ist bedauerlich.
Es besteht vollkommene Eintracht zwischen uns.
Der Krieg endete mit der vollkommenen Vernichtung des Feindes.
Sie brauchen vollkommene Ruhe.
Die Aufführung war ein vollkommener Erfolg (not *völlig*; but *ein völliger Mißerfolg*).
Eine Minute nach dem Alarm lag die Stadt vollkommen im Dunkeln.
Die Stadt ist vollkommen zerstört.
Sie haben mich vollkommen mißverstanden.
Es ist vollkommen unmöglich, ihm zu helfen.
Das Rätsel ist vollkommen gelöst (not *völlig*).
Sein Vorgehen war vollkommen berechtigt.
Der Plan hat vollkommen versagt.

2. **Vollständig:**[1] having all the parts, items, etc. necessary for a thing to fulfil its purpose. The whole thus formed need not be organic, it may be, e.g., of a merely numerical kind. When not combined with a noun (or adverbially with a verb) which denotes an object, it means 'complete in every respect, aspect'. In concentrating attention on the parts it differs from *vollkommen*, which suggests the whole as something more than the sum of its parts. It cannot be applied to a person.

As the sense of 'complete in all parts' is clearest in the predicative position, it should be avoided in this use with expressions which denote the absence of a thing. Thus while it is correct to say: *ihre vollständige Unkenntnis der Lage ist mir bekannt*, it is not possible, not even ironically, to use *vollständig* to translate 'their ignorance of the situation is complete'.

Die Liste der Namen ist noch nicht vollständig.
Ein vollständiges Gebiß.
Die Niederlage des Feindes ist vollständig.
Es besteht vollständige Eintracht zwischen uns.
Der Krieg endete mit der vollständigen Vernichtung des Feindes.
Das ist ein vollständiges Abrücken von Ihrem früheren Standpunkt.
Sie brauchen vollständige Ruhe.
Die Stadt ist vollständig zerstört.
Sie haben mich vollständig mißverstanden.
Das Rätsel ist vollständig gelöst.
Sein Vorgehen war vollständig berechtigt.
Der Plan hat vollständig versagt.
Das Haus wurde vollständig durchsucht.

[1] See also *vervollständigen* under 'finish, complete'.

3. **Völlig** expresses a subjective, often emotional, interest on the part of the speaker and therefore lacks the convincing sense of finality conveyed by *vollkommen*. This subjectivity makes it more dynamic than *vollkommen* and *vollständig*. Although the objective fact may be felt more strongly, this is, of course, not more complete in an objective sense.

Used adjectivally, *völlig* cannot be applied to concrete objects, and can qualify a noun denoting a person only if this noun is really equivalent to an adjective, i.e. indicates a quality capable of provoking a subjective interest. Predicative use is not possible.

Er ist ein völliger Narr, ein völliges Kind.
Ihre Antwort zeigt nichts als eine völlige Unkenntnis der Lage.
Es besteht völlige Eintracht zwischen uns.
Das ist ja ein völliges Abrücken von Ihrem früheren Standpunkt. (The subjective interest is expressed also by *ja*.)
Die Stadt ist völlig zerstört.
Sie haben mich ja völlig mißverstanden.
Es ist völlig unmöglich, ihm zu helfen.
Er ist völlig verschwunden.
Das ist mir völlig gleichgültig.
Er trat auf den völlig menschenleeren Platz.
Sie haben das Feuerzeug nun völlig kaputt gemacht (colloquial).
Ich kann Ihre Schwierigkeiten völlig nachfühlen.
Wir tappen völlig im Dunkeln.
Er ist ein völlig unbrauchbarer Mensch.

4. **Vollends** denotes the final stages of completion and suggests a contrast with preceding stages. It is only used adverbially.

Jetzt ist es aber vollends dunkel (it was dark before, but not completely).
Eine zweite Welle genügte, um das Boot vollends zum Kentern zu bringen.

5. **Gänzlich** is an emphatic word and thus has an emotional connotation. 'Utter' and 'entire' are often closer approximations than 'complete'. As an adjective (it is not used predicatively) it can be combined only with abstract or verbal nouns.

Die gänzliche Harmlosigkeit des Mannes sollte doch klar sein.
Das gänzliche Ausbleiben der gewöhnlichen Stürme war eine angenehme Überraschung.
Er ist gänzlich ohne Schuld.
Ich verlasse mich gänzlich auf Sie.
Er ist gänzlich zu Grunde gerichtet.
Seine Worte wurden gänzlich verdreht.

Es ist gänzlich überflüssig, zu dem schon Gesagten noch mehr hinzuzufügen.
Die Symptome sind gänzlich verschwunden.

6. 'Complete' used in the sense of 'completed' must be translated by *fertig, vollendet* or the other terms discussed under 'finish, complete' (see article).

Mein Bericht ist noch nicht fertig.
Das ist ein unvollendeter Satz.

CONFESS, ADMIT, CONCEDE[1] All these terms imply varying degrees of reluctance. 'Confess' normally suggests an admission of wrong-doing, either in a religious sense, i.e. to a priest and the like, or to others. It is also used as a polite way of registering dislike (e.g. I confess, I don't care for it much). 'Admit'[2] suggests an absence of wholeheartedness, and is often followed by 'but', irrespective of the truth. 'Concede' expresses a recognition of one's opponent's point of view despite reluctance.

1. **Beichten:** to confess in a religious sense, the only German term used in this way.

Er hat dem Priester alles gebeichtet.

2. **Zugeben** is the most general term, and suggests no more than that one refrains from disputing a point of view, i.e. it does not necessarily imply acceptance. 'Admit' is the closest English equivalent.

Geben Sie mal zu, daß die Aufgabe kompliziert ist.
Zugegeben, daß er es ehrlich meint... (admitting).

3. **Gestehen** and its compounds imply a recognition of the truth or justice of a statement and the like, and therefore approximate closely to 'confess'. *Gestehen* means 'to confess' or 'reveal' a fault, a misdemeanour, crime. Like 'confess', it can also be used as a polite expression of dislike. It suggests in general an emotional state of mind, reluctance, hesitancy. As object, a clause is more frequently found than a noun.

Er hat gestanden (a fixed phrase).
Ich gestehe meine Schuld.
Er gestand, daß er die Frau ermordet hatte.
Ich gestehe, daß ich mir keine Mühe gegeben habe.
Ich gestehe, daß ich keine Freude daran finde.

[1] 'Grant' is also used in the sense of 'to admit the truth or justice of' a statement, and implies greater readiness to recognize this than the other terms. For its use in the sense of 'accede to' a request see separate article.

[2] 'Admit' is also used in the sense of 'to let into' a place ((*her*)*einlassen*) and 'to accept into' an institution and the like (e.g. *zum Universitätsstudium zugelassen werden*).

4. **Eingestehen** is more common with a noun object in the sense of 'to confess' a fault, crime. It must be accompanied in normal use by the reflexive dative when followed by a *daß* clause. It implies a fuller recognition of the truth than *gestehen.*

Er hat seine Schuld eingestanden.
Endlich mußte er sich eingestehen, daß er sich zu viel zugemutet hatte.

5. **Zugestehen** implies a qualified recognition of an opponent's point of view, and therefore means 'to concede'.

Sie gestehen mir zu, daß das zuviel verlangt wäre.

6. **Bekennen** differs from the other terms in suggesting a full, unreserved, and spontaneous confession.[1] It has no close English equivalent.

Ich bekenne offen meine Schuld.
Ich bekenne, daß ich Wein gerne trinke.
Er bekannte, daß er seine Gedichte erst in Prosa geschrieben hatte.

CONSIDER 1. **Sich überlegen** is the most general term in the sense of 'apply the mind to, give thought to', a matter. While the thinking is carried on with a view to arriving at a judgment, whether purely intellectual or with reference to action, this judgment is stressed less than the thinking itself. Since the meaning is 'to think about',[2] it is, for example, inappropriate when 'consider' means to consider the granting of a request, an application, and the like. The activity of thinking is suggested only in a general way, without reference to the close examination of details. The addition of the reflexive dative suggests more careful, its omission more superficial, thought, but both forms are often used indiscriminately, the omission, however, only being possible when the object is a clause, i.e. not a noun, or when it is used absolutely.

Ich werde mir die Frage, den Plan, Ihren Vorschlag, überlegen.
Er überlegte einen Augenblick, bevor er antwortete.
Ich überlege mir, wo ich meine Ferien verbringen könnte.
Er überlegte (sich), ob er das Angebot annehmen sollte.
Ein wohlüberlegter Plan.

2. **Erwägen,** to weigh, suggests a close examination of all details, factors, with regard to their relative importance. It is used particularly with reference to requests. When the weighing of point against point is stressed, **abwägen** is the preferred term. See 'weigh'.

[1] Hence the much-used expression *sich zu etwas bekennen,* to declare oneself, to make a profession of faith in something.

[2] To reflect, ponder, i.e. protracted thinking, is *nachdenken.* See 'think'.

Ich habe alle Möglichkeiten erwogen.
Sie müssen die Kosten erwägen, bevor Sie sich entscheiden.
Die Regierung erwägt gewisse Maßnahmen, um den Handel mit Südamerika zu beleben.
Der Senat erwägt Ihr Gesuch.
Er hat das Für und das Wider gegeneinander abgewogen.

3. **In Erwägung ziehen** suggests that the consideration is given more hesitantly or reluctantly than is the case with *erwägen*. Similarly, if used in making a request, it implies that the latter is put forward more humbly.

Ich werde Ihren Vorschlag in Erwägung ziehen.
Würden Sie folgendes in Erwägung ziehen?

4. **Bedenken:** to think a thing all over (i.e. the force of *be-*), in the sense of 'to realize its consequences, results', 'to bear these in mind'. Because of this reference to consequences it conveys a suggestion of hesitation, of stopping to think.[1] The noun *Bedenken* means 'misgiving'.

Sie müssen die Wirkung, die Folgen, eines solchen Schrittes bedenken.
Ich hatte die Schwierigkeiten nicht bedacht, als ich den Vorschlag machte.
Bedenken Sie, was ich ihnen gesagt habe.
Wenn man bedenkt, daß er fast keine Schulung gehabt hat, muß man seine Leistung bewundern.

5. **Prüfen:** to examine, scrutinize, as the action of an authoritative body.[2]

Die Regierung prüft die Ernährungslage.
Der Senat prüft Ihr Gesuch.

6. **Betrachten** (a) only translates 'consider' in reference to thought[3] when it is accompanied by some phrase which denotes the angle, point of view, from which a matter is seen.

Er betrachtet das Problem von diesem Standpunkt aus, unter diesem Gesichtspunkt, von allen Seiten, in einem falschen Licht.

[1] *Sich besinnen* is 'to stop to think' in the sense of 'to try to remember'. The success of this effort, i.e. to remember, is expressed by *sich entsinnen, sich erinnern*. The latter is the more general term in the sense 'to recall', while *sich entsinnen* suggests more forcibly the re-awakening to consciousness of something forgotten. 'Remember' in the imperative in the sense of bearing in mind, not forgetting, is sometimes translated by *bedenken Sie*, particularly in reference to a warning about consequences, but in general by *vergessen Sie nicht!*

[2] *Sich befassen mit* is a close synonym.

[3] *Betrachten* also means 'to contemplate', 'to gaze at' a thing in such a way as to be absorbed in it in mind and spirit. *Besehen, besichtigen* (view, inspect) suggest merely that the intellect is brought to bear on a thing in order to discover some external characteristic of it.

(b) Followed by *als* it also means 'to regard as', 'to take to be'. It differs from **halten für** in suggesting finality and conviction, while the latter states an opinion in a more argumentative way, and so is a closer equivalent of 'consider'.

Wir können die Verhandlungen als abgeschlossen betrachten.
Ich betrachte ihn als einen Freund.
Betrachten Sie sich als entlassen (not *halten*, since there can be no question of opinion).
Ich halte den Preis für zu hoch.
Ich halte ihn für unzuverlässig.

7. In the sense of 'to be of the opinion', when this phrase is followed by a 'that' clause, 'consider' can only be translated by **der Meinung, Ansicht, sein,** and the like. '*Dafür halten, daß...*' is rare.

Ich bin der Ansicht, daß Sie zuviel verlangen.

8. In the sense of 'to examine' a person or thing with a view to acceptance or rejection or suitability the following phrases are used: **in Betracht ziehen; in Betracht, Frage, kommen.**

Ich würde ihn nie für den Posten in Betracht ziehen (consider as suitable).
Eine Gehaltserhöhung kommt nicht in Betracht.
Würde Donnerstag eventuell für Sie in Frage kommen? (would you consider...as suitable, acceptable?)

9. **Berücksichtigen:** to take into account, to pay due attention to a thing as a determining factor. It does not mean 'to be sympathetic', and cannot therefore be interchanged with *Rücksicht nehmen.*

Sie müssen diese beiden Momente berücksichtigen, bevor Sie sich entscheiden.
Er hat den Einfluß des Klimas nicht genügend berücksichtigt.
Haben Sie das Risiko, das damit verbunden ist, berücksichtigt?

10. **Rücksicht nehmen auf:** to show sympathetic consideration, to be considerate towards.[1]

Er nimmt keine Rücksicht auf andere.
Auf seine Wünsche hat man keine Rücksicht genommen.

CONSOLIDATE Frequently, the German words here discussed are better rendered into English by terms other than 'consolidate'.

[1] *Du bist dem alten Herrn auf den Fuß getreten, das war eine Rücksichtslosigkeit* (a lack of consideration).

CONSOLIDATE

Befestigen[1] is 'to consolidate' a place in the sense of fortifying it against military attack. It also means 'to consolidate' such intangibles as fame, power, in an external way. When followed by 'in' it can mean 'to confirm' someone in a habit of mind.[2] **Festigen** is 'to consolidate, fortify inwardly', particularly with reference to an attitude of mind. The inner strength and coherence of the person or thing is emphasized more than the means by which this is accomplished.

In reflexive use both can mean 'to become stabilized', of prices and the like. If there is any distinction, it is that *sich festigen* suggests greater permanence because its reference is inward.

Die Stadt, die neuen Gebiete, wurden schnell befestigt.
Diese Maßnahmen haben die Macht des Regimes befestigt.
Eine kluge Politik hat die Stellung der Kirche befestigt.
Er hat seinen Ruhm durch neue Leistungen befestigt.
Dieses Erlebnis hat ihn in seinem Glauben befestigt.
Die Preise haben sich befestigt (gefestigt).
Er hat eine gefestigte Lebensauffassung.
Innerlich gefestigt, rief er das Volk zum Protest gegen das Vorgehen der Regierung auf.
Das Verhalten vieler Ausländer hat in nicht geringem Maße dazu beigetragen, den Nationalsozialismus in Deutschland zu festigen.
Jeder Kompromiß konnte die Herrschaft der Gewalt und des Unrechts in Deutschland nur festigen.

CONSTANT, PERMANENT, PERSISTENT[3] **1. Ständig:** continuing, without end, whether applied to a thing or to activities or facts connected with a person. If the noun to which it refers is a person, the noun denotes the activity of the person (e.g. *ein ständiger Begleiter*). *Ständig* thus translates 'permanent' as well as 'constant'. It differs from **beständig** in that the latter denotes not merely continuance, but also an attitude of mind which does not relax its efforts or vigilance. This holds good, too, when the accompanying noun denotes not persons, but the actions of persons. Applied to things, it implies that these have the capacity to vary, but do not, i.e. are persistent. *Ständig* draws attention not to an inner quality or attitude, but to the mere fact of continued existence. It comes from *stehen* and means 'standing', 'continuing', while *beständig* comes from *bestehen* used in the sense of 'persist'. *Ständig* is not emphatic and cannot be used predicatively. It concentrates attention on the action or fact, *beständig* on the person.

[1] *Befestigen* also means 'to fasten' one thing on to another.
[2] See also 'strengthen'.
[3] See also *dauernd* and *andauernd* as footnote to 'last' (p. 188, n. 1).

Eine ständige Adresse.
Eine ständige Drohung.
Die Zeitungen melden ständige Durchbrüche zum Rhein hin.
Eine ständige Zufuhr von Waffen.
Ein ständiges Mitglied.
Er ist ständig hier.
Die Beurteilung der Lage bedarf der ständigen Korrektur.
Ein beständiger Mensch.
Ein beständiger Liebhaber.
Beständige Schmerzen.
Ein beständiger Wind.
Ihre beständigen Nörgeleien gehen mir auf die Nerven (persistent, whereas *ständig* would be more objective and less of a reproach).
Die Helden fast aller romantischen Bücher sind beständig auf Reisen (*ständig* would tend to make them real people).

2. Both **stet** and **stetig** mean 'unvarying' and therefore 'uninterrupted', particularly with regard to intensity, whereas *ständig* and *beständig* merely denote continued existence and do not exclude fluctuations, pauses, even if they do not necessarily imply them. *Stetig* is the normal prose term and is used both adjectivally and adverbially, *stet* occurring only in poetry and elevated prose and only as an adjective. *Stets*, the adverbial form derived from it is, however, used in ordinary prose. It means 'invariably'.

Ein stetiges (stetes) Herz; sein steter, stetiger, Herrscherwille; ein stetiges Fieber; ein stetiger Regen; stetiges Wachstum.

CONTINUE A. Transitive.

1. **Fortsetzen** is used, with a noun object, only in the sense of continuing an action or an activity.[1]

Nach dem Kriege setzte er seine Studien fort.
Wir können das Gespräch nun ungestört fortsetzen.
Er setzte seinen Weg durch den Wald fort.

2. **Weiterführen:** to extend an object or a line.

Die Straße ist um 100 Kilometer weitergeführt worden.
Der Bau ist seit letztem Winter nicht weitergeführt worden.

[1] *Weitermachen* is much used in conversation, like 'to go on', mostly intransitively, but also transitively with neuter pronoun objects such as *es*, *das*, and with nouns which mean 'work, activity'. *Wir können nicht weitermachen. Machen Sie Ihre Arbeit weiter.*

CONTINUE

B. Intransitive.

1. Followed by the infinitive or the gerund.

(a) **Fortfahren** is used only of a continuous activity, whether resumption after a pause is implied or not. It is not applied to the repetition of an activity from time to time.

Nach einer kurzen Pause fuhr er zu schreiben, zu essen, fort.
Nach der Unterbrechung fuhr er zu sprechen fort.

(b) In the sense of 'to repeat an action from time to time' **weiter** should be used with an appropriate verb. It includes also the meaning of *fortfahren.*

Er drängte weiter auf Änderungen.
Er bekämpft den Plan weiter.
Sein Zustand bleibt weiter kritisch.

2. In other intransitive uses more specific terms must be used. The commonest are equivalents of 'to last' (see article) and **weitergehen,** 'to go on', of a line or an activity.

Sein Glück kann nicht dauern.
Der Regen hielt drei Tage an.
Der Weg geht noch einige Kilometer weiter.
Der Krieg muß weitergehen.

COOK, BOIL, SEETHE 'Cook' means 'to apply heat to a substance so as to remove it from the state of rawness'. 'Boil' means 'to heat liquid to the point where it is converted into gas'.

1. **Kochen** generally means 'to boil' liquids. It is applied transitively and intransitively, to the cooking of food only in reference to the preparation of the whole meal, but never to any particular item of food unless these are cooked by boiling (e.g. *Erbsen*). For 'cook' in reference to particular items of food German can only use specific terms which indicate the method of preparation.

2. **Sieden** can mean 'to bring a liquid to a point of heat where it leaps or spouts' up, i.e. to seethe. In addition it is sometimes applied to describe the state and movement of water just before the boiling point, i.e. it is used to denote a subjective impression rather than an objective condition. Expressions in which it is applied to the boiling of food exist, but are rarely used (e.g. *gesottene Eier, gesottenes Huhn*).

Sie hat das Essen schon gekocht.
Sie kocht ausgezeichnet.
Zum Abendessen haben wir gekochtes Huhn.
Kochst du die Kartoffeln oder brätst du sie?
Siedend heißes Öl.

CORNER **Ecke** is the general term. **Winkel** means primarily 'angle'. In the sense of 'corner' it refers only to one that is remote or secluded.

Er stellte seinen Regenschirm in die Ecke.
Er bog plötzlich um die Ecke.
Ich habe Sie in jeder Ecke gesucht.
Sie wohnen in einem verborgenen Winkel des Waldes.

CORPSE **Leiche** is the ordinary, **Leichnam** a more dignified, term. **Leiche** must also be used to translate 'dead body'.[1]

Die Leiche wurde verbrannt, war verstümmelt.
Der Leichnam wurde feierlich aufgebahrt.

COSTLY, EXPENSIVE, PRECIOUS, DEAR **Kostspielig** is 'costly' or 'expensive' in the sense of costing more than one estimates the thing to be worth. It is applied, like 'costly', mainly to what is elaborate, particularly activities. **Kostbar**[2] implies great expense, but denotes primarily that which has great value, especially when it is gorgeous, sumptuous. It corresponds to 'costly' only when this primary meaning is present. 'Precious' is its most common equivalent. **Preziös** means 'precious' only in the sense of 'artificial'. **Teuer** corresponds exactly to 'dear' in reference to the cost of an object.[3]

Das Reisen ist ein kostspieliges Vergnügen.
Es war ein kostspieliges Unternehmen.
Sie besitzt allerlei kostbare Edelsteine.
Er hat viel kostbare Zeit verschwendet.
Seine Ausdrucksweise ist manchmal preziös.
Ich kann mir den Wagen nicht leisten, er ist zu teuer.
Alle Lebensmittel sind viel teurer als vor dem Kriege.

COST(S), EXPENSE(S) **Kosten** denotes in general what a thing costs, whether in money, time, energy, or the like. It may be followed by the genitive of the noun, representing the thing purchased, the activity carried out. **Unkosten,** which cannot be followed by the genitive in this sense, means 'expenses' for which one feels one has no positive return, e.g. as involved in the removal or alleviation of an evil (e.g. in an accident),

[1] Both terms once had the meaning of 'body' in general. *Leichnam* has survived in this sense in a few fixed phrases.

[2] Do not confuse with *köstlich* which has the general sense of 'lovely' as a term of praise and in reference to food means 'delicious'. *Der Hering war köstlich.*

[3] In the sense of 'held in affection', *teuer* is used only to show an awareness of what the person so addressed means to one (e.g. *ein teurer Freund*). Otherwise 'dear' must be rendered by the more general term *lieb*.

needless expense. As a commercial term it differs in no appreciable way from *Kosten*. **Ausgabe(n)** refers to expense(s) which yield(s) a positive return. **Spesen** is exclusively a commercial term which does not differ in meaning from *Kosten* and *Unkosten* used in this sense.

Er berechnete die Kosten, und fand, daß sie zu hoch waren.
Ich kann die Kosten des Umbaus nicht bestreiten.
Es tut mir leid, Ihrer Bitte um Hilfe nicht stattgeben zu können, aber ich habe in letzter Zeit allerlei Unkosten gehabt.
Durch den Autounfall sind mir ziemliche Unkosten entstanden.
Stürzen Sie sich nicht meinetwegen in Unkosten.
Wir müssen unsere Ausgaben stark einschränken.
Die beiden Firmen haben die Spesen geteilt.

COURSE (in the course of) **Im Lauf** implies that something is done or happens once, at one point during the course of an activity. It need not be the result of what precedes. Only in this sense does *Lauf* mean 'course'. **Verlauf,** on the other hand, refers to the whole action and is consequently freely used (*der Verlauf der Verhandlungen*), often being translated into English by some other word (e.g. *nach Verlauf vieler Jahre*, 'lapse').[1] *Im Verlauf* is applied to something that takes place or emerges as a result of what has preceded, or is thought of in connection with the action as a whole.

Im Laufe der Operation fuhr dem Arzt der Gedanke durch den Kopf, daß die Zahl der Lungenkranken im Steigen sei.
Im Verlauf der Operation hat sich der Zustand des Patienten erheblich verschlechtert.
Im Laufe des Gesprächs erwähnte er, daß seine Frau krank sei.
Im Verlauf des Gesprächs stellte sich heraus, daß er ein paar Unwahrheiten gesagt hatte.

COVER 1. **Bedecken** is the ordinary prosaic term. It suggests no interest or emotional participation on the part of the speaker, but concentrates attention on the action. The force of the prefix *be* is that the covering is 'all over'.

Der Schnee bedeckt die Berge.
Der Himmel ist mit Wolken bedeckt.

2. **Decken** conveys secondary associations. In the active, though rarely in the passive, voice it suggests in elevated or poetical diction to 'cover

[1] *Ablauf*: the lapse or course of a fixed period in relation to a pre-determined end. Thus *im Ablauf des Gesprächs* means 'while the conversation is moving to a known end or goal'.

here and there'. It can also suggest the performing of an action in stages. Further, it means 'to protect', literally and figuratively.[1]

Der Schnee deckt die Berge (here and there).

'*Die Treppen deckten sie zuletzt auch schwarz, ich sah es wohl*' (Goethe, *Egmont*).

Das Dach wird mit Schiefern gedeckt.

Unsere Stellungen sind vor der Bombardierung gedeckt.

In diesem Unternehmen bin ich genügend gedeckt (financially).

3. **Zudecken:** to cover up, on all sides. It can suggest emotional participation.

Sie deckten den Sarg mit Blumen zu.

CROSS 1. **Kreuzen:** to place one thing crosswise over another, e.g. parts of the body, streets, lines (i.e. which intersect). Extended senses are: the mutual passing of objects without actually touching (e.g. trains, letters); to thwart plans, etc. (more commonly *durchkreuzen*); to clash, of interests.

2. **Überqueren** is little used.[2] It suggests an elaborate operation (e.g. the mountains, ocean). In most cases German uses the equivalents of 'to go across'.

'*Gegen Mitte März bricht die Stellung der Wehrmacht...so jäh zusammen, daß...die Alliierten ungefähr gleichzeitig mit dem Rheinübergang Montgomerys und Bradleys den Strom bei Oppenheim fast spielend überqueren.*' (From a German newspaper. Surprise is indicated, because the crossing would in most cases be difficult.)

3. To go across, when the points of departure and arrival are outside the limits of the space crossed. See 'go'.

Ich ging über die Straße.[3]

Hannibal ging über die Alpen.

Der Zug fuhr über die Brücke.

Wir flogen über den Kanal.

Wolken ziehen über die Sonne (pass across).

4. To cross a space when the points of departure and arrival are within its limits.

Er ging auf die andere Seite des Zimmers (he crossed the room).

[1] Note further: *die beiden Begriffe decken sich durchaus* (coincide completely).

[2] *Durchqueren*: to traverse (e.g. *die Wüste*).

[3] *Quer* should only be added in the sense of 'obliquely'.

5. **Überschreiten:** to cross a line or anything conceived as a line.

Die Grenze überschreiten.
Das Überschreiten der Gleise ist verboten.
Die Alliierten haben den Rhein auf breiter Front überschritten.

6. Example of a more specific term:

Die Brücke führt über den Fluß.

CURSE, SWEAR **Fluchen** generally means 'to curse' or 'to swear' in the sense of 'to use profane oaths'. In this sense it is used absolutely or followed by *auf* (to swear at a person). Followed by the dative it occurs in elevated language in the sense of 'to utter an invocation of destruction or punishment' on a person or thing. **Verfluchen** is only used in the latter sense, and may indicate either momentary annoyance or a solemn imprecation. **Verwünschen** also has this sense, but is less strong. It suggests: to wish a person ill. **Schwören** has as its only meaning: to swear a solemn oath.

Er flucht unaufhörlich (swears).
Er hat schrecklich auf mich geflucht (swore at).
Er fluchte den Göttern in seinem unendlichen Schmerz (cursed).
Der Vater verfluchte seinen Sohn.
Er wurde wegen seiner Willkür von seinen Untertanen verflucht.
Er verwünschte sein Schicksal.
Er schwor, sein Leben für die gute Sache einzusetzen.

CUT Sense: literal, to part something with pressure of an edge (*P.O.D.*).

1. **Schneiden** is 'to cut' by any instrument or means which does not require great force on the part of the person performing the act. It is therefore not applied to the cutting down of trees or the cutting of firewood.[1]

Er hat das Brot, das Fleisch, das Tuch, das Gras, das Korn, das Glas, geschnitten.
Er hat sich die Haare, die Nägel, in den Finger, geschnitten.

2. **Aufschneiden:** to cut open. It should be used when 'open' is implied.

Schneiden Sie die Seiten des Buches auf.
Die Leiche wurde aufgeschnitten.

[1] *Beschneiden* is 'to trim', 'to lop'; also 'to circumcise'. Figuratively: to curtail. *Verschneiden* is 'to cut wrongly'; also 'to fortify' wine. *Zerschneiden* is 'to sever', particularly of things that should remain whole. Examples: *der Arzt zerschnitt den Nerv; das Band zwischen ihnen wurde zerschnitten.*

3. **Durchschneiden:** to intersect.

Die Landschaft ist von Kanälen durchschnitten.

4. Both **hauen** and **spalten** imply the expenditure of force. The former approximates to 'hew', 'chop', and suggests the hewing out or away of pieces from an object by repeated blows. The latter approximates to 'split', and suggests that the instrument goes clean through the object and severs it.

Wir müssen ein Loch in das Eis hauen.
Er haut Holz für den Winter (from trees).
Er spaltet Holz, um ein Feuer zu machen (e.g. large blocks into smaller pieces).[1]

DAMAGE 1. **Beschädigen:** to cause actual physical damage.

Das Haus ist von dem Sturm schwer beschädigt worden.
Kriegsbeschädigte (cripples and the like).
Die Feuchtigkeit hat das Klavier beschädigt.
Der Regen hat das Obst beschädigt.

2. **Schaden:** to damage in any way, externally or internally, physically or morally, directly or indirectly. The harm is more potential than actual. The sense is therefore 'to be bad for' in a vague, indefinite way.

Zu viel Regen schadet dem Hause.
Das Trinken wird Ihrer Gesundheit schaden.
Der Preissturz hat meinem Geschäft sehr geschadet.
Das Eingreifen der Regierung schadet nur dem Kulturleben eines Landes.
Zuviel Regen schadet dem Obst.
Es schadet seinem Ruf.

3. **Schädigen** means 'to cause loss to' a person, in two ways. (*a*) By far the commonest use, in reference to property or money. (*b*) A rarer use: to damage the inner principle or vitality of a person or thing, generally in a psychological or spiritual sense.

Kriegsgeschädigte, Bombengeschädigte (those who have suffered loss or destruction of property through war or bombs).
Der Preissturz hat mein Geschäft geschädigt.
Durch diese Transaktion bin ich geschädigt worden.
Er hat mich geschädigt.
Meinungsverschiedenheiten schädigen ihre Freundschaft nicht.
Die systematische Philosophie hat nach Nietzsches Ansicht das Leben schwer geschädigt.

[1] *Fällen* is 'to cut down' trees, 'to fell'.

DARE 1. **Wagen:** to venture, to have the audacity, spontaneously, from within oneself.[1]

Er wagte nicht, zu widersprechen.

2. **Dürfen** is used negatively and interrogatively when 'dare' denotes a prohibition from without. It is often accompanied by a statement of the consequences which would result from an ignoring of the prohibition. The third person singular of 'dare' is in this sense 'dare' (i.e. not 'dares').

Er darf das nicht tun, es würde sicher seine Aussichten verderben ('dare' or 'must not').

DATE **Datum** is used only in giving the calendar date and in a few fixed phrases (e.g. *neuesten Datums sein*). Otherwise such terms as **Zeit(punkt), Termin** (a fixed point of time by which a thing is required to be done) must be used.

Welches Datum haben wir heute?
Wir können die Zeit, den Zeitpunkt, später bestimmen.
Er hat den Termin für das Belegen der Vorlesungen schon überschritten.

DECEIVE, CHEAT, DELUDE 1. **Trügen** can have only a thing as subject and therefore cannot indicate deliberate deception. The thing deceives because of its nature, i.e. because it is such that human beings are prone to error when confronted by it. *Trügen* is normally intransitive (but Kleist uses it transitively in *Die Verlobung in St. Domingo*: '*Wenn mich nicht alles trügt*').

Der Schein, das Gedächtnis trügt.
Wenn nicht alle Anzeichen trügen... (see 'sign').
Derartige Gesichter trügen.

2. **Betrügen** always implies deception or disappointment in an expectation or conviction, whether in material things or otherwise. It does not mean simply 'to tell a lie'. It is frequently followed by an expression denoting what one has lost (with *um*), and is often best translated by 'cheat (of)'.[2] Furthermore it need not be deliberate, and the deception can be in act as well as in word.

Er wurde um seine Erbschaft betrogen.
Er hat mich in der Frage des Gehalts betrogen.
Seine Versprechen haben mich betrogen.

[1] In this sense *wagen* also means 'risk'.

[2] In this sense *betrügen* also translates 'swindle'. *Schwindeln* means 'to tell tall stories'. 'To cheat' in the sense of using dishonest means (e.g. at an examination), but not robbing a person of anything, is in popular language *mogeln, schummeln.*

3. **Täuschen:** to cause to mistake the false for the real, to involve in a delusion, illusion,[1] hallucination. It frequently, but not necessarily, suggests an optical delusion (*vortäuschen*). The subject, i.e. what causes the delusion, can be the same as that of *trügen*, but, unlike the latter, *täuschen* may be used transitively. The deception can be deliberate or otherwise.

Mein Gedächtnis hat mich getäuscht.
Er hat mich mit seinen Schilderungen vollkommen getäuscht.
Ich hielt ihn für einen Schauspieler, aber ich habe mich vielleicht getäuscht.
Ich habe mich in ihm getäuscht.
Ich tat es nicht, um Sie zu täuschen (very close to *irreführen*).

4. **Belügen** must be used when 'deceive' means 'deliberately to tell a lie', without further implication.[2]

Warum hast du mich belogen?

DECIDE, RESOLVE, DETERMINE 1. **Sich entschließen, entschlossen sein** (to be resolved, determined) imply strong determination, will-power. The original meaning of *entschließen* was 'unlock', i.e. unlock one's mind, clarify, make definite one's thoughts.

Nach langem Zögern entschloß ich mich, seinem Rat zu folgen.
Er ist entschlossen, alles zu riskieren.
Er kann sich nicht entschließen.

2. **Beschließen** is used in two ways: (*a*) when no particular exercise of will-power is implied, i.e. as the ordinary term for 'decide'; (*b*) when it is a question of decisions or resolutions which are enforced by virtue of authority. The passive is possible only with a non-personal subject. Reflexive use is not possible.

Ich habe beschlossen, meine Ferien am Meer zu verbringen.
Ich beschloß, mich nicht von seinen Einwänden beeinflussen zu lassen.
Der Senat hat beschlossen, daß die Prüfung früher stattfinden soll.
Es ist beschlossen worden, die Steuern herabzusetzen.

3. **Entscheiden:** to settle a question intellectually, to choose between various possibilities. It may be used reflexively in this sense. *Sich entscheiden für*: to decide on.

Die Frage, ob wir diesen Sommer verreisen, ist noch nicht entschieden worden.

[1] See Fowler's *Modern English Usage* for the distinction between 'delusion' and 'illusion'.

[2] *Anlügen* means 'to lie to a person on a vast scale'. For a similar use of *an* see *anschuldigen* under 'accuse'.

DECIDE

Der Streit ist entschieden worden.
Wir haben uns schließlich entschieden, ins Theater zu gehen.
Ich habe mich für diesen Mantel entschieden.

4. **Bestimmen** is used with a non-personal subject and a personal object in the sense of inducing a person to a course of action. It also translates 'determine' when the object is a thing.

Die Aussichten auf eine bessere Stellung haben ihn bestimmt, nach London zu fahren.
Die Größe des Hauses hat die Zahl der Gäste bestimmt.
Haben Sie den Treffpunkt schon bestimmt?

DEMAND (noun) 1. **Forderung:** a demand made by a person.

Er stellte viele Forderungen an mich.
Ich habe alle seine Forderungen erfüllt.

2. **Anforderung:** a demand made by a thing.

Die Vollendung der Sixtinischen Kapelle stellte große Anforderungen an die Arbeitskraft Michelangelos.
Die Anforderungen der Lage sind erfüllt worden.
Er ist den Anforderungen nicht gewachsen.

3. Economic terms: **Bedarf, Nachfrage.**

Den Bedarf decken, eine starke Nachfrage nach gewissen Waren.

DEMAND[1] (verb) 1. **Fordern** is used with a personal subject or with things which stand for persons, and is the general term for to demand peremptorily.

Sie fordern zu viel von mir.
Die Generale forderten mehr Truppen.
Die Schlacht forderte viele Opfer.

2. **Erfordern** is used with a non-personal subject.

Die Lage erfordert harte Maßnahmen.

3. **Anfordern,** with a personal subject, is only used in the sense of 'to demand by virtue of powers vested in one' and then only in an administrative capacity. It is most common in contexts referring to the number of men or the amount of material required for specific work.

Er forderte 17 Leute an, um diese Arbeit auszuführen.

[1] See also *verlangen* under 'ask'.

DENY A. Sense: declare untrue or non-existent, disavow or repudiate.

1. **Leugnen** means 'to declare' a statement (mostly in the form of an accusation) 'to be untrue' or, less often, a thing 'to be non-existent'. It refers to matters which can be accepted as facts (e.g. doings or happenings) and religious beliefs, only to opinions when used negatively. Thus, it is possible in the sentence 'I don't deny that it is a good poem', but is less common in the positive form of this statement. In this sense it is perhaps more frequent with a following *daß* clause than with a noun object.

Leugnen is connected etymologically with *lügen*, and refusal to admit a fact is its commonest sense. The etymology suggests why *leugnen* is used with reference to religious matters (i.e. the denial of God's existence was once regarded as a lie), and with reference to opinions in the negative (i.e. one cannot deny or tell a lie about something obvious).

Der Angeklagte leugnet.
Er leugnete, daß er den Mord begangen hätte. Er leugnete den Diebstahl.
Er leugnet das Dasein Gottes.
Er leugnet das Vorhandensein einer Gefahr, die Absicht einer Beleidigung.
Die Regierung leugnet ihre Verantwortlichkeit (denies theoretically, not in any specific case, the existence of its responsibility).
Ich will garnicht leugnen, daß es ein gutes Bild ist.

2. **Bestreiten,** to dispute, contest, argue, is used in statements which must be taken as matters of opinion and which refer to any matter which is disputed. It is obligatory when 'deny' is used positively, optional when used negatively (see *leugnen*).

Ich bestreite (nicht), daß es ein gutes Bild ist.
Ich bestreite, daß Goethe das meinte.

3. **Verneinen** only means 'deny' in the sense of a categorical contradiction of the validity of an affirmation or of the value of a thing. It governs a noun object, but not a clause. In other cases it corresponds to 'say no', 'negate', etc.

Ich verneinte seine Behauptung, diese Anschauung, die Gültigkeit dieser Theorie.
Er verneint alle bestehenden Werte.
Die Weltschmerzler verneinen überhaupt den Sinn des Daseins

4. **Ableugnen:** to deny emphatically an assertion, mostly something imputed to oneself, an accusation.[1] It is normally used with a noun object

which denotes the specific accusation (i.e. where *leugnen* is impossible) and with a following *daß* clause. In the latter case it differs from *leugnen* in being more emphatic and referring to more important matters.[2]

Der Angeklagte leugnete die Tat, den ihm zur Last gelegten Diebstahl, den Mord, ab.

Er leugnete die Schuld, die Verantwortung, ab.

Der Minister leugnete energisch ab, daß solche Maßnahmen ins Auge gefaßt worden seien.

5. **Dementieren:** to deny officially a report, a rumour.

Der Bericht ist von der Regierung schon zweimal dementiert worden.

6. **Verleugnen:** as a rendering of 'deny', to be able to make a personal trait appear to others different from what it is, or as non-existent. It is mostly used with *nicht können.* The object must be a noun, not a clause.

Er kann seine Nationalität, niedrige Herkunft, nicht verleugnen.

'*Es* (= *das Blatt*) *war von Larkens, wie er augenblicklich sah, wie selbst die angenommene Handschrift kaum verleugnen wollte*' (Mörike, *Maler Nolten*).

7. **Absprechen** is followed by a double object, dative and accusative, and means 'to deny' that a person possesses a quality. It is often translated by other terms than 'deny'.

Kunstsinn kann man ihm nicht absprechen.

B. Sense: to withhold something from a person. **Versagen.**[3]

Ich versagte ihm meine Unterstützung.

Er muß sich den Luxus nun versagen.

DESTROY, ANNIHILATE[4] **Zerstören** implies the violent wrenching asunder of the parts of an object, not necessarily its complete disappearance without trace. When only the latter is meant, **vernichten** must be used. It is also the appropriate term when utter annihilation (i.e. without

[1] With the words *Anschuldigung, Beschuldigung, zurückweisen* is used, with words which denote the specific charge *ableugnen.*

[2] *In Abrede stellen* is a close synonym of *ableugnen.*

[3] See also 'fail'.

[4] *Vertilgen* is 'to obliterate', 'to destroy all trace of' a thing, generally by devouring it, literally or figuratively. *Die Spinne vertilgt eine Menge Ungeziefer. Ungeziefer vertilgte die Obsternte. Tilgen* is 'to wipe out', 'to annul' in technical senses. *Eine Schuld tilgen. Austilgen*: to wipe out by a process, to extirpate, particularly large sections of people. *Die russische Revolution hat das Bürgertum systematisch ausgetilgt.*

surviving traces) involving violence is suggested. In figurative use *vernichten* is stronger than *zerstören*. **Zunichte machen** is used figuratively in the sense of 'to annul', 'to rob of existence'. It is less emphatic than *vernichten*.

'To destroy' not wanted animals can be translated by *vernichten* if it is done on a large scale and by officials, as at a zoo. In reference to private animals *erschießen* (see article on 'shoot') or some other specific term must be used.

Die Stadt wurde durch die wiederholten Bombardierungen fast gänzlich zerstört.
Der Hagel hat die Ernte zerstört.
Sie müssen alle belastenden Dokumente vernichten (not *zerstören*).
Hitler wollte Polen vernichten.
Sie zerstören den guten Eindruck, den ich von Ihnen bekommen habe (*vernichten* would be too emphatic).
Das hat meine Hoffnungen zerstört (more emphatic: *vernichtet*).
Der Krieg hat meine Pläne zunichte gemacht.
Die Tiere müssen vernichtet werden, da sie nicht mehr gefüttert werden können.
Wir müssen das Pferd erschießen.

DIFFERENT 1. **Verschieden** is used when two or more persons or things are described as having different attributes which distinguish them from each other. The adjective *verschieden* is, according to the sense, attached to the persons or things on the one hand, or to the attribute on the other.

Die Brüder sind verschieden.
Die zwei Stühle sind nur in der Farbe verschieden.
Wir sind verschiedener Ansicht.
Verschiedene Leute haben verschiedene Interessen.
Sie faßten die Arbeit verschieden an.
Er ist verschieden von seinem Bruder.

2. **Ander** (*anders* in predicative and adverbial use).

(a) A different person or thing from that mentioned before.

(b) A person or thing is different, has changed from what he or it was before. *Ander* does not distinguish from each other the persons or things of whom a change is predicated.

Die Brüder sind jetzt anders.
Wir sind jetzt anderer Ansicht geworden.
Andere Leute haben andere Interessen.
Sie faßten die Arbeit anders an.

DIFFICULT 1. **Schwierig** denotes an objective quality in the person, thing, action, to which it is applied, and means 'complicated', 'intricate', 'involved'. In the case of a person it has the sense of inwardly complicated in such a way as to be difficult to have dealings with. In all cases the complication distinctly implies a process with all its stages and details. It is the normal rendering of 'difficult' when the latter qualifies nouns or pronouns.

2. **Schwer** refers in the first place to the effect on the subject, and means 'arduous' for him, whether it is or is not so for others. The object is apprehended in a general way as difficult, but without reference to details or the relationship between its parts. It thus approximates more closely to 'hard' than to 'difficult'. It is a widely used term, its fundamental meaning being 'grievous', 'hard to bear'. Accordingly, it is not the normal word for 'difficult' as applied to nouns and pronouns. With nouns which in themselves denote an ordeal and the like it can only mean 'grievous', 'severe', etc. and therefore must not be used in the sense of 'difficult' (*eine schwere Prüfung* = a severe ordeal; *eine schwierige Prüfung* = a difficult examination). With nouns which in themselves do not suggest the sense of 'grievous' both terms may be used, the distinction being approximately the same as between 'hard' and 'difficult', *schwer*, however, being less colloquial than 'hard' (*ein schwieriges, schweres Examen*).

Schwer cannot be applied to a person in the sense of 'difficult' (*ein schwerer Junge* = a criminal).

3. 'Difficult' followed by the infinitive ('it is difficult to see'; 'he is difficult to catch') requires special attention. Since in this construction the meaning is generally that the difficulty lies with the subject and is not a quality of the object, *schwer* is the normal term and can always be used, even in those cases where *schwierig* would be more discriminating. *Schwierig* does not often occur in this combination. It may be used, provided an involved process, extended in time (e.g. manœuvres, a technical process, an action requiring constant readaptation) is indicated. The examples show that in cases where a verb alone does not convey this sense, the substitution of a phrase can do so.

(a) *Ein schweres Problem.*

Ein schwerer Vortrag (the speaker thinks of his trouble in following, but not of any objective characteristic of the lecture).

Es ist eine schwere Aufgabe, den Schutt der zerstörten Stadt wegzuschaffen.

Ein schwerer Krieg.

(b) *Ein schwieriger Mensch.*
Ein schwieriger Dichter.
Ein schwieriges Gelände zum Kämpfen.
Ein schwieriges Problem.
Ein schwieriger Vortrag.
Es ist eine schwierige Aufgabe, den Schutt der zerstörten Stadt wegzubringen.
Ein schwieriger Feldzug.
Eine schwierige Stelle.

(c) *Es ist schwer, ihn zu befriedigen.*
Er ist schwer zu befriedigen.
Es ist schwer, den Umzug unter solchen Umständen zu veranstalten.
Das Kind ist ein schwieriger Fall und daher schwer zu behandeln.
Die Einwendung ist schwer zu verstehen.
Es ist schwer, mit ihr zu leben.
Es ist schwer, diese beiden Wörter zu unterscheiden.
Es fällt mir schwer, das zu glauben.

(d) *Es war höchst schwierig, diesen Feldzug zu planen und auszuführen.*
Es war schwierig, bei derartigen Einschränkungen immer die richtigen Grenzen zu beobachten.
Es ist schwierig, das Geschäft wieder in Gang zu bringen.
Es ist schwierig, eine Lebensgemeinschaft mit ihr aufrechtzuerhalten (not: *zu leben*).
Es ist schwierig, zwischen diesen beiden Wörtern einen Unterschied zu machen.
Es ist schwierig, den Vortrag zu verstehen.
'*...viel schwieriger schien es mir, die Geldangelegenheit zu lösen*' (Ricarda Huch, *Fra Celeste*).
'*Deshalb war ihm eine Last Goldes nicht so begehrenswert wie ein menschlicher Körper für eine Untersuchung, wie denn in der Tat ein solcher schwieriger zu erhalten war, da man es in der Christenwelt für sündlich hielt, das zur Auferstehung und Verwandlung bestimmte Kleid der unsterblichen Seele zu zerstören*' (Ricarda Huch, *Der Arme Heinrich*).

DISAPPEAR **Verschwinden** is the general term and means 'to become invisible'. **Schwinden** means 'to dwindle away and cease to exist'. It emphasizes the process, not sudden extinction. *Verschwinden* sometimes implies cessation of existence, and stresses the result, not the process. **Entschwinden** is not used in everyday prose, and is often followed by phrases such as *dem Auge, den Blicken.* It means 'to disappear', not 'to cease to exist', and stresses the stages in which a person or thing disappears from sight.

Die Kerze ist verschwunden.
Die Kerze schwindet.
Er verschwand unter der Oberfläche.
Er verschwand um die Ecke.
Mein Vermögen verschwindet (either: someone is taking it away, or: it is being used up; *schwindet* being also possible in the latter sense, with emphasis on the process).
Der Winter verschwand (there was no trace of it left; also *schwand* and, in elevated style, *entschwand*).
Die Vorräte verschwinden dauernd.
Die Vorräte schwinden.
Mein Mut, meine Hoffnung, schwindet (*verschwindet* not possible).
Er entschwand dem Auge, den Blicken.

DIVE In the intransitive sense, **tauchen** means 'to dive' from the surface of the water in which one is already immersed.[1,2]

Springen is 'to dive' from a height, often as a feat of skill. Only the context can show whether 'dive' or 'jump' is meant.

Er tauchte so tief, daß er nicht mehr sichtbar war.
Er springt gut.
Er sprang vom Deck ins Wasser (dived or jumped).

DO **A.** Sense: perform, execute, carry out, bring about, effect, cause, accomplish.

Tun, machen[3]

1. With an indefinite pronoun as object.

Tun refers to acts that are viewed as serious or important or thought of with precision, *machen* to those that are regarded as trivial or unimportant

[1] In transitive use *tauchen* means 'to plunge' or 'to dip'. *Tunken* also means 'to dip', in reference to light objects.

[2] The direction of *tauchen* can be changed by the prefix (e.g. *umhertauchen, auftauchen*, particularly of submarines).

[3] Some close approximations to this sense are: (*a*) *Anfangen* (followed by *mit*, and taking *nichts, wenig, etwas, nicht viel* and the like as object): achieve something with, get somewhere with, find some use for. *In Italien konnte ich mit meinen paar Brocken Italienisch nichts* (*wenig*) *anfangen. Was kann man mit solchen Studenten anfangen? Können Sie mit diesen Fleischresten irgendwas anfangen?* (*machen aus* = make out of). (*b*) *Anstellen* suggests half-humorously what one ought not to do (to be up to). *Was haben Sie bloß angestellt?* (*c*) *Schaffen* (weak): get through work, get done. As object: *viel, wenig*, etc. It is widely used in south Germany. *Heute habe ich recht wenig geschafft.*

or thought of only vaguely. In tone *machen* is lighter, more familiar than *tun*.[1]

This distinction means that in general *tun* is used to express the idea of being busy, *machen* that of spending one's leisure, filling in time. *Tun* refers to important, *machen* to humbler work. The border-line is vague. Only *tun* can ask what right a person has to be in a stated place (*was tut er hier?*).

With an adverb of appraisal (e.g. well, badly, brilliantly) only *machen* can be used.

The following sentences contain examples in which both *tun* and *machen* are possible, with the distinction explained above, examples in which *tun* alone is correct, examples of *machen* with an adverb of appraisal.[2,3]

(a) *Was tut er im Büro* (what is his work or what right has he to be in the office)?

Was macht er im Büro (what is his work or what does he happen to be doing there at the moment)?

Was tun Sie da (presses for a serious answer)?

Was machen Sie da (lightly)?

Was tun Sie heute abend (expects a precise answer or implies a more serious pursuit)?

Was machen Sie heute abend (how are you spending..., amusing yourself)?

Was tun Sie mit Ihrer Freizeit (what serious use do you find for...)?

Was machen Sie mit Ihrer Freizeit?

Was kann man tun, um die Schmerzen etwas zu betäuben (expects a full explanation)?

Was kann man machen, um die Schmerzen etwas zu betäuben (expects a quick or simple remedy)?

Wer hat das getan?

Wer hat das gemacht?

Wie tust du das nur?

Wie macht man das (e.g. cracking one's fingers)?

Sowas tut man doch nicht!

Sowas macht man doch nicht (said lightly, e.g. of an old woman who tries to look young).

Sonntag taten wir nichts als zu Haus faulenzen (we ought to have done something more useful).

[1] The same type of distinction exists between *aufmachen* and *auftun* (see 'open').

[2] If *tun* is combined with such adverbs they acquire a moral connotation (e.g. *das war schlecht von dir getan*).

[3] 'To do well' followed by the infinitive: *gut daran tun* (e.g. *Sie täten gut daran, es zu gestehen*).

Sonntag machten wir nichts als zu Hause faulenzen (we spent our leisure in this way).
Was haben Sie mit Ihrem Bein getan (a more serious injury)?
Was haben Sie mit Ihrem Bein gemacht (e.g. a scratch)?
Ich habe etwas Dummes gemacht (*getan* is possible but is more appropriate with a serious adjective such as *töricht*).

(b) *Ich habe morgen* (*viel*) *zu tun* (busy).
Im Augenblick tut er nichts, er könnte Ihnen helfen.
Dieser Student hat das ganze Jahr nichts getan.
Tu' doch mal was, sitz' doch nicht da, wenn alles schief geht.
Das englische Volk fragt sich, was es getan hat, um solche Vorwürfe zu verdienen.
Kulturell hat der Adel in Deutschland wenig getan.
Das Kind tut nichts als schreien.
Er tat alles, was ihm befohlen wurde.
Ich will nichts mit einem derartigen Vorschlag zu tun haben.

(c) *Das haben Sie gut* (*schlecht, richtig, falsch, verkehrt, glänzend, besser als er*) *gemacht.*

2. With a noun object.

(a) In this combination *machen* is familiar and conversational in tone in the sense that a more precise term would in most cases be used in serious writing (e.g. *einen Aufsatz schreiben, ein Examen bestehen* (pass), *den Dr. phil. erlangen, die Klassik behandeln, studieren*). Its use is practically limited to the following senses and types of nouns:

(i) To perform, to carry out, with *Sache* (not *Ding*) preceded by an adjective or with a noun which is an equivalent.

Sie haben dumme Sachen gemacht (or: *Dummheiten gemacht*).
Sie haben tolle Streiche gemacht.

(ii) To produce, fabricate a thing, particularly an academic exercise. With other types of writing (e.g. a leading article, correspondence) the use of *machen* is slovenly.

Haben Sie Ihre Arbeit (e.g. an essay), *Ihren Aufsatz, die Übersetzung, Ihre Aufgabe* (home-work) *gemacht?*
Machen Sie sechs Durchschläge ('do' or 'make').

(iii) To sit for, study for, pass an examination.

Er hat in letzter Zeit sein Examen gemacht ('sat for' or 'passed').
Er macht den Dr. phil., seinen B.A. ('is working for' or 'sitting for').

(iv) With the noun *Arbeit* when stating the nature of one's job.

Er macht die Gartenarbeit für X.

(v) In the sense of 'teach, lecture on', 'study' (from the point of view of the student) a subject or a branch of a subject. It should not be used with a proper name (*er behandelt, studiert Goethe*), and sounds slovenly with the name of a faculty (*er treibt Medizin, Jura*).

Ich mache die Klassik, er die Romantik ('lecture on' or 'study').
Er macht dieses Jahr Latein mit den Jungens (teaches).
Wir machen Deutsch mit ihm (study).
In diesem Semester machen wir Lyrik, Metrik.
Im vorigen Jahr hat er Strafprozeß gemacht.

(b) *Tun* is used with most other types of nouns.

Seine Pflicht, schreckliche Dinge, Wunder, Schaden tun.
Er hat gute, wichtige, Arbeit getan.

It is used, too, with neuter substantival adjectives.

Sein Bestes, Möglichstes; Gutes, Böses, tun.

B. Sense: operate on, deal with, prepare, put in order.

1. In this sense *machen* is only used in a few well-defined senses, mostly 'to clean', 'to tidy up' a room (*sie hat das Zimmer, die Küche, die Bibliothek schon gemacht*). Also: *die Haare machen, den Weg* (but not: *die Gasse*) *machen* (do up), *Reparaturen machen*. Most other uses of *machen* with the thing operated on as object sound slovenly.

2. In other cases *besorgen, erledigen* (attend to) or a specific term should be used.

Er besorgt die Korrespondenz im Büro (*macht* sounds slovenly).
Sie hat das Aufwaschen, die Wäsche, schon besorgt.
Haben Sie meine Schuhe besohlt?
Sie sind der Nächste an der Reihe (I'll do you next, e.g. said by the hairdresser).
Sie schnippelt die Bohnen.

C. To cause harm and the like. Accompanied by an indefinite neuter pronoun (e.g. *nichts, was*) and the dative case. **Tun** is obligatory in direct statements (e.g. *ich habe dir nichts getan*) and is usual in direct questions (*was haben Sie ihm getan?*). **Antun** must be used in indirect statements and questions (*ich erzählte ihnen, was er mir angetan hatte; wer weiß, was er mir noch alles antun wird?*), and is possible in a direct question (*was haben Sie ihm angetan?*).

D. In cases where a verb substitute is needed, this must be *tun*.

Wer wäre bereit, ihm die Nachricht beizubringen? Ich habe es schon getan.
Sie sang besser, als sie es je getan.

E. Other senses.

1. Fare: *gehen, machen* (in the form: *was macht...?*).

Es geht dem Patienten besser.
Was macht das Bein, die Arbeit?

2. To serve the purpose, to be permissible, to suit: *gehen.*

Dieses Wort geht nicht.
Geht das?
Es geht nicht, daß er mit solchen Forderungen kommt.

3. To study: *studieren, treiben.*[1]

Er studiert Medizin, treibt Sprachen.

4. To be able to manage, to be good at: *fertig werden mit.*

Mit Latein werde ich nicht fertig.

5. To cover a distance: *zurücklegen.*

Wir haben heute 400 Kilometer zurückgelegt.

6. To be travelling at a certain speed: *fahren.*

Das Auto fuhr mit 80 Kilometer Geschwindigkeit.

7. To be able to achieve a speed: *schaffen, leisten.*

Dieses Auto kann 150 Kilometer die Stunde schaffen (leisten).

8. To serve time: *absitzen, abdienen,* both as a part of the time.

Er hat ein Jahr im Gefängnis abgesessen (im Heer abgedient).

9. To play a role: *spielen.*

Er hat den Hamlet gut gespielt.

10. To achieve: *ausrichten* (stronger than *tun*).

Versuchen Sie, was freundliche Worte bei ihm ausrichten können.

[1] *Betreiben* is also used in the sense of 'to carry on' a thing (e.g. *ein Geschäft betreiben*), including studies. In reference to the latter it is an intensive, and is often accompanied by an adverbial phrase to make this clear. *Er betreibt Medizin, seine Studien, mit Eifer.* '*Keine (Fassung) konnte der Selbstkritik des Dichters, der die Kunst schließlich mit einer beinahe wissenschaftlichen Grübelei betrieb, voll genügen*' (J. Petersen, *Die Wissenschaft von der Dichtung*). Again, *betreiben* can mean: to endeavour to bring a thing off successfully (e.g. *eine Heirat betreiben*).

11. To have finished with: *fertig sein mit.*
Ich bin mit der Zeitung fertig.

12. To bestow, cause to have, affect favourably or unfavourably: *tun.*
Die Medizin hat mir gut getan.
Er hat mir Unrecht getan.

DOUBT 1. With a noun object.
Bezweifeln presupposes an argument or statement to the contrary. It therefore comes as an objection. **Zweifeln** (followed by *an* with the dative) does not imply any such preceding assertion.

Ich bezweifle seinen guten Willen. *Ich bezweifle seine Ehrlichkeit.*
Ich zweifle an seinem guten Willen. *Ich zweifle an seiner Ehrlichkeit.*

2. Followed by a clause.
The distinction explained above means that *bezweifeln* is followed by a *daß* clause, *zweifeln* by an *ob* clause or a clause introduced by an interrogative pronoun (*was*). It also means that *zweifeln* is usual when there is a negative and a 'daß' clause follows. *Bezweifeln* with a negative and a direct noun or pronoun object follows.

Ich zweifle, ob er rechtzeitig ankommt.
Ich bezweifle, daß er rechtzeitig ankommt.
Ich zweifle nicht, daß er es schaffen wird.
Ich bezweifle es nicht.

DRESS, CLOTHE, INVEST[1] 1. **Sich anziehen** is the normal prose term. **Sich ankleiden** is more dignified, though it is often used in the same way as *sich anziehen.* The same implication is conveyed by *anziehen* when it is used without *sich,* i.e. in reference to individual items of clothing in the sense of 'put on'.[2] The more elevated term in this meaning is *anlegen* (e.g. *Geschmeide*). *Ankleiden* is not used in this way. **Sich kleiden** can only refer to the way one dresses (e.g. *gut, auffällig*).

Ich mußte mich schnell anziehen. *Er kleidet sich elegant, schlecht.*
Sie kleidete sich für den Ball an. *Er ist immer sorgfältig gekleidet.*

2. **Bekleiden** is, in its literal sense, 'to clothe' as a contrast to the unclothed state, therefore often 'to provide the essentials of clothing'. It is

[1] *Verkleiden* means 'to disguise', but normally only where the disguise is effected by clothing in the literal sense (e.g. *er verkleidete sich als Mönch*) or in the sense of 'to choose words which hide one's real meaning' (e.g. *er verkleidete seine wahren Absichten in schön klingenden Worten*). But: *er machte seine Schrift unkenntlich.*

[2] *Anziehen* in the sense of 'put on' can only be applied to articles of clothing that are 'pulled on'. Otherwise: *aufsetzen* (a hat); *umbinden* (a tie).

then extended to mean: to cover any object as with clothes (e.g. to drape). Another sense is: to invest with the insignia of office; and in figurative extension of this: (*a*) to invest with the office itself; (*b*) to occupy the office.

Es ist eine ungeheure Aufgabe, die Bevölkerung Europas auch nur notdürftig zu bekleiden und zu ernähren.
Es ist nicht erlaubt, hier unbekleidet herumzuliegen.
Der Bischof wurde mit Ring und Stab bekleidet.
Er wurde mit einem hohen Amt bekleidet.

3. **Einkleiden** is 'to clothe as befits one's office , therefore 'to put into the uniform of this office'. Figuratively, it refers to the clothing of thoughts in suitable words.

Er wurde als Mönch eingekleidet.
Es gelingt ihm immer, solche Bemerkungen in freundliche Worte einzukleiden.

DRINK 1. **Getränk** is the general term for any kind of beverage, whether taken for pleasure or to slake thirst, and whether intoxicating or not.

Tee ist ein angenehmes Getränk.
Allerlei Getränke standen auf dem Tisch.

2. **Trank** is a more special term for beverage. On the one hand it can be an elevated term, on the other it can denote a drink prepared for a special purpose, particularly a concoction, in which case it often expresses a subjective attitude to the beverage in question. In the second application it occurs frequently in compounds.

Das ist ein göttlicher Trank.
Versuch' mal meinen Trank (concoction).
Ein Fruchttrank, ein Liebestrank.

3. **Trunk** means (*a*) a draught, a gulp. It translates 'to take a drink' of a beverage, only in a few fixed phrases. (See also **4**.) (*b*) In a few fixed phrases, mostly only in literary use, it means excessive drinking of intoxicating liquors. (See also **5**.)

(*a*) *Das war ein erfrischender Trunk* (in literary language).
Er hat einen Trunk Wein getan.
(*b*) *Er ist dem Trunk ergeben.*

4. In the sense of 'draught', in such phrases as 'to take, ask for, give, a drink', without mention of the beverage, German uses **etwas zu trinken**. The omission of *etwas* is possible only in exalted, e.g. biblical style.

Er verlangte etwas zu trinken.
Er gab dem Kind etwas zu trinken.

5. In the sense of the excessive drinking of intoxicating liquors **Alkohol** is generally used. **Trinken** is possible where 'drinking' could be used in English.

Die Alkoholfrage wurde lebhaft debattiert.
Der Alkohol hat viele Ehen zerstört.
Er hat sich dem Alkohol, dem Trinken, ergeben.

DRUNK **Betrunken** is the literal term, i.e. intoxicated through indulgence in alcohol. **Trunken** is mostly figurative, i.e. intoxicated in mind, spirit, and is used only in exalted language. Only in elevated style can it be used in the literal sense. 'Drunken', i.e. a permanent characteristic, cannot be translated by these terms without their modification.[1,2]

Er kam betrunken nach Hause.
Man sieht ihn kaum, ohne daß er betrunken ist.
'Wo bist du? Trunken dämmert die Seele mir
Von aller deiner Wonne....' (Hölderlin, *Dem Sonnengott.*)

EDUCATE **Erziehen**[3] refers to the process, **bilden**[4] to the result of the process of educating.

Er wurde in dieser Schule erzogen.
Er wurde schlecht erzogen.
Er ist ein gebildeter Mensch.

[1] *Trunkenbold*: drunkard.

[2] *Berauscht* is used literally and figuratively. In the literal sense it does not necessarily assign the cause of drunkenness to alcohol. Drugs and the like may be the cause. *Besoffen*, a somewhat vulgar term, suggests the consumption of vast quantities of alcohol. *Saufen*, normally applied to animals, suggests immoderate drinking when used of human beings. *Er säuft wie ein Loch.*

[3] *Aufziehen* refers to the care bestowed on the physical growth of persons, animals, plants, and means 'to bring up', 'to rear', 'to raise'. *Großziehen* is a general term (used mostly in the passive voice) for the bringing up of children. *Ein unerzogenes Kind* = a naughty, ill-bred, child. *Ziehen* is used transitively in the related sense of 'to grow' plants, vegetables, etc. (e.g. *er zieht Tomaten*). *Anbauen* is used of cereals. *Wachsen* can only be used intransitively. 'To grow up' = *aufwachsen, heranwachsen*, the latter denoting only the process, and therefore is not used in the past participle (e.g. *heranwachsende Kinder*). *Groß werden* is used in compound tenses in the sense of 'grow up' (e.g. *sie sind auf dem Lande groß geworden*).

[4] The same distinction applies to the nouns *Erziehung, Bildung* (e.g. *er hat eine schlechte Erziehung gehabt, er hat keine Bildung*), though at times the distinction tends to disappear (e.g. *Erziehungs-, Bildungsanstalten*). *Bildung* now means exclusively 'education'. In the classical and romantic periods it meant 'culture', which is now expressed by *Kultur*. *Kultur* also means 'civilization', *Zivilisation* referring mainly to mechanical inventions as the result of industrial progress. The two stand in sharp contrast to each other, unlike the English and the French terms. Some of the implications of civilization cannot therefore be expressed succinctly in German. *Gesittung* = civilized behaviour. Often 'Schulen' must be used for 'education' (*Staatsunterstützung für Schulen*).

EMBITTER i.e. a lasting state, is **Verbittern.**

It should not be confused with **erbittern,** to incense, to provoke, to make fierce, i.e. a temporary state.

Der Mißerfolg seines Buches hat ihn, ihm das Leben, verbittert.
Die Demütigung hat ihn erbittert.
Es wurde erbittert gekämpft.

ENJOY 1. Genießen.

Unlike 'enjoy', *genießen* cannot be used in generalizations as a synonym of 'like' (e.g. I enjoy good conversation), but only in reference to a particular occasion (e.g. I enjoyed the music). Nor can it be used as a synonym of 'have' (e.g. we are enjoying the first holiday in five years; last week we enjoyed a spell of good weather). In the latter sense only *haben* is possible in German.

When the object of *genießen* is a noun denoting food or drink, its meaning is not 'enjoy' (see 'taste', *schmecken*), but 'partake of', 'consume'. This use is, however, apt to sound affected.

Genießen translates 'enjoy' in the following senses:

(a) To possess something that is of benefit to one, to have the use of, to have as one's lot.[1,2]

Er genießt die Achtung seiner Mitbürger.
Er genießt keinen guten Ruf.
Er hat einen gründlichen Unterricht genossen.
Er genießt dieselben Rechte wie wir.
Er genießt die Zinsen des Vermögens seiner Frau.

(b) With things that have the power to absorb one emotionally, sensuously or spiritually *genießen* means 'to enjoy intensely' by surrendering oneself to this power. Such things include: (i) states of being, feelings and words that indirectly stand for these (e.g. *Gegenwart*); (ii) words that denote sight and sound, i.e. sense-perceptions, and the objects of these if they suggest vastness, the illimitable (e.g. *Landschaft*); (iii) a few activities which possess this power of absorption, mostly artistic performances.

Das Leben, das Landleben, den Aufenthalt (i.e. being somewhere), *die Freude des Wiedersehens, das Glück, das Alleinsein, seine Jugend, die Ruhe nach der Arbeit, den Humor einer Situation, den Anblick* (e.g. *einer Statue, des Meeres*), *die Natur, den Sonnenaufgang, das Licht, die Luft, die Musik, das Rauschen* (*der Wellen*), *die Schönheit* (*des Waldes*),

[1] *Genießen* is etymologically connected with *nutzen* (compare *Nutznießer*).
[2] *Sich einer Sache erfreuen,* to rejoice in the possession of a thing, is a close synonym.

die Klarheit eines Stils, die Aufführung eines Theaterstücks, das Spiel (of music).

'*Trägheit fesselte den Geist, indes die Sinne die ungeheure und betäubende Unterhaltung der Meeresstille genossen*' (Thomas Mann, *Der Tod in Venedig*). (*Genießen* could not be used with *Unterhaltung* in its ordinary sense.)

(c) **It** is used with other words if it is emphasized either (i) by emphasis in the spoken word; (ii) by the addition of some adverb such as *wirklich* or *sehr*; (iii) by being used in certain constructions that have this force (e.g. the imperative, the purpose infinitive with *um...zu*, a contrast).

Ich habe den Spaziergang wirklich genossen.
Wir haben den Vortrag, den Film, das Konzert, aber sehr genossen.
Wir genießen den Feiertag in vollen Zügen.
Genießen Sie Ihre Ferien, den Ausflug!
Genießen Sie das schöne Wetter, solange es anhält.
Wir gingen aus, um das schöne Wetter zu genießen.
Heute ist das erste Mal, daß wir die Fahrt genossen haben.
Gestern haben wir den Ritt genossen, aber nicht heute.
Er fand den Vortrag schlecht, ich habe ihn aber genossen.

(d) With reference to smoking.

Ein Pfeifchen, eine Zigarre, eine Zigarette genießen.

2. To enjoy oneself: **sich amüsieren.**

Instead of this verb, however, the verbs treated in the next section are more commonly used.

Ich habe mich auf der Reise gut, köstlich, amüsiert.

3. When *genießen* is not possible, 'enjoy' must be rendered by terms such as: *schmecken* (food and drink); *gefallen* (often stronger than 'please'); *einem Freude, Vergnügen, Spaß, machen, bereiten; Freude, Vergnügen, Spaß haben, finden an; ein (Hoch)genuß sein, schön sein.*[1]

Der Wein hat mir geschmeckt.
Das Konzert hat mir gut gefallen, Freude gemacht; war ein Genuß.

[1] *Sich freuen an* suggests the enjoyment of something before one's senses. *Er freute sich an den Klängen der Musik, am Anblick des Bildes, an meiner Verlegenheit, an dem Grün der Wiese. Freuen* is mostly used reflexively or with the impersonal *es* as subject, and means that joy is given by the presence or existence of a thing. For distinctions between it and *erfreuen* see Paul and Euling, *Deutsches Wörterbuch*. To the explanations given in that work can be added that when the subject is a thing (e.g. *Nachricht*) the distinction is generally that *freuen* expresses a simple impulsive feeling, whereas *erfreuen* suggests detachment (e.g. *die Nachricht hat mich gefreut, erfreut*). *Sich freuen über* means 'to rejoice at' a fact, *sich freuen auf* refers to the future and means 'to look forward' to a thing with pleasure.

ENJOY

Ich habe viel Freude an seinem Besuch gehabt.
Wie hat Ihnen Ihr Aufenthalt auf dem Lande gefallen?
Ich kann an einem Gespräch, das immer wieder abschweift, keine Freude finden.

ENTER Literal sense.

'Enter' is often interchanged with 'go into'. In discriminating use it suggests with a personal subject something special about the circumstances of entry, e.g. the state or attitude of mind of the person who enters, the effect on others present. With a thing as subject, it suggests a passage through a medium, sometimes a resisting medium.

The use of the German terms is determined in particular by the following factors: (*a*) whether the space entered is enclosed or not; (*b*) whether an official (i.e. permission to enter) or a human term is required.

1. **Gehen** (*fahren, reiten, fließen,* etc., see 'go') must be used when 'enter' does not suggest anything special about the circumstances of 'entry', i.e. when it is interchangeable with 'go'.

Hinein is added to these verbs only (*a*) if it is desired to give a vivid picture of the space entered or to express violent motion; (*b*) to render the intransitive use of 'enter' (to go inside). In (*a*) the prefix really suggests a stage after entry. Thus: *wir fuhren in die Hauptstraße* (turned into it); *wir fuhren in die Hauptstraße hinein* (a picture of the whole street). Further: *wir fuhren in den Hafen* (the normal statement); *wir fuhren in den Hafen hinein* (a picture of a stretch of water with its shores); '*Ich ging also in das alte Haus hinein und holte meine Geige*' (Eichendorff, *Aus dem Leben eines Taugenichts*) (a picture of the *Taugenichts* in the house); *wir fuhren blindlings in die Menge hinein* (violent movement).

Er ging ins Zimmer und legte sich hin.
Er ging durch eine Seitentür ins Theater (hinein).
Der Strom fließt hier in das Meer.

2. **Treten** and its compounds. These primarily mean 'to step', and should only be used when this meaning is present, i.e. to put one's foot across the threshold. *Treten* and *eintreten* as renderings of 'enter' can be applied only to entry into an enclosed space.

(a) **Treten,** used in the sense of 'enter', always suggests a circumscribed space, mostly a room, but sometimes merely a part of a larger area. It conveys an impression of the manner of entry, e.g. by a description of the effect on others. It must always be followed by *in,* i.e. it cannot be used absolutely.

(iii) **Entweichen:** to escape silently, stealthily.

Der Gefangene ist entwichen.

(iv) **Entwischen** suggests that the escape is effected by seizing the right moment, so that one cheats one's would-be capturer.[1] It thus approximates to *entschlüpfen* and 'elude', but has a somewhat colloquial flavour.

Der Täter ist im letzten Augenblick entwischt.

(v) **Entfliehen,** which is much used, means 'to escape by flight', and suggests distance.

Nachdem er seinen Wächter niedergeschlagen hatte, konnte er entfliehen.

(vi) **Entrinnen** is an elevated term and used figuratively, particularly with the noun *Gefahr.*

(vii) **Entgehen:** to escape being caught or involved in a situation, generally by a wide margin.[2]

Er ist dem Schiffbruch entgangen (by not travelling on the wrecked ship).

Er ist dem Tode, der Gefahr, der Entdeckung, entgangen.

2. To escape from something which holds the body, e.g. a trap, net, chains. **Sich befreien** can be used when a struggle with the trap, etc. is implied. Otherwise specific terms such as *springen, kriechen* must be employed.

Die Ratte befreite sich aus der Falle.
Er hat sich aus dem Netz, seinen Ketten, befreit.
Die Katze sprang aus dem Sack.

3. Simple verbs (*schlüpfen, springen,* etc.) should be used where the action is stressed as much as or more than the result, and where the context makes it clear that the purpose of the action is escape.

Der Fisch ist durch das Netz geschlüpft.
Sieh mal, der Gefangene springt aus dem Zug.

4. **Sich retten** is used particularly in reference to shipwreck. It can be followed by a prepositional phrase denoting separation or destination.

Er hat sich aus dem Schiffbruch, ans Ufer, gerettet.

5. **Fliehen,** to flee, does not denote the success of the action of flight (contrast *entfliehen*) unless accompanied by a phrase which makes this

[1] The time-factor is also uppermost in *erwischen* (see 'catch').
[2] There exist a number of other verbs compounded with *ent,* not treated here (e.g. *entlaufen, entfliegen*). *Der Hund ist entlaufen. Unser Vogel ist uns entflogen.*

Er trat in das Zimmer, und alle verstummten sofort.
Als er in die Versammlung trat, horchten alle auf.
In andächtiger Stimmung traten wir in die Kapelle.
Er trat behutsam ins Wasser.

(b) **Eintreten** is used in three ways. (*a*) In the sense of 'step into' it implies a contrast with the space outside. (*b*) In the sense of 'enter' it refers almost exclusively to a room, and suggests a more intimate relation with the person in the room than *treten.* (*c*) It can be used absolutely.

Wir traten in das Gebäude ein, um uns vor dem Regen zu schützen (stepped into).
Vom Garten aus tritt man gleich in sein Arbeitszimmer ein (steps into).
Mein alter Freund Karl trat ganz unerwartet in mein Arbeitszimmer ein und wollte mich zu einem Spaziergang abholen (entered).
Er trat ein.

(c) **Hineintreten** suggests a certain hesitation at the threshold.

Er zögerte eine Weile vor der Tür und trat dann hinein.

(d) **Betreten** is used in two ways. (*a*) It suggests on the part of the person who enters a strong emotional attitude or an awareness that the entry is or has proved to be a fateful step. 'To set foot in, on' is the closest English equivalent. (*b*) As an official term it refers to the right or permission to enter.[1] In neither case is it applied solely to a confined or enclosed space.

Ich werde sein Haus nie wieder betreten.
Voll Ehrfurcht betrat er das Heiligtum.
Als er deutschen Boden betrat, hatte er keine Ahnung, daß er ihn nie wieder verlassen würde.
Bevor man eine Moschee betritt, muß man die Schuhe ausziehen.
Sie haben keinen Haftbefehl, der Sie berechtigt, dieses Haus zu betreten.

3. **Hinein-, hereinkommen** are used in the sense of 'to enter' a large area, e.g. a country, a town, a harbour, i.e. to get into.

Hereinkommen is used, though not as a formal, official term, in reference to permission to enter. It suggests in a general way the steps necessary to enter, e.g. the obtaining of permission, but less clearly the specific act of attempting to enter. The latter is expressed by *hineinkommen.* Neither of these words can be used when the place of entry is mentioned (e.g. I entered Germany at Basel).

Es ist schwer, in die Schweiz hereinzukommen (generally, and in particular: to get permission).

[1] The English equivalent is often 'to walk on'. *Das Betreten des Rasens ist verboten.*

Es ist schwer, in die Schweiz hineinzukommen (difficulties at the frontier itself).

Sobald Sie nach Holland hereinkommen, fühlen Sie sich in einer anderen Welt.

4. Words compounded with **ein**.

Einziehen is used of a body of people which enters an area, e.g. an army, a procession. See article on 'move'. **Einsteigen:** to climb into a thing, particularly into a vehicle as a passenger. **Einreise** and the verb **einreisen** are official terms which refer to permission to enter a country.[1, 2]

Das Heer zog in die Stadt ein.
Als Sieger zog er in Wien ein.
Er stieg in den Zug ein.
Der Dieb stieg durch das Fenster ein.
Die Einreiseerlaubnis für Deutschland wurde ihm nicht bewilligt.
Er ist am 13ten März nach Deutschland eingereist.
Seine Einreise nach Deutschland erfolgte am 3ten September.

5. Both **dringen** and **eindringen** are used with a person or a thing as subject. They correspond more closely to 'penetrate' than to 'enter', but in the absence of a more exact term must be used to translate the latter. With a non-personal subject, both can refer, amongst other things, to the entry of objects into the human body and to the entry of gases, liquids and the like into a confined space. The distinction between the two terms is that *eindringen* suggests greater difficulty in entry than *dringen*, often a burrowing action.

Die Kugel, der Dolch, drang in seine Brust.
Der rostige Nagel drang in seinen Schenkel ein.
Das Gift drang in den Blutstrom.
Der Blutklumpen drang in sein Herz ein.
Der Rauch drang ins Zimmer (the addition of *ein* would suggest clouds of smoke billowing at the door or window).
Der Rauch drang in meine Nase.
Die Sonne dringt kaum in das Dickicht (*ein*).
Der Regen dringt in meine Schuhe.
Der Feind dringt in die Festung (the addition of *ein* would clearly denote difficulty).

[1] *Ausreise* is the official term for 'exit' from a country.

[2] Further verbs compounded with *ein* are: *einrücken* (see 'move'); *einmünden*, to empty into, of water, streets and the like; *einbrechen*, to burgle, to irrupt into. *Einfahren* and *einlaufen* mean 'to arrive'.

ESCAPE **A.** Of living beings.

1. Verbs compounded with *ent*. Of these *entkommen* is the most ger while the others suggest the particular manner of escape. With exception of *entgehen* all mean 'to escape from' the power of a perso thing into which one has fallen or is about to fall. When the escape made from a place, this can be a building, a restricted area such as a tow but can be neither an area as large as a country nor a thing which gri or entangles the body (e.g. a trap, a net, chains, a small bag). *Entkomm* suggests that one escapes from something which has held one in its grip not that one avoids a thing by not being near it.

(a) **Entkommen**

Er entkam aus dem Konzentrationslager.
Er ist seinen Wächtern entkommen.
Er ist nach den Bergen entkommen.
Er ist der Gefahr entkommen.
Er entkam aus dem brennenden Gebäude.

(b) The others compounded with *ent* suggest the manner of escape. This reference is, however, often more figurative than literal. Therefore these verbs are not normally used when the concrete situation with reference to its details (e.g. the thing from which the escape is made) is visually evoked. They would, for instance, be inappropriate to call attention to an escape which is being effected before one's eyes. Thus while it is possible to say: *er ist aus dem Gefängnis, dem Zug, entsprungen* (an event in the past), this verb would be unsuitable to translate 'escape' in the sentence: look, he's escaping from the train. Since an escape from small objects emphasizes the concrete and realistic character of the situation, these verbs should not be used in such cases (e.g. to render: the cat escaped from the sack). *Ent* generally suggests that the act is viewed from a certain distance. Hence its tendency towards figurative application.[1]

(i) **Entspringen:** to escape by jumping (*aus einem Zug*) or by a sudden coup (*aus dem Gefängnis*). In all cases actual captivity is implied.[2]

(ii) **Entschlüpfen** is used in the figurative sense of slipping through one's fingers, i.e. nimbly and adroitly. It approximates to 'elude', i.e. to escape capture by a hair's breadth. It is used particularly of animals.

Der Verbrecher, der Hase, die Schlange, ist uns entschlüpft.

[1] *Ent* stresses separation as a result more forcibly than the action of separating (e.g. *er entnahm es der Schublade* is less concrete than *er nahm es aus der Schublade*). This characteristic makes these verbs elevated in tone or, if misapplied, precious (e.g. *er ist dem Zug enstiegen*).

[2] *Ausbrechen* is often used of escaping from prison (e.g. *ein ausgebrochener Häftling*).

Er trat in das Zimmer, und alle verstummten sofort.
Als er in die Versammlung trat, horchten alle auf.
In andächtiger Stimmung traten wir in die Kapelle.
Er trat behutsam ins Wasser.

(b) **Eintreten** is used in three ways. (*a*) In the sense of 'step into' it implies a contrast with the space outside. (*b*) In the sense of 'enter' it refers almost exclusively to a room, and suggests a more intimate relation with the person in the room than *treten*. (*c*) It can be used absolutely.

Wir traten in das Gebäude ein, um uns vor dem Regen zu schützen (stepped into).
Vom Garten aus tritt man gleich in sein Arbeitszimmer ein (steps into).
Mein alter Freund Karl trat ganz unerwartet in mein Arbeitszimmer ein und wollte mich zu einem Spaziergang abholen (entered).
Er trat ein.

(c) **Hineintreten** suggests a certain hesitation at the threshold.

Er zögerte eine Weile vor der Tür und trat dann hinein.

(d) **Betreten** is used in two ways. (*a*) It suggests on the part of the person who enters a strong emotional attitude or an awareness that the entry is or has proved to be a fateful step. 'To set foot in, on' is the closest English equivalent. (*b*) As an official term it refers to the right or permission to enter.[1] In neither case is it applied solely to a confined or enclosed space.

Ich werde sein Haus nie wieder betreten.
Voll Ehrfurcht betrat er das Heiligtum.
Als er deutschen Boden betrat, hatte er keine Ahnung, daß er ihn nie wieder verlassen würde.
Bevor man eine Moschee betritt, muß man die Schuhe ausziehen.
Sie haben keinen Haftbefehl, der Sie berechtigt, dieses Haus zu betreten.

3. **Hinein-, hereinkommen** are used in the sense of 'to enter' a large area, e.g. a country, a town, a harbour, i.e. to get into.

Hereinkommen is used, though not as a formal, official term, in reference to permission to enter. It suggests in a general way the steps necessary to enter, e.g. the obtaining of permission, but less clearly the specific act of attempting to enter. The latter is expressed by *hineinkommen*. Neither of these words can be used when the place of entry is mentioned (e.g. I entered Germany at Basel).

Es ist schwer, in die Schweiz hereinzukommen (generally, and in particular: to get permission).

[1] The English equivalent is often 'to walk on'. *Das Betreten des Rasens ist verboten.*

Es ist schwer, in die Schweiz hineinzukommen (difficulties at the frontier itself).

Sobald Sie nach Holland hereinkommen, fühlen Sie sich in einer anderen Welt.

4. Words compounded with **ein**.

Einziehen is used of a body of people which enters an area, e.g. an army, a procession. See article on 'move'. **Einsteigen:** to climb into a thing, particularly into a vehicle as a passenger. **Einreise** and the verb **einreisen** are official terms which refer to permission to enter a country.[1, 2]

Das Heer zog in die Stadt ein.
Als Sieger zog er in Wien ein.
Er stieg in den Zug ein.
Der Dieb stieg durch das Fenster ein.
Die Einreiseerlaubnis für Deutschland wurde ihm nicht bewilligt.
Er ist am 13ten März nach Deutschland eingereist.
Seine Einreise nach Deutschland erfolgte am 3ten September.

5. Both **dringen** and **eindringen** are used with a person or a thing as subject. They correspond more closely to 'penetrate' than to 'enter', but in the absence of a more exact term must be used to translate the latter. With a non-personal subject, both can refer, amongst other things, to the entry of objects into the human body and to the entry of gases, liquids and the like into a confined space. The distinction between the two terms is that *eindringen* suggests greater difficulty in entry than *dringen*, often a burrowing action.

Die Kugel, der Dolch, drang in seine Brust.
Der rostige Nagel drang in seinen Schenkel ein.
Das Gift drang in den Blutstrom.
Der Blutklumpen drang in sein Herz ein.
Der Rauch drang ins Zimmer (the addition of *ein* would suggest clouds of smoke billowing at the door or window).
Der Rauch drang in meine Nase.
Die Sonne dringt kaum in das Dickicht (*ein*).
Der Regen dringt in meine Schuhe.
Der Feind dringt in die Festung (the addition of *ein* would clearly denote difficulty).

[1] *Ausreise* is the official term for 'exit' from a country.

[2] Further verbs compounded with *ein* are: *einrücken* (see 'move'); *einmünden*, to empty into, of water, streets and the like; *einbrechen*, to burgle, to irrupt into. *Einfahren* and *einlaufen* mean 'to arrive'.

ESCAPE A. Of living beings.

1. Verbs compounded with *ent*. Of these *entkommen* is the most ger while the others suggest the particular manner of escape. With exception of *entgehen* all mean 'to escape from' the power of a perso thing into which one has fallen or is about to fall. When the escape made from a place, this can be a building, a restricted area such as a tow but can be neither an area as large as a country nor a thing which grip or entangles the body (e.g. a trap, a net, chains, a small bag). *Entkomme* suggests that one escapes from something which has held one in its grip, not that one avoids a thing by not being near it.

(a) **Entkommen**

Er entkam aus dem Konzentrationslager.
Er ist seinen Wächtern entkommen.
Er ist nach den Bergen entkommen.
Er ist der Gefahr entkommen.
Er entkam aus dem brennenden Gebäude.

(b) The others compounded with *ent* suggest the manner of escape. This reference is, however, often more figurative than literal. Therefore these verbs are not normally used when the concrete situation with reference to its details (e.g. the thing from which the escape is made) is visually evoked. They would, for instance, be inappropriate to call attention to an escape which is being effected before one's eyes. Thus while it is possible to say: *er ist aus dem Gefängnis, dem Zug, entsprungen* (an event in the past), this verb would be unsuitable to translate 'escape' in the sentence: look, he's escaping from the train. Since an escape from small objects emphasizes the concrete and realistic character of the situation, these verbs should not be used in such cases (e.g. to render: the cat escaped from the sack). *Ent* generally suggests that the act is viewed from a certain distance. Hence its tendency towards figurative application.[1]

(i) **Entspringen:** to escape by jumping (*aus einem Zug*) or by a sudden coup (*aus dem Gefängnis*). In all cases actual captivity is implied.[2]

(ii) **Entschlüpfen** is used in the figurative sense of slipping through one's fingers, i.e. nimbly and adroitly. It approximates to 'elude', i.e. to escape capture by a hair's breadth. It is used particularly of animals.

Der Verbrecher, der Hase, die Schlange, ist uns entschlüpft.

[1] *Ent* stresses separation as a result more forcibly than the action of separating (e.g. *er entnahm es der Schublade* is less concrete than *er nahm es aus der Schublade*). This characteristic makes these verbs elevated in tone or, if misapplied, precious (e.g. *er ist dem Zug enstiegen*).

[2] *Ausbrechen* is often used of escaping from prison (e.g. *ein ausgebrochener Häftling*).

(iii) **Entweichen:** to escape silently, stealthily.

Der Gefangene ist entwichen.

(iv) **Entwischen** suggests that the escape is effected by seizing the right moment, so that one cheats one's would-be capturer.[1] It thus approximates to *entschlüpfen* and 'elude', but has a somewhat colloquial flavour.

Der Täter ist im letzten Augenblick entwischt.

(v) **Entfliehen,** which is much used, means 'to escape by flight', and suggests distance.

Nachdem er seinen Wächter niedergeschlagen hatte, konnte er entfliehen.

(vi) **Entrinnen** is an elevated term and used figuratively, particularly with the noun *Gefahr.*

(vii) **Entgehen:** to escape being caught or involved in a situation, generally by a wide margin.[2]

Er ist dem Schiffbruch entgangen (by not travelling on the wrecked ship).

Er ist dem Tode, der Gefahr, der Entdeckung, entgangen.

2. To escape from something which holds the body, e.g. a trap, net, chains. **Sich befreien** can be used when a struggle with the trap, etc. is implied. Otherwise specific terms such as *springen, kriechen* must be employed.

Die Ratte befreite sich aus der Falle.
Er hat sich aus dem Netz, seinen Ketten, befreit.
Die Katze sprang aus dem Sack.

3. Simple verbs (*schlüpfen, springen,* etc.) should be used where the action is stressed as much as or more than the result, and where the context makes it clear that the purpose of the action is escape.

Der Fisch ist durch das Netz geschlüpft.
Sieh mal, der Gefangene springt aus dem Zug.

4. **Sich retten** is used particularly in reference to shipwreck. It can be followed by a prepositional phrase denoting separation or destination.

Er hat sich aus dem Schiffbruch, ans Ufer, gerettet.

5. **Fliehen,** to flee, does not denote the success of the action of flight (contrast *entfliehen*) unless accompanied by a phrase which makes this

[1] The time-factor is also uppermost in *erwischen* (see 'catch').

[2] There exist a number of other verbs compounded with *ent,* not treated here (e.g. *entlaufen, entfliegen*). *Der Hund ist entlaufen. Unser Vogel ist uns entflogen.*

clear. It is used particularly of escape from a wide area (e.g. a country). **Flüchten** differs from it in that it means 'to seek refuge' and thus stresses the goal rather than the attempt to get away from the pursuer. It can, however, be accompanied by a phrase meaning 'from', whereas *sich flüchten* only suggests the goal and is followed by *in* or an equivalent.

Er ist aus Deutschland geflohen.
Er ist in die Schweiz geflüchtet.
Er hat sich in das Haus geflüchtet.

6. **Davonkommen:** to escape, get off, with less injury than might be expected.

Er ist mit dem Schrecken, mit einem gebrochenen Arm, davongekommen.

B. Of gases, liquids, things.

1. **Entweichen** is the normal term in reference to gas.[1]

Das Gas entweicht aus dem Ofen.

2. **Ausströmen, ausfließen** (in smaller quantities), **rinnen** (trickle) are used of escaping liquids.

Das Benzin fließt aus; das Gas strömt aus.

3. In reference to things the appropriate specific term must be used.

Das Mehl rinnt aus dem Sack.

C. Figurative use. The subject is a thing.

1. **Entgehen:** to escape the mind, observation, appreciation.[2]

Der Sinn Ihrer Bemerkung ist mir entgangen (I missed).
Die Schönheit der Landschaft entging ihm nicht.

2. **Entschlüpfen** is used of remarks that one makes inadvertently.

Die Bemerkung entschlüpfte ihm.

3. **Entfallen:** to escape the memory.

Sein Name ist mir entfallen.

ESTIMATE[3] **Schätzen:**[4] to estimate roughly.[5] **Einschätzen:** to estimate exactly. 'To estimate at' followed by a numeral can only be *schätzen auf* (with the accusative) or **abschätzen auf,** which is used to

[1] More popularly: *herauskommen.*
[2] *Sich eine Gelegenheit entgehen lassen*: to let an opportunity slip.
[3] Study together with 'evaluate'.
[4] See also 'appreciate'. With a personal object it can only mean 'appreciate' or 'esteem'.
[5] *Schätzungsweise*: at a rough estimate, guess.

estimate distances and prices of articles and is more exact than *schätzen*. It cannot be followed by a personal object.

Wie hoch schätzen Sie den Verlust?
Wie hoch schätzen Sie den Verlust ein?
Ich schätze, die Brücke ist 3 Kilometer entfernt.
Ich habe ihn immer so eingeschätzt.
Er hat sich genau so betragen, wie ich ihn eingeschätzt habe.
Ich habe die Entfernung bis auf 1 Kilometer, die Möbel auf 750 D.M., abgeschätzt.

EVALUATE **Werten** is only used in contexts which are concerned with basic principles. **Bewerten** suggests an evaluation carried out according to standards of measurement already established. Its purpose may be purely practical. In reference to numbers it implies exactness, unlike the synonymous term *schätzen* (see article on 'estimate'). Both verbs are used transitively and intransitively, but the transitive use of *werten* is becoming obsolete except in the infinitive. In conversation *bewerten* tends to be used in both senses.

Wie haben Sie den Aufsatz bewertet (what numerical mark did you award)?
Er wertet nach strengen Gesichtspunkten.
Verschiedene Generationen werten Kunstwerke anders.
Dieses Bild ist höher zu werten als jenes.
'*Völlig falsch ist es, dies zugleich eiskalte und brennende Werk als ein dichterisches Weltbild, als Ausdruck einer Lebensanschauung zu werten*' (Gundolf, *Heinrich von Kleist*).
Ein ehrlicher Materialist ist höher zu werten als ein wurzelloser Idealist.
Das Kommittee hat die Bilder schon bewertet (judged their merit, fixed a price, and the like).
Der deutsche Generalstab hat die Macht der englischen Luftwaffe bei Dünkirchen falsch bewertet.
Wie bewerten Sie die Geschäftskapazität dieses Unternehmens?
Die zum Verkauf stehenden Autos müssen heute offiziell bewertet werden.

EVEN (adverb) **Sogar** and **selbst** are often interchangeable. Where, however, emphasis is required, as in a climax or a contrast, *sogar* should be used.[1] When 'even' modifies a verb, *selbst* is impossible in this sense, since it would mean 'self'.

With *nicht* **(ein)mal** is usual, except in emphatic contexts, in which case *sogar* is preferable. *Nicht* retains its ordinary position in the sentence; it does not precede *sogar*.

[1] In this sense it approximates closely to 'indeed', 'in fact'.

Auch nur is used in phrases or clauses depending on a negative, e.g. after *ohne* (=without so much as what is stated, let alone more). *Sogar* is also possible in this combination where great emphasis is desired.

Sogar, selbst, seine Freunde haben sich von ihm abgewandt.
Sogar, selbst, mit Geld ist hier nichts zu machen.
Ich mag den Mann nicht, und sogar sein Name ist mir verhaßt (*selbst* would be too weak).
Selbst im Frieden können Sie das nicht kaufen (unemphatic).
Sie sagen, der Mann ist nicht ganz ehrlich, er ist sogar ein ausgesprochener Betrüger (*selbst* would be impossible).
Wegen seiner Verspätung wurde er sogar entlassen (*sogar* modifies the verb, *selbst* is therefore impossible).
Nicht einmal Brot war zu haben.
Das Dorf war derartig ausgeplündert, daß sogar Brot nicht mehr aufzutreiben war (*sogar* preferable to *nicht einmal* because of the emphasis).
Er blieb eine Woche in der Stadt, ohne uns auch nur anzurufen.
Ich hätte nicht gemeint, daß er sich des Abends auch nur erinnerte.

EVENT, INCIDENT 1. **Ereignis** is the most general term. It is connected with *Auge*, and means that which becomes visible, real ('*Das Unzulängliche, Hier wird's Ereignis*', Goethe, *Faust II*). Since it conveys the idea of 'become visible', it can only refer to definite, specific events, not to vague or obscure happenings.

Die Ereignisse haben uns recht gegeben.
Diese Konferenz ist ein wichtiges Ereignis.
Das ist schon ein wirkliches Ereignis.
Die Ereignisse der letzten Woche waren gradezu katastrophal.
Die Reihenfolge der Ereignisse ist wichtig.

2. **Begebenheit** is something out of the ordinary, whether some dramatic manifestations of Nature, something in the human world that strikes us by its dimensions, or something in the realm of fancy. It has a strong subjective colouring.

Erzählen Sie uns eine Begebenheit aus dem 14. Jahrhundert!
'*Was ist eine Novelle anders als eine sich ereignete, unerhörte Begebenheit?*' (Goethe to Eckermann, 1827).

3. **Vorgang** refers to something changing, evolving, a process. The plural is used of a vague, undefined series of happenings. It thus contrasts with the specific term *Ereignis*.

Die Vorgänge in Europa sind nicht ermutigend.
Die Vorgänge jenes Tages bleiben mir ein Geheimnis.

4. **Vorfall:** a sudden happening, often unpleasant. It corresponds to 'incident' in all senses except that treated under 5.

Dieser Vorfall hat die ganze Situation geändert.

5. **Zwischenfall:** an incident in a diplomatic sense, i.e. fraught with dangerous possibilities.

Der Zwischenfall an der deutschen Grenze.

6. **Geschehnis** is the most abstract term for 'happening'. Its use is confined to the written word.

Vorgänge sind eine Reihe von Geschehnissen.

EXCITE 1. **Aufregen** refers to excitement which is visible, i.e. manifested externally, in act or gesture, and is therefore the common equivalent of 'excite'.

Regen Sie sich nicht so auf.
Er war so aufgeregt, daß er kaum sprechen konnte.
Das Schließen der Banken hat die Bevölkerung sehr aufgeregt.
Das Kind regt sich zu sehr auf, wenn es ins Kino geht.

2. **Erregen** has no precise equivalent in English. Its meaning is to excite inwardly, to throw into an emotional state, particularly in reference to anger, indignation, and the like. It is sometimes better rendered into English by 'stir', 'work up'.[1] When a feeling or state of mind is the object it is the normal translation of 'excite', i.e. in the sense of 'cause'. It is always used to render the electrical sense (cf. *Erregerkreis* = exciter circuit).

Er war furchtbar erregt, als er die Nachricht hörte.
Er sprach mit erregter Stimme (*aufgeregt* is impossible).
Zuviel Alkohol erregt das Gehirn.
Er hat meinen Haß, Neid erregt.
Hunger, Durst erregen.[2]
Das Ereignis hat mein Interesse, meine Neugierde erregt.
'*Der Geselligkeitsdunst hat sich verstärkt — dieser trockensüßliche, verdickte, erregende, an Ingredienzien reiche Festbrodem...*' (Thomas Mann, *Unordnung und Frühes Leid*).

3. **Anregen** means 'to stimulate'. It must be used to render 'excite' when the latter is followed by 'to' plus a noun or an infinitive.[3]

Seine Rede hat die Bevölkerung zur Tat angeregt (excited...to action).

[1] *Erregung* comes very close to 'emotion'.
[2] But *den Appetit anregen, Appetit* being too weak to use with *erregen*.
[3] In older German *aufregen* was sometimes used in the sense of *anregen*.

EXPERIENCE **A.** Verb.

1. **Erleben:** to pass through an experience without necessarily more than witnessing it.[1] It can thus be ambiguous.

Er hat die Schrecken des Krieges erlebt.
Die Firma erlebt einen neuen Aufschwung.
Ich habe Wutausbrüche von ihm erlebt (not necessarily directed against oneself).
Tu's, sonst wirst du was erleben.

2. **Erfahren:** to receive, be subjected to a thing,[2] often but not invariably unpleasant, i.e. in the sense of 'befall'. It never means merely 'to witness'.

Sie haben eine schwere Enttäuschung erfahren.

B. Noun.

1. **Erlebnis:** something that is lived inwardly and intensely. Its permanent effects, if any, are changes in the inner, emotional life. It can be used absolutely in the sense of an intense imaginative or spiritual experience. Thus used it is stronger than 'experience' which tends to be more external.

Das Erlebnis der Wüste ist unvergeßlich.
Von seinen Kriegserlebnissen wollte er nichts erzählen.
Für Rilke war die Reise nach Rußland das erste, große Erlebnis seines Lebens.
Das Konzert war wirklich ein Erlebnis.

2. **Erfahrung** refers to external happenings and to the wisdom, practical knowledge, general rules drawn from them.

Ich weiß es aus Erfahrung.
Auf Grund meiner Erfahrung habe ich den Vorschlag abgelehnt.
Ich habe schlechte Erfahrungen mit ihm gemacht.[3]

EXPRESS 1. **Ausdrücken** is only used when the manner or form is stated or clearly implied or intensity is suggested.

Drücken Sie sich etwas deutlicher aus.
Er drückt sich schlecht aus.

[1] Similarly: *ich habe es erlebt, daß er zwanzig Stunden hintereinander geschlafen hat* (I have known him to sleep...). A related sense is: to live to see. *Er wird seinen* 80. *Geburtstag sicher noch erleben.*

[2] *Erfahren* can also mean 'to be subjected to' a process, a treatment. *Eine Zubereitung erfahren.*

[3] *Die Erfahrung machen* combines the ideas of having the experience and making the discovery.

EXPRESS

Wie soll man diesen Gedanken ausdrücken?
Dieses Gedicht drückt Körners Begeisterung für den Freiheitsgedanken aus.
Ich habe ganz offen mein Mißfallen ausgedrückt.
Darf ich Ihnen mein Beileid ausdrücken?
Ich habe ihm meinen aufrichtigen Dank ausgedrückt.
Er drückte seinen Zweifel in nicht mißzuverstehender Weise aus.
Seine ganze Haltung, sein Gesicht, drückt Freude aus.

2. **Äußern** and **aussprechen** (the latter of something important) mean 'to make the content of a thing known'.[1] It is also used of emotions and the like in so far as they manifest themselves in action, not only in language.

Äußern Sie sich etwas deutlicher (tell me what you really mean, i.e. in content).
Er äußerte den Wunsch, hier bleiben zu dürfen.
Er äußerte seine Zweifel darüber, ob der Bericht in jeder Einzelheit stimme.
Er sprach die Überzeugung, die Meinung, aus, daß der Krieg noch lange dauern würde.
Wer kann umhin, die Treue der Neger zu bewundern, auch wenn sie sich in so furchtbarer Weise äußert?

3. **Zum Ausdruck bringen** is fuller, more plastic with regard to manner and is used of something vaster in content.

In grandioser Weise hat Michelangelo den Geist der Renaissance zum Ausdruck gebracht.
Das Volk brachte seine Entrüstung über die Politik seiner Führer energisch zum Ausdruck.

EXTENT, DEGREE, MEASURE, SCALE 1. **Maß** corresponds closely to 'measure', and can translate 'extent' and 'degree' only when these are close synonyms of 'measure'. In a measure = *in einem Maß*. 'Great' as an adjective qualifying 'measure' must be translated by *hoch*. In all uses *Maß*, like 'measure', suggests definite limits. *Gewissermaßen* = in some measure.[2]

Sie haben in hohem Maße recht.
Er hat das volle Maß seiner Macht noch nicht erreicht.
Das Maß seiner Sünden ist voll.

[1] In fixed phrases other words are found; e.g. *ich möchte Ihnen für Ihre Unterstützung unseren Dank sagen.*
[2] For *einigermassen* see footnote to 'mind' (p. 225, n. 5).

2. **Grad** corresponds closely to 'degree'. To a degree = *in einem Grade*, up to = *bis zu*. 'Great' as an adjective qualifying 'degree' is translated by *hoch*.

Das ist mir im höchsten Grade verhaßt.
Die Skandinavier sind in hohem Grade zivilisiert.

3. **Ausmaß** suggests absence of limits, and corresponds to 'extent', 'scale', 'magnitude' thus used, particularly in reference to intangibles. To an extent = *in einem Ausmaß*.

Das Ausmaß seines Größenwahns ist gradezu unheimlich.
Das Ausmaß seiner Verschwendungssucht steht in gar keinem Verhältnis zu seinem Einkommen.
Das Ausmaß seiner Verbrechen ist noch nicht bekannt.
Das Ausmaß des Schadens ist unübersehbar.
Solche Verbrechen kommen jetzt in geringerem Ausmaß vor.

4. **Umfang** means primarily 'circumference', which suggests the idea of limits in the sense of 'extent'.

Der Umfang des Schadens ist gering.
Der Umfang unseres Handels mit Südamerika ist befriedigend.
'*Hier ruht zunächst, von dem Ausmaß und Umfang seines Wesens abgesehen, Stefan Georges geschichtlicher Sinn: er allein beherrscht heute die neue Ebene die Nietzsche zuerst wieder sah, die Ebene des ewigen Menschen, nicht die der modernen Menschheit*' (F. Gundolf, *George*).

5. **Ausdehnung** is 'extent' in one dimension, i.e. in reference to something stretched out. See article on 'spread'.

Die Ausdehnung der Stadt hat mich überrascht.

6. 'To an extent' presents difficulties in translation. When the above terms are inapplicable, use may often be made of *Teil* and of such formations as *großenteils* (largely), *größtenteils* (for the most part).

Ein großer Teil des Heeres wurde vernichtet (to a large extent).
Es ist großenteils seine Schuld.

EXTINGUISH (something burning) **Löschen** is the ordinary term in reference to any fire except a small one. **Auslöschen:** to put out a flame or embers which are burning a small object, to snuff out a candle. 'Put out' is therefore translated by both verbs.[1]

Die Feuerwehr löschte den Brand.
Er löschte die Kerze aus.

[1] Both verbs are used figuratively. *Löschen* refers more to the action, *auslöschen* stresses complete cessation of existence. The former is used sometimes as a legal and

FAIL A. To prove unequal to the demands made on a person or thing with reference to a specific occasion or situation.

1. **Versagen** implies the disappointment of expectations and emphasizes the inner weakness or defect which causes the failure rather than the collapse of an undertaking during its execution.

Meine Kräfte haben versagt.
Die Stimme versagte ihr.
Seine Anstrengungen haben versagt.
Der Plan zur Regelung des Verkehrs hat versagt.
Das Gewehr, die Maschine, hat völlig versagt (i.e. *den Dienst versagt*).
Das Licht versagte (electric light, lamp, etc., not day-light).
Diese Anlage wird sicher versagen.
Er versagte in seinem Beruf.
Der Lehrer hat versagt.

2. **Scheitern:** to crash completely in the execution or in action, whether owing to internal weakness or not.

Der feindliche Angriff ist gescheitert.
Das Unternehmen wird aus Mangel an Vorbereitung scheitern.
Der Plan zur Regelung des Verkehrs ist gescheitert (suggests, unlike *versagen*, an external cause).
Alle unsere Hoffnungen sind gescheitert.

3. **Fehlschlagen:** to go awry, to miscarry, at some point or with reference to some detail. The failure need not be absolute, but may be retrieved. It can be coupled with the same nouns as *scheitern*. A further example:

Der Versuch ist fehlgeschlagen.

4. **Durchfallen:** to fail in an examination.

Der Kandidat ist in allen Prüfungen durchgefallen.

B. Not to come, not to eventuate, of something expected.

Ausbleiben can often be used,[1] particularly with reference to the phenomena of nature. Sometimes 'fail to come' or some such equivalent is a more appropriate translation.

Die Weizenernte ist ausgeblieben.[2]

commercial, the latter only as a human term. *Die Eintragung wird gelöscht; eine Schuld löschen; den Durst löschen* (slake, quench); *jeden Verdacht löschen. Das löscht seine Schuld nicht aus; diese Tatsache ist wie ausgelöscht.*

[1] Also in the phrase *es kann nicht ausbleiben, daß* (*die Regierung gestürzt wird*), i.e. the Government cannot fail to fall. See 'fail' followed by the infinitive.

[2] Or *ist ausgefallen* (of something which otherwise recurs regularly).

Der Wind, der Regen, der Sturm, ist ausgeblieben.
Die unheilvollen Folgen dieser Handlungsweise werden nicht ausbleiben.
Ihm blieb der Atem aus.

C. To become weaker or less, with reference to things. German has no general term to render this use as the following examples show.

Seine Geisteskräfte nehmen ab (his mind is failing).
Sein Gedächtnis wird schwach.
Seine Augen werden schlecht.
Seine Gesundheit läßt sehr nach.
Die Vorräte werden knapp.
Der Brunnen ist versiegt.

D. 'Fail' followed by the infinitive.[1]

1. When failure in conscious effort or purpose is implied, **nicht gelingen**[2] is the most common rendering.

Es ist mir nicht gelungen, ihn zu überzeugen.
Den Truppen gelang es nicht, die feindlichen Stellungen einzunehmen.
Es gelang mir nicht, die Zigarette selbst zu drehen.

2. With phrases denoting mental perceptions conscious effort may or may not be implied. For the latter case, which is merely equivalent to a strong negative, German lacks a general term. Somewhat colloquially the emphatic *gar* may be added to the negative. *Entgehen* (to escape[3] one's notice) can indicate conscious effort or its absence. With sense perceptions *übersehen* (fail to see) and *überhören* (fail to hear) are often appropriate terms to denote absence of effort. Frequently an emphatic phrase is the only solution.

Ich sehe garnicht ein, warum das verlangt wird (I fail to see).
Der Witz entging mir.
Es entging mir, daß er nicht da war.
Ich übersah die Zeitungsnotiz.
Ich überhörte seine Bemerkung.
Seine Handlungsweise ist mir vollkommen unbegreiflich.

3. 'Fail' can also indicate that something expected or desired of the subject, who may even be unaware of it, does not eventuate. The subject may be a thing as well as a person. German lacks a term for this use. Examples: I failed to react to his threats, I failed to feel impressed, they

[1] See also footnote 1, p. 122.
[2] *Mißlingen* means 'fail' with reference to something attempted. It is not normally followed by the infinitive, and is more common without than with an accompanying dative. Example: *der Versuch mißlang* (*ihm*).
[3] See 'escape'.

failed to get my letter, the letter failed to arrive. This sense cannot be translated into German, unless somewhat colloquially by *garnicht*, as with **2**.

4. Vernachlässigen (to neglect) and **unterlassen** (to omit, to abstain) are often close approximations to 'fail'. *Unterlassen* implies conscious abstention, but says nothing about the reasons for this, nor the type of action from which one abstains. **Ermangeln:** not to do a thing which is expected of us and which is often, but not exclusively, conceived as an obligation. It is confined to negative use, and occurs mainly in the future tense. Conversational use is apt to sound servile or precious.[1]

Er hat es vernachlässigt, mich zu verständigen.
Er hat es unterlassen, uns diese Woche zu besuchen.
Ich werde nicht ermangeln, mich nach seinem Befinden zu erkundigen; alle in seinem Brief enthaltenen Fragen zu beantworten.
'*. . . zu seinem Erstaunen blieb darauf Olympia bei jedem Tanze sitzen, und er ermangelte nicht, immer wieder sie aufzuziehen*' (E. T. A. Hoffmann, *Der Sandmann*).

5. The following verbs, which primarily mean 'to miss' (see article on 'miss') may sometimes be used to translate 'fail': **versäumen, verfehlen, verpassen**. All three may be followed by the infinitive, which is, however, less common with *verpassen*. To translate 'fail' with the infinitive, it is sometimes not only possible but preferable to use these verbs in the sense of 'miss' with a noun object.

Er hat es versäumt, seine Schulden zu bezahlen.
Er versäumte es nicht, mich zu benachrichtigen.
Er verfehlte den richtigen Weg (or: *den richtigen Weg einzuschlagen*).
Die Kugel verfehlte ihn.
Ich werde nicht verfehlen, ihm alles mitzuteilen.
Die Uhr verfehlte zu schlagen (in this and the following example *nicht* would be more usual).
Die Bombe verfehlte zu explodieren.
Die Medizin verfehlte ihre Wirkung.
Ich verpaßte, ihm auf Wiedersehen zu sagen.
Der Bote verpaßte mich (failed to reach me, i.e. missed me).

6. 'Cannot fail' with the infinitive as a synonym of 'cannot help' must be variously translated. Common renderings are: *müssen, nicht anders können als, unfehlbar, nicht* strengthened by an appropriate adverb.[2]

[1] See 'lack'.
[2] *Nicht umhin können* is now apt to sound out of place, unless used in eloquent or emotional diction.

Er muß, kann nicht anders als, dem Plan zustimmen.
Er wird dem Plan unfehlbar zustimmen.
Er wird sich dem Einfluß seines Vaters einfach nicht entziehen können.

FALL 1. Sense: literal, to come to the ground, of persons.

Fallen indicates nothing more than downward movement, either from a height or from a level with the ground. In the sense of 'to crash violently and to sustain injuries' **stürzen** must be used.[1] *Fallen* does not exclude abrasions, particularly in cases of tripping and slipping, but does not necessarily imply them.

Er fiel von der Leiter, aus dem Fenster (leaves open the question of injuries).
Beim Tennis bin ich gefallen.
Er glitt aus und fiel auf den Rücken.
Ich bin da scheußlich hingefallen (*hin* = lengthwise).
Er stürzte von der Leiter, aus dem Fenster (crashed violently).
Ich bin mit meinem Motorrad gestürzt (*fallen* would be out of place with *Motorrad*).

2. Sense: to pass, lapse, into a subjective[2] state.[3]

This sense is generally rendered by **verfallen**. When followed by *in*, the implication is that the state expresses itself actively. A following dative without preposition gives the meaning of 'to fall a victim to a state'.

Es liegt in der menschlichen Natur, immer wieder in die alten Fehler, den alten Fehlern, zu verfallen.
Er ist in Wahnsinn, in seine alten Gewohnheiten, verfallen (suggests activity).
Er ist seinen alten Wutanfällen, seinen alten Gewohnheiten, verfallen (these things have a hold of him).

3. Sense: to divide into parts.

This sense is rendered by **zerfallen**[4] and **sich gliedern**.

Der Aufsatz, die Stadt, zerfällt, gliedert sich, in drei Teile.

[1] *Abstürzen* is often used in the sense of 'to crash from a height', particularly when the destination is not given. It is the regular term in reference to an aeroplane crash. *Das Flugzeug ist abgestürzt.*

[2] For a state or condition which is not subjective *fallen* is used. *In Ungnade fallen.*

[3] 'To get into a state, condition', is *geraten*. *Er gerät sehr leicht in Wut.*

[4] Both *verfallen* and *zerfallen* are used in the sense of 'to decay'. The latter indicates complete disintegration of the parts of a thing, and can therefore only be used of a dead, not a living, body. *Verfallen* means 'to fall, waste away', i.e. to a point approaching disintegration, but short of the latter. *Das Haus, die Leiche, zerfiel. Das Haus, der Mensch verfällt. Ein verfallenes Gesicht.*

FALSIFY, FORGE, ADULTERATE **Fälschen** means (1) to put something spurious in place of the genuine article, i.e. to forge (e.g. a document, a signature); (2) to falsify, corrupt, adulterate a thing by mixing something else with it (e.g. a text, wine). **Verfälschen** has only the second meaning of *fälschen*. If there is any distinction between the two terms used in this sense, it is that *verfälschen* denotes more the result, *fälschen* the action. But this distinction is not rigidly observed.[1]

Das Geld ist gefälscht (counterfeit).
Der Text, der Wein, ist gefälscht, verfälscht.
Er hat die Tatsachen gefälscht, verfälscht.

FATE[2] **Schicksal** denotes both the power which predetermines events and these events themselves. **Geschick** refers only to the latter. **Verhängnis,** that which is decreed, inflicted, is always used in an unfavourable sense, i.e. an untoward fate.[3] The first two terms may be used in the plural.

Das Schicksal hat es gut mit ihm gemeint.
Er hat ein furchtbares Schicksal erlitten.
Er bejammert sein widriges Geschick.
Es war sein Verhängnis, daß er in seinen eindrucksfähigen Jahren in üble Gesellschaft geriet.

FEAR (verb) 1. **Fürchten** is 'to feel real fear, dread of' someone or something, but is also used as a polite formula. **Befürchten** does not express the emotion of fear, but means 'to be convinced that something that one dislikes or is contrary to what one wants will take place'. It is therefore the only appropriate term to translate 'it is to be feared that...', 'it is feared that...', since these impersonal phrases do not strongly suggest the emotion of fear. *Fürchten* does not in itself imply expectation that a thing will take place. *Befürchten* cannot because of its meaning take a personal object.

Ich fürchte ihn, seine Wutausbrüche.
Er wird (or: *ist*) *überall gefürchtet.*
Ich fürchte für seine Sicherheit.
Ich fürchte, daß es zum Schlimmsten kommen wird.
Ich fürchte, Sie sind falsch verbunden (polite).
Ich fürchte seinen Besuch.

[1] *Ein gedokterter, ungedokterter, Wein.*
[2] *Los* corresponds exactly to 'lot'.
[3] The phrase *einem zum Verhängnis werden* means 'to prove fatal to someone'. *Sein Erfolg wurde ihm zum Verhängnis.*

Ich befürchte das Schlimmste (since the meaning is 'I am convinced the worst will happen', *fürchten* is impossible).
Es wird in London befürchtet, daß bald ein Krieg ausbricht.
Ich befürchte seinen Besuch.
Ich befürchte das Gegenteil von dem, was Sie behaupten.

2. **Sich fürchten vor jemandem (etwas)** is an emotionally stronger expression and suggests the concrete presence of danger.

Ich fürchte mich vor ihm, vor seinen Wutausbrüchen, vor seinem Besuch (one visualizes the situation).

3. **Angst haben** is used colloquially in the sense of *fürchten*. It is, however, weaker and suggests an uneasy feeling.

Ich habe Angst vor ihm, seinen Wutausbrüchen, seinem Besuch.
Ich habe Angst, daß es zum Schlimmsten kommt.

FEED 1. **Nähren** can only translate 'feed' in the sense of 'nourish', i.e. out of the substance of the feeder. It can also be used figuratively in this way.

Die Mutter nährt ihr Kind (at the breast).
Die Truppen sehen gut genährt aus.
Das wird seinen Rachedurst nur nähren.
Den Geist des Widerstands nähren.

2. **Ernähren**: to support, to provide for. It often implies the organization and distribution of food.

Der Vater ernährt seine Kinder, eine zahlreiche Familie.
Wir mußten ein ganzes Heer von Arbeitslosen ernähren.
Die Vorräte, die noch übrigbleiben, werden wohl kaum reichen, um auch nur die Ausgebombten zu ernähren.
Dieses Gut kann so viele Menschen nicht ernähren.

3. **Zu essen geben, das (sein, ihr) Essen geben, zu essen (das Essen) bekommen.** These expressions must be used when the number of meals or the time of feeding is referred to.

Die Mutter gibt den Kindern um 6 Uhr zu essen.
Den Gefangenen wird nur einmal täglich zu essen gegeben.
Unter den Umständen bekamen die Truppen erst um Mitternacht ihr Essen (zu essen).

4. **Speisen**: to dine (intransitive only). Its use is often a sign of false refinement. Correct use: *Majestät haben gespeist.* It is the normal term in technology (e.g. *mit Strom speisen*).

5. **Beköstigen, verpflegen** (see 'food'). *Die Pensionsmutter muß 30 Gäste beköstigen* (cater for). *In diesem Hotel wird man gut verpflegt.* **Verköstigen** implies large numbers.

6. **Füttern:** to feed animals. *Dick füttern*: feed, fatten up.

7. **Abfüttern:** to feed masses of people in a rough-and-ready way.

Horden von Flüchtlingen wurden abgefüttert.
Eine Schule abfüttern.

FEEL 1. **Fühlen** is the most general term in the meaning: to be aware of a thing through no special sense,[1] but generally several at once and sometimes including that of touch. It must be distinguished from **empfinden**. *Fühlen* refers simply to the strength or weakness of the feeling, *empfinden* to one's capacity to react to or to be aware of stimuli, therefore to one's sensitiveness[2] and powers of subtle discrimination, particularly (*a*) with regard to pain; (*b*) aesthetic experience. At times 'to be sensitive to' is a more suitable English equivalent than 'to feel'.[3]

Ich fühlte etwas unter meinem Fuß.
Ich habe keine Schmerzen gefühlt.
Er fühlte die Kälte sehr.
Er fühlte ein starkes Bedürfnis nach Ausspannung.
Ich fühlte die Macht seiner Argumente.
Seine Worte ließen mich fühlen, wie töricht ich gehandelt hatte.
Ich fühle, daß ich genug gesagt habe.[4]
Ich empfinde die Kälte sehr.
Sie empfindet sein weiteres Fortbleiben als schmerzlich.
Ich empfand seine Worte als wohltuend.
Ich empfinde Verehrung für ihn.
Ich empfinde diese Farbenmischung als eine Störung der Harmonie.

2. When 'feel' means 'to exercise deliberately one's sense of touch' the following verbs are used: **fühlen, befühlen, nachfühlen, tasten, betasten, abtasten**. *Fühlen* and its compounds mean 'to touch' a thing in order to ascertain something through it, but not to test its quality.

[1] In earlier German *fühlen* meant only 'to be aware through the sense of touch'.

[2] *Empfindlich* means 'sensitive' to pain, also 'touchy', and further 'sore'. See footnote to 'severe' (p. 318, n. 2).

[3] Close synonyms of *fühlen* in the sense of 'to notice a thing as an effect' are *spüren* and *verspüren*. *Spüren* is the general term and suggests merely ordinary intensity (e.g. *Hunger, Schmerzen, spüren*). *Verspüren* is an intensive and means to feel something that is strong or insistent (e.g. *Hunger, Schmerz, Übelkeit, verspüren*).

[4] The sense is 'to be emotionally aware'. *Fühlen* cannot be used in the sense of 'to hold a conviction' when it is desired to express this tentatively (e.g. I feel we ought to do something to help him).

Fühlen, which can also refer to awareness which comes from accidental contact (see first example under **1**) means '**to** touch in one spot', *befühlen* 'to touch in many, all over', while *nachfühlen* may imply one or many places, but in this sense always takes a clause (generally *ob*) as its object.[1] *Tasten* and its compounds suggest still more definitely the use of the sense of touch, a fingering of objects. *Tasten* is generally intransitive and mostly means 'to search' for a thing by using one's sense of touch. It often suggests 'groping'. *Betasten* is 'to touch' a thing in a number of places, often in order to test its quality. *Abtasten* is 'to touch up and down', mostly in the meaning of 'to search thoroughly all over'.

Der Arzt fühlte seinen Puls (one spot).
Der Arzt befühlte seine Lunge (here and there).
Er fühlte nach, ob noch etwas Tabak in seiner Tasche wäre.
Er tastete im Dunkel nach seinem Hut.
Er betastete das Tuch (to test its quality).
Er betastete den Hund (e.g. to see whether it had ticks on it).
Der Detektiv tastete ihn ab.

3. Sich fühlen with a following adjective or past participle has the sense of 'to be consciously'. It can only be used with a person, i.e. unlike 'feel' (e.g. 'my feet feel sore') not with a specific part of the body, as subject. Furthermore: (*a*) it can only be followed by such adjectives as can also be combined with the verb *sein* used personally, i.e. not to translate 'I feel hot' and the like (*mir ist heiß*); (*b*) it is not normally used with adjectives expressing anger, indignation, curiosity.[2]

It is also used with *wie* and a following noun in the sense of 'to feel that one resembles' something.[3]

Ich fühle mich glücklich, traurig, krank, müde, schwach, betrogen, befangen.
Ich fühle mich wie ein geschorenes Schaf.

4. Sich anfühlen with an adverb of manner and a thing as subject is used to denote the kind of tactile sensation communicated by a thing. This must not be confused with non-tactile sensations as, e.g., with parts of the body (e.g. my brow feels hot, feverish).

Das Tuch fühlt sich hart, weich, an.

FEW 1. With animate beings and objects the inflected form **wenige,** which individualizes, must be used, except in statements about the

[1] Except in the sense of 'sympathize'. *Das kann ich Ihnen nachfühlen.*
[2] For 'to feel sure' see 'sure'.
[3] In this sense *vorkommen* with the reflexive dative is more common. It suggests rather 'to have a certain impression of oneself' than real feeling. *Ich komme mir wie ein geschorenes Schaf vor.*

existence of a species. In the latter case the uninflected form **wenig** is normal.

Auf dieser Insel gab es nur wenige Menschen, Tiere.
Auf dieser Insel gab es nur wenig Menschen, Tiere.
In dieser Gegend habe ich wenige Eingeborene gesehen.
Es gibt heute nur noch wenig Eingeborene in Australien.
'*Ein von wenig Menschen besuchtes Tal*' (Kleist, *Das Erdbeben in Chili*).

2. With nouns which do not denote animate beings or objects **wenig** is the usual form. **Wenige** individualizes and expects an enumeration.[1]

Es sind wenig Fehler in dem Aufsatz.
Sie haben nur wenige Fehler gemacht (with a following enumeration).
Es hat mir wenig Schwierigkeiten gemacht.
Der Junge hat mir wenig Sorgen gemacht.

FIGHT 'Fight' is used intransitively, transitively, with a cognate accusative. The third use involves mostly fixed phrases, the German equivalents of which are given in dictionaries.

1. **Kämpfen** implies great effort. It is applied (*a*) to participation in battle, both by the individual and the group (e.g. a nation); (*b*) to boxing; (*c*) to the action of struggling against anything that threatens to overwhelm us or defeat our purposes, both physically and morally. This latter meaning includes fighting for a cause. (*d*) It may be followed by *Kampf* as a cognate accusative. (*e*) In the animal world it is applied to stags. (Otherwise terms such as *aufeinander losgehen, sich herumbeißen* are used of animals. *Es gab eine Beißerei zwischen den Hunden.*)

Er hat in drei Kriegen gekämpft.
Hitler irrte sich in seiner Annahme, daß England nicht kämpfen würde.
Die Boxer kämpften wie besessen.
Ich kämpfe seit Tagen gegen einen Schnupfen.
Wir kämpfen gegen unerhörte Schwierigkeiten.
Er kämpfte hartnäckig gegen den Vorschlag.
Er kämpft für die Wahrheit, seinen Glauben.
Wir haben einen harten Kampf gekämpft.

2. **Ankämpfen** emphasizes the action of fighting against that which threatens to overwhelm us or which is greater than we. It is used of a struggle against institutions, ideas, the elements of nature, and, unlike

[1] The distinction between the two forms *wenig* and *wenige* also applies to *viel, viele* (many), but is less strictly observed. *In diesem Teich gibt's viel(e) Fische. Es hat viel(e) Schwierigkeiten bereitet. Er bewilligte es, ohne viel(e) Worte zu machen.*

kämpfen, against feelings, but not against persons. It is always followed by *gegen*.

Er kämpfte gegen die Lehren der Kirche, gegen diesen Unsinn, an.
Es hat keinen Zweck, gegen einen solchen Standpunkt anzukämpfen.
Auf unserer Bergtour hatten wir uns verirrt und mußten 3 Stunden gegen ein schweres Schneegestöber ankämpfen.
Er kämpfte gegen seine Müdigkeit, seine melancholischen Anwandlungen, an.

3. **Bekämpfen:** to combat something one wants to kill. It suggests an effective use of the means of combat, but less the exertion of the struggle itself. Hence 'to combat' and 'to oppose' are often close equivalents. It governs the same type of object as *ankämpfen*. A personal object (in the sense of 'oppose') is rare.

Wir müssen diesen Vorschlag, diese Maßnahmen, diese Ideen, bekämpfen.
Wir bekämpften das Feuer mit aller Macht.
Ich bekämpfe meine Müdigkeit mit Mengen schwarzen Kaffees.

4. **Fechten,**[1] strictly used, means only 'to fence'. In colloquial speech, particularly university students' slang, it can, however, be applied to the participation by a country in warfare. In his book *Vom anderen Deutschland* von Hassel uses it continually in this sense.

5. To come to fisticuffs.

None of the above terms can be used in this sense. The commonest are:

(a) **Sich schlagen,** which is very strong and implies a high degree of animosity.[2]

Die zwei Männer schlugen sich zehn Minuten lang vor dem Gerichtshof (the addition of *herum* makes it less serious).

(b) **Sich hauen**[3] (a brief scrap); (c) **sich in den Haaren liegen** (to quarrel either with physical violence or a dispute); (d) **sich balgen,** more playful, to scuffle.

Die beiden Jungens haben sich gehauen, liegen sich dauernd in den Haaren, balgen sich.

6. To scramble in order to seize a thing, i.e. of a number of people, a crowd.

(a) **Sich reißen um:** to try to snatch, tear, a thing from each other's hand.

Sie reißen sich um die Zeitungen, die Lebensmittelpakete.

[1] *Verfechten* is 'to fight for' in the sense of 'to champion' an idea or cause.
[2] Compare the noun *Schlägerei*. *Im Wirtshaus entwickelte sich eine Schlägerei.*
[3] *Verhauen* in the sense of 'to give a hiding' cannot be reflexive. In the latter use it means 'to make a blunder'.

(b) **Sich drängen und schubsen:** to push, to elbow and the like, in order to get a seat or a desired position.

Sie drängten und schubsten sich, um die besten Plätze zu bekommen.

7. To quarrel[1] over the possession of a thing, by argument or physical violence.

(a) **Streiten**[2] can imply physical violence, but more often suggests a dispute with words. It may be for the possession of a thing or to establish truth. (b) **Sich in den Haaren liegen, haben** (see above) is a more colloquial expression, in reference to both physical violence and a dispute with words.

Die beiden Kinder stritten sich um das Buch.
Sie stritten sich um die väterliche Erbschaft.

FILL 1. **Füllen:** (*a*) to fill in the literal sense; (*b*) to fill a period of time; (*c*) to fill with emotions, thoughts, when the seat of these is mentioned. It is uncommon in the passive voice, except in the literal sense (coupled with *werden*, not *sein*).

Er füllte das Faß mit Wasser.
Das Faß wurde mit Wasser gefüllt.
Dieses Zeug füllt das ganze Haus.
Der Theaterdirektor füllte das Theater mit Inhabern von Freikarten.
Er hat ganze Hefte mit Zeichnungen gefüllt.
Das Theater war vollkommen gefüllt.
Dieses Programm füllt den ganzen Abend.
Ein abendfüllendes Stück (a technical term).
Ihre Augen füllten sich mit Tränen.
Warum füllen Sie sich den Kopf mit solchen Gedanken?
Sein Herz füllte sich mit Dankbarkeit.
Der Anblick solcher Schönheit füllte unser Herz mit Ehrfurcht.

2. **Erfüllen:**[3] (*a*) to fill a person, his doings, utterances (as distinct from the localized seat of these) with strong[4] emotion, his thoughts with meaning; (*b*) to fill a large space with sound, light, smoke, and the like.[5]

[1] *Zanken* means 'to quarrel' when accusations and abuse are hurled to and fro.
[2] For *bestreiten* see 'deny'.
[3] Another meaning is 'fulfil'.
[4] If the emotion is not intense other verbs are preferred (*die Nachricht erweckte Freude in uns*).
[5] Goethe in *Faust* uses *erfüllen* in the literal sense:

'*Hier ist ein Saft, der eilig trunken macht.*
Mit brauner Flut erfüllt er Deine Höhle' (i.e. of a beaker).

Die Nachricht erfüllte mich mit Abscheu.
Er war von Wut erfüllt (with = *von* after the passive voice).
Das waren haßerfüllte Ausbrüche.
Der Anblick solcher Schönheit erfüllte uns mit Ehrfurcht.
Bei Versen muß jede Silbe sinnerfüllt sein.
Das Zimmer war von Sonne erfüllt.
Die Luft war von wilden Schmerzensschreien erfüllt.

3. **Voll** is commonly used for 'filled' instead of *gefüllt sein.* See 'full'.

Der Wartesaal war voll von Passagieren.
Die Stadt war voll von amerikanischen Soldaten.
Sein Leben war voller Vorfälle derartiger Natur.
Die Zeitungen waren gradezu voll von solchen Anschuldigungen.

4. **Anfüllen:** to fill up, to the brim. It is occasionally used figuratively in the passive voice.

Füllen Sie die Gläser an.
Sein Kopf ist mit solchen Gedanken angefüllt.

5. **Ausfüllen:** The literal sense is to make one thing fit exactly into another. The figurative use preserves this image. It also translates 'fill in' (e.g. a form).

Das Schwert füllt die Scheide aus.
Er füllt den Stuhl aus.
Meine Zeit ist mit allen meinen Beschäftigungen sowieso schon ausgefüllt.
Er füllt seine Stellung wunderbar aus.
Wir haben nicht genug Rekruten, um die Reihen auszufüllen.

6. **Überfüllen** is used mostly with the verb *sein* in the sense of 'crowded'.

Die Straßen waren mit Soldaten überfüllt.

7. **Besetzen:** in reference to appointment to a position.

Alle Posten sind schon besetzt.

FIND In phrases of the type 'I find it difficult, painful, gratifying, cold', **finden** can only be used to express a judgment. Its meaning is 'to consider'. When 'find' suggests an experience, impersonal phrases formed with **sein, fallen** and the like, or **empfinden** (see 'feel') when emotional experience is implied, must be used. **Befinden** suggests an expert judgment.

Ich finde das Gedicht sehr schön.
Ich finde die Prüfung schwierig.

Die Prüfung fiel mir sehr schwer.
Es fällt mir schwer, ihn zu überzeugen.
Ich fand es kalt.
Es war mir kalt.
Es ist mir peinlich, ihn auf solche Sachen aufmerksam machen zu müssen.
Ich empfand den Sonnenschein als wohltuend.
Sie empfindet es als sehr schmerzlich, daß er noch länger wegbleiben soll.
Der Plan wurde für gut befunden.

FINISH,[1] END, COMPLETE[2] 'Finish' may be followed by a noun object or by a gerund. In some cases the former implies the latter (e.g. he finished his meal, finished eating his meal). Sometimes the omission of the gerund produces ambiguity (e.g. he finished the book, i.e. reading or writing).

1. **Fertig** means 'ready'[3] for something by virtue of having done the necessary work required. It thus comes to mean: having done (with) (active), being done (passive). In these senses it is used in the following combinations:

(a) **Fertig machen** suggests the making or production of an object. If the noun it governs denotes an activity, the results of this activity must be visible as a thing, i.e. it cannot govern a noun which expresses merely an activity (e.g. to finish a game). It is normally used only of simple, everyday things.

Ein Kleid, das Essen (preparing, not eating), *einen Aufsatz, seine Arbeit, fertig machen.*

(b) **Fertig sein**[4] **(mit)** means 'to have finished, to have done', in the sense of finishing an activity, finishing the making of a thing, 'not to need any longer', 'to have consumed'. Without *mit* it can also mean 'to be finished' in the passive as well as the active sense.

Ich bin fertig (have, am, finished; am ready).
Das Haus, die Arbeit, ist nun fertig.
Sind Sie mit Ihrem Koffer fertig (packing or using it)?
Sind Sie mit Ihrer Toilette fertig?
Er ist mit dem Buch fertig (writing or reading it).

[1] For 'finish' see Webster's *Dictionary of Synonyms*. The sense of 'kill' is not discussed in this article.

[2] See also the adjective 'complete'.

[3] *Bereit* means 'ready' in the sense of 'prepared, willing'. *Fertig* meant originally 'ready for a journey'. It cannot be followed by an infinitive. Other senses are (*a*) dexterous, (*b*) done for (in the sense of *erledigt*).

[4] *Fertig werden* (*mit*) means 'to get a thing finished', 'to manage'.

Er ist mit dem Gemälde noch nicht fertig (painting or using it).
Er war schon vor zwei Jahren mit der Schule fertig.
Er war mit dem Abschreiben des Briefes nicht fertig.
Sind Sie mit dem Rasieren schon fertig?

(c) *Fertig* can be combined adverbially with a small number of specific verbs, but not with every verb. Either the point of time when the action is finished is stated or inferable, or the completion of the thing which is being made is stressed, i.e. this is not left unfinished. The following is not a complete list.

Der Koch hat den Kuchen fertig gebacken.
Er hat den Roman, Brief, fertig geschrieben.
Nach vielen Schwierigkeiten (or: *endlich*) *haben sie das Haus fertig gebaut.*
In dieser Woche werden wir das Haus fertig gebaut haben.
Er hat den Tisch soeben fertig gezimmert.
Er hat sich fertig angezogen.
Er hat das Buch fertig gelesen.
Er hat sich nicht fertig rasiert.

(d) *Fertig sein* and *fertig werden* are not used in the imperative.

2. **Zu Ende** is used with a number of verbs in the sense of carrying the activity to a conclusive finish, covering all the ground, i.e. not ceasing before the end. It can only be used where (in English) 'to an end' or 'at an end' expresses the sense.

Den Krieg zu Ende kämpfen.
Das Lied zu Ende singen.
Die Zeitung zu Ende lesen.
Er hat die Verhandlungen erfolgreich zu Ende geführt.
Das Konzert ist jetzt zu Ende.

3. Compound verbs.

(a) Of the prefixes which express the sense of finishing *aus* is the most common. It can be combined with some verbs that denote an activity.

Ich habe die Zeitung noch nicht ausgelesen.
Lassen Sie mich ausreden.
Er trank seinen Wein aus und ging zu Bett.
Schlafen Sie sich ordentlich aus.

(b) Examples of other compounds (with the meaning of 'consume') are:

Essen Sie die Bratkartoffeln auf.
Wir haben unsere Vorräte schon längst verbraucht.

4. **Alle** (used predicatively and therefore undeclined) means 'finished' in the sense of 'all gone'.

Der Wein, das Fleisch, ist alle.

5. **Beenden, beendigen.**

Like 'end' these verbs mean 'to add (or to perform) the last part', and refer more often to an activity (e.g. to end a game) than to the production of a thing (e.g. to end a book). With the latter they are practically restricted to writing, speeches, and the like, where the sense of a development in time is strong. Both the English and the German terms convey a heightened sense of finality of action as compared with 'finish'. None of them is applied to trivial activities (e.g. washing-up).

Beenden suggests less forcibly than 'end' the sense of 'putting an end, a stop to', i.e. before the natural end except in the sense of 'to terminate officially'.

Beendigen is a more recent formation than *beenden*, and is often used colloquially instead of the latter. In colloquial speech only *beendigen* supplies the imperative mood. In discriminating use it is often accompanied by a statement as to what the last stage of the action is, e.g. a statement introduced by *mit* or some equivalent. But it can also be used without any such phrase in the emphatic sense of 'to put an end to'.

'Egmont' wurde in Frankfurt begonnen und erst in Italien beendet.
Er hat seine Studien, seine Grammatik, seinen Ferienaufenthalt, den Abend mit einem Spaziergang, beendet.
Der Krieg wurde nur nach schweren Anstrengungen und Verlusten beendet.
Er wird die Besichtigung des Lagers bis 12 Uhr beendet haben.
Er hat seine Rede mit einem Appell an das ganze Land beendet, beendigt.
Er beendigte seine Reise mit einem kurzen Aufenthalt an der See.
Beendigen Sie Ihren Aufsatz mit einer Zusammenfassung der Hauptpunkte.
Wir müssen diesen unhaltbaren Zustand beendigen.

6. **Ein Ende machen (bereiten):**[1] to put an end, a stop, to something undesirable (see also 'stop'). It suggests forceful intervention rather than an official act of the kind implied by 'terminate'.

Wir müssen seinem Treiben, dem Unsinn, ein Ende machen (bereiten).
Er machte seinem Leben ein Ende (beenden is impossible in the sense of suicide).

7. **Vollenden** corresponds to 'complete' in the sense of finishing a thing, an activity in such a way that one thinks of the whole and its effect, not

[1] More colloquially: *Schluß machen (mit).*

merely the addition of the final section (see *beenden*). It is only applied to things or activities in so far as their completion adds to their quality, suggests perfection or maturity of what is produced, or the value and thoroughness of what has been done. *Vollendet* is used adjectivally in the sense of 'perfect', 'consummate'.

Er hat den Aufsatz vollendet.
Der Maler hat sein Bild vollendet.
Er hat seine Schulbildung vollendet.
Er hat seine Aufgabe glänzend vollendet.
Er hat trotz allem seine Reise vollendet.
Er hat sein dreißigstes Jahr vollendet.
Ein vollendetes Kunstwerk.

8. **Vervollständigen** means 'to add a part or parts' necessary to form a whole, the nature of which is numerical, inorganic. Unlike *vollenden* it does not imply inner value, but a mere accumulation of parts.

Haben Sie Ihre Briefmarkensammlung vervollständigt?
Er ist bemüht, sein Verständnis der Theorie zu vervollständigen.
Um mein Bild vom amerikanischen Leben zu vervollständigen, muß ich noch ein Jahr im Lande bleiben.

9. **Ergänzen:** to add a missing part or parts necessary to form an inner unity, particularly with reference to meaning. It suggests more strongly than *vervollständigen* that the idea of a given whole is present to the mind.[1]

Einen Satz, einen Gedanken, den Sinn ergänzen, eine Briefmarkensammlung, ergänzen.

10. **Voll machen** is used figuratively in the sense of intensifying or multiplying emotional experiences.

Sein Unglück, seine Leiden, seine Freude, voll machen.

11. The sense of 'do', i.e. without particular merit or distinction, 'fulfil requirements', must be variously translated. Examples are:

Er hat alle Anforderungen erfüllt.
Er hat alle Fächer absolviert.

FIRE 1. **Feuer** means (*a*) the element fire; (*b*) the state of combustion; (*c*) burning fuel in a grate and the like. It can be used in the sense of a 'conflagration, destructive burning', only when this sense is

[1] A related sense is 'to restore a missing part' (e.g. *ein Standbild ergänzen*). It can also mean simply 'to supplement' (e.g. *sein Einkommen ergänzen*).

interchangeable with those listed. In a sentence such as *Waren im Werte von* 100 000 *D.M. sind vom Feuer zerstört worden* the meaning is 'by fire' as opposed, e.g., to flood. *Feuer* does not admit of a plural.

Das Feuer reinigt.
In dem Zimmer brennt ein Feuer (im Kamin).
Wir hatten ein Feuer, ein kleines Feuer, in der Fabrik.

2. **Brand** means 'destructive burning'. **Feuersbrunst** is always on a large scale, e.g. a whole street.

In der Fabrik ist ein Brand ausgebrochen.
Der Brand wurde auf seinen Herd beschränkt.

3. **Brennen** is the commonest term in the sense of 'there is a fire', 'to be on fire'. It is used with the thing or the impersonal *es* as subject.

Es brennt in der Scheune.
In der letzten Zeit hat es in der Stadt oft gebrannt.
Das Haus brennt.

FIRST, AT FIRST 1. **Zuerst** means (*a*) in the beginning, in the first stages, i.e. at first; (*b*) for the first time; (*c*) before anyone, anything else in a sequence, whether this refer to time, rank, or the like, the order being external and therefore indicating no inner dependence of the second on the first such as a condition. This meaning can be translated also by the more emphatic **als erst-er, -e, -es** (compare *zuletzt* and *als letzt-er, -e, -es*).[1]

Zuerst habe ich das anders beurteilt, aber jetzt sehe ich ein, daß Sie recht haben.
Ich möchte Sie auf das aufmerksam machen, was ich zuerst sagte.
Wann haben Sie ihn zuerst gesehen?
Als er zuerst in den Krieg zog, hatte er keine klare Vorstellung, was Krieg bedeutet.
Er kam zuerst, als erster, an.
Wer spielt zuerst?
Tun Sie das zuerst, als erstes.
Gehen Sie zuerst zum Arzt und dann zu Ihrem Rechtsanwalt (a mere time-table, without inner necessity in the order).

2. **Erst** never means 'at first'. As an equivalent of 'first',[2] it can only mean 'first' in a sequence. In this sense it must be used if the second

[1] 'To go first', i.e. to lead the way, is *vorangehen*. In stepping aside to allow someone else to go ahead, *vorgehen* is usual, particularly in the imperative. *Gehen Sie vor!*
[2] For another meaning of *erst* see 'only'.

action is dependent on the first. It may, however, be used, like *zuerst*, when there is no such dependence, provided a second action is reported (mostly with the imperative mood).

Sehen Sie erst mal den Arzt, und dann können wir entscheiden, ob die Arbeit Sie überanstrengen würde oder nicht (*zuerst* impossible).

Erst iß mal deine Suppe auf, dann kannst du die Erdbeeren haben (*zuerst* impossible because the order given in the first clause is a condition of the fulfilment of the promise given in the second).

Setzen Sie sich erst mal hin, dann bringe ich Ihnen eine Tasse Tee (or *zuerst* because the order is casual, not an absolute condition).

3. **Zunächst** means 'first', 'first of all', 'in the first place'. It indicates concentration on a given matter and suggests that what follows is or seems to be of less importance. A close German equivalent is *in erster Linie*.

Tun wir zunächst mal dies, wir können immer noch sehen, ob wir Zeit für das andere haben.

Er behauptet, zunächst Weltbürger und erst in zweiter Linie Deutscher zu sein.

Das Angebot sah zunächst sehr verlockend aus.

FLAT **Flach** is a more objective term than **platt**, which can suggest an impression of flatness, particularly that of being pressed flat. Thus: *ein Boxer hat oft eine platte Nase; platt auf dem Boden liegen* (pressed against the ground). *Er mußte flach liegen*, merely suggests a horizontal position. Both terms are applied in the literal sense to the same objects, but *platt* is more vivid because of its subjective connotation (e.g. *platt wie ein Pfannkuchen*, a fixed phrase). In figurative use *flach* means 'shallow' (i.e. *oberflächlich*), which meaning it also has in literal application (e.g. *die Ruhr ist flach*). In figurative use *platt* indicates lifelessness.

FLOAT (intransitive) 1. **Treiben** means 'to drift', and is used of inanimate objects. It implies (*a*) motion over, not rest on, the surface of water or through the air; (*b*) involuntary, and sometimes aimless, action. If a decision to drift or (in this sense) to float is meant, as in the case of a person, **sich treiben lassen** must be used.

Das Schiff trieb weit von der Küste ab, auf Felsenriffe.

Wolken treiben am Himmel.

Wir können uns (vom Winde) treiben lassen.

Er ließ sich den Strom hinunter treiben.

2. **Schwimmen** is used of objects and substances in contrast to 'sink', i.e. to indicate that they are capable of remaining on the surface of liquid.[1]

Ein schwimmender Palast.
Allerlei Schutt, Öl, schwimmt auf der Oberfläche des Wassers.

3. In reference to water sports German can only say *auf dem Rücken liegen* to express the idea of floating without movement.

Er liegt (regungslos) auf dem Rücken.

4. **Schweben** means in its literal sense 'to float' through or 'hover' in the air.

Der Ballon schwebt hoch über der Erde.
Töne schwebten durch die Luft, den Raum.

FOLLOW, PURSUE, ENSUE 1. **Folgen,** like 'follow', is the most comprehensive term. Its use in the passive voice is mostly limited in literary German to the past participle without the auxiliary verb (e.g.: *von seinem Assistenten gefolgt, trat er ins Zimmer*). It occurs in the following senses:

(a) To go, come after, to move in the same direction.

Der Detektiv folgte dem Dieb.

(b) To keep to a direction, road, etc.

Folgen Sie dieser Straße bis zur Ecke.

(c) To come after in a sequence or series, whether in time, in rank, or as effect after cause. With reference to time or to cause of effect *auf* with the accusative (cf. English 'on') or the dative without preposition may be used.

Ein Unglück folgte dem, auf den, Beschluß.
Georg der Fünfte folgte auf Eduard den Siebenten.
Auf die Verlängerung der Arbeitszeit folgten Streiks.

(d) To take as a leader, to accept as an authority.

Die Massen folgten blind dem Führer.
Ich folge dem Kritiker Gundolf in seiner Deutung Kleists.

(e) To act in accordance with, to obey (conjugated with *haben* in the sense of 'obey').

Ich folgte seinem Rat, der Regel, diesen Richtlinien.
Er hat in dieser Angelegenheit seinem Vater nur gefolgt (a rare use).

[1] In reference to a ship *flott sein, werden* is used to indicate that it is seaworthy (e.g. *Das Schiff ist wieder flott*). Similarly: *flott machen.*

(f) To pursue a line of conduct, work.

Er folgt Kursen an der technischen Hochschule.
Die Regierung folgt der Politik der Gewerkschaften.

(g) To watch the progress or course of a thing, literally and figuratively.

Ich folgte dem Flugzeug mit den Augen, bis es verschwand.
Er folgt aufmerksam der politischen Entwicklung.
Er folgt mit Interesse den neuesten literarischen Veröffentlichungen.

(h) To understand.

Ich folge Ihnen ganz gut.
Ich kann seinen Gedankengängen nicht folgen.
Er kann genug Deutsch, um den Vorlesungen zu folgen.

(i) To emerge as a conclusion.

Aus Ihrer Behauptung folgt, daß Sie diese Ansicht nie geteilt haben.

2. Verfolgen

The prefix *ver* has here an intensive force and gives the meaning of 'pursue', 'prosecute'[1] in all senses of these terms. It must be used to translate 'follow' when intensified mental activity is implied, i.e. in the sense of tracing, tracking down, or of attending alertly and critically, not merely in understanding the words of others (contrast **1** (h)).

Um sein Buch zu schreiben, mußte er die ganze Entwicklung der Klassik verfolgen.
Es ist reizvoll zu verfolgen, wie allmählich der Spieß umgedreht wird.
Er verfolgte die Vorgänge mit Interesse.
Die Regierung verfolgt eine kühne Politik.
Er verfolgt seine Studien mit Eifer.
Die Abstimmung hat bewiesen, mit wie kritischem Blick das Volk die Arbeiten seiner Gesetzgeber verfolgt.

3. Nachfolgen: to follow or succeed a person in office and to follow in death.

Er ist seinem Vater als Chef der Firma nachgefolgt.
Er ist seiner Frau bald nachgefolgt.

4. Befolgen has only one meaning: to act in accordance with (see *folgen* (e)). Unlike *folgen* it does not mean 'to obey' a person.

Er hat die Vorschriften des Arztes genau befolgt.

[1] *Verfolgen* also means 'to persecute'.

5. **Erfolgen:** to follow as the effect of a cause, particularly as the result of the fulfilment of a condition. The subject cannot be a person.

Seine Zulassung erfolgte sofort.
Seine Entlassung ist wider alles Erwarten nicht erfolgt.

6. **Nachkommen** is used in reference to arrangements for one person to go ahead and for another to follow later. In colloquial language, it, not *folgen*, is the normal term in this sense.

Gehen Sie vor, ich komme nach.

FOOD (with notes on 'nourishment', 'nutrition', 'fare', 'meal', 'provisions'). 1. **Nahrung** translates 'food' only with reference to its capacity to maintain life, to promote growth and energy, i.e. when 'food' is a synonym of 'nourishment', which is itself translated by *Nahrung*. It is also used figuratively in the same way.

Seit drei Tagen hat er keine Nahrung zu sich genommen (only in the sense that he is too ill to eat or drink, not because no food is available; see *essen* for the latter).
Die Nahrung, die er bekommt, genügt nicht.
Der Nahrungswert von Kartoffeln.
Das ist nur Nahrung für seinen Verdacht.
Wir gehen ohne Nahrung, ohne Heizung und ohne warme Kleidung dem Winter entgegen.

2. **Lebensmittel** ('provisions') and **Nahrungsmittel** (both plural) are sometimes, but not always, interchangeable. The distinction is that *Nahrungsmittel* is vaguer, more general, and refers more to the raw material of food and to its growing, while *Lebensmittel* suggests food in relation to its purchase. It is the appropriate term when food is thought of as tinned.[1] Thus one can only speak of a *Lebensmittelgeschäft*. *Nahrungsmitteleinfuhr* suggests meat, wheat, potatoes, and the like; *Lebensmitteleinfuhr*, butter, bacon, tinned food (though no hard and fast dividing line can be drawn). Again *Lebensmittelkontrolle* is the accepted term because the distribution and purchasing of food is meant. When the type of food is not specified the choice of term depends on whether the context suggests the purchase of food or its properties.[2]

The plural 'foods' is translated by *Nahrungsmittel* when the variety produced is indicated.[3]

Die Mutter besorgt die Lebensmittel für das Wochenende.

[1] To translate 'tinned food' the kind must be specified. *Fleisch- und Gemüsekonserven.*
[2] A food-producing land = *ein Rohstofferzeuger.*
[3] The ugly term *Nahrungssorten* is also used.

Unsere Lebensmittel reichen kaum für eine Woche (or: *Nahrungsmittel*).
Die Lebensmittel sind in dem Korb.
In diesem Sack sind nur Nahrungsmittel.
Deutschland muß seine Nahrungsmittelproduktion steigern (or: *Lebensmittel-*).
Halten Sie die Nahrungsmittel kühl in dem Schrank (better than *Lebensmittel*).
Diese Nahrungsmittel werden in Java erzeugt.

3. **Essen** (both as noun and verb) must be used in the sense of 'meal'.[1] It includes everything that comprises a meal. It is used freely with reference to the type or quality of food that is or should be eaten.

Seit drei Tagen hat er nichts gegessen.
Das Essen steht schon auf dem Tisch.
Wir haben das Essen auf unseren Ausflug mitgebracht.
An kalten Tagen muß man etwas Warmes essen.
Wie war das Essen in London?
Das Essen in diesem Hotel ist schlecht.
Man ißt sehr gut in diesem Restaurant.

4. **Speise** may be prepared or unprepared, and often approximates to 'dish' (*Gericht*). It is used for 'food' as opposed to 'drink' (*Speise und Trank*), and is sometimes an abbreviation for *Mehlspeise*. The use of *Speise* sometimes savours of a genteelism (e.g. *diese Speise ist zu scharf für mich*).

Diese Speise ist angegangen, ungenießbar.
Speiseschrank, Speisekammer.

5. **Kost** approximates to 'fare', i.e. a type of food, particularly in reference to its effect on health. It is always simple in character and therefore used only in connection with small hotels, restaurants, and boarding-houses. It refers only to food and drink, i.e. it excludes board.

In dieser Pension gibt man uns nahrhafte Kost.
Vegetarische Kost (Rohkost) esse ich gern.

6. **Verpflegung** refers exclusively to food and drink, i.e. not board. It is restricted in its reference to one's permanent place of residence, which may be either a cheap or an expensive hotel.

In diesem Hotel ist die Verpflegung gut.

[1] *Essen* is the commonest word for 'meal'. *Mahl* is an elevated term. *Mahlzeit* is used in reference to the number of meals taken or the hour when they are taken.

7. **Ernährung** (see 'feed'): 'feeding' in the sense of 'providing for'. It must be used for 'food' when by the latter its administration, organization, distribution is referred to.

Die Ernährungslage ist befriedigend.
Der Reichsernährungsminister.
Das Reichsernährungsamt.

FOOL 1. **Tor** and **Narr**. A man may be a *Tor* because he is inexperienced (compare the conception of *der reine Tor* in *Parzival*), or because he has made mistakes, applied the wrong means in pursuing some serious purpose. Such a person does not necessarily lack intelligence. If, on the other hand, his doings and sayings are so devoid of intelligence as to appear clownish or grotesque, he is a *Narr*.

Tor is now exclusively, and *Narr* (except in southern Germany) mostly, a literary term. Used in conversation *Narr* is very strong.

'Da steh' ich nun, ich armer Tor,
Und bin so klug als wie zuvor.' (Goethe, *Faust I.*)

Du bist doch ein Narr, dich so zu benehmen.

2. 'Fool' as a familiar term must be translated by adjectives meaning foolish, mad, crazy, etc.

Sei doch nicht so verrückt.
Ich war sehr dumm, mein Geld so anzulegen.

FOUND Sense: to call into existence an institution, school of thought, etc.

1. In this sense German uses **gründen** and **begründen**. The distinction is that *gründen* suggests one clear act, therefore an official ceremony or act, or at most a few of the stages involved in founding an institution.[1] *Begründen*, which is less common, is wider in its implications and is not limited to any official act or to particular stages. It suggests both the idea from which the foundation sprang and also consolidation. Through the latter reference it approaches the sense of 'establish', when this is used as a synonymous term. When reference is solely to ideas, *gründen* is impossible.

Despite the implication of consolidation conveyed by *begründen*, it is possible to say *fest gegründet*.

To found on, i.e. base, ground on = *gründen auf*[2] (followed by the accusative case).

[1] See 'found' in Webster's *Dictionary of Synonyms*.

[2] *Gründen auf* is also used in reference to ideas in the sense of 'to base on'. *Begründen*, applied to ideas, points of view, means 'to substantiate, to give reasons for'.

2. When 'found' means 'endow', i.e. provide funds, it must be translated by **stiften.**[1]

Er hat verschiedene Schulen, Vereine, Firmen, Zeitungen, gegründet (or: *begründet*).
Bismarck hat das zweite Reich gegründet (or: *fest begründet*).
Er hat einen Geheimkult begründet (*gegründet* could suggest a ceremony).
Friedrich Schlegel begründete die romantische Welt- und Kunstanschauung.
Er hat verschiedene Stipendien, einen Lehrstuhl, gestiftet.

FREEZE 1. **Frieren** is used of persons and of Nature. Applied to persons it means, whether used impersonally or with a personal subject, and whether in reference to the whole body or only a part, no more than 'to be very cold'. Of things it means 'to turn to ice' (i.e. of liquids) or 'to be covered with ice'.[2] Used of persons, a personal subject is in present-day German more usual than the impersonal form.

Ich friere; habe (*furchtbar, arg*) *gefroren.*
Meine Hände frieren.
Es friert mich (*an den Händen*).
Das Wasser, der Fluß, ist gefroren.
Das Glas im Fenster ist gefroren.

2. **Zufrieren:** to freeze all over, of large areas of water, such as a lake.[3]

Der See, der Fluß, ist zugefroren.

3. **Erfrieren** has intensive force, and means, applied in the active voice to persons, 'to freeze to death'. In the passive with *sein* it means, used either of the whole person or a part of the body, 'to be numbed and rigid with cold'.

Noch so ein Winter, und wir erfrieren alle.
Er war ganz erfroren.
Mein kleiner Finger ist erfroren.

4. **Einfrieren is** used of things which are either ice-bound themselves or filled with ice. It is also applied figuratively to the freezing of money.

Das Schiff im Hafen, die Wasserleitung, ist eingefroren.
Die Regierung hat alle Kredite eingefroren.

[1] In its wider sense *stiften* means 'to bring about' something intended to be permanent (e.g. *Frieden, eine Versöhnung*). It is used also in reference to what is bad, i.e. to instigate (cf. *anstiften*).

[2] *Tiefgefroren*: quick-frozen, of fruit, fish. *Gefrierfleisch*: frozen meat.

[3] *Gerinnen*, to coagulate, is used freely in Holstein of the sea in the sense of starting to freeze.

FRIENDLY[1] **1. Freundlich:** kindly, affable, displaying friendly feelings, showing these by smiling, etc.

Er ist ein freundlicher Typ.
In diesem Dorfe wohnen freundliche Leute.
Der Wirt war sehr freundlich zu uns.
Wir wurden im Ausland sehr freundlich behandelt.

2. Freundschaftlich must be used in the sense of 'bearing the relation of friendship, as a friend'.

Es bestehen freundschaftliche Beziehungen zwischen den beiden.
Er hat sich mir gegenüber sehr freundschaftlich verhalten.

3. Befreundet mit: friendly with.

Ich bin mit ihm befreundet.

FRIGHTEN, CAUSE ANXIETY, WORRY The following verbs are derivatives of *Angst* (from *eng*),[2] correspond to 'frighten' only in the sense of 'to put into a state of anxiety', i.e. not in that of 'to give a sudden fright', which is *erschrecken, einen Schreck geben.* The accepted term for Freud's use of *Angst* as opposed to *Furcht* is 'anxiety'.[3] The German terms approximate closely to 'worry', but refer to the psychological state rather than to thoughts associated with it. When 'worry' implies the latter it is translated by *sich Sorge machen,*[4] or, when it implies little more than 'thinking about', *sich Gedanken machen.*[5]

1. Ängstigen emphasizes the state rather than the capacity of the agent to cause the state. It therefore often suggests unfounded anxiety or unawareness of the cause. It is most common in reflexive use.

Er ängstigte mich mit seinen erdichteten Geschichten.
Ein böser Traum hat mich geängstigt (example from Duden, the anxiety arising from the unconscious).
Du brauchst dich meinethalben nicht zu ängstigen.
Sie ängstigte sich sehr um die Gesundheit ihres Kindes.

[1] Friend. *Freund* is only an intimate friend. When 'friend' means casual friend, it must be translated by *Bekannte(r).* *Freund* and *Freundin,* applied to the opposite sex, mean 'sweetheart'. To avoid this sense 'friend' must be rendered by *guter Freund, gute Freundin* (e.g. *Frau X ist eine gute Freundin von ihm*). Note further: *ich bin gut Freund mit dem Bäcker* (I am good friends with...).

[2] See also article on 'to fear'.

[3] *Bange* and *Bangigkeit* express a lesser degree of anxiety than *Angst,* and correspond roughly to 'apprehensive', 'uneasy'.

[4] *Sorge* means a definite, often rational 'care' or 'worry', and may refer to the agent as well as the feeling.

[5] See also *sich (be)kümmern* under 'bother'.

2. **Beängstigen** suggests the capacity of the agent to produce the state of anxiety. For this reason it is used freely in the present participle as an adjective, but rarely as a reflexive verb.

Seine erdichteten Geschichten haben mich beängstigt.
Sein ungewisses Schicksal beängstigt mich.
Seine Drohungen beängstigen mich nicht.
Er hat beängstigende Geschichten erzählt.
Seine Worte sind beängstigend.

3. **Verängstigen** draws attention to the result as one of complete anxiety, and can for this reason only be used in the past participle, either as this appears in the perfect tenses or as an adjective.

Seine Geschichten haben uns ganz verängstigt.
Das Benehmen des Vaters hat die Kinder vollkommen verängstigt.

FULL (adjective)[1] Full of.

(*a*) *Voll* followed by *von* is the most objective term, and emphasizes the absence of everything else except that with which a given thing is said to be filled. If it is used otherwise than in the literal sense, it indicates a superabundance. (*b*) Followed by a noun in apposition, *voll* merely denotes a large number or quantity. (*c*) The form *voller* suggests a subjective impression or emotional participation.

Das Beet war voll von Unkraut.
Das Beet war voll Unkraut.
Das Beet war voller Unkraut.
Das Zimmer ist voll Ungeziefer. (*Voll von* is not possible, because it would mean literally 'full', with nothing else there.)
Das Zimmer ist voller Ungeziefer.
Der Zug ist voll von Flüchtlingen.
Der Zug ist voller Flüchtlinge.
Die Kiste ist voll von Büchern.
Sein Herz war voll von Liebe.
Sein Herz war voller Liebe.
Die Eltern waren voller Liebe für ihre Kinder.

FUNNY[2] The term is applied to someone or something which raises laughter in the sense of pure fun or because of an element of queerness

[1] *Voll* is used adverbially practically only in the senses of (*a*) without reservation (e.g. *ich weiss das voll zu würdigen*); (*b*) in full (e.g. *er hat es voll bezahlt*). Otherwise the German terms for 'quite' or 'complete' (see articles) or 'in detail' (*ausführlich*) must be used. Example: *ich bin restlos, völlig, davon überzeugt.*

[2] Study together with 'strange'.

or incomprehensibility. One aspect alone or both can be present. The German term **komisch** rarely suggests pure fun, at least not in a naïve, innocent way. Its most characteristic feature is a twist, a touch even of the ironical or grotesque. A regular meaning is: not understood and not expected (also: 'funny' or 'strange': it's funny that he did not keep the appointment). For lack of a closer equivalent *komisch* must, however, be used in most senses of 'funny', except where exclusively pure fun is meant. In such cases *lustig* (see 'merry', 'gay') is often used (e.g. *er unterhielt uns mit lustigen Kunststücken*).

Er erzählt dauernd komische Geschichten.
Er sah urkomisch aus.
Er sieht immer die komische Seite der Dinge.
Er ist immer sehr komisch (queer, or funny with a twist of irony and the like).

GATHER, COLLECT, ASSEMBLE 1. **Sammeln** is the normal term for gathering or collecting things in the sense of bringing them together in the same place, particularly in reference to the action of a collector of interesting objects (e.g. pictures, stamps, butterflies) and to appeals for charitable purposes, but also more generally (e.g. *die gesammelten Werke eines Dichters*).

Used with a personal object it differs slightly according to whether it is reflexive or not. Reflexively it means: (*a*) in the literal sense, to come along to a place casually, a few at a time without any set purpose; (*b*) figuratively, to rally round someone.[1] With a non-reflexive object it means: to gather what lies apart in order to build the parts into a solid whole. It must be carefully distinguished from *versammeln*.

Ich sammle Material für ein Buch.
Er sammelt Münzen.
Er sammelt Äußerungen über die sozialistischen Maßnahmen der Regierung.
Es wird für ein Waisenheim gesammelt.
Eine Menschenmenge sammelte sich am Ort des Unfalls.
Die Ausgebombten sammelten sich auf dem Marktplatz.
Er hat viele tüchtige Menschen um sich gesammelt.
Der Feldherr sammelte die Reste seiner Armee um sich.

2. **Versammeln** is used only with a personal object. As a reflexive verb it emphasizes the idea of purpose, i.e. it does not suggest casual appearance as *sammeln* does. In non-reflexive use it means: to summon, to call together for a purpose.

[1] *Sich sammeln* also has the special sense of 'to collect one's thoughts, to pull oneself together emotionally'.

Die Teilnehmer am Umzug versammelten sich auf dem Marktplatz.
Der Minister versammelte seine Berater zu einer Besprechung.
Der Alte versammelte seine Freunde um sich, um seinen achtzigsten Geburtstag zu feiern.

3. **Einsammeln** particularly stresses the length or the extent of the process.

Ich sammle meine Außenstände ein, um mein Geschäft zu verkaufen.

4. **Ansammeln** means 'to accumulate', when a heap is actually present, and can refer to a crowd of people. 'Tartar has accumulated, collected, on my teeth' (i.e. just a coating) would, however, be: *Zahnstein hat sich... angesetzt.*[1]

Ihre Briefe haben sich hier angesammelt.
An der Unfallstelle sammelten sich viele Menschen an.

5. Some other senses of 'collect', 'gather'.

(a) 'To collect', in the sense of 'to go and get' one or more things already in the same place, can only be rendered by **abholen**.

Vergessen Sie nicht, Ihre Pakete bei mir abzuholen!

(b) 'To gather together (a few things) quickly' is generally translated by verbs compounded with *zusammen*. *Er packte seine Sachen zusammen und reiste ab*. *Sammeln* implies a process extended in time and in space. *Aufsammeln* does not, however, necessarily suggest length of time, but means 'to pick up' things scattered over an area. *Auflesen*: to pick up what lies close to one. 'To gather' in the sense of 'to pick', but not 'to seek far and wide': *pflücken*.

GET (sense: receive, come by, go and get, obtain).[2] 1. **Bekommen:** to come by a thing passively. Since it mostly suggests inactivity on the part of the subject, it cannot be used in the imperative or in the sense of getting a thing for someone else, which would imply effort. If activity is expressed, it is either of an inner, unconscious kind, or movement conveyed by some prefix such as *ab*, or mental activity (*herausbekommen*).

Ich habe das Buch bekommen.
Wir haben gestern Schnee bekommen.
Er hat drei Wochen Ferien bekommen.
Er bekam Hunger.

[1] Figuratively, 'accumulate' is often translated by *häufen* and its compounds. *Die Beispiele, die Schulden, häufen sich.*

[2] For 'get' used causatively see 'make'. See also 'go' for its use as a synonym of the latter.

Können Sie überseeische Funkstationen mit Ihrem Apparat bekommen?
Die Erde hat große Risse bekommen.
Der Baum bekommt jetzt neue Blätter.
Mit den Jahren bekommt er mehr Weisheit.
Ich kann den Deckel nicht abbekommen (get off).
Haben Sie die Antwort schon herausbekommen?

2. **Kriegen** is often a colloquial equivalent of *bekommen*. Apart from this popular use it suggests activity, effort, vigour.

Ich habe diesen Tisch billig gekriegt (suggests bargaining).
Ich muß den 8 Uhr Zug kriegen.
Ich werde dich schon kriegen.
Können Sie überseeische Funkstationen mit Ihrem Apparat kriegen?
Er kriegte ein Messer in die Rippen (*bekam* would be colourless).
Haben Sie die Antwort schon herausgekriegt?

3. **Verschaffen:**[1] to procure for oneself or for others. It suggests the trouble one takes, the ways and means one adopts, often tactics or manœuvres, to make it possible to come by a thing. It does not mean 'to fetch', and should not be used where the operation is so simple as to require no effort or contrivance. The object need not be a thing that can be moved, but may be something intangible (contrast *beschaffen*).

Verschaffen Sie mir bitte das Buch (not 'fetch', but adopt the necessary measures to obtain it).
Könnten Sie mir eine Stellung in diesem Geschäft verschaffen (e.g. by negotiations, influence)?
Ich habe ihm ein Zimmer in einem entlegenen Teil der Stadt verschafft (by my enquiries I put him on to the track of a room).
Ich werde Ihnen schon die Erlaubnis verschaffen.
Seine Tüchtigkeit verschaffte ihm Zutritt zum Direktor.

4. **Anschaffen:** to purchase. It stresses possession and is used mostly of big or important objects or of things in bulk.

Wir haben uns einen Wagen, neue Geräte, neue Vorräte, angeschafft.

5. **Beschaffen:** to obtain a thing, particularly a concrete object, and also to bring it to where it is required. The latter idea is prominent and is expressed by the prefix *be*. Unlike *verschaffen* it does not imply tactics.

Ich werde mich bemühen, die Bücher neu oder antiquarisch zu beschaffen.
Er hat uns das Material, die Instrumente beschafft.
Sie besprachen, wie sie ein neues Boot beschaffen könnten.

[1] For *schaffen* as a rendering of 'get' in the sense of 'move' see the latter verb.

6. **Besorgen** suggests the buying of and paying for things[1] for other people. (Compare *sorgen für* under 'provide'.) Though very common, it is not well used in reference to single articles which cost only a few pence (e.g. a newspaper), or with words which do not denote things (e.g. a doctor, permission). It is, however, used indiscriminately for both *verschaffen* and *beschaffen* (see above).

Die Hausfrau hat die Lebensmittel für Sonntag besorgt.
Ich habe ihm ein Zimmer in einem entlegenen Teil der Stadt besorgt.
Besorgen Sie mir bitte die Theaterkarten, wenn Sie in der Stadt sind.
Ich werde Ihnen eine Zeitung, die Erlaubnis, besorgen.

7. **Holen** must be used to translate 'get' in the sense of 'fetch', 'go for'. It also means 'to catch' an infectious illness.

Holen Sie bitte die Stühle aus dem Nebenzimmer.
Er hat sich eine Erkältung geholt.

8. **Gewinnen:**[2] to obtain products from the earth or substances from other substances by chemical process.

Gold, Salz wird in diesen Bergen gewonnen.
Petroleum aus Kohle gewinnen.

9. **Hernehmen** is used in a question with *wo* in the sense of 'look for', 'find'.

Wo soll ich das Geld hernehmen?

GIVE The following are the commonest senses of 'give' in which *geben* is not used.[3]

1. **Schenken:** to make a personal gift to someone.[4]

Er hat mir zu Weihnachten ein Buch geschenkt.
Was soll ich ihr zu Weihnachten schenken?

2. **Bereiten** or **machen:** to cause a continued state of being or of mind to a person.[5]

Es hat mir Vergnügen, Kummer, bereitet, gemacht.

[1] *Besorgungen machen:* to go shopping. *Besorgen*, apart from its meaning of 'to fear', also means 'to attend to' duties (e.g. *die Küche besorgen*).

[2] *Gewinnen* has a wider range of application than the English 'win'. It often translates 'gain', 'obtain'. The latter is also rendered by *verschaffen, erlangen. Erlangen* is now becoming old-fashioned except as an official, chiefly legal term (e.g. *eine Scheidung, einen Aufschub, Gebiete bei einer Friedenskonferenz, den Doktorgrad, erlangen*). *Erreichen* is 'to reach' something desired, strived after, and implies effort on the part of the subject. It translates 'achieve', 'attain'.

[3] For *geben* used in other senses than 'give' see e.g. 'put'.

[4] *Geben* is used in the sense of 'to give to charity' or 'to make bequests'.

[5] *Geben* is used in reference to a sharp, momentary reaction (e.g. *einen Schreck, Schock, geben*).

3. **Hingeben** (reflexive) or **widmen:** to devote oneself to a task. *Hingeben* is also used reflexively in the sense of 'to give oneself up' to pleasurable states of mind.

Er hat sich der Aufgabe hingegeben, gewidmet.
Er gibt sich Illusionen, süßen Träumen, hin.

4. **Hergeben:** to lend oneself, to stoop, to a course of action.

Dazu gebe ich mich, meinen Namen, nicht her.

GLAD, JOYFUL **A.** To be glad.

1. **Es freut mich (dich,** etc.) is a polite, conventional expression, and is therefore weak.

Es freut mich, Sie zu sehen, kennen zu lernen.
Es freut mich, daß ich es ihm gesagt habe.

2. **Sich freuen** expresses a genuine feeling of joy, and is therefore more intimate.

Ich freue mich aber wirklich, Sie zu sehen.
Wir haben keinen Grund, uns zu freuen.

3. **Froh:** relieved that something important has not been missed or that something unpleasant has been avoided.

Ich bin froh, daß ich Sie zu Hause treffe.
Ich war froh, nicht länger bleiben zu müssen.
Seien Sie froh, daß Sie rechtzeitig weggekommen sind.

B. In other combinations.

1. **Froh** suggests here, too, the absence of any cause for depressing feelings. It is used particularly, but not exclusively, in biblical and elevated style.

Ein froher Mensch (inwardly).[1]
Eine frohe Botschaft, Nachricht (e.g. the birth of Christ).
Ein frohes Ereignis.
Die Musik Bachs stimmt einen froh (suggests a catharsis).

2. **Freudig:** causing joy. It therefore corresponds more closely to 'joyful', 'joyous' than to 'glad'. It is mostly applied to actions, to persons only in so far as they imply activity.[2] It suggests strong joy, but not the religious implication of *froh*.

[1] *Fröhlich*: showing joy outwardly, merry. See 'merry'.
[2] *Ein freudiger Arbeiter*: one who finds cause for joy in his work.

Eine freudige Botschaft, Nachricht.
Ein freudiges Ereignis (e.g. the birth of a child).
Er ging freudig in den Tod.
Die Nachricht hat mich freudig gestimmt.

GO (literal sense) 1. To go on foot, to walk:[1] **gehen.**

Ich gehe, ich fahre nicht.
Ich gehe jetzt nach Hause.

2. **Kommen** must be used instead of *gehen* to translate 'go' when the place of arrival is not, or only weakly, vaguely, conceived as a goal purposefully pursued, i.e. when arrival is conceived as accidental or incidental. English uses 'get'[2] even more frequently than 'go' in this sense and sometimes the perfect tense of 'to be' followed by the preposition 'to' (e.g. have you ever been to Munich?).

Wie weit sind Sie nach Norden gekommen?
Sind Sie schon mal nach München gekommen?
Auf meiner Reise bin ich nicht nach Wien gekommen.
Ich bin sehr spät ins Bett gekommen.
Er kommt sehr viel herum (*geht* would mean 'walks').
Er ist sehr viel in Deutschland herumgekommen.

3. To go in a vehicle.

Fahren must be used when the means of transport, the time of departure or the actual journey is prominent in one's mind. See also footnote to 'leave' (p. 191, n. 2). **Gehen** concentrates attention on what one intends to do on reaching one's destination (e.g. a holiday, to see someone, to do business, to settle permanently).[3,4]

Ich muß morgen nach Melbourne fahren.
Ich muß morgen in die Stadt gehen.
Wollen Sie jetzt nach Sydney fahren?
Gehen Sie heute abend nach Sydney?

[1] *Zu Fuß* may be added to *gehen* for clarity or emphasis (e.g. *sind Sie zu Fuß gegangen?*), but *gehen* itself means 'walk' as a contrast to transport. *Laufen* means 'to walk much' and can imply haste (e.g. *ich laufe sehr gerne, ich bin den ganzen Tag gelaufen*). See 'run'. *Wandeln* is 'to walk without effort'. It is used in elevated and biblical style, and in the phrase *im Schlafe wandeln.*

[2] *Geraten,* like 'get', expresses still more strongly the accidental result of an action or movement, sometimes in an unfavourable sense (e.g. *er ist in die falsche Straße geraten*). It also means 'to get into a state, condition' (e.g. *in Wut geraten*).

[3] *Reisen*: to travel.

[4] *Gehen* may be used of a passenger on a ship, unless the means of transport is emphasized. *Mit welchem Schiff gehen Sie nach England?* (casually). *Mit diesem Schiff bin ich nicht nach England gefahren* (more emphatic).

Ich fahre jetzt zur Universität.
Wir fuhren bei Basel über die Grenze.
Als wir von Griechenland nach der Türkei fuhren, erlebten wir ein Gewitter.
Ich fahre morgen zu meinem Vetter in Hamburg.
Wie lange fahren Sie nach Hause?
Ich muß morgen zur Universität gehen, um Bücher zu holen.
Ich gehe zu meinem Vetter in Hamburg.
Er ist ins Ausland gegangen.
Er ging nach Wien, um Kunstgeschichte zu studieren.

4. The means of transport as subject.

With phrases indicating destination or time of departure *gehen* may be used except with *Autobus* and *Strassenbahn* in phrases of destination. *Fahren* is always possible.

Wann geht der Zug?
Das Schiff geht nach Indien.
Dieses Flugzeug geht nach Rom.
Die Straßenbahn, der Autobus, fährt nach Chelsea.

5. **Reiten, fliegen,** etc. must be used when these methods of movement are indicated.

GRANT,[1] ALLOW[2] The object of 'grant' can be either the thing requested or the term 'request' itself (or a synonym).

1. **Bewilligen** is the most general term in the sense of 'to grant' the thing requested or the term 'request'. It means: to give approval,[3] particularly as an official or administrative act, to accept or pass a motion.

Seine Einreise in die U.S.A. ist bewilligt worden.
Für die Ausstattung des Saals ist eine beträchtliche Geldsumme bewilligt worden.
Sein Gesuch ist nicht bewilligt worden.

2. **Gewähren** implies a gracious act by a superior or by a person in a position of vantage.[4]

Der König gewährte ihm eine Unterredung.
Sein Gesuch, seine Bitte, wurde ihm gewährt.

[1] See also 'admit' and related synonyms dealt with in the same article. Further: *genehmigen*, to sanction; *erhören*, to grant, hear, a prayer.

[2] *Erlauben* is 'to allow' only as a synonym of 'to permit', not, e.g., to grant a sum of money.

[3] 'To approve' is *billigen* and *gutheißen*. *Billigen* suggests unqualified approval, *gutheißen* a subjective attitude which may imply reservations. See *heißen* under 'call'.

[4] The subject may also be a thing. *Dieser Kurs gewährt manche Vorteile.*

3. **Gestatten** is simply 'not to prevent', particularly in reference to what is allowed by officialdom. It can suggest, particularly in the imperative, a polite request to allow the speaker to trouble the addressee. It translates 'allow' rather than 'grant'.

Das Betreten des Rasens ist nicht gestattet.
Allerlei Freiheiten wurden uns gestattet.
Gestatten Sie bitte! (e.g. when pushing past others to take a seat in the theatre or a vehicle).

4. **Verstatten** suggests that permission is given after deliberation and then without qualification.

Der Vater verstattete seinem Sohn allerlei Vergnügungen.

5. **Vergönnen** is an elevated term and suggests that one is singled out as a special favour, particularly by fate.[1]

Das Schicksal hat es uns nicht vergönnt, uns wiederzusehen.

6. **Einräumen** suggests a concession. What is granted is therefore partial, qualified.

Unter einer Diktatur wird der Presse so gut wie keine Freiheit eingeräumt.
Sogar besiegten Völkern müssen gewisse Rechte eingeräumt werden.

GREET 1. **Grüßen:** to hail, to salute with words or gestures, to say good-day to a person in passing;[2] also figuratively with a subject such as the phenomena of nature.

Er grüßte mich freundlich, als ich ihn an der Ecke traf.
Die Sonne grüßte uns.

2. **Begrüßen:** to greet someone expected, to welcome, to receive (the act of a host).[3]

Die Dame begrüßte ihre Gäste.

GUARD 1. **Posten** is a sentry, whether armed or not; normally placed outside a building or an enclosed area.[4]

Bei Regen tritt der Posten ins Schilderhäuschen.
Der Posten schoß auf eine verdächtige Figur, die sich in seiner Nähe bewegte.
Das Konzentrationslager wurde von zahlreichen Posten bewacht.
Die Diebe haben einen Posten ausgestellt.

[1] *Gönnen* means 'not to begrudge', 'to be glad' that something has befallen a person, both in a favourable and an unfavourable sense. The latter may at times be translated by 'to serve a person right'. *Ich gönne ihm sein Schicksal* (which may be good or bad).
[2] *Jemand grüßen lassen*: to send regards.
[3] Also 'to welcome' in figurative use. *Ich würde etwas mehr Rücksicht begrüßen.*
[4] *Streikposten*: picket.

2. **Wache** generally refers to a body of men, but can also be applied to one man in so far as he is considered as a representative, not as an individual. In the latter sense it is preceded by the definite, but never the indefinite, article.[1] The compound term **Wachposten** is also used in reference to one man.

Die Leibwache des Führers.
Die Wache mußte verstärkt werden.
Die Wachen sind pünktlich abgelöst worden.
Die Wache am Kasernentor wollte das Auto nicht passieren lassen (one man as a representative or a body of men).
Der Wachposten wurde ermordet.
Ich hatte eine Auseinandersetzung mit dem Wachposten.

3. **Wächter** generally refers to a man who keeps watch or guard inside a building. It refers particularly to a (night) watchman or a warder, jailor.

Der Wächter machte die Runde durch die Bank.
Der Zuchthäusler wurde von seinen Wächtern erschossen.

4. **Wärter** is an attendant or a caretaker rather than a guard, i.e. one whose sole duty is to keep watch. It implies, however, that certain things are entrusted to him for safe keeping.

Er ist Wärter in einer Irrenanstalt.
Der Bahnwärter.[2]

5. **Garde** is only used, collectively, to denote the guard of an exalted personage and particularly in connection with a ceremonious occasion. It is the military term for names of traditional regiments. **Gardist** is a member of such a guard.

Eine Ehrengarde wurde für den französischen Ministerpräsidenten bestellt.

HABIT, CUSTOM[3] 1. **Gewohnheit** is that which by repetition has become second nature. It corresponds exactly to 'habit', and is ac-

[1] *Wache* also means: vigil (*die Nachtwache, Wache halten*); an official station (*Polizeiwache*). The alternative form *Wacht* is generally confined to elevated diction, except in compounds (*die Wacht am Rhein; der Wachtmeister*). The verb *wachen* means 'to be watchful, on the alert'.

[2] The fare-collector on a vehicle is *Schaffner*.

[3] The adjectives *gewöhnlich, gebräuchlich, üblich* are distinguished as follows. *Gewöhnlich*, the most general term, means 'done' or 'happening' in most cases. It corresponds most closely to 'ordinary' (also in the sense of 'vulgar'; see 'common') and 'usual'. It is used freely both as an adjective and an adverb, but is uncommon in the predicative position except in the sense of vulgar. Examples: *das ist der gewöhnliche Preis; wir essen gewöhnlich zu Hause. Gebräuchlich*, which is only used as an adjective, simply means 'in use', particularly of words, idioms, and the like. Example: *diese Redensart*

cordingly applied in the first place to the activities of individuals, not of groups. **Angewohnheit** is only a habit that has become so ingrained that one cannot resist it. While *Gewohnheit* can express this sense, it does not stress it.

Er hat die Gewohnheit, morgens um 5 Uhr aufzustehen.
Er kann diese schlechte Gewohnheit nicht mehr ablegen.
Das Lügen ist bei ihm zur Gewohnheit geworden.
Rauchen ist eine üble Angewohnheit.

2. **Sitte,** custom, is the most general term for anything that is habitually practised by a group and has grown spontaneously. It is applied particularly to the customs of such groups as a country, a class, a family. It may be morally good or bad. In the plural it corresponds in this sense also to 'ways'.[1]

Die Sitten und Gebräuche eines Volkes.
In Deutschland ist es Sitte, den Hut abzunehmen, wenn zwei Herren sich grüßen.
Es ist in Deutschland eine alte Sitte, daß der Heilige Abend zu Hause gefeiert wird.

3. **Gebrauch** mostly means 'use'.[2] In the meaning of 'custom' it is rare, particularly in the singular, in which it occurs mainly in fixed phrases. It refers to a way of doing things that has been agreed upon by a number of people.

Die Diplomatie hat Gebräuche, an denen sie festhält.
Dies sind hier die Gebräuche.

4. **Brauch** is used in reference to time-honoured and ceremonious occasions.

Es ist ein alter Brauch, daß am Weihnachtstag Puter gegessen wird.

5. 'Custom' when applied to an individual, particularly in the phrase 'it is my (his, etc.) custom to...', cannot be rendered by any of the above

ist nicht mehr gebräuchlich. It implies: used on certain occasions, in certain places. *Üblich*, on the other hand, means 'practised at all times' (*üben* = practise). *Dann kamen die üblichen Entschuldigungen. Es ist üblich, vorher anzurufen, wenn man einen Besuch machen will. Üblich* is free from all suggestion of vulgarity. It is used only as an adjective.

[1] In the singular *Sitte* can also mean 'decorum, propriety', either as correct or polished behaviour (c.g. *die Sitte verlangt es; ein Verstoß gegen die Sitte*). In the plural *Sitten* can also mean (*a*) 'manners' in the sense of customary ways, (*b*) the 'morals' of an individual. See also footnote to 'educate' (p. 107, n. 4).

[2] Compare: *im Gebrauch sein*, to be in use, to be customary. *Gebrauch* approximates closely to 'usage', either as an established way of behaviour that serves as a guide, or in reference to the correct meaning of words.

terms. **Pflegen** or a synonymous verb should be used. It is applied only to an activity which is careful, controlled, not to what is wild, unrestrained. Thus it cannot be used to translate the synonym 'would' in the following sentence: They would push and scramble to get a seat. The same implication is associated with the other meaning of *pflegen*, 'to look after, to nurse, to tend, to bestow care on'. *Ein gepflegter Garten*: trim, well looked after.

Er pflegt, an seinem Geburtstage seine Freunde um sich zu sammeln.
Ich pflege nicht, solche Angebote anzunehmen.

HANG (to put to death) **1. Hängen** or **henken:** the normal literary terms.[1]

Der Mörder wurde gehängt (gehenkt).

2. Aufhängen is a popular term for *hängen, henken* or *erhängen* (cf. 'string up').

Ich hoffe, daß die ganze Bande aufgehängt wird.

3. Erhängen is in careful use only reflexive.

Er hat sich erhängt.

HEAD In the literal sense **Kopf** (cognate with middle L. *coppa*) is the ordinary term. **Haupt** (L. *caput*) is more dignified, and is normally restricted to human beings.[2] L. *coppa* denotes a drinking vessel and *Kopf* suggests shape or form in both literal and figurative senses. In the latter it is applied only to the top of an object which has a form of this kind. *Haupt* in figurative use refers to what is most important, particularly to the chief of an organization.

Er hat einen runden, schönen, Kopf.
Ich musterte ihn vom Kopf bis zu den Füßen.
Er neigte das Haupt vor dem König.
Die gekrönten Häupter Europas.
Der Kopf eines Nagels.
Das Haupt der Familie.

HEAR (of, from) **Hören von** means 'to hear of, about', unless it is followed by a statement giving information (mostly a *daß* clause), in which case it can mean 'to hear from'. In the sense of 'to receive letters, a message', or the like, from a person, when this is not followed by the

[1] *Durch den Strang hinrichten* is common in legal language.

[2] Hence *enthaupten*, to execute, behead, is a more elevated term than the usual *hinrichten*.

content of the letter or message, phrases such as **Nachricht bekommen von** should be used.

Haben Sie von ihm gehört? (of).
Ich hörte von ihm, daß wir Ihren Besuch bald erwarten können (from).
Haben Sie in letzter Zeit Nachricht von ihm bekommen?
Hat er in letzter Zeit von sich hören lassen?

HEART In compounds *Herz-* is a physiological term, *Herzens-* is regarded as the seat of the emotions.

Er hat einen Herzfehler. *Er zeigte wirkliche Herzensgüte.*

HEARTY **Herzlich** means 'heartfelt', i.e. it stresses inner feeling, without, however, excluding reference to its outward expression. **Herzhaft** refers primarily to the outward manifestation of heartiness conceived as zest, robust enjoyment. It is not, however, applied adjectivally to a person.

Er dankte mir, grüßte mich, herzlich. *Er lachte herzhaft.*
Er lachte herzlich. *Er griff herzhaft zu.*

HEAT **Heizen** is used transitively and intransitively of heating a hollow space, particularly a room. **Einheizen** is applied in its literal sense only to the latter, *ein* having intensive force. **Erhitzen** means in its literal application 'to heat to a given degree', figuratively it refers to feelings. 'To heat' food or water for ordinary domestic purposes is **heiß machen**.

Wir müssen das Zimmer, den Ofen, heizen.
Ich habe tüchtig eingeheizt.
Ich habe das Wasser auf 80 *Grad erhitzt.*
Bei einer Diskussion erhitzt er sich immer.
Bitte, machen Sie etwas Wasser heiß.

HIDE 1. **Verstecken** suggests the putting away of a thing in order to outwit the seeker, i.e. a purely practical purpose. As with *stecken* one thinks of the object to be hidden as being put *into* something else, although this is not necessarily the case. The action itself is emphasized. While what is hidden is generally a concrete object, it may also in the past participle, i.e. as an adjective, be applied to something intangible (e.g. *Absichten*).

Sie versteckte den Schlüssel.
Er mußte sich vor der Polizei versteckt halten.

Die Kunstschätze des Landes wurden kurz vor dem Einmarsch des Feindes so weit wie möglich versteckt.

Die Sonne versteckte sich hinter den Wolken. (But *verstecken* could not translate literally 'the clouds hid the sun', since *verstecken*, used actively, so strongly suggests the action of putting away by a person.)
Er hegte versteckte Absichten. (Since *verstecken* used actively has the literal sense, it cannot be used to translate: he hid his intentions.)

2. **Verbergen** refers to the hiding of anything about one's person or anything connected with one's inner self. The action it suggests is frequently that of putting one thing over another in order to protect it (*bergen* means 'to bring to safety'). It is used also of things hidden by nature, not by man.

Er verbarg das Papier in seiner Manschette.
Er versuchte, seine linke Hand zu verbergen, weil ein Finger fehlte.
Sie verbarg ihr Gesicht.
Ein Tuch verbarg sein Gesicht.
Er verbarg sich vor dem Überfall.
Wir müssen die Flüchtlinge verbergen.
Er verbarg sich vor dem Gesetz.
Die Mauer verbirgt das Haus vor unserem Blick.[1]
In dieser Gegend sind viele Naturschätze in der Erde verborgen.
Ich habe einige verborgene Zigaretten (saved up).
Die Wolken verbargen die Sonne.
Ich konnte meine Freude kaum verbergen.
Du sollst mir Deine Gedanken, Absichten, nicht verbergen.
Sie verbarg das Geheimnis im Innersten ihres Herzens.

3. **Verhehlen** suggests dissimulation and often an accusation. It is not used of concrete objects.

Verhehle mir nichts!
Sie haben mir die Wahrheit verhehlt.
Er verhehlte ihr, daß er schon zweimal verheiratet gewesen war.
Er kann beim besten Willen den Nazi nicht verhehlen (the Nazi in him).

HOWEVER, NEVERTHELESS, YET, ALL THE SAME 1. **Jedoch** is only used as a qualification of a preceding absolute statement, and corresponds to this sense of 'however'.

Er ist schwer verwundet, es besteht jedoch keine Gefahr, daß er stirbt.
Er hat triftige Gründe vorgebracht, hat mich jedoch nicht überzeugt.

[1] But: *die Mauer versperrt die Aussicht* (see article on 'block'). The above verbs are impossible, because German has no term which corresponds exactly to 'view' in the sentence: the wall hides the view. See article on 'view'.

Es gab unzählige Gegner des Nazi-Regimes, jedoch war nur eine Handvoll organisiert.

2. **Dennoch** indicates a contrast between the result and what the preceding clause leads one to expect. It does not express a qualification, but is a direct and emphatic adversative, often following a concessive clause. The meaning is really 'even then', i.e. *dann noch.*

Alle Voraussetzungen für den Erfolg des Unternehmens waren da, und dennoch ist es mißlungen.

Wenn er mir auch 1000 *Mark anbieten würde, gebe ich mich dennoch nicht dazu her.*

3. **Doch** is also an adversative and indicates a contrast between the result and what the preceding clause leads one to expect, but is much less emphatic than *dennoch.*[1] If it stands at the beginning of the clause it normally requires the inversion of subject and verb. There are, however, cases, particularly in literature, of non-inversion. The closest English equivalent is 'yet'.

Er meldete sich freiwillig für den Dienst im Ausland, doch ließ seine Begeisterung rasch nach.

Er ist reich, doch keineswegs zufrieden.

Sie haben noch nicht Ihre früheren Schulden zurückgezahlt und bitten doch um eine weitere Anleihe.

4. **Trotzdem** (i.e. despite that) and the more literary **dessenungeachtet** (i.e. notwithstanding) imply that the preceding statement, the truth of which is indisputable, is to be left out of account.

Er hat mich mehrere Male im Stich gelassen, aber ich werde mich heute trotzdem auf ihn verlassen.

5. **Immerhin,** like *trotzdem,* implies that the preceding statement, which is indisputable, can be left out of account. It often has a strong emotive value and stresses a redeeming feature in an apparently hopeless situation. The closest English equivalent is 'all the same'.

Das Stück ist ungünstig beurteilt worden, aber ich möchte es mir immerhin ansehen.

6. **Allerdings** and **Freilich** approach some uses of 'however', though more closely 'certainly', 'it is true' when these denote a concession in

[1] *Doch* frequently, particularly in the body of a clause, denotes an opposition to something felt and not expressed in a preceding clause. Its shades of meaning are numerous. It can, e.g., express uncertainty that seeks confirmation in a question (e.g. *du hast es ihm doch nicht gesagt,* i.e. I hope), an unfulfilled wish (e.g. *wenn ich es doch nur wüßte*).

the form of a qualification. When they express a concession not in the form of a qualification they are often followed by 'aber'.

Er ist ein reicher Mann, allerdings nicht so reich wie sein Vater.
Er hat es mir allerdings schon gesagt, aber nicht deutlich genug.

HURRY, HASTEN The distinction between 'hurry' and 'hasten' is that the first is prompted primarily by an external, the second by an inner cause (e.g. an emotion). The German *hasten* resembles the English 'hasten' in this point, but is confined to a few special uses. *Hastig* too indicates a lack of inner composure, whereas *eilig* indicates external needs.

This article deals with the translation of the intransitive uses of the English terms and then offers a few suggestions about the transitive uses.

A. Eilen denotes primarily a change of position, i.e. hurrying or hastening from one place to another.[1] In reflexive use it is now limited to the imperative, with the sense of *sich beeilen.* **Sich beeilen:** to do something speedily or to make haste to do something. In the imperative it is more common than *sich eilen.*

Er eilte nach Hause, ihr zu Hilfe.
Er beeilte sich, es zu leugnen.
Beeilen Sie sich (or less commonly: *eilen Sie sich*).
Sie müssen sich mit dem Abendessen beeilen.

B. Transitive uses.

(a) **Übereilen:** to do a thing before the time is ripe or too quickly. **Überstürzen:** also, to precipitate or to do a thing so quickly that it becomes confused (particularly with regard to speech). These verbs are used reflexively and in the past participle when 'hurry' and 'hasten' denote excess. Apart from the reflexive use, the object cannot be a person.

Übereilen Sie sich nicht mit der Arbeit.
Der Entschluß, die Arbeit, hätte nicht übereilt werden sollen.
Seine Reden sind immer überstürzt.

(b) Frequently a specific term must be used (often *eilig* with an appropriate verb). The following is not an exhaustive list.

Sorgen haben seinen Tod beschleunigt.
Dränge mich nicht so!
Truppen wurden eilig an die Front geworfen.
Er hat sein Frühstück hinuntergestürzt.

IDEA, CONCEPT, CONCEPTION[2] 1. **Idee** has all meanings of 'idea', from its philosophic use to that of 'notion', whether vague or clear,

[1] *Eilen* with a thing or the impersonal *es* as subject means 'to be urgent'. *Die Sache eilt nicht. Es eilt nicht mit der Sache.* [2] See also 'view'.

'belief', 'fancy', 'plan'. It is, however, often preferable to use a native German term such as *Vorstellung*.[1]

Die platonischen Ideen.
Die Gottesidee.
Eingeborene Ideen.
Das entspricht nicht meiner Idee der königlichen Würde.
Das ist eine vernünftige Idee.
Er ist auf die Idee verfallen, daß wir ihn loswerden wollen.
Er ist voller Ideen.
Meine Idee war, ein Zimmer hier anbauen zu lassen.

2. **Vorstellung** is a mental picture of a thing. It draws attention less to the thing in its objective aspects than to the state of mind of the subject, particularly with regard to the intensity, vividness, clarity, persistence or otherwise of the image. Hence: *er leidet an Zwangsvorstellungen*, fixed ideas (or *an fixen Ideen*). It should not be used when this subjective element is absent. Hence: *seine* (but not *die*) *Vorstellung der Pflicht.*

Er hat klare, verworrene, Vorstellungen.
Die Vorstellung, daß er eine unheilbare Krankheit hat, beherrscht ihn ganz und gar.
Stefan George hat seiner Zeit strengere Vorstellungen der Dichtkunst entgegengehalten als die, welche in der zweiten Hälfte des 19ten Jahrhunderts gang und gäbe waren.

3. **Begriff** means both 'concept', i.e. the typical or generic idea of a thing divested of all its accidental features, and 'conception', particularly in the sense of 'ability to conceive, to represent to the mind'.[2]

Der Gottesbegriff.
Der Begriff des Staates.
Klare, feste, Begriffe.
Das ist ein überwundener Begriff.

[1] Further: *ich hatte keine Ahnung* (inkling), *daß Sie hier waren; er hat manchmal gute Einfälle* (only in sense of 'brain-waves'); *der Gedanke, meine Ferien dort zu verbringen, ist mir nie vorher eingefallen* (*Gedanke* refers to something more normal, obvious, *Idee* can be sudden, ingenious; see also 'thought').

[2] *Konzeption* means 'conception' only in the sense of the actual process of conceiving, bringing to birth, a product of the mind such as a work of art (e.g. *die Konzeption des 'Faust' war schon früh in großen Zügen fertig; bei der Konzeption dieses Gedichts*). *Konzept* does not mean 'concept'. It is used only in a few fixed phrases meaning 'train of thought' (e.g. *Sie bringen mich aus dem Konzept, Sie verderben mir das Konzept*). In Goethe's day it means a 'rough draft' of a letter. *Empfängnis* is the physiological term for 'conception'.

Nach seinen Begriffen von dem, was schicklich ist.
Ich kann mir keinen rechten Begriff von den dort herrschenden Verhältnissen machen.

ILLUMINATE In literal application **beleuchten** is a purely objective term, while **erleuchten** refers to an impression. In figurative use *beleuchten* is 'to throw light on' a thing, *erleuchten* denotes the illumination or inspiration of the mind.

Gut beleuchtete Straßen.
Die hell erleuchtete Stadt.
Die Scheinwerfer beleuchteten den Hafen.
Das Schloß war hell erleuchtet.
'*Den andern Abend nach seiner Rückkehr waren Krespels Fenster ungewöhnlich erleuchtet...*' (Hoffmann, *Rat Krespel*).
Wir gingen in den festlich erleuchteten Saal.
Er beleuchtete seine These mit einer Fülle von Beispielen.
Er ist ein erleuchteter Geist.

IMAGINE[1] **1. Sich vorstellen:** to make a conscious effort to picture a thing to oneself, whether real or unreal.

Stellen Sie sich vor, Sie wären ein reicher Mann.
Ich kann mir den Ort ganz schön vorstellen.

2. Sich einbilden denotes an involuntary act, and often an illusion. As it is involuntary it cannot be used in the imperative.

Das haben Sie sich nur eingebildet.
Er bildet sich ein, er sei ein Genie.

IMPROVE[2] **1. Bessern:** to bring about a limited, but unspecified, degree of improvement with regard to (*a*) health; (*b*) behaviour, conceived in a wide sense including both moral and intellectual aspects; (*c*) social conditions. It occurs mainly in the reflexive form. With a personal object in non-reflexive use, which in present-day German is less common than formerly, it refers to morals, not to health, and comes to mean 'to reform to a certain degree, but not completely'. Non-personal objects are generally words referring to the moral side of man (e.g. *Charakter*,

[1] *Einbildungskraft, Vorstellungskraft:* the faculty of imagination. These terms are used chiefly in analyses of the nature of this faculty. Otherwise *Phantasie* is the usual equivalent of 'imagination' (e.g. *er hat eine rege Phantasie; ein mit Phantasie begabter Mensch*). *Einbildung* is the specific content of any act of the imagination, often 'imaginitis' (e.g. *das ist doch nur Einbildung!*).

[2] *Ausbessern*: to mend (shoes, streets, etc.).

Betragen) or *Zustand, Lage* or equivalents.[1] A process, not a brief act, is suggested, which explains the prevalence of the reflexive use.

Bessern an, followed by the dative, denotes, however, a series of brief acts, and means 'to effect improvements in' an object by alterations, by removing errors or other imperfections. It is applied particularly to writing.

Sein Gesundheitszustand hat sich erheblich gebessert.[2]
Er hat sich politisch nicht gebessert.
Er hat sich in der Schule nicht gebessert.
Die sozialen Verhältnisse haben sich in der letzten Zeit kaum gebessert.
Der Weltverbesserer sagt: Ich habe die Lage der Arbeiterschaft gebessert.
Gewisse Maßnahmen, die in letzter Zeit ergriffen worden sind, haben den Gesundheitszustand des Volkes gebessert.
Früher starben viele Frauen am Kindbettfieber, die Einführung antiseptischer Mittel durch Lord Lister hat diesen Zustand gebessert.

'*Bilde mir nicht ein, ich könnte was lehren,*
Die Menschen zu bessern und zu bekehren.' (*Faust I*, ll. 372–3.)

'*Euphemie ist religiös schon aus Temperament, vielleicht gelingt es ihrer besonderen Rednergabe, tief in ihr Herz zu dringen, sie zu erschüttern und zu bessern, daß sie den Verrat am Freunde,. . .unterläßt.*' (E. T. A. Hoffmann, *Die Elixiere des Teufels.*)

'*Ich finde mich erst wieder, als die Mutter meinen Anzug, soviel es ihr möglich war, besserte und ordnete.*' (E. T. A. Hoffmann, *Die Elixiere des Teufels.* Not possible in present-day German.)

2. **Verbessern:** to bring a thing closer to the ideal type by raising it to a standard which is objectively recognized as a step towards the ideal and which, in some cases, is capable of being tested by measurement. It is therefore applied particularly to things which can be improved as types, often in accordance with specifications and by a technical process. As objective recognition tends to be accorded to public or large-scale institutions, inventions and enterprises which are in the hands of experts more than to small private objects and activities with which one 'muddles through', *verbessern* is more often applied to the former than the latter. It thus corresponds to 'improve' as a close synonym of 'to improve on', which it also translates.[3] Since it should only be used when the reference to an objective standard is clear, the nature of the improvement must in

[1] *Die Gehälter bessern* is somewhat colloquial, as is also *er wurde aufgebessert* (=he was raised, i.e. in salary).

[2] Compare the use of the corresponding noun in the expression *gute Besserung.*

[3] 'To improve' mostly implies changes in the same object, but is also used in the sense of 'to improve on', which implies another object that is compared with the first. Example: to improve (on) a record.

some cases be indicated, e.g. by mention of the process. Thus while the sentence 'the park has been improved' cannot be translated by *verbessern*, the addition of a phrase such as 'by building a playing area for children' or 'by the addition of fountains' makes its use possible. The addition brings the park more into conformity with the ideal of a park. With reference to the economic circumstances or the social standing of an individual, the meaning is 'to raise (them) to a standard recognized as satisfactory'.

The changes necessary to bring a thing closer to the ideal type can imply 'correction' of errors, and 'to correct' is a meaning of *verbessern*, particularly with reference to errors in writing. The object may be the piece of writing itself (short rather than long pieces), the error, or the person who makes the error. With writing therefore *verbessern* means 'to correct', i.e. to eliminate errors, not 'to improve' in the sense of removing other types of imperfection.[1]

Reflexive use with a personal subject is limited to the following meanings: (*a*) to correct a slip of the tongue, i.e. to correct oneself; (*b*) to seek a better job, i.e. to better oneself.

In all cases a deliberate act, not an unconscious process, is implied.

Die öffentlichen Anlagen wurden durch einen Spielplatz für Kinder verbessert.

Um den allgemeinen Gesundheitszustand zu verbessern, wurde dem Wasser Jod entzogen.

Der Geschmack des Weins wurde durch gewisse Zusätze verbessert.

Die Befestigungswerke, die Museen, müssen verbessert werden.

In den letzten Jahren sind die Unterrichtsmethoden fast überall verbessert worden (improved or improved on).[2]

'*Ehe wir mit der Aufklärung vorschreiten, d.h. ehe wir die Wälder umhauen, den Strom schiffbar machen, Kartoffeln anbauen, die Dorfschulen verbessern,...ist es nötig, alle Leute von gefährlichen Gesinnungen, die keiner Vernunft Gehör geben und das Volk durch lauter Albernheiten verführen, aus dem Staate zu verbannen*' (E. T. A. Hoffmann, *Klein Zaches*).

Dieser Mann hat die Rechtsprechung des Landes verbessert.

Er hat seinen eigenen Rekord, eine Spitzenleistung, verbessert.

Er war in der Lage, seine gesellschaftliche Stellung zu verbessern.

Er hat sich verbessert (corrected or bettered himself).

3. In other cases, which are numerous, German uses more specific terms. Common amongst these are *steigern* (see 'increase'), *heben* (see 'raise'),

[1] *Verbessern* also means 'to amend', and 'to emend'.
[2] Also 'to reform', with reference to an institution.

verstärken (see 'strengthen'), *veredeln, verfeinern, vertiefen, erweitern, fördern.* With an object such as 'things', 'the state of affairs', *besser machen* may be used. *Meliorieren* means to improve the value of land property.[1]

Die Leistungsfähigkeit der Arbeiter steigern.
Das Niveau der Volksgesundheit heben (with *Zustand, bessern* and *verbessern* could be used).
Sie müssen Ihre Kenntnisse des Deutschen zu vertiefen, erweitern, versuchen.
Ein Aufenthalt in den Bergen wird Ihrer Gesundheit zugute kommen.
Das wird Ihre Chancen kaum fördern.
Das wird die Sache nicht besser machen.

INCREASE 1. **Mehren** is only used reflexively and in reference to the numerical increase of things. Though the Bible has '*Seid fruchtbar und mehret euch*', it is in present use rarely applied in ordinary prose to the increase of population.

Die Beschwerden, seine Sorgen, mehren sich.
Die Fehler in dieser Arbeit mehren sich ganz bedenklich.
Die Anzeichen einer Krise, die Anfragen, mehren sich.

2. **Vermehren**: to increase in number. With other objects, particularly feelings, it is now common only in elevated or poetic diction, except occasionally in the past participle. In reflexive use it commonly refers to an increase in population. Other reflexive uses in reference to number should not be imitated. It cannot be followed by a prepositional phrase meaning 'to a level'.

Die Eingeborenen vermehren sich schnell.
Er hat die Zahl der Polizisten, der Beispiele, vermehrt.
'*Selbst ihre Unruhe schien ihre Zärtlichkeit zu vermehren*' (Goethe, *Wilhelm Meisters Lehrjahre*; no longer normal usage).

3. **Steigern** and **erhöhen** both mean 'to increase in intensity to a higher level'. *Steigern* is 'to increase to a maximum or to an unlimited extent'. *Erhöhen* is weaker and denotes a definite level.[2] 'To' is translated by *bis zu* after *steigern*, and by *auf* after *erhöhen*.

Die Preise erhöhen.
Die Preise steigern.
Ich habe meine Ansprüche, meine Anforderungen, erhöht (not *gesteigert*).
Der Wert des Grundstücks wurde durch diese Maßnahme erhöht (not *gesteigert*).

[1] Note also *ameliorieren* (=ameliorate).
[2] See also *erhöhen* under 'raise'.

Die Rationen wurden erhöht (not *gesteigert*).
Er hat seine Technik bis zur vollkommenen Beherrschung des Instruments gesteigert.
Der Beifall steigerte sich bis zur Begeisterung.

4. Examples of more specific terms are: *einen Verdacht verstärken* (see 'strengthen'); *eine Strafe verschärfen* (to make more severe; see footnote to 'severe', p. 316, n. 4).

5. **Zunehmen,** only in intransitive use, is 'to increase in numbers or intensity'.[1]

Die Zahl der Einwohner nimmt rasch zu.
Das Gewitter nimmt an Heftigkeit zu.

INHABITANT 1. **Einwohner** suggests the idea of a community, and approximates to 'citizen'. It must therefore be used in reference to the number of inhabitants of a place; also with a following genitive which denotes a community settlement (e.g. *Stadt, Stadtviertel, Ort, Dorf*).

London ist eine Stadt von 8 Millionen Einwohnern.
Die Einwohner dieses Dorfes haben bei den Wahlen fast alle sozialdemokratisch gestimmt.

2. **Bewohner** is applied to people who are thought of as happening to be in a place, to have their dwellings there. It must be used with a following genitive which denotes a house or a street, and also with a land or region when the people there are thought of merely as inhabiting these.

Die Bewohner dieses Hauses, dieses Schloßes, sind augenblicklich verreist.
Fast alle Bewohner dieser Straße sind Ausländer.
Die Bewohner dieser nördlichen Gegenden sind zu einem schweren Leben verurteilt.

3. **Bevölkerung,** population, should be used in reference to the human characteristics, customs, and attitudes of a group of people settled in a place.

Die Bevölkerung dieses Dorfes ist degeneriert.
Die Bevölkerung des Spreewaldes hat ihre alte Sprache erhalten.
Die Bevölkerung dieses Ortes war feindlich eingestellt (a border-line case for *Einwohner*).

INHERIT **Erben** is the general term, both literally and figuratively. It stresses the possession of a thing which has, so to speak, been handed to one. **Ererben** refers to what is handed down, often through generations, and of which the possessor may be unaware, particularly in reference to

[1] *Zunehmen* is used also in the sense of 'put on weight'. *Er hat stark zugenommen.*

a cultural inheritance. It is common only in the past participle and has adjectival force, corresponding to 'hereditary'. The process of passing from generation to generation, rather than the act of reception, is emphasized. Goethe uses it verbally in this sense. '*Was du ererbt von deinen Vätern hast, erwirb es, um es zu besitzen.*' The second part of this quotation is based on the implications of *ererbt*, i.e. that what is handed down is not thought of in close association with the receiver, as a conscious part of him. *Erben* used adjectivally in the past participle is more active.[1]

Er hat ein beträchtliches Vermögen, den Jähzorn seines Vaters, geerbt.
Eine geerbte Krankheit.
Eine ererbte Krankheit, Sünde.
Sein Jähzorn ist ererbt.
Das ererbte Traditionsgefühl der Hansastädte.

INHERITANCE, LEGACY, BEQUEST, ESTATE **Erbschaft** may or may not be bequeathed by deed of will. **Vermächtnis** always implies in the literal sense a deed of will, often to someone who is not the natural heir, and thus corresponds most closely to 'legacy', sometimes to 'bequest' (*vermachen* = bequeath). Figuratively, it denotes something expressly addressed to someone (e.g. words of advice). **Hinterlassenschaft** is simply what is left behind, i.e. the testator's estate.[2] *Erbschaft* is the normal term for 'inheritance' in reference to property, but is also used figuratively in an unfavourable sense, i.e. as something that is a handicap, or as a disorderly state of affairs that has to be straightened out. **Erbe**[3] is used in reference to both material and spiritual goods, but more often to the latter. Applied to material goods, it suggests moral or sentimental ideas associated with inheritance, while *Erbschaft* is purely objective.

Er hat zugunsten seines Bruders auf seine Erbschaft verzichtet.
Die Sünden der Väter werden oft zu einer Erbschaft für die Kinder.
Er trug ein Leben lang an der Erbschaft seines Vaters.
Die Männer, die die Nazi-Erbschaft angetreten haben, stehen vor kaum zu bewältigenden Problemen.
Goethes Vermächtnis an das deutsche Volk ist von diesem nicht immer geschätzt worden.
Seine Hinterlassenschaft war nicht beträchtlich.
Das Kulturerbe der Deutschen ist vom Nationalsozialismus mißverstanden worden.

[1] *Vererben*: to bequeath, to transmit (a quality, disease, or the like).
[2] *Nachlaß*: (1) the posthumous works of a writer; (2) the 'effects' of an unknown dead person (e.g. a deceased soldier). Nowadays also used for *Hinterlassenschaft*.
[3] *Der Erbe:* the heir.

INTERESTED IN **Sich interessieren für** refers to an intellectual or emotional interest. Without qualification it is not strong, merely indicating the direction or object of an interest. **Interessiert sein an** denotes (*a*) a more intense and active interest of an intellectual or emotional kind; (*b*) a commercial interest. The same distinction holds good for these prepositions when they follow the noun *Interesse.*

Er interessiert sich für Kunst, Blumenzucht, die Frau.
Er ist an Kunst, Blumenzucht, der Frau, interessiert.
Er ist an dem Unternehmen interessiert.

INTERPRET **Deuten** should only be used in reference to lofty or important matters. **Auslegen** is applied to humbler or everyday matters. **Interpretieren** is used in both ways. **Dolmetschen** means only 'to translate orally' from a foreign language for two or more people who are ignorant of one of the languages concerned.

Er hat Goethes 'Faust' neu gedeutet, interpretiert.
Wie legen Sie seine Absage, diese Stelle, aus?
Er hat die Rede falsch interpretiert, ausgelegt.
Wie würden Sie seinen Besuch interpretieren?
Er hat für die beiden Staatsmänner gedolmetscht.

INTRODUCE 1. **Vorstellen** refers only to the act of presenting one person to another.[1]

Darf ich Sie vorstellen?
Ich bin ihm noch nicht vorgestellt worden.

2. **Einführen** means (*a*) to bring about an association between people, but without reference to formal presentation. It is followed by a preposition such as *in* or *bei.* (*b*) To introduce a person to something abstract, e.g. a world of thought. (*c*) To establish a thing as a practice.

Er führte mich bei Schmidts, in diese Gesellschaft, ein.
Er, dieses Buch, führte mich in die romantische Gedankenwelt ein.
Er hat eine neue Mode, Sitte, Russisch in den Schulplan, eingeführt.

[1] *Vorstellen* also means 'to represent' in reference to art. It differs from *darstellen* which also means 'to represent', in that it means no more than 'to convey the idea of' a thing (*Vorstellung* = idea), while *darstellen* suggests the evocation of a thing with a wealth of sensuous detail. *Das Bild stellt einen Hafen vor*, i.e. is meant to convey the idea of a harbour, though the resemblance may not be striking. *Das Bild stellt einen Hafen dar*, i.e. in its sensuous reality. *Darstellung* has as one of its meanings 'performance', 'impersonation', in reference to theatrical art. *Vorstellung* in the sense of a theatrical performance and the like means 'session' (e.g. *seine Darstellung von Hamlet, die 5 Uhr-Vorstellung*).

3. **Einleiten** is 'to take the preliminary or first steps', particularly in reference to something written or spoken.[1]

Er leitete das Buch mit einer propagandistischen Vorrede ein.
Er leitete das Thema mit einigen Anekdoten ein.
Das Schuljahr wurde von dem Direktor mit einer feierlichen Ansprache eingeleitet.

4. **Bekannt machen** can mean (*a*) to present one person to another, but is less formal than *vorstellen*; (*b*) to introduce a person to a thing.

Darf ich Sie bekannt machen?
Ich habe ihn schon mit unseren Weinen bekannt gemacht.

5. **Einbringen:** to submit a bill to Parliament for approval.

Ein neuer Antrag, eine Gesetzesvorlage, wurde heute eingebracht.

JOIN A. Of persons, to come into contact, association, etc.

1. German has no special term for 'join' with reference to social entertainment and the like.

Gehen wir zu den Damen hinüber.
Wir treffen uns in London (I'll join you...).[2]
Ich treffe Sie zum Frühstück.
Setzen Sie sich zu uns (when seated).
Trinken Sie ein Glas Bier mit uns (see **A. 6**).

2. **Beitreten:** to join a club or a school as a teacher. In suggesting free association it differs from **eintreten**,[3] which implies more rigid compliance with a code of rules (particularly with reference to business and military organizations).

Er trat dem Verein bei.
Er trat der Schule als Hilfslehrer bei.
Er trat in den Verein ein.
Er trat in die Firma, ins Heer, in die Luftwaffe, ein.

3. **Sich anschließen:** to join a person or a group of persons with the purpose of doing something or going somewhere; also to associate oneself with the expression of a point of view (i.e. join in).

[1] The introduction to a book in the sense of a preliminary chapter is *Einleitung*. *Einführung* is the introduction to a subject and may consist of an entire book (e.g. *eine Einführung in die griechische Sprache*). The distinction between *führen* and *leiten* is as follows. *Führen* implies the absolute subordination of those led, *leiten* means 'to give general directions' how an activity is to be carried out, hence 'to direct, to guide'. *Lenken* means 'to guide every step, every change of direction', 'to steer'.

[2] See 'meet'. [3] See 'enter'.

Schließen Sie sich der Reihe an (or: *an die Reihe*; the queue).
Er hat sich der Expedition angeschlossen.
Sie schlossen sich den Rebellen an.
Darf ich mich Ihnen anschließen? (e.g. on a walk, in some action).
Ich möchte mich dem Protest, Ihnen bei Ihrem P., anschließen.

4. **Stoßen zu** is used of joining a person after encountering difficulties (e.g. traversing difficult country).

Als wir ankamen, stieß eine Abteilung Kavallerie zu uns.
Er stieß zu uns auf der anderen Seite des Gebirges.

5. **Zusteigen:** to board a conveyance at a stopping place and so join people already there.

Er ist in Wannsee zugestiegen.

6. 'To join in' an activity can sometimes be translated by verbs with the prefix *mit*, particularly *mitmachen* (which has the extended sense of to be a party to a thing).

Wir müssen mitmachen.
Er macht den Ausflug, jeden Unsinn, mit.
Singen Sie mit.
Er lachte mit.

B. To put things together. The commonest terms are:

1. **Fügen** (*an...*, *zusammen...*): to make fit exactly, to dovetail, in order to make two things one.[1]

Er fügte die beiden Bretter aneinander, zusammen.
Versuchen Sie, die zerbrochenen Teile wieder zusammenzufügen.

2. **Verbinden** in some uses corresponds closely to 'connect', i.e. by some intermediary link, so that the two things retain their identity.[2]

Die zwei Häuser sind durch einen Gang verbunden.
Die wichtigen Städte sind durch erstklassige Autostraßen verbunden.
Der Hals verbindet Kopf und Körper.

[1] See also 'add'.

[2] The main figurative uses of *verbinden* are: (*a*) to combine qualities (e.g. *Strenge mit einem Gerechtigkeitsgefühl v.*); (*b*) to combine substances chemically; (*c*) to associate in an emotional bond or as allies (e.g. *sie sind freundschaftlich miteinander verbunden*); (*d*) to associate mentally one thing with another (e.g. *ich verbinde keinen bösen Zweck mit seiner Bemerkung*); (*e*) of things, in passive with *sein* and followed by *mit*: to be associated with, involved in, bound up with (e.g. *mit Ihrem Vorschlag sind gewisse Vorteile, Gefahren, verbunden*); (*f*) followed by *zu* in the sense of to bind to an obligation; a rare use and weaker than *verpflichten*.

Binden is also used figuratively in the sense of 'to bind, tie down' someone to a thing,

3. **Vereinigen:** to 'unite' various units so that they function as one, but not in the sense of physical contiguity.[1]

Die britische und französische Flotte wurden im zweiten Weltkrieg unter einer Führung vereinigt.

4. **Zusammenlegen:** to unite in a whole things already joined, i.e. to remove the artificial dividing line.

Er legte die beiden Felder, Grundstücke, zusammen.

5. Examples of specific terms (formed with *zusammen*) are:

Sie nähte die Fetzen zusammen und machte ein Kleid daraus.
Die Wagen wurden zusammengekoppelt (or: *gekuppelt*).
Er hat die Seile zusammengeknotet.

C. Of things, to be, come, together.

Grenzen an (to border on), **stoßen an** (to adjoin) may be used of land and buildings lying side by side, **fließen** (or *münden in*) with reference to rivers.

Bei Basel grenzt Deutschland an die Schweiz.
Die Wiese grenzt, stößt, an dieser Stelle einen halben Kilometer lang an die Straße.

JUDGE Sense: to form or to pronounce an opinion.[2]

1. **Urteilen** suggests an expert or at least highly qualified judge, and therefore a thorough study of the matter judged. Both the matter examined and the formulation of the judgment are mostly weighty. Modification by an adverb which denotes the opposite of an intensive study is,

with the implication of restricting his free movement. 'To' here is normally *an* (e.g. *an einen Eid binden, an eine Aufgabe binden*).

Verknüpfen indicates a closer connection than *verbinden*. When applied to thought, it therefore denotes a logical connection, not a casual association (e.g. *logisch verknüpfte Gedanken*).

'Connect' and 'combine' are often translated by compounds with *zusammen*. *Zusammentun* and *zusammenstellen* suggest the gathering together of various things into a heap. *Zusammensetzen* suggests the fitting together of parts so that they function as a whole while retaining their separate identity (e.g. to connect parts of machinery, to combine classes of a school, units of an army).

[1] Distinguish *vereinigen* from *einigen*, which means 'to unite' in the sense of 'unify', i.e. 'to make a true whole of the parts, to integrate', not merely 'to bring separate things together' (e.g. *ein geeinigtes Volk*). See also 'agree'.

[2] To judge in a court of law: *richten*. Followed by an adjective and an infinitive in the sense of 'deem', 'consider', it must be translated by equivalents of the latter. See article.

however, possible in order to indicate that the judgment is contrary to expectation (e.g. *er urteilt oberflächlich*). It is followed by *über* to render the transitive use of 'judge'.

Goethe urteilte sehr hart über die Romantiker.
Er urteilt sehr ruhig, sehr klar.
Nach seinem Erfolg zu urteilen, muß er ein tüchtiger Mann sein (the reference to the judge is less audible in this expression).
Wie urteilt er über die Lage?

2. **Beurteilen** differs from *urteilen* in that it does not draw attention to the qualifications of the judge. The opinion may be that of the man on the street. Neither weightiness in formulation of the judgment nor in the matter judged is necessarily implied. On the other hand, attention is concentrated on the judgment, i.e. not on the judge as with *urteilen*. This is particularly noticeable in questions beginning with *wie*. Intransitive use is possible when it is accompanied by an adverb of manner. 'To criticize' is a common rendering and clearly shows the reference to the merits or defects of a thing.

Goethe beurteilte die Romantiker sehr hart.
Er beurteilt alles sehr ruhig, sehr klar.
Wie beurteilt er die Lage?
Er hat die Aufführung günstig beurteilt.

KEEP, MAINTAIN, PRESERVE 1. Retain in one's possession, custody or control: **behalten** (literally or figuratively).

Sie können das Buch behalten.
Er hat seinen einfachen religiösen Glauben behalten.
Ich kann ihn nicht länger in meinem Büro behalten.
Sie wird das Kind für einen Monat im Hause behalten.
Behalten Sie Platz.
Er kann so viele Regeln nicht im Kopf behalten.

2. Preserve from decay, deterioration, destruction, maintain alive (for this sense when followed by an adverb or adverbial phrase of manner see next section).

Erhalten can, but need not, suggest active measures to ensure preservation, but, as it points to the result, use in the passive is more common. It is used mainly with persons and things subject to decay, deterioration, destruction, but also with inner possessions. Reflexive use is possible. **Wahren** suggests watching over, guarding, an attitude of preparedness to take action if necessary. It is a more elevated term than *bewahren*. **Bewahren** is less active, meaning no more than 'not to lose'. Only *bewahren*, however, can be followed by *vor* in the sense of 'preserve from', even when activity is implied. Both *wahren* and *bewahren* convey the idea of preserving something regarded as precious, particularly inner possessions or concrete objects regarded as such.

Gott erhalte den König!
Die meisten Gebäude sind in diesem Stadtviertel erhalten geblieben.
Nur eine einzige Handschrift des Werkes ist uns erhalten geblieben.
Sie müssen versuchen, sein Interesse zu erhalten.
Trotz allen Mißgeschicks hat er seinen Humor erhalten.
Erhalten Sie Ihren Humor, was immer kommen mag.
Erhalte mir deine Freundschaft (actively).
Diese Sitten haben sich jahrhundertelang erhalten.
Völker Europas, wahret eure heiligsten Güter! (but: *bewahret...vor dem Verfall*).
Sie wahrt ihre Tugend.
In einer schwierigen Situation hat er seine Würde, seine Ehre, den Anstand, gewahrt.
Wahren Sie dieses Geheimnis.
Er hat seine Passivität bewahrt.
Er hat seinen Humor bewahrt (simply: not lost it).
Er hat sein Gleichgewicht bewahrt.
Er hat seine Fassung, Haltung, bewahrt.
Bewahre mir deine Freundschaft (don't forget me).
Bewahren Sie dieses Geheimnis (don't talk).
Unsere Vernunft bewahrt uns vor dem Irrtum.
Sein Rat bewahrte uns davor, uns lächerlich zu machen.

3. With an adverb or adverbial phrase indicating condition.

Erhalten should only be used in the sense of keeping alive, preserving from decay and the like. It draws attention to the result. Otherwise **halten**[1] must be used in the sense of 'to keep in a state, at a level' (but see section 4). *Erhalten*, however, is sometimes found where good usage requires *halten* (e.g. *seine Leistungen auf einem hohen Niveau erhalten*, instead of the more correct *halten*). *Erhalten* is also used with the phrase *in einem...Zustand*, whereas only *halten* is possible with the simple adverb (e.g. *frisch halten* but *in frischem Zustand erhalten*). **Bewahren** suggests an absence of effort, nature often being the cause which keeps a person or thing in the given condition.

Halten replaces *erhalten* in the imperative and in rapid questions in the meaning of the latter.

Wir müssen ihn am Leben erhalten.

[1] See under 'last' for a closely related meaning.

Das Haus ist gut erhalten (preserved from decay).
Die Blumen wurden frisch erhalten (but: *Halten Sie mir die Blumen frisch, in frischem Zustand*).
Österreichs Grenzen müssen unversehrt erhalten werden.
Ich habe die Erinnerung an dich ungetrübt erhalten.
Er hat die Tradition seiner Familie unverfälscht erhalten (or *gehalten*, a border-line case).
Sie hat ihre Figur, ihr Aussehen, gut, jugendlich, erhalten.
Die Straßen dieser Stadt werden in gehörigem Stand erhalten (or: *gehalten*).
Das Haus ist gut gehalten (clean, tidy).
Sie hielt ihm sein Essen warm.
Die Regierung hat das Volk in völliger Unwissenheit gehalten.
Der Eisschrank hält das Fleisch frisch (but: *erhält in frischem Zustande*).
Er hat seine Ausgaben niedrig gehalten.
Halten Sie sich den Mittwoch frei.
Der Bericht hat uns in Spannung gehalten.
Er hat sein Gewissen, seine Seele, rein gehalten (*bewahrt*) (less correctly: *erhalten*).
Sie hat ihre jugendliche Figur, ihr jugendliches Aussehen, gut bewahrt.

4. Keep (up), maintain (in synonymous use). An extension of section **3**.

To keep up or to maintain at a certain standard, level: **aufrechterhalten.** In this combination the simple verb *halten* is uncommon.

Das Niveau (standard), *die Moral* (morale), *das Interesse* (or *erhalten* alone, i.e. to keep alive), *die Ordnung, die Disziplin, die Blockade, die Beziehungen, den Frieden, ein mörderisches Feuer, stundenlang aufrechterhalten.*

When 'keep (up)', 'maintain' suggest no more than 'carrying on', 'having', 'keeping going', without particular effort, **unterhalten** must be used (to maintain, support a family: see **11**). It is also applied in this sense to the maintenance, the keeping in order of streets, parks, and the like.

Ein Gespräch, einen Briefwechsel, Beziehungen (little more than 'have'), *ein Feuer* (merely keep from going out) *unterhalten; gut unterhaltene Straßen.*

5. To keep in, not to remove from, a place or position.

(a) When 'keep' implies effort, however slight, **halten** is used. In this sense it also translates 'hold'[1] with which it is practically interchangeable.

[1] The figurative uses of 'hold' rarely correspond to those of *halten*. The compound *abhalten* means 'to hold' a function (e.g. *eine Versammlung, eine Parade, eine Prüfung*). Often *haben* must be used (e.g. *Ansichten*).

Er hielt seine Hände in den Taschen.
Halten Sie die Hände hoch.
Halten Sie den Finger auf diese Stelle.
Er hielt den Fuß gegen die Tür.
Er hielt die Gefangenen in einem kleinen Saal.
Ich rate Ihnen, sich ihn vom Leibe zu halten.
Die Rebellen wurden durch Maschinengewehrfeuer ferngehalten.

(b) When it is necessary to distinguish between 'keep' and 'hold', the former must be translated by **behalten** (e.g. with clothing and in figurative senses).

Er behielt den Hut auf dem Kopf (*hielt* = held).
Behalten Sie Ihren Mantel an.
Das werde ich im Auge behalten.

(c) When no activity is implied **lassen** (really short for: *sein, bleiben lassen*; see 'leave') must be used.

Wir ließen das Verdunklungspapier während des ganzen Krieges auf den Fenstern.
Ich werde Ihren Namen auf der Liste lassen (or: *stehen lassen*).
Sie müssen die Tür offen lassen (*halten* – hold).
Wir können es uns nicht leisten, den Jungen noch länger in der Schule zu lassen.
Wir lassen nachts die Fenster immer auf.

6. To keep a thing in a place where it is normally stored or housed: **halten.** This sense should be carefully distinguished from that of 'have available', a sense which mentions the place incidentally (see **7**).

Wir halten die Teller in diesem Schrank.
Ich halte mein Geld immer im Schreibtisch.
Wir halten den Hund nachts in der Waschküche.

7. To keep something for use or pleasure sometimes with incidental mention of the place.

(a) When expense is implied, **sich** (*etwas*) **halten** is used, mostly with servants, animals, vehicles.

Wir können uns nur einen Diener halten.
Er hält sich einen Hund, zwei Pferde und einen Wagen.

(b) When little or no activity is implied, only **haben** is possible. *Immer* or an equivalent is generally added.

Ich habe immer Geld im Hause.
Ich habe immer ein Wörterbuch auf meinem Schreibtisch.

Um nicht von Einbrechern überrascht zu werden, habe ich immer einen Revolver in meiner Nähe.
Wir haben ständig ein Thermometer auf der offenen Veranda.

8. To keep safe, with mention of the place.

Both **bewahren** and **verwahren** refer to things considered as valuables and mean 'to keep (them) in a safe place'. They are thus distinguished from *halten*, which suggests neither valuables nor the safety of the place. *Verwahren* is the stronger of the two and can imply 'under lock and key', for which reason it cannot be used with a person or an animal. It is most common in the past participle after *sein* and with some adverb such as *gut*.

Wo bewahren Sie Ihre Geldscheine, Ihr Geld, Ihre silbernen Teller (but: *wo halten Sie Ihr Kleingeld, Ihre Teller*)?
Ihre Wertpapiere, Juwelen, sind in meinem Schrank gut verwahrt.

9. To keep a thing which is to be called for later: **aufbewahren**.

This need not refer to valuables. It suggests a relatively short period. Note the phrase: (*Gepäck*) *in Aufbewahrung geben* (at luggage rooms on railway stations and the like). A safe place is implied, even if not stated.

Ich kann Ihre Wertsachen für Sie aufbewahren, während Sie verreist sind.
Wollen Sie mir diese Bücher etwas aufbewahren?
Bewahren Sie uns etwas warmes Essen (*im Ofen*) *auf.*

10. To keep, to reserve for later use (i.e. not to use up, throw away): **aufheben**.

This meaning is also expressed by *aufbewahren* (see last section), the distinction being that with *aufbewahren* the idea of place is important, while *aufheben* stresses that of not using or losing at the moment, and does not imply that the place, if mentioned, is of consequence.

Die Mutter versprach, dem Kind etwas Kuchen aufzuheben.
Heben Sie mir meine Ringe auf.
Sie hat ihm sein Essen (*im Eisschrank*) *aufgehoben.*
Den zweiten Band dieses Romans hebe ich mir für später auf (since place is not implied, *aufbewahren* would sound unnatural).
Ich hebe mir meinen Urlaub für nächstes Jahr auf.

11. Maintain, support, provide for (with the necessities of life).

Unterhalten: to support the person one is normally expected to support, without undue strain. It is a close synonym of *ernähren*. **Erhalten:** to support as an additional burden.

Er muß eine zahlreiche Familie unterhalten.
Er unterhält seine Familie in einer gradezu luxuriösen Weise.
Er hat drei Kinder seines Bruders, eine kranke Schwester zu erhalten.

12. To keep a person, oneself in a commodity. Use must be made of the various verbs meaning 'to provide'.

Der Junge sorgt für seine eigenen Kleider.

13. To abide by laws, rules, agreements.

Halten: to keep, in general. **Einhalten:** to keep, with regard to details. With a general term such as *Vertrag, halten* is used. If details are implied by some word such as *Einzelheiten, genau, strikt, einhalten* is necessary. In some case either term is possible according to the point of view.

Er hat den Vertrag, sein Wort, seinen Eid, die Gesetze, die Gebote gehalten.
Er hat jede Bestimmung des Vertrages, alle Paragraphen der Gesetze eingehalten.
Er hat alle Vorschriften genau eingehalten.
Er hat zwei Drittel des Versprochenen gehalten (or: *eingehalten*).

14. To keep a line of goods: **führen** (e.g. *Kämme, die Frankfurter Zeitung*).

15. To keep accounts, a diary, etc.: **führen** (e.g. *ein Tagebuch*).

16. To keep, run, a business, shop: **betreiben** suggests activity (cf. 'run'), otherwise **haben** (e.g. *er betreibt zwei blühende Kolonialwarengeschäfte*).

17. To detain: **halten,** which is normally followed by an adverb of place. If emphasis is desired: **festhalten** or **aufhalten** (hold up, delay). (To keep in at school, i.e. detention: *nachsitzen lassen.*)

Die Mutter hat ihn zu Hause gehalten.
Die Gefangenen sind Monate lang in Ketten gehalten worden.
Ich will Sie nicht länger aufhalten.
Er ist durch Geschäfte hier festgehalten worden.
Nichts kann mich länger in England festhalten.
Ich habe Sie zu lange (fest)gehalten (aufgehalten).

KILL A. Literal.

1. Töten.

(a) With a personal subject and object *töten* is much less used than 'kill'. It mostly suggests savagery, even butchery, but not what is legally known as murder. With a personal object it is rarely used in the first person. It occurs in the following ways:

(i) In elevated language and with reference to the gods and the like.

'*Du sollst nicht töten*' (biblical).
Die Götter töteten ihren Liebling.

(ii) With reference to accidents in which only persons (e.g. not vehicles) are concerned; particularly with scuffles, collisions, blows and the like.

Er wurde bei einem Straßenkrawall getötet.

In meiner Wut packte ich ihn an der Gurgel, und fand zu meinem Entsetzen, daß ich ihn getötet hatte.

Bei dem Eisenbahnunglück sind 40 *Menschen getötet worden.*

(iii) Deliberately, with reference to a threat which may be legal (e.g. in self-protection). In this sense it is mostly intransitive and used as an infinitive of purpose.

Ich schieße mit der Absicht zu töten.

(iv) Deliberately, with reference to mercy killings.

Er tötete seine Frau, um sie von ihren entsetzlichen Leiden zu befreien.

(b) To kill a person by one's behaviour and the like.

Er hat seine Frau durch seine Herzlosigkeit getötet.

(c) With a thing or a feeling, habit, etc., as subject.

Das Trinken, das Gift, der Kummer, ein Schlag des Propellers, hat ihn getötet.

2. Other renderings. These occur with a personal subject and object.

(a) **Ermorden** must be used with any act officially classified as murder (see 'murder').

(b) **Umbringen** is used of acts of violence which may or may not be murder. It is not a legal term for 'murder'. It denotes intention and is only used of persons.

Er hat seine Frau in einer eifersüchtigen Anwandlung umgebracht.

Sie haben ihre Gefangenen umgebracht.

Der Vater brachte seine Tochter um, weil er sie nicht entehrt sehen wollte.

Er brachte sich um, als ihm klar wurde, daß er gefoltert werden würde.

(c) **Totschlagen** suggests violence of feeling and of act, normally a blow from a heavy instrument. At times, e.g. in poetry, violence in general is suggested, not necessarily a heavy instrument.

Er hat ihn mit einem Hammer totgeschlagen.

Ich lasse mich totschlagen, bevor ich so was unterzeichne.

'*Schlagt ihn tot! das Weltgericht*
Fragt euch nach den Gründen nicht.' (Kleist, *Die Hermannsschlacht*).

(d) **Umkommen:** to be killed in an accident, in which a person and a thing, often a means of conveyance, are involved.

Er ist in einem Eisenbahnunglück umgekommen.

(e) **Fallen** must be used, even in conversation, in the sense of 'to be killed on the field of battle'.

Drei von seinen Söhnen sind in Afrika gefallen.

(f) **Den Tod finden** is used in official statements and in 'journalese' in the sense of 'to be killed accidentally'. Compare 'to meet one's death'.

Bei einem Autozusammenstoß fand er den Tod.

(g) Often it is preferable to use specific terms such as: *erschießen; erdolchen; zu Tode prügeln, quetschen.*

B. Figurative.

Töten is used in the sense of killing anything which has vitality (e.g. feelings), also in a number of idioms (but less widely than 'kill').

Das hat alle Hoffnung, mein Interesse, das Stück, getötet.
Er tötet die Zeit mit Gartenarbeit.

KIND, SPECIES, SORT, TYPE[1] **1. Art**[2] primarily means 'species', i.e. a subdivision of a 'genus',[3] and translates 'kind', when the latter is a close synonym of 'species'. Like 'kind', though not to the same extent, it has been extended to denote mere similarity, being applied to inanimate objects and to actions, states and the like as well as to living structures. The plural *Arten* rarely has the looser sense. In the singular note particularly the following loose uses: *eine Art von* (i.e. something like); *so eine Art von*; *aller Art* (genitive; i.e. of all kinds); *in dieser Art.*

Difficulties in the plural, 'kinds'. *Pflanzen aller Art*: all manner of plants, plants of every kind. *Pflanzen aller Arten*: of all species. *Alle Arten von Pflanzen waren in seiner Sammlung vertreten*: all species.... *Allerlei*[4] *Pflanzen waren*...all kinds, sorts of....

Difficulties in the singular. The loose uses of 'kind' are rendered by the following terms (amongst others): *solch, so ein, derartig, so etwas, was für ein.* E.g. this kind of rain, wind.

'*Die Entstehung der Arten*' (the origin of species).
Welche Art Baum ist das? (what species...?).
Was für ein Baum ist das? (what kind, sort...?).
Menschen aller Art.
Menschen aller Arten (whites, negroes, etc.).

[1] *Schlag* is used as a vigorous term for 'kind', 'stamp' (e.g. *Menschenschlag*), and particularly in the genitive case (e.g. *Leute seines Schlages*).
[2] See also 'way'.
[3] *Gattung* = genus.
[4] *Allerhand* means 'many and varied' and stresses subjectively the idea of number.

Diese Art Vogel ist mir unbekannt.
Diese Art Männer haben Deutschland ins Unglück gebracht.
Diese Art Bücher lese ich sehr gerne.
Ich mag diese Art Kuchen, Menschen, nicht.
Das ist eine Art Kuchen.
Er fühlte eine Art Besorgnis.
Sie hat eine Art Kranz geflochten.
'*Es gibt sehr verschiedene Arten Einsamkeit*' (F. Gundolf, *Heinrich von Kleist*).
Das Bild ist vollkommen in seiner Art.
Einen solchen Regen haben die Bauern gern (that's the kind of rain...).
Ein solcher Wind macht einen verrückt (that, this kind of wind...).
Und Sie wollen sich so einen langweiligen Menschen anhören!
Ich habe so eine Idee, daß....
So einer ist er! (that's the kind, sort, of person he is!).
So etwas kann ich nicht ausstehen.
Etwas derartiges meine ich!
Allerlei Kunst- und Kitschgegenstände standen auf dem Kaminsims.

2. **Sorte** is limited to two uses. (*a*) It is applied to things, particularly food, in so far as they are bought and sold. (*b*) It is a term of contempt applied particularly to persons.

Sie verkaufen die besten Obstsorten.
Diese Sorte Bücher sollte man nicht lesen.
Diese Sorte Menschen liegt mir gar nicht.
Das ist eine furchtbare Menschensorte.

3. **Typ, Typus** (plural of both: *Typen*).

The distinction between these two forms, both of which mean 'type', is that the former is looser and more familiar, the latter more scientific. *Typ* is, however, frequently used in reference to a particular model of a thing.

Er ist ein preußischer Typ.
'*Guter Typ des Wirtschaftskapitäns seiner Generation*' (reference to Bosch in U. von Hassel's *Vom Anderen Deutschland*).
'*Der Typus des dämonischen Müssers*' (reference to Kleist in F. Gundolf's work on that poet).
'*Der dritte Typus ist ja der Typus dieser Gotik, der erste der Typus des klassisch-antiken Menschen, des Lateiners*' (O. Walzel, *Gehalt und Gestalt im dichterischen Kunstwerk*).
Das ist ein ganz verschiedener Strukturtypus.
Ein neuer Wagentyp (model).

KIND, KINDLY 1. **Gütig** means 'kindly' (i.e. in inner disposition) rather than 'kind' (i.e. in act) and refers to the manner of oldish people and to young women who have something motherly about them. It can also be applied to the powers that influence human life, e.g. fate. As a polite, almost over-deferential, formula, it occurs in the phrase: *Seien Sie so gütig...*, and as a superlative adverb in requests (e.g. *wollen Sie gütigst...?*).

Ein gütiger alter Herr.
'*Was soll der gütige Blick, mit dem sie mich oft...ansieht*' (Goethe, *Werthers Leiden*, applied to Lotte).
Ein gütiges Schicksal.

2. When 'kind' is followed by 'to' or 'towards', or by the infinitive (e.g. be so kind as to...) it is translated by **gut, freundlich, liebenswürdig**. The last two are also used in polite formulas.

Er ist sehr gut zu seiner Mutter.
Bitte seien Sie so freundlich, dieses Paket für mich auf die Post zu tragen.
Ich danke Ihnen für Ihre freundliche Einladung, Ihre freundlichen Worte.
Wollen Sie so liebenswürdig sein und mir das Buch leihen?
Das war sehr liebenswürdig von Ihnen.

3. When 'kind' is not followed by 'to' or 'towards' or used in a polite phrase, it is generally best rendered by **gutherzig**. As the meaning of *liebenswürdig* has been watered down by its use in conventional expressions, it mostly lacks the full sense of 'kind'.

Ein gutherziger Mensch.
Er ist sehr gutherzig.

KNOW[1] 1. **Kennen:** to be acquainted, familiar, with a person or thing. Direct experience and retention in the memory of the distinguishing marks of the person or thing are implied. **Wissen:** to be aware (of), to have information (of), as a fact. While *wissen* does not exclude experience, it must be used whenever knowledge is conceived of as fact, therefore before a following *daß* clause and the like (e.g. *ich weiß aus Erfahrung, daß...*).

Wissen is in ordinary prose followed by a noun in the accusative case only when this refers to something intangible (e.g. *Ich weiß ein Mittel, wie...*), but not to a person or an object.[2] In reference to the latter, 'to know' in the sense of 'to know of' must be *wissen von*.

[1] See also 'knowledge'.

[2] It is sometimes used without a noun object somewhat poetically or in reference to something remote or mysterious. *Ich weiß einen schönen Platz, Ort, wo...; ich weiß ein Haus im Walde.*

Neither *kennen* nor *wissen* is used in the passive voice. In this construction **bekannt** has the meanings of both *kennen* and *wissen*.[1] It can also mean 'well-known' without the addition of *wohl*.

Ich kenne den Mann, den Ort, die Musik.
Ich kenne das Gedicht auswendig.
Ich kenne seine Launen, seine Ansichten.
Er kennt keine Grenzen.
Er kennt die Geschichte des 17. Jahrhunderts sehr gut.
Ich weiß nicht, worauf Sie hinaus wollen.
Das weiß ich ganz genau.
Ich weiß ein gutes Mittel gegen Rheumatismus.
Ich weiß von einem Hotel, wo man Sie bestimmt unterbringen kann.
Der Mann ist mir schon lange bekannt.
Er ist ein bekannter Schriftsteller.
Es ist bekannt, daß die beiden sich nicht vertragen.

2. 'To know how to' is translated by *wissen, wie . . . sollen*, when knowledge of a method is implied. *Wissen* followed by *zu* and the infinitive refers rather to an innate capacity and often approximates to 'can'.[2]

Ich weiß nicht, wie man mit ihm fertig werden soll.
Er weiß zu schweigen, wenn es nötig ist.
Er weiß sich nicht zu beherrschen.

3. For **erkennen** used in the sense of 'know' see 'recognize'.

4. 'To know' an academic subject of study is **können,** in so far as the use of it is implied, particularly for examination purposes. It is most common in reference to a language, since in this case use is generally meant. In the sense of 'to be familiar with' *kennen*, however, is used.

Er kann Deutsch, nicht viel Deutsch.
Er kann nicht viel Geschichte.
Er kennt die deutsche Sprache gründlich.

5. When 'know' is followed by the accusative and the infinitive in the sense of 'to come at some time within one's experience that . . .', it must be translated by **erleben, daß . . .** (see 'experience').

Ich habe es niemals erlebt, daß er zu viel verlangt hätte (I have never known him to . . .).

[1] *Bewußt* is also used with an impersonal subject and the dative of the person in the sense of 'to be aware', and particularly to emphasize that one is not unaware of a fact. *Es ist mir ja bewußt, daß er solche Absichten hegt.* With a personal subject and the dative of the person *bewußt* means 'to be conscious' of a thing. *Er ist sich seiner Schuld bewußt.*

[2] See also 'appreciate'.

6. **Sich auskennen in:** to know one's way about, both in a place and in a field of study. **Bescheid wissen:**[1] to know all about a matter and to know one's way about in a place.

Er kennt sich in der Stadt, in der Geschichte Spaniens, aus.
Ich weiß Bescheid über seine Pläne.
Ich weiß Bescheid in der Stadt.

KNOWLEDGE 1. **Kenntnis** (singular) is used in the sense of 'cognizance, awareness', of a specific fact. It occurs mainly in set phrases.

Ich spreche mit voller Kenntnis von dem, was geschehen ist.

2. **Kenntnisse** (plural) suggests detailed knowledge (i.e. pieces, items of knowledge) of (*a*) any specified matter, whether of ordinary matters or in a branch of learning; (*b*) unspecified general knowledge. It must be used in the sense of (*a*) to translate 'knowledge' followed by a genitive.

Seine Kenntnisse der russischen Sprache reichen nicht sehr weit.
Seine Kenntnisse des Dramas zeigen viele Lücken auf.
Er hat ungeheure Kenntnisse.

3. **Wissen** means 'general knowledge or awareness', but unlike *Kenntnisse* does not strongly suggest items of knowledge. It can be interchanged with *Kenntnisse* when not followed by a phrase denoting a specific matter or field of knowledge. When such a specific matter or field is stated, *Wissen* cannot be followed by the genitive. *In* and such phrases as *auf dem Gebiet* are common. When followed by *von* and *um* intimate or secret knowledge is implied.

Wissen must be used in general statements about the nature and purpose of knowledge.

Er hat ein ungeheures Wissen.
Sein Wissen auf dem Gebiet des Dramas hat viele Lücken.
Sein Wissen von dem Mord.
Sein Wissen um Gott.
Wissen ist Macht.
Wissen ist ein mächtiges Werkzeug.

4. **Erkenntnis:** philosophical, scientific knowledge, i.e. of the real nature of things.

Die Erkenntnistheorie (epistemology).
Diese Betrachtungsweise besitzt keinen Erkenntniswert.
Auf diesem Wege wird er kaum zur Erkenntnis des Wesens der Kunst gelangen.

[1] *Bescheid*, which is mostly used in fixed phrases, means 'information' (e.g. *ich sagte ihm Bescheid*), or 'official notification' (e.g. *ich erhielt Bescheid von dem Auswärtigen Amt*).

LACK[1] 1. **Fehlen** denotes the complete absence of a thing. In the sense of 'lack' its subject can only be impersonal.[2] When the thing lacking is put in the nominative case, the lack is thought of in relation to a specific purpose.[3] Thus *mir fehlt Geld* is practically equivalent to *das nötige Geld* and expresses this specific reference. If, however, the thing occurs in the dative case preceded by *an*, the lack is conceived as more general, i.e. with no implication of a specific purpose. In practice, the two are often interchanged.

Ihm fehlt die nötige Erfahrung, eine solche Anstalt zu leiten.
Es fehlt ihm noch an Erfahrung.
Es fehlt ihm der Mut dazu.
Es fehlt ihm an Mut.
Es fehlt ihm die Kraft, sich weiter zu schleppen (*an Kraft* also possible, but less correct).

'*Den Köchen tut kein Mangel wehe;*
Wildschweine, Hirsche, Hasen, Rehe,...
Sie gehen noch so ziemlich ein,
Jedoch am Ende fehlt's an Wein.' (*Faust II*, ll. 4856 ff.)

2. **Mangeln** expresses not complete absence, but a deficiency, whether in quantity or quality. In present-day German the thing is put in the dative case preceded by *an*, its occurrence in the nominative is obsolete or confined to poetry and archaic style.[4]

Es mangelt mir an Geld.
Es mangelt ihm an Takt.

3. **Ermangeln** denotes, like *mangeln*, a deficiency, but implies more strongly that a serious view is taken of it.[5] It is hardly used in conversation or everyday prose. It is followed by the genitive of the thing lacking.[6]

Seine Worte ermangelten der Überzeugungskraft.

[1] In a few phrases *entbehren* followed by the genitive means 'to lack' something considered necessary. *Das Gerücht entbehrt jeder Grundlage. Sie entbehrt jeden Reizes.* With the accusative case and a personal subject the sense is 'to do without', 'to dispense with', often with the idea of suffering privations. See also 'spare'.

[2] *Du fehlst mir* = I miss you (see 'miss'). *Er fehlt* = he is absent.

[3] With this construction the meaning can also be 'to miss' in the sense of 'to notice the absence of a thing'. *Mir fehlen 2 Pfund* (I had them before).

[4] Examples: (i) '*Der Herr ist mein Hirt, mir wird nichts mangeln*' (Luther, Psalm xxiii. 1).
(ii) '*Wenn sie den Stein der Weisen hätten,*
Der Weise mangelte dem Stein.' (*Faust II*, ll. 5063–4.)

[5] Its most characteristic use is therefore to express a determination not to be found wanting with regard to an obligation, i.e. when followed by an infinitive in the sense of 'fail' (see 'fail').

[6] *Mangeln* with the genitive is obsolete. '*Sie sind allzumal Sünder und mangeln des Ruhmes.*' (Luther, Romans iii. 23.)

LAST 1. **Dauern** suggests primarily that the duration of a thing or an action is due to its nature. In reference to the durability of things[1] it is used in the following ways.

(a) Of things that 'endure' because of their spiritual qualities, although they may be subject to physical destruction.

Die Werte der Kunst werden ewig dauern.
Ihre Freundschaft hat nicht lange gedauert.

(b) Of things that are subject to decay, particularly those conceived as having life, or in reference to the 'season' of flowers and fruits.

Die Blumen haben nicht lange gedauert.
Die Apfelsinen haben dieses Jahr bis in den Sommer hinein gedauert.

(c) Of things that withstand the ravages of time in so far as long periods are meant.

Großmutters Hochzeitskleid hat schon mehr als 60 Jahre gedauert.
Eine gute Lederhose dauert ein Leben lang.
Moderne Häuser dauern nicht wie die aus früheren Zeiten.

(d) In reference to the consumption of commodities *dauern* should only be used when the dwindling of supplies or of a heap is implied, i.e. not with single objects (e.g. a pair of shoes).

Die Kohlen, die Lebensmittelvorräte, müssen für 2 Monate dauern.

(e) Applied to activities, *dauern* can imply that these, because of their character, take, require a certain time.[2]

Der Vortrag dauerte zwei Stunden.
Der Ausbildungskursus dauert ein Jahr.
Die Probezeit hat 6 Monate gedauert.

(f) It can refer to a period of time the limits of which have been fixed.

Wie lange dauert Ihr Urlaub?

(g) Finally, it is used of the mere passing of time, in the sense of 'go on', without the activity requiring the stated time. This is the only meaning of the less common **währen**.

Der Lärm dauerte, währte, bis Tagesanbruch.
Die Mahlzeit dauerte, währte, zwei Stunden.

2. **Andauern** suggests persistence or duration despite difficulties or despite what is expected. The subject may be an activity, a condition,

[1] *Dauerhaft*: lasting, enduring.

[2] With a non-personal subject *dauern* regularly translates 'take' used in this sense. *Die Wiederherstellung der Kirche wird Jahre dauern. Es dauerte lange, bevor er sich zu der Tat entschließen konnte.* See 'take'.

either of man or of Nature, but it cannot be a person. Emotional emphasis, whether pleasurable or otherwise, is expressed.[1] **Anhalten,** which is a close synonym, is purely objective. See also 'continue'.

Der Streik, die Unruhe, das Fieber, der Regen, der Frost, dauert, hält, noch an.

Unsere Freundschaft hat ein Leben lang angedauert (said, e.g. in a funeral speech, and therefore not replaceable by *anhalten*).

In vielen Ländern Europas haben alte Volkstrachten angedauert.

Für Sonntag wird anhaltender Regen gemeldet.

3. **Halten** is used of things in reference to their use as wear and tear, particularly in the sense of 'hold' when resistance to strain on joins, seams and the like is implied. In reference to things which are subject to decay, **sich halten** should be used, although the reflexive pronoun is sometimes dropped. See also 'keep'.

Die Schuhe, die Möbel, die Reifen, haben nicht lange gehalten.

Dieser Stoff, dieser Anzug, dieses Segeltuch, hat gut gehalten.

Der Anzug wird jahrelang halten müssen.

Wie lange halten sich diese Blumen?

Bei warmem Wetter hält (sich) die Butter nicht lange.

4. **Vorhalten** is used of things which imply the using up of a reservoir. These may be (*a*) things which are conceived as having strength, intensity, particularly effects; (*b*) commodities which are thought of as supplies, not as single objects. This use is closely synonymous with that of *dauern* as explained in 1 (d).

Das Betäubungsmittel hat nur eine Stunde vorgehalten.

Wie lange kann seine Kraft noch vorhalten?

Meine Ermahnungen haben nicht lange vorgehalten.

Die Vorräte werden noch eine Weile vorhalten.

Wird das Holz für den Winter vorhalten?

Das Geld hielt nicht lange vor.

5. **Reichen** refers to the consumption of commodities in the sense of 'to be sufficient' for a given purpose. It carries no implication of time or resistance to decay or disintegration, and approximates more closely to 'suffice' or 'do' than to 'last'.

[1] The present participles of both *dauern* and *andauern* are used adjectivally and adverbially. *Dauernd* means 'continuous, permanent, constant' (e.g. *ein dauernder Wohnsitz, dauernde Liebe*) and also 'continual, frequent' (e.g. *er reist dauernd zwischen Wien und Berlin*). *Andauernd* adds to both these meanings that of persistence, often in an unwelcome form (e.g. *er ist andauernd hier*; *er redet andauernd von sich selbst*). It has therefore an emotional connotation.

Der Wein wird für den ganzen Abend, für so viele Menschen, kaum reichen.
Das Fleisch muß für zwei Tage reichen.
Das Holz muß für den Winter reichen.

6. Auskommen mit, to manage, to make do, with, can be used when the capacity of the person to make a thing last is stressed.

Werden Sie für das ganze Jahr mit zwei Hemden auskommen? (Can you make them last?)

LAST, AT LAST, FINALLY, IN THE END[1] **1. Endlich** means (*a*) after a long time, particularly of expectation or hesitation, corresponding to 'at last', 'at length', and (*b*) after a long time and followed by nothing further, corresponding to 'at last', 'finally', 'in the end'. It does not mean 'finally', in the sense of 'decisively', 'irrevocably' unless the lapse of a long time is implied.

Er hat endlich von sich hören lassen (at last, at length).
Sie haben uns allerhand Scherereien gemacht, bis wir endlich mit ihnen fertig wurden.

2. Zuletzt, used only as an adverb, means (*a*) as the last of a series without any inner connection between the units (compare *zuerst*). It is a close synonym of the more emphatic **als letzter, letzte, letztes.** (*b*) On the last occasion before the present. Both these meanings correspond to 'last'. (*c*) 'Finally', 'in the end'. It differs from the second meaning of *endlich* in drawing attention to the number of things that have preceded rather than to the length of time that has elapsed.[2]

Er sprach, kam, zuletzt, als letzter.
Tun Sie das zuletzt, als letztes.
Wann haben wir uns zuletzt gesehen?
Zuletzt mußten wir unabhängig handeln.

3. Schließlich corresponds to 'finally', 'in the end', and draws attention more to the various stages of what precedes than to the length of time that has elapsed. It differs from the third meaning of *zuletzt*, with which

[1] The synonymous term *eventual* (i.e. bound to follow from causes already operating, or which is bound to follow if certain causes operate) can only be translated (approximately) by *endlich, schließlich*, or if the result is strongly hypothetical, by *etwaig*. *Eventuell*, mostly used as an adverb, means only 'possibly'. *Endlich* as a rendering of 'final' in the sense of *endgültig* is antiquated. Similarly 'ultimate', which stresses all that has preceded, must be translated by *endlich* and *schließlich*.

[2] *Zu guter Letzt* denotes a conclusion which is satisfying because of either its friendliness or its reasonableness. *Zu guter Letzt tranken wir alle noch einmal auf sein Wohl. Zu guter Letzt hat er seinen Fehler doch zugegeben.*

it is closely synonymous, in presenting the final point and the preceding stages as parts of a whole. Because it suggests a whole, *schließlich* often implies a calculation or an inference.[1]

Schließlich haben wir uns doch geeinigt.
Schließlich möchte ich noch sagen....
Er wird schließlich doch recht behalten.

4. **Am Ende** merely denotes what the end is, often despite what reason suggests, i.e. 'in the end'. Similarly **zum Schluss** means 'in conclusion'.

Am Ende wird er wohl doch noch recht behalten.
Zum Schluß möchte ich sagen... (does not necessarily imply a summing-up of what precedes).

5. **Zum letzten Mal** must be used for 'finally' in warnings and the like when reference is less to what precedes than to the future, i.e. not again.

Ich warne Sie zum letzten Mal.

6. **Endgültig** means 'finally' in the sense of 'decisively', 'irrevocably', i.e. more in reference to the future than to the past.

Er hat endgültig mit ihm gebrochen.

LAZY, SLUGGISH **Faul**[2] corresponds closely to 'lazy', i.e. averse to effort, **träge** to 'sluggish', i.e. slow in moving.

Der Lehrer sagte zu dem Jungen: 'Du bist faul!'
Er ist von Natur aus träge.
Träge Darmtätigkeit.

LEARN 1. **Lernen** can refer to both process and result, but stresses the former more than the latter. It therefore sometimes means 'to study'.[3] When the result is emphasized as complete mastery of the material **erlernen** must be used. The latter is never followed by the infinitive.

Er lernt Deutsch, Mathematik.
Er hat die Verse auswendig gelernt.
Sie lernt singen, Klavier spielen.
Sie müssen lernen, wie man sich in diplomatischen Kreisen benimmt.

[1] In this sense it mostly corresponds to 'after all', 'in the last resort', 'in the last analysis'. *Wir haben uns schließlich nichts vorzuwerfen. Letzten Endes* is a close synonym.

[2] *Faul* also means 'rotten', i.e. decayed, and 'foul' in reference to the smell, taste, and the like caused by decaying matter.

[3] *Studieren* is only applied to university students (e.g. *er studiert Germanistik*). Of school-boys and girls *lernen* must be used in the sense of 'study' (e.g. *er lernt sehr fleißig.*)

Er hat viele Tricks von ihm gelernt.
Wer eine Fremdsprache erlernen will, muß nicht nur in dem fremden Land leben, sondern die Sprache bewußt analysieren.

2. Neither of the above terms can be used in the sense of 'to receive information'. *Hören, erfahren,* and the like must be used (see 'hear').

Ich habe gehört, daß Sie bald verreisen.
Ich habe es von ihm erfahren.

AT LEAST **Wenigstens** indicates a lower limit which one is prepared to accept, even though it is far from the ideal. It has a subjective colouring. **Mindestens** refers, on the other hand, to an objectively established indispensable minimum. The estimate it expresses is therefore exact, mostly, though not exclusively, in numerical form.[1] **Zumindest** is an intensive of *mindestens,* i.e. in no case less, rather more; English: at the very least.

Geben Sie mir wenigstens 3 *Pfund für die Reise* (I am prepared to accept as little as this).
Ich brauche mindestens 3 *Pfund für die Reise* (I could not do it with less).
Er hat wenigstens drei Monate daran gearbeitet.
Er hat mindestens drei Monate daran gearbeitet.
Laden Sie ihn doch wenigstens einmal ein!
Sie müssen ihn mindestens einmal einladen.
Hitler mußte mindestens Frankreich besiegen, bevor er Rußland angreifen konnte.
Man muß zumindest sechs Semester studiert haben, bevor man das Examen machen darf.

LEAVE[2] **A.** To depart from a person, place, activity, the person or thing that departs and the separation of subject and object being emphasized.

Verlassen translates 'leave' in this sense, whether the departure is temporary or permanent, whether it means simply 'to go away' or carries the implications of 'abandon',[3] 'desert'.

Ich verließ ihn an der Ecke.
Ich verließ das Haus um 8 *Uhr.*

[1] *Minder* and *mindest,* used adjectivally, are close synonyms of *geringer* and *geringst,* from *gering,* 'slight in value, importance'.

[2] 'Leave' is etymologically connected with *bleiben* (O.H.G. *be-lîban*) and means fundamentally 'to let remain'. The primary sense of *lassen,* on the other hand, is 'to let'. When it means 'leave' some following infinitive such as *sein* or *bleiben* is understood. See also under 'keep'.

[3] But: *sie ließ alles stehen und liegen, um ihm zu folgen* (left everything, i.e. gave up).

Er hat das Land verlassen.
Er verließ den Klub sehr früh.
Er hat die Schule schon verlassen.
Warum hat er seine Arbeit, Ihren Dienst, verlassen?
Sein Verstand, die Besinnung, hat ihn verlassen.

B. To allow, to cause to remain, in a place or condition, or to put into a new condition, the person or thing left and the condition being emphasized rather than the departure of the subject. The activity of 'put' and the inactivity of 'allow' or 'cause to remain' must be clearly distinguished. 'Leave' followed by an infinitive or a present participle, or gerund requires special attention, since each of these constructions admits of various meanings and must be variously translated. 'Leave' followed by 'with' also has numerous senses, all of which must be differently rendered into German. Of the German verbs treated in this article only *zurücklassen* and *sitzenlassen* can be followed by *mit*.

1. **Lassen:** to allow to remain in a place or condition, i.e. inactively, *sein* or *bleiben* being understood (i.e. to let be, remain). It must be followed by a complement (which may be a prefix; see compounds). If a place is implied but not mentioned with 'leave', *lassen* is impossible (see *zurücklassen*). The idea of departure is not expressed prominently. The act of leaving can be deliberate or accidental.

Ich ließ den Brief auf dem Tisch.
Ich muß meine Tasche in der Bahn gelassen haben.
Ich ließ ihn an der Ecke stehen.
Sie ließ das Kind im Kinderwagen und besorgte die Hausarbeit.
Können wir das Kind bei Ihnen lassen?
Ich ließ mein Gepäck im Wartesaal.
Er ließ die Tür offen.
Lassen Sie mich in Ruhe.
Das Konzert ließ mich kalt, gleichgültig.
Diese Erklärung hat mich ganz verwirrt, konfus, unbefriedigt, gelassen.
Das hat meine Sehnsucht ungestillt gelassen.
Alles beim Alten lassen (leave things as they are).
Er ließ die Stadt hinter sich.

2. **Liegen-, stehen-, sitzen-** (etc.), **lassen.**[1]

These expressions translate 'to leave lying, standing', sitting, etc. in the literal sense. They are also preferred at times as a translation of the literal sense of 'leave'. *Stehen lassen* refers particularly to things that

[1] Compare further: *es dabei bewenden lassen, es auf sich beruhen lassen* (leave it at that).

cannot be carried by hand. Sometimes they have special meanings (e.g. *sitzen lassen*: jilt, leave stranded).

Ich ließ meinen Wagen an der Ecke stehen.
Er ließ das Fleisch stehen (at table).
Er ließ sein Kapital stehen.
Er ließ mich auf der Bank sitzen.
Er ließ sie mit den Kindern sitzen (deserted her and left her to care for the children).
Ich ließ ihn mit der Korrekturarbeit sitzen (left him to do it and went away).

3. **Zurücklassen** is used in a number of ways. In each case it is clearly implied that the subject departs, moves away.

(a) Used literally, with a place as object, *hinter sich* (*mir*, etc.) must be added (though *zurück* may be omitted; see *lassen*). The phrase also has the figurative sense of 'outstrip'.

Wir ließen die Stadt hinter uns zurück und strebten den Bergen zu.
Er ist so begabt, daß er alle anderen Studenten weit hinter sich zurückgelassen hat.

(b) To leave in a place, which is stated or implied. *Zurücklassen* must be used when the place is not stated, but implied, or when English adds 'behind'. When the place is mentioned, it is also the correct term to express a deliberate leaving, i.e. for some purpose. It also stresses the distance between subject and object. With words such as *Nachricht*, *Anweisungen*, it suggests a material object, i.e. that these are written on paper. With a non-personal subject, the action is, of course, not deliberate.

Sie liessen ihn tot zurück (they left him dead; *zurück* being necessary, since a place is implied but not stated).
Er hat sein Gepäck am Bahnhof zurückgelassen.
Er hat seine Uhr als Pfand zurückgelassen.
Ich ließ einen Zettel für ihn zurück.
Ich werde Ihnen Anweisungen zurücklassen (on paper, see *hinterlassen*).
Das Obst ließ große Flecken auf der Jacke zurück.

(c) 'To leave' with and without a following 'with'. Sense: to leave in a condition. *Zurücklassen* is used if (i) the cause, i.e. the subject, moves on; (ii) the condition is inactive (e.g. a feeling, not an act of willing).

Die Feuersbrunst ließ die Fabrik in Trümmern zurück.
Ein Sturm fuhr über das Land und ließ die Gärten in chaotischem Zustand zurück.

Er ließ sie als unbemittelte Witwe zurück.
Der Krieg ließ die Besiegten mit einem blinden Haß gegen die Sieger zurück.
Er ließ sie mit dem Gefühl zurück, daß ihr übel mitgespielt worden war.
Er ließ mich mit dem Eindruck zurück, daß es ihm nicht ernst war.
Das Schauspiel ließ uns mit dem Gefühl zurück, daß es nicht genug eingeübt worden war.

(d) Neither *lassen* nor *zurücklassen* is possible in the sense of 'put' into a condition when (i) the subject does not move on; (ii) the object by his activity has brought about his condition; (iii) the condition is active (e.g. an act of willing). German uses an active verb, often *machen.*

Die vier Treppen haben mich ermüdet.
Der Ausbruch des Vulkans machte die Stadt zu einer Ruine.
Der Krieg ließ in vielen Menschen den Entschluß reifen, eine neue Ordnung zu schaffen.
Der erste Teil der Oper machte mir wenig Appetit auf den Rest.

4. **Hinterlassen:** (*a*) to leave behind after death what belongs to one, either material possessions (i.e. bequeath) or a family; (*b*) to leave intangible things (e.g. *Eindruck, Spur, Nachricht, Anweisungen*). Since what is left must be intangible, *Nachricht* and *Anweisungen* refer to spoken, not to written messages. (Contrast *zurücklassen.*)

Er hinterließ seinem Sohn sein ganzes Vermögen.
Er hinterließ eine Frau und zwei Kinder.
Er hinterließ einen starken Eindruck auf mich.
Er hat mir Anweisungen hinterlassen.

5. **Überlassen:** (*a*) 'To commit, refer to another person or agent instead of oneself' (*S.O.D.*). In this sense it is followed by an accusative and a dative, and may be followed by an infinitive (i.e. to hand over a thing to a person to do, for it to be done). (*b*) To abandon a person, a thing, to another person, another thing. A dative and an accusative must follow.

In the imperative *überlassen* tends to refer to important matters, while for trivial things *lassen* is widely used.[1]

Ich überlasse Ihnen die Korrektur dieser Bogen.
Ich überlasse es Ihnen, uns das nötige Material zu verschaffen.
Ich überlasse es ihm, den Brief zu schreiben.
Er wurde seinem Schicksal überlassen.
Überlassen Sie mir das (e.g. paying heavy costs).
Lassen Sie mir das (e.g. washing up).

[1] The same distinction exists between *lassen* and *überlassen* in the sense of 'let have'. *Er ließ mir das Buch für ein paar Tage. Er überließ mir seine Notizen über Kant.*

6. **Belassen:** to leave in a place or condition. It must be followed by *in*. The distinction between it and *lassen* is that it stresses the intention of the subject, while *lassen* may imply an intention or not.

Er beließ uns in dem Wahn, daß wir das Schlimmste schon hinter uns hätten.

Er wurde im Amt belassen.

7. **Übriglassen:** to leave, yield as a remainder after deduction (leave over). *Übrigbleiben* is often used as a substitute for the passive.

Der Tod des ältesten Sohnes läßt nur noch die Tochter übrig.

Es bleibt sehr wenig von meinem Gehalt übrig, wenn so viel für Steuern abgezogen wird.

8. **Loslassen** may be used negatively with reference to a thought or feeling in the sense of 'not to let go'.

Das Gefühl ließ ihn nicht los, daß man ihm sein Verhalten übelgenommen hätte.

9. 'Leave' in the sense of 'go away' or 'abandon' followed by the accusative and the infinitive. Here English gives equal prominence to the action of going away, abandoning, and the action which the object is left to perform. This sense must be distinguished from that of 'let remain' (*lassen*) and 'hand over' (*überlassen*). (She left the clothes on the line to dry = *Sie ließ die Kleider auf der Wäscheleine zum Trocknen*; I left him (= it to him) to write the letter = *Ich überließ es ihm, den Brief zu schreiben*). Since German has no standardized way of expressing this meaning, only a few hints can be given.

(a) When the context allows 'let' to be substituted for 'leave' *lassen* may be used, but does not render the idea of going away.

Sie ließen ihn verhungern (left him to starve).

(b) *Sie überließen ihn dem Hungertod* (left him to starve).

(c) *Sitzen laßen.* The use of this expression is limited by the type of adverbial phrase possible with *sitzen.*

Ich ließ ihn damit sitzen (I left him to get it done unaided, i.e. I dissociated myself from him so that, if he did it, he would have to do it alone).

Er ließ sie mit den Kindern sitzen.

Er ließ sie mit den Kindern fast ohne Geld sitzen.

10. 'Leave' followed by the gerund. German cannot express by one verb the two ideas of going away and causing sometimes contained in 'leave'.

LEAVE

Die Flieger ließen die Stadt in Flammen (left the town burning).
Sie ließ das Gas brennen (left burning, or let burn).
Ich verließ ihn, als er dabei war, das Haus zu streichen (I left him painting).

C. Intransitive use of 'leave'.

1. By transport.

(a) **(Ab)fahren** is only used when thinking of the time of departure of the means of transport. The use or omission of *ab* fluctuates. It can, however, only be dropped if the context makes it clear that departure is meant. In general, its use is more common when the means of conveyance is the subject, and is then obligatory in the perfect tenses. With persons it is less common.

Der Zug ist schon abgefahren.
Der Zug fährt gleich ab (*ab* usual, but could be omitted).
Wann fährt (see 'go') *der Zug?* (*ab* could be added, but is less usual).
Ich fahre morgen um 9 Uhr (*ab* possible, but unusual).
Wann fahren Sie? (*ab* not used).

(b) **(Ab)reisen** concentrates attention on the fact that a journey is being made and emphasizes the leaving of a place, whether this be a town, country, hotel, or the like. In the perfect tenses *ab* must be used. Otherwise, the use of *ab* suggests that departure is imminent, its omission that it is more remote.

Er ist schon abgereist.
Wann reisen Sie (*ab*)*?*

2. When walking is implied, **gehen** (see 'go') is used with the addition of *weg* if the context does not in itself make the idea of departure. Instead of the perfect tenses **weg sein** is usual.

Wir müssen jetzt gehen.
Er ging früher als ich (*weg*).
Er ist schon längst weg.

LEND, BORROW 1. (a) **Leihen** is the act of lending, not the state of being lent. In the passive it is therefore used with *werden* (i.e. the action of handing over), but not with *sein*. It must be followed by the dative of the person in order to indicate the particular act.

Ich habe ihm ein Buch geliehen.
Können Sie mir 100 Mark leihen?
Das Auto wurde uns geliehen.

(b) *Leihen* also has regularly the meaning of 'borrow', with or without the reflexive dative. To avoid ambiguity the latter can be added. Except in reference to money *leihen* is more common than *borgen* in the sense of 'borrow'.

Ich habe seinen Wagen geliehen (to translate 'I have *lent* his car', German must add to whom, if *leihen* is to be used).
Ich leihe Bücher grundsätzlich nicht (contrast example with *verleihen*).

2. Verleihen.

(a) In the literal sense *verleihen* expresses (i) a generalization, often as a principle; (ii) in the passive voice (with *sein*) a state. It is followed by *an* and the accusative in order to denote the receiver. The dative is impossible in this sense.

Ich verleihe Bücher grundsätzlich nicht.
Bücher soll man nicht an fremde Leute verleihen.
Das Buch ist verliehen.

(b) *Verleihen* has also the figurative sense of 'lend': bestow, impart a quality to something. In this use it is followed by the dative.[1]

Das verleiht seinem Verhalten eine gewisse Würde.

3. Ausleihen: to lend or (with reflexive dative) to borrow, in reference to libraries and the commercial hiring and lending out of objects (not money).

Dieses Buch ist ausgeliehen.
Wir haben uns einen Wagen ausgeliehen.

4. Borgen: to borrow and, less frequently, to lend, money or other things that are consumed by use. It is not in careful use applied to objects which in themselves are valuable, and, suggesting a casual arrangement, is therefore inappropriate in elevated contexts.[2]

Ich habe 10 *Mark geborgt.*
Können Sie mir 10 *Mark borgen?*

5. Entlehnen and **entleihen** are dignified terms, which only mean 'borrow'. The former is used particularly of ideas, and does not suggest the obligation to repay.

Milton hat viele Ausdrücke und Bilder aus der Dichtung des klassischen Altertums entlehnt.
Ich habe viele wertvolle Bücher von ihm entliehen.

[1] *Verleihen* also means 'to bestow', 'to confer' orders, decorations, and the like.
[2] *Pumpen* is a slang term for *borgen*.

LIMIT, RESTRICT[1] **1. Einschränken:** to reduce, curtail, retrench, i.e. to make a thing less than it was before. It can only be used when the following factors are present. (*a*) The reduction is brought about by a deliberate act of intervention (i.e. by a person or his actions, e.g. a decree). This being so, its use in the passive voice requires *werden*, not *sein*. (*b*) Its noun object mostly refers to material goods, but may also be such things as power, authority, concrete freedoms. (*c*) It can only be followed by *auf* when the noun governed by *auf* refers to material goods (i.e. not power, etc.). (*d*) Used reflexively it can only indicate material goods (*sich einschränken* = tighten the belt). (*e*) It is always emphatic and so it is used characteristically with adverbs such as *stark, wesentlich, noch weiter*. When its object is not material goods, it is generally accompanied by some such phrase.[2]

Wir können unseren Gasverbrauch nicht weiter einschränken.
Die Kontinentalsperre schränkte den deutschen Handel ein.
Als das geschah, haben wir unseren Milchverbrauch auf 5 Liter wöchentlich eingeschränkt.
Der Betrieb schränkte seine Produktion auf 1000 Lokomotiven ein.
Wir müssen unsere Mahlzeiten auf täglich 2 einschränken.
Infolge meines Augenleidens mußte ich meine Lektüre stark einschränken.
Der Krieg hat die Zahl[3] *der verfügbaren Ärzte wesentlich eingeschränkt.*
Die neue Verfassung schränkt die Macht des Königs noch weiter ein (or: *derartig ein, daß er nur noch Ratschläge erteilen darf*).
Während des Krieges wurde die Bewegungsfreiheit feindlicher Ausländer eingeschränkt.
Wir genießen noch das uneingeschränkte Vertrauen des Königs (emphatic).
Ich habe, sage ich Ihnen, uneingeschränkte Vollmacht (emphatic).

2. Beschränken has the definite meaning of 'not to allow a thing to exceed a certain limit'. It can, however, also mean 'to reduce', but rather by implication, without emphasis and without necessarily suggesting

[1] *Begrenzen* means no more than 'to draw boundaries' (e.g. *die Mauer begrenzt unsere Aussicht*). The past participle *begrenzt* can be used in a derogatory way with reference to the mind. Unlimited possibilities = *unbegrenzte Möglichkeiten*.

[2] *Einschränken* was formerly used more extensively. The following examples are from Goethe's *Werther*: '*Der alte M. ist ein geiziger rangiger Filz, der seine Frau im Leben was rechts geplagt und eingeschränkt hat....*' '*Und dann, so eingeschränkt* (i.e. from without) *er ist, hält er doch immer im Herzen das süße Gefühl der Freiheit, und daß er diesen Kerker verlassen kann, wann er will.*' '*Der Fürst fühlt in der Kunst, und würde noch stärker fühlen, wenn er nicht durch das garstige wissenschaftliche Wesen und durch die gewöhnliche Terminologie eingeschränkt wäre.*' The explanation of *beschränken* is sufficient to show that it could not be used in these cases either.

[3] *Herabsetzen, kürzen* are mostly used when *Zahl* is the object. See 'reduce' and 'shorten'.

a deliberate act of intervention. The latter is implied if the passive voice formed with *werden* is used, *sein* indicating a continuing state. It is used freely with non-material things in the sense of 'reduce'. It may be followed by *auf*, whatever the type of noun governed by the latter (i.e. not only a noun denoting material goods as in the case of *einschränken*). The use of *auf* often makes *beschränken* necessary, even if without it *einschränken* would be possible (e.g. *die Pressefreiheit wurde stark eingeschränkt*; but: *die Pressefreiheit wurde auf ein Minimum beschränkt*).

Sich beschränken, used absolutely, has a moral signification. *Beschränkt*, applied to persons, means 'limited intellectually', almost 'stupid'.

Wir haben unseren Gasverbrauch beschränkt.
Die Kontinentalsperre beschränkte den deutschen Handel auf das Festland.
Wir haben unseren Milchverbrauch auf 5 Liter wöchentlich beschränkt.
Wir müssen unsere Mahlzeiten auf täglich zwei beschränken.
Früher habe ich Wein getrunken, jetzt beschränke ich mich auf Wasser.
Infolge meines Augenleidens mußte ich meine Lektüre beschränken.
Ich mußte meine Unterstützung auf 20 Mark monatlich beschränken.
Früher bin ich 3 Kilometer gegangen, jetzt beschränkte ich mich auf zwei (*einschränken* impossible).
Infolge dieses Ereignisses haben wir unseren Aufenthalt auf eine Woche beschränkt (*einschränken* impossible).
Die schwierigen Verhältnisse veranlaßten mich, die Zahl der wöchentlichen Artikel auf zwei zu beschränken (*einschränken* impossible).
Die neue Verfassung beschränkt die Macht des Königs auf Erteilung von Ratschlägen (*einschränken* impossible because of the *auf* phrase).
Während des Krieges wurde die Bewegungsfreiheit feindlicher Ausländer auf die Vorstädte beschränkt (see comment on previous example).
Unsere Freiheit ist beschränkt (*einschränken* impossible).
Die Macht des Parlaments ist durch das neue Gesetz beschränkt (or: *wird eingeschränkt*).
Sie können Ihre Pflicht nicht so beschränken (*einschränken* impossible).
Sie müssen sich auf das Notwendigste beschränken (*einschränken* impossible).
Ich schenke ihm unbeschränktes Vertrauen.
Ich habe unbeschränkte Vollmacht.

LISTEN 1. **Hören** is used in generalizations and intransitively in the imperative, either as a remonstrance or as a request for attention.

Ich höre Radio, klassische Musik, gern.
Hören Sie mal!

2. **Zuhören:** (*a*) to listen passively, without taking part, transitively and intransitively; (*b*) to surrender oneself to sound as a sensuous, spiritual experience.[1]

Ich war bei der Sitzung und hörte zu.
Ich hörte (ihm) zu, während er mir seine Pläne auseinandersetzte.
Ich hörte der Debatte zu.
Ich hörte dem Rauschen des Wassers zu.
Mit geschlossenen Augen hörte ich der Musik zu.

3. **Anhören:** (*a*) to give a fair hearing (only transitively); (*b*) with the reflexive dative the sense is 'to want to hear', 'to go to hear', particularly as pleasure, entertainment.

Hören Sie mich an!
Ich hörte seinen Rat an, aber fand ihn nicht klug.
Ich danke Ihnen dafür, daß Sie mich so freundlich angehört haben.

4. **Hören auf:** to listen actively and intently, often with a view to action, and therefore sometimes with the implication of responding to a suggestion, order, and the like.

Er wollte nicht auf meinen Rat hören.
Hören Sie auf meine Worte.
Er hört nie auf das, was ich sage.
Ich höre gespannt auf die Klänge der Violine.

LIVE **Wohnen** means 'to dwell', 'to be domiciled'. It is used (*a*) in giving one's address; (*b*) in reference to larger areas, e.g. a country, when the ties of home or occupation are emphasized; (*c*) when the circumstances of occupying a house are stressed. **Leben** (*a*) means 'to be alive', i.e. not dead; (*b*) refers to the way one spends one's life.

Während meines Urlaubs werde ich im Hotel Bristol wohnen.
Er wohnt in London.
Sie wohnen zu viert.
Sie leben augenblicklich in Frankreich, aber sie wohnen eigentlich in Italien.
Viele Ausländer leben augenblicklich in Deutschland als Mitglieder der Besatzungsarmeen (not *wohnen*, which would suggest the idea of 'home').
Er lebt noch.
Er lebt zurückgezogen.
Er lebt nur der Kunst.

[1] *Lauschen* to listen intently, with all one's senses alert, to drink in sounds. It is much used in poetical language.

LIVELY **Lebendig:** full of life, vital, i.e. more than simply 'not dead'. In this intensive sense it also corresponds to 'living' (e.g. *ein lebendiger Glaube*). While *lebendig* refers more to inner vitality, though not excluding its external manifestations, **lebhaft** denotes a heightening of the external manifestation in such a way as to strike one forcibly. Both words often need to be translated by some term other than 'lively'.

Eine lebendige Phantasie.
Eine lebhafte Phantasie.
Ein lebendiges Kind.
Ein lebhaftes Kind.
Eine lebendige, lebhafte, Beschreibung.
Lebhafte Farben.
Ich bedaure lebhaft.
Ein sehr lebendiger Stil.
Eine sehr lebhafte Art.

LOCK 1. **Schließen** means (*a*) both 'to close'[1] and 'to lock' a house, room, door, etc. but should not be used when the idea of locking with a key or bolt is stressed. It is, however, regularly used in reference to the locking of windows. (*b*) It is also used in the sense of locking something to be guarded in a place or a container. (*c*) It can be used intransitively.[2]

Schließen Sie das Fenster.
Er schloß das Geld in den Kasten (ein).
Dieser Schlüssel, diese Dose, diese Tür, schließt nicht.

2. The following compounds of *schließen* stress the idea of locking.
(a) **Zuschließen** suggests the turning of a key, the shooting of a bolt, and the like, and is used more of single objects than larger complexes such as a room, a house.

Ich habe die Tür schon zugeschlossen.

(b) **Abschließen** means 'to lock up' (i.e. something consisting of a number of parts).[3]

Schließen Sie hier ab! (intransitive in the sense of 'lock every door or opening').
Ich habe den Wagen abgeschlossen (all doors and windows).

[1] To use *schließen* for *zumachen* is as much a genteelism as 'close' for 'shut'. *Zumachen* and 'shut' emphasize the action, *schließen* and 'close' the permanent state, official action, the closing of gaps.

[2] *Schließen* also means 'to lock' in the sense of 'to join by interlacing parts', 'to clasp' (e.g. *jemand in seine Arme schließen*); also figuratively (e.g. *in sein Herz schließen*).

[3] *Schließen, abschließen, beschließen* also mean 'to end', 'to close', 'to conclude'. Like 'close' *schließen* suggests little more than the opposite of 'open' (e.g. *er schloß seinen Vortrag mit der Bemerkung*...). *Abschließen* suggests greater finality, often a formal

(c) **Verschließen** is an intensive and is used (*a*) of an enclosed space (a room, house, safe). In this use it is more common in the passive with *sein* (i.e. to indicate a state) than in the active. In the latter mood *gut* or an equivalent is often added. (*b*) With doors and windows it is emphatic, i.e. not the normal term. (*c*) The object may also be a thing guarded in the locked room, safe, etc.

Ich habe den Schrank, das Geld, gut verschlossen.
Ich fand das Zimmer verschlossen.
Die Tür ist verschlossen.
Sie müssen alle Türen und Fenster unbedingt verschließen, bevor Sie ausgehen.

LONGER (NO), NO MORE In reference to duration of time, the distinction between **nicht länger** and **nicht mehr** differs somewhat from that between the English expressions. *Nicht mehr* simply denotes a cessation and is the general term. *Nicht länger* suggests (*a*) an emotional attitude towards the fact of cessation, or (*b*), particularly when followed by *als*, at least a heightened awareness of the limits of the period in question. It is therefore more emphatic than *nicht mehr*. In reference to the frequency with which an action or state is repeated, German only uses *nicht mehr*.

Ich bin sein Freund nicht mehr, nicht länger.
Ich kann es nicht länger aushalten (*nicht mehr* would be weak in such an emotional context, but not impossible).
Er arbeitet nicht mehr, nicht länger, als 2 Stunden pro Tag.
Er war nicht mehr, nicht länger, als 3 Jahre weg.
Er kommt nicht mehr hierher (*nicht länger* impossible because frequency is meant).

LOOK AT[1] 1. **Ansehen** is used when only the eye, i.e. not the mind, is engaged. It suggests that the object is at close quarters and is looked at

ending, and corresponds closely to 'conclude' (e.g. *ich habe meine Untersuchungen, die Verhandlungen, abgeschlossen*). *Beschließen* means 'to mark the end' by some special feature and is frequently followed by a *mit* phrase or some equivalent (e.g. *sie beschlossen die Versammlung mit der Nationalhymne*; *wir beschlossen den Tag mit einem Konzert*; *er beschloß seine Rede mit einem weiteren Appell*; *hiermit ist die Vortragsreihe abgeschlossen*). Both *schließen* and *abschließen* are also used in the sense of concluding, bringing about an agreement, *schließen* meaning little more than 'make', *abschließen* 'to finalize' (e.g. *einen Vertrag schließen, abschließen*).

[1] *Schauen*, when strictly used, stresses the intensity of the action, not the result. Only *sehen*, therefore, can be used in the following: *ich sah sofort, worauf er hinaus wollte.* To denote the action *schauen* is used in southern Germany and Austria without any implication of intensity, where standard German requires *sehen.* In northern Germany *gucken* or *kucken* is used colloquially in reference to the action.

steadily, i.e. for more than the duration of a glance. Combination with an adverb such as *lange* clearly reveals these implications. These also make its use in the imperative unusual, i.e. except when a certain intensity is to be conveyed (e.g. *sehen Sie das nur mal an*, where *nur* suggests intensity). In the interrogative form *ansehen* is also rare.

Ich sah ihn an, aber erkannte ihn nicht.
Sie hat ihn nicht mehr angesehen.
Er sah ihn schief, argwöhnisch, mit Verachtung, an.
Es hingen wunderbare Bilder im Zimmer, aber er sah sie nicht mal an.
Ich sah ihn forschend an.
Das Haus ist schön anzusehen, aber nicht sehr fest gebaut.

2. **Sich etwas ansehen** implies an enquiry by the mind into the object looked at, an effort to form an idea about it. Only adverbs which suggest such an examination can be combined with it.[1]

Ich habe mir den Aufsatz angesehen und finde ihn gut.
Sehen Sie sich das Kleid genau an.
Ich muß mir das Auto ansehen, bevor ich es kaufe.

3. **Sehen** with a direct object or with a preposition must be used to translate 'look at', when *ansehen* and *sich etwas ansehen* as explained above are inapplicable. The direct object is usual with the imperative, the choice of preposition is determined by the implications conveyed by the verb.

Sehen Sie mal das Flugzeug da (*an* cannot be added).
Wonach sehen Sie? (What are you looking at?)
Ich sah auf meine Uhr und stellte fest, daß ich schon seit einer Stunde wartete.

LOOSE A. Some literal senses.

1. **Locker** is the more general term. It can refer (*a*) to objects which are not firmly fixed into or on to each other, but should be; (*b*) to objects which are not taut, i.e. slack; (*c*) to objects the parts of which do not cohere, i.e. are not compact.

(a) *Ein lockerer Zahn.*
Die Backsteine sind locker geworden.
Das Tischbein ist locker.

(b) *Ein lockeres Seil.*

(c) *Lockere Erde.*

[1] *Sich ansehen* is also used in reference to entertainment, e.g. the drama, the film. *Ich muß mir diesen Film ansehen.*

2. **Lose** is applied to objects (which may be of the same kind) which lie separately, often close to each other, but not bound or tied together at all, or at least not tightly. A contrast is often implied to the tying together of things in a bundle or parcel.

Ich habe nur lose Blätter.
Die Backsteine lagen lose aufeinander.
Die Waren sind nur lose zusammengepackt.

3. **Los** as a translation of 'loose' is only applied to persons, animals or things that have broken away from chains and the like. It is confined to predicative use.

Der Hund, die Mine, ist los.

B. Some figurative senses.

Both *locker* and *lose* are used figuratively in reference to (*a*) morals, (*b*) the connection between thoughts. *Lose* is stronger, and conveys more forcibly the sensuous impression. Sometimes, particularly when applied attributively to persons, they form fixed expressions, and cannot then be interchanged.

Die Gedanken sind nur locker, lose, aneinandergereiht.
Lockere, lose, Sitten.
Ein loses Mädchen.
Ein lockerer, loser, Vogel.

MAKE, GET, LET, HAVE,[1] CAUSE[2] (used causatively) In some cases English makes a clear distinction between 'make', 'get' and 'let' (e.g. despite his protests I made him rewrite his report; after much effort I got him to rewrite his report; I let him rewrite his report, even though it meant a delay). In other cases the distinction between these terms is so slight that they are practically interchangeable (e.g. I'll make the firm pay all expenses; I'll get the firm to pay all expenses; I'll let the firm pay all expenses). Often two, if not three, are interchangeable (e.g. he made, let, me feel my inferiority; he made, let, his eyes roll; I can't make (get...to) the engine start).

The following examples illustrate 'let' used in the sense of 'cause', and reveal the transition in meaning from 'not to prevent' to 'to make' and 'to have'.

[1] For 'have' in the sense of 'suffer' there is no general term in German. You'll have the roof falling down if you don't do something about it = *das Dach wird Ihnen zusammenstürzen, wenn Sie untätig zusehen.*

[2] 'Leave', 'keep', 'set', 'send' are also used causatively (e.g. to send somebody flying). They must be rendered by the German verbs explained in this article or by some specific verb (e.g. to set moving = *in Bewegung setzen*).

I let him see he was not wanted.

Let me know as soon as possible (French: *faire savoir*).

Let the prisoner come, be brought, before me (the regular use of 'let' in the 3rd person imperative).

'Get' and 'have' can be followed by the infinitive, the present or past participle. 'Make' can be followed by the past participle[1] as well as the infinitive.

In the causative sense 'make', 'get' and 'let' can be used in the passive voice. *Lassen* can be used passively only in the meaning of 'let', *machen* only actively. The other German verbs treated are capable of passive use.

'Cause' should in this construction be translated by *verursachen*, which can be followed by a *daß* clause, but not by the infinitive. When the idea of causation is not emphasized and no infinitive follows, other terms (e.g. *bewirken*) are more usual.

A. Lassen translates 'make' in the senses explained below and also 'get', 'have' and 'let' when they are practically interchangeable with 'make'.

1. *Lassen* cannot emphasize the idea of insistence or force which is sometimes expressed by 'make'. Nor can it suggest any activity of the will (in the form of resistance) or deliberation on the part of the person on whom pressure is brought to bear.

It can, however, be used in a context denoting insistence or even force, if it stands in an unemphatic part of the sentence. 'The strong current made them turn back' = *die starke Strömung machte sie umkehren*. But: *es war die starke Strömung, die sie umkehren ließ* (*machte* is, of course, possible). Here the fact of turning back is already known, the point of the sentence being to draw attention to the cause.[2]

The style in which *lassen* is used is that of report, of plain objective statement. It does not indicate any emotional participation on the part of the speaker (contrast *machen*).

2. The constructions used with *lassen*.

The infinitive depending on *lassen* can only be passive in a few fixed phrases where *lassen* means 'let' (e.g. *ich ließ es mir gesagt sein*). Otherwise the dependent infinitive must (except in old-fashioned diction) be active in form, even though it be passive in sense (e.g. *ich ließ das alte Haus abreißen* = had . . . pulled down).

[1] The past participle is translated variously, generally by an adjective: *sich verhaßt* (hated), *fühlbar* (felt, of a thing), *beliebt* (liked), *bekannt* (known), *verständlich* (understood) *machen*. Note also: *ich werde mich schon fürchten machen* (feared; but more commonly: *ich werde mir schon Respekt verschaffen*).

[2] For the importance of emphasis see also 'prevent'.

The origin of this construction is probably to be found in the desire to leave vague the agent of the action expressed by the infinitive (i.e. I had someone pull down the old house). The feeling of such an omission must have been lost by the time it became possible to insert *von* or *durch* to denote the agent.

When the object of the infinitive depending on 'make', 'get', 'have' is a pronoun referring to the subject of these verbs, the *von* or *durch* construction is generally used in German, i.e. the object of the dependent infinitive in English becomes in German the reflexive pronoun[1] and the object of 'make', etc., is turned by the *von* or *durch* phrase. The same construction is possible in English after 'get', 'have', though followed by the past participle, not the infinitive (e.g. he had, got, himself carried over the river by the natives).

Ich ließ mir den Vorfall von ihnen schildern.
Lassen Sie sich von Ihrem Vorgesetzten die nötigen Anweisungen geben.

The two constructions exist in German. The distinction, which is often ignored, is that the less usual form (i.e. *ich ließ ihn mir den Vorfall schildern*) tends to mean 'let'. It suggests that the subject lets the object have his way. The more usual form is, on the other hand, more energetic and implies that the subject acts in his own interest, i.e. it tends to mean 'get'. *Lassen* may be stressed in the sense of 'let'.

Laß dir doch mal von ihm die Geschichte erzählen.
Laß ihn dir doch mal die Geschichte erzählen.

While these constructions are possible with the first and second person pronoun, only the *von* or *durch* form can be used with the third person if the subject of 'make', 'let', etc. and the object of the dependent infinitive refer to the same person.

Ich ließ sie mich tragen ('let').
Er ließ sich von ihnen tragen ('let', 'made', 'got').

A reflexive infinitive depending on *lassen* is mostly avoided and is impossible if it would involve the repetition of the same pronoun (i.e. in the first and second persons). The object of the infinitive must then be dropped or another verb used. For example: it made me wonder = *es ließ mich wundern* (or *staunen*).

3. *Lassen* can best be understood by considering it in the following combinations:

[1] *Sich lassen* is widely used: in the sense of 'to be able' followed by the passive infinitive, in which it often acquires idiomatic force (e.g. *der Vorschlag läßt sich hören, der Film läßt sich sehen,* is worth listening to, seeing; *er läßt mit sich reden* = is a reasonable man).

(a) Both subject and object are persons, the dependent infinitive denoting a conscious act.

In this case *lassen* translates 'make' in the sense of 'order'. The order may amount to little more than a request or even a suggestion, it may be given by virtue of authority accepted as a matter of course. On the other hand, it may be accompanied by a threat of force, even with a gun in the hand. In all circumstances the giver of the order expects this to be complied with unquestioningly.

If a phrase indicating opposition and implying the need for insistence or the application (as distinct from the threat) of force (see *zwingen*, p. 211 (**D**)) is added, *lassen* is no longer possible. Frequently, expressions formed with 'can' and 'must' convey the idea of insistence (I can't make him wear a hat, if he doesn't want to).

When 'have' implies an order it, too, is translated by *lassen*.

Ambiguity in this use of *lassen* can arise, since the meaning can be 'let' as well as 'make'.[1]

Ich ließ ihn Platz nehmen (made, got, let).
Ich ließ ihn die Zeitung holen (made, got).
Laß sie um die Zugeständnisse bitten ('make' and 'let' interchangeable).
Ehe er den Studenten erlaubte, den Umzug abzuhalten, ließ der Rektor sie versprechen, daß sie sich ordentlich verhalten würden.[2]
Sein Vater ließ ihn Latein studieren (made, got, let).
Die Mutter ließ ihre Tochter Klavier lernen, obschon diese wenig Begabung dafür hatte.
Er ließ mich für das Telephon zahlen.
Der Offizier ließ die Kompanie stramm stehen.
Der Offizier ließ seine Leute in den sicheren Tod marschieren.
Die Gestapo ließ ihn zwei Stunden lang auf einem Bein stehen.
Laß ihn doch für ein paar Minuten den Mund halten.
Abends läßt die Mutter die Kinder aufwaschen.
Durch Vorhalten der Pistole ließ er ihn sein Geld aushändigen.
Der Lehrer ließ das Kind in der Ecke stehen.
Der Lehrer läßt die Schüler fleißig arbeiten.
Er hat nicht das Recht, uns das Haus räumen zu lassen.
Ich bin entschlossen, sie für ihren Unterhalt arbeiten zu lassen ('let' and 'make' interchangeable).
Ich drohte, ihn das Schuljahr wiederholen zu lassen.

[1] To avoid ambiguity *zulassen* can be used (e.g. *die Mutter ließ zu, daß ihre Tochter Klavier lernte*).

[2] *Versprechen* combined with *lassen* is somewhat solemn. In trivial matters use would be made of *müssen* (e.g. *ich mußte ihm versprechen, ihm das Buch in* 8 *Tagen zurückzugeben* =he made me promise). Similarly with many other words.

Er ließ uns stundenlang warten ('make', 'let', 'leave', 'keep' interchangeable).

Er läßt den Hund durch den Reifen springen.

(b) The subject is a person, the object his creation. Here 'make' and 'let' are interchangeable.

Im 'Werther' läßt Goethe den Helden sterben.

In diesem Stücke läßt der Dichter Szene auf Szene ohne Einteilung in Akte folgen.

(c) The subject is animate or inanimate, the object animate, the infinitive denotes something between a voluntary and an involuntary act, one carried out under the stress of some emotion and not after reflection, or as a result of a free decision.[1] Here, again, 'get' and 'make' will sometimes be interchangeable.

Lassen is at times used in the sense of 'make' when the action denoted by the infinitive is the result of a decision rather than prompted by emotion (see *veranlassen*, p. 210(C)). The cause is, however, always a compelling one.

Der Hunger ließ ihn stehlen.

Die plötzliche Hitze ließ mich vom Ofen zurückspringen.

Die Hitze ließ mich schlaflos im Bett hin und her wälzen.

Die Hitze ließ uns die Jacke ausziehen.

Seine Willkür ließ mich Widerspruch erheben.

Der Anblick des Flugzeugs ließ sie alle fliehen.

Was ließ Sie damit herausplatzen?

Die Entdeckung von einigen roten Flecken am Körper ließ ihn sofort zum Arzt laufen.

Die Angst vor Dieben ließ sie die ganze Nacht aufsitzen.

Diese Erwägung ließ die Behörden gegen X. einschreiten.

Das Außermenschliche in Kleist ließ Goethe die 'Penthesilea' völlig ablehnen.

(d) The subject is animate or inanimate, the object a person, the dependent infinitive denotes an involuntary mental or emotional reaction.[2]

Lassen is only possible when the infinitive denotes an involuntary reaction or a passive state of being (but not with thought as an active,

[1] *Lassen* is rare with reflex action denoted by a single verb, but it occurs in phrases such as: *die Hitze ließ ihn in Schweiß ausbrechen* (or: *machte schwitzen*).

[2] To make feel. *Ich ließ ihn meinen Ärger fühlen.* But when 'to make feel' is followed by a predicative adjective *lassen* cannot be used. His treachery made me feel sick = *bei seinem Verrat wurde mir übel.* His success made me feel happy = . . . *machte mich glücklich, beglückte mich* ('feel' in this expression is often redundant).

willing process).[1] When 'let' and 'make' are interchangeable, both may be translated by *lassen*.

Since *lassen* is weak, it should not be used in a statement made under the impression of an emotion, e.g. in the present tense (e.g. the incident makes me wonder...).

Der Wein ließ ihn seine Sorgen vergessen.
Seine Tüchtigkeit läßt (=lets) *mich hoffen, daß ihm irgendein einflußreicher Posten übertragen wird.*
Seine Kritik ließ mich fühlen (or: *durch seine Kritik ließ er*), *daß ich zum Versemachen ganz unbegabt bin.*
Sein Treiben läßt mich den Verdacht schöpfen (*den Verdacht in mir aufkommen*), *daß er dunkle Pläne hegt.*
Seine Worte ließen mich fürchten, daß es um meine Aussichten nicht zum besten bestellt sei.
Seine Schilderung ließ den Wunsch in mir aufkommen (made me want), *das Land selbst zu sehen.*[2]
Laß (=let) *ihn glauben, daß es dir ernst mit dem Vorschlag ist.*[3]
Ihre Freundlichkeit läßt (=lets) *mich manche Kränkung vergessen.*
Sein Fieberzustand ließ ihn sich allerhand Dinge einbilden.
Seine Arbeitsweise ließ mich staunen, daß ihm eine so wichtige Arbeit anvertraut worden war.

(e) Both subject and object are things or forces that belong to the world of nature. The subject may also be God. *Lassen* is used regularly in this combination, unless exceptional force is indicated or unless the action resembles a reflex action of persons (see *machen*, p. 210(**B**)).

Der anhaltende Regen ließ den Fluß über seine Ufer treten.
Der Wind hat den Schornstein herunterpurzeln lassen.
Der starke Seegang ließ das Boot umkippen.
Die Hitze ließ die Blätter gelb werden.
Die Mauer ließ die Kugeln zurückprallen.
Gott ließ sein Herz erweichen.

(f) The subject is a person, the object a thing.

Lassen can only be used in the sense of 'make' or 'get' if these are interchangeable with 'let'. For other renderings of 'make', 'get' in this combination see *bringen* (p. 210(**E**)).

Er läßt die Augen rollen.

[1] Expressions such as 'to make see' (with the mind), 'to make understand', which imply effort, are translated variously. *Ich machte ihm klar* (*verständlich*) (*brachte ihm bei*), *daß er sich geirrt hatte.*
[2] 'To make want' is often translated by *reizen*.
[3] 'To make believe' in the sense of 'deceive' is often *vormachen*.

Er läßt die Geige singen.
Er ließ seine Stimme ertönen.
Durch Andrehen einer Schraube ließ er das Wasser nach allen Seiten spritzen.
Sie müssen es so aussehen lassen, als ob Sie alles schon wüßten.
Lassen Sie die Rosen das Spalier hinaufklettern.

B. Machen, used in this sense, is now antiquated except in reflex actions, certain mental reactions, and short, vigorous exclamations, and even here in more or less fixed phrases, which are survivals of an earlier, more extensive use. Apart from this, it is a stylistic device and makes for vividness in the hands of an accomplished writer.

Die Kälte machte mich zittern (reflex action).
Er machte mich lachen.[1]
Er machte sie erröten.
Sie machen mich zweifeln, ob Sie ehrlich sind (involuntary mental reaction).
Ich kann ihn nicht glauben machen, daß es mir ernst mit dem Vorschlag ist.
Den mach' ich schon gehorchen (a short, vigorous phrase).
'*...als noch Ihr Vater neben Ihnen stand und seine Geige jene Töne singen ließ, die Sie weinen machten*' (Thomas Mann, *Tristan*).
'*...weil es auf Erden mein unausweichlicher Beruf ist, die Dinge bei Namen zu nennen, sie reden zu machen*' (Thomas Mann, *Tristan*).
'*Vielleicht war es das Erbteil seines Vaters in ihm...das ihn dort unten leiden machte und manchmal eine schwache, sehnsüchtige Erinnerung in ihm sich regen ließ an eine Lust der Seele, die einstmals sein eigen gewesen war*' (Thomas Mann, *Tonio Kröger*).

C. Veranlassen implies reflection before the performing of the action expressed by the infinitive. A decision, which presupposes a measure of free will, is taken. This term thus corresponds to both 'make' and 'get' thus used.

Was hat sie veranlaßt, das zu sagen (*ließ* would suggest impulse)?
Seine Willkür veranlaßte mich zum Protest.
Sie veranlaßte ihren Mann, zu Bett zu gehen und seine Arbeit auf den nächsten Tag zu verschieben (got).
Diese Überlegung veranlaßte mich, nach Paris zu fahren.
Die Hitze veranlaßte uns, die Jacke auszuziehen.
Durch freundliche Überredung veranlaßte sie ihn, das Geheimnis preiszugeben.

[1] Also: *er brachte mich zum Lachen* (as a report, without emotional colouring); *ich mußte aber lachen* (conversational with emotional participation).

Ehe sie die neue Vorlage unterstützten, veranlaßten sie die Regierung, der Verfassung eine Klausel hinzuzufügen, welche die Redefreiheit gewährleisten sollte.

D. Zwingen must be used when the application of force is implied. When 'made' is in the passive voice, it is often the only possibility.

Ich kann Sie nicht zwingen, die Poesie zu lieben.
Wir zwangen den Feind zum Rückzug.
Durch die Folter zwangen sie ihn, seine Mitarbeiter zu verraten.
Die Deutschen wurden gezwungen, bis zum letzten zu kämpfen.

E. Bringen is used in a number of combinations, with differing shades of meaning, to express the idea of difficulty and effort in bringing about an effect. It translates 'make' and 'get'. Both subject and object may be either animate or inanimate. It occurs in the following combinations:

1. With *zum* and the substantival infinitive.

The substantival infinitive denotes an action which comes dramatically as a climax or represents a final development. When the object is a person, this noun often, but not necessarily, suggests a reflex action or an uncontrollable action (e.g. an outburst of emotion). A typical example would be: *der Witz brachte mich zum Lachen.* On the other hand *Lächeln* would here be impossible, as it would be an anticlimax. Such a weak term could only be used in a phrase of the type: *seine Witze brachten mich nicht einmal zum Lächeln*; i.e. in a phrase which indicates that the cause did not produce a lesser, let alone the desired, effect.

When the object is a thing, the substantival infinitive may have the character of a climax (e.g. *zum Kochen bringen*), or simply indicate perfect functioning (e.g. *zum Rotieren bringen*), or the cessation of movement (e.g. *zum Stehen bringen*).

The substantival infinitive may be compounded of various parts of speech (e.g. *zum Reißausnehmen bringen*), and it may be followed by a genitive (see examples under 2).

Mit meinen Sticheleien brachte ich ihn zum Weinen, Rasen, Schreien, Verzweifeln.
Der Minister brachte den König zum Unterschreiben des Todesurteils.
Ich brachte ihn endlich zum Reden.
Ich werde versuchen, ihn endlich zum Schweigen zu bringen.
Ich kann das Rad nicht zum Rotieren bringen.
Können Sie das Auto nicht zum Laufen bringen? (*lassen* = let).
Es gelingt mir nicht, den Ball zum Wirbeln zu bringen.
Durch die richtige Behandlungsweise brachte er die Rosen schnell zum Blühen.

Durch Nachlegen vieler Zweige brachte er das Feuer bald zum Brennen.
Nur mit großer Mühe brachten wir das Feuer zum Erlöschen.

2. With an infinitive or a *daß* clause preceded by *dazu, dahin, so weit.*

The infinitive is possible only in the case of a verb which implies a free decision (normally a verb of external action, not of emotion).

The *daß* clause, on the other hand, merely indicates a result and may be substituted for the infinitive as well as used in all other cases.

The distinctions between *dazu, dahin* and *so weit* are, if made, as follows. *Dazu* is used when no special effort is suggested and the result may be looked upon as an ordinary, normal action. It cannot be stressed. *Dahin* presents the result as the accomplishment of a goal, which may be followed by further action, without this, however, being the concern of the speaker. The result may be an attitude of mind in which a person is favourably or unfavourably disposed towards a thing. *So weit,* which is not normally followed by the infinitive, can imply that a stage that is not conclusive has been reached. Again, it can imply that the result is something unusual, difficult, unexpected or extreme.

(a) Examples of the infinitive.

Ich habe ihn dazu gebracht, ja zu unserem Plan zu sagen.

'Er (Hitler) werde als größter Feldherr in die Geschichte eingehen und bei einer Offensive den Feind dahin bringen, grade an die Stelle zu marschieren, wo er ihn haben wolle' (U. von Hassel, *Vom Anderen Deutschland*).

Ich habe ihn dahin gebracht, in Ruhe darüber nachzudenken.

(b) Examples of a *daß* clause.

In the examples of the preceding section a *daß* clause could be substituted for the infinitive. A *daß* clause must, however, be used in the case of an involuntary action or an emotion. *Sie brachte ihn so weit, daß er bei seinem Nachbarn einbrach* could mean that he performed this act under the stress of emotion. The infinitive would clearly indicate a decision.

Er hat sie so weit gebracht, daß sie ihn haßt.

Er hat ihn so weit gebracht, daß er die Schönheit der Bachschen Musik empfindet.

Sie brachte ihn so weit, daß er sich aus dem Fenster stürzte.

3. Other expressions formed with *bringen.* In these *bringen* governs not a person or a thing, but a *daß* clause anticipated by *es.*

Es dahin (soweit) bringen, daß . . . ; es fertig bringen (kriegen), daß . . . ; es zustande (zuwege) bringen, daß . . . .

Ich will es schon dahin bringen, daß sie mich fürchten (make them fear me).

Ich kriege es nicht fertig, daß der Pfahl aufrecht steht (I can't get the post to stand up straight).

Er hat es zustande gebracht, daß die Arbeiter in seiner Fabrik nicht mehr streiken.

F. Examples of other renderings which involve a *daß* clause. These can often be used when the object of 'make' or 'get' is a thing. They are frequent in familiar style.

Sehen Sie mal zu, daß der Pfahl aufrecht steht.

Sie müssen dafür sorgen, daß die beiden Bretter sich berühren.

Können Sie es nicht so machen, daß die zwei Wege sich kreuzen? (make the two paths cross).

MAN 1. **Mann:** a member of the male sex. It is only used in this sense, i.e. in contrast to woman. The form *Mann* may, however, stand as plural, when preceded by a numeral, in reference to the numerical strength of a team, squad, army, or the like.

Er ist ein kluger Mann.

Der Mann hat vielseitige Interessen.

Die Männer sind spät gekommen.

Ich brauche 1000 *Mann, um das Manöver durchzuführen.*

2. **Mensch:**[1] human being, the human race.

Der Mensch ist sterblich.

Der Mensch braucht Beschäftigung.

Kein Mensch weiß das.

3. In the sense of 'servant', 'worker', 'soldier', 'sailor', and the like, whether singular or plural, German can only use the specific term.

Die Arbeiter verließen die Fabrik um 4 *Uhr* (the men).

MARRY 1. **Heiraten** refers to the act by which the two parties marry each other. It cannot be used in the passive voice.

Er hat sie geheiratet.

Sie hat ihn geheiratet.

Er hat geheiratet.

Sie haben geheiratet.

[1] See also 'people'. *Mensch* must also be used to translate 'individual' and 'person' when these are synonymous terms. The German *Person* denotes: (i) human beings as contrasted with things; (ii) persons of rank (i.e. personage); (ii) females, mostly of the lower orders and often in a disparaging sense; (iv) the characters of a play.

2. **Verheiraten** draws attention to the state of matrimony, not the act of marrying. It is used passively, reflexively, and, in the sense of 'to give in marriage', actively.

Er ist verheiratet.
Sie haben sich verheiratet.
Sie hat sich mit einem alten Bekannten verheiratet.
Der Vater hat seine Tochter mit seinem Geschäftspartner verheiratet.

3. **(Sich) vermählen** is a dignified term for *verheiraten*, and is applied to important personages. It is also used figuratively.

Hoheit haben sich vermählt.

4. **Trauen** is used of the official who performs the marriage ceremony.

Der Geistliche hat das Paar getraut.

MAY, MIGHT **A.** The meanings of 'may' and 'can'.

'May' is related to the noun 'might' (=power), as *mögen* is with *Macht*. The original meaning of both 'may' and *mögen* was 'to have power', i.e. to have ability, to be able. 'Can' and *können* also denote ability in persons,[1] capacity in things. In addition, they express possibility.[2] 'Can' expresses it not in the sense of uncertainty whether a thing will be, happen, etc., but of capability of being, happening, etc. under certain circumstances. The *S.O.D.* defines this meaning (II. 3) as follows: 'Expressing possibility: *can you . . . ?* = is it possible for you . . . ?' It gives the examples: 'And can you blame them' (Stubbes); 'Thy way thou canst not miss' (Milton). The connection between these two senses of possibility, 'capability of being' and 'uncertainty of being', is close. In other words, it is a short step from the type of possibility expressed by 'can' to that expressed by 'may' (i.e. uncertainty). This becomes particularly clear in questions (e.g. can it be that . . . ?, may it be that . . . ?). It will be seen later that *können* expresses both types of possibility.

'May' can denote both power or ability and possibility in the sense of uncertainty, one sense predominating sometimes to the exclusion of the other. Thus, 'may' sometimes means 'may be able', as in the sentence: you may win the prize, if you work hard. In the following example 'the University may, if it thinks fit, dispense students from examinations', the sense is 'has the power, though it may not exercise it'. Such a use clearly contains also the germs of the idea of permission. The sense is seen more clearly in the following: 'this passage may be interpreted in two ways'. The meaning is: I regard these two interpretations as possible, but I state

[1] 'Can' like *können* formerly meant also 'know' (*Ich kann Deutsch*). Both are related to *kennen*. Compare also English 'ken', 'uncouth'.

[2] 'Possibility' comes from Latin *posse*, to be able.

this as my own opinion, i.e. subjectively, not as an objective fact. The latter would be expressed by 'can'. Again, 'may', used in purpose clauses or depending on a verb such as 'hope', combines the ideas of ability and possibility (e.g. work that you may succeed; I hope our association may endure).

The various senses of 'may' in present-day use all express the idea of possibility (uncertainty) with or without some other idea. The *P.O.D.* classifies them as follows: possibility, permission, request, reproach, aim, wish.

'Possibility' may be apprehended more objectively or more subjectively. The use of 'may' in concessive clauses is an instance of the latter.

Both *mögen* and *können* originally had the same meanings as 'may' and 'can' respectively. In the course of development the German words, while retaining some meanings of the English words, have lost others. These losses have been offset by the growth of new meanings (e.g. *mögen* in the sense of 'like').

B. Mögen meant in the Middle High German period 'to be able'. This meaning is now extinct[1] as a primary sense, and, as a secondary sense, has survived in fewer uses than is the case with 'may'. In reference to possibility as a primary meaning and when combined with other ideas (e.g. request), it is also less widely used than 'may'. On the other hand, it has acquired the sense of 'like'.[2]

1. Possibility as the primary meaning. Here *mögen* has to a varying extent a subjective colouring. It can indicate an inclination to regard the possibility as a probability (in English 'well' is often added to 'may' in this sense, in German *wohl*, *ja*, or *schon* may, but need not be added to *mögen*). From the idea of probability it is a short step to that of concession (expressed by *mögen*), i.e. an admission that a thing is a fact, or at least highly probable, though without bearing on something else. In this sense *mögen* is practically confined to literature, conversational use[3] being extremely rare. Even in writing it is often apt to sound precious. Examples that require no further explanation are:

Das mag schon sein (that may well be).

Gewisse Kreise in Deutschland mögen wegen der Spannung zwischen Rußland und den Westmächten auf mildere Friedensbedingungen rechnen.

[1] It is preserved in *vermögen*, which generally refers to inner ability, particularly of an emotional, ethical character; less to external skills, and not to external circumstances.

[2] The connection between the idea of possibility and that of liking is seen in a sentence such as: I suggest you might see this play. In the sense of 'like' *mögen* may take a direct object or be followed by an infinitive. See also footnote to 'anxious' (p. 24, n. 1).

[3] Examples, which are all border-line cases, are: *das mag sein, er mag wollen oder nicht.*

Ich bin gespannt, was das wohl sein mag.
Ich war mir nicht klar darüber, was das sein mochte.
Was er auch immer tun mag, ich weiß, daß es mit den besten Absichten geschieht.

(a) A limitation to the use of *mögen* in the above sense is that apart from subordinate clauses in strictly concessive form *mögen* can be used freely in the positive and the negative interrogative, but not at all in the negative indicative, and only in certain circumstances in the interrogative. In the latter it occurs only in conjunction with an interrogative pronoun or adverb (e.g. *wer, was, wie, wann*), and imparts to the phrase a kind of poetic wonder. The English 'may' is used 'to render a question less abrupt or pointed' (*S.O.D.* II. 6). For 'may' in questions see also *können* (below, **C**); for its use with a negative, see **D**.

Was mag das wohl sein?
Mag es nicht auch sein, daß er es schon weiß?

(b) The translation of the compound tenses (may have been, might have been) presents special difficulties. The forms *mag gewesen sein, mochte sein* and *mochte gewesen sein* must be distinguished. *Mag gewesen sein* records a judgment or impression made at the moment of speaking, i.e. from the point of view of the present. *Mochte sein* records a judgment or impression already made, and implies that the action or state expressed by the infinitive was contemporaneous with this judgment. It is therefore used in connected historical narrative. *Mochte gewesen sein* records a judgment or impression made in the past about an action or state anterior to the making of the judgment.

Mochte sein translates 'may have been', i.e. the distinction between the English terms does not correspond to that between the German. As an equivalent of 'might' *mochte* can only refer to what is contemporaneous, i.e. not to the future (for 'might' in the latter sense see *können*, below, **C**).

In this combination *mochte* never becomes *möchte*, which can refer to the future, even in indirect speech.

Es mögen insgesamt 30 *Personen dagewesen sein.*
Er berichtete, es mochten insgesamt 30 *Personen da sein.*
Er berichtete, es mochten insgesamt 30 *Personen dagewesen sein.*
Ich ging spazieren und sah einen Mann, der bessere Zeiten gesehen haben mag.
Ich ging spazieren und sah einen Mann, der bessere Zeiten gesehen haben mochte.
Er schrieb, er habe einen Mann getroffen, der in seiner Jugend bessere Zeiten gesehen haben mochte (not *möchte* despite indirect speech).

2. *Mögen* is used in literature, but not in conversation, in subordinate clauses after verbs which express emotional states of mind, e.g. verbs of wishing, fearing, hoping. Also in purpose clauses and in indirect question (expressing wonder in the latter case). Except in indirect question this use serves as a periphrastic subjunctive (*S.O.D.* II. 7, *a*). After verbs of wishing, fearing, and in purpose clauses the subjunctive of *mögen* is usual (mostly *möchte*).

Ich wünschte, er möchte kommen.
Ich fürchte, es möchte schon zu spät sein.
Ich hoffe, daß die Verbindung zwischen uns noch weiterhin bestehen mag.
Ich nahm das Angebot an, damit es nicht aussehen möchte, daß es mir gleichgültig war.

3. In principal clauses *mögen* is used in the present subjunctive[1] as an equivalent of *mag* to express a wish.

Möge Gott dich erhalten!

4. *Mögen* is used in conversation as well as in literature in indirect command, request. This use is general in German, whereas 'may' in English is confined to a few verbs such as 'request'.[2]

Ich bat ihn, er möchte doch nicht annehmen, daß ich den Plan unbedingt ablehnen würde.
Ich schlug vor, er möchte das im Auge behalten.

C. Können expresses possibility in an objective way. It is, however, also used in conversation and in ordinary prose where *mögen* would be used in literature, except in clauses which are strictly concessive in form. In the concessive sense *wohl, ja, schon* may be added. It is used similarly after verbs of fearing, hoping and in purpose clauses, though not to express a wish, an indirect command, or an indirect question. It must be used when 'may' combines the senses of ability and possibility (see the examples under **A**).

Since *können* also means 'to be able' ambiguity is possible, particularly in the present tense *kann*. In conversation this ambiguity can be eliminated by the inflection of the voice. In writing the ambiguity remains. See **D** for renderings which avoid it. As 'might' and 'could' are often practically interchangeable, unlike 'may' and 'can', *könnte* can mostly be used to translate both terms.

[1] *Möchte* in this sense is rendered into English by 'would'. *Möchte er doch bald kommen!*

[2] *Mögen* in the present indicative and present subjunctive also expresses a command which is expressed in English by 'let'. *Er mag, möge, nur sagen.* The indicative makes the command shorter.

MAY

With a negative, *können* can only mean 'to be able'. In the positive, interrogative, and negative interrogative it can mean both 'may' and 'can'.

Vielleicht is often added in a question and with the conditional tenses: *könnte* (*sein*), *hätte* (*sein*) *können*.

Können is used to translate 'might' when it denotes a reproach. It is unusual in conjunction with another modal verb (e.g. he may have to leave).

Es kann heute regnen.
Er kann heute kommen (may or can).
Das kann wahr sein.
Das kann vorkommen (may or can).
Das kann wohl, ja, schon, sein.
Er kann das gesagt haben.
Kann er das gesagt haben?
Glauben Sie, daß wir noch Erfolg haben können?
Es können insgesamt 30 *Personen dagewesen sein.*
Ich weiß nicht, wie er sich zu dem Vorschlag stellt, er könnte ihn zu radikal finden.
Ich fürchte, Sie können sich zuviel zugemutet haben.
Kann das vielleicht die Ursache des Fiaskos sein?
Er hätte vielleicht den Preis gewinnen können, wenn er gearbeitet hätte.
Sie hätten es mir doch sagen können! (a reproach).
Sie könnten mich vielleicht verständigen, wenn das Buch ankommt (a request).

D. Other renderings of 'may' in the sense of 'possibility'. To avoid the ambiguity admitted by *können* and to render 'may' accompanied by a negative, resort may be had to such phrases as *vielleicht, es kann sein, daß*. . . . These are used as commonly as *können*.

Vielleicht kommt er heute.
Vielleicht regnet es heute nicht mehr.
Er hätte es vielleicht getan, wenn sie ihn gebeten hätten.
Es kann sein, daß wir zu hart gewesen sind.

E. Permission.

Dürfen expresses permission, both with regard to the asking for and the granting of it, and whether the request is justified or not. It refers to important matters without taking the granting of the permission as a matter of course. **Können** expresses the idea more familiarly, and is used particularly when asking permission to do something for someone else. Though 'can' is sometimes used in the same way, it is still accepted by many authorities as good English only when accompanied by a negative. *Dürfen* with a negative (but not the negative interrogative) indicates a strong denial of permission, which is expressed in English by 'must not'.[1,2]

Darf ich auf Ihre Hilfe rechnen?
Sie dürfen gehen.
Sie dürfen annehmen, daß Ihnen keine Schwierigkeiten in den Weg gelegt werden.
Kann ich dieses Buch borgen?
Kann ich Ihnen dabei behilflich sein?
Sie können das Buch mitnehmen.
Der Stuhl kann hier bleiben.

MEAN[3] 1. **Meinen:** to intend, to indicate or to convey a certain sense, or to intend a remark to have a particular reference. In the sense of 'to be disposed' (e.g. to mean ill) it can like 'mean' be used only in a few fixed expressions. In all uses except those in the passive voice, the subject must be a person, the object may be a person or a thing.[4]

Was meinen Sie?
Ich meine, daß unsere Aussichten schlecht sind.
Er meint Sie.
Sind Sie gemeint?
Das Gesetz ist mit diesem Hinweis gemeint.
Er meint es gut (mit Ihnen).

2. **Bedeuten.** Applied to things[5] this term means 'to have a certain signification, import', 'to portend'. With a personal subject the meaning is 'to be of importance' to another person. See also under next section.[6]

Was bedeutet dieses Wort?
Der Name bedeutet mir nichts.
Diese Hilfe bedeutet mir sehr viel.

[1] *Nicht müssen* corresponds to 'need not', 'not to have to', or 'must not' when this is no stronger than 'need not'.

[2] *Mögen* only expresses permission in the sense that the person who grants it places no obstacle in the way because he is indifferent to what happens. English expresses this by 'let...' (for all I care).

[3] The sense of 'intend' is not treated in this article.

[4] Followed by the infinitive *meinen* means not 'intend' but 'to be of the opinion' that a thing, denoted by the infinitive, is possible. *Ich meinte, dir damit zu helfen.*

[5] With a personal subject and followed by a dative denoting a person, the sense is 'to intimate to a person' that he must do a certain thing. *Ich bedeutete ihm, daß er auf seinen Plan verzichten müsse.*

[6] For *Bedeutung* see 'sense'.

Es bedeutet wenig, daß er mir so viel versprochen hat.
Diese Wolken bedeuten Regen.
Eine solche Politik bedeutet Krieg.
Er bedeutet sehr viel für mich.

3. **Heißen** implies a categorical assertion that such and such is the meaning of something previously referred to. It is final, while *bedeuten* leaves room for doubt, for other interpretations. It can only be followed by a clause, i.e. not a noun.

Die Regierung hat das Benzin rationiert. Das heißt, wir können Sonntags nicht mehr ausfahren.

4. **Besagen** is 'to make clear' something that is unclear or not definite. It is more tentative than *heißen*. In reference to a preceding word or statement it comes close to 'imply'.[1] Its subject can be personal only in combination with a modal verb such as *wollen* (see example below). When it does not refer to any specific preceding word or words, it can mean 'to tell', 'to reveal' something that was not known or apparent before.[2]

Die Rationierung des Benzins besagt, daß der Handel mit Amerika ins Stocken geraten ist.
Willst du damit besagen, daß ich das Geld gestohlen habe? (*Besagen* suggests more strongly than *sagen* that the accusation was expressed indirectly.)
Es ist ein Name, der mir nichts besagt.[3]

MEET A. Of persons: to come into each other's presence or company (without secondary associations such as 'receive', 'get to know').

1. **Begegnen** is, strictly speaking, used of people coming from opposite directions, and indicates a chance encounter (i.e. to run across). It frequently suggests that the persons are known only casually to each other, or that the encounter is unwelcome to one or more of the persons. Generally subject and object can be interchanged without any perceptible difference in meaning.

Ich bin ihm nie begegnet.
Ich bin ihm heute auf der Brücke begegnet (or: *er ist mir . . . begegnet*).
Der ist mir verschiedentlich in London begegnet.
Die D-Züge von und nach Berlin begegnen sich in Hannover.
Er ist der letzte Mensch, dem ich begegnen will.

[1] German has no general term for 'imply'. In reference to the implications of a word considered as a term in a dictionary the following phrases are common: *in dem Wort ist (mit) enthalten, daß . . .*; or more colloquially: *in dem Wort steckt (noch), daß . . . .*

[2] Example: *ein Blick in den Raum besagt alles.*

[3] *Es ist ein Name, der mir nichts sagt*: which conveys nothing to me.

2. **Treffen**[1] can denote a chance or an arranged meeting. While not excluding casual acquaintance, it more often suggests closer relations and the spending of a certain time in each other's company.

In arranging meetings *sich treffen* is more common than *Sie*, etc. as object (e.g. *wir treffen uns vor dem Rathaus* = I'll meet you...). *Uns* conveys no implication of intimacy.

To emphasize that a meeting is arranged, often for an important discussion, and is not accidental, *sich treffen mit jdm.* is sometimes used. It is unnecessary to use it with reference to the future.

Wir haben uns heute auf der Brücke getroffen.
Ich habe ihn ganz zufällig in der Bahn getroffen.
Wir treffen uns heute abend.
Ich habe mich mit ihm im Wirtshaus getroffen.

3. **Zusammentreffen**[2] is used (*a*) to emphasize the place at which a number of people coming from opposite directions meet; (*b*) of a meeting which has results (often momentous).

Die Ausflügler trafen auf dem Marktplatz zusammen.
Immer wenn wir zusammentrafen, heckten wir irgendwelchen Unsinn aus.
Als Churchill mit Roosevelt im Atlantischen Ozean zusammentraf, ahnte die Welt kaum, wie folgenschwer ihre Besprechungen sein sollten.

4. **Entgegengehen:** to go to meet, in the sense of 'to go forward a few steps to meet' someone approaching. Similarly *entgegenkommen, -eilen*, etc.

Er ging seinen Gästen entgegen.

B. Of persons with secondary associations. Some common uses are:

1. **Zusammentreten,** of deliberative bodies.

Das Parlament, das Kommittee, tritt heute zusammen.

2. **Empfangen:** to receive, sometimes for the purpose of discussion.

Der Außenminister empfing den neuen Botschafter am Bahnhof.
Der Premierminister empfängt heute die Gewerkschaftsführer.

3. **Abholen** (to go for a person); **erwarten** (to await a person): to meet a person on his arrival and take him to some destination.

Er holte meinen Bruder am Bahnhof ab (*erwartete*...).

[1] *Treffen* also means to 'hit the target' (see 'strike' and footnote to 'affect', p. 12, n. 3). *Treffen auf* means to 'come, hap upon'. *Antreffen*: to find a person in a place or condition. An adverbial phrase of place or condition often follows.

[2] *Zusammentreffen* can also mean a 'clash'. Compare *Treffen*, which can mean an 'engagement' in the sense of combat.

4. **Kennen lernen:** to get to know, to make the acquaintance of.

Möchten Sie den neuen Konsul kennen lernen?
Er lernte seine Frau in Paris kennen.[1]

C. Of things.

1. Of vehicles.

Verschiedene internationale Züge begegnen sich in Basel (coming from different directions).
Ein Autobus wartet auf den 10 *Uhr Zug.*

2. Of geographical features. See 'touch', 'join'.

Die Linien berühren sich in diesem Punkt.
Die beiden Grundstücke stoßen hier aneinander.
Bei Koblenz fließt die Mosel in den Rhein.

D. Figurative. Some common renderings are:

1. **Begegnen**

(a) To counter. *Einwänden begegnen.*

(b) To comply with a wish. *Er ist immer bestrebt, meinen Wünschen zu begegnen.*

(c) To return one kind of treatment for another. *Feindschaft mit Freundschaft begegnen.*

(d) To come upon examples of a thing. *Beispiele dieses Wortes begegnen uns bei Goethe* (occur, i.e. the thing as subject).

(e) To meet the gaze. *Eine grauenhafte Szene begegnete unserem Blick.*[2]

2. **Entgegenkommen:** to arrive at a compromise with a person.

Ich werde mein Bestes tun, Ihnen in dieser Sache entgegenzukommen.

3. 'To satisfy demands, needs' and the like, is translated by **erfüllen** (fulfil), **nachkommen** (comply with), **entsprechen** (comply with).[3] Other, less frequent renderings are given by the dictionaries.

Er hat meinen Forderungen, Wünschen, nicht entsprochen (*hat sie nicht erfüllt, ist ihnen nicht nachgekommen*).

4. 'To meet (with)' in the sense of 'to receive', 'to experience', a certain treatment or fate must be variously translated. Sometimes *finden, erfahren* (see 'experience'), *erleiden* (see 'suffer') are used.

[1] 'To meet one's spouse for the first time' can also be translated by *treffen.*
[2] But: *das Ohr treffen.*
[3] These verbs, like the English equivalents given, are wider in application than this meaning of 'meet'.

Das Stück fand eine gute Aufnahme.
Er hat viel Freundlichkeit von dir erfahren.
Er hat schwere Verluste erlitten.

MERRY, GAY, CHEERFUL, SPRIGHTLY 'Merry' suggests uninhibited enjoyment, festivity, fun, animal spirits; 'gay' a carefree state of mind overflowing with good humour, laughter, and the like; 'cheerful' a disposition to look on the bright side of things and not to yield easily to depression (e.g. the English have a cheerful temperament). The German terms are not close equivalents.[1]

1. **Lustig** is a wide term and suggests an uninhibited outward expression of high spirits, divorced from all reflection. It can be applied to loud merriment, practical jokes, the romping of children, and the like. See also article on 'funny'.

Er hat viele lustige Geschichten erzählt.
Es war ein sehr lustiger Abend.
Die Kinder sind heute abend sehr lustig.
Ein lustiges Feuer brennt im Kamin.

2. **Fröhlich** suggests laughter and good spirits as these are manifested in talk, singing, dancing, in association with festivity. Unlike *lustig* it excludes wild, unrestrained actions, but not reflection. See also footnote to article on 'glad' (p. 152, n. 1).

Das war ein fröhlicher Tanz.
Ich wünsch Ihnen ein fröhliches Weihnachtsfest.
Er ist wieder der alte, fröhliche Mensch, den alle liebten.

3. **Heiter** is applied to a state of mind which manifests itself inwardly more than outwardly and which is unclouded, serene. It can be applied to the higher activities of the mind, e.g. art (e.g. *die Heiterkeit der klassischen Kunst*), and also to its state in relation to everyday tasks and events. In the first case 'serene', 'bright'[2] must often be used in English for lack of closer equivalents. In the latter case it approximates to 'cheerful'. Common to both *heiter* and 'cheerful' are harmony and balance. The German term tends, however, to say more than the English. *Ein heiterer Abend* could mean 'exhilarating to the mind'.

Er hat ein heiteres Wesen.

[1] *Freudig* (see article on 'glad') sometimes approximates to 'cheerful', e.g. *eine freudige Nachricht*, i.e. causing joy, but suggests more positive joy than the English term. *Ein freudiger Spender.*

[2] The normal prose term for 'bright' in reference to light is *hell*. *Licht* as an adjective in this sense is a more elevated word.

Der Engländer bleibt sogar in Kriegszeiten heiter.
Er hat ein heiteres Zimmer (*heiter* can refer to the appearance of things, e.g. *ein heiterer Himmel*, serene).

4. **Munter** suggests animation which expresses itself in movement, particularly in play. Its closest equivalent in English is perhaps 'sprightly' (in German often *lebhaft*) (see article on 'lively'). It implies too much activity to be translated by 'cheerful'.

Das muntere Spiel der Kinder (suggests running, jumping about).
Sie hat muntere Augen (mobile).

MIND[1] 1. When the verb makes the reference to the mind clear, it is sufficient to translate 'mind' by the person to whom it is attributed.

Die Propaganda verwirrt die Menschen (confuses people's minds).
Beruhigen Sie sich (set your mind at rest).
Er ist auf andere Dinge bedacht (his mind is taken up with other things).

2. **Geist** corresponds to 'spirit' more frequently than to 'mind'. As an equivalent of the latter when this refers to the thinking faculty, *Geist* is generally a lofty term and inclines more to abstract than to concrete use. It is thus to be found more often with the definite article than with the possessive adjective, which, however, is possible.

Der Geist ist der kostbarste Besitz des Menschen.
Der deutsche Geist.
Sein Geist war auf höhere Dinge gerichtet.
Das Allumfassende seines Geistes.

Though the most characteristic use of *Geist* is to suggest loftiness and range of content, it is occasionally qualified by adjectives which denote the opposite.

Ein beschränkter Geist.

Since in the meaning of 'spirit' it can denote life, vitality,[2] particularly the subtle, invisible essence of a thing, it can also, as an equivalent of 'mind', be qualified by adjectives which express vitality and be used in contexts which by implication attribute this characteristic to the mind.[3,4]

[1] '...in all cases, despite a difference in stress on certain qualities, it denotes a complex of powers of which man is conscious and which includes the perceiving, the remembering, the thinking, and less often, the feeling and willing powers or functions' (Webster's *Dictionary of Synonyms*).

[2] Examples: *den Geist aufgeben, die erschlafften Geister erfrischen.*

[3] In this sentence *Geisteskräfte* or *geistige Kräfte* is sometimes used for 'mind'. Example: *seine geistigen Kräfte haben nachgelassen.*

[4] An extension of this characteristic leads to wit, which meaning *Geist* has in a few

Ein reger, lebhafter, Geist.

'*Der Pfarrer war die Güte selbst, er wußte meinen lebhaften Geist zu fesseln...*' (E. T. A. Hoffmann, *Die Elixiere des Teufels*).

'*Du weißt, mein lieber Rufin, daß ich nichts in der Welt so fürchte und scheue, als die brennenden Sonnenstrahlen des Tages, welche die Kräfte meines Körpers aufzehren und meinen Geist dermaßen abspannen und ermatten, daß...*' (E. T. A. Hoffmann, *Klein Zaches*).

Geist is used much less with *haben* than 'mind' with 'have'.[1] The following examples are fairly common.

Er hat einen regen, lebhaften, zersetzenden, Geist.

3. **Geistig** (intellectual,[2] spiritual) can often be used in phrases which describe the characteristics or power of an individual's mind.[3]

Er ist seinem Bruder geistig überlegen (has a better mind than...).

4. **Verstand** is the 'faculty of understanding',[4] 'reason',[5] and may be used to translate 'mind' when the reference contained in the latter is to logic

expressions (e.g. *Geist haben*). Compare French *esprit, spirituel*, Dutch *geestig*. Similarly *geistreich* suggests a brilliance, cleverness of mind that is akin to wit.

[1] *Geist* is used freely with the verb *sein*, but the reference is less to the thinking faculty than to the person in general. Thus *er ist ein edler, lebhafter, Geist* suggests the nature of the person's actions more than his thoughts.

[2] Since *geistig* combines the meanings of intellectual and spiritual, it is a wider term than either and has no exact equivalent in English.

[3] *Geistig*, used adjectivally, can be coupled with a thing, but not a person, except in the case of *Mensch* (e.g. *der geistige Mensch*). Examples: *eine geistige Kunst, geistige Interessen.*

[4] See 'understanding'.

[5] Kant's distinction between *Verstand* (the faculty of clear and logical thinking on sensuous material) and *Vernunft* (the faculty of perceiving the relationships in non-sensuous material and of integrating them into a whole) is not observed in the everyday use of these terms. *Verstand* is more widely used and translates 'mind', 'understanding', 'reason', 'sense' (often expanded to *gesunder Menschenverstand*, i.e. common sense). It suggests the operation of the mind on specific material more forcibly than *Vernunft*, which refers more exclusively to a state of mind, i.e. reasonableness, sensibleness, and is mostly, though not entirely, restricted to fixed phrases. *Vernunft* is, however, the appropriate term for 'reason' conceived as an attribute that ennobles man. Compare *Faust I* (ll. 283–6):

> '*Ein wenig besser würd' er leben,*
> *Hätt'st du ihm nicht den Schein des Himmelslichts gegeben;*
> *Er nennt's Vernunft und braucht's allein,*
> *Nur tierischer als jedes Tier zu sein.*'

The adjective *vernünftig* translates 'sensible' and sometimes 'reasonable'. In many cases, however, the latter cannot be rendered by *vernünftig*, particularly as an adverb (e.g. *er weiß einigermaßen Bescheid*). 'Reasonable' differs from 'sensible' in emphasizing the exercise of a sense of measure. For example: Please return the book in a reasonable time (*in absehbarer Zeit*). While *vernünftig* refers to an attitude or state of mind, *verständig* draws more attention to the object on which the mind operates, and means 'displaying intelligence' (logic or commonsense) in dealing with this object. *Sachverständig* = expert.

and clarity of thought. Unlike *Geist* which is mostly directed to elevated spheres, it can operate on any kind of material: it can be combined freely with *haben* and with any adjective that can be associated with the term intellect.

Its additional meaning of 'common sense',[1] 'practical sense', has given rise to a number of fixed expressions which, mostly negative, denote the absence of this quality. They may be translated by 'mind' or 'wits'.

Er hat einen klaren, scharfen, durchdringenden, Verstand.
Er hat seinen Verstand an den verschiedenartigsten Problemen ausgebildet.
Sie haben Ihren Verstand gar nicht gebraucht.
Der Verstand stand ihm still.
Er ist nicht recht bei Verstand.

5. **Kopf** is used in much the same way as 'head', though perhaps more extensively so, in the sense of 'mind'. Like *Verstand,* it refers to capacity for clear, logical thought, and, preceded by an appropriate adjective, is used with both *haben* and *sein.*

Like 'head', it is also used, mostly in fixed expressions, as the place where thoughts reside, without reference to the activity or the quality of the mind. Compare *Sinn.*

Er ist ein hervorragender, schlauer, gescheiter, Kopf.
Man braucht die besten Köpfe, um so schwierige Probleme zu bewältigen.
Ich kann so viele Tatsachen nicht im Kopf behalten.
Der Gedanke ging, schoß, fuhr, mir durch den Kopf.
Er hat es sich in den Kopf gesetzt, daß man sich über ihn lustig mache.
Schlagen Sie sich den Gedanken aus dem Kopf.
Sein Kopf steckt voller dunkler Pläne.

6. **Gedanken** should be used to refer to the content of the mind at any given moment.

Seine Gedanken sind verwirrt.
Richten Sie Ihre Gedanken auf diese wichtige Angelegenheit.
Seine Gedanken kehren immer zu demselben Punkt zurück.
Seine Gedanken schweifen ab.
Ihre Gedanken sind nicht bei der Arbeit.
Ich war anderswo mit meinen Gedanken, als Sie mich anredeten.

7. **Sinn** is the faculty which makes consciousness of external and internal impressions possible. It refers to any of the special organs of sense[2]

[1] See footnote 5, p. 225. [2] See 'sense'.

through which these impressions pass, and to consciousness in general. In the latter case it is often associated with one of the faculties of thinking, feeling or willing. In earlier German[1] it was used in this way more freely than at the present day, when it is mostly confined to fixed expressions. As a translation of 'mind' it occurs in the following senses.

(a) Consciousness of the most general kind. Compare *Kopf*.

Die Idee kam mir in den Sinn.
Der Gedanke fuhr mir durch den Sinn.
Ich werde Ihre Wünsche im Sinne behalten.
Schlagen Sie sich den Plan aus dem Sinn.
Die Sinne vergingen ihm (his mind became a blank, i.e. in the sense of a mental black-out).

(b) Wits, sanity. Compare *Verstand*.

Bei Sinnen sein (in one's right mind).
Von Sinnen sein (out of one's mind).
Seine fünf Sinne beisammen haben.

(c) Opinion, intention.

Anderen Sinnes werden (change one's mind, either opinion or intention).
Wir waren eines Sinnes (of one mind).

[1] The following examples, which would not now be used in ordinary prose are taken from the works of E. T. A. Hoffmann. From *Meister Martin*: (i) '*Ich bin ein Küfer worden . . . aber einer andern, wohl schönern Kunst war mein ganzer Sinn zugewandt von Kindheit auf*' (mind in the sense of 'desire' and 'will'). (ii) '*Wessen Sinn jemals ein böser Traum verwirrte, daß er glaubte in tiefer Nacht zu liegen . . .*' (wits, reason). From *Die Elixiere des Teufels*: (i) '*Ach wie ein fernes herrliches Land, wo die Freude wohnt und die ungetrübte Heiterkeit des kindlichen unbefangenen Sinns, liegt die Heimat weit, weit hinter mir . . .*' (disposition). (ii) '*Aber finstre Gestalten steigen auf, und . . . versperren . . . die Aussicht und befangen meinen Sinn mit den Drangsalen der Gegenwart . . .*' (thoughts and feelings). From *Der Sandmann*: (i) '*Haben wir festen, durch das heitre Leben gestärkten Sinn genug, um fremdes feindliches Einwirken als solches stets zu erkennen . . .*' (will and intellect). (ii) '*Sage du mir, Sigmund, wie deinem sonst alles Schöne klar auffassenden Blick, deinem regen Sinn Olimpias himmlischer Liebreiz entgehen konnte?*' (sensibility). (iii) '*Es wäre daraus zu schließen, daß Clara das ruhige häusliche Glück noch fand, das ihrem heitern lebenslustigen Sinn zusagte . . .*' (disposition). From Kleist's *Robert Guiskard* (ll. 511–12):

'Ja, in des Sinns entsetzlicher Verwirrung
Die ihn zuletzt befällt . . .'

From Friedrich Schlegel: '*Künstler ist ein jeder, dem es Ziel und Mitte des Daseins ist, seinen Sinn zu bilden*' (*Athenäum*, 20). Gundolf's use of the term in the following passage from his *Heinrich von Kleist* is only possible in elevated diction of this kind. '*Der Kurfürst . . . kämpft gelassenen Sinns in sich das aus was der Prinz im Tatenfeuer und in Todesqual auszukämpfen hat.*' The following use from Mörike's *Maler Nolten* is obsolete: '*. . . sie selbst gab sich eigentlich mehr aus Gutmütigkeit zu alledem her, als daß sie ungeteilten Sinnes dabei gewesen wäre.*'

8. **Gemüt** is the seat of certain types of feelings, particularly those which embrace the world and its objects with warmth and affection.[1,2] It excludes sexual emotion and, though it may be deeply moved, violent feelings. The sanity, stability, equilibrium, excitement of the mind may, however, be implied. It is, further, sometimes conceived as the source of poetry, particularly of the romantic order.[3] English lacks an equivalent term and resorts to approximations such as 'soul', 'heart', 'disposition'. If 'mind' is used, the reference must be to its emotional side, to feelings of the type described above.

The plural is used in the sense of 'people's minds'.

'*Und ganz von selbst umkreiste sein Gemüt — besessen von Wunschbildern äußerster Jugendschönheit, Manneswildheit und Götterhuld — den homerischen Achill, das unausweichliche Ideal solcher Träume*' (Friedrich Gundolf, *Heinrich von Kleist*).

'*...und gleich, als ob der eine plötzliche Eindruck, der sich seinem Gemüt eingeprägt hatte, alle früheren daraus verdrängt hätte, weinte er vor Lust, daß er sich des lieblichen Lebens voller bunter Erscheinungen, noch erfreute*' (Kleist, *Das Erdbeben in Chili*).

'*Die Oper stimmt durch die Macht der Musik und durch eine freiere*

[1] *Ein hartes Gemüt* as well as *ein weiches Gemüt.* Compare the use of *Geist* which attributes to it characteristics which are the opposite of its essential nature.

[2] The expression *das deutsche Gemüt* cannot be paralleled by the use of an adjective which denotes another nationality.

[3] Compare Novalis: (i) '*Poesie ist Darstellung des Gemüts, der inneren Welt in ihrer Gesamtheit.*' (ii) '*Es ist höchst begreiflich warum am Ende alles Poesie wird. Wird nicht die Welt am Ende Gemüt?*' It would be inappropriate, however, to ascribe *Gemüt* to a poet such as Stefan George. See Gundolf's judgment in his *George*, p. 25: '*Seinem stetig tiefen Herzen, weiten Geist und mächtigen Willen...mangeln alle die deutschen Lieblingseigenschaften, die eben jener Zwiespalt erst zeitigt: das "Gemüt", das wohlige oder schmerzlich-dumpfe Überwölken des Zwiespalts....*' But Gundolf, in his essay on Mörike (*Romantiker, Neue Folge*), writes: '*Eichendorff, der beschwingte Sänger von Wald und Wandern, Genius nur, wo dieses Erscheinen und Geschehen ein ward mit seinem Gemüte....*' The writings of the romantics abound in the description and evocation of feelings, and the term *Gemüt* occurs again and again. Examples from E. T. A. Hoffmann are: (i) '*...aber den Gläubigen, der ohne zu grübeln sein ganzes Gemüt darauf richtet, erfüllt bald eine überirdische Begeisterung, die ihm das Reich der Seligkeit erschließt, das er hienieden nur geahnt...*' (*Die Elixiere des Teufels*). '*...du mögest mit recht heitrem, unbefangenem Gemüt es dir gefallen lassen, die seltsamen Gestaltungen zu betrachten, ja dich mit ihnen zu befreunden, die der Dichter der Eingebung des spukhaften Geistes, Phantasus geheißen, verdankt...*' (*Der Sandmann*). The word is used to-day more in critical than in narrative prose. Goethe felt called upon to protest against its excessive use by the romantics, since, according to him, it had come to denote nothing but indulgence with weakness. The following is an example of Goethe's use of the term in *Werther:* '*Das klare Wetter konnte wenig auf sein trübes Gemüt wirken, ein dumpfer Druck lag auf seiner Seele, die traurigen Bilder hatten sich bei ihm festgesetzt, und sein Gemüt kannte keine Bewegung als von einem schmerzlichen Gedanken zum andern.*'

harmonische Reizung der Sinnlichkeit das Gemüt zu einer schöneren Empfänglichkeit' (Schiller in a letter to Goethe).

Um die Gemüter zu beruhigen, sagte er, daß die Gefahr nicht ernst sei.
Die Propaganda hat die Gemüter entflammt.
Er ist gemütskrank.
Er hat seine Gemütsruhe verloren.

9. **Seele** is used in a few fixed expressions which suggest worry or stress of soul.

Seine Untreue lastet, liegt, ihm auf der Seele.

10. Examples of other terms that must sometimes be used are:

Er hat eine sprunghafte Denkart.
Er denkt sehr schnell.
Er hat eine rasche Auffassungsgabe.

MISS 1. **Vermissen:**[1] to notice or to regret the absence of a person or a thing.[2]

Ich vermißte mein Gepäck, als ich wieder in das Coupé zurückging.
Ich vermisse jetzt Ihren Gruß, wenn ich im Büro ankomme.
Ich habe Sie in der letzten Zeit sehr vermißt.
Er wurde beim Appell vermißt.
Die Vermißten (missing, i.e. a casualty list).

2. **Versäumen:**[3] to let something that is regarded by oneself or by others as valuable or necessary pass by without either (*a*) taking, using, being present at it, or (*b*) doing it. The cause may be remissness, in which case it implies blame more strongly than *verpassen* and *verfehlen*, or adverse circumstances. Like *verpassen*, but unlike *verfehlen* it can suggest tardiness, i.e. being too late to take or do a thing.[4] It must have a person as subject, a thing as object, and cannot therefore mean to miss, i.e. fail to meet, a person.

Er hat den Zug, die Gelegenheit, den richtigen Augenblick, den Vortrag, seine Pflicht, versäumt.
Sie haben nichts versäumt (nothing worth while).

3. **Verpassen** is said more lightly than *versäumen* and therefore implies a less serious situation and less blame. The cause is inattentiveness[5] or

[1] *Missen* means 'to do without'.
[2] *Fehlen* can also have this meaning. *Du fehlst mir sehr.* See 'lack'.
[3] *Verabsäumen* is a commercial term.
[4] *Säumen* means 'to delay' and may be followed by the infinitive.
[5] *Passen auf* means 'to watch for', *aufpassen* is 'to pay attention'.

a piece of bad luck (e.g. absence, tardiness) at the crucial moment. Like *versäumen* it implies the missing of something wanted or worth while, but, unlike it, does not mean to neglect the doing of something considered as a duty. Its object may be a person as well as a thing (in the sense of 'to fail to meet a person'), while the subject can sometimes—loosely used—be a thing (particularly something sent to a person such as a letter). It is never a dignified term.

Er hat den Zug, die Gelegenheit, den richtigen Augenblick, den Vortrag, den Anschluß, verpaßt.
Ich kam zu spät und verpaßte ihn (him).
Der Brief hat mich verpaßt.

4. **Verfehlen:** to miss by reason of a mistake made. The object may be not only a thing, but also a person or a place, in which case the meaning is 'to miss by going to the wrong place', or it may be anything else that is conceived as a goal, the implication being that failure to reach it is due to error. The error rather that the value of the goal is stressed.

Wir haben uns, den Weg, verfehlt.
Er hat seinen Beruf verfehlt.
Die Rede hat ihren Zweck, ihre Wirkung verfehlt.

5. A number of verbs (see dictionaries) may be compounded with the prefix *vorbei* and followed by the preposition *an* in the sense of going past the goal, not hitting it.[1]

Er schoß an der Scheibe vorbei.
Sie reden an der Sache vorbei (you are missing the point, i.e. talking irrelevantly).

6. Very often German requires a specific verb used negatively or a verb meaning 'to fail'.[2] At times the English is ambiguous (e.g. 'to miss the ball' can mean: not to hit, not to catch). If 'miss' is followed by the gerund of the verb, the ambiguity is removed. Of the verbs treated in this article only *versäumen, verpassen, verfehlen* cannot be used with the infinitive. Examples of specific verbs are:

Er hat die fünfte Seite übersprungen, ausgelassen.
In seiner Beschreibung des Vorfalls hat er die richtige Stimmung nicht getroffen.

[1] Colloquialisms compounded with *vorbei* and *daneben* and meaning 'to miss' are: *vorbei (daneben) gelingen, vorbei (daneben) greifen, vorbei (daneben) hauen. Er hat arg danebengehauen.*
[2] See 'fail'.

7. 'Just to miss' with the gerund (i.e. by a narrow margin) may in the past tense be translated by *wenig fehlte*. This expression occurs only in literature, and even here is inclined to be archaic.

Wenig fehlte, so wäre er gewählt worden.

MISTAKE, ERROR[1] **Fehler** is a definite imperfection in a thing which ought not to be there. In this sense it translates both 'mistake' and 'error'.[2] **Irrtum** corresponds to 'mistake' only in the sense of 'misunderstanding', 'misconception', 'mistaken judgment', i.e. which is confined to the mind, not embodied in something done or made.[3,4]

Die Übersetzung hat zu viele Fehler.
Sie machen beim Sprechen zu viele grobe Fehler.
Diese Annahme war ein Irrtum meinerseits.

MIX, MINGLE, BLEND 1. **Mischen** generally means 'to mix' elements in such a way that they are indistinguishable in the product. It thus corresponds to 'mix' rather than to 'mingle', and is applied characteristically to liquids, colours, and substances which can merge by the addition of liquid.

It is, however, also applied to substances such as ingredients of food dishes (e.g. a salad) which do not lose their identity though they are meant to form a harmonious whole. With reference to the act of mixing such ingredients, *zusammenmischen* is common.[5]

It is applied to feelings, though less frequently than *vermischen*.

In the sense of mixing with people, it is used of mixing with a crowd and of mixing or mingling races, but not of association with individuals in society.

The past participle occurs in a number of fixed expressions (see dictionaries).

Wein und (or: *mit*) *Wasser mischen.*
Mischen Sie die Farben gut.
Ich habe den Salat ordentlich gemischt.

[1] 'Error' expresses a more severe criticism than 'mistake .

[2] *Fehler* is also a positive fault or flaw in a person or a thing with regard to right and wrong. *Mangel* is a deficiency, an absence of something, but also a visible flaw, blemish, in an aesthetic sense.

[3] *Versehen* is a petty mistake, an oversight, a slip due to inadvertence. *Aus Versehen* =by mistake. *Mißgriff* and *Fehlgriff* are mistakes in doing a thing as the result of an error in judgment.

[4] 'To make a mistake, to be mistaken', in the sense of 'to be the victim of a delusion', is generally *sich täuschen*. See 'deceive'.

[5] With cocktails: *mixen*.

Er hat sich unter die Menge gemischt.
Die beiden Völker haben sich gemischt.
Gemischte Gefühle.

2. **Vermischen.**

Ver suggests completeness in the result, often shown by the addition of some adverb such as *gut* or *stark*. Sometimes a deliberate, careful process is suggested, sometimes the sense is pejorative (e.g. to confuse ideas). It is applied to liquids, to metals, to feelings, to the mixing of races, to the confusing of ideas. The past participle used adjectivally means 'miscellaneous'.

Wasser und Öl vermischen (or: *mischen*) *sich nicht* (given by Duden).
Vermischen Sie diese Farben gut.
'*Das Märchen des Frühlings...vermischte sich mit dem Zauber der heiligen Legende von Jesus*' (Hauptmann, *Der Narr in Christo*).
'*Wie im deutschen Geistesleben überhaupt die Empfindsamkeit zwei ganz verschiedene Ströme hatte, die sich indessen bald vermischten und vereinigten, nämlich das beseelte Christentum und die humanisierte Natur...*' (Gundolf, *Goethe*).
'*...so war der Schmerz in jeder Menschenbrust mit so vieler süßer Lust vermischt, daß...*' (Kleist, *Das Erdbeben in Chili*).
Diese Völker sind stark vermischt.
Sie haben diese beiden Begriffe ganz und gar vermischt.

3. **Mengen** generally means 'to combine' things so that they remain distinguishable in the result, and is therefore mostly applied to solid substances, or at least to one substance which is kneaded with liquid. In poetry it is sometimes applied solely to liquids. It also means 'to confuse', 'to mix up'; and further (in the reflexive) 'to mix' among a crowd (but in the latter sense is less common than *mischen*).

Vermengen has intensive force, is often used with *stark*, etc. and is applied to the mixing of solid substances and to the confusing of ideas.

Neither verb is used as commonly as *mischen* and *vermischen*.

Sie mengte die verschiedenen Ingredienzien in einem Topf.
Er hat die beiden Begriffe vermengt.

4. In the sense of 'associate with': **verkehren.**

Er verkehrt in guter Gesellschaft.

5. In the sense of 'to be involved' (i.e. mixed up in, with): **verwickelt sein.**

Er ist in die Angelegenheit verwickelt.

MOVE[1] **A.** To be, to set in motion as opposed to a state of rest.

1. Sich bewegen.

The character of the movement suggested by *bewegen* is that it is round about, to and fro, i.e. it does not indicate primarily a change of position towards a destination, whether this be remote or close at hand. This characteristic can imply sustained motion, but does not exclude a single movement. Applied to a person it denotes only physical movement of the limbs without secondary associations (contrast *rühren*). From this fundamental meaning arises that of taking physical exercises, which may be confined to the movement of the limbs without change of position or include such exercises as marching, running about. To give *bewegen* the sense of 'move' care should be taken that the context excludes that of 'exercise'. (Note also *sich Bewegung machen*, to take exercise).

In its application to persons, whether reflexive or with a part of the body as object it therefore means (i) positively: to move the body or a part of it about; (ii) negatively: not to move so much as a muscle. When the object is a person other than the subject, *bewegen* is mostly combined with *von der Stelle* (see **B**).

Ich kann mich nicht bewegen (I am paralysed or bound, and in the idiomatic sense of *gauche* in society).

Ich kann den Arm jetzt wieder bewegen.

Seine Lippen bewegten sich kaum.

Bewegen Sie sich (move your limbs to show that they are capable of movement, contrast *rühren*).

Bewegen Sie sich nicht (don't move even a muscle, e.g. when being photographed).

2. *Bewegen* can be accompanied by a phrase denoting direction (to or from), destination, provided the manner of the movement is stated or clearly implied. It is never the equivalent of 'go' when the manner of going is not specified (contrast **A, 6**). *Bewegen* rarely suggests a straight line, but rather 'hither and thither'. In reference to means of transport

[1] 'To move emotionally' is *bewegen* when the emotion is strong (*der Tod ihrer Mutter hat sie sehr bewegt*; *der Entschluß, die Nachricht, die Aufführung hat mich bewegt*; *ich war gradezu bewegt*). *Bewegen* cannot, however, be used in this sense in the present participle (use *ergreifend, erregend*). For the gentler emotions (e.g. tenderness, melancholy) *rühren* is used. In other figurative uses *bewegen* suggests turbulence (e.g. *ein bewegtes Meer, bewegte Zeiten*). To move to a decision, i.e. 'to induce' is *bewegen* conjugated as a strong verb.

'To move' in the sense of 'to force (someone) to abandon a position, an attitude', 'to yield', can only be translated by *bewegen* in the combinations *zu bewegen sein, sich bewegen lassen. Er war durch Drohungen nicht zu bewegen. Er ließ sich durch Drohungen nicht bewegen* (I, they, etc., could not move him by threats).

it can be applied only to boats (i.e. not with trains, cars; see section **A, 6**).

Das Schiff bewegte sich langsam aus dem Hafen.
Langsam bewegte sie sich von mir fort.
Nur mit Schwierigkeit konnte er sich von der Stelle fortbewegen, die unter feindlichem Feuer lag.
Tanzend, mit leichten Schritten, bewegte sie sich von der Bühne weg.
Sie bot ein liebliches Bild, wie sie sich zwischen den Blumen bewegte.
In voller Natürlichkeit (ganz ungezwungen) bewegte sich die Königin unter ihren Gästen.
Die Menge der Streikenden bewegte sich unruhig auf den Straßen hin und her.
Der Trauerzug bewegte sich zum Friedhof.
Die Herde bewegte sich in der Richtung auf den Fluß.

3. A special application of this fundamental sense of *bewegen* is 'to make go, run' (i.e. to keep in motion) of machinery, a boat.[1] The subject can only be the force that provides the impetus, not a person.

Die Elektrizität bewegt die Maschine.
Der Wind bewegt das Boot.
Die Uhr wird durch eine Feder bewegt.

4. *Sich bewegen* is used in the figurative sense of 'live, have one's being' in a certain sphere. Distinguish from the sense of 'move' explained in **A, 2** and in the last example of **A, 6**.

Er bewegt sich viel in musikalischen (politischen) Kreisen.

5. **Rühren** can suggest not only physical movement of the body, but also any activity that may accompany it, and furthermore a change of place. This is its meaning when applied to persons, whether used reflexively or with a part of the body as object, whereas *bewegen* is primarily limited to physical movement of the limbs without a change of place. In the positive the sense is predominantly 'to bestir oneself' (*rührt euch!* = 'bestir yourselves' or 'stand at ease'; *er will keinen Finger rühren* = he won't lift a finger, do a tap of work). The negative means 'not to change one's position and at the same time to remain inactive'.

Rühren (with or without *von der Stelle*) is not used transitively with a personal object other than the reflexive pronoun in the sense of 'move'.

Der Dieb sagte: 'Rühren Sie sich nicht, oder ich schieße.'
Ich konnte kein Glied rühren.

[1] In this sense *bewegen* means 'to keep a thing moving'. *In Bewegung setzen* (or stressing the change from absolute rest: *versetzen*) is 'to set moving'.

When the object is not a person or a part of the body, but something in the world of nature, *rühren* in the sense of 'move' suggests greater freedom than *regen* (stir, i.e. the beginning of a movement), but less than *bewegen*.

Der Wind rührt die Blätter.
Es rührt sich kein Lüftchen (*bewegt* is impossible; *rührt* is here almost identical with *regt*).

6. To set in movement, to move about, without reference to the manner of movement.

In this case 'move' must be translated by the various German equivalents of 'go' (see article on 'go'). It occurs mainly in two types: (i) with reference to the means of locomotion; (ii) in the sense of 'to go, to walk about' amongst people.

Das Auto fährt sehr schnell.
Das Auto läuft schon.
Der Zug fährt (*geht*) *jetzt.*
Der König geht viel unter die Armen.

B. To move away, out of the way, the new position being unimportant and not mentioned. Specific terms (for some of them see **C**) are mainly used, the commonest being:

1. To get out of the way, of persons.

(a) Positive: *zur Seite treten, rücken, Platz machen, weitergehen* (move on), *verschwinden.*

Bitte, Platz machen.
Er trat beiseite, um mich vorbeigehen zu lassen.

(b) Negative.

Rühre dich nicht (don't change your position).
Bleiben Sie da (*sitzen*, etc.).

2. To move a thing out of the way.

(a) *Nehmen Sie Ihren Arm, den Stuhl, weg.*

(b) To move a little: *zur Seite* (*weg*) *schieben, rücken* (see **C**).

Rücken Sie den Schrank von der Wand weg.
Schieben Sie den Tisch zur Seite.

3. To budge, to make budge: (*sich*) (*von der Stelle*) *bewegen, rühren, rücken, kommen.*

Drei Krankenschwestern waren nötig, um ihn von der Stelle zu bewegen.
Das Auto, rührt (*bewegt*) *sich nicht* (*von der Stelle*).
Wir versuchten, den Stein fortzurollen, aber er rührte, bewegte, sich nicht.

C. To change position, posture, place, abode, the destination being mentioned or clearly implied.

The most general terms are the German equivalents of 'take' and 'put', which must be used when the more specific terms are inapplicable. The verbs compounded with *ver* denote a change of position (transfer), those with *um* either a change or interchange, rearrangement, generally in a confined space, e.g. a room, *ver* suggesting a wider area.

(a) Verbs meaning 'take' and 'put' (see articles on these words). All these verbs, with the exception of *bringen*, suggest that the object moved is either in one's hands, arms, or near by, and that it is moved only a short distance. The destination must be stated, unless some adverb such as *weg* (see **B**) is added.

Ich trug die Pakete auf den Stuhl (or *legte, tat*).
Ich tat meinen Regenschirm in die Ecke.
Tragen Sie den Kohlenkasten auf die andere Seite des Kamins.
Wir brachten unsere Möbel in die neue Wohnung.

(b) **Verlegen** (transfer) often suggests the moving of things which consist of a number of units (e.g. complex masses), also the transfer of one's official abode or the seat of one's activities. The destination need not be stated.

Die Geschäftsführung hat ihre Verwaltungsräume in ein anderes Stadtviertel verlegt.
Die Betriebsverwaltung ist in andere Räume verlegt worden.
Die Hälfte der fünften Armee ist an eine andere Front verlegt worden.
Das Lager ist verlegt worden.
Die Ostgrenze Deutschlands ist an die Oder verlegt worden.
Die Universität wurde während des Krieges nach einer Kleinstadt verlegt.

(c) **Versetzen** frequently refers to the transferring of a person from one place to another where he will carry on the same work or occupation and to the promotion of school children. It can also denote the transposing of things in a pattern and the moving of things to another fixed position (e.g. plants). The destination need not be stated.

Der Gesandte, der Lehrer, wurde nach Berlin versetzt.
Die Bäume müssen versetzt werden, bevor sie höher wachsen.
Der Grenzstein ist versetzt worden.

(d) **Verpflanzen:** to move plants and the like, to uproot people and settle them elsewhere. The destination need not be mentioned.

Wir müssen die Lilien an einen kühlen Ort verpflanzen.
Unzählige Menschen wurden während des Krieges (nach fremden Ländern) verpflanzt.

(e) **Verrücken:** (i) to move a thing elsewhere by stages (see *rücken*), particularly things which have to be moved in parts. It points to the result, i.e. the new position, while *rücken* denotes the action of moving. (ii) Since the new position can be desired or otherwise, *verrücken* can also mean 'displace', 'disarrange'. The past participle should be used warily because of its frequent use in the sense of 'crazy'. The destination need not be mentioned.

Da wir ein neues Stück Land gekauft haben, müssen wir den Zaun etwas verrücken.
Verrücken Sie nichts.

(f) **Verschieben:** to move masses of people, complex or heavy things.

Juden sind während des Krieges massenhaft nach Polen verschoben worden.
Wir haben den Schrank, das Sofa, ein bißchen verschoben.
Die Grenze ist 100 *Kilometer nach Westen verschoben worden.*

(g) **Verstellen:** to move objects that are thought of as standing.

Einen Zaun, die Kulissen verstellen.
Sie haben überall die Möbel verstellt (e.g. in the house, i.e. over a wider area than *umstellen*).
Sie haben das Schilderhaus verstellt.

(h) Verbs compounded with *um* mostly denote a rearrangement, an interchange of position in some pattern which can be surveyed, whereas those with *ver* suggest no arrangement.

Wir sollten die Möbel in diesem Zimmer umstellen.
Legen Sie den Schlauch um.
Die Bilder wurden in dem Museum umgehängt.
Die Klasse wurde in ein anderes Zimmer umquartiert.

(i) **Rücken** (transitive and intransitive): to move gradually or in short stages (*der Ruck*=jerk). It is used characteristically of furniture, which must be moved in this way, or of things set in some order (e.g. words). In intransitive use it generally suggests movement to a fixed position within some formation or scheme (e.g. in a row), a sudden step in some direction or the marching of troops (i.e. as a stage of a march). It must be followed by a phrase denoting destination, or *weg, fort.*

Er rückte seinen Stuhl an den Tisch heran.
Rücken Sie den Schrank in die Ecke.
Rücken Sie bitte eins weiter.
Rücken Sie hier (in diese Reihe) ein.
Er rückte an die Wand, einen Schritt zur Seite.
Die Truppen rücken in die Stadt.

Der Uhrzeiger rückt vorwärts.
Rücken Sie diesen Ausdruck an den Anfang des Satzes (*stellen* would not clearly indicate a change of position).

(j) **Ziehen** in intransitive use suggests a long line (from the idea of drawing denoted by its literal transitive sense). Unlike *bewegen* it can imply speed and conveys the idea of passing on, even wandering, without interruption, to some distant destination. It is used widely with persons or natural phenomena. It also means 'to move one's place of abode', the compounds *ein-*, *aus-*, *umziehen* (used intransitively) being the normal terms for moving oneself and one's goods from one dwelling to another.

Das Heer zog über den Fluß in, durch, die Stadt.
Die Burschen zogen an dem Wirtshaus vorbei.
Die Schafe zogen über das Feld.
Die Vögel ziehen im Winter nach wärmeren Ländern.
Die Wolken ziehen über den Himmel.
Der Nebel zieht nach Westen.
Die französische Regierung zog nach Bordeaux, als die Deutschen in Paris einbrachen.
Sie sind in eine ganz neue Wohnung eingezogen.

(k) **Schaffen** (when conjugated as a weak verb) can mean 'to cause something to be done or to be made available'. The sense of 'move' is an extension of this causative use and comes closest to 'get', thus applied. The overcoming of some difficulty, sometimes by quick or rough means, or the remedying of a situation, the averting of a danger is often implied. The act of moving itself may involve difficulty. It is frequently combined with *zur Stelle* and *aus dem Wege*.

Schaffen Sie das brennende Holz weg.
Wir müssen die Urkunden an irgend einen sicheren Ort schaffen.
Wir haben unsere Möbel noch nicht in die neue Wohnung geschafft.
Wollen Sie bitte mein Gepäck in das nächste Abteil schaffen?
Schaffen Sie den Schlauch nach hinten.

(l) **Schieben** can translate 'move' in the sense of 'push' or 'shove'. It is also the correct term (not colloquial like 'push' or 'shove') for moving masses of people about.

Wir müssen das Klavier in das Wohnzimmer hinüberschieben.
Während des Krieges wurden Millionen von Menschen umhergeschoben.
Diese Truppen werden morgen näher an die Front geschoben.

MUCH, VERY MUCH **Sehr** refers to intensity, **viel** to quantity, frequency.

Meine sehr geliebte Mutter (I love her deeply).
Meine vielgeliebte Mutter (many people love her).
Er hat sich sehr getäuscht (a serious mistake).
Er hat sich viel getäuscht (often).
Das wird sehr bewundert.
Das wird viel bewundert.

MURDER 1. **Ermorden** is the normal equivalent of 'murder' used transitively and in its literal sense.

Er hat ihn ermordet.

2. **Morden** is used in several ways: (*a*) Intransitively in the literal sense. (*b*) Sometimes in the literal sense with a direct object such as *niemand*, this being practically equivalent to the intransitive use with *nicht*, and in the sense of murdering on a large scale. (*c*) Poetically for *ermorden*. (*d*) In the sense of 'to murder a person indirectly' by one's behaviour towards him, not by direct action. (*e*) Figuratively.

Sie plündern und morden überall.
'*Wir haben niemand gemordet*' (Martin Niemöller, *Deutsche Blätter*).
Frauen und Kinder sind gemordet worden (on a vast scale).
'*Nicht Ihr habt ihn gemordet! Andre taten's*' (Kennedy to Maria; Schiller, *Maria Stuart*).
Du mordest mich noch mit der Geschichte.
Er hat sie durch sein Verhalten gemordet.
Mordet die Unschuld nicht (poetic, figurative diction).

NARROW 1. **Schmal** in its literal sense means 'of small width in proportion to length'.

Ein schmaler Weg, ein schmales Tal.

2. **Eng** means both literally and figuratively 'confined', i.e. without particular reference to any dimension, though the object so described may be of small width.[1]

Der Weg ist hier sehr eng.
Ein enges Tal.
Im engeren Sinne des Wortes.

3. **Knapp** means 'with little margin'.

Eine knappe Mehrheit.
Mit knapper Not entkommen.

[1] In the sense of 'confined', 'cramping' or 'cramped', *eng* also translates 'tight' (e.g. *die Schuhe sind mir zu eng*), 'close' (e.g. *er schreibt sehr eng*), 'poky' (e.g. *ein enges Zimmer*).

4. In the sense of 'illiberal', *engherzig, engstirnig, beschränkt, begrenzt* (see 'limit') must be used.

Ein engherziger, beschränkter, Mann.

NATURE 1. **Natur** is ascribed (*a*) to what is animate (e.g. human beings, animals, vegetation) and to things in so far as they are thought of in relation to what is animate (i.e. unlike the English 'nature', not in relation to their purely physical structure or properties). The term denotes qualities, characteristics, character and is applied to persons in the sense of the character they possess. (*b*) It is used to refer to the phenomena of the material world as a whole and to the physical power which produces this world (i.e. nature). (*c*) It denotes what is unspoilt in contrast to the artificial products of civilization (e.g. in the state of nature; back to Nature!).

Es widerspricht der menschlichen Natur.
Er ist eine robuste, gesunde, faustische, Natur.
Er ist von Natur aus grausam.
Die Liebe ist von Natur aus eifersüchtig.
Es liegt in der Natur der Dinge, daß der Mensch ewig unbefriedigt ist.
Es lag in der Natur des römischen Reiches, daß er früher oder später zusammenbrechen mußte.
Er liebt die Natur.
Die Natur ist weich und lieblich in diesem Tal.
Der unerschöpfliche Schoß der Natur.
Naturvölker (i.e. not *Kulturvölker*).
Zurück zur Natur!

2. In the sense 1 (*a*) *Natur* must be distinguished from **Wesen**. The latter means 'being',[1] 'essence' (from Latin *esse*, to be) and refers to the inner, particularly spiritual, principle of things.[2] Thus: *das Wesen der Planwirtschaft*; *das Wesen der Einbildungskraft*. *Natur*, on the other hand, refers more to the character of a thing as it manifests itself externally, as it functions.

Es liegt im Wesen der westlichen Kultur, daß sie die Freiheit des Menschen achtet.
Es liegt in der Natur der westlichen Kultur, daß sie eine Beschneidung der menschlichen Freiheit nicht dulden kann.
Es liegt in der Natur des Krieges, Länder zu zerstören, die Menschen grausam zu machen.
Das Wesen des Krieges hat niemand bis jetzt verstanden.

[1] *Wesen* also means 'being' in the sense of 'person'. *Ein armseliges Wesen. Alle Wesen* can mean 'all creation, all created things'.

[2] It can, however, refer also to the way a person expresses, conducts, himself. *Sein Wesen ist mir unangenehm. Sein unberechenbares Wesen.*

3. In reference to an analysis of the physical structure or elements of a thing only **Beschaffenheit** (i.e. the way a thing is created, made) can be used.

Die Beschaffenheit des Bodens, des Klimas, des menschlichen Gehirns.

4. In the sense of 'kind' *Natur* can only be used when it itself is in the genitive case and accompanied by an adjective, otherwise **Art**[1] must be used.

Dinge so grauenhafter Natur haben sich ereignet, daß wir sie uns kaum vorstellen können.

Nach der Art des Verbrechens zu urteilen, muß ein Irrsinniger es begangen haben.

NECESSARY 1. **Nötig:** necessary in a subjective sense, for some personal purpose, which may even be an arbitrary one.

Ihre Hilfe ist garnicht nötig, ich kann nämlich das Fenster selbst aufmachen.

Es ist nötig, den Treffpunkt klar zu bestimmen, wenn Sie ihn nicht verfehlen wollen.

2. **Notwendig.**

(a) Necessary in the nature of things.

Es ist notwendig, daß der Mensch sich dauernd wandelt (otherwise he would not be man).

(b) Necessary in an objective sense, though not in the nature of things. In this sense it is often used indiscriminately with *nötig*.

Dieses Gesetz ist unbedingt notwendig in solchen Zeiten.

NEED, NECESSITY 1. **Not:** 'need' in the sense of 'distress, want'. It means 'need for something to be done' only in the expression *not tun*. This can be followed by a *daß* clause, but not by a genitive or prepositional phrase.

Sie haben ihm in seiner Not beigestanden.

Sie hat große Not gelitten.

Vorsicht tut hier not (elevated diction).

2. **Notwendigkeit** means (*a*) the power, both material and moral, which acts as compulsion; (*b*) imperative need. It thus corresponds to 'necessity', never to 'need'. It is used in the same formal combinations as

[1] See 'kind'.

'necessity', not as 'need', e.g. a following genitive denotes the thing necessary, not the person on whom the necessity is imposed.

Die Macht der Notwendigkeit.
Die Notwendigkeit seines Todes.
Es besteht immer noch die Notwendigkeit, eine sichere Grundlage für den Frieden zu finden.
Der sibirische Winter macht warme Kleidung zur absoluten Notwendigkeit.
Es besteht gar keine Notwendigkeit für Sie, heute in die Stadt zu gehen.
Die Notwendigkeit dieser Maßnahmen sieht er jetzt ein.
Er betrachtet es als eine Notwendigkeit, Lebensmittel nach dem hungernden Europa zu schicken.

3. **Bedürfnis** is a subjectively felt want, desire, whether physical, emotional, or intellectual, for something, not an objective necessity. It is followed characteristically by *nach* (=for).

Er hat ein starkes Bedürfnis nach Ruhe.
Ich verstehe sein Bedürfnis nach solcher Lektüre nicht.
Seine Bedürfnisse sind unersättlich.

4. **Bedarf** (without plural): need or needs for material things, particularly in the economic sense of 'demand'.

Unser Bedarf ist nicht gedeckt.
Der Bedarf an Lebensmitteln ist sehr stark.
Bürobedarf.

5. It will be seen that apart from the terms explained under 1, 2, 4, German has no word for 'need'. This means that many uses of 'need', particularly in fixed expressions such as 'to be in need of', 'to have need of', 'there is (no) need of (to)' must be translated by such phrases as *nötig haben; nötig, notwendig sein; brauchen; benötigen; müssen.* The phrase 'in need of' can sometimes be rendered by a compound, the second part being *bedürftig* (e.g. *reparaturbedürftig, ruhebedürftig*). If a sentence such as 'the need of teachers to read widely' is rendered by *die Notwendigkeit für Lehrer, gut belesen zu sein,* 'necessity' rather than 'need' has been translated.

NOTICE (verb)[1] 1. **Merken** suggests alertness of the senses, that the mental realization comes immediately through these, i.e. without reflection. It is therefore the only term that can be applied to animals.

[1] *Auffallen,* to strike, to attract attention, is widely used as a close synonym of 'notice', and approximates more to *merken* than to *bemerken. Ist Ihnen etwas Sonderbares an ihm aufgefallen?*

Negatively, it implies that one is not sufficiently alert to notice what is obvious.[1]

Since it so strongly suggests the activity of the senses, a word denoting a smell can be the object. On the other hand, the object cannot be a person.

In general, only *merken* is possible when 'notice' is followed by 'from'.[2]

Heute nacht waren Einbrecher bei uns im Haus, und wir haben nichts gemerkt.

Obgleich der Mann eine Stunde bei mir war, habe ich nicht gemerkt, daß er ein Snob ist.

Ich trat ins Zimmer und merkte sofort, daß die Möbel umgestellt waren.

Er merkte nicht, daß er seinen Geldbeutel hatte fallen lassen.

Haben Sie gemerkt, daß er schielt?

Ich merkte an seinem Gesichtsausdruck, daß er einen Schreck gekriegt hatte.

Haben Sie gemerkt, daß er hinkt?

'*Überall merkt man die zufallsfeindliche Gesinnung, deren dichtester Ausdruck "Die Wahlverwandtschaften" sind*' (Gundolf, *Goethe*).

'*Engel nicht, Menschen nicht,*
Und die findigen Tiere merken es schon,
daß wir nicht sehr verläßlich zu Haus sind
in der gedeuteten Welt.' (Rilke, *Duineser Elegie I.*)

Ich merkte einen üblen Geruch.

2. Bemerken[3] is less vivid and sensuous than *merken*. It implies mental activity, however brief, after the sense perception, and an inference from the sense material, the meaning of which is not immediately obvious. The observation is therefore more subtle than with *merken*.

A personal object may follow, but only to indicate that something special, noteworthy, attaches to the presence of a person in a certain place.[4] A smell cannot be the object.

Bemerken cannot be used in the imperative.

Ich habe nicht bemerkt, daß er ein Snob ist.

Ich glaubte zu bemerken, daß die Möbel umgestellt waren.

[1] *Sich etwas merken* means 'to note a thing', i.e. to record it in one's memory.

[2] But compare the following from Goethe's *Werthers Leiden*: '*Was mich am meisten betrübte, war, daß ich an seinen Gesichtszügen zu bemerken schien, es sei mehr Eigensinn und übler Humor als Eingeschränktheit des Verstandes, der ihn sich mitzuteilen hinderte.*' If *merken* were used, *schien* would contradict the force and directness of the impression it should convey.

[3] *Bemerken* also means 'to remark', i.e. to say something.

[4] Otherwise *sehen* should be used.

NOTICE

Ich habe oft bemerkt, daß Vorträge in diesem Saal gehalten werden.
Haben Sie seinen Gesichtsausdruck bemerkt?
Haben Sie bemerkt, daß er hinkt?
Unter den Anwesenden bemerkten wir den Präsidenten.
Zufällig habe ich ihn im Theater bemerkt (but: *ich habe ihn im Theater gesehen*).

3. **Spüren:** to feel bodily sensations, atmospheres, to detect a smell. See 'feel'.

Ich habe einen üblen Geruch gespürt.
Ich spüre Schmerzen im linken Arm.
Ich spürte sofort die Feindlichkeit der Atmosphäre, als ich in den Raum trat.

NOW (in temporal sense) 1. **Jetzt** means 'at this moment', without reference to any other unless it be as contrast. It can, however, refer to the immediate past and the immediate future in so far as these are felt to be present. It is emphatic.

It can be preceded by prepositions, e.g. *bis jetzt, von jetzt an.*

Jetzt ist der Augenblick gekommen, wo wir uns verabschieden müssen.
Soll ich es jetzt oder später tun?
Jetzt müssen Sie aber gehen.
Er war eben jetzt hier (just now, i.e. the immediate past).
Er wird jetzt gleich kommen (the immediate future).

2. **Nun** expresses a relation of the present to what precedes and views the present as the result of a development. It is therefore less emphatic than *jetzt*, and tends to combine the idea of 'so', 'accordingly' with its time sense. At times it is no more than a vague connecting link (e.g. *es gibt nun verschiedene Gründe dafür*).

It can be preceded by prepositions, though not by *bis* (e.g. *von nun an*).

Er ist nun endlich gekommen.
Siehst du nun ein, wie schwierig die Aufgabe ist?
Es wird nun allmählich Zeit, daß wir gehen.
Wir können uns nun etwas Ruhe gönnen (combines the idea 'that being so' with the temporal sense).

3. **Nunmehr** is used in the sense of 'now' decisively, without possibility of return to the previous state of affairs. *Nun* can be substituted, but without expressing the idea as definitely.

Nach all dem bleibt uns nunmehr keine andere Wahl.
Die Gefahr ist nunmehr vorüber.

NUMBER 1. **Zahl** means a 'definite or fairly definite number'. It must be used when the number is stated, and may be used when preceded by the definite article and followed by the genitive.

Wir waren drei an der Zahl.
Die Zahl der Teilnehmer ist sehr beschränkt.

2. **Anzahl** means an 'indefinite number'. It must be used when preceded by the indefinite article and followed by the genitive, and may be used when preceded by the definite article and followed by the genitive.

Eine, die, große Anzahl von Büchern.

3. **Nummer:** a number in a series.

Die Nummer des Hauses, des Regiments.
Welche Nummer haben Sie gewählt?

OBJECT, OBJECTION, PROTEST 1. A stated, formulated objection.

(a) **Einwand** is a general objection to a matter as a whole, **Einwendung** to a specific point. The distinction is often ignored. Combined with *machen* and *erheben* (*Einwendung* generally only with *machen*) they translate 'to object'. They are rarely used in the first person, present tense (i.e. they do not translate 'I object').

Er erhob Einwände gegen den Plan.
Was für Einwendungen hat er gegen den Plan gemacht?
Das sind keine stichhaltigen Einwendungen.
Es ist bei ihm zur Gewohnheit geworden, Einwände zu erheben.

(b) **Einspruch** is a stated, formal objection or protest made during discussion. It is generally combined with *erheben*. It translates 'I object' in this formal sense.

Ich erhebe Einspruch gegen den Vorschlag, gegen seine Ernennung.

(c) **Einwenden:** to object in the sense of (a). It is followed by a *daß* clause, or by an indefinite pronoun (e.g. *vieles, nichts*). It is rare in the first person present tense.

Ich wandte (dagegen) ein, daß er die nötigen Schritte noch nicht getan habe.

(d) **Sich etwas verbitten:** to object in a subjective way, to resent something felt to be offensive. It translates 'I object'.

Ich verbitte mir eine solche Bemerkung.

(e) **Sich verwahren** denotes an objective objection. It translates 'I object', 'I protest'.

Ich verwahre mich gegen Ihr Benehmen.

2. An unstated objection which approximates to a mere feeling.

(a) **Was, etwas, vieles, nichts, (einzuwenden) haben gegen....**
These expressions are used in this weaker sense of 'object', i.e. 'to mind'. The addition of *einzuwenden* suggests a more serious context and more reasoned objections.

Was haben Sie dagegen, gegen ihn? (what's your objection to...?)
Haben Sie etwas dagegen, daß ich das Fenster aufmache?
Ich habe nichts dagegen, daß er hier übernachtet.
Ich habe nichts dagegen einzuwenden, daß Sie das Geld so anlegen.
Es ist nichts dagegen einzuwenden (there is no objection to it).

(b) **Gegen sein:** to be opposed, averse, to. It is common as a translation of 'object' in conjunction with 'why'.

Warum sind Sie gegen den Verkauf des Autos?

3. When 'objection' denotes an emotional reaction rather than a reasoned argument, German uses terms such as *Abneigung* (dislike, aversion).

Ich habe eine eingewurzelte Abneigung gegen diesen Baustil.

4. Followed by the gerund, the implied subject being the same as that of the object (e.g. I object to doing it). This use can only be translated by a paraphrase, as the following suggestions show.

Ich bin nicht gesonnen, ich weigere mich, mir das noch länger anzuhören (I object to listening...).
Ich lasse mich doch nicht so behandeln (I object to being treated like that).

OCCUR **Vorkommen** can only be applied to things or acts which are conceived as instances or cases of a species,[1] i.e. not simply as an equivalent of 'happen'. For the latter see 'event'.

Solche Fehler kommen häufig vor.
So etwas ist hier nie vorgekommen.
Das darf nicht wieder vorkommen.

OFFER 1. With a noun object.

(a) **Anbieten** carries the implication of handing a thing over to a person as a conscious act, sometimes with the idea of pressing it on the person. The object may also be a noun denoting an action that one intends to

[1] The addition of *mir* means: as far as my experience goes. *So etwas ist mir nie vorgekommen*: I have never known, heard of, such a thing. It can also give *vorkommen* the meaning of 'seem'.

perform for the person in question. The subject is a person or something which stands for a person. The intended receiver must be mentioned (in the dative case).

Sie bot mir eine Tasse Tee an.
Ich bot ihm meine Hilfe an.
Die Universität Berlin bietet ausländischen Studenten größere Vorteile als Jena an (the suggestion is that Berlin takes active steps to attract such students).

(b) **Bieten** in its commonest use suggests not a conscious act of offering, but that what is offered is simply available. A frequent synonym is 'present'. The subject here is generally not a person. When the subject is a person, the object is generally a part of the body (e.g. *Arm, Hand*).[1]

Der Hügel bietet einen weiten Blick über die Stadt.
Die Universität Berlin bietet ausländischen Studenten größere Vorteile als Jena (the advantages are there, without any suggestion that the university authorities take steps to bring them before the notice of such students).
Er bot ihr seinen Arm.

2. With a following infinitive.
Anbieten refers to ordinary acts or to contracts. **Sich erbieten:** to volunteer in bigger matters.

Ich habe ihm angeboten, den Brief für ihn zu übersetzen.
Er hat uns angeboten, unseren Wagen für 2000 Mark zu kaufen.
Sie hat sich erboten, die Diphtheriekranken zu pflegen.

ONLY (adverb) The uses treated refer to time, number, or quantity.
Erst[2] in reference to numbers or quantity implies that more are to come. **Nur** means 'not more' or 'not other than' that indicated, and makes no reference to anything outside this. Applied to a point of time *erst* means 'not before', *nur*, 'on that occasion only'.

Der Junge ist erst 10 Jahre alt, erwarte nicht zu viel von ihm.
Von einem Jungen, der nur 10 Jahre alt ist, kann man nicht zu viel erwarten.
Erst drei Schiffe haben den Hafen verlassen.
Nur drei Schiffe haben den Hafen verlassen.
Ich bin erst am 22. September nach Berlin gefahren.
Ich bin nur am 22. September nach Berlin gefahren.

[1] *Bieten* is also 'to bid' at an auction.
[2] See also 'first'.

OPEN (verb)[1] 1. **Aufmachen** is the general prose term which translates 'open' in its literal sense.[2] In particular, it is applied to small things, and without any suggestion beyond the action of opening itself. It is also the familiar term for opening a small business.

Das Fenster, die Tür, die Kiste, die Schublade, den Brief, den Mund, die Augen, aufmachen.
Er hat ein kleines Geschäft in der Nähe aufgemacht.

2. **Auftun** is used only in more elevated diction. It implies the opening of something inward through externals, and so is not normally applied to inanimate objects. It thus easily passes over into figurative use.[3]

Die Augen, die Lippen, auftun.
'*Gleichwie in Wollust und kaltem Entsetzen waren die Münder weit aufgetan*' (Gerhart Hauptmann, *Der Narr in Christo*).
Die Blumen tun sich am Morgen auf.
Das Erlebnis hat ihm Herz und Sinne aufgetan.

3. **Öffnen** is mostly a literary term. It is, however, still the preferred term in reference to the opening of something big, particularly when associated with the idea of some ensuing activity. Applied to small things it is affected or old-fashioned. It is the normal term for 'to be open' in reference to a public building.

Er öffnete feierlich das Testament.
Die Türen der Halle werden um 8 Uhr geöffnet.
Die Bank ist von 10 bis 3 Uhr geöffnet.

4. **Eröffnen:** (*a*) to start an activity, proceedings; (*b*) to establish a business or an institution of some size.

Die Sitzung wurde um 3 Uhr eröffnet.
Feindseligkeiten wurden plötzlich eröffnet.
Er hat ein neues Konto in dieser Bank eröffnet.
Er wird bald ein großes Warenhaus eröffnen.

5. **Aufschlagen** is used mainly in fixed phrases (e.g. *ein Buch, die Augen,* the latter only in elevated diction).

OPINION, VIEW, CONCEPTION 1. **Meinung** stresses the personal element and the possibility of error in the conclusion reached about a

[1] *Aufschließen*: unlock (*die Tür, sein Herz*). *Erschließen*: open up, in the sense of 'explore' (*das Innere Australiens*); make available for use (*einen neuen Markt*).

[2] To open a bottle: *entkorken.*

[3] Similarly *zumachen* is the general term for 'shut'. *Schließen* like *öffnen* is applied to bigger things. The past participle *geschlossen* is mostly used in the sense of 'firmly', 'permanently closed'.

matter. It is held sincerely and seriously, without thought of display. It cannot, however, unlike 'opinion', be applied to an expert judgment.

It can, on the other hand, be used, like 'opinion', in phrases meaning 'to esteem' (*eine hohe, schlechte, Meinung von jemand haben*), i.e. when a judgment of value about a person or his abilities and the like is implied, but not where a mere estimate of probabilities is meant (e.g. in the sentence: what's your opinion of his chances?).

Ist das Ihre Meinung?
Ich bin der Meinung, daß es keine Gefahr gibt.
Nach meiner Meinung müssen wir abwarten.
Ich bin ganz und gar Ihrer Meinung.
Er äußerte vorsichtig seine Meinung.
Er hat seine Meinung geändert.
Ich habe keine große Meinung von ihm, von seinem Talent.

2. **Gutachten** is an expert opinion of any kind, given professionally and used in a formal context. While it can be used in this way of a medical opinion, a term such as *Urteil* would be preferred in reference to the everyday relationship between doctor and patient.

Nach dem Gutachten eines Sachverständigen ist mein Auto 20 000 Mark wert.
Der Arzt gab ein Gutachten über die Gesundheit des Angeklagten ab.
Ich habe einige Gutachten über den Fall eingezogen.
Das Urteil des Arztes über die Möglichkeit einer völligen Wiederherstellung meiner Gesundheit ist günstig.

3. **Beurteilen** (see article on 'judge') refers to an estimate of probability and in this sense translates phrases such as: what is your opinion of...? See also *Urteil* in the previous section.[1]

Wie beurteilen Sie meine Chancen?

4. **Erachten** is only used in a few fixed phrases (*meines Erachtens, nach meinem Erachten*) and is apt to sound pretentious since it claims a thorough scrutiny of the grounds for an opinion.

5. **Ansicht** corresponds to only one meaning of 'view' as a synonym of 'opinion'. It cannot be used like the English term to denote a theory of a matter (e.g. Schiller's view of art). It suggests rather an attitude to, a judgment about, a thing, often in relation to something extraneous to it, than an understanding, a conception, of the matter itself. It is often superficial, particularly in the plural. The title of E. T. A. Hoffmann's novel *Die Lebensansichten des Kater Murr* is ironical. The singular

[1] See also *halten* under 'think'.

Ansicht refers to a specific question, not a whole field of knowledge for which the plural must be used.

'To take a view' cannot be translated literally. 'Hold' with 'view' is *haben.*

Was ist Ihre Ansicht über das Buch?
Nach meiner Ansicht kann der Plan nicht gelingen.
Die Ansicht der Kirche über Ehescheidung.
Der Mann hat merkwürdige Ansichten.
Er teilte mir seine Ansichten über die Demokratie mit.
Ich will keine Ansichten, sondern Begründungen hören.

6. **Anschauung** means 'view' in the sense of a 'conception' and can include a theory. This meaning is connected with other uses of the term: (i) contemplation in the sense of seeing into the inside of things; (ii) 'intuition' as a philosophical term (e.g. Fichte's '*intellektuelle Anschauung*'); (iii) experience of the concrete, the visible, mainly in fixed phrases (e.g. *Anschauungsunterricht; seine Sprache kommt aus der Anschauung*). In the sense of 'view' it suggests origin in the inner life, the workings of intuition on experience, although it does not exclude a certain amount of analytical thought. In strict use it is applied to the great spheres of knowledge and experience (e.g. life, art, love, and the like), but is also used loosely and popularly in much the same way as *Ansicht.*

Eine Lebensanschauung, Weltanschauung.
Schillers Kunstanschauung.
Ich teile diese Anschauung nicht.
Er hat komische Anschauungen.
Sag' mir mal ein bißchen deine Anschauungen darüber.

7. **Auffassung** approximates more closely to 'conception' than to 'view'. It denotes a personal way of conceiving, understanding, a matter,[1] particularly important spheres of knowledge, i.e. it is a way of understanding, taking the matter itself, not an attitude to it.[2]

Schillers Auffassung der Kunst.
Die Staatsauffassung der deutschen Romantik unterschied sich stark von der westlichen Demokratie.

ORDER Sense of 'command', 'instruct', 'bid'.

In this sense the verb of motion (e.g. go, come) may be omitted after 'order' if a phrase expressing destination follows (e.g. he was ordered to the front, to Paris, back). Of the German verbs treated in this article only *beordern, ausweisen* and *verweisen* dispense with the verb of motion.

[1] See *auffassen* under 'take'. [2] See also *Begriff* under 'idea'.

1. **Befehlen** should only be used when 'order' is practically interchangeable with 'command', to which it more closely approximates. It suggests the formal exercise of authority by virtue of an exalted position (e.g. a king, general, government, but not a parent or schoolteacher), and is only appropriate in reference to matters dealt with officially and solemnly by high personages. Its object may be the person commanded or the action to be performed.[1,2]

Der General befahl dem Heer, die Waffen zu strecken.
Die Regierung befahl, die Stadt zu räumen.
Der Richter befahl, den Gefangenen abzuführen.
Die Regierung befahl eine allgemeine Säuberungsaktion.

2. German has no exact term to translate 'order' used peremptorily and suggesting opposition or at least doubt as to whether compliance will follow. **Auffordern,** to call upon a person to do a thing, sometimes approximates to this sense. In addressing the person ordered, **verlangen** (followed by a *daß* clause) may be used (see 'ask' and footnote to 'anxious', p. 23, n. 1).

Er forderte den Dieb auf, stehen zu bleiben.
Die Festung wurde zur Übergabe aufgefordert.
Ich verlange, daß Sie das Zimmer aufräumen.

3. To instruct, direct, bid.[3,4]

(a) **Anordnen** is used of the orders given by persons possessed of official authority and tends to refer to actions carried out by a number of people. The object can only be the action performed, expressed by a clause, an infinitive or a noun, i.e. it cannot be the persons required to act. It approaches the meaning of 'decree' (*verfügen, bestimmen*).

Die Regierung ordnete an, daß die Streikenden zur Arbeit zurückkehren sollten.
Der Gewerkschaftsführer ordnete einen Streik an.

(b) **Anweisen** corresponds exactly to 'instruct', and must be used to translate 'order' when the two are close equivalents.

Sie werden hiermit angewiesen, sich alle 14 Tage bei der Polizei zu melden.

[1] *Befehlen* is also used as a polite or deferential term, mostly in fixed expressions. See dictionaries.

[2] *Gebieten* is used in the sense of 'command', 'enjoin' in lofty contexts. It suggests that refusal is impossible.

[3] *Lassen* (see 'make') may also be used in this sense. In the past tense it means that the order was obeyed. *Der Lehrer ließ das Kind in der Ecke stehen. Laß die Pferde satteln.*

[4] *Heißen,* to bid, suggests that the order is given orally. It can be more familiar than 'bid'.

(c) **Beordern:** to order a person to proceed to a place in an official capacity. The verb of motion is omitted.

Der Gesandte wurde nach Hause, an den Hof des Königs, beordert.

(d) **Auferlegen,** to impose, is used as a legal term in the sense of 'to order to pay'.

Ihm wird auferlegt, die Kosten zu zahlen.

4. Sense of 'prescribe' (medically).

(a) **Vorschreiben** suggests the prescription (often in writing) of the details of a course of action.

Der Arzt schrieb ihm eine neue Diät vor.

(b) **Verordnen:** to prescribe in general, without reference to detail.

Der Arzt verordnete einen Luftwechsel.

5. Sense of 'to direct (a thing) to be furnished or supplied' (*S.O.D.* II, 3): **bestellen.**

Haben Sie schon bestellt? (a waiter to guests).
Er hat einen neuen Anzug bestellt.
Ich habe den Wagen für 8 Uhr bestellt.

OTHER **Ander** can be used to translate 'another' only in the sense of 'different' from the one mentioned or implied. See article on 'different'. In the sense of 'additional' to the first, but not different from it, **noch ein, weiter,** or **zweit** must be used. The idea of difference conveyed by *ander* may be no more than 'better', i.e. not necessarily different in kind, e.g. *geben Sie mir ein anderes Streichholz*, which could imply: better than the first, which broke, or which would not strike. The other terms suggest the idea of addition, which may imply retention of the first. *Geben Sie mir ein weiteres Streichholz*, which could mean: I need two. *Weiter* carries this implication more clearly than the other terms.[1]

Geben Sie mir noch ein Stück Brot.
Ich habe noch eine Frage an Sie.
Er machte eine weitere Bedingung.
Ich möchte das kein zweites Mal erleben.

PAINFUL 1. **Schmerzhaft** refers only to physical pain.

Die Wunde ist sehr schmerzhaft.
'*Es schwoll darin von schmerzhaft entzückter Sehnsucht nach...*' (G. Hauptmann, *Der Narr in Christo*).

[1] *Noch* is also used to translate 'more' preceded by a numeral or by 'some', 'a few', in the sense of additional. *Geben Sie mir noch etwas Wein, noch drei Pfund. Es kommen noch einige Leute.*

2. **Schmerzlich** refers to mental anguish springing from the sense of loss.

Er hat einen schmerzlichen Verlust erlitten.
Ich habe mich zu der schmerzlichen Erkenntnis durchgerungen, daß das Leben einen Kompromiß mit unseren Idealen erfordert.
Die Nachricht hat mich schmerzlich berührt.
Er wurde von dem Vorfall schmerzlich betroffen.
'"*Mir ist das All, ich bin mir selbst verloren*"—*ein schmerzliches Bekenntnis bei jedem Menschen, ein erschütterndes bei einem dessen All und dessen Selbst Goethe war*' (Gundolf, *Goethe*).

3. **Peinlich** is applied (*a*) to that which embarrasses one or wounds, grates on one's sensibilities or aesthetic feeling; (*b*) in the sense of over-exact, punctilious, which it also translates.[1]

Es war eine peinliche Begegnung, ein peinlicher Augenblick.
Es ist mir peinlich, das sagen zu müssen.
Es ist höchst peinlich, so etwas mitansehen zu müssen.
Wir können es nur als eine peinliche Pflicht betrachten.
Es herrschte eine peinliche Stimmung.
Er hat eine peinliche Stimme.
Ich fühle mich von der Angelegenheit peinlich betroffen.
Er spricht sogar von alltäglichen Sachen mit peinlicher Präzision.

4. **Mühselig, mühsam, beschwerlich:** laborious, arduous, onerous, with reference to work, effort, and to ways (literally, and figuratively in the sense of 'courses of action'). *Beschwerlich*: attended with physical discomfort, hardship, difficulty.

Es war ein ganz kleiner Staat, der mühselig bestrebt war, sich gegen ungünstige Umstände durchzusetzen.
Er kroch mühsam aus den Trümmern hervor.
Das Gehen fällt ihm beschwerlich.

PALE, PALLID **Blaß** indicates an absence of colour greater than what is regarded as normal and approaching white. It corresponds to 'pale'. **Bleich** is stronger and means 'pallid'. *Erbleichen*: to blanch.

Er war blaß vor Angst.
Das ist ein blasses Blau.
Ihr Gesicht ist bleich.
Er war bleich vor Schrecken.

[1] *Penibel* (French: *pénible*) is used in the sense of *peinlich*, particularly in the sense of 'over-punctilious', 'fastidious'. It is more commonly applied to a person than *peinlich* (e.g. *er ist sehr penibel*).

PAY **Zahlen** denotes simply the operation of handing over money or any other form of payment. **Bezahlen** adds to this the idea of discharging an obligation. When the object is what is paid, i.e. the money, or the account, etc., both verbs are used, but with the distinction indicated. When the object is a person, *bezahlen* must be used with a direct object, or *zahlen* with the dative of the person and with mention of what is paid or paid for. In the figurative sense (e.g. to pay for one's folly) only *bezahlen* is possible.

'To pay for' may be translated by *bezahlen* with the thing acquired as direct object, or *für* may be added; also: *zahlen für*.

Ich habe das Geld, die 100 Mark, schon gezahlt.
Zahlen, bitte, Herr Ober!
Wollen Sie bitte mittels Scheck zahlen.
Sie müssen endlich mal das Geld bezahlen, das Sie ihm schulden.
Ich habe alle meine Rechnungen bezahlt.
Du kannst für den Wein, ich werde für das Essen zahlen.
Du mußt den Wein jetzt bezahlen, du hast den Mann schon lange genug warten lassen.
Ich werde Sie gleich bezahlen.
Ich habe ihm drei Mark dafür gezahlt.
Er hat seine Dummheiten teuer bezahlen müssen.
Wir haben den Wagen noch nicht bezahlt (or: *für den Wagen*).

PEOPLE 1. **Menschen:** human beings. It is used when the general characteristics of human beings as such are thought of; often, therefore, in opposition to other animate beings or to things.

Wieviele Menschen wohnen in London?
Sie müssen die Menschen verstehen, ehe Sie ein Urteil über sie fällen können.
Leider vergessen die Menschen sehr schnell.
Was für Menschen haben Sie dort gefunden?
Es geschah zu einer Zeit, wo die Menschen normalerweise im Bett sind.
Seine Menschenkenntnis geht nicht sehr weit.

2. **Leute:** any odd group or class of people that one thinks of in connection with some specific matter, but not in reference to their general characteristics as human beings. It is not a dignified term and can often be disparaging.[1] *Die Leute* is sometimes used colloquially for *die Menschen*. It can also mean 'men' in the sense of 'workers' or 'followers'.[2]

Die Leute drüben machen sehr viel Lärm.

[1] Applied to servants it is free from disparaging suggestions.
[2] Example: *wir haben 3 Leute im Garten.*

Es waren fünf Leute im Zimmer.
Kleider machen Leute.
Was für Leute haben Sie dort getroffen?
Reiche, arme, kluge Leute.
Die Leute wollen das nicht glauben (colloquial for *die Menschen*).
Die Partei hat ihre Leute überall.

3. Volk.

(a) 'People' in the sense of a 'community' bound together by common customs, sentiments, language.

Das deutsche Volk.
Die Völker der Erde.

(b) 'People' in the sense of the 'common people' as distinct from their leaders.

Das Volk muß politisch erzogen werden.

PLACE 1. **Ort** is the most general term. It can therefore indicate in the most general way existence in space (e.g. *Ort und Zeit angeben*; *er hat keinen Ortssinn*). Only in this sense can it denote a building, e.g. in definitions (e.g. *eine Bibliothek ist ein Ort, wo Bücher gelesen oder ausgeliehen werden*). It can also refer to (*a*) an inhabited locality (e.g. town, village); (*b*) a more circumscribed area, e.g. the scene of some happening, but vaguely, never an exact point (therefore never a place, spot, on the body); (*c*) the place where a thing belongs, in which use it denotes position more exactly; (*d*) figuratively: the proper place.

Wir müssen den Ort ausfindig machen, wo er sich versteckt hat.
Berlin ist sein Geburtsort.
Die Einwohner dieses Ortes sind alle sehr arm.
Sie wohnen in einem sehr schönen Ort.
An diesem Ort habe ich ihn zuerst getroffen.
Das ist ein geheiligter Ort.
Stellen Sie Ihr Fahrrad, das Buch, an den richtigen Ort zurück.
Hier ist nicht der Ort, solche Bemerkungen zu machen.

2. **Stelle**[1] denotes a more exact point, and so approximates to 'spot'.[2] It can therefore refer to a point in an area, on the body, in a book, speech and the like,[3] place where a thing belongs, ordinal position. It also

[1] See also 'position'.
[2] *Der Fleck* is 'spot' both in the sense of 'highly circumscribed area' and 'stain'. *Der Flecken* is 'spot' in the sense of 'blemish'. *Der Flecken auf seiner Ehre.*
[3] *Stelle* can also mean 'passage' in a book, speech, musical composition, and the like.

corresponds to 'place' used in the sense of 'stead' (e.g. in place of you, in your place). It never denotes a building.

Hier ist die Stelle, wo er ermordet wurde.
Ich sah ihn an der Stelle, wo der Pfad abbiegt.
Das ist eine empfindliche Stelle an meinem Arm.
An dieser Stelle spricht der Dichter von seiner Jugend.
Bringen Sie das Buch an die richtige Stelle zurück.
Ich würde das an zweiter Stelle erwähnen.
An Ihrer Stelle würde ich das nicht tun.

3. **Platz** denotes (*a*) primarily a place made for the carrying on of some activity, and is frequently translated by 'square', 'ground' as well as 'place' (e.g. *Marktplatz* = market place, *Spielplatz* = playing ground). (*b*) It then means 'place' in the sense of 'room, accommodation' for sitting, standing, or the like;[1] (*c*) further, the place where a thing belongs, and (*d*) figuratively: the proper place; (*e*) finally, the position obtained in competitive activities.

Ist da Platz für mich?
Hier ist noch Platz für den Schrank.
Der Platz an der Sonne (figuratively).
Stellen Sie das Fahrrad an den richtigen Platz zurück.
Hier ist nicht der Platz, solche Bemerkungen zu machen.
Die Bemerkung war nicht am Platz (an idiom, 'in place').
Er gewann den dritten Platz bei dem Preisausschreiben.

4. **Stätte,** which was originally the plural of *Statt* but subsequently became a singular, is an elevated term and often suggests a place that endures and possesses spiritual associations. It can denote a building.

Eine heilige, geweihte, Stätte.

POPULAR 1. **Beliebt** means 'liked'. In the attributive position, it can qualify only nouns which indicate a middle-brow level of entertainment unless it is accompanied by an intensifying adverb such as *sehr* or *allgemein*.

Franz Lehar ist ein beliebter Komponist.
Er ist ein beliebter Artist, Clown.
In meiner Jugend war Whist ein beliebtes Kartenspiel.
Das ist ein beliebter Schlager, ein beliebtes Lied.
Er ist ein allgemein, sehr, beliebter Redner, Prediger, General (*allgemein* or *sehr* must be added).
Er ist bei jedem beliebt (liked by everyone).

[1] *Platz* further means 'seat' in so far as its occupation or the intention, right, and the like, to occupy it, and not the object itself, is meant. *Seinen Platz verlassen, einen Platz belegen.*

2. **Populär** is used in various ways: (*a*) in the sense of 'non-expert', mostly in fixed phrases; (*b*) popular because of a certain heartiness, often in a slightly derogatory sense; (*c*) accepted, mostly negative.

Die Populärphilosophen (e.g. Nicolai).
Ein populärwissenschaftliches Werk.
Populärwissenschaftliche Aufsätze.
Göring war in weiten Kreisen des Volkes sehr populär (because of his hearty and clownish manner).
Gewisse amerikanische Ausdrücke sind sehr populär unter der jüngeren Generation.
Ich meine nicht den populären Sinn des Wortes Romantik.
Der Krieg war wenig populär in Italien (not *beliebt*).
Das ist keine populäre Maßnahme (not *beliebt*).

3. **Volkstümlich:** partaking of the characteristics of the *Volk*; appealing through such characteristics; used by the *Volk*. Unlike *populär*, which can suggest superficiality, it is always used in a good sense and denotes the simplicity, vigour, and freshness of the *Volk*.

Volk is used in a few fixed compounds (e.g. *Volksausgabe*).
Ein volkstümlicher Redner, Prediger, Schriftsteller, Ausdruck.

4. For many uses of 'popular' German has no well defined term, particularly in reference to political life. 'Popular government' could be paraphrased as *Regierung durch das Volk*. (*Regierung des Volkes* is a leftist government.) Popular election = *allgemeine Wahl*. The popular cry for victims: *der Schrei der Menge, der Massen, nach Opfern*. With reference to the popularization of knowledge: *allgemeinverständlich* (*allgemeinverständliche Vorträge*). A popular fallacy: *ein allgemeiner Irrglaube* (i.e. universal).

POSITION,[1] **SITUATION** (in space) 'Position' suggests an occupied place, and can mean 'position in relation to something else' in terms of strict measurement or more vaguely the 'position relative to other things', or again, still more vaguely, the 'whereabouts' of a thing. 'Situation' suggests relation to the surrounding district or countryside, often in reference to its picturesqueness.

The German nouns are strictly limited in their range of application, and are never identical with 'place' (*Ort, Stelle, Platz*). When those listed are inappropriate, verbs must be used.

[1] The *Fremdwort 'Position'* in reference to space is used in the same way as English 'position'. See also footnote (p. 261, n. 1) to 'position' and 'situation' in the sense of external circumstances.

POSITION

1. **Lage** denotes the position of an object in a district or landscape, and therefore corresponds most closely to 'situation'. It is applied only to objects which are more or less broad-based, i.e. which appear to lie. Thus it can refer to a building, even if tall, but not to a tree, to heavy machinery but not to furniture. It also translates 'position' as a relation expressed in exact measurement or in general directions. The position is in each case fixed. Hence expressions such as: *aus der gehörigen Lage bringen.*

It is applied to persons only in so far as 'lying' is meant, and then only in reference to comfort and the like.

Das Haus, der Garten, hat eine schöne Lage.
Durch seine Lage war Leningrad einem Angriff aus dem Westen ausgesetzt.
Durch seine Lage ist der Busch scharfen Winden ausgesetzt.
Den Fliegern wurde die Lage des Bahnhofs genau erklärt.
Er hat die Maschine aus der gehörigen Lage gebracht.
Der Kranke hat eine unbequeme Lage im Bett.

2. (a) **Stellung** refers not to where, but to how a thing is placed, either in relation to surrounding persons or things or in the relation of its parts to each other.[1] In the first case the angle at which one object points to another is implied. No other kind of relationship is expressed. Thus it cannot translate 'his position on the stage gave him a good view of the artist', because there is no question here of angle, but of proximity. In a sentence such as 'he chose a position from which he could see everything clearly', *Stellung* would be possible if a crouching, squatting, leaning position, or the like, is meant, but not if position refers, for example, to a hill, i.e. merely a place.

(b) *Stellung* can refer to the position or order of words in a sentence.

(c) As a military term *Stellung* refers to an entrenched or in mobile warfare a heavily fortified position.

Er blieb eine Stunde lang in liegender, knieender, gekrümmter, Stellung.
In vorgebeugter Stellung kann ich besser sehen.
Der Hund hob das rechte Bein und verharrte eine Minute lang in dieser Stellung.
Wenn Sie das Klavier in dieser Stellung belassen, werden Sie die Tür nicht öffnen können. (Although such a sentence is possible, *an dieser Stelle*, i.e. place, would be more usual.)
Alle feindlichen Stellungen wurden erobert.
Die Stellung dieses Wortes macht den ganzen Satz unklar.

[1] *Haltung* as applied to the body means 'carriage, attitude', in so far as it expresses an inner state. See article on 'attitude'.

3. **Stand** is regarded as a fixed position as far as one is concerned with the object at the moment, though this may move. It is little used,[1] being applied only in a few cases with which the verb *stehen* is regularly associated. It implies measurement. As a hunting term it denotes not only position, but also a 'stand' in the sense of an 'object'.[2]

Der Stand der Sonne (considered as a fixed point at any given moment).
Der Stand des Beobachters.

4. **Stelle** and other terms which mean 'place' (see article) can be used when 'position' does not stress the idea of relationship, i.e. when 'place', 'spot' would be more appropriate in English.

Setzen Sie den Strauch an eine andere Stelle.
Ich suchte mir eine schattige Stelle aus, wo ich ungestört lesen konnte.
Wer diese Stelle für den Brunnen wählte, hat nicht viel Kunstsinn an den Tag gelegt.
Von meinem Platz auf dem Podium konnte ich den Redner gut beobachten.

5. The verbs *liegen, gelegen sein* (to be situated), *sein, stehen, stellen,* and others are often used, when the above nouns are inapplicable.

Die Stadt liegt sehr schön.
Ich kann Ihnen nicht sagen, wo die dritte Armee sich im Augenblick befindet.
So wie das Klavier steht, stört es die Harmonie des Zimmers.

POSITION, SITUATION 'Position' is vague in its reference to external circumstances, but suggests the interest of the person in dealing with them. It forms a number of fixed phrases. Examples: That's the position! The position is that.... The (beer, food) position is.... The position with (your application) is.... What is the position with...? 'Situation' does not in itself suggest action on the part of the person, and in this sense it is more objective than 'position'. It can refer (*a*) to a wide set of external circumstances (e.g. the political, military, situation) or (*b*) to a moment characterized by the interplay of human personality, emotion, the dramatic (e.g. I found myself in a ludicrous situation).

German has no term of German origin for 'position' thus used.[3]

[1] The idea of a fixed point is always present, no matter what the English translation is. Sometimes it corresponds to 'level', 'mark'. *Der Stand des Wassers, des Getreides.* See also article on 'state', 'condition'.

[2] Further: *Standort* in military contexts (e.g. in reference to aircraft, the position of a ship in convoy) corresponds to 'location'. It is also used as a gardening term for the position of shrubs and the like.

[3] *Position* is used as a *Fremdwort* in many of the senses of the English term, except in fixed phrases, particularly as 'job'; 'place from which one can survey a scene'; 'point of

POSITION

1. **Lage** corresponds to 'situation' in its reference to a set of circumstances, i.e. meaning **2** (*a*). It suggests that these have come about gradually, that they hold the person, and does not stress human intervention in order to change them, i.e. the person tends to be thought of as a victim. 'Plight' is sometimes an English equivalent. 'Position' must be translated by *Lage* when it is practically interchangeable with 'situation' (e.g. the food position, situation: *die Lebensmittellage, die Ernährungslage*). *Lage* is in general combined only with a few fundamental commodities (e.g. *Brennstofflage, Brotlage,* not with *Butter, Wein,* though, exceptionally, with *Zigaretten*). *Lage* cannot be used to translate the other fixed expressions formed with 'position'.

2. **Situation** corresponds to the English 'situation' only in the second sense as described above. It is applied typically to a situation which arises suddenly, is of short duration, and in which the interest is in the human element, not the external circumstances as such.

(a) *Die militärische Lage ist sehr ernst.*
Die politische Lage kann sich grundlegend ändern.
Die Ernährungslage hat sich verschlechtert.
Ich bin in einer wenig beneidenswerten Lage, ich soll die beiden wieder versöhnen (position or situation).
Die Lage ist für einen weiteren Appell an seine Freigebigkeit sehr ungünstig.
In Ihrer Lage würde ich die Wahlergebnisse abwarten.

(b) *Eine tragische Situation* (e.g. in a drama, novel).
Ich befand mich in einer peinlichen, lächerlichen, Situation (*sich befinden* goes well with *Situation* because it expresses the mental and emotional reaction of the person).
In dieser Situation kann ich nichts tun.

3. Some translations of 'position' used to form fixed expressions.

(a) The most general are: *wie steht, ist, es mit...?* (what is the position with...?); *es ist so mit...* (the position with...is...).[1]
Wie steht (ist) es mit dem Ausflug? Findet er statt?

view'; and more generally in the sense treated in this article. Examples: (*a*) *Wir hatten eine gute Position und konnten von da aus die ganze Rennbahn überblicken.* (*b*) '*Freilich hat Goethe dadurch auch seine Position aus Höflichkeit selbst geschwächt...*' (Gundolf on Kleist, referring to Goethe's criticism of Kleist). (*c*) '*Das ist ja die günstige Position dieser hohen Funktionäre der braunen Revolution, daß sie abstreiten oder behaupten können, was ihnen für ihre Unschuldslegende paßt, weil die Belastungszeugen beseitigt sind*' (H. B. Gisevius, *Bis Zum Bitteren Ende*, vol. 2).

[1] *Die Sache ist die, daß...* means: the point is that....

Wie steht es denn mit der Gehaltserhöhung? (What stage of the negotiations has been reached? what are the chances?)
Es ist so, daß wir Ihnen die versprochene Reise nicht mehr bezahlen können.
Es ist also so! (So that's the position!) *Die Rationen müssen wieder gekürzt werden.*

(b) *Es verhält sich mit..., wie verhält es sich mit...?* are used to give or ask for details or clarification of something obscure or not understood.

Wie verhält es sich nun eigentlich mit dem Mann?
Wie verhält es sich mit Ihrer Reise, Ihren Ferienplänen?

(c) *Es ist...bestellt mit..., wie ist es mit...bestellt?* are used typically with *gut* or *schlecht* of persons and their interests rather than of external circumstances. With the latter they are apt to sound precious.

Wie ist es mit deinen Zigaretten bestellt?
Wie ist es mit seiner Professur bestellt?
Es ist schlecht um ihn, mit ihm, bestellt.

POSITION, SITUATION, JOB **Stellung** is the most general term and suggests the person[1] in relation to the position more than the nature of the position itself. **Stelle,** on the other hand, emphasizes the nature of the position, which is thought of as having real existence, even if vacant. For this reason it is often extended, particularly in compounds, to mean 'office', 'board', and the like. If there is no indication to the contrary, it tends, however, to denote a humble job. *Stellenangebot*, as the heading of an advertisement column, refers to jobs of this kind. **Posten** is an already created position into which a person moves. It strongly suggests either his suitability for the position or the material advantages it brings, or the opposite of these. It is most common in reference to administration or business, but is not applied to the professions or labourers' jobs. **Arbeit** and the verb *arbeiten* are often used for a labourer's job, particularly in reference to the seeking or finding of it. **Platz,** which is little used, is a small job, generally in the commercial world. **Anstellung** corresponds rather to 'appointment' than to any of the above terms (see article on 'appoint').

Er hat eine hohe Stellung im Heer, in der Verwaltung, im Geschäft.
Er ist auf der Suche nach einer neuen Stellung.
Er nahm die erste freigewordene Stellung an.

[1] Since *Stellung* concentrates attention on the person, it is also used of social rank, standing in any group, professional or otherwise. *Seine Stellung in der Gesellschaft verbietet ihm, unvorsichtige Äußerungen zu machen.* 'Position' thus used should be distinguished from the sense of external circumstances (see article on 'position', 'situation' in this sense).

POSITION

Er eignet sich nicht für diese Stelle.
Diese Stelle ist freigeworden.
Er bewirbt sich um diese Stelle.
Er eignet sich in hohem Grade zum Posten des Vize-Kanzlers.
Er hat einen Posten in einer Bank gefunden.
Er sucht Arbeit in einer Fabrik (job).
Seine Arbeit behagt ihm nicht.
Er arbeitet in einer Mehlfabrik (has a job).
Er hat jetzt einen Platz in einem Exportgeschäft.
Seine Anstellung erfolgte sofort.

POSSIBLY 1. **Möglicherweise**[1] is used in the sense of *vielleicht*, but is more strongly concessive, and at the same time implies a nicer weighing up of possibilities than the latter.[2]

Möglicherweise haben wir zuviel verlangt.

2. In the sense of 'in accordance with what is possible' (*P.O.D.*) **nur** (colloquially **bloß**) is used,[3] except when 'possibly' is accompanied by 'not'. In this case German uses *unmöglich.*

Er braucht den besten Arzt, den man nur finden kann.
Wie können Sie so was nur (bloß) sagen?

POWER, STRENGTH, FORCE A. Sense: ability to exert effort; person or thing possessing such ability.

1. **Macht,** when held by persons, suggests a position of power by means of which we are enabled to exert influence, control over people and things. In reference to political power it implies this weight of influence, whether legal or illegal, not the specific organs of power (see **Gewalt**). Attributed to things, it likewise suggests power to influence. Further, a person, a country, and, with personification, a thing, a natural or supernatural force may be termed as **Macht**. Used in the plural, it only has this latter application.

[1] The adverbial form compounded with *weise* must be used when the adverb modifies the whole clause, not one word. *Er hat vernünftigerweise nicht zu viel angestrebt. Er hat mir seltsamerweise nichts davon gesagt.*

[2] *Eventuell*, though sometimes translated by 'possibly', has a more special meaning than the latter. While 'possibly' simply denotes a concession that a thing may be as indicated as the alternative to its not being so, *eventuell* means that a thing may be as indicated in the event of certain circumstances operating. It is most commonly used to indicate a second possibility, in the sense of 'or', and 'in a certain contingency'. *Ich fahre Montag, eventuell Dienstag. Er wird eine Gehaltserhöhung von 20, eventuell 25 R.M. pro Woche, bekommen.* It refers to the future. See also footnote to 'at last' (p. 189, n. 1).

[3] A close synonym is *irgend* (at all), which is used in this way in *wenn* clauses. *Wenn ich irgend kann.* Often it is combined with *nur.*

It will be seen that compared with 'power' its range of meaning is limited, and that it corresponds more exactly to the cognate term 'might', which, however, tends to be used exclusively in elevated diction or in reference to the supernatural.

Er besitzt fast unbeschränkte Macht.
Er hat Macht über ihn gewonnen.
Er mißbraucht seine Macht.
Die absolute Macht verdirbt den, der sie besitzt.
Ich bin in seine Macht geraten.
Er hat sich in eine Machtstellung hineinmanövriert.
Eine revolutionäre Partei hat die Macht an sich gerissen.
Das steht, liegt, nicht in meiner Macht.
Die Macht der Liebe, des Hasses, der Musik, der Gewohnheit.
Er ist eine Macht im Lande.
Machtpolitik ist untrennbar von dem Begriff 'Großmacht'.
Wissen, Geld, ist Macht.
Die Mächte der Hölle.

2. **Gewalt** is power to force people to do one's will. It suggests more definitely than *Macht* the actual application of power, force, the overcoming of resistance, and therefore corresponds closely to both 'power' and 'force' used in this sense. With the implication of overwhelming[1] power it can also be attributed to things (e.g. *die Gewalt der Musik, des Sturmes*). A close synonym is 'violence', which it sometimes, but by no means invariably, translates.[2]

Ich bin in seine Gewalt geraten.
Er hat mich in seiner Gewalt.
Sie müssen Gewalt anwenden.
Er hat es mit Gewalt durchgesetzt.
Die Gegensätze wurden durch Waffengewalt entschieden.
Er schrie mit aller Gewalt.
Die Gewalt des Windes war unbeschreiblich.
Die Gewalt seiner Sprache ist gradezu hinreißend.

3. **Kraft** is the energy, physical or moral, in persons or things which produces an effect. In this sense of 'energy, vigour, vitality', it translates 'power' (e.g. *elektrische Kraft, seine geistigen Kräfte*), 'strength' (e.g. *das geht über meine Kraft*), 'force' as a close synonym of 'strength' and in the sense of 'efficacy, cogency' (e.g. *die Kraft eines Arguments*) and 'validity' (only in fixed phrases; e.g. *das Gesetz ist in Kraft getreten*).

[1] *Überwältigen*, to overwhelm, contains the same root.

[2] Mostly in fixed phrases, e.g. *Gewalt antun*. 'Violence' is generally *Gewaltsamkeit, Gewalttätigkeit, Heftigkeit*. See 'violent'.

With reference to bodily strength, the plural *Kräfte* is used when the waxing or waning of the energy of the mind and body as a whole is meant (e.g. *seine Kräfte nehmen rasch ab*, of a dying person). As an equivalent of 'strength' distinguish from *Stärke* (see **A**, **4**).

For *Kraft* in the sense of 'faculty of the mind' see section **B**, **3**.[1]

Pferdekraft, Dampfkraft.
Die Kräfte der Natur der Menschheit dienstbar machen.
Ich werde alles tun, was in meiner Kraft liegt.
Die Kraft des Widerstandes ist gebrochen.
Es steckt eine unheimliche Kraft in seiner Sprache.
Ihre Stimme hat keine Kraft.
Die Suppe hat keine Kraft.
Er ist wieder zu Kräften gekommen (has regained his strength).
Das Gesetz bleibt noch weiter in Kraft.

4. Stärke is not strength in the sense of 'energy' (see *Kraft*), but strength which can be more or less measured. It can be applied to the human body and to things.[2]

Die Stärke seines Arms, der feindlichen Armee, der Festung, des Biers, des Fiebers, seiner Stellung.

5. Wucht: weight,[3] weightiness, which is forcibly felt, either literally or as an impression on the mind. As a rendering of 'force' it refers to an impact.

Er fiel mit voller Wucht auf das Pflaster.
Die Wucht seiner Argumente.

B. Sense: 'a faculty[4] or active property' (*S.O.D.*).

1. Vermögen is applied now only to persons and denotes the inner structure or disposition which enables us to produce an effect. It suggests a latent state[5] rather than the actual expression or functioning of this disposition, and so approximates more to 'capacity' than to 'ability'. It is applied mainly, but not exclusively, to well-defined faculties of the mind

[1] In reference to a body of men German only has the term *Streitkräfte*. For air force, police force, etc. see section **D**.

[2] *Stärke* also means 'intensity'. See *stark* under 'severe'. Another sense is 'stark'. While *Stärke* is used less than 'strength', the opposite is true of the frequency of *stark* as compared with 'strong'.

[3] *Gewicht* is weight as a measurement, also 'importance' of persons, and weight, e.g. of an argument, which appeals to reason.

[4] The terms discussed in this section also translate 'faculty' of the mind. Other terms sometimes found are: (*Unterhaltungs*)*talent*, (*Überredungs*)*gabe*.

[5] As is also *Anlage* which is a potentiality, a disposition, a capacity which requires development.

(frequently in compounds) such as: *Empfindungsvermögen* (= sensibility), *Sehvermögen, Fassungsvermögen.* But its use with a following infinitive to denote less well-defined, but generally possessed, capacities is also possible, though it occurs mostly in generalizations about human beings and only when the idea of a capacity as such is stressed. Thus, while the term *Sprachvermögen* exists, it would be pedantic to use it to translate such a sentence as: he has lost the power of speech (*er hat die Sprache verloren*). Similarly it is possible to say: *sein Konzentrationsvermögen* (power of concentration) *nimmt ab*; but, unless special prominence is to be given to the idea of a capacity, the normal statement would be: *er kann sich nicht konzentrieren.*

Vermögen is applied only to conscious actions, i.e. not to purely physiological functions or reflex actions (e.g. the power to digest food, the power of blushing).

Sein Ausdrucksvermögen ist beschränkt.
Sein Vorstellungsvermögen ist sehr gut.
Sie besitzt ein starkes Ahnungsvermögen.
Der Mensch hat das Vermögen, das Zusammenleben der Völker friedlich zu gestalten, aber er macht oft keinen Gebrauch davon.
Das Vermögen, sich in jeder Lage zurechtzufinden, ist sehr nützlich.
Ich habe alles getan, was in meinem Vermögen stand.

2. **Fähigkeit** suggests a special ability or gift and its actual expression or functioning, whereas *Vermögen* is more general and tends to be latent. 'Ability' is therefore a closer equivalent than 'capacity'.[1] A high degree of consciousness and control in its exercise is implied. It is accordingly only applied to persons.[2]

Er hat die Fähigkeit, rasche Entschlüße zu fassen.
Nicht viele Menschen besitzen die Fähigkeit, den Wortlaut eines Gedichts nach der ersten Lektüre zu behalten.

3. **Kraft** means energy, and by extension can refer to the source of this, i.e. to the faculty or capacity from which flows the energy that produces an effect. Its meaning of 'energy, force, strength' (see **A, 3**) must be distinguished from that of 'source', i.e. faculty. In the latter sense it refers

[1] 'Capacity' is, however, sometimes translated by *Fähigkeit*; e.g. in its sense of receptiveness as applied to persons. Examples: *Eindrucksfähigkeit, Aufnahmefähigkeit. Kapazität* refers to (*a*) the holding power of things, particularly as a chemical term; (*b*) occasionally to the mental power of persons, particularly in the phrase *er ist eine Kapazität.*

[2] It is sometimes applied in compounds to the holding power of things in the sense of 'capacity' (e.g. *Ladefähigkeit*—of ships). The adjective *fähig* is applied regularly to things (e.g. *diese Maschine ist fähig,* 1000 *Kilogramm zu heben*).

only to the well-defined faculties of the mind, and has in this use come to be practically synonymous with *Vermögen*.

It can also denote an active property in a thing (e.g. *die Brennkraft der Kohle*). The property is normally expressed by compounding the term in question with *Kraft*.

A following infinitive to denote the activity of the property is impossible when 'power' is thought of as a capacity, a source of energy, i.e. after the combination in which *Kraft* is followed by the thing in the genitive case (*die Kraft der Hitze, Sonne*). In other words, the English 'the power of heat, of the sun, to burn' is untranslatable. On the other hand, when 'power' is thought of, not as a capacity, but as actual functioning, i.e. 'strength', a following infinitive is admissible; i.e. after such combinations as: *die Sonne hat die Kraft zu brennen.*

Einbildungskraft, Vorstellungskraft, Urteilskraft, Fassungskraft, Geisteskräfte.

Die Heilkraft gewisser Kräuter, des Schlafes.

4. **Eigenschaft,** quality, property, may be used for 'power' in the sense of 'active property' when applied to things.[1]

The explanation of the use of the infinitive after *Kraft* holds good for *Eigenschaft* too.

Diese Medizin hat die Eigenschaft, die Infektionsgefahr zu verringern.

5. To denote an involuntary action (e.g. a reflex action) or a purely physiological function, none of the above terms is applicable. *Können* as a verb is often the only possible rendering.

Sie kann nicht mehr gehen, erröten (has lost the power to walk, to blush).
Sein Magen kann solche Speisen nicht verdauen.

C. Sense: delegated authority.[2]

1. **Gewalt,** in addition to its meaning of 'overwhelming force', can denote legal, constitutional power, in which case it always refers to the organs of power through which the state functions or to the power exercised by an officer appointed to such organs.[3] In this sense it occurs mainly in fixed phrases.[4]

[1] *Wirkung* (effect) may be used as a close synonym.

[2] *Autorität* is only used in the sense of 'power, influence'. It cannot stand for persons themselves.

[3] *Walten* = to rule (now used only in fixed phrases or figuratively). *Verwalten* = to administer.

[4] *Gewalt* can mean 'control' in fixed phrases, mostly 'self-control'. *Er hat sich in der Gewalt. Er hat die Gewalt über sich verloren. Kontrolle* only means 'administrative supervision which acts as a check'. Similarly *kontrollieren.*

Die Staatsgewalt, die kaiserliche Gewalt.
Die gesetzgebende, vollziehende, Gewalt.
Unter einer Diktatur gibt es keine Trennung der Gewalten.
Ich habe nicht die Gewalt, diesen Mann verhaften zu lassen.

2. **Befugnis** is a formal, official term, and means the 'power to act' conferred legally, constitutionally on an individual or a body by virtue of his office, or special circumstances. It should only be used in a formal discussion or statement which seeks to define specific powers, i.e. not in an informal conversation.

The verb *befugt sein* is used in the same sense.[1]

Die Befugnisse des Vize-Kanzlers sind ganz empfindlich gekürzt worden.
Er hat seine Befugnisse überschritten.
Der Vize-Kanzler sagte, er habe nicht die Befugnis, das zu tun.
Das gehört nicht zu meinen Befugnissen (a common expression).

3. **Berechtigt sein,** to be entitled, is a more general term which can denote human rights[2] as well as specially conferred power, and can be used informally as well as formally.

The noun *Berechtigung* is used, though less frequently, in the same sense.

Ist der Senat berechtigt, das zu tun?
Wir sind berechtigt, Anleihen vorzunehmen.
Sind Sie berechtigt, mich zu fragen?
Die Treuhänder sind berechtigt, ihn zum Vormund zu bestellen.

4. **Ermächtigung, ermächtigt sein,**[3] denote the exercise of power allowed by a higher authority. Power in a specific matter is implied, whereas *berechtigt sein* can refer in a more general way to the possession of power.

Sind Sie ermächtigt, mich zu fragen? (i.e. in this specific matter, whereas *berechtigt* would ask if this was amongst the powers of the interrogator).
Der Kanzler hat mich ermächtigt, nach Gutdünken zu handeln.

5. **Vollmacht** means exclusively 'power of attorney'. It is used also in the plural without distinction of meaning.

Vollmacht zu verhandeln ist ihm erteilt worden.
Er hat seine Vollmachten überschritten.

[1] *Fug* is now only used in fixed phrases (e.g. *mit Fug und Recht*). It is connected with *fügen*, and so has the fundamental sense of 'what is fitting, suitable'.

[2] *Recht* = (i) a right; (ii) 'law' as a principle.

[3] *Sich ermächtigen* is now obsolete. It means 'to usurp power', 'to seize possession' of a thing (i.e. *sich bemächtigen*; see 'seize').

D. Some other senses of 'power' and 'force'.

Electric current: *Strom.* A body of men: *Luftwaffe* (air force); *die Polizei* (police force). *Potenz* (in mathematical sense). German has no exact term for 'force' in the sense of 'real import of a word or document'.

PRACTISE, EXERCISE 1. **Üben:** (*a*) to practise in order to acquire proficiency, mastery; (*b*) do, perform, carry out.

Sie übt zehn Stunden täglich Klavier.
Er übt sich im Reden.
Ein geübtes Auge.
Er hat Gnade, Gerechtigkeit, geübt (exercised).

2. **Ausüben:** (*a*) to carry on, exercise something in which one is already proficient; (*b*) to put into practice, into action, to make use of something one already has.

Er übt seinen Beruf, sein Amt, seine Kunst aus.
Seine Worte übten einen starken Einfluß aus.
Er hat sein Stimmrecht nicht ausgeübt.

3. **Einüben:** to study thoroughly, particularly a role in a play.

Er hat seine Rolle gut eingeübt.

PRAISE, EXTOL 1. **Loben,** like praise, is the general term, the sense of which is 'to express a favourable judgment on' a person or thing.

Der Lehrer lobte ihn, seine Arbeit.
Das Stück wurde in den Zeitungen sehr gelobt.

2. **Beloben** is 'to say so much in praise of a thing (not a person) that the result is practically a speech of praise'. A formal occasion is often suggested.

Er wurde wegen seines mutigen Verhaltens belobt.
'*Ich ließ mir herzlich dankbar alles und jedes wohl gefallen, belobte und pries; nur nahm es mich wunder, wozu er das Gartengerät gekauft*' (Mörike, *Mozart auf der Reise nach Prag*).

3. **Preisen:** to draw the attention of other people emphatically to the qualities of a person or thing so that he or it becomes known. Unlike *loben*, it does not mean to praise a person to himself.[1]

[1] *Anpreisen* has a commercial sense, and means 'to recommend', 'to urge a person to take a thing'. The object is generally a thing (e.g. *Waren anpreisen*).

Er pries das Buch, den Wein, die Kochkunst der Frau.
Er hat den Redner sehr gepriesen.

4. **Rühmen** suggests even more strongly than *preisen* the spreading of the fame of a person or thing.[1]

Seine Taten wurden von der Presse gerühmt.

PREPARE[2] 1. With a noun object.

(a) **Bereiten** is only regularly used in present-day German[3] in reference to the mixing of substances. It is short for **zubereiten** which is used in the same way. Both the skilled process of preparation and the result are stressed.

Er hat das Essen, eine Medizin, die richtige Mischung von Farben bereitet, zubereitet.
Sie hat ein wunderbares Essen bereitet.

(b) **Vorbereiten** is used in all other senses of 'prepare'. It includes every action, however trivial, involved in any preparation.

Ich habe die Berichte für meinen Vorgesetzten schon vorbereitet.
Sie bereitet das Essen vor (the stages before the blending of the substances, e.g. getting the materials, cleaning, cutting them).
Er bereitet sich auf das Abitur vor.
Wir waren auf die schlechte Nachricht nicht vorbereitet.

2. With the following infinitive.

(a) **Sich vorbereiten** can only be used in reference to elaborate preparations.

Er bereitet sich auf sein Examen vor.
Ich bereite mich jetzt schon darauf vor, das nächste Jahr in China zu verbringen.

(b) **Sich anschicken** is used of small adjustments for immediate action of a limited character.

Ich schickte mich an zu gehen, seine Frage zu beantworten, als das Telephon klingelte.

3. 'To be prepared' followed by the infinitive can be translated by *vorbereitet sein* in the sense described in the preceding section. In the

[1] *Sich rühmen* followed by the genitive means 'to boast of a thing'.
[2] *Präparieren* refers only to a technical process.
[3] The use of *bereiten* with such words as *Bad, Bett* is old-fashioned or rarefied.

sense of 'to be willing'[1] (under conditions or with tacit reservations, or the like) its only equivalent is **bereit,** i.e. ready.[2]

Ich bin bereit, Ihren Plan zu unterstützen.
Ich bin bereit, das Risiko auf mich zu nehmen.

PRESS, SQUEEZE, URGE, DEPRESS, OPPRESS 1. In the literal sense of 'press' and 'squeeze' **drücken** is the general term. **Pressen** denotes very strong pressure, sometimes 'to press both sides of a thing together', often by means of machines. The figurative sense of both verbs is 'to weigh heavily upon', 'to oppress', of feelings, conditions, or circumstances. Here too *pressen* is stronger than *drücken.*

Er drückte sie an seine Brust.
Er drückte ihm eine Mark in die Hand.
Er drückte auf den Knopf.
Er preßte sie an seine Brust.
Er preßte so viel in den Koffer hinein, daß er platzte.
Er preßte den Saft der Zitrone in ein Glas.[3] (*Drücken* cannot mean 'to squeeze out the contents'.)
Der Kummer, die Not, drückt, preßt, ihn sehr.
Drückende Hitze (the present participle of *pressen* is not used adjectivally).

2. In the sense of 'to urge', 'press for a thing', 'press a person to do a thing', both **dringen** and **drängen** are used. The distinction is that *dringen* means to insist in general, while *drängen* suggests a demand for immediate action. Both are followed by *auf* when the object is a thing, *dringen* by *in* when the object is a person. **Bedrängen** is sometimes, though infrequently, used in this sense. It stresses the emotional state into which one is thrown, the subject being a person close to one. See also next section.

[1] In synonymous use 'willing' is also translated by *bereit. Willig* suggests absence of compulsion, but not eagerness. *Bereitwillig* suggests a certain amount of the latter. *Gern* is 'gladly' or 'willingly' when this implies the former. *Willig* is only followed by an infinitive when inactivity or submission is stressed (e.g. *willig, den Tod zu erleiden*). Further, it is applied to persons only in more or less fixed phrases (e.g. *er ist nicht recht willig*). 'To be willing' can sometimes be translated by *wollen*, but not, of course, when the latter means 'to insist'. See article on 'want'. Similarly, 'unwilling' is rendered by *nicht bereit, nicht wollen. Unwillig* means 'indignant'. *Widerwillig* means 'reluctant', but cannot be applied directly to persons in any combination.

[2] 'Ready' in the sense of 'having made all the necessary preparations' is *fertig*, which, however, cannot be followed by the infinitive. *Bereit* must be used in this case.

[3] To press grapes: *keltern.* 'To press' in reference to technical processes differs from case to case.

Die Gläubiger drangen, drängten, auf Zahlung.
Er drang in mich, drängte mich, den Mann zu entlassen.
Sie bedrängen mich, meine Aktien zu verkaufen.

3. **Bedrängen:** to press hard, to beset, i.e. from all sides. Used of emotions it means to cause concern, not 'to depress' (see *bedrücken*). The past participle is used adjectivally, particularly with reference to circumstances that press hard upon one.

Sie bedrängen mich mit ihren Ansprüchen.
Er befindet sich in einer bedrängten Lage.
Das Elend meiner Geschwister bedrängte mich.

4. **Bedrücken** means 'to depress' the spirits. It also means 'to oppress' in the sense of 'to pinch, to squeeze' taxes and the like out of a population. In the more general sense of 'to govern tyrannically', **unterdrücken** (which also means 'to suppress') is the normal term.

Daß es ihm schlecht geht, bedrückt mich sehr (depress).
Eroberte Länder werden von ihren Eroberern immer bedrückt.
Die militärische Besetzung wurde als bedrückend empfunden.
Die Nazis unterdrückten ihr eigenes Volk.

5. **Quetschen** is 'to squeeze' or 'to crush' a thing from both sides so that it becomes flattened, both literally and figuratively. It approaches the meaning of 'squash'.[1]

Die Früchte sind auf dem Transport gequetscht worden.
Ich habe meine Hand in der Tür gequetscht.
Ich quetschte mich noch in die übervolle Straßenbahn.

PREVENT 1. **Hindern, verhindern**[2] with the following infinitive.

Hindern concentrates attention on the act of preventing itself, and is therefore more dramatic and vivid than *verhindern*, which emphasizes not the act but the result, i.e. that the act did not take place. *Hindern* suggests physical intervention on the part of a person by an act that is characteristically brief and sometimes sudden. With a personal subject *verhindern*, correctly used, suggests less an act of intervention than the mere existence or presence of the person or something about him that acts as a deterrent. The deterrent operates not in one brief act, but gradually, after the lapse of time, or permanently though weakly. It is

[1] *Zerquetschen* is 'to squash completely'.

[2] *Abhalten*: deter from some act that the object, which must be a person, consciously means to carry out. In this sense it is used as commonly as 'stop'. *Lassen Sie sich dadurch nicht abhalten* (don't let it stop, deter, you).

thus appropriate in generalizations about the permanent or repeated operation of a deterrent, or when the deterrent functions indirectly.

(a) Examples with a personal subject:

Er trat ihr in den Weg und hinderte sie daran, in den Saal zu treten.

Er schloß ihre Kleider in den Schrank und verhinderte sie dadurch, den Ball zu besuchen.

(b) When the subject is not a person, but, for example a motive, emotion, idea, and the like, the same distinction holds good. *Verhindern* is more usual, since *hindern* indicates a sudden and forceful assertion of the motive or emotion.

'*...so schien ein Etwas in seiner Haltung auszudrücken, daß nur Erziehung ihn hinderte, sich umzuwenden*' (Thomas Mann, *Der Tod in Venedig*).

Seine Erziehung verhinderte ihn, die Leute anzustarren.

Meine Grundsätze haben mich verhindert, auf seinen Vorschlag einzugehen.

(c) German regards the following forms of the verb as having something of the dramatic: the imperative, the interrogative form (but not a mere rhetorical question), often the infinitive in combination with modal verbs. *Hindern* is therefore more usual.

Hindern Sie ihn daran, das Zimmer zu verlassen.

Wer wird mich daran hindern, das Zimmer zu verlassen?

Was hindert Sie daran, das Zimmer zu verlassen (what is there to prevent...)?

Ich mußte ihn daran hindern, was sollte mich daran hindern, das Zimmer zu verlassen?

'*Ich mußte den Molch in der Hand halten und am Weglaufen verhindern*' (Ricarda Huch, *Teufeleien*).

(d) *Verhindern* is used with the effect of a mere report in unstressed, undramatic parts of a statement, even when the same idea, emphasized, would be expressed by *hindern*. In such cases some other word in the sentence (often the subject) bears the stress, particularly when it is already known that an action has been prevented and it is decided to draw attention to the cause.

Er sagte: 'Ich will ihn totschlagen und niemand wird (or: *wer kann*) *mich daran hindern.' Der Schutzmann hat ihn aber daran verhindert.*

Er trat vor mich, was mich verhinderte, weiterzugehen.

Ihr Mann war es, der sie verhinderte, in den Saal zu treten.

(e) The infinitive after these verbs is only possible, if it denotes a conscious, deliberate act.

Daran is generally used to anticipate the following infinitive, though it is sometimes omitted for reasons of rhythm (see the above example under 1(*b*) from *Der Tod in Venedig*). It is obligatory when *verhindern* is used absolutely (e.g. *er hat mich daran verhindert*).

Further examples are:

Er hat sie daran gehindert, Selbstmord zu begehen.
Seine Überredungskraft hat sie verhindert, Selbstmord zu begehen.
Das Parlament hat den König daran gehindert, Krieg zu erklären (actively intervened).
Das Parlament hat den König verhindert, Krieg zu erklären (by its mere existence).
Die Wachen hinderten den Gefangenen daran, zu entkommen.
Die Wachen verhinderten den Gefangenen zu entkommen (with stress on *Wachen*, not *verhinderten*).
Der Lärm hinderte mich, seine Worte deutlich zu hören (die Musik zu genießen).
Der Lärm der Straßenbahnen verhindert mich, in diesem Zimmer geistige Arbeit zu leisten.
Wir haben den Feind daran gehindert, den Fluß zu überschreiten.
Kein Gesetz kann uns daran hindern, ein neues Haus zu bauen.
Die Schmerzen hinderten mich daran, fest zu schlafen.
Könnte seine Liebe zu ihr ihn verhindern wegzufahren?
Ich habe so lange mit ihr gesprochen, daß ich sie dadurch verhindert habe, den Zug zu erreichen.
Seine Eifersucht verhinderte ihn, sie in ihrem wahren Licht zu erkennen.
Seine Liebe zu ihr verhinderte ihn wegzufahren.
Der niedrige Stand meines Bankkontos hat mich verhindert, die Reise zu unternehmen.
Sie haben ihn doch hoffentlich nicht verhindert, den Garten zu verlassen (a mild rhetorical question, stressing the result rather than the action).
Es war der Regen, der uns verhinderte, die Reise anzutreten.
Ich war geschäftlich verhindert, das Büro früh zu verlassen.

2. *Verhindern* with a *daß* clause.

The preceding account of *verhindern* with the infinitive largely applies to its use with a *daß* clause. In general, the prevention is still less active and direct than with the infinitive construction.

(a) It is therefore more appropriate, though not obligatory, in the following cases:

(i) When the activity on the part of the subject (i.e. the author of the preventing) is absent or weak. A negative frequently has this effect.

Der Mißerfolg der anderen verhinderte nicht, daß er selbst den Versuch machte.

Die Unerreichbarkeit des Ziels verhinderte nicht, daß er Zeit und Geld dafür opferte.

Sein Wissen um die Absichten, die sie gegen ihn hegen, verhindert nicht, daß er noch mit ihnen verkehrt.

(ii) When the whole action (both the action of preventing and that prevented) is vast, complicated, and indirect, so that it cannot be seen as a single act; the subject or object or both being frequently not one person, but a group.

Bei all ihrer Tüchtigkeit konnten die deutschen Generale nicht verhindern, daß die Heere der vereinigten Nationen an allen Fronten siegreich durchbrachen.

Er konnte nicht verhindern, daß Spanien dazu überging, eine selbstständige Politik zu treiben.

Der Westen kann nicht verhindern, daß Rußland in Osteuropa nach Gutdünken waltet.

(b) The *daß* construction is normally obligatory in the following cases:

(i) When the whole action (both subject and object) belong to the world of inanimate nature. *Hindern* with the infinitive would be unusual in so far as it would personify the action.

Die Gebirge verhinderten, daß die Gewässer weiterflossen.

Die Bäume verhindern, daß die Sonne zu den Pflanzen dringt.

(ii) When the action prevented is involuntary, i.e. in the sense of 'save'.

Der Felsvorsprung verhinderte, daß er tiefer abstürzte.

Das Betäubungsmittel verhinderte, daß ich Schmerzen empfand.

Further examples are:

Das Fehlen eines wohlhabenden Mittelstandes in gewissen Ländern hat verhindert, daß ein liberales Regierungssystem aufkam.

Seine Hilflosigkeit verhinderte nicht, daß sie ihn übel zurichteten.

Der starke Donner verhinderte, daß ich den Ruf meines Kameraden hörte.

Der Nebel verhinderte, daß er den Graben sah, und so stürzte er hinein.

3. A noun or verbal noun (or corresponding pronoun), that refers to the action prevented, as the object of *(ver)hindern.*

In this case 'prevent' is mostly translated by *verhindern. Hindern* fluctuates between the meanings of 'prevent' and 'hinder'[1] (impede,

[1] *Behindern*, which takes a personal object, means 'to hinder'. *Seine Gicht behindert ihn beim Gehen. Er kann die nötigen Bücher nicht bekommen und findet sich deswegen in*

delay). If the verbal noun is accompanied by an adjective meaning 'quick', or the like, it tends to mean 'hinder'. In terse statements coloured by emotion it is the preferred term for 'prevent'.

Die Ausführung des Plans hat er verhindert, wurde verhindert.
Den Verrat müssen wir um jeden Preis verhindern.
Das werde ich zu verhindern wissen.
Der Fluß verhinderte das Heranführen von Verstärkungen (prevented).
Der Fluß hinderte das schnelle Heranführen von Verstärkungen (hindered, impeded).
Wenn du in dein Unglück rennen willst, ich kann's nicht hindern (prevent).

PROTECT **Beschützen** stresses the personal nature of the protection extended to one. **Schützen** is used in all other cases.

Fühlen Sie sich beschützt, wenn er in der Nähe ist?
Während der ersten Jahre seiner Kindheit wurde er geliebt und beschützt.
Diese warmen Kleider werden Sie vor der Kälte schützen.
Australien glaubte lange Zeit, es sei durch seine geographische Lage vor feindlichen Angriffen geschützt.
Sie müssen sich vor seinen Anschuldigungen schützen.

PROVIDE[1] 1. **Versehen** can only be used in the sense of 'equip',[2] whether literal or figurative, i.e. when 'equip' could be substituted in English. It is always followed by a phrase with *mit* denoting the thing provided. With intangibles *versehen* is more common in the passive than the active voice.

In the sentence 'Can you provide us with beds?' the sense of equipment is present if the question is addressed to a house-agent. The German is therefore *können Sie uns mit Betten versehen?* If, however, it is a request for accommodation, this sense is absent, so that German would say: *können Sie uns für die Nacht unterbringen?*

Das Heer wurde mit den neuesten Waffen versehen.
Die Kandidaten wurden mit Papier versehen.

seiner Arbeit behindert. Hindern can mean 'hinder', generally with a personal, but sometimes with a non-personal object, and therefore admits ambiguity. *Behindern* is more common in the passive than in the active voice, while the reverse is true of *hindern* in the sense of 'hinder'.

[1] *Ausrüsten* is 'to equip for action', whether physical (e.g. *ein Kriegsschiff ausrüsten*), or mental (e.g. *mit guten Kenntnissen ausgerüstet*). *Ausstatten* means 'to endow' a person with natural gifts and 'to furnish' or 'fit out' a thing with features that enhance its appearance (e.g. *ein schön ausgestattetes Buch* = a beautifully got-up book). Compare 'well-appointed'.

[2] *Versehen* is often better translated by 'equip'. *Der Wagen ist mit einer neuen Bremse versehen.*

Das Haus ist mit Betten, Tischen, Stühlen wohl versehen.
Die Firma versah ihn mit einer Schreibmaschine.
Er versah uns mit dem nötigen Geld, mit warmen Kleidern.
Bevor er nach London fuhr, versah er sich mit ein paar guten Empfehlungsbriefen.
Er war mit einer guten Entschuldigung versehen.

2. **Versorgen** refers only to the necessities of life, food, clothing, etc. Used absolutely without a *mit* phrase, it translates 'to provide for'. In this use it is best preceded by some adverb such as *gut, reichlich* (see *sorgen für*).[1]

Der Staat muß die Arbeitslosen mit Nahrung und Kleidung versorgen.
Die Witwe ist gut versorgt.

3. **Sorgen für:** (*a*) to provide permanently for a person, i.e. to supply the necessities of life. Unlike *versorgen*, this expression requires no adverb such as *gut*. (*b*) To see that something is done or made available.

Für die Witwe ist gesorgt.
Der Staat wird für Arbeit sorgen.
Für Luftschutzkeller wurde in diesem Viertel nicht gesorgt.
Die Firma wird für Schadenersatz sorgen.

4. **Liefern:** (*a*) to make goods available, by placing them ready to hand, delivering them; (*b*) to provide something needed by producing it (as from the earth); (*c*) to furnish something intangible which is sought after.

(a) *Können Sie hundert Exemplare dieses Buches liefern?*
Amerika hat die neuesten Waffen geliefert.

(b) *Der russische Boden liefert fast alles, was die Wirtschaft braucht.*

(c) *Seine Taten liefern einen Beweis für seine Einstellung.*
Seine Saumseligkeit lieferte mir den Vorwand, den ich suchte.

5. **Stellen** is used to denote contributions made by two or more persons.

Ich stelle die Pferde, wenn Sie einen Wagen haben.
Er wird das Benzin stellen, aber Sie müssen für alles andere bezahlen.
Bei dem Aufmarsch wird dieses Regiment die Musik stellen.

6. **Aufkommen für:** accept the responsibility for financing a thing.

Der Staat wird für das Geld aufkommen.
Wenn Sie für die Nahrungsmittel sorgen, bin ich bereit, für den Wein aufzukommen.

[1] Some such adverb as *gut* tends to be necessary with many other verbs compounded with *ver-* (e.g. *gut verpackt, gut verwahrt*).

7. In other cases a more specific term must be used as in the following:

Sein Besuch bietet uns die Gelegenheit, die Frage aufzuwerfen (approximates to 'liefern'; see 'offer').

Sie müssen ihm Arbeit verschaffen (procure).

Es hat uns viel Vergnügen bereitet.

Die Firma hat ihm einen Sekretär zur Verfügung gestellt.

Ich kann es mir nur leisten, meinen Gästen ein einfaches Essen vorzusetzen.

Wir müssen gegen solche Vorkommnisse Vorkehrungen treffen.

PUBLIC **Öffentlichkeit** means 'the community at large',[1] but is used much less than 'public' as a political concept to refer to a body of opinion which addresses demands to its rulers. For this meaning German has no distinct term.[2] **Publikum** is generally a specific part of the community; particularly an audience or concourse of people or a section of the community that follows some particular activity, e.g. one that is interested in art, literature, racing.

Ich spreche im Namen der Öffentlichkeit.

Der Minister muß sich vor der Öffentlichkeit rechtfertigen.

Die Polizei richtete einen Appell an die Öffentlichkeit.

Das Publikum zeigte sich sehr ungeduldig über den späten Beginn des Konzerts.

PULL, DRAW, DRAG, TUG, TEAR German has no term as general as 'pull', and so uses the equivalents of 'draw', 'drag', 'tug', 'tear', etc.

1. **Ziehen** is 'to draw', i.e. either when the effort required is not stressed or control is implied.

Er zog das Hemd aus der Schublade, den Kork aus der Flasche.

Ich muß mir einen Zahn ziehen lassen.

Das Pferd zieht den Karren.

Die Lokomotive zieht den Zug.

Ziehen Sie den Stuhl weg.

Er zog die Glocke.

Ziehen Sie das Seil fester.

2. **Schleppen** is 'to drag', i.e. behind one and when a heavy object is implied.[3]

Die Fischer schleppten den Haifisch, das Boot, ans Ufer.

[1] It also means the 'publicness' of a thing (e.g. *die Öffentlichkeit der Verhandlungen*).

[2] *Volk* (see 'people') is sometimes used.

[3] *Verschleppen* has as one of its meanings 'to drag a person or thing away to an unknown destination' so that he, she, or it is to be regarded as lost. *Die Verschleppten*: displaced persons, i.e. dragged off into slavery in war.

3. **Zerren** suggests a violent or convulsive pulling or tugging by the subject and resistance on the part of the object pulled or tugged.[1]

Er zerrte die Kiste an die Oberfläche des Wassers.
Sie zerrten den Baumstamm in die Scheune hinein.
Sie zerrten ihn aus dem Schlamm.

4. **Zupfen** is 'to pluck' at a thing, mostly a part of the body, as an expression or sign of an attitude or meaning, but not in order to detach one thing from another.

Er zupfte ihn bei den Haaren, am Ärmel.

5. **Reißen** implies not only force on the part of the subject and resistance on that of the object, but, in certain cases, unlike *zerren*, also a tearing or wrenching of one thing from another.[2]

Er riß sie an sich, an seine Brust.
Er riß die Pflanzen mit allen Wurzeln heraus.
Er riß die Tapete von der Wand.

PUNISH 1. **Bestrafen** is the ordinary term. It means to make the penalty fit the offence.

Ein faules Kind muß bestraft werden.
Zuwiderhandelnde werden bestraft.
Jeder Mißbrauch wird bestraft.

2. **Strafen** is also 'to punish for an offence', but it suggests punishment by God or by Nemesis. It is therefore mostly used in elevated and emotional diction.

'*Gott strafe England*' (said by the Germans in the 1914–18 war).
Gott straft den Sünder.
Die ganze Familie ist gestraft worden.

PUT (literal sense) 1. **Tun** is the most general term[3] and translates 'put' in many of its literal senses when a thing is the object. It differs from 'put' in the following ways: (*a*) it does not suggest firmness of position, and therefore cannot normally be substituted for *setzen*; (*b*) it does not carry any implication of effort or difficulty, and accordingly should not be used when these are emphasized (e.g. when attention is focused on

[1] *Verzerren* is 'to distort' or 'to contort', particularly the face.

[2] In the sense of 'to tear a thing into two or more parts' *zerreißen* is generally used. Example: *ich habe meine Schuhriemen zerrißen.* It does not necessarily suggest tearing to shreds. *Reißen* is rather 'to tear' one thing from another. Example: *er riß mir die Zeitung aus der Hand.* See also 'break'.

[3] In Austria *geben* is used instead of *tun. Geben Sie die Papiere dahin.*

the act of putting, carrying, as opposed to the result); (*c*) it is more off-hand than 'put'; (*d*) it cannot normally govern a person or a part of the body as object; (*e*) it is not freely combined with prefixes (mostly only with *weg, hinein, hinaus*); (*f*) it is rarely used figuratively[1] in the sense of 'put'; (*g*) it is used less for *stellen* and *legen*, though this use is possible, than 'put' for such specific terms as 'lay', 'set', 'stand'.[2]

Tun Sie die Papiere auf den Stuhl, in die Schublade.
Er tat den Anzug in den Kleiderschrank.
Wir haben eine ganze Menge Möbel in dieses Zimmer getan.
Tun Sie etwas Butter auf das Brot.
Ich habe zwei Briefmarken drauf getan.

2. **Legen** means *liegen machen*, to make lie, to lay flat. It suggests care, solicitude and the like.

Er legte das Buch auf den Tisch.
Sie legte die Decken auf das Bett.
Er legte die Hand aufs Herz.
Der Kranke wurde aufs Bett gelegt.

3. **Stellen** means *stehen machen*, i.e. to make stand, to place upright on the narrowest base, to stand (used transitively).

Er stellte die Flasche auf den Tisch.
Er stellte das Buch in den Bücherschrank.
Sie stellte den Kessel auf den Herd.
Sie stellte den Regenschirm in die Ecke.
Wir haben das Klavier in dieses Zimmer gestellt.

4. **Setzen** is *sitzen machen*, to make sit, to set, to sit (used transitively). It suggests that one thing is made to fit into, on to another, and sometimes that it 'sits' firmly or permanently in position. It must also be used when 'put' means 'to sit' (transitive) or when the putting of one edge to another is strongly suggested (e.g. *er setzte den Becher an den Mund, ihm das Messer an die Kehle*). Because of its reference to fixed position it is used for all matters pertaining to writing.

Er setzte den Fuß auf den Stuhl.
Sie setzte das Kind auf den Stuhl (sat).

[1] Examples are: *hinzutun* (see 'add'); *Geld auf die Bank tun*. The explanations given of the literal uses of *legen, stellen, setzen, stecken* do not always hold good for the figurative uses (e.g. *er legte mir die Worte in den Mund*; not *steckte*). Further, the figurative uses of 'put' are most frequently not rendered by these terms at all. For example: *Das ist milde ausgedrückt* (putting it mildly); *seine Gedanken zu Papier bringen.*

[2] Certain compounds of *machen* are used colloquially in the sense of 'put'. *Wir könnten das Bild in diesen Rahmen hereinmachen.*

Setzen Sie Ihren Freund hinten in den Wagen.
Er setzte das Gebiß in ihren Mund (ein).
Er setzte die Pflanzen in weiten Abständen voneinander.
Er hat sich den Hut aufgesetzt.
Setzen Sie Ihre Unterschrift hierhin.
Setzen Sie das Wort hier herein.
Muß ich ein Komma setzen?

5. **Stecken:** (*a*) to put one thing into another which covers or encloses it;[1] (*b*) to put a thing on another thing so that it encircles it; (*c*) it has the meaning of 'stick' (though not in the sense of make adhere with gum and the like),[2] but unlike 'stick' it is not colloquial.

Er steckte die Hand in die Tasche, die Papiere in die Schublade, das Schwert in die Scheide, eine Zigarette in den Mund, den Brief in den Briefkasten.
Er steckte den Ring an den Finger.

6. **Hängen** should be used when the idea of hanging is emphasized. Otherwise *tun* is possible.

Hängen wir die Bilder an diese Wand.

QUALITY 1. **Qualität** means (*a*) degree of excellence, relative nature; (*b*) general excellence. It is generally used in a material, particularly a commercial sense, though it is sometimes applied —loosely—to spiritual qualities. It means 'attribute' (e.g. *Eigenschaft*) only as a philosophical term.

Dieser Stoff ist von erstklassiger, schlechter, Qualität.
Wir haben Anzüge in allen Qualitäten.
Bei der Herstellung unserer Waren sind wir immer auf Qualität bedacht (general excellence).

2. In the sense of 'attribute, characteristic, property', **Eigenschaft** must be used. It does not in itself denote excellence.

Der Sinn für Humor ist eine besondere Eigenschaft der Engländer.
Intoleranz ist eine Eigenschaft aller Diktatoren.
Er hat gute, schlechte, Eigenschaften.

3. **Vorzug** is an excellence, merit, of any kind, whether material or spiritual.

Seine Vorzüge sind bekannt.
Dieses System hat den Vorzug, daß es schnell funktioniert.

[1] *Stecken bleiben* = to get stuck (see 'catch'); *stecken* in intransitive use and as a weak verb means 'to be' in the sense of 'not visible, hidden' (e.g. *wo stecken Sie denn so lange?*) or 'in the inner being, at the core' (e.g. *es steckt sehr viel in ihm*).

[2] 'To stick' in this sense is *kleben*.

4. In the sense of 'faculty', 'gift', and the like, the German equivalents of these terms must be used.

Er hat das Vermögen, Ungläubige zu bekehren (*Vermögen* can suggest an act of will, see 'power').

Er hat die Gabe, Vertrauen zu erwecken (*Gabe* is a more unconscious quality than *Vermögen*).

QUITE, ENTIRELY 1. **Ganz** has as its primary meaning 'entire', 'whole',[1] and is less used than 'quite' in other senses. Accompanied by a negative it invariably means 'entirely' (e.g. *es ist nicht ganz klar, es ist ganz unmöglich*). This is also the meaning when in positive use it modifies a verb (e.g. *ich verstehe es ganz*) or a prepositional phrase (e.g. *es ist ganz in Ordnung*).[2]

Another use it has—in common with 'quite'—with certain adjectives and adverbs is to indicate that one concedes to a thing the quality attributed to it by the adjectives, but not in the highest degree, i.e. not entirely. It thus expresses a reservation (e.g. *er ist ganz nett, ich finde Ihre Arbeit ganz schön*).

Used adjectively with the indefinite article it means 'whole' in all senses of this term. It is frequently an equivalent of 'quite' (e.g. *eine ganze Meile*, a whole mile, quite a mile;[3] *eine ganze Menge*, a whole lot, quite a lot; *ein ganzes Ende*, quite a way). Generally, however, when 'quite' is accompanied by the indefinite article it must be otherwise translated (e.g. he is quite an expert, a celebrity).

It cannot be used apart from these meanings, e.g. as an affirmation that a thing is as it is stated to be (e.g. it is quite possible, that is quite sufficient). Further: quite soon, quite recently.[4]

Der Tisch ist ganz von dem Tuch bedeckt.
Ich verstehe nicht ganz, worauf Sie hinaus wollen.
Er hat sich ganz unvernünftig benommen.
Er blieb ganz still.
Er ist ganz bereit, Ihnen zu helfen.
Ich bin ganz Ihrer Meinung.
Ich habe es ganz vergessen.
Die Stadt ist ganz zerstört.
Es liegt ganz außerhalb meiner Sphäre.
Es ist heute ganz warm.
Ich habe es ganz gern.

[1] See 'all'.
[2] More emphatically *ganz und gar*. For *gänzlich* see 'complete'.
[3] Or: *eine gute Meile.*
[4] *Recht bald, erst neulich.*

2. **Durchaus** is accented either on the first or on the second syllable. When accented on the first the meaning is 'in every respect, through and through'; when accented on the second it is an affirmation that a thing is as it is stated to be. In the latter sense it corresponds to 'quite', e.g. before a verb, an adjective or adverb, before a superlative adjective.

Durchaus is not normally used (*a*) with adjectives or adverbs combined with the prefix *un* or the suffix *los* (but can be used with *nicht*) (e.g. *ganz unzweifelhaft, ganz würdelos*); (*b*) with adjectives denoting qualities in persons or things considered in themselves (e.g. he is quite clever, bold). It is possible, however, if these adjectives have an impersonal subject (e.g. *es ist durchaus klug, das zu tun*; *das ist durchaus irreführend, widersinnig*).

Es ist durchaus möglich.
Was Sie getan haben, genügt durchaus.
Das ist durchaus der beste Bericht über den Vorgang.
Ich habe durchaus Lust, dahin zu gehen.
Ich sehe durchaus ein, warum Sie darauf bestehen.
Ich bin durchaus Ihrer Meinung (or *ganz*).

3. When 'quite' is followed by the indefinite article and has the sense of 'real', it can generally be translated by **richtig** (more objective) or **recht** (with subjective emphasis).[1]

Das Stück war ein richtiger Erfolg.
Es hat richtiges Aufsehen erregt (quite a stir).
Er ist ein richtiger, rechter, Narr.
Es war ein richtiges, rechtes, Vergnügen.

RAISE, LIFT, HEIGHTEN **A.** Literal sense.

1. **Heben**[2] is the general term. It means 'to lift a thing higher than before', not 'to add to its height'.

Er hob das Glas zum Mund.
Er hob den Deckel seines Koffers.
Er hob sein Gepäck vom Wagen.
Das Schiff wurde vom Meeresgrund gehoben.
Der Kran hob die schweren Maschinen aus dem Schiff.
Er hob die Hand, das Bein, den Kopf, die Augen.

2. **Erheben** is a more dignified term and often suggests emotional or symbolical gestures. Similarly *sich erheben* (to arise).

[1] A synonym is *ziemlich* (e.g. *ein ziemlicher Erfolg, ein ziemliches Aufsehen*).
[2] *Aufheben* and, more colloquially, *hoch heben* are used in the sense of 'lift' and 'lift up'.

Er erhebt die Hände (e.g. in prayer or supplication).
Er erhebt das Glas (e.g. solemnly).
Er erhob den Blick gen Himmel.

3. **Erhöhen** is sometimes used in the sense of adding to an object in order to make it higher.

Die Mauer ist etwas erhöht worden.
Das Gebäude ist um ein Stockwerk erhöht worden.

4. **Aufziehen** should be used in the sense of 'draw up'.

Der Vorhang, die Zugbrücke, wurde aufgezogen.

B. Figurative senses.

1. **Heben:** to improve. It cannot be followed by any prepositional phrase meaning 'to a level, standard'.

Die Gesundheit, den Geschmack, die Leistungsfähigkeit, das Niveau der allgemeinen Bildung, den Mut der Truppen heben.

2. **Erheben.**

(a) To elevate a person to a higher rank.

Er wurde in den Adelsstand erhoben.
Die Gesandtschaft wurde zur Botschaft erhoben.

(b) To start[1] vigorously,[2] particularly with reference to sound.

Ein Geschrei, die Stimme erheben.

(c) To make known, particularly a point of view.

Zweifel, Einwände, Ansprüche erheben.

(d) To collect money.

Steuern erheben.

3. **Erhöhen.**[3]

(a) To raise a thing to a higher level, standard (not to raise a person to a higher rank). As in the literal use, the sense is 'to add to, to increase', i.e. not simply 'to lift' from a lower to a higher position. It cannot be followed by any prepositional phrase meaning 'to a level, standard'.

Die Produktion, die Wohlfahrt des Landes, das schulpflichtige Alter, Preise, die erlaubte Geschwindigkeit, erhöhen.

[1] Compare *anheben* (to start).
[2] Reflexively: *ein Sturm, ein Streit erhebt sich.*
[3] See also *steigern* under 'increase'.

(b) To heighten, to intensify a thing so that it is more readily apprehended or felt.

Die Wirkung, seine Freude, wurde erhöht.

4. **Bringen:** to raise to a certain level. It is followed by such phrases as *auf ein Niveau.*

Das Volk muß auf ein höheres Bildungsniveau gebracht werden.

REAL, TRUE, GENUINE 1. **Wirklich** means 'existing in actuality and effect' as opposed to something which exists in name or mere possibility. It lacks the other sense of 'real' defined by *P.O.D.* as: genuine, rightly so called, natural, sincere.

Das ist ein wirkliches Ereignis (not imaginary).
Ein wirklicher Professor, eine wirkliche Kultur.

2. **Wahr** means 'corresponding to the prototype' and 'conforming with the real idea of the thing as it should be', opposed to the false and apparent. It can thus translate 'real' and 'genuine' as well as 'true'. For the rendering of the adverb 'truly' see *wahrhaft.*

Ein wahrer Professor, eine wahre Kultur.

3. **Echt** is 'genuine' only in the sense of 'unadulterated', 'not spurious'.[1] Thus while both *wahr* and *echt* can mean 'genuine', *echt* goes further than *wahr* in suggesting the idea of greater or more typical perfection.

Ein echter Professor, eine echte Kultur.

4. **Wahrhaft,** used adjectively, normally means 'truth-loving', 'sincere'. Its use in the sense of 'conforming to the real idea of a thing', 'not a sham, is rare'. It must be used to translate all senses of 'truly'.[2]

Ein wahrhafter Mensch.
Er ist ein wahrhaft großer Mann.

REALLY 1. **Wirklich:** in reality, as opposed to illusion, a fiction of the mind. It is often used to persuade the listener that one's statement is a fact.

Er steht wirklich da.
Er ist wirklich krank.
Er wohnt wirklich in Berlin.

[1] See also *ernstlich* under 'serious'.

[2] *Wahrhaftig* expresses in present-day German an affirmation of a statement, and sometimes corresponds to 'veritable'. *Wahrlich,* mostly an adverb, is used only in exalted style and often corresponds to 'verily'.

2. **Eigentlich:** in reality, at bottom, though this may not be apparent because of external or superficial departures from the fundamental reality. The departure is often expressed in a following *aber* clause.

Er wohnt eigentlich in München, verbringt aber viel Zeit in Nürnberg.
Er ist eigentlich ganz zuverlässig, wenn er auch diesmal sein Versprechen nicht erfüllte.

RECEIVE 1. **Erhalten** suggests, like *bekommen*, that the receiver is passive, but unlike the latter is used almost exclusively in writing. Apart from its use with persons, the subject may be a thing, the object some treatment it receives.

Einen Brief, ein Geschenk, eine Antwort, einen Befehl, eine Strafe, eine gute Schulbildung erhalten.
Er hat einen Schlag, einen Hieb, einen Stich erhalten.
Die Maschinen haben eine gründliche Ausbesserung erhalten.

2. **Empfangen** draws attention to the act of receiving. This is mostly ceremonious (the conferring of distinctions, the welcoming of guests). If the implication of ceremony is absent, either the manner of reception must be stated or the context must suggest activity on the part of the receiver.

Aus den Händen des Kaisers empfing er das eiserne Kreuz.
Er hat einen hohen Orden empfangen.
Er hat ein Diplom empfangen.
Er empfing den Preis.
Er hat die Sterbesakramente, das Abendmahl empfangen.
Die Hausfrau empfing die Gäste.
Er hat den Befehl voll Mißtrauen empfangen.
Er hat einen Schlag, einen Hieb, empfangen.

3. **In Empfang nehmen:** to take delivery of goods. A formal term.

Wollen Sie die Kiste in Empfang nehmen?

4. **Aufnehmen.**

(a) To accept,[1] admit into an organization, a society, as a member.

Er wurde in unseren Verein aufgenommen.

(b) To receive with a mental attitude.

Das Stück wurde mit Begeisterung aufgenommen.

5. **Finden:** to meet with some specified kind of treatment or attitude of mind.

Der Plan fand seine Billigung, keine Beachtung.

[1] See 'accept'.

RECENTLY 1. Both **kürzlich** and **neulich** refer to a point of time in the past, the former being more precise.[1] *Neulich* translates 'the other day'.[2] It looks at the action from the point of view of the present moment of speaking or writing. *Kürzlich* must also be used in cases of historical narrative, i.e. in the meaning of a short time before the present denoted by the past narrative, e.g. with the pluperfect tense.

Er nat kürzlich promoviert.
Ich war neulich im Theater.
Ich hatte kürzlich darum gebeten (before the moment of asking).

2. **In letzter Zeit** is used in cases where the action continues up to the present.[3]

Ich bin in letzter Zeit sehr beschäftigt gewesen.

RECOGNIZE, ACKNOWLEDGE 1. Recognize: to know again with the senses, either through having seen, heard, etc. the person or object before, or through distinguishing features, of which one is aware, but without such previous experience.

Erkennen translates this sense. If it is desired to make clear that the recognition is due to one's having seen, heard, the person or object before and not merely to a knowledge of distinguishing features, *wieder* is normally added.

Ich habe ihn an seinem Mantel erkannt.
Ich habe ihn gleich wiedererkannt.
Ich erkenne Sie nicht wieder.

2. *Erkennen* also 'means to come to a mental understanding, realization', with regard both to trivial matters and to the pursuit of scientific truth.[4, 5]

Ich habe meinen Irrtum erkannt.
Ich habe allmählich erkannt, daß ich mich gründlich in Ihnen getäuscht habe.
Er hat den Ernst der Lage erkannt.
Er hat diese Wahrheit noch nicht erkannt.

3. **Anerkennen** translates both 'recognize' in the sense of 'to acknowledge by special notice, approval or sanction; to treat as valid, as having existence or entitled to consideration; to take notice of (a thing or person)

[1] *Jüngst*, 'recently', is somewhat old-fashioned.
[2] *Den anderen Tag*: the next day.
[3] Until recently: *bis vor kurzem.*
[4] Since *erkennen* means 'to come to know', it must be used to translate 'know' in this sense, e.g. in the imperative. *Erkenne dich selbst* (see 'knowledge').
[5] See also *erkennen* under 'see'.

in some way' (*S.O.D.*); and 'acknowledge'[1] in the sense of 'to recognize or confess' (a person or thing, to be something); or, simply, 'to own the claims of' (*S.O.D.*).

When these terms come into comparison, 'recognize' denotes a more formal according of standing, validity, and the like, and its translation into practice, while 'acknowledge' may imply nothing more than a mental attitude of acceptance. *Erkennen* translates both, except in sentences where English uses both in deliberate contrast (e.g. 'The ladies never acted so well as when they were in the presence of a fact which they acknowledged but did not recognize', Meredith, quoted in Webster's *Dictionary of Synonyms*). In such cases 'acknowledge' must be rendered by *gelten lassen* (see 'accept') and the like.

Man muß seine hohe Begabung anerkennen.
Der Anschluß Oesterreichs an Deutschland wurde von den meisten Regierungen anerkannt.
Goethe wird allgemein als der größte deutsche Dichter anerkannt.
Seine Ansprüche wurden anerkannt.
Der Papst ist das anerkannte Haupt der römisch-katholischen Kirche.

REDUCE, LESSEN[2] 'Reduce' suggests much more strongly than 'lessen' the deliberate intervention of a personal agent.[3]

1. **Vermindern** and **verringern** (i.e. *geringer machen*[4]) are sometimes used interchangeably, but in discriminating use the following distinctions are observed. *Vermindern* is more serious, more accurate, and denotes a more drastic reduction than *verringern*, which means 'to take a little less of a substance', 'to relax', 'to lessen gradually'. Further, *vermindern* suggests more clearly a deliberate act, a decision. *Verringern* is therefore more common than *vermindern* when the subject is a thing (e.g. *das Auto verringerte seine Geschwindigkeit*; but, *der Fahrer verminderte die Geschwindigkeit des Autos*). Both verbs are used reflexively, but this use is more common with *verringern*, unless a drastic reduction is implied, since it does not strongly suggest deliberate intervention.

[1] 'Acknowledge' in the sense of 'signify the receipt of' a thing is *bestätigen* (e.g. *den Empfang eines Briefes bestätigen*). In the sense of 'admit': *eingestehen*, etc.

[2] See also *kürzen* (under 'shorten') and *einschränken* (under 'limit') which frequently translate 'to reduce' in the sense of a deliberate act on the part of a person. *Die Löhne, die Forderungen, sind gekürzt worden. Die Hausarbeiten wurden stark eingeschränkt.*

[3] Further synonyms are: 'diminish', which strongly suggests 'loss' and therefore corresponds more closely to *verringern* than to the other terms; 'lower', i.e. to a certain level; 'decrease', by a gradual process.

[4] *Gering* means 'slight, of little importance, negligible, trifling' (compare *geringfügig*), *klein* means 'small' without specific implications. *Das Bild hat nur einen geringen Wert* (in a bad sense). *Die Arbeit stellte nur geringe Anforderungen an ihn* (in a neutral sense).

'Undiminished' is, however, *unvermindert*; *un* cannot be combined with *verringert*.

It will be seen that these distinctions are only tendencies, which sometimes cut across each other.

Neither verb can be followed by a preposition to translate 'to reduce to', but *um*, meaning 'by' may follow.

Die Zahl der Unterrichtsstunden wurde vermindert, verringert.
Die Medizin hat die Schmerzen vermindert, verringert.
Wir haben die Zahl unserer Angestellten verringert.
Wir müssen unsere Ausgaben vermindern.
Wir müssen die Unkosten verringern.
Durch die Abwesenheit der Kinder haben sich unsere Ausgaben verringert.
Vermindern Sie die Zahl der Zigaretten, die Sie täglich rauchen.
Unsere Vorräte verringerten sich zusehends (not *verminderten*, because a gradual reduction is implied).
Durch die vielen verlorenen Schlachten verminderten sich die deutschen Reserven (not *verringerten*).
Sein Gewicht verringerte sich (not *verminderte*).
Ich habe die Menge des Phosphats, das ich für den Garten gebrauche, verringert.
Verringere die Medizinmenge um zwei Tropfen pro Stunde.

2. **Mindern** is applied particularly to the weakening of a feeling or sentiment. It can also be used for *vermindern* in elevated prose and in poetry, which generally prefers the forms without the prefix, since they are more direct and vivid. Otherwise *mindern* is little used.

Das mindert nicht die Hochachtung, die ich vor ihm habe.
Das mindert meine Vaterlandsliebe nicht.

3. **Verkleinern**[1] (i.e. *klein machen*), is primarily applied to the reduction of size, but also to numbers where these imply size. It cannot be followed by a preposition to translate 'reduce to'.

Das Lehrpersonal wurde verkleinert.
Die Zahl der Banken hat sich verkleinert.
Der Ertrag des Grundstücks hat sich verkleinert.

4. **Herabsetzen** (i.e. to put down) generally implies the intervention of a personal agent. It is not used of size or intensity. It may be followed by *auf* to translate 'reduce to'.

Die Regierung hat die Steuern, die Löhne, herabgesetzt.
Er hat seine Forderungen herabgesetzt.

[1] *Verkleinern* also means 'to disparage, belittle'.

Wir müssen die Zahl der Sitzungen auf die Hälfte herabsetzen.
Die Preise[1] *der Autos sind noch nicht herabgesetzt worden.*

5. **Herunterbringen** means 'to get down', generally by an effort, but also more generally 'to bring down'.

Sie müssen versuchen, Ihre Temperatur, Ihren Blutdruck, herunterzubringen (or: *kriegen*).
Diese Politik hat den Lebensstandard heruntergebracht.

REFER 1. **Sich beziehen** is used of words, statements, thoughts in the sense of 'to be related, directed to'. With a personal subject it can only mean to 'link up' something previously said or written with a present statement, e.g. in support of it; i.e. it cannot be generally used in the sense of 'allude to'.[2]

Seine Bemerkung bezog sich auf den schon erwähnten Plan, auf Sie.
Ich beziehe mich auf meinen Brief vom 5. Mai.
Zum Beweis bezog er sich auf zwei Dokumente, auf die schon zitierte Stelle.

2. In the general sense of 'allude to', **sprechen von** or some synonym such as *anspielen auf* must be used.

Ich spreche nicht von Ihnen.
Er spricht dauernd von seinen Kriegserlebnissen.

3. **Verweisen** means (*a*) to direct a person to someone as an authority; (*b*) to direct someone's attention to a thing. In the first case 'to' is translated by *an*, in the second by *auf*.

Ich verwies ihn an meinen Vorgesetzten.
Ich verwies ihn auf einige wichtige Stellen in der Rede.

4. Used intransitively in the sense of 'consult', 'refer' must be translated by equivalents of the latter.

Sie müssen das Lexikon zu Rate ziehen, zu Hilfe nehmen.

5. **Weitergeben, übergeben** have the meaning of 'to pass on', 'to hand over', a matter to an authority.

Wir können die Angelegenheit nur an den Minister weitergeben.

[1] *Ermäßigen* means 'to reduce' prices, as a concession. *Dieses Theater hat auch Eintrittskarten zu ermäßigten Preisen.*

[2] *Beziehen* is also used non-reflexively in the sense of 'to relate one thing to another' or 'to make one statement apply to a further case'. '*Was ich in Nürnberg naturgemäß nur vom ersten Band sagen konnte, möchte ich hiermit auch auf den zweiten beziehen...*' (Gisevius, *Bis Zum Bitteren Ende*).

REFUSE, DECLINE 1. **Sich weigern** is generally only followed by an infinitive and means 'to refuse'. *Weigern* is occasionally used transitively in the sense of *verweigern*, but unlike the latter stresses the force of the action, not the result.

Er weigerte sich, dem Befehl zu gehorchen.
Er weigerte ihm den Gehorsam.

2. **Verweigern** means 'to refuse' only in the sense of 'withhold, not to grant'. It is commonly used of the withholding of what is rightly or lawfully demanded (e.g. *den Gehorsam, den Eid*). It is not normally followed by the infinitive. Used reflexively, it can have a sexual implication.

Er verweigerte den Dienst, ihnen seine Hilfe.

3. **Abschlagen** and **ausschlagen** translate 'refuse' only in the sense of 'to reject' a thing. Both are stronger terms than 'refuse' and suggest a flat, brusque refusal. *Abschlagen* is used more of a request, *ausschlagen* of an offer.[1] Neither term admits a person as direct object.

Er schlug mir meine Bitte, mein Gesuch, ab.
Sein Angebot wurde ausgeschlagen.

4. **Ablehnen** means 'to decline' and is therefore a less harsh expression than those treated under **1, 2, 3**. It should therefore be used to translate 'refuse' when this conveys no implication of brusqueness. It can refer to a request or to an offer, and can be followed by the infinitive.

Er lehnte die Bitte, das Angebot, die Einladung, ab.
Der Vorschlag wurde abgelehnt.
Er wurde als Lehrer abgelehnt.
Ich lehne es ab, die Verantwortung dafür zu übernehmen.

5. **Abweisen:** to reject firmly and definitely[2] a thing or a person who makes a request. With a thing as subject it frequently implies its rejection by an authority as inadmissible.

Sein Gesuch, seine Ansprüche, wurden abgewiesen.
Ich wurde abgewiesen.

6. When a thing is the subject of 'refuse', **wollen** (or some other term such as *sich sträuben*) may be used negatively. *Sich weigern* is here impossible.

Mein Haar will durchaus nicht flach liegen.
Die Tür will nicht offen bleiben.

[1] For *versagen* used synonymously, see 'deny'.
[2] *Einen kurz abweisen* = to send one about one's business.

RELATION(SHIP), CONNECTION, RATIO, PROPORTION

1. (a) **Verhältnis**[1] means primarily 'ratio' and 'proportion'. Applied to a 'relation' between things, it can only mean that they stand in a certain ratio to each other, i.e. that the relation is fixed in this way. It is not used in a general way to indicate a vague connection. It is the regular philosophical term (*das Leib-Seele-Verhältnis*). **Beziehung** is a relationship in which one thing influences the other, or where there is an interaction, therefore often in reference to two events. Further, in the phrase: *in dieser Beziehung*, i.e. in this connection, respect. The plural *Verhältnisse* is not used in this sense of the singular.[2]

Das Verhältnis zwischen Ursache und Wirkung.
Im Verhältnis zum Gewinn waren die Kosten zu hoch.
Die Sensationsnachrichten, die die Zeitungen bringen, stehen häufig in gar keinem Verhältnis zu der Wichtigkeit der Ereignisse.
Das Steigen des Yen stand in direkter Beziehung (not *Verhältnis*) *zur amerikanischen Präsidentenwahl im Jahre* 1936.

(b) In the sense of relations between people *Verhältnis* is much deeper and more intimate than *Beziehung*. Thus *ein freundschaftliches Verhältnis* means much more than *freundschaftliche Beziehungen*. *Beziehungen*, mostly plural in this sense, draws attention to externals, such as what people do, *Verhältnis* to the inner attitude. Though generally singular, the latter may be plural in this sense.[3] In reference to countries, however, *Beziehung* is stronger, since it denotes concrete realities, whereas *Verhältnis* is formal.

Es besteht ein freundschaftliches Verhältnis zwischen England und Frankreich.
Es bestehen freundschaftliche Beziehungen zwischen England und Frankreich.
Das Verhältnis zwischen ihnen war gespannt.
Ich habe alle Beziehungen zu ihm abgebrochen.
Er hat viele Beziehungen zur diplomatischen Welt.

2. **Zusammenhang** indicates in a general way a close relationship between things or ideas, but not personal relations. In reference to ideas the relation is logical and necessary.[4]

[1] See also 'behave', 'attitude'.
[2] See 'state', 'condition'.
[3] *Verhältnis* also means 'liaison'. Vulgarly: *sie ist sein Verhältnis.* See also 'appreciate', p. 31, 3(*c*).
[4] *Im Zusammenhang*: in the context. Similarly: (*einen Gedanken*) *aus dem Zusammenhang reißen.* The plural is used idiomatically, and without an English equivalent. *Die großen Zusammenhänge erklären*, i.e. not details. *Das Buch läßt hinter die Kulissen schauen und deckt unbekannte Zusammenhänge auf.*

RELATION(SHIP)

Der Zusammenhang zwischen Ursache und Wirkung.
Was damals geschah, steht in keinem Zusammenhang mit der gegenwärtigen Lage.
Der dramatische Dichter muß bestrebt sein, den Zusammenhang zwischen den verschiedenen Vorgängen seines Werkes klar zu machen.
Ihre Antwort steht in gar keinem Zusammenhang mit der gestellten Frage.

3. **Verbindung** is a loose connection either between thoughts, things or persons.[1] In reference to thoughts it means no more than 'association', and applied to persons it denotes no more than the existence of channels of communication.

Die Verbindung zwischen diesen beiden Gedanken ist phantastisch.
Er hat während des Krieges seine Verbindungen mit dem Feind aufrechterhalten.

REPEAT **Wiederholen** means 'to do or to say a thing again'. It cannot be used in the following senses: (*a*) to pass on information, which is **weitersagen**; (*b*) to say a thing over and over to oneself in order to memorize it, which is **aufsagen**.

Er wiederholte, daß er den Vorschlag ablehnen müsse.
Er wiederholte seine Frage.
Sie dürfen das Experiment nicht wiederholen.
Sagen Sie es nicht weiter.
Er sagte sich stundenlang die unregelmäßigen Verben auf.

RESPONSIBILITY 1. **Verantwortung** is the state of being responsible. The reference to the person who bears it is stressed. **Verantwortlichkeit,** a rarer term, draws attention to the nature of the objective obligation, the charge itself. Both *Verantwortung* and *Verantwortlichkeit* can mean 'sense of responsibility'.

Sie müssen die Verantwortung dafür übernehmen.
Er lehnt die Verantwortung dafür ab.
'*Auf Ihnen ruht eine große Verantwortlichkeit, und ich würde Sie um keine Gefälligkeit bitten, die Sie mit Ihrer Pflicht in Konflikt brächte*' (R. Huch, *Weiße Nächte*). (*Verantwortung* also possible, if it is thought of in close association with the person, and not as detached from him).
Das Prinzip der Verantwortlichkeit.
Ärzte müssen sich der Verantwortlichkeit bewußt sein, die ihr Beruf in sich schließt.
Das Wichtige ist, daß man dem Schüler die Verantwortung überträgt, um ihn zur Verantwortlichkeit zu erziehen (sense of responsibility).

[1] See 'join'.

2. The plural 'responsibilities' can only be translated by **Verpflichtungen**, i.e. obligations.

Er versucht dauernd, sich seinen Verpflichtungen zu entziehen.

REST (noun) 1. Followed by 'of' (which may be implied).

Rest is used in the same way as English 'rest',[1] and must be distinguished from **übrig**. The distinction is not concerned with size, except that with countries *Rest* mostly refers to the smaller, *übrig* to the larger area. In general, *übrig* suggests that which lacks or loses value[2] in our eyes, either absolutely or with regard to a specific matter.

Übrig presents special difficulty when it qualifies a singular noun. It is only used with such nouns as can be conceived in terms of units, as consisting of items (e.g. a concert, which has numbers).

Essen Sie den Rest des Fleisches auf!

Wir behalten zehn Mark von Ihrem Gehalt, den Rest können Sie gleich haben.

Ich nehme ein Zimmer, der Rest des Hauses gehört Ihnen.[3]

Er ist in einem Fach durchgefallen, aber den Rest der Prüfung hat er gut bestanden.

Beethoven wurde entsetzlich gespielt, der Rest des Konzerts war prachtvoll.

Wir verbrachten den Rest des Abends zu Hause.

Westlich der Oder hat Deutschland keine Gebietsverluste erlitten, der Rest ist an Polen und Rußland gefallen.

Wenn die Ostgebiete endgültig verloren sind, wird das übrige Deutschland sich kaum ernähren können.

Beethoven wurde prachtvoll gespielt, das übrige Konzert war entsetzlich.

Zwei Gäste blieben im Wohnzimmer, die übrige Gesellschaft ging in den Garten (or, of course: *der Rest der Gesellschaft*).

Das übrige Programm bot nichts Besonderes.

Die übrige Saison war ein Fiasko.

Dezember war erträglich, aber der übrige Winter war schauderhaft.

Einige Bilder waren gut, aber die übrige Ausstellung war unter aller Kritik.

[1] *Rest* can, unlike its English equivalent, be (*a*) preceded by the indefinite article, (*b*) pluralized. In these cases it means 'remainder' (also in a mathematical sense), 'bit', 'scrap' (e.g. *es bleibt nur ein kleiner Rest übrig*; *die Diener bekamen den Rest der Mahlzeit*). The plural *Rester* is often used (particularly in Saxony) for 'remnants', in a draper's shop, etc. *Überrest* (often pluralized) is a smaller and more insignificant part, often corresponding to 'remains' (e.g. *die Überreste der Mahlzeit frassen die Hunde*). *Überbleibsel* is what is worthless, unusable.

[2] Similarly: *was übrig bleibt* (e.g. *was...interessiert mich nicht*).

[3] Colloquially *sonst* is often used in this sense. *Ich nehme ein Zimmer, sonst gehört das Haus Ihnen.*

Er verbrachte die übrige Zeit im Gefängnis.
'Den übrigen Abend zersplitterte ich wieder Willen da und dort in Gesellschaft' (Mörike, *Lucie Gelmeroth*).

2. Referring to a plural noun previously mentioned: **die anderen, die übrigen** (i.e. the remaining ones). For an explanation of *übrig* see the preceding section.

Um die anderen brauchen wir uns nicht zu kümmern, sie wissen sich im Notfall schon zu helfen.
Diese Möbel werden wir benutzen, die übrigen stelle ich unter.

REST (verb) **1.** With reference to the physical resting of persons **ruhen** suggests sleep, while **sich ausruhen** means 'to relax', 'to refresh oneself by rest' whether through sleep or by lying down or merely by avoiding tiring activity. *Sich ausruhen* can apply to a part of, as well as to the whole, body. The reflexive pronoun can be omitted in exalted style, but also in ordinary prose to refer to 'rest' in general as distinct from a specific moment.

In a question designed to ascertain whether a person is resting or engaging in some activity *ruhen* is used (*sich ausruhen* referring to the result, i.e. recuperation, not the attempt to rest, unless accompanied by some verb such as *wollen*). If *ruhen* in such a question is felt to be ambiguous by referring to 'sleep', when it is desired only to indicate an attempt to rest, *ein bißchen* can be added.

Kinder, macht keinen Lärm, ich ruhe jetzt!
Haben Sie ein bißchen geruht oder Ihre Korrespondenz erledigt?
Ich wünsche, wohl geruht zu haben (said by a servant to his master in old-fashioned style).
Kinder, macht keinen Lärm, ich will mich ausruhen.
Haben Sie sich (gut, ein bißchen) ausgeruht?
Ruhen Sie sich in den Ferien aus.
Der Arzt sagte: 'Ruhen Sie erst mal aus.'
Man muß die Truppen ausruhen lassen.
Sie müssen die Augen ausruhen lassen.

2. Figurative senses.

(a) **Ruhen** denotes a state which is the opposite of activity or movement. Of a person it means 'to do nothing', of a thing (or a dead body) 'to remain in a certain position' or 'to lean on' anything that acts as a support. It is used also of a responsibility or a task. Applied to aspects of nature or inner states of being it means 'to be still, peaceful'.

Er ruht nie, er arbeitet wie besessen.

Er ruht auf seinen Lorbeeren.
Der Abend, der Wald, ruht.
Seine Hand ruhte auf dem Fensterbrett.
Mein Blick ruhte auf der Schönheit der Landschaft.
Das Dach ruht auf Säulen.
Napoleon ruht im Hôtel des Invalides.
Eine schwierige Aufgabe ruht auf Ihnen.

(b) **Rasten** suggests more definitely than *ruhen* a pause in the course of an activity.

Er kann nie rasten, er muß immer weiter.

(c) **Beruhen:** (i) to be based on; (ii) *etwas auf sich beruhen lassen* = to let a thing rest at that.

Die Klage gegen ihn beruht auf der Aussage zweier Zeugen.
Der Beweis beruht auf diesen Tatsachen.

REVEAL, DISCLOSE, DIVULGE 1. **Offenbaren** can only be used (*a*) of lofty truths that come to one as though by inspiration, and of matters so intimate as to be regarded as sacred or as concerned with one's deepest self; (*b*) of some deficiency about oneself.

Die (ge)offenbarte Religion.
Große Männer offenbaren der Menschheit neue Wege, neue Ideale.
In diesem Gedicht offenbart der Dichter seine innerste Seele.
Damit offenbart er nur seine Schwächen.

2. **Enthüllen,** i.e. to remove the covering,[1] is the most general term in the sense of 'to reveal what is hidden'.

Er hat das Geheimnis, seine Pläne, enthüllt.
Deine Bemerkung hat alles, deinen ganzen Charakter, enthüllt.

3. **Entdecken** means 'to discover' and, figuratively, 'to uncover', i.e. what is hidden. It may be used of what is bad as well as of what is good, but in both cases this is regarded as important.

Er hat ihr seine Liebe entdeckt.
Er hat uns den ganzen Betrug entdeckt.

4. **Eröffnen,** i.e. to open what is closed,[2] is used only of important matters, particularly intentions, plans and the like, and implies a trustworthy recipient of the disclosure.

Der Minister eröffnete seinen Kollegen seine Pläne.

[1] *Enthüllen* also means 'to unveil' a monument, statue and the like. *Entschleiern* means literally 'to unveil' a picture, figuratively 'to unveil' something mysterious. It is a less prosaic term than *enthüllen.*

[2] See also 'open'.

ROLL **Rollen** (transitive and intransitive) is 'to roll smoothly, without impediment', of both light and heavy bodies. **Wälzen** (only transitive) is 'to roll with difficulty', or erratically, with contortions,[1] either forwards or about, and of bodies that are too heavy to roll or revolve easily.

Er rollte das Faß hinunter.
Der Ball, der Stein, rollte den Abhang hinunter.
Er rollte seine Augen.
Der Donner rollt.
Der Fluß rollt dem Meere zu.
Der Sturzbach wälzte große Baumstämme über den Damm.
Er wälzte sich stundenlang im Bett, ohne schlafen zu können.

ROOM, SPACE **Raum,** like 'space', is the wider term. In the sense of 'available space', it also corresponds to 'space', while the equivalent of the more limited 'room' is **Platz.**[2] In reference to measurement *Raum* and 'space' are the more objective terms.

Ich habe hier nicht genug Platz zum Stehen, geschweige denn zum Liegen.
Die Universität hat nicht genug Raum, um so viele Studenten aufzunehmen.
Wieviel Schiffsraum wird für das Gepäck erlaubt.

RUN (literal) **Rennen** is 'to run with great speed', whether in a race or otherwise.[3] **Laufen** is 'to run at a moderate speed', often implying little more than 'hurry', or intermittent running while moving about. It cannot therefore be applied to a race. In northern Germany *laufen* often means 'to walk'.[4,5]

Das Pferderennen.
Er rannte so schnell, daß niemand ihn einholen konnte.
Er rannte spornstreichs gegen den Feind.
Sie müssen rennen, wenn Sie nicht vom Regen überrascht werden wollen.
Als der Detektiv auf ihn zuging, lief er weg.
Laufen Sie, sonst werden Sie den Zug verpassen.
Trotz seines Gewichts läuft er sehr behende auf dem Tennisplatz herum.
Diese Kinder laufen in Lumpen herum.

[1] Hence also 'to writhe' (e.g. *sich vor Lachen wälzen*).
[2] See also 'place'.
[3] *Rinnen* is 'to run or flow in drops', particularly from leaky vessels. *Der Sand rinnt ihm durch die Finger*; *das Bier rinnt aus dem Faß.*
[4] Examples: *ich laufe sehr gern*; *wie lange sind Sie gelaufen?*
[5] *Rennen* being applied exclusively to persons or in reference to racing also to animals, lacks the wide figurative application of *laufen.*

SAFE, SECURE, SURE 1. **Sicher** corresponds closely to 'secure'[1,2] and 'sure', but means 'safe' almost only when this is practically interchangeable with 'secure' or 'sure'.

In the sense of 'free from doubt' it means 'sure'. From this it is a small step to the sense of 'free from anxiety, care, or danger', i.e. secure. In reference to a person and in combination with the verb *sein* it means 'sure', unless some phrase is added (e.g. *vor*, i.e. from), or a place which definitely gives it the meaning of 'secure' (or 'safe'). *Ich bin sicher* = I am sure. *Ich bin hier sicher vor einem Angriff* = secure, safe from.... On the other hand, with many other verbs *sicher* tends to mean 'secure', 'safe'. *Mein Kapital steht sicher. Ich fühle mich sicher.*[3] *Ist der Wagen ganz sicher?*

In reference to things, places, courses of action, and the like, *sicher* means 'secure', 'not exposed to danger' in the sense given by the *P.O.D.*, 'impregnable, certain not to fail or give way or get loose or be lost'. To this could be added 'certain not to be stolen', a common sense of *sicher*. This is the primary meaning. The sense of 'affording protection' and 'not actively involving in or exposing to danger' is present only in a secondary way and not independently of the primary sense. Thus *die Brücke ist ganz sicher* means in the first place 'secure against collapse' because the foundations, etc. are solid. Only because of its own security is it able not to expose to danger those who use it. For the sentence 'my car is safe' *sicher* could only be used in the sense of 'secure against theft', and the addition of *vor Dieben* would be necessary. *Dieser Strand ist sicher* could only mean 'secure against hostile attack' during a war, not 'safe (for swimming)', i.e. 'not presenting dangers through its own nature or structure'.

When 'safe' and 'sure' are practically interchangeable in the sense of 'reliable', both can be translated by *sicher. Sichere Methoden. Ich weiß es aus sicherer Quelle. Sicheres Geleit.* Similarly, 'secure of' = 'sure of' and may be rendered by *sicher*.

Sicher cannot be used in the sense of 'unscathed after passing through real or imagined danger', i.e. in the original meaning of 'safe': well, sound (e.g. to arrive safe and sound). Nor can it be used with *es ist* and

[1] *Sichern* = to secure (i.e. make secure, safe); to ensure, to assure, in the sense of 'to make a thing certain'. *Versichern* = to insure (life, property, etc.); to assure (i.e. remove doubt from the mind). In the latter sense it now governs the dative case, except in the combination 'to assure someone of something', where it is followed by the accusative and the genitive. *Ich versichere Ihnen, daß Sie sich irren. Ich versicherte ihn meiner Hilfe.*

[2] *Sicher* comes from Latin *securus*.

[3] Both 'I feel sure' and 'I am sure' must therefore be translated by *ich bin sicher*. 'Sure' followed by the infinitive in the sense of 'bound to' must be translated by the adverb *sicher* (e.g. *er wird sicher kommen* = he is sure to come). He is sure of coming = *er ist sicher, kommen zu können*. 'Surely', when it expresses a doubt and seeks for confirmation, is *doch sicher* (e.g. *er wird doch sicher kommen*).

a following infinitive (e.g. it is safe to walk there) or with an infinitive of the type: a gun safe to handle. It is possible, on the other hand, to say: *das Sicherste ist...zu...* (i.e. the surest thing, course, is to...).

Wir sind hier sicher vor einem Überfall, vor Verfolgung.
Das Geld ist in Ihren Händen ganz sicher.
Das Geld ist in sicheren Händen.
Eine sichere Anlage (secure, sure, reliable investment).
Eine sichere Straße (safe from thieves and the like; not 'so constructed as to eliminate accidents').
Ein sicherer Hafen.
Ein sicheres Türschloß.
Ist das Dokument sicher?
Er befindet sich in sicherer Entfernung.

2. In the sense of 'unscathed after passing through real or imagined dangers' **gut** is normally used to express the idea of safe arrival. In other combinations the sense of 'unscathed' requires a specific term.

Er ist gut angekommen.
Er hat sie gut nach Hause gebracht.
Eine gute Überfahrt.
Seine Ehre ist unbefleckt, gerettet.

3. When 'safe' is followed by an infinitive, use may be made of **Gefahr, ungefährlich**, etc. or the phrase may be recast.

Dort können Sie ohne Gefahr gehen (it is safe to walk there).
Sie sind ganz sicher, wenn Sie dort gehen.
Es ist gefährlich, zu nahe an den Rand zu gehen.

4. In the sense of 'not exposing to danger', particularly with reference to a place **ungefährlich,** etc. may be used, but often other terms are more appropriate.

Das ist ein Strand, der für Kinder ungefährlich ist.
Kann man sich auf Ihren Wagen verlassen? (is your car safe, trustworthy?).

5. **In Sicherheit:** in safety. **Mit Sicherheit:** with surety (certainty), safety, security (often interchangeable meanings).

Wir sind jetzt in Sicherheit (secure, safe).
Sie wurden in Sicherheit gebracht.
Man kann mit Sicherheit behaupten, daß der Preis nicht zu hoch war (it is safe to say...).

SATISFY In the sense of 'convince' only **überzeugen** is possible. **Befriedigen** is 'to satisfy' a wish, feeling, sensation, or demand.[1] **Genügen** is 'to comply with' a standard.

Ich habe mich überzeugt, daß er sein Bestes getan hat.
Er hat seine Wünsche, seine Neugier, seinen Hunger, seinen Ehrgeiz, befriedigt.
Seine Arbeit ist befriedigend.
Er hat allen Anforderungen genügt.

SEAL **Siegeln** is 'to stamp a seal on' a document. It is no longer in common use. **Versiegeln** means, literally and figuratively, 'to close a thing with a seal so as to keep secret its contents'. Since it includes the meaning of *siegeln*, it is often used for the latter. **Besiegeln** is only used figuratively, in the sense of 'to decide', 'to settle finally'.

Die Urkunde wurde gesiegelt.
Er hat den Brief versiegelt.
Alle Türen des Hauses wurden versiegelt (a police action).
Meine Lippen sind versiegelt.
Sein Schicksal ist besiegelt.

SECRET **Geheim** is applied to that which is deliberately kept secret, particularly to matters from which the State excludes the public. **Heimlich** can also imply deliberate exclusion, but never in relation to state matters, and not with the verb *halten*.[2] It is more frequently applied to that which happens to be hidden or is by its nature hidden. It evokes the atmosphere of secrecy or seclusion both in persons and in things, and in persons sometimes stealth.

Geheimpolizei, ein Geheimbund.
Die Pläne müssen geheim gehalten werden.
Sie hat einen geheimen Kummer.
Er ist ein geheimer Säufer.
Er hegt den heimlichen Wunsch, Schauspieler zu werden.
Ein heimliches Laster, ein heimlicher Platz.
Er sagte es ihm heimlich ins Ohr.

SEE ('I see' used absolutely in conversation is treated in section 5).

1. **Sehen** denotes: (*a*) physical sight;[3] (*b*) perception with the mind. It expresses the latter only when understanding is immediate and implies no

[1] *Befrieden*, to impose peace on, to pacify.
[2] 'To keep secret' is often *verheimlichen*.
[3] Also in memory and in imagination.

process of thought, i.e. not as an equivalent of 'realize'. A visual act may or may not accompany the mental perception. *Sehen* is used in fewer extended senses than 'see'. See also section 5.

Der Nebel ist so dicht, daß ich nicht sehen kann.
Ich sehe schon meinen Fehler (e.g. a visible error in a piece of writing, or purely in the mind).
Ich sehe, daß ich mich geirrt habe.
Er sah gleich, daß hier nichts zu erreichen war.
Ich seh' schon, worauf Sie hinaus wollen.
Ich sehe die Wahrheit (only as a vision in a biblical sense).

2. **Einsehen:** to come to an understanding of a thing after a process of thought, to realize. Insight into causal relationships, into the why and wherefore of things, is implied. (*Ich sehe nicht ein, warum...* is a very common phrase.) It can refer to everyday matters no less than to philosophic and scientific truths. It must be followed by an object (a noun or a clause).

Ich sehe jetzt meinen Fehler ein.
Ich sehe jetzt ein, daß ich mich geirrt habe.
Ich sehe nicht ein, warum Sie zögern.
Er sah ein, daß hier nichts zu erreichen war.
Ich sehe den Grund nicht ein, warum Sie so handeln mußten.
Ich sehe die Notwendigkeit dieser Maßnahmen nicht ein.

3. **Verstehen:** to understand.[1] A clear grasp of a thing as a whole in a general way, but no necessary reference to any preceding process of thought is implied. It translates 'see' in the above sense, particularly: (*a*) when the latter refers to the meaning of something said or written; (*b*) when it is used absolutely (see section 5).

Ich verstehe den Sinn dieser Stelle nicht (it is unintelligible; *einsehen* would imply insight into its why and wherefore).
Ich verstehe meinen Fehler.

4. **Erkennen** is a close synonym of *einsehen* in so far as it indicates a process of realization, a coming to know.[2]

Er erkennt seinen Fehler.
Er erkannte die Notwendigkeit dieser Maßnahmen.
Er erkannte, daß er sich geirrt hatte.

5. 'I see', used absolutely as an interjection or a comment. German uses *ich verstehe, ich seh' schon* (*schon* must be added) to indicate that one

[1] *Verstehen* is the most general term. *Begreifen* is 'to comprehend' a thing in all its aspects and in its causal relations with other things. See 'understand'.
[2] See 'recognize' and 'know'.

already sees. If a sudden realization accompanied by surprise is meant, German says: *So! Ach so!* (the second denoting a higher degree of surprise).

Ja, ich seh' schon (ich verstehe), das ginge nicht.
So (Ach so)! Dann hat er das nicht ernst gemeint.

6. **Absehen:** to form an estimate of some kind in relation to what is remote. It is used therefore with terms such as *Ende, Folgen.*

Ich kann das Ende, die Folgen, nicht absehen.
Es ist nicht abzusehen, was die Zukunft bringen wird.

7. Other compounds of *sehen* are **nachsehen** (to ascertain by inspection, to check); **zusehen** (to take care that...).[1]

Sehen Sie mal nach, ob das Buch in der Bibliothek steht.
Sehen Sie mal zu, daß Sie rechtzeitig ankommen.

8. Examples of terms that occur in less frequent senses are:

(a) *Dem leuchtet niemals ein Witz ein* (*einleuchten* means that the meaning or the rightness of a thing occurs to one in a flash).

Ihm leuchtete die Erklärung sofort ein.

(b) In the sense of 'to perceive' something good or bad about a thing *finden* is sometimes used.

Er findet viel an Paris, aber nichts an London.
Da finde ich nichts Schlimmes dabei (see no harm in it).
Ich finde keinen Sinn darin, daß Sie solche Ansprüche stellen.

(c) *Kann ich Herrn Schmidt sprechen?* (interview). *Ich werde Sie zur Tür, nach Hause, begleiten* (see to the door, home).

SEIZE A. Literal sense. In this sense it is synonymous with one of the uses of 'catch', which must be translated by the same German terms.

1. **Ergreifen** is restricted to such actions as can be performed by the hand and imply suddenness, impulsiveness, or violence, and, frequently, accompanying emotion. It stresses the act of seizing more than the retaining of one's hold on the object, and cannot be used in contexts which emphasize the latter.

Sie ergriff den Eimer, um das Feuer zu löschen.
Er ergriff das Gewehr und schoß auf den Feind.
Er ergriff die Feder und unterzeichnete das Todesurteil.
Er ergriff meine Hand und dankte mir.
Die Polizei ergriff den Dieb.

[1] See 'careful'.

2. **Fassen:** to seize, grasp firmly and retain one's hold.[1] It thus approximates more closely to 'catch' than does *ergreifen.*

Fassen Sie das Seil (e.g. said to a drowning person).
Er faßte das Fensterbrett und zog sich hinauf.

3. **Packen** suggests not only greater violence and effort in the act of seizing, but a firmer grip on retaining one's hold.[2] It is particularly appropriate where a struggle is implied.

Er packte den Ertrinkenden am Arm.
Er packte ihn bei der Kehle und schüttelte ihn tüchtig.

4. When 'seize' is followed by 'from' (i.e. snatch from), **entreißen** is used, both with small and big things.

Er hat mir das Messer entrissen.
Er entriß seinem Bruder den Thron.

5. **Sich bemächtigen:** to secure control of, power over, a person or thing by effort or violence.

Der Feind hat sich sofort aller Flottenstützpunkte bemächtigt.[3]
Die revolutionäre Partei hat sich des Staatsapparates bemächtigt.

6. **Beschlagnahmen** must be used in the sense of 'confiscate'.

Die Polizei hat seinen Briefwechsel, die gestohlenen Waren, beschlagnahmt.

7. Special senses of 'seize' must be translated by specific terms, e.g. *erbeuten,* to steal as booty.

Die Diebe haben große Mengen von Kleidern erbeutet.

B. Figurative uses.

1. **Ergreifen.**

(a) The idea of stretching out one's hand and grasping what one wants appears in such phrases as: *die Gelegenheit, die Initiative, ergreifen.*

(b) To grip suddenly and violently, with a strong or impulsive feeling as subject.[4,5]

Die Sehnsucht ergriff ihn, seine Heimat noch einmal zu sehen.
Die Furcht ergriff ihn, daß er die Gelegenheit schon versäumt habe.

[1] *Anfassen* means no more than 'to touch'. *Fassen Sie den Ofen nicht an. Den Hund können Sie ruhig anfassen.*

[2] *Anpacken* is only used figuratively. *Er hat die Sache richtig angepackt* (tackled).

[3] *Besetzen,* 'to occupy', is more common with reference to military or any other armed occupation, but does not in itself suggest force.

[4] *Ergreifen* with a personal object also means 'to move', i.e. emotionally. See 'move'.

[5] With weaker feelings *ergreifen* is inappropriate. *Der Wunsch, das Verlangen, überkam ihn.*

2. **Packen** is used of sudden, paralysing feelings such as terror, and of thoughts which suddenly and forcibly take possession of one.[1]

Eine plötzliche Angst hat ihn gepackt.
Der Gedanke packte ihn, daß sein Leben in Gefahr sei.

3. **Erfassen:** to comprehend, to lay hold of a matter.

Er hat den wesentlichen Unterschied sofort erfaßt.

SELF-CONSCIOUS, SELF-ASSURED 'Self-conscious' must be translated by such terms as **befangen** (embarrassed), **sich genieren** (to feel awkward). **Selbstbewußt** only means 'self-assured'.[2]

Er fühlt sich befangen, wenn er Fremde empfangen muß.
Er geniert sich zu fragen.
Er trat sehr selbstbewußt auf.

SELFISH *Selbstsüchtig* and *selbstisch*, which can also mean 'self-centred', 'absorbed with self', are little used in conversation, the common terms being *egoistisch* and *an sich selbst denken.*

Seien Sie nicht immer so egoistisch.
Er denkt immer nur an sich selbst.

SEND 1. **Senden** is a more dignified term than the more common **schicken**[3] and refers to the sending of persons and things of importance, particularly on a mission. *Schicken* is an almost exclusively human term, while 'send' is also applied to the world of nature (e.g. *die Sonne sendet ihre Strahlen zur Erde*) and to such utilizations of the forces of nature as radio, electricity, telegraph. Only *schicken* means 'to send away' in the sense of 'to get rid of'.[4]

Er wurde als Botschafter nach Paris gesandt.
Schicken Sie den Brief per Luftpost.
Ich habe ein Telegramm an ihn geschickt.
Schicken Sie die Kinder weg, sie machen zu viel Lärm.
Wir senden Ihnen einen Katalog der in diesem Jahr erschienenen Bücher.

2. **Abschicken** should be used when it is a question of whether a thing has been sent or not.

Ich habe den Brief schon abgeschickt.

[1] *Packen* also means 'to grip' one's interest. *Das Stück hat mich sehr gepackt.*

[2] Similarly *selbstbesessen* means 'unduly occupied with oneself', not 'self-possessed', which is *selbstbeherrscht.*

[3] *Schicken* is the factitive verb to *(ge)schehen* and originally meant 'to make happen', then 'to arrange, to dispose one's affairs'.

[4] Neither *schicken* nor *senden* corresponds to 'send' used figuratively. I sent him word = *ich ließ ihm sagen.* To send regards = *grüßen lassen.*

3. **Zuschicken,** followed by the dative, suggests more definitely a personal interest in the receiver than *schicken,* often a good turn. It is, however, never obligatory.

Ich kann Ihnen das Buch zuschicken lassen.

4. **Verschicken** and **versenden** are commercial terms and are used particularly in reference to bulk. *Verschicken* is also used of sending people away, particularly for reasons of health.[1]

Der Verlag schrieb mir, daß die Bücher baldigst versandt würden.
Die Kinder wurden schon vor den schweren Bombenangriffen aufs Land verschickt.

5. **Entsenden** is a dignified term used only in the sense of despatching someone on an important mission.

Ist es im gegenwärtigen Augenblick Amerika möglich, Truppen nach Europa zu entsenden?

SENSE 1. As a synonym of 'meaning', 'point'.

Sinn differs from **Bedeutung,** as 'sense' does from 'meaning', in that *Bedeutung* is more objective and more exact, whereas *Sinn* is more subjective and often refers rather to one interpretation of a word or phrase amongst a number of possible others.

Sinn differs from 'sense' in one point. While it is possible to refer to the 'sense' of a word or its various senses as listed in a dictionary, *Sinn* only denotes the sense of a word either in a context or in reference to an idea as conceived by a person or a group of persons.

In certain fixed expressions *Sinn* means 'sense' in the meaning of 'point'. *Sinn* in this use cannot be pluralized.

Der Sinn einer Stelle, einer Bemerkung.
Im wahrsten Sinne des Wortes.
Schönheit im Sinne, wie die Griechen sie auffaßten.
In diesem Zusammenhang hat das Wort folgenden Sinn....
Dieses Wort hat fünf verschiedene Bedeutungen.
In der ersten Bedeutung des Wortes (as defined in a dictionary).
Was er sagt, hat keinen Sinn (point).
Es hat keinen Sinn, die Sache weiter zu verfolgen.

2. With reference to the five senses, seeing, hearing, etc., **Sinn** is used.

Die fünf Sinne.
Der Geruchssinn.
Die Vergnügungen der Sinne.
Seine Sinne waren wach.

[1] *Verschicken* can also mean to deport undesirable subjects.

3. **Sinn** in the sense of 'capacity for perception, appreciation of a thing', 'sensibility'. At times the thing for which one has sensibility must be defined more specifically than in English, e.g. by an adjective (e.g. *der Sinn für künstlerische, menschliche, Werte* = a sense of values).

Der Schönheitssinn.
Er hat Sinn für Schönheit.
Er hat Sinn für Humor.
Ihm fehlt der Sinn für die Kunst des Barock.

4. **Gefühl** translates 'sense' in a use allied to 3, but, unlike *Sinn*, excludes subtle appreciation and sensibility. It should be used when feeling or mere awareness predominates. Most of the meanings of 'sense' given by *S.O.D.* under II are translated by *Gefühl.*

Ein Gefühl des Schmerzes, der Müdigkeit, der Sicherheit, der Dankbarkeit, der Leere, das Gefühl einer bevorstehenden Katastrophe, das Pflichtgefühl.

5. In the meaning of 'sanity', 'sense' occurs in a number of fixed phrases, translated by *Sinn, Verstand, vernünftig.* For examples see dictionaries.

SEPARATE(LY) 1. **Einzeln** translates 'separate(ly)' in reference to the individual parts of a whole or a group. See article on 'single'.

Sie können die Gedichte dieses Zyklus einzeln lesen, da jedes in sich ein Ganzes darstellt.
Die Zeugen kamen einzeln herein.

2. **Verschieden.** For an explanation of this word see 'different'.

Wir brauchen verschiedene Gläser für den Wein und das Bier.
Dieser Roman hat zwei verschiedene Handlungen.
Das sind zwei verschiedene Probleme.
Sie kamen durch verschiedene Türen herein.
Die Zahlen wurden in verschiedene Spalten eingetragen.

3. **Unabhängig** emphasizes that the two things in question have nothing to do with one another.

Ägypten war ein unabhängiges Mitglied des Völkerbundes.
Das sind zwei unabhängige Probleme.
Der Mensch, der leidet, und der Künstler, der schafft, scheinen oft zwei unabhängige Wesen zu sein.

4. **Eigen:** of one's own, not shared. In this sense it must be clearly referable to the person who owns or enjoys the use of the article in

question. Thus: *sie haben eigene Betten.* But it cannot translate: it is a room with separate beds. Unlike 'own' it can be preceded by the indefinite article.

Jedes der Kinder hatte sein eigenes Zimmer.
Jedes Studienfach braucht eigene Räume.
Ich habe einen eigenen Eingang zu meiner Wohnung.

5. **Für sich** is often attached to nouns or referable to them in the sense of (*a*) for oneself; (*b*) in itself, i.e. not connected with other things of its kind. In the second sense it is linked only to nouns preceded by the verb *sein.*

Jeder braucht ein Zimmer für sich.
Das ist ein Problem für sich.

6. **Getrennt,** separated, is applied to things which are deliberately separated because separation is desired.[1]

Sie haben getrennte Interessensphären.
Sie handelten getrennt.
'*Getrennt marschieren und gemeinsam schlagen.*'

7. **Gesondert** is a term common among tradespeople and used of despatching or taking goods, letters, and the like, separately. It can, however, also be used in its more general sense, particularly in reference to the separate examination of problems.[2]

Schicken Sie mir bitte das Rindfleisch, und dann gesondert zwei Pfund Leber.
Der Brief wurde in gesondertem Umschlag abgeschickt.
Wir wollen die zwei Fragen gesondert betrachten.

8. **Besonder(s)** can mean both 'special' and 'separate', the former being by far the commonest meaning.

Ich habe die Bücher schon abgeschickt und werde Ihnen die Broschüren besonders zuschicken.

9. **Sonder** is used in a number of compounds, sometimes in the sense of 'separate', sometimes in that of 'special'. Thus: *ein Sondervertrag* (separate), but: *ein Sonderzug* (special).

[1] *Der Einzelne* is the general term for 'the individual'. *Das Individuum* is used in more strictly philosophical contexts, and not like English 'individual' in the sense of 'person'.

[2] *Trennen* is 'to separate or cut off' a part from something to which the part is joined. *Scheiden* is 'to part or dissolve' things or parts of things inwardly united or fused. Hence *Scheidung* = divorce, *Trennung* = separation. *Sondern*: to sort out like things or parts in a medley.

10. **Extra** is used adverbially of the wrapping and taking of parcels separately.

Ich nehme das Kalbfleisch extra ('separately', not 'extra').

SERIOUS, GRAVE None of the German words treated in this article corresponds exactly to the English. *Schwer* is the strongest and comes closest to 'grave', when this does not refer to appearance. *Ernst* is 'serious' or 'grave' according to the context and is stronger than *ernsthaft* and *ernstlich*. In some uses *schlimm* and *arg* (the latter when used adverbially) approach the sense of 'serious' (see 'bad').[1]

The idea of ardent conviction in and devotion to a cause expressed by 'earnest' is lacking in the German words. With nouns or verbs which in themselves suggest such moral fervour *ernst*, *ernsthaft* and *ernstlich* acquire by attraction something of the sense of 'earnest'. In most cases, however, this term can only be rendered approximately into German.[2]

Ernst and **schlimm** can be used adverbially only in a few of the senses corresponding to their adjectival use.

1. 'To be serious, in earnest about a thing' is translated by the impersonal phrase: *es ist einem ernst mit (um)....*

Ist es Ihnen ernst mit dem Vorschlag?

2. **Ernst** means 'serious' or 'grave' in reality, not in appearance.

(a) Applied to persons it means 'serious in mind', 'having a serious content of mind', 'not gay'. It also corresponds to 'serious' when applied to any direct bodily expression of this temper of mind (mostly 'face', 'eye', 'look') or to thoughts, sayings, actions, works, and the like which proceed from and indicate it. It thus refers to inner content, not to external appearances.

Ein ernster Mann (serious, not gay by nature).
Ein ernster Wissenschaftler (takes science seriously).
Ein ernster Bewerber (serious in himself, not 'to be taken seriously').
Ein ernstes Gesicht.
Ernste Gedanken.
Ernste Musik (not jazz and the like).
Ernste Worte.
Ein ernstes Buch.

[1] *Seriös* is used mainly in the sense of 'to be taken seriously' or 'wanting to be taken seriously'. *Dieser Student ist nicht ganz seriös. Nur seriöse Künstler sollten sich um den Preis bewerben. Seriöse Kunden.* It is often interchangeable with *ernsthaft.*

[2] Examples of renderings of 'earnest': *ein wahrhafter Christ, ein gewissenhafter Student* (*ein ernster Student* is one who is serious as a human being); *es muß unser ernstes Bestreben sein..., ich hege die ernstliche Hoffnung..., Ihr ernstliches Ansuchen....*

Er hat ernste Absichten (normally refers to intentions of marriage and should not be used in any other way).
Trotz ernsten Nachdenkens habe ich die Lösung nicht finden können.
Ziehen Sie die Angelegenheit in ernste Erwägung.
Seit Monaten habe ich keine ernste Arbeit geleistet.
Ich habe in diesem Jahre nichts Ernstes gelesen.
Wir sind in eine ernste Auseinandersetzung verwickelt.

(b) Applied to an attitude of mind or a feeling (e.g. doubt, fear) arising from the awareness of an 'evil', actions taken, or warnings given because of an 'evil' and proceeding from this attitude of mind, *ernst* is very strong and comes closer to 'grave' than 'serious'.

Ich hege ernste Bedenken, ernsten Verdacht, gegen seine Ehrlichkeit.
Ich hege ernste Besorgnisse für seine Sicherheit.
Eine ernste Warnung, Ermahnung.
Das heißt einen ernsten Schritt tun.

(c) Applied to things which induce a serious or grave attitude of mind.

(i) With words denoting a situation, a condition, state,[1] *ernst* suggests that a recognition of the possibility of disaster induces a grave attitude of mind. It thus corresponds more closely to 'grave' than to 'serious'. As with 'grave', the probability of disaster is emphasized by the predicative position, which in this sense is used as freely as the attributive position. Words in this section denote an evil which is conceived as a situation or a condition and are to be distinguished from the evils treated under (ii).

Eine ernste Lage. Die Lage ist ernst.
Die Stunde ist für Europa ernst.
Ernste Symptome haben sich gezeigt.
Die Nachrichten von der Front lauten ernst.
Sein Leben schwebt in ernster Gefahr.
Wir haben ernste Verluste erlitten.
Der Verlust eines Gliedes ist ernst.
Seine Erkrankung ist ernst.
Er hat eine ernste Verletzung erhalten.
Die Niederlage hatte ernste Folgen.

(ii) *Ernst*, like 'grave', is applied attributively, but not predicatively, to a few evils not accounted for under (i). Since the predicative use emphasizes the probability of disaster, it is meaningless with a word which in itself indicates disaster as an accomplished fact, unless followed by some such phrases as *für jemanden.*

[1] Note the synonym *kritisch* (*eine kritische Lage*). It cannot be used adverbially.

In the phrases *als ernst ansehen, betrachten, ernst* refers to the idea contained in the verb (i.e. *Ansicht*) and may refer to nouns which do not admit it predicatively after *sein*.

Ein ernster Schaden wurde ihm zugefügt.
Er leidet an einer ernsten Krankheit.
Das war ein ernster Unfall.
Er hat eine ernste Halsentzündung.
Die Niederlage ist sehr ernst für ihn.
Die Wunde, die Niederlage, ist als ernst anzusehen.

(d) The use of *ernst* as an adverb is limited to its combination with verbs of saying and looking (compare (a) for the corresponding use of the adjective). A verb of saying, thus used, cannot be followed by a *mit* phrase (see *ernsthaft*). In a sentence such as *er ging ernst neben mir her, ernst* refers to *er*, not to 'going', i.e. it does not describe the manner of walking. It refers to the subject, too, when used with *meinen* and *nehmen*.

Er sprach ernst.
Er blickte sie ernst an.
Er sah ernst zur Decke empor, vor sich hin.
Er meint es ernst.
Er nimmt es, das Leben, seine Pflichten, ernst.

3. **Ernsthaft:** having the manner or the appearance of seriousness, serious-looking, while not necessarily excluding the inner reality. In emphasizing appearance it differs from *ernst*, which refers only to inner reality. Applied to facial expression, gestures, movements, bearing, tone of voice, and the like it covers not only 'serious' but 'grave', when this suggests appearance. Unlike *ernst*, it is not limited in the sphere of physical appearance to such expressions as proceed directly from an inner state of mind. It can even suggest appearance as opposed to reality (e.g. *trotz der Lächerlichkeit der Lage setzte er eine ernsthafte Miene auf*).

It differs from *ernst* in suggesting a judgment based on appearances (e.g. *wir hielten die Wunde nicht für ernsthaft*). It characteristically presupposes an observer who is asked to accept a thing as serious, not as a joke.

Its character as a judgment based on impressions normally precludes its use in the predicative position after *sein*, unless this is combined with a modal verb or *scheinen* (see 'appear'). It may be used predicatively after *werden*, since such a judgment is less categorical than in the case of *sein*, and occasionally after *sein* when followed by some phrase denoting the effect (e.g. *die Beweggründe, die er anführt, sind ernsthaft genug, um mich zum Nachdenken zu veranlassen*).

It cannot be used with the type of noun discussed in **2** (b) (i.e. words which exclude the idea of appearance), or the type described in **2** (c) (i.e. an objective situation, condition, evil, not a person).

Used adverbially, *ernsthaft* also refers to the manner and appearance of the subject and may include his attitude of mind. This restricts its range of application. It is closely connected with the manner or attitude of mind of the subject, not with the degree of vigour, the intensiveness with which the action of the verb is carried out (see: *ernstlich*). There is a tendency to limit its use as an adverb to cases where the verb excludes the idea of intensiveness. Conversely, *ernstlich* is the preferred term when this type of verb is used. This means that in translation from English into German *ernstlich* is sometimes obligatory, even though the idea to be expressed may refer to the manner, appearance or attitude of mind of the subject. It means also that, whereas *ernsthaft* is used with certain nouns, *ernstlich* is required with the corresponding verb. Thus: *er ist ein ernsthafter* (serious, earnest) *Bewerber für diesen Posten*; but: *er bewirbt sich ernstlich um diesen Posten. Ernstlich* here means 'intensively'.

The term 'tendency' was used above to describe this characteristic of *ernsthaft* and *ernstlich.* Germans exhibit, however, a measure of uncertainty in handling *ernsthaft.* Though no one would use *ernsthaft* in the sentence *ich ersuche Sie ernstlich*, one finds it combined with a word like *Warnung*, even though *ernstlich* is felt to be more correct. Similarly, though it is more natural to say *wir müssen uns ernstlich mit Latein beschäftigen* and *Sie müssen ernstlich darüber nachdenken, ernsthaft* would not be impossible. On the other hand, *ernsthaft* is sometimes used, not as in the preceding examples, where it can refer to the subject, but where there is no justification for it at all. Thus *Paris ist ernstlich gefährdet* (degree of danger) is the only correct way of expressing this idea. *Ernsthaft*, however, appeared in a number of German accounts of this phase of the 1939–45 war.[1]

'*Da räusperte sich der ernsthafte Mann und sprach, indem er sich bemühte, in den Ton seiner Stimme recht viel Gewichtiges zu legen*' (E. T. A. Hoffmann, *Die Elixiere des Teufels*).

Ein ernsthafter Mann ist niemals auffällig angezogen (an *ernster Mann* might or might not be *auffällig angezogen*).

Das ist ein ernsthafter Bewerber (he appears not to be playing with the girl, but to intend marriage).

Mach' doch kein so ernsthaftes Gesicht (said lightly to a child).

[1] In *Egmont* Goethe makes the character of this name say: '*Wenn ihr das Leben gar zu ernsthaft nehmt, was ist denn dran?*' Referring to *ihr*, not to *Leben, ernsthaft* expresses more clearly a reproach than *ernst* would. In present-day German, however, only *ernst* is normally used with *nehmen.*

Das ist aber ein ernsthafter Blick, den Sie auf mich richten.
Der hat schon ernsthafte Absichten (impression of observer).
Ziehen Sie die Angelegenheit in ernsthafte Erwägung (in such a way as to convince others that you are seriously considering it).
Das war eine ernsthafte Frage und ich erwarte eine ernsthafte Antwort (not a joke).
Seit Monaten habe ich keine ernsthafte Arbeit geleistet (the results of which could be taken seriously).
Wir sind in eine ernsthafte Auseinandersetzung verwickelt (in form, e.g. externally dramatic).
Ernsthafte Symptome haben sich gezeigt (visible to anyone, e.g. inflammation; a doctor would say *ernst*).
Mir als Laien scheint das eine ernsthafte Krankheit zu sein (but: *der Arzt hat dies für eine ernste Krankheit erklärt*).
Ihre Halsentzündung dürfte ernsthaft sein, wird ernsthaft.
Er sprach ernsthaft mit ihr (*ernst* impossible because of the addition of *mit ihr*).
Erst wagte er nicht, ihren Augen zu begegnen, dann blickte er sie ernsthaft an (with verbs of seeing, looking, *ernst* is more usual as the adverb).
Er nickte ernsthaft.
Er tat ernsthaft bemüht, uns zu helfen (*ernsthaft* not *ernstlich* because *tat* suggests appearance).
Er ging ernsthaft an die Arbeit.
Aber, ernsthaft gesprochen, wären Sie bereit, einen solchen Schritt zu unternehmen?
Nur drei nahmen an der Besprechung ernsthaft teil (refers to earnestness of purpose, not the vigour of discussion).
Er hat ganz ernsthaft geantwortet.

4. **Ernstlich** differs from *ernsthaft* in that it does not refer to the manner or attitude of mind of the subject (the person), but to the object. It means 'serious' only in the sense that the noun, verb, or adjective to which it is attached is to be taken in its full, intensive sense. This reference to the object makes *ernstlich* a synonym of 'real', 'genuine'[1] (*ernstlich krank* is hardly more than 'genuinely ill'). Its meaning can thus be explained as 'sufficient', 'appreciable in amount', 'considerable' (e.g. *wir können uns keine ernstliche Herabsetzung der Steuern versprechen*).

For the preferment of *ernstlich* to *ernsthaft* with words which admit the idea of intensity, see *ernsthaft* in **3** above.

Ernstlich is much weaker than *ernst* (which can be applied to the object as well as to the subject) (contrast: *ernste und ernstliche Bedenken*).

[1] *Echt* corresponds to 'genuine' only in the sense of 'not spurious'. See 'real'.

Consequently it can never mean 'grave'. From its exclusive application to the object it is obvious that it has nothing of the meaning of 'earnest'. It must, however, for lack of a closer equivalent be used to translate 'earnest' with words which in themselves can imply 'earnestness' (e.g. *Ermahnung*).

The meaning of *ernstlich* precludes its application to a person. It is, furthermore, too weak to be used as a predicative adjective.

Ziehen Sie die Angelegenheit in ernstliche Erwägung (real, adequate consideration).

Ich hege ernstliche Bedenken, ernstlichen Verdacht, gegen seine Ehrlichkeit.

Ich hege ernstliche Besorgnisse für seine Sicherheit.

Eine ernstliche Warnung, Ermahnung.

Er hat ernstliche Schritte unternommen, um den Verbrecher der Strafe zuzuführen.

Sein Leben schwebt in ernstlicher Gefahr.

Wir sind in einer ernstlichen Auseinandersetzung begriffen.

Der Wind hat ernstlichen Schaden verursacht.

Ich habe ernstliche Gründe, das zu bezweifeln.

Sein Leben ist ernstlich gefährdet.

Die Stadt ist ernstlich bedroht.

Nur drei nahmen ernstlich an der Besprechung teil (contrast example with *ernsthaft*).

Wenn Sie es ernstlich hätten sehen wollen, dann hätte ich es Ihnen gezeigt.

Er hat ernstlich Lust, dahin zu gehen.

Ich habe ihn ernstlich dazu angehalten, die Stellung anzunehmen (vigorously; 'earnestly' would be *ernsthaft*).

5. **Schwer** is a much used term and translates 'severe' (see article) as well as 'serious' and 'grave'. It is stronger than *ernst, ernstlich, ernsthaft, schlimm, arg* and is combined with the following types of words:

(a) With a word denoting wrong-doing, a mistake, or an accusation with regard to these. It is the only translation of 'serious' and 'grave' used in this combination.

Sie haben einen schweren Fehler, Verstoß, begangen.

Er hat sich eines schweren Vertrauensbruches schuldig gemacht.

Sie haben eine schwere Anklage gegen ihn erhoben.

Er hat schwere Schuld auf sich geladen.

(b) *Schwer* is used of other evils including those to which *ernst* is not applicable and indicates that they are highly oppressive. With regard to sickness it is a medical term (German does not distinguish in this case between 'serious' and 'grave').

Schaden, Verlust, Niederlage, Unglück, Unheil.

(c) As an adverb it is used with verbs of wrong-doing and verbs denoting an objective evil.

Er hat schwer gesündigt.
Er ist schwer verwundet.
Sein Bein ist schwer beschädigt.
Die Schwerkranken.

SERVANT **Dienstbote** in the singular is not used in reference to any specific individual, but in general statements about servants. In the plural it can refer to females. **Dienstmädchen** is a servant girl. It is often abbreviated to *Mädchen*, as the English term is to 'girl', when referring to a specific individual. **Diener** is used only of a big private house; **Bediente(r)**[1] of the house of an important public figure. *Diener* is the only term used metaphorically. **Hausangestellte(r)** is the official term for a domestic, used as a classification. **Personal:** servants, i.e. as a staff.

Seit März haben wir keinen ständigen Dienstboten, kein ständiges Dienstmädchen, bekommen können.
Die Dienstboten haben heute Ausgang.
Der Diener hat gekündigt.
Er ist ein Diener seines Volkes.
Die Schloßbedienten sind augenblicklich mit den Vorbereitungen für das Fest beschäftigt.
Sie ist Hausangestellte.
Das Personal ist mit den Arbeitsbedingungen unzufrieden.

SERVE 1. **Dienen:** to carry out generally the will of a superior; to help a purpose or cause. It is used of persons and things.

Er hat seinem Herrn treu gedient.
Er hat jahrelang dem Staat gedient.
Er dient in der Armee.
Ihre Bemerkungen dienten dazu, viele Irrtümer zu berichtigen.

2. **Bedienen** is only used in the specific senses of attending to customers, acting as waiter at table.[2]

Er hat mich sehr schnell bedient.

SERVICE 1. **Dienst:** work, labour, effort.

Seine Dienste an der guten Sache.
Er bot der Regierung seine Dienste an.
Heeresdienst, Kriegsdienst, Staatsdienst.

[1] The older form is: *Bedienstete(r)*.
[2] *Bedienen* also means 'to service' machinery. *Er bedient die Flugzeuge.*

2. **Verdienst** (neuter)[1] stresses the achievements that result from labour. *Seine Verdienste um das Vaterland.*[2]

SEVERE,[3] STERN, STRICT While 'stern' draws attention to a temper, an attitude of mind, which is characterized by inflexibility, 'severe', even when applied to persons, suggests their acts and the effects of these on a sufferer. It is also used of impersonal agencies which cause pain, distress, and the like. Thus 'stern discipline' makes one think of a temper of mind, while 'severe discipline' makes one think of the effect on those on whom it is imposed.

1. **Streng** denotes a temper of mind that manifests itself in the character, appearance, utterances, and acts for which a person is responsible. This attitude or temper of mind is, or believes itself to be, in accordance with strict standards. The closest English equivalent is therefore 'stern'. 'Severe' can only be rendered—approximately—by *streng* when it qualifies words which include a reference to a temper of mind as well to the effects of an action. Since these words are, generally speaking, only those to which 'stern' can be applied, 'severe' does not really correspond to *streng*. Thus: *ein strenger Richter, ein strenger Vater, ein strenges Gesicht,*[4] *ein strenges Urteil, ein strenger Verweis, eine strenge Kritik,* all suggest the temper of mind described above and are more accurately rendered by 'stern' than by 'severe'.

The latter cannot be translated by *streng* in reference to impersonal agencies except those relating to the characteristics and phenomena of winter that are felt as severe or rigorous. The origin of this use is clearly metaphorical and can be seen in the English use of 'stern' as well as 'severe' to characterize winter. For this reason *streng*, unlike 'severe', is not applicable to summer and to heat.

Streng differs, however, from 'stern' in not suggesting the lack of sympathy[5] which can be implied by the latter. It can thus be applied in a good sense to art (e.g. *die Strenge des Georgeschen Stils*; *Bach komponierte in strengem Kontrapunkt*).

[1] *Der Verdienst*: earnings, gain.

[2] *Sich ein großes Verdienst um etwas erwerben, sich verdient um etwas machen*: to deserve well of.

[3] Study in conjunction with 'serious' and 'bad'.

[4] *Streng* also translates, as here, 'austere' as a term of praise denoting simplicity, self-denial, self-discipline and the like. This sense, as also that of 'strict' (see later in the article), widens the range of *streng* as compared with 'stern', and at the same time softens some of the implications conveyed forcibly by the latter.

[5] It implies less of admonition, rebuke, and threat than 'stern'. Thus in diplomatic language 'a stern note, warning, answer to Franco' would be normally translated by *scharf*. In human relations however, with stress on the moral aspect of the rebuke: *das sei dir eine strenge Warnung.*

The last example could be rendered by 'strict', which is a regular meaning of *streng*. In this sense it implies the same attitude of rigid adherence to a standard.[1] *Ein strenger Lehrer* can thus mean 'a stern' or 'a strict teacher'. Extended to the products of the mind: *im strengen Sinne des Wortes*; *eine strenge Einteilung in Akte.*

Strenge Disziplin (stern, strict).
Eine strenge Strafe.
Ein strenger Befehl.
Eine strenge Regel.
Streng verboten (strictly).
Streng sein gegen, verfahren mit, jemand.
Ein strenger Winter.
Strenge Kälte.
Ein strenger Frost.
Ein strenges Klima.
Eine strenge Prüfung[2] (stern ordeal or strict examination).
Strenger Gehorsam.
Der Befehl wurde streng befolgt.
Das Dokument muß streng geheimgehalten werden.

2. **Hart,** like *streng*, refers to an attitude of mind, and only by inference to unpleasant effects. 'Hard' and even 'harsh'[3,4] are generally closer equivalents than 'severe'. Thus: *eine harte Kritik* (hard, harsh, severe criticism). But it could not be used to translate 'severe damage'. On the other hand, it can, like 'hard', refer to effects which are arduous, painful and the like, provided its use with such nouns expresses one of its other senses, e.g. violence of impact (e.g. *ein harter Schlag*).

[1] 'Strict' can only be used with reference to the giving or carrying out of orders, instructions (e.g. *der Befehl wurde strikt befolgt*). It cannot be applied to persons to characterize their disposition.

[2] See also examples of *Prüfung* with *schwer* (section 3) and *genau* (section 6).

[3] *Harsch*, and *verharscht* are applied only to the outer surface, crust or covering of things, particularly to snow.

[4] The adverbial uses of *hart* rarely correspond to those of 'hard', and mostly mean 'harshly' (e.g. *er behandelte mich sehr hart*; *er spricht hart*). The following are common equivalents of 'hard' used adverbially. (*a*) *Fest*, which should be used when 'hard' means 'firm' (e.g. *etwas fest anfassen*; *jemand fest ansehen*; *fest bei der Arbeit sein*). (*b*) *Tüchtig*, which combines the meanings of 'capable', 'efficient', 'energetic', when applied to persons and their activities, can also, somewhat colloquially, combine the ideas of intensity and amount when applied to words which admit of this combination of meaning. *Er hat seinen Bruder tüchtig geschlagen. Er hat tüchtig gelogen.* It is used in this sense, both adjectivally and adverbially, more widely than 'hard' as the following examples show: *es ist tüchtig warm*; *geben Sie mir tüchtig davon*; *essen Sie tüchtig.* (*c*) *Schwer* (see section 3) or *sauer* must be used in the sense of 'arduously' (e.g. *schwer, sauer, arbeiten*; *schwer, sauer, verdientes Geld*). (*d*) See also footnote to *stark* (section 5).

Ein harter Mann.
Eine harte Strafe.
Ein hartes Urteil.
Harte Bedingungen.
Einen harten Fall tun.
Hartes Kämpfen.
Ein harter Marsch.
Er ist hart bestraft worden.

3. **Schwer** is a widely used term, which from its literal meaning of 'heavy'[1] develops those of 'difficult to do, to understand, to bear' (physically, mentally, emotionally, morally).[2] It always stresses the effect, which is injurious, onerous, not the attitude of mind of the agent, and corresponds most closely to 'grievous', which is, however, less commonly used than 'severe'. In this sense it is applied not to persons, but to actions and their effects as conditions and the like caused by persons or by impersonal agencies. In accordance with the fundamental meaning of *schwer*, the sufferer feels the effects as a crushing weight, which presses heavily on him, rather than a sharp, intense pain. It is not applied to words meaning 'acute pain' (as distinct from mental suffering). Most of the terms, however, to which it is applicable, are either evils in themselves or clearly imply evil effects.[3] It is therefore not used with words such as *Kälte, Kritik.*

Das sind schwere Bedingungen.
Er hat eine schwere Prüfung (ordeal, not examination), *Krankheit, überstanden.*
Er hat eine schwere Strafe erhalten.
Sie haben eine schwere Niederlage, schwere Verluste, erlitten.
Das war ein schwerer Schlag für ihn.
Der Sturm hat schweren Schaden verursacht.
Er ist schwer verwundet worden.
Die Stadt wurde schwer bombardiert.
Er hat schwer gelitten.

4. **Scharf** has a wider range of application than 'sharp'.[4] As an approximation to 'severe' it denotes primarily an effect that is felt as sharp or

[1] 'Heavy', though it rather suggests bulk, can approximate in meaning to 'severe' (e.g. *eine schwere Geldstrafe*, heavy or severe). Other examples of *schwer* can also be translated by both terms (e.g. *schwere Verluste, schwer bombardiert*). When 'heavy' refers to clumsiness of the mind or of its expression it should be translated by *schwerfällig* (e.g. *ein schwerfälliger Stil*). For *stark* as a common equivalent see footnote to section 5.

[2] See 'difficult' and 'serious'.

[3] See also *schlimm* and *arg* under 'bad' as approximate renderings.

[4] *Verschärfen* means 'to intensify' in the sense of 'to make more severe, aggravate'

biting. It is applied mainly to the utterances of persons and, to a lesser extent, their actions. In so far as it suggests their attitude, this is subjective,[1] i.e. unlike *streng*, without consciousness of an objective norm, and concerned only with the intensity of the effect on the sufferer. Impersonal agencies with which it may be used must suggest an effect that is biting in its intensity, and are not numerous, principally cold and pain.

Ein scharfer Tadel.
Ein scharfes Urteil abgeben.
Scharfe Kritik.
Eine scharfe Zunge.
Scharfe Maßnahmen.
Das Einfuhrverbot wirkt sich immer schärfer aus.
Scharfe Kälte.
Ein scharfer Schmerz.

5. **Stark** is a more widely used term than 'strong(ly)' and can express intensity.[2] With words which in themselves admit of this conception it can mean 'severe'. These are mainly (*a*) certain ills of the body, (*b*) natural phenomena such as heat and cold.

Starke Schmerzen.
Starkes Kopfweh.
Starke Kälte.
Eine starke Erkältung.
Starke Hitze.
Ein starker Frost.
Ein starker Hustenanfall.
Er hat stark gelitten.

6. The preceding articles will have shown that the suggested renderings of 'severe' are mere approximations and that in some cases closer English equivalents can be found for the German terms. Examples of the latter

(e.g. *Maßnahmen verschärfen, das Übel verschärfen*). It must be distinguished from *schärfen*, which means: (*a*) to sharpen in the literal sense (e.g. *ein Messer*); (*b*) to sharpen the faculties of the mind.

[1] It is used, for example, with *Hohn, Spott*, but would be translated by 'sharp', 'acid', etc. rather than by 'severe'.

[2] The idea of intensity is also present when *stark* translates 'heavy' and 'hard'. As an equivalent of 'hard' it suggests energy alone. When it renders 'heavy' it combines the idea of mass, quantity with that of energy, pressure. Examples: *es regnet, schneit, friert, stark*; *eine starke Forderung, Nachfrage*; *es bläst sehr stark. Stark* is so widely used in this sense that it must often be translated by other English terms (often 'badly', e.g. *er zitterte sehr stark*). Further: *stark geschwollen, erregt, bewegt, sinnlich.* 'Intense', referring to the inner life, is *innig* (e.g. *innige Freude, innig lieben*).

not yet noted are: *genau*,[1] *gründlich* in reference to an examination; *anstrengend* (i.e. strenuous) with reference to physical or mental effort (e.g. *ein anstrengender Marsch*); *gänzlich* to translate 'leave severely alone' (see Fowler's comment on this phrase in *Modern English Usage*); *empfindlich*, which means not only 'sensitive' (to stimuli or to pain), 'touchy'[2] with reference to persons, their mind and body (e.g. *eine empfindliche Stelle*, i.e. 'sore') but applies also to the evils which cause intense suffering or pain (e.g. with: *Schaden, Verluste, Kälte, Schmerzen, Schlag*).

With reference to style, aesthetic effect, whether this be pleasing or otherwise, 'severe' is untranslatable (e.g. a severe face, a severe style, severely plain). The dictionaries offer approximations.

SHAKE **1. Schütteln:** to shake about freely, without encountering much resistance. It is said frequently, though not exclusively, of things which can be moved, carried about, i.e. offering no resistance. Applied to emotions it means 'to give a shock, a scare'. It may be followed by prepositional phrases.

Er schüttelte die Erbsen im Topf (or: *aus dem Topf*).
Sie schüttelten den Teppich (or: *den Staub aus dem Teppich*).
Der Wind schüttelte die Bäume.
Der Wind schüttelte die Äpfel vom Baume.
Er schüttelte den Kopf.
Er ergriff den Dieb am Genick und schüttelte ihn heftig.
Der alte Wagen schüttelte uns tüchtig.
Sie schüttelten ihn aus dem Schlaf.

2. Rütteln: to shake something which stands firmly on its base and offers resistance, the sense being 'to try to shake loose, to move'. When the object is a thing of considerable size this verb is normally followed by *an* (i.e. to shake at). With a personal object it is followed by the accusative, often accompanied by a prepositional phrase with *aus* denoting the result of the action.

Er rüttelte an der Tür (to force it open).
Die Krise rüttelt an der bestehenden Ordnung.
Sie rüttelten ihn aus dem Schlaf (stresses the effort more than *schütteln*).

3. Erschüttern: to shake from within, to make the foundations totter, to undermine, with stress on the violence of the action. Its most common

[1] *Genau* means 'exact', but can also indicate the habit of mind called 'punctilious'.
[2] Applied to persons *empfindlich* generally has a bad sense, i.e. 'touchy', but rarely 'sensitive' to beauty, etc. *Empfindsam* is now rarely used, but was common in Goethe's day. It meant 'sentimental' (e.g. *der empfindsame Roman, Werther*, the novels of Richardson).

use is figurative. When applied to emotions, it means 'to move profoundly', 'to cause an emotional upheaval'.

Ein Erdbeben erschütterte die ganze Stadt.
Der Krieg hat die bestehende Gesellschaftsordnung in ihren Grundfesten erschüttert.
Mein Glaube an ihn ist erschüttert.
Die Nachricht von seinem Tode, der Anblick der Verwüstung, die Schönheit des Sonnenunterganges, hat ihn tief erschüttert.

SHAME (noun and verb), DISGRACE, ASHAMED, SHAMELESS, SHAMEFUL, DISGRACEFUL, BAREFACED

A. Nouns.

1. Scham, Schamgefühl refer to the feeling of humiliation which springs from a consciousness of having offended against standards of propriety, etc.; also to the restraint produced by fear of such humiliation. *Schamgefühl* is more common than *Scham*, except in prepositional phrases (e.g. *vor*, *aus*, *Scham*). Where 'sense of shame' is possible in English, *Schamgefühl* is generally used, *Scham* being more elevated in tone.

Scham in the sense of 'disgrace' is obsolete.
Sie errötete vor Scham.
Er hat kein Schamgefühl.
Er hat alles Schamgefühl verloren.

2. Schande is shame in the sense of 'disgrace' (which it also translates),[1] i.e. loss of reputation,[2] also, in predicative use, in the sense of 'a circumstance which brings disgrace to a person', 'a matter for reproach' (it is a shame, disgrace, that...); also 'a person or thing that is a cause or source of disgrace' (*S.O.D.* 6).

Sie lebt in Schande.
Er hat seine ganze Familie in Schande gebracht.
Zu meiner Schande muß ich es gestehen.
Es ist eine Schande, daß er nicht freigesprochen wurde.
Er ist die Schande seiner Familie.

3. Schade, in predicative use, translates 'shame' in its weaker use, i.e. when it approximates to 'pity'[3] (which it also translates).

Wie schade!
Es ist schade, daß wir Sie zu spät verständigten.

[1] 'Disgrace' in the weaker and older sense of 'disfavour' must be translated by *Ungnade*.

[2] *Schmach* is a synonymous term meaning 'ignominy', i.e. the state of being exposed to an extreme degree of contempt. *Schimpf* is 'insult to one's honour, self-esteem', etc.

[3] Also: *es ist ein Jammer, daß...*, i.e. something to be regretted.

SHAME

B. Verbs.

1. **Sich schämen:** to be ashamed. 'Ashamed', used otherwise than predicatively after the verb 'to be', must be translated by *beschämt* (see next section).

Ich schäme mich, es gestehen zu müssen.

2. **Beschämen:** to make ashamed, i.e. to arouse a feeling of shame in a person. The past participle *beschämt* must be used to translate 'ashamed' when not preceded by the verb 'to be'.

Er sah tief beschämt aus.
Beschämt ließ er den Kopf hängen.
Sie beschämen mich (make me feel ashamed, or put me to shame).
Sie beschämen mich mit Ihren Kenntnissen (shame me, put me to shame).

C. Adjectives.

1. **Schamlos** means 'shameless', i.e. it suggests indifference to disgrace.

Ein schamloser Kerl.
Das ist eine schamlose Forderung.
Er hat ganz schamlos gehandelt.

2. **Unverschämt**[1] corresponds closely to 'barefaced' and 'brazen', i.e. effrontery in taking or demanding and absence of any attempt to disguise it. It draws attention more to the act, *schamlos* to the attitude of mind behind it.

Ein unverschämter Kerl.
Das ist eine unverschämte Forderung, Lüge.
Er benimmt sich ganz unverschämt.

3. 'Shameful' and 'disgraceful' in its stronger sense are close synonyms. They are translated by **schändlich,** i.e. meriting opprobrium.

Ein schändliches Leben führen.
Eine schändliche Tat.
Ein schändlicher Betrug.

SHARE **A.** Noun.

1. Both **Teil** and **Anteil**[2] are used in the sense of what is due from one as well as to one. *Anteil* is only possible where the division can be measured exactly or clearly discerned, i.e. with concrete objects and with

[1] *Verschämt* means 'feeling shame unnecessarily' mostly in the sense of 'bashful'. *Verschämte Arme,* too proud to beg.
[2] *Anteil* can also mean 'sympathy'.

some activities. *Teil* is vaguer and more general and can therefore refer to intangibles (e.g. qualities). In the sense of 'share' it is neuter.

(a) *Die Frau erhielt ihren Anteil aus dem Vermögen ihres Mannes.*
Er hat seinen Anteil aus der Erbschaft seines Vaters verpraßt.
Ich verlange meinen Anteil an der Beute, an der Geschäftsführung.
Haben Sie Ihren Anteil an dem Wein bekommen?
Er hat seinen Anteil an den Kosten getragen.
Sein Anteil an dem Verbrechen beschränkte sich auf Mitwisserschaft.
Ich habe nur geringen Anteil daran gehabt, ihn durch sein Examen zu bringen.

(b) *Du mußt dein Teil der Arbeit leisten.* (*Anteil* would be more precise.)
Sie haben ihr Teil zu dem Siege beigetragen. (*Anteil* is too precise to be used in such a context.)

2. **Portion** is common in reference to food.

Er hat seine Portion des Kuchens schon gegessen.

3. **Entfallen** (without a precise equivalent in English) is often used in the precise sense of *Anteil* in reference both to what one receives and to what is expected of one.

Dieses Stück Kuchen entfällt auf mich.
Die Hälfte der Kosten entfällt auf mich.

4. Note the idiom: *ich habe mein gerüttelt Maß an Leiden gehabt* (my share of suffering).

B. Verb.

Sich teilen in: to share equally. Otherwise **teilen** is used. **Repartieren** is a colloquialism for 'to share equally'.

Wir müssen uns in die Ausgaben teilen (*die Ausgaben repartieren*).
Wir teilten uns in das Zimmer.
Wir wollen uns in die Verantwortung teilen.
Ich mußte das Zimmer mit ihm teilen.
Wir teilen die Verantwortung für das, was geschehen ist.
Ich teile viele von Ihren Ansichten (*sich teilen in* is impossible).
Wir haben viele Erlebnisse miteinander geteilt (*sich teilen in* is impossible).

SHOOT It must be made clear in German whether 'shoot' means 'wound' or 'kill'.

1. **Schießen** means 'to shoot dead' only as a hunting term (see also *erschießen* in reference to animals, birds, etc.). A personal object must

be accompanied by a phrase indicating where the person is shot. It is both transitive and intransitive. When transitive the object can be the missile as well as the person or thing shot at. In intransitive use it has most of the figurative senses of 'shoot'. The subject can also be the weapon. To shoot at = *schießen auf.*

Still, oder ich schieße!
Ich schoß den Vogel, das Kaninchen, den Löwen.
Er wurde in den Rücken, in den Arm, geschossen.
Er schoß die Pfeile durch die Luft.
Der Gedanke schoß mir durch den Kopf.
Ich schoß auf ihn.
Das Blut schießt ihm zu Kopf.

2. **Erschießen:** to shoot dead (*totschießen*), whether deliberately or by accident. It is applied to animals, birds, and the like in all circumstances other than the hunt.

Er wurde als Spion erschossen.
Ich habe ihn mit Absicht erschossen.
Wir mußten den Hund erschießen.

3. **Anschießen:** to wound on the surface by a bullet (for other uses see the dictionary). Intention is not necessarily implied.

Er ist angeschossen worden.

SHORTEN, ABBREVIATE, ABRIDGE, CURTAIL 1. **Kürzen** strongly suggests direct intervention, particularly, not exclusively, in an unfavourable sense, and generally with a personal subject. The implication is thus frequently: to reduce, to cut down, to curtail,[1] a thing in a way unwelcome to a person. But in reference to written material it can be used without these implications in the sense of 'to abridge'. Used of objects, e.g., it simply means 'to cut a piece off'.

Verkürzen often suggests that the reduction is the result of circumstances, habit, or the like, rather than of direct personal intervention.[2] In this case the subject is normally a thing. When the subject is a person, the reduction is more often favourable than the reverse, particularly with reference to time, i.e. to shorten a period of time for someone. Applied

[1] *Kürzen* is in this sense a common equivalent of 'to reduce', 'cut', i.e. in reference to an allowance or share of a thing. *Die Löhne, die Rationen, sind wieder gekürzt worden.* By transference it is also applied occasionally—somewhat loosely—to the person. *Wir sind wieder gekürzt worden.* See 'reduce'.

[2] *Verkürzen* also translates 'reduce' as a result of circumstances. *Scharfe Konkurrenz verkürzte das Einkommen aller Geschäftsleute* (here in an unfavourable sense).

to objects *verkürzen* suggests an adjustment, not simply the cutting-off of a piece. In adjectival use, the distinction tends to be obliterated.

In reference to objects, in the sense of 'to cut off a piece', **kürzer machen** is more common, particularly in conversation.

Er hat das Tuch, den Mantel, gekürzt, kürzer gemacht.

'*...man verlängerte, man verkürzte die Steigbügel*' (Goethe, *Novelle*) (*kürzte* could only mean: cut off a piece).

Sie müssen Ihren Artikel kürzen (not *verkürzen*, because drastic intervention is implied).

Der Artikel erschien in gekürzter, verkürzter, Form.

Neue gekürzte Ausgabe (abridged).

Das Stück wurde in gekürzter Form gespielt (abridged).

Ich muß Ihnen leider Ihre Ferien, Ihren Urlaub, kürzen.

Wir haben Ihnen die Wartezeit, die Dienstzeit, verkürzt.

Durch den Erlaß des Königs wurde dem Gefangenen die Gefängnisstrafe verkürzt (*gekürzt* impossible).

Der Alkohol hat ihm das Leben verkürzt (*gekürzt* impossible).

Sein munteres Treiben verkürzte uns die Zeit.

2. **Abkürzen** is used in two ways. (*a*) To abbreviate, i.e. to represent the whole by a part, which becomes either a sign or the skeleton of the whole. (*b*) To cut a thing short in time so that it remains incomplete.[1]

Kürzen Sie dieses Wort ab.

Das ist ein abgekürztes Verfahren (e.g. legal procedure as shortened in a court martial).

Das Drama wurde in abgekürzter Form gespielt (only in skeleton outline, more drastic than 'abridge').

Ich mußte leider die Unterredung, meinen Aufenthalt, abkürzen.

3. **Zusammenstreichen** implies a radical cut in reference to written matter.

Sie müssen den Artikel, das Stück, stark zusammenstreichen.

SHOW: *Zeigen* and its compounds refer to the external act, while *weisen* and *erweisen* stress the content or attitude of mind from which an act proceeds.[2]

[1] With other objects 'curtail' is often translated by *einschränken* (e.g. *Ausgaben, Rechte, einschränken*). See 'limit'.

[2] This distinction is evident also in *hinzeigen auf* and *hinweisen auf etwas*. Both mean 'to point out', 'to point to...', the first more in reference to a visible thing, the second to a fact, truth, etc.

SHOW

1. **Zeigen** is the most general term. It means primarily 'to bring a thing before a person's eye', or 'a quality, etc. before one's notice', and then 'to show how a thing is done', whether this be a physical or mental operation, 'to make a truth manifest'. The subject can be a person or a thing.

Ich zeigte ihm das Buch.
Er zeigte viel Begabung fürs Zeichnen.
Er hat sich sehr dankbar gezeigt.
Ich zeigte ihm, wie ich zu dem Ergebnis kam.
Die Folgen zeigen, daß er sehr unbedacht handelte.

2. **Bezeigen** only means 'to make an emotion or an attitude visible'. In drawing attention to the external act or token by which this is done it approximates to 'evince'. It sometimes suggests ceremony. *Zeigen* can also be used in this case, but does not emphasize the manner of the act.

Er bezeigte ein großes Verlangen, die Heimat wieder zu sehen.
Sie bezeigten ihm viel Ehre.

3. **Erzeigen** and **erweisen,** which are often interchanged, mean 'to show a person one's attitude' by doing something for him. In some cases 'do' is a more appropriate translation. In discriminating use the following distinction can be made: *erzeigen* concentrates attention rather on the external act, which is mostly ceremonial, *erweisen* on the attitude of mind. A noun which denotes one clear act is therefore preferable (though not obligatory) with *erzeigen.*[1]

Sie haben ihm Barmherzigkeit, viel Gefälligkeit, erwiesen.
Sie haben ihm Ehre erwiesen, erzeigt.

4. **Weisen** is 'to impart instruction by showing', and is generally translated by 'direct', 'instruct'.[2] It is rendered by 'show' only in the sense of 'show out', i.e. expel.[3]

Er wurde zur Tür hinaus, aus dem Hause, gewiesen.

SIGN **Zeichen** is a 'clear sign' of any kind, the meaning of which is understood or established. **Anzeichen** is a 'symptom', an 'intimation' of

[1] *Erweisen* also means 'to prove', and differs from *beweisen* in stressing the result (i.e. one of the senses of *er*). The meaning is thus 'to prove a thing so that it becomes absolutely clear, evident' (e.g. *seine Schuld ist einwandfrei, klar, erwiesen*). In this use it is commonest in the passive voice. *Sich erweisen als* = to prove, turn out, to be; particularly in reference to a quality. *Nachweisen* means 'to prove step by step', by tracing, tracking down evidence, by demonstration, particularly by furnishing evidence in the form of documents (e.g. *seine Herkunft nachweisen*). Sometimes 'demonstrate' is a more appropriate equivalent than 'prove'.

[2] Hence *anweisen* (to instruct), *zurechtweisen, verweisen* (to reprimand).

[3] Hence *ausweisen, verweisen* (to expel).

something to come which may or may not be recognized and interpreted aright.

Das Licht gab das Zeichen zum Weiterfahren.
Was bedeuten die verschiedenen Zeichen auf diesem Blatt?
Wenn nicht alle Anzeichen trügen, wird es bald eine Lebensmittelknappheit geben.
Die Anzeichen einer politischen Krise häufen sich.
Das sind die Zeichen einer politischen Krise.

SILENCE **Stillschweigen** is used of deliberate silence, often enjoined on one, in order to exclude others from knowledge of a matter, and therefore only of human beings. **Schweigen** is a more general term, and can be applied to any kind of silence, deliberate (in which case it is unemphatic), of human beings, animals, or nature.[1]

Er hat Stillschweigen darüber bewahrt.
Stillschweigen wurde ihm auferlegt.
Ich kann mir sein Schweigen nicht erklären.
Er hat sich in Schweigen gehüllt.
Das Schweigen des Waldes ließ phantastische Bilder in seiner Seele aufsteigen.

SIMPLE **Einfach** has all the meanings of 'simple' except (*a*) that of guileless (with heart, soul, and the like), and (*b*) that of simple-minded. These meanings are both rendered by **einfältig**.[2] In reference to the heart and the mind *einfach* only means uncomplicated.

Er ist eine einfältige Seele.
Er ist ein einfältiger Mensch (simple-minded; *einfach* would mean 'uncomplicated' or 'unpretentious' or refer to class).

Schlicht means 'simple' with reference to the sensuous impression given off by a person or thing, while *einfach* is purely objective. *Schlicht* can therefore mean 'simple' in appearance but not necessarily in reality.

Er ist ein schlichter Mann.
Die Königin trug ein schlichtes Kleid (*einfach* would mean simple as an objective fact).
Er hat einen schlichten Glauben (*einfach*: uncomplicated, easy to understand).

[1] As a verb *stillschweigen* is both more emphatic and more familiar than *schweigen*, and like the noun most commonly suggests an order. *Schweig'still*, e.g. said to a child. *Stillschweigend* used adjectivally means 'tacit' (e.g. *ein stillschweigendes Abkommen*). *Schweigsam*, silent, refers to a trait of character.

[2] Distinguish from *albern*, which means 'silly in a drivelling way, fatuous'.

SINGLE

SINGLE[1] **1. Einzig** means 'one only'.[2] In this sense it also translates 'only' (used adjectivally) and 'sole'.

Ein einziges Beispiel genügt.
Er ist von einem einzigen Gedanken beherrscht.
Er hat kein einziges Wort gesagt.
Nach dem Luftangriff blieb kein einziges Haus unversehrt.

2. Einzeln means 'individual', i.e. taken separately, by itself, in relation to the parts of a whole or to a number. See article on 'separate'.

Die Bände werden einzeln verkauft (singly or separately).
Die Zeugen wurden einzeln verhört.

3. Einzel is also used in a number of compound nouns in the sense: for or with one person or thing. *Einzelteile* means 'single parts' in the sense of *Ersatzteile*.

Einzelzimmer, Einzelkabine, Einzelbett, Einzelgänger.

4. In the sense of 'not double' or 'multiple' **einfach** is used.[3] *Ein einfaches Geleise, eine einfache Fahrkarte* (not return), *eine einfache Nelke.* **Ein** occurs in a number of compound adjectives. *Eingleisig* (e.g. *Strecke*), *einäugig, einbettig.*

5. In the sense of 'unmarried' **unverheiratet** (see article on 'marry') is the most general term. **Alleinstehend** is often used officially of a woman,[4] less commonly of a man.

SINK 1. Intransitive.

(a) **Sinken** is used literally and figuratively in most senses of 'sink'.

Das Schiff, die Temperatur, die Sonne (poetically), *sinkt.*
Er ist in meiner Achtung gesunken.
Dein Mut ist gesunken.

(b) **Versinken** is used (*a*) literally in the sense of 'to disappear beneath the surface' of a thing, particularly by being sucked under; (*b*) figuratively in the sense of 'to be completely absorbed into a state and to lose consciousness of everything else'. When the preposition *in* follows in the literal sense, it governs the dative case.

Er ist im Schlamm, im Flugsand, versunken.
Er ist in Melancholie, in die Betrachtung der Landschaft, versunken.

[1] German has no close equivalent for the sense of 'sincere', e.g. single-hearted.
[2] *Einzigartig* means 'unique'.
[3] See article on 'simple'.
[4] *Ledig* is used in fixed combinations.

2. Transitive.

(a) **Senken:** to lower a thing gradually, both literally and figuratively. It must frequently be rendered into English by 'lower'.[1]

Er senkte die Angel ins Wasser, den Kopf.
Der Baum senkt seine Wurzeln in die Erde.

(b) **Versenken:** to sink a thing so that it disappears completely and irrevocably.[2] It does not necessarily suggest gradualness of the process, but rather the result. In figurative use it is reflexive, and means 'to allow oneself to be absorbed' in a thing (compare *versinken* (*b*)).

Nach dem ersten Weltkrieg wurde die deutsche Flotte bei Scapa Flow versenkt.
Er versenkte sich in seine Arbeit.

SLIP (literal sense) 1. To loose one's footing: **ausgleiten.**[3] More colloquially **(aus)rutschen** (also = skid).

Er glitt auf dem Eise aus.

2. To move easily, often unobserved, into or through a thing: **schlüpfen.**

Er schlüpfte in das Loch, in seine Kleider.
Der Gefangene schlüpfte an der Wache vorbei.
Der Aal schlüpfte ihm durch die Finger.

SOFT, GENTLE, TENDER, DELICATE, MILD 1. **Weich** means in its literal sense 'yielding to pressure, soft as a tactile sensation', i.e. not hard. Applied to the impression of the other senses and to feelings it conveys the same suggestion. In reference to sound it thus means 'insinuating', 'not harsh'. It does not mean 'low, not loud' (e.g. he spoke softly).

Weiches Haar, weich wie Seide, ein weiches Bett, ein weiches Ei, weiche Wiesen, ein weicher Himmel, ein weiches Blau, weiche Linien, eine weiche Stimme, weiche Klänge, weich sprechen (see *leise*), *ein weiches Herz.*

2. **Sanft** suggests in both literal and figurative use (*a*) lightness of contact, and (*b*) pleasurable, often soothing,[4] sensations arising from such contact. Its closest English equivalent is 'gentle', i.e. not rough, violent.

Er berührte sie sanft.

[1] Example: *er senkte den Eimer in den Brunnen.*

[2] As with *senken* 'lower' is a more frequent English equivalent. *Der Sarg wurde in die Erde versenkt.*

[3] Glide: *gleiten.* 'Slide' has no exact equivalent in German and must be translated according to whether it approximates closer to 'slip' or 'glide'.

[4] *Besänftigen*: to soothe.

Ein sanfter Druck, sanfte Gewalt.
Er klopfte sanft an die Tür.
Eine sanfte Stimme, ein sanftes Blau, ein sanfter Wind, ein sanfter Regen.

3. **Sacht** is the Low German form of *sanft* (both cognate with 'soft'), but is not always interchangeable with it. In reference to gentle contact it is a more popular and vigorous term than *sanft*, and, unlike the latter, can also be applied to movement or activity in the sense of 'steady', 'not precipitate'.

Er berührte sie sachte.
Sachte, sachte! Nicht übereilt!

4. **Zart** means in the literal sense 'fragile, easily cut or broken', and figuratively 'impressionable', particularly in the sense of 'vulnerable', 'sensitive to pain'. Its chief implication is passive receptivity, and in this sense it corresponds closely to 'tender' and 'delicate'.[1] It does not mean 'tender' in the active sense of 'loving, affectionate'.

Zartes Fleisch, zarte Haut, eine zarte Gesundheit,[2] *ein zartes Gewebe, ein zartes Gemüt, eine zarte Stimmung, zarte Farben, eine zarte Stimme, ein zartes Gedicht.*
Sie müssen ihn zart behandeln.

5. **Zärtlich** means 'tender' only in the sense of 'loving, affectionate'.

Zärtliche Gefühle, Liebe.
Sie flüsterten zärtlich miteinander.

6. **Leise** has the general sense of 'barely perceptible', faint. Applied to sound it means 'soft' in the sense of 'low, not loud'.

Ein leises Geräusch, eine leise Stimme, leise Musik.
Er sprach, klopfte, leise.

7. **Mild,** like English 'mild', means 'not severe or harsh'.[3] It is applied to an agent which because of its lack of intensity or severity affects us painlessly or even pleasurably.

Mildes Wetter, ein mildes Klima, milde Luft, eine milde Strafe.
Er urteilt sehr mild.

[1] *Delikat* in figurative use means 'delicate' in the sense of 'tactful' (applied to persons) and 'requiring tact' (applied to things). Examples: *Sie müssen hier sehr delikat vorgehen*; *eine delikate Angelegenheit.* In literal use it is applied to food and drink.

[2] 'To be delicate', i.e. of frail constitution, is *schwächlich sein.* 'Tender' in the sense of 'sore' is *empfindlich.* Example: *Die Haut ist an dieser Stelle sehr empfindlich.* See 'severe'.

[3] *Mild,* unlike the English term, can in certain combinations mean 'kind, charitable'. Example: *milde Gaben.*

8. **Gelind(e)** means 'gentle or mild enough to cause no pain',[1] but not 'pleasurable' (contrast *sanft*). Attention is concentrated more on the effect, whereas *mild* suggests rather a property of the agent.

Ein gelinder Wind, Regen, Verweis, eine gelinde Strafe.

SOME (adjective) 1. With singular nouns.

Sense: a certain unspecified amount, part, degree, or extent of something, frequently implying 'not a little, considerable'. See *S.O.D.*

(a) **Etwas** suggests a quantity that is more or less measurable, while **einig** is much vaguer. The result of this distinction is that *etwas* is generally restrictive, meaning 'just a little', whereas *einig* means 'more than a little'. Hence, only *einig* is possible in such sentences as: *eine Stadt von einiger Bedeutung*; *er stand in einiger Entfernung*; *nach einiger Zeit.* The sense here approaches 'considerable'. On the other hand only *etwas* is correct in a sentence such as: *haben Sie doch etwas Mitleid mit ihm* (a plea for just a little pity).

Applied to substances, *etwas* is the normal term. *Einig* is sometimes used, but generally only of things that do not form one compact mass, but consist of separate parts (e.g. *einiges Geld, einiges Getreide*).

Er braucht noch etwas Übung (just a little).
Er braucht noch einige Übung (more than a little).
Geben Sie mir noch etwas Zeit, und ich werde alles erledigen (*einig* is impossible in a restrictive statement of this kind).
Es wird noch einige Zeit dauern, bis ich Ihre Angelegenheit erledigen kann.
Bei einigem Fleiß werden Sie es erreichen.
Mit etwas mehr Fleiß werden Sie es erreichen.
Ich habe die Sache mit etwas, einiger, Besorgnis beobachtet.
Ich brauche etwas Fleisch, Brot, Butter, für das Mittagessen.
In der Kanne ist noch etwas Tee.

(b) In some cases neither of the above terms is applicable. The sentence may be turned to use *etwas* as a pronoun or an adverb.

Es wäre gut, schon etwas über den Vorfall zu berichten (to give some account).
Sie müssen ihm das schon etwas auseinandersetzen, aber sagen Sie nicht zu viel (some explanation is necessary).

2. With plural nouns.

Sense: A certain number of; a few at least. See *S.O.D.*

Einige in the plural is more restrictive than in the singular. It corresponds to 'a few' and is used when 'some' is practically interchangeable

[1] *Lindern*: to assuage pain.

with 'a few'. **Manche** means 'a considerable number', and is used when the intention is not to restrict the reference to a few.[1]

Die Regierung beklagte sich darüber, daß manche Mitglieder der Opposition aus jeder Angelegenheit eine Parteifrage machen wollen.
Manche müssen sterben, damit andere leben.
Ich weiß, daß manche Studenten mit dem Lehrplan unzufrieden sind.
Einige Worte über den Plan müssen genügen.
In jedem Jahrgang gibt es nur einige Studenten, die wirklich begabt sind.
Ich habe diese Woche einige Briefe aus Deutschland bekommen.

SOUND, NOISE 1. **Schall** denotes primarily any sound in so far as it is thought of as vibrations which impinge on the ear. It is therefore used in scientific statements on the nature of sound. Apart from this in contexts which deal with the audibility of sounds it can refer to a clear and strong sound, i.e. ringing or pealing, or to a sound which would have these qualities if it had an unimpeded passage, but which has become muffled (e.g. *ein dumpfer Schall*). In phonetic contexts it means 'a continuous stream of sound'. Finally, it is used figuratively in the sense of 'empty, meaningless sound'.

Die Geschwindigkeit des Schalles ist kleiner als die des Lichts.
Schallanalyse (i.e. a field of study).
Er entfernte sich, so daß der Schall seiner Stimme nicht mehr zu hören war.
Schallmasse.

2. **Laut** is the most general term for sound in so far as it is made by a living being, particularly the human voice. It refers exclusively to audibility, except in the science of phonetics, where qualities may be ascribed to it. In phonetic contexts it means 'individual sound'.

Ich hörte plötzlich einen Laut, und gleich darauf erschien ein Mann.
Er gab keinen Laut von sich.
Sprechen Sie diese Laute nach!
Lauttafel (in phonetics).

3. **Klang** is a musical sound which is distinct and rings and whose vibrations are of equal duration. It is also used within this general sense of the total effect of a number of sounds, in so far as their sensuous quality is thought of as colouring (compare *Klangfarbe*). It is the normal term for the 'sound' of artistic prose and verse. **Ton,** as a musical term,

[1] *Manche* does not mean 'many'. *Manchmal* means 'sometimes', and can be modified by *nur*. It does not mean 'often', as is wrongly stated in some dictionaries and grammars. *Einigemal*: a few times.

refers to pitch, and corresponds to English 'tone'. When applied outside music to the human voice, it differs from *Klang* in suggesting an emotional attitude, often one felt as unpleasant,[1] whereas *Klang* evokes a sensuous impression that tends to be agreeable.

Der Klang der Geige hielt mich gebannt.
Seine Stimme hat einen warmen Klang.
Der Klang seiner Stimme gefällt mir.
Der Klang dieses Verses erinnert an das Plätschern eines Springbrunnens.
Er untersucht die Klangwerte von Hölderlins Dichtung.
Ich kann schrille Töne nicht ertragen.
Der Ton seiner Stimme geht mir auf die Nerven.
Der Ton der preußischen Stimme liegt dem Süddeutschen nicht.

4. **Geräusch** is indistinct and not loud. It is the most general term for both 'sound' and 'noise' when these terms have such properties.

Ich hörte ein Geräusch unter meinem Fenster.
Das Geräusch des Telephons weckte mich aus einem tiefen Schlaf. (*Geräusch* can only be applied to the telephone in so far as it is confused or indistinct, e.g. as heard in a semi-conscious state.)
Das Geräusch des Hagels auf dem Dach ist nicht unangenehm.

5. **Lärm** is 'noise' in so far as the latter is loud and continuous.

Der Lärm auf den Straßen läßt mich nachts nicht schlafen.
Es entstand ein ohrenbetäubender Lärm in dem Haus.

6. When the above terms are inapplicable, a specific term must be used. This will most often be a substantival infinitive, e.g. *Dröhnen, Klingeln, Läuten,*[2] *Rauschen, Brausen.*

Das Rauschen der Wellen am Strand regt immer meine Phantasie an.

SPARE Many former senses of 'spare' have now become obsolete. In a number of cases it has survived more in the negative than in the positive use (e.g. he does not spare himself, he spared no efforts). In certain negative uses, too, it only appears in fixed phrases.

A connection in meaning exists between *sparen* in the sense of 'save' and the practically obsolete sense of 'spare': 'not to use'.

A. To abstain from hurting, damaging, destroying, inflicting evils of any kind on people.

[1] *Ton* can also refer to the manner of speaking, the actual sound not being given prominence. In this use it need not be unpleasant. *Er antwortete in ruhigem Tone.*

[2] *Klingeln*: 'ringing' in the sense of a series of sounds in quick succession, as the buzzing of a telephone. *Läuten*: 'ringing' as separate strokes, as of a church bell.

SPARE

1. With one object.

(a) **Schonen:** to treat carefully (really *schön behandeln*). It suggests actual doing, using, and in such a way that one abstains from inflicting harm, etc. on the object (contrast the idea of abstention implied in *verschonen*).

It translates 'spare' only with a personal object or a word meaning 'feelings' in the sense of 'to spare a person's feelings'. Used reflexively or with a thing as object it means 'to look after'.[1]

Sie müssen ihn, seine Gefühle, schonen.

(b) **Verschonen:** to abstain from inflicting physical harm, destruction which one is in a position to inflict. It can imply the sparing of a person's life.[2] Whereas *schonen* suggests treatment with care or consideration, *verschonen* emphasizes abstention from all action. It is not used reflexively.

Der Sieger verschonte die Besiegten.
Der Krieg verschonte diese schöne Stadt nicht.
Der Tod verschont niemanden.

2. With two objects (to spare someone something).

(a) **Verschonen:** to abstain from bothering, boring a person with a thing. It is used mainly in reference to trivial matters.

Verschonen Sie mich mit diesem Geschwätz (said impatiently).

(b) **Ersparen** is used in more serious matters and where deep feeling is involved. As a reflexive verb it cannot be used in the imperative (see *sparen*).

Ersparen Sie mir die Erzählung vom Tode Ihres Kindes (the story would affect me too deeply; *verschonen Sie mich mit . . .* : it would bore me).
Ersparen Sie mir den Verdruß, diesen Kummer.
Er hätte sich die Unannehmlichkeiten, die Mühe, die Kosten, ersparen können.

(c) **Sparen** is in this sense only used reflexively. It suggests something of a reproach or a rebuke, whereas *ersparen* makes a simple statement, which may be friendly in tone.[3] However, as a translation of the English reflexive imperative, only *sparen* is possible.

Er hätte sich die Mühe, die Kosten sparen können.
Sparen Sie sich den Verdruß.

[1] *Er schont sich* (his health), *seine Gesundheit, ein Buch.*

[2] When the idea of 'sparing one's life' is to be made explicit German uses a specific term. *Schenken Sie mir das Leben* (spare me my life). *Wenn ihm noch einige Monate geschenkt sind* (if he is spared . . .).

[3] Both *sparen* and *ersparen* are also used in the sense of 'to save money', the former being an objective statement, the latter suggesting the attitude of mind or manner of living associated with the action of saving.

B. To abstain from using.

'Spare' and *sparen mit* are sometimes used negatively in this sense, *sparen mit* also positively in contexts with a more emotional connotation (mostly with immaterial things). To translate the positive sense English uses 'to be sparing with', German *sparsam umgehen mit.*

Sparen Sie nicht mit der Butter.
Gehen Sie sparsam mit der Butter um.

C. To abstain from expending. *Sparen* is used negatively (with *kein*) with words such as *Kosten, Aufwand, Mühe, Fleiß.* In this sense *scheuen* is a synonymous term.

Er hat keine Mühe gespart (*gescheut*).

D. To abstain from demanding exhausting efforts from a person (mostly negative). German uses specific terms.

Er ist hart gegen sich selbst; *mutet sich sehr viel zu* (he doesn't spare himself).
Er stellt starke Ansprüche an seine Truppen (does not spare).

E. To give, to lend, out of a sufficiency or superabundance. German uses specific terms such as *übrig haben, entbehren.*

Haben Sie ein paar Minuten für mich übrig?
Können Sie das Buch bis morgen entbehren?

SPEND (time) 1. **Verbringen** is the general term. It cannot, however, be used with *wie lange* as object.

Ich habe meine Ferien am Meer verbracht.
Er hat eine schlaflose Nacht verbracht.
Er hat drei Jahre im Gefängnis verbracht.
Ich verbringe jeden Sonntag bei ihnen.

2. **Zubringen** suggests that what one does or thinks absorbs one. It cannot, therefore, be used with phrases that suggest inactivity or idle pursuits. It is normal with *wie lange* as object.

Er hat 5 Jahre mit seiner Doktorarbeit zugebracht.
'*Die letzte Nacht, die ich in dem großen Spiegelsaale zubrachte, wo die Leiche des Prinzen aufgebahrt stand, lag mir eine liebliche, oder soll ich sagen traurige oder lächerliche Szene im Sinne, ich spreche von der Maiwiese*' (R. Huch, *Die Maiwiese*).
Wie lange haben Sie in Rom zugebracht?

SPIT **Spucken** is the normal term in the sense of 'to eject saliva or anything else from the mouth'. **Speien** means in its literal sense 'to vomit'. Figuratively, as applied to persons, mainly in fixed phrases it means 'to spit, emit' fire, sparks, and the like, as an expression of a feeling. It is used, further, of things which seem to do this.

Er spuckte auf den Fußboden, ohne sich um andere Leute zu kümmern.
Er spie Gift und Galle.
Er hat Galle gespieen.
Die Geschütze spieen Feuer und Flamme.

SPREAD With each of the following verbs it is necessary to determine whether the sense is (*a*) to extend over an area, without increasing the area, or (*b*) to increase the area concerned.

1. **Breiten, ausbreiten:** to spread one thing over another, the form with *aus*, like 'out' in English heightening the impression of extent. Only the context can decide whether an increase in area is meant. *Feuer*, e.g. admits only the idea of increase. Whether the increase is real or imaginary, it proceeds on all sides, i.e. not only in one direction, unless this is expressly stated. Both simple verb and compound suggest something poetical, ceremonious, or at least of considerable proportions, or that the action is performed with care and with attention to the various parts of the object (e.g. a map). Another sense of *sich ausbreiten* is 'to spread oneself' over a subject.

Der Baum breitet seine Zweige über die Rasenfläche.
Der Teppich wurde ausgebreitet.
Der Vogel breitet seine Flügel aus.
Das Feuer hat sich ausgebreitet.
Der Wald breitet sich bis zum Fluß aus.
Das Meer breitete sich vor uns aus.
Wir breiteten die Karte aus.
Breiten Sie sich nicht zu sehr aus.

2. **Légen** or a similar verb must be used in reference to trivial things.

Wir legten den Teppich auf den Fußboden, die Decken auf das Bett, die Taschentücher auf das Gras.

3. **Streichen** and **schmieren:** to spread a substance over a thing, e.g. butter on bread, ointment on a wound.

4. **Übergreifen auf:** to spread from one thing to another, rather in one direction than in all, unless the latter is stated. It is used of such things as fire, disease, i.e. whose advance it is difficult to halt.

Das Feuer greift auf das Nebengebäude über.
Der Krebs greift auf andere Organe über.

5. **Verbreiten:** to diffuse,[1] to disseminate over a wide area, mostly with spaces between the points which diffusion reaches (unlike *ausbreiten*). It is applied to intangibles as well as to people and things. *Sich verbreiten über*... also has the meaning of 'to spread oneself at great length over' a subject.

Meine Freunde sind über das ganze Land verbreitet.
Die Angelsachsen haben sich fast über die ganze Erde verbreitet.
Er hat das Gerücht, die Nachricht, in weiten Kreisen verbreitet.
Diese Sitte hat sich überall verbreitet.
Der Geruch verbreitete sich sehr schnell.

6. **Verteilen:** to distribute at fixed intervals over space or time.[2] *Verbreiten* does not suggest deliberately fixed intervals, but the vague idea of diffusion.

Die Befestigungen waren über eine weite Fläche verteilt.
Sie können die Zahlungen über einige Jahre verteilen.

7. **Dehnen** means in its literal sense 'to stretch[3] a thing lengthwise so that it becomes longer' (e.g. elastic). In figurative use it does not mean 'to increase the length', but 'to be so extensive as to call for comment'. There may be spaces between the various parts.

Das britische Reich dehnt sich über die halbe Welt.

8. **Ausdehnen:** to increase the size of, to extend, to expand.[4] It is used particularly of land and of spheres of power, of operation.

Rußland dehnt sich mehr und mehr nach Europa hin aus.

9. **Streuen** must be used to translate 'spread' in the sense of 'strew', i.e. with masses of loose particles such as sand.

Er streute Sand über das Blut.

STATE, CONDITION 'State' is the general term. 'Condition' draws attention to the causes, the circumstances which bring about the condition. It is therefore the appropriate term where accurate measurement is involved (e.g. the patient's condition; the condition of the roads, in

[1] *Breit* means in figurative use 'diffuse' (e.g. of a style).

[2] 'To spread out' in reference to small things is rarely *verteilen*. *Machen Sie die Abstände zwischen den Pflanzen größer* (spread the plants out more).

[3] *Sich erstrecken*: to extend or stretch lengthwise, without increase. It is used of large geographical features and of time. *Reichen*: to stretch or reach, of smaller things. *Der Garten reicht bis zum Fluß. Das Seil reicht nicht weit genug.*

[4] *Erweitern*: to extend, to expand, i.e. with increase. It is used mainly of intangibles (e.g. *Kenntnisse, Machtsphäre*).

the eyes of a road-engineer; the state of the roads, in the eyes of the public). 'Condition' can, unlike 'state', stand for the external circumstances themselves, particularly in the plural.

1. **Zustand** is the general term, wider than both 'state' and 'condition', but cannot stand directly for external circumstances.[1] In the sense of 'conditions' it is thought of in relation to persons. It is casual and changeable. While it is applied to a person's physical or mental state or condition as controlled by medical intervention, it is not used of activities and operations in so far as they are consciously planned and controlled and conceived of as moving from stage to stage towards a goal, or as it is measured according to an objective standard of fitness, perfection, or the like. In this sense **Stand** (see article on 'position') is the appropriate term. It refers to things and activities, not to persons themselves.

Stand is used in a number of fixed phrases which suggest an objective standard, a level. In reference to things or animals: *gut, schlecht, im Stande sein*; *in gutem, schlechtem, gehörigem* (and the like) *Stande sein*; (*gut*) *im Stande* (*er*)*halten*; *in den* (*alten*) *Stand setzen*. In reference to persons: *imstande sein, in den Stand setzen...zu. In der Lage sein...zu* refers rather to the nature of external circumstances.

Der Zustand seiner Gesundheit ist besorgniserregend.
Der Zustand der Straßen ist gefährlich.
Er befindet sich in einem Zustand der höchsten Aufregung.
Der Stand der Forschung ist befriedigend (the stage it has reached; but: *die Forschung befindet sich in einem beklagenswerten Zustand*).
Der Stand der Rüstungen läßt zu wünschen übrig (*Zustand* would indicate a less accurate assessment).
Das Pferd ist gut im Stand (in good condition).
Das Haus wird gut im Stand gehalten.
Obgleich das Haus seit 20 Jahren unbewohnt ist, ist es in gutem Zustand.
Die Zustände im Gestapogefängnis sind haarsträubend.

2. **Verhältnisse,** plural (see article on 'relation'), refers to external circumstances in the sense of 'a state of affairs', the nature of the elements or parts of these in relation to each other. It is used particularly of the important activities of life.

Wie sind die Verhältnisse in China?
Die Wohnverhältnisse sind jetzt überall sehr schwierig.
Die kulturellen Verhältnisse in Deutschland sind als Folge der langen Nazi-Herrschaft sehr verworren.

[1] 'Circumstances' are *Umstände*.

Unter den gegenwärtigen Verhältnissen bereitet einem das Reisen wenig Freude.
Er lebt über seine Verhältnisse.

STOP[1] **A.** To bring, come, to a motionless state, of a person, vehicle or any other object in motion.

1. **Halten** (intransitive only).

Applied to vehicles *halten* suggests a regular, prescribed stop. Applied to persons, it leaves open the question of whether the stop is prescribed or not and also that of its duration.

Die Straßenbahn hält hier.
Ich hielt auf meinem Spaziergang vor dem Schloß.
Halt!
Wir können hier für das Mittagessen halten.

2. **Anhalten** (transitive and intransitive).

Applied to persons *anhalten* definitely suggests a temporary stop (generally short). With vehicles it indicates in intransitive use a stop that is not prescribed, in transitive use one that is either prescribed or not.

Die Straßenbahn hielt zwischen zwei Haltestellen an.
Das Auto hat vor der Tür angehalten.
Ich hielt vor dem Schloß an und sah mich einen Augenblick um.
Der Lokomotivführer hielt den Zug an.
Ich wurde an der Ecke von einem Bekannten angehalten.

3. **Aufhalten** (transitive only): either 'to stop permanently', 'to check' or 'to delay', 'to hold up'. Only the context can indicate which sense is intended. The agency which causes the stopping can be an irresistible force or the intervention of authority.

Wir müssen den Feind mit allen Mitteln aufhalten.
Stürmisches Wetter hat das Schiff aufgehalten (held up; see *zurückhalten*).
Der Scheck, der Brief, wurde aufgehalten (held up in transit, e.g. by the censor; see *zurückhalten*).

4. **Abhalten** (transitive only): to intercept an object or something

[1] 'Stop' comes from the popular Latin *stuppare* = 'to stuff' with oakum or tow (as does 'stuff', German *stopfen*). When it retains this original sense of 'stuff (up)', 'block', it must be translated by such verbs as *(ver)stopfen, füllen. Stoppen* tends to be colloquial in the sense of 'stop', but is becoming more and more prevalent. It is used intransitively of a person or thing in quick motion (e.g. of machinery), transitively of a vehicle and of some activities which involve motion.

intangible (often moving through the air) and prevent it from reaching, hitting, or penetrating to its goal.

Die Säcke hielten die Kugeln ab.
Die Mauern sind dick genug, um jeden Lärm abzuhalten.
Wir brauchen Vorhänge, die das Licht abhalten.

5. **Halt machen** suggests a more or less final stop, at any rate a lengthy one.

Die Soldaten mußten vor den Barrikaden haltmachen.
Wir machten beim Wirtshaus halt.

6. **Stehen bleiben,** applied to persons and other animate beings, leaves open the question of whether the stop is momentary or not and intentional or not. It definitely implies standing, i.e. not sitting, lying. Applied to vehicles and other machinery, it implies a defect or breaking-down of the machinery (but see **B** for another use).

Ich blieb an der Ecke stehen und sah mich um.
Er blieb stehen und legte sich nach einiger Zeit hin.
Nach einer tollen Jagd blieben die Pferde stehen.
Mein Auto ist plötzlich stehen geblieben.
Die Uhr, die Maschine, ist stehen geblieben.

7. **Zum Stehen (Stillstand) bringen (kommen).** The phrase with *stehen* means 'to stop a person or a thing in headlong motion' (see *bringen* under 'make'), the one formed with *Stillstand* is applied to objects such as machinery that revolve regularly.

Mit Müh' und Not brachte er das Auto zum Stehen.
Er brachte die Maschine, das Mühlrad, zum Stillstand.

B. 'Not to (be allowed to) begin moving, to leave' (a sense more correctly conveyed by 'stay' in the case of persons).[1]

1. **Bleiben, stehen (sitzen,** etc.) **bleiben.**

Bleiben Sie zum Mittagessen.
Bleiben Sie sitzen.
Dieser Wagen bleibt hier stehen (will not leave).

2. **Zurückhalten:** not to allow a thing to start, to be sent.

Das Schiff wurde vom stürmischen Wetter im Hafen zurückgehalten.
Der Scheck, der Brief, wurde zurückgehalten.

[1] Used loosely in the sense of 'sojourn', 'stop' is *sich aufhalten.* To stop and spend some time at an inn = *einkehren.*

C. To cease from an activity. Distinguish whether one stops (*a*) one's own activity, or (*b*) that of someone else. The subject may be animate or inanimate.

1. To stop one's own activity.

(a) **Aufhören** is the most general term and can mean 'to stop' finally or for a certain time. It is used with the infinitive and with *mit* followed by a noun. In combination with *mit* and a verbal noun it is more familiar than with the infinitive.[1]

Er hörte auf, zu fragen.
Es hat zu regnen aufgehört.
Hören Sie mit dem Nörgeln auf.
Hören Sie mit dem Unsinn auf.
Der Regen hat aufgehört.

(b) As a familiar equivalent of 'prevent' in the imperative mood.

Tu' doch was, damit das Kind nicht mehr schreit (*damit die Tür keinen Lärm mehr macht*).

(c) Each of the following compounds of *halten* has a specific sense.

(i) **Einhalten** is used only of something explosive or violent.

Er hielt mit dem Fluchen ein.
Die Wilden hielten mit dem Gemetzel, Gebrüll, ein.

(ii) **Innehalten** denotes an involuntary, often sudden, cessation. In other uses it has an old-fashioned flavour.

Als er Schüsse von der Straße hörte, hielt er in seiner Rede inne.

(iii) **Anhalten** denotes an act of will.

Er hielt in seiner Rede an, um sich an den Vorsitzenden zu wenden.

2. To stop the activity of someone or something else. German mostly uses specific terms, the only more general ones being *ein Ende machen* (put an end to), *Einhalt tun, gebieten* (stop someone's machinations, manœuvres, and the like in an authoritative way).

Wir müssen ihren Umtrieben ein Ende machen.
Man hätte Hitler gleich am Anfang Einhalt gebieten sollen.
Die Polizei löste die Versammlung auf (dissolved).
Die Polizei verbot die Versammlung (before it started).
Der Regen unterbrach das Spiel (finally or temporarily).
Das Spiel mußte abgebrochen werden (finally).

[1] *Schluß machen* (*mit*) indicates a sharp and final stopping. *Lassen* (only in the imperative) is familiar. *Lassen Sie das* (*das Heulen*).

STOP

Das Feuer wurde rechtzeitig gelöscht.
Der Strom wurde abgeschnitten.
Die Zahlungen sind eingestellt worden (suspended).
Sein Gehalt ist suspendiert worden.
Sein Herz hörte zu schlagen auf (elliptical use of 'stopped' in English).
Sein Herz setzte aus (temporarily) (*aussetzen* also of breath and the like).

STRANGE[1] 1. **Fremd:** unknown to one, not one's own, out of one's element. It does not necessarily mean 'foreign'.

Diese Handschrift ist mir fremd.
Ich schlief in einem fremden Haus.
Ich sah viele fremde Gesichter.
Er kann nicht auf einem fremden Klavier spielen.
Ich bin hier fremd (a stranger).
Es läuft ein fremder Hund im Garten herum.

2. **Sonderbar** is a stronger term than **seltsam** (which is connected with *selten*). The latter means little more than 'surprising, unexpected', sometimes with the suggestion that a thing is so because it is rare. No desire to fathom causes or reasons is implied. 'Odd' is sometimes an appropriate translation. *Sonderbar*, on the other hand, strongly suggests this desire, or, again unlike *seltsam*, evokes the sensuous impression of strangeness in the appearance of persons and things and in actions. Thus: *er ist heute etwas sonderbar gewesen* (*seltsam* impossible). *Sonderbar* can mean 'queer'.

The phrases 'it is strange that...', 'I find it strange that...' can be translated by either adjective, but both are strong in this context. *Sonderbar* often implies a reproach. *Ich finde es sonderbar, daß er das verschwieg*, suggests both a reproach and a search for an explanation. *Es ist seltsam, daß er sich zu dem Handel bereit gefunden hat*, means that I would not from my knowledge of him have expected this, but do not rack my brains for the reason. More commonly used terms, are: *merkwürdig* (as weak as 'peculiar'), *komisch* (see article on 'funny'). What is laughable, amusing in its strangeness is expressed by *komisch*, not by *sonderbar* or *seltsam* (e.g. *sie trägt die komischsten Hüte*, the strangest hats).[2]

Er sieht sonderbar aus.
Sein Benehmen ist höchst sonderbar.
Ein seltsamer Fremder.
Das ist eine seltsame Beschäftigung.

[1] Study together with 'funny'.
[2] *Wunderlich* also means 'strange', 'queer'. Do not confuse with *wunderbar* (wonderful).

Das ist ein seltsamer Befehl (*sonderbar* would engage one's thoughts much more intensively).

Es ist merkwürdig, daß er nicht geschrieben hat (the most commonly used term in conversation).

STREET, ROAD, PATH 1. **Straße** translates both 'street' and 'road', i.e. in the city and in the open country.[1]

Die Straßen dieser Stadt sind sehr eng.

In dieser Gegend gibt es schöne, breite Autostraßen.

2. **Weg** translates only 'path', or 'way' in the sense of 'direction', i.e. not 'road'. It mostly denotes a made path.

Ein Gartenweg.

'*Der Weg Zurück*' (title of a novel by Remarque).

Den falschen Weg einschlagen.

Alle Wege führen nach Rom.

3. **Pfad** is a path worn by being trodden on, not one marked out and constructed with implements.

Ein Pfad durch den Wald, die Wiese.

STRENGTHEN 1. **Stärken:** to restore from weakness to normal strength. It is applied particularly to the strengthening of limbs. *Sich stärken* used absolutely means 'to strengthen oneself by liquor'.

Diese Übungen werden Ihr Bein stärken.

Stärken Sie sich ein bißchen, bevor Sie die Reise antreten.

Ich möchte, daß meine Ausführungen dazu beitragen, Ihren Entschluß zu stärken.

2. **Verstärken:** to strengthen further what is already strong, i.e. to reinforce, the commonest sense of 'strengthen'.

Die Regierung muß durch eine Umbildung des Kabinetts verstärkt werden.

Ein Regiment verstärken (*Verstärkungstruppen* = reinforcements).

Das wird Ihre Sache (= cause) *verstärken.*

Das verstärkt nur noch meine Entschlossenheit.

3. **Bestärken:** to strengthen, to confirm in an attitude of mind. It is generally followed by *in* when the object is a person. The object may also be a word meaning 'belief', 'view' and the like.

Das bestärkt ihn in seinem Glauben, Wahn, Entschluß.

Das bestärkt meine Auffassung.

[1] In Vienna *Gasse* is regularly used in the sense of 'street'.

4. **Kräftigen:**[1] to increase physical energy.

Die Suppe wird Sie schon kräftigen.
Sie müssen sich etwas kräftigen, bevor Sie die Reise antreten.

STRIKE, HIT[2] (literal sense)[3] 1. **Schlagen** with a direct object can mean 'to deal deliberately a blow to' a person, animal or thing with the intention of doing harm.[4] It also means 'to propel' a thing with a part of the body or an instrument.

Er schlug ihn so hart, wie er nur konnte.
Er schlug ihn (or: *ihm*) *ins Gesicht.*
Er schlug das arme Tier.
Er schlug den Baum mit der Axt.
Er schlug den Ball.

2. **Schlagen** with a prepositional phrase denoting the person or thing struck means (*a*) to strike deliberately, but without necessarily intending harm; (*b*) collision or contact[5,6] which is not deliberate. It does not, however, refer to a collision of vehicles or ships.

Er schlug mit der Faust auf das Pult.
Er schlug mit der Rute auf die Erde.
Er schlug mit dem Kopf auf den Boden.
Er schlug mit dem Kopf gegen die Wand.
Die Bombe, der Blitz, schlug in das Gebäude.
Die Wellen schlagen ans Ufer.

3. Collide,[7] with reference to vehicles, etc. Here German uses a variety of terms.

[1] *Bekräftigen* is now used only metaphorically in the sense of confirming an agreement by some gesture. *Sie haben ihre Versöhnung durch einen Handschlag bekräftigt.*

[2] 'Hit' is treated here as a more colloquial equivalent of 'strike'. If there is any other distinction, it is that 'strike' stresses more the dealing of the blow, 'hit' more the force of the impact. When 'hit' refers exclusively to the reaching of the mark aimed at, it must be translated by *treffen*. See footnote to 'affect'.

[3] Though both 'strike' and *schlagen* are much used figuratively, these uses rarely correspond.

[4] *Hauen* is a more colloquial term for 'hit', 'punch', etc. *Prügeln*: to beat, to give a thrashing. *Klopfen* indicates a more gentle contact, 'to rap', 'to tap', 'to knock at the door'. *Pochen*: to knock with insistence, to thump.

[5] Also in the less literal sense of 'impinge'. *Der Lärm schlug an mein Ohr.*

[6] *Stoßen*: to collide with a sharp jerk or knock. It therefore translates 'knock' thus used (e.g. *er stieß mit dem Kopf gegen die Wand*) and 'thrust' (e.g. *er stieß ihm den Dolch ins Herz*).

[7] To collide: *zusammenstoßen*. *Kollidieren* is used of two moving objects (ships, aircraft); also of a clash of lectures. 'To collide' with an iceberg is *zusammenstoßen* since the iceberg is not conceived as moving in the same way as the ship.

(a) **Fassen** is used of two vehicles, one of which normally runs on rails. Its subject must be the bigger of the two, i.e. ordinarily the one on rails.

Der Zug faßte das Auto.
Das Auto wurde von der Eisenbahn gefaßt.

(b) **Fahren in** is used if the smaller strikes the side of the bigger vehicle on rails or if two vehicles not on rails collide.

Mein Auto fuhr in die Eisenbahn.
Sein Auto fuhr direckt in meines.

(c) **Anfahren** is used of a vehicle which strikes a person or another vehicle.

Er wurde von der Straßenbahn angefahren.
Ich habe das andere Auto leicht angefahren.

(d) **Auflaufen** followed by *auf* is used when a vehicle or a ship collides with a stationary object which juts up in its path.

Das Schiff lief auf einen Felsen auf.

SUFFER 1. Leiden.

(a) To suffer pain (mental or physical), damage, or the like. In this sense it may be transitive or intransitive. *An* or *unter* may follow, the distinction being that with an ailment, whether physical or mental, *an* tends to suggest a permanent state, whereas *unter* suggests 'on one or more occasions'. The distinction is, however, not rigidly observed, *an* only being possible with *Kopfschmerzen*, both with *Halsschmerzen*. With physical ailments *an* tends to prevail. When mental distress is caused by an external agency, i.e. not an illness, only *unter* is used.

Er hat starke Schmerzen, Hunger und Durst, gelitten.
Die Gärten haben in den letzten Wochen gelitten.
Er leidet an Arterienverkalkung (*unter* impossible).
Er leidet an Größenwahn (*unter* impossible).
Er leidet an, unter, Größenwahnanfällen.
Er leidet an, unter, Wahnvorstellungen.
Sie leidet unter seinen Sticheleien.

(b) *Leiden*, like 'suffer', also has the sense of 'tolerate', 'allow', 'brook'. In this sense both *leiden* and 'suffer' are somewhat old-fashioned in flavour.[1]

Er leidet keinen Widerspruch.
Die Sache leidet keinen Aufschub.

[1] *Dulden* is more commonly used in this sense. It means 'to tolerate', 'to endure patiently, with mildness of spirit'. See also 'bear'.

2. **Erleiden:** to undergo, to be subjected to an external evil. Only transitive use is possible.

Sie haben eine Niederlage, Verluste, Schaden,[1] *Schiffbruch, erlitten.*

SUGGEST Most of the German terms are no more than approximations.

1. Sense: to propose for acceptance.

Vorschlagen corresponds to 'propose' rather than 'suggest', but for lack of any other German term must be used to translate the latter.

Er schlug einen Spaziergang, neue Bedingungen, diese Auslegung, vor.
Er schlug mir einen Ausweg aus dem Dilemma vor.
Er schlug vor, daß wir uns um 4 Uhr treffen sollten.

2. Sense: to cause an idea, which may initiate a train of thought, awaken a desire, lead to action, or the like, to present itself to the mind.[2]

(a) **Bringen** (*auf einen Gedanken, eine Idee,* or the like) is the most general term.

Was hat Sie auf diesen Gedanken, diesen Plan gebracht?
Seine Geschichten brachten mich darauf, daß ich als Textilfabrikant viel Geld verdienen könnte.
Der Rauch brachte uns auf den Gedanken, daß Menschen in der Nähe seien.

(b) **Nahelegen:** to suggest something to someone as the obvious or natural thing to do.[3] The subject is normally, but not always, a person.

Ich legte ihm nahe, daß er sein Geschäft erweitern solle.
Es wurde ihm nahegelegt, daß er sein Amt niederlegen solle.
Dieses Ereignis legt ein Wort des Dankes nahe.

(c) **Suggerieren** can only be used in the sense of insinuating a thing into a person's mind by, as it were, hypnotic methods, or by the use of tricks.

Sie hat ihm suggeriert, daß er sie heiraten solle.

(d) **Eingeben** is 'to inspire', i.e. in reference to a suggestion which comes as an inspiration.

Ein Erlebnis als Feldarzt hat ihm den Grundgedanken des Gedichts eingegeben.
'*...seine Durchtriebenheit, die ihm eingab, jeweils nur die dunkelsten Schleichwege zu benutzen*' (Gisevius, *Bis Zum Bitteren Ende*).

[1] With *Schaden, leiden* can also be used.

[2] 'A solution suggested itself to me' (i.e. reflexive use): *eine Lösung fiel mir (ohne weiteres) ein.*

[3] *Naheliegen*: to be obvious, to be the natural thing to do. *Die Lösung liegt nahe. Es liegt nahe, ihn des Verbrechens zu beschuldigen.*

(e) **Anregen** means primarily 'to stimulate' (see article on 'excite'). As a rendering of 'suggest' it can only mean 'to prompt the doing or the production of' a thing by stimulating suggestions, i.e. the suggestion must lead to production.

Er hat meinen Aufsatz über Rilke, diese Politik, angeregt.

(f) **Andeuten** is a closer equivalent of 'to indicate' than of 'to suggest', i.e. it is more definite than the latter, and can even convey an order.

Er deutete die Form an, die der Artikel haben sollte.
Er deutete mir an, daß ich das Geld sofort abholen sollte.
'...denn man kann einem Menschen ohne Brutalität andeuten daß er nicht in die Zeit paßt, aber nicht, daß er nicht in die Welt paßt' (F. Gundolf, *Heinrich von Kleist*).

(g) **Deuten auf:** to point to the existence of something not fully revealed or to something which is likely to become a reality, as knowledge, not as a sensuous experience (see **3**).[1]

Die letzte Entscheidung deutet auf Krieg.
Sein Gesichtsausdruck deutete darauf, daß er Angst hatte.

(h) **Schließen lassen auf:** to allow an inference, which is presented as more definite than with *deuten auf*.

Sein Gesichtsausdruck läßt darauf schließen, daß er Angst hat.
Schon der Preis läßt darauf schließen, daß Eier sehr knapp geworden sind.

(i) When 'suggest' implies 'to suggest the desirability or advisability of' a thing **erscheinen lassen als** (see 'appear') with an appropriate adjective may be used.

Die Vorsicht läßt diese Maßnahme als ratsam erscheinen.
Die Schönheit des Ortes ließ einen längeren Aufenthalt als wünschenswert erscheinen.

3. Sense: to evoke as a sensuous experience.

(a) **Erinnern an** may be used in the sense that one thing because of its sensuous properties makes one think of another.

Seine Nase und seine Ohren erinnern an ein Kaninchen.
Der Wind erinnerte an einen schluchzenden Menschen.

(b) In reference to the suggestive power of art phrases involving **suggestiv** may be used.

Es ist das Wesen der Kunst, suggestiv zu wirken (to suggest).
Das Suggestiv-Machen einer Stimmung, nicht deren Ausdruck, ist der Lyrik eigen.

[1] *Deuten auf* also means 'to point to' a thing in the literal sense.

(c) **Ahnen lassen** may be used in the sense of 'to suggest as a sensuous experience, particularly in art, the existence of something not fully revealed'. For *ahnen* see footnote to 'suspect' (p. 350, n. 1).

Mörikes Nachtgedichte lassen das Geheimnisvolle der werdenden Natur ahnen.
Das Bild läßt mehr ahnen, als es deutlich darstellt.

4. In reference to an accusation **unterstellen** is used in the sense of 'to impute', 'to insinuate'.

Wollen Sie mir unterstellen, daß ich lüge?[1]

SUIT, FIT A. Passen.

1. Used absolutely its general sense is: to be the right thing, either in respect to the requirements of a thing or of circumstances or to the wants of a person. Thus: *ich habe nichts, was passen würde*, which would do, i.e. meet your requirements or those of a thing. This meaning could also imply 'fit'. As an intransitive verb, mostly accompanied by an adverb such as *gut* or *schlecht*, it means 'fit' in a general way in reference to clothes (e.g. *der Anzug, der Hut, paßt gut, schlecht*). The meaning of 'fit' as applied to clothes is given more precisely by *sitzen* (e.g. *der Anzug sitzt gut*). *Paßt dir der Anzug?* = is the suit what you want? (not: does it fit you?). See **A, 2.**

Passen is followed by the simple dative or by prepositions with the shades of meaning explained in the following sections.

2. Followed by the simple dative of the person without preposition *passen* means: to be convenient, either as an arrangement of circumstances or in reference to the structure and the like of a thing.

Die Zeit, die Sie vorschlagen, paßt mir schlecht.
Es paßt mir gar nicht, hier übernachten zu müssen.
Das Haus paßt mir nicht.
Eine solche Stellung würde mir ausgezeichnet passen.

3. Followed by *zu* it is used in two closely related ways:

(a) To match, to harmonize with, i.e. one person or thing with another. Do not confuse with **B**.

Diese Eheleute passen nicht zueinander.
Rot paßt nicht zu ihrer Gesichtsfarbe.

(b) To be suitable[2] in, for, a certain capacity, function. A close synonym

[1] More familiar: *soll das heißen, wollen Sie damit sagen, daß ich lüge?*
[2] The adjectives 'suitable' and 'appropriate' are translated by *passend* and *geeignet*,

is *sich eignen*. The distinction is that while *sich eignen* stresses inherent qualities, *passen* draws attention to these as they manifest themselves in practice.

Er paßt, eignet sich, nicht für die Rolle.
Er paßt, eignet sich, nicht zum Lehrer.

4. Followed by other prepositions *passen* means 'to fit', i.e. to be of the right size and shape.

Der Deckel paßt genau auf den Topf.
Die Schublade paßt nicht in den Schrank.
Seine Hand paßt nicht in den Handschuh.

B. In reference to clothes 'to suit' in the sense of 'to become' is normally **stehen**. It is generally accompanied by an adverb. A dative of the person follows.

Das Kleid steht ihr gut, schlecht.

C. To agree with, in reference to food: **bekommen**. A dative of the person follows.

Gewürzte Speisen bekommen mir nicht.

D. Transitively, in the sense of 'to adapt' one thing to another: **anpassen**.

Er paßte seine Worte dem Ernst der Lage an.

SUPPORT Stützen, unterstützen.

1. Sense: to prop up an object by another in order to keep it from falling. *Stützen* is much more common than *unterstützen*. It is also more active and more vivid. It occurs frequently in the phrase *sich stützen auf*, to support oneself, to be supported, on, by.

Die Brücke, der Stollen, mußte gestützt werden.
Der schwere Zweig wurde von einem Pfahl gestützt.
Ein Haus wird mit Balken gestützt.
Er stützte seine alte Mutter, damit sie leichter die Treppen steigen konnte.
Der Krüppel stützte sich auf seinen Sohn.

2. Figurative sense: to give strength to a plan, argument, and the like. *Unterstützen* is more common than the more active *stützen*. (*Sich*)

which derive their meanings from their corresponding verbs. *Passend*, accompanied by an adverb such as *gut* or *schlecht*, can therefore mean 'fitting' in reference to clothes (e.g. *ein gut passendes Kleid*, or more commonly: *ein gut sitzendes Kleid*). 'Fitting' in the sense of 'befitting', 'meet' is *schicklich* (e.g. *eine schickliche Antwort*). *Angemessen*, which is much used, has rather the meaning of 'commensurate' (e.g. *ein angemessener Lohn*).

stützen auf is, however, freely used in the sense of 'to base on', 'to be based on'.

Er hat den Plan tatkräftig unterstützt.
Ich unterstütze sein Gesuch.
Er hat seinen Standpunkt mit wohlfundierten Beweisen gestützt.
Er stützte seine Argumente auf zweifelhaftes Material.
Sein Standpunkt stützt sich auf folgende Tatsache.
'*Ich war nicht unschuldig daran, seine Kandidatur gegen manche Bedenken im anderen Lager gestützt zu haben*' (Schlange-Schöningen, *Am Tage Danach*).

3. Sense: to supply with the necessaries of life. Only *unterstützen* is possible. But see also 'keep' and 'provide'.

Er muß seine Eltern unterstützen.

SUSPICION, SUSPICIOUS, SUSPECT (verb) **A.** Suspicion. For 'to have a suspicion' see also 'suspect', **C.**

1. With reference to wrong-doing.

(a) **Verdacht** is a suspicion based on the observation of signs in the object suspected. It therefore tends towards objectivity. It cannot be pluralized.

Er begründete seinen Verdacht mit einer Reihe von Argumenten.
Sein Zögern erregte meinen Verdacht.
Mein Verdacht, daß er es getan hatte, erwies sich als begründet.

(b) **Argwohn,** i.e. *arger Wohn*, is a subjective state of mind due more to character, temperament, prejudice, and the like than to objective signs.

Er hat, hegt, einen unbestimmten Argwohn gegen mich.

2. With reference to a fact, which need not be wrong-doing.
Ahnung: inkling, presentiment. It suggests a glimpse, not a prolonged feeling.

Ich habe eine Ahnung, daß er ungern gekommen ist.
Ich hatte keine Ahnung von dem, was geschehen war.

B. Suspicious.

1. **Verdächtig** is used only in the sense of the adjective 'suspect', i.e. arousing suspicion.

Ein verdächtiger Typ.
Er sieht verdächtig aus.
Seine Beteuerungen kommen mir sehr verdächtig vor.

2. **Argwöhnisch:**[1] inclined to suspicion, as a permanent characteristic of a person.

Er ist in seinem Alter argwöhnisch geworden.
Er ist so argwöhnisch, daß man ihn nicht belügen kann.

3. **Mißtrauisch:** suspicious, in the active sense of 'distrustful', with reference to the existence of a thing or to intentions.

Ich bin immer mißtrauisch, wenn er so redet.
Ich war vielleicht zu mißtrauisch gegen ihn.
Ich bin sehr mißtrauisch seinen vorgeblichen Sprachkenntnissen gegenüber.

4. **Stutzig,** mostly with *werden* or *machen* suggests that one is made or becomes suddenly distrustful. It is somewhat popular.

Die Bemerkung machte mich stutzig.

C. To suspect, to be suspicious of, to have a suspicion. See the meanings of 'suspect' given in *P.O.D.*

1. **Im Verdacht haben:**[2] to accuse mentally of wrong-doing. The passive 'to be suspected' is translated by *im Verdacht stehen, in Verdacht kommen.* It may be followed by the accusative of the person and the genitive of the thing, a *daß* clause, an infinitive.

Ich habe ihn, seine Motive, schwer im Verdacht.
Ich habe ihn im Verdacht des Diebstahls.
Er steht im Verdacht des Mordes.
Er wurde in der Nähe der Leiche gesehen und kam folglich in Verdacht des Mordes.
Ich habe ihn im Verdacht, daß er ein Gewohnheitsverbrecher ist.
Ich habe ihn im Verdacht, das Geld gestohlen zu haben.

2. **Argwöhnen, beargwöhnen.** To be disposed, because of one's nature or condition, to see evil, to think evil of. *Beargwöhnen* requires a noun or pronoun object, even when followed by a *daß* clause. *Argwöhnen* can only be followed by a *daß* clause. Neither verb is in common use.

Er beargwöhnt mich des Diebstahls.
Sie beargwöhnen und bestehlen sich gegenseitig.
Er argwöhnt, daß sie böse Absichten haben.
'*Ich redete mit Lotte über die unglaubliche Verblendung des Menschensinns, daß einer nicht argwöhnen soll, dahinter müsse was anders stecken, wenn...*' (Goethe, *Werthers Leiden*).

[1] *Arglos,* 'unsuspecting', is old-fashioned except in a few expressions such as *ein argloses Geschöpf.*

[2] *Verdächtigen*: to throw suspicion on. *Er verdächtigt meine Absichten.* It is, however, used loosely, actively, and particularly passively, in the sense of 'suspect'.

3. **Mißtrauen:** 'doubt the innocence of, doubt the genuineness or truth of' (*P.O.D.*). This is a common meaning of suspect.

Ich mißtraue seinen Plänen, seinem Urteil, seinen Fähigkeiten, dem Text.

4. **Vermuten:** to regard it as probable that a thing is a fact or a truth.[1] It is frequently, but not exclusively, used of wrong-doing.

Ich vermutete eine neue Tücke seinerseits.
Er vermutet sofort böse Absichten unsererseits.
Es wird Mord vermutet.
Ich vermute, daß er nicht kommen wird.
Man würde nichts Ungewöhnliches dahinter vermuten.

SWALLOW 1. **Schlucken** is the normal verb meaning 'to swallow' in the literal sense, i.e. the action of letting something pass from the mouth to the stomach. It is also used figuratively in the sense of accepting something unpleasant aimed at one from without.

Ich habe beim Schwimmen viel Wasser geschluckt.
Er schluckte die Medizin, obwohl sie bitter war.
Beim Schlucken tun mir die Mandeln weh.
Schluck' mal endlich die Pille.
Er mußte die Vorwürfe schlucken.

2. **Schlingen:** to swallow ravenously or greedily, without chewing, in a manner suggesting an animal. Manner, not quantity is stressed.

Er schlingt alles, was man ihm vorsetzt, herunter.
Schling' doch nicht so schrecklich (to a child).

3. **Verschlucken** denotes the completed action, whereas *schlucken* emphasizes the action itself. In the literal sense *verschlucken* therefore means 'to get rid of' a thing, especially when it is unpleasant, or 'to swallow inadvertently'. Figuratively it is used in three main ways: (*a*) to make disappear by opening, metaphorically speaking, the jaws and closing them again (see *verschlingen*); (*b*) to repress feelings, from within; (*c*) to slur sounds.

Sich verschlucken: to swallow the wrong way.
Verschluck' mal endlich die Pille.
Er hat den Kern verschluckt.
Die Wellen verschluckten ihn.
Die Dunkelheit verschluckte ihn.

[1] *Vermuten* requires to be distinguished from *ahnen*, which means to have an inkling and suggests that one regards the thing suspected as real or true, not, as with *vermuten*, only probably true. *Ich ahne so etwas wie eine Verschwörung.*

Seine Spielsucht verschluckte sein ganzes Vermögen.
Er verschluckt Worte, wenn er schnell spricht.

4. **Verschlingen** suggests, like *schlingen*, great avidity, but stresses the completed action and therefore conveys the idea of making a thing disappear quickly. Both literally and figuratively it means 'to devour'. It differs from *verschlucken* in implying, figuratively, greater activity, a reaching forward to seize the object.

Er war so hungrig, daß er alles verschlang, was man ihm vorsetzte.
Ein großer Konzern verschlingt viele kleine Betriebe.
Das Feuer verschlang eine Reihe von Häusern.
Rauchwolken verschlangen ihn.
Die Wellen verschlangen ihn.
Er verschlingt Bücher haufenweise.
Seine Spielsucht verschlang sein ganzes Vermögen.

TAKE I. Nehmen.

A. Literal. The fundamental meaning of *nehmen* is 'to take' something or someone from a place or another person to oneself with one's hand or into one's hand. Some degree of activity, however slight, is generally implied, whether mere voluntary acceptance or, on the other hand, reaching for or going and getting. With the action (in the literal sense) 'to oneself' is associated the purpose 'for oneself'. In extended use the latter idea is more easily perceptible than the former.

The idea of 'to' and 'for' oneself can recede before that of removal from the original position, i.e. before the idea of 'away', which is to be conceived in its vaguest sense, i.e. with no implication whatsoever of destination (unlike 'take' in some important uses). German equivalents of 'from' are accordingly common after *nehmen*. The sense may be (i) that of removal in space, (ii) deprivation. The latter is translated by the simple dative without preposition. *Von* with a person indicates acceptance.

The addition of the dative reflexive pronoun emphasizes the idea of conscious purpose, i.e. for oneself, for one's own use, interest.

The taking of food and drink[1] are considered here as instances of the literal meaning, despite additional associations, because of the distinct action of taking a thing from a place to oneself.

Er nahm das Geld, das ihm gereicht wurde.
Er nahm den Teller vom Tisch.
Er nahm die Briefe aus der Schublade.

[1] To ask whether one takes tea or coffee or the like, *trinken* is normally used.

Er nahm den Korb auf den Rücken.
Er nahm die Hand aus der Tasche.
Sie nahm das Kind auf die Knie, in ihre Arme.
Das Klavier wurde aus dem Wohnzimmer genommen.
Nehmen Sie diese Stühle weg.
Der Polizist nahm dem Verhafteten seine Pistole.
Er nahm die Pistole von ihm.
Ich werde mir eine zweite Portion nehmen.
Ich habe Medizin genommen.

B. Some extended uses.

(i) The sense is 'deprive', the idea 'to oneself' being absent, since the subject is not personal.

Ihre schwer erkämpften Rechte wurden ihnen wieder genommen.
Wir dürfen uns unsere Freiheit nicht ein zweites Mal nehmen lassen.
Die Nachricht hat mir alle Freude an dem Ausflug genommen.

(ii) The sense: take for use or interest. 'Take' is, however, more widely employed in this sense.

(a) To hire, to engage, to buy, a person or thing; to occupy; to accept; to seize; to capture; to steal; to seize something non-tangible; to borrow words, ideas, and the like; to ascertain a measurement. The manner of taking is left vague.

Wir nahmen das Haus auf drei Wochen.
Ich habe einen neuen Sekretär genommen.
Er nahm einen Autobus zum Bahnhof.
Er nahm sie zur Frau.
Nehmen Sie Platz.
Die Stadt ist genommen worden.
Die Diebe nahmen alles, was sie nur finden konnten.
Er nahm eine Karte für die Oper, eine Fahrkarte nach Berlin.
Sie nahm den Schleier.
Er nimmt Stunden, Unterricht.
Diese Stelle wurde aus einem früheren Werk genommen.
Dieses Wort wurde aus dem Lateinischen genommen.
Ich habe mir die Freiheit genommen, den Fehler zu verbessern.

(b) To perform an action denoted or suggested by the noun objects. The range of such expressions is less wide than in the case of 'take', partly because of the capacity of English to use verbs as nouns (e.g. to take a look,[1] a kick at...). Even where a suitable German noun exists, some

[1] But Middle High German: *er nam im mange schouwe/an mislichen buochen* (*Der Arme Heinrich*).

verb other than *nehmen* is, however, often preferred (e.g. *Maßnahmen treffen*,[1] *Schritte tun*).

Ein Bad, eine Wendung, einen Anlauf, den Weg nach dem Fluß, nehmen.

(c) A mental or emotional attitude. The sense is passive rather than active.

(i) To accept as (not to be confused with *halten für*, i.e. consider as).

Ich nehme ihn als vollgültig.
Ich nehme ihn so wie er ist.
Ich nehme es für ein günstiges Zeichen.

(ii) To react in an emotional way, in fixed phrases. This sense needs to be distinguished carefully from that of interpreting in a certain way (see *auffassen*, **IV**(*a*) below).

Etwas ernst, leicht, schwer, (sich) zu Herzen, nehmen.
Anstoß, Ärgernis nehmen.

(d) *Nehmen* is sometimes followed by a preposition and the reflexive pronoun where English can either add or omit the prepositional phrase. The following are common:[2]

(i) *An sich* in the sense of 'to arrogate to oneself'.

Er hat alle Macht an sich genommen.

(ii) *Auf sich* in the sense of 'to accept', 'to assume', something onerous.

Die Verantwortung, die Folgen, auf sich nehmen.

(iii) *Zu sich* in the meaning of 'to eat', and in a number of fixed expressions (e.g. *der Herr hat ihn zu sich genommen*).

II. Some compounds of *nehmen*.

In certain cases German uses only a specific term (here a compound) where English uses either the general term 'take' or a specific verb (e.g. to take, to accept a challenge). Thus while it is possible to say in English: 'he took, accepted, adopted, the suggestion' (with differing shades of meaning), German only says: *er nahm den Vorschlag an.* In other cases German, like English, uses both the simple verb and the compound (with differing shades of meaning). In the following list indications as to whether the simple verb can also be used are added.[3]

[1] *Nehmen* is sometimes found with *Maßnahmen*, but is clumsy because of its relation to *nahme*.

[2] *Nehmen* is of course used to form numerous fixed phrases. Expressions involving the preposition *in* are common (e.g. *in Anspruch, Schutz, Miete nehmen*).

[3] *Abnehmen* is normally rendered into English by 'relieve', the sense being 'to take from'. *Kann ich Ihnen einige Pakete abnehmen?*

(a) **Annehmen:** to take on, to accept, to adopt, to assume, to absorb on to the outside of a thing. The addition of *an* often suggests beyond the act of taking that of keeping. See article on 'accept'.

Eine Herausforderung annehmen.
Einen anderen Namen annehmen.
Einen anderen Glauben annehmen.
Der Stoff nimmt die Farbe gut an.

(b) **Aufnehmen** implies the taking of someone or something into something else or something connected with the subject, whether this idea is made explicit in a prepositional phrase or not. See article on 'accept'.

Er nahm ihn in sein Geschäft auf (also *nahm*).
Das Protokoll aufnehmen (also *nehmen*).
Der Saal nimmt niemand mehr auf.

(c) **Benehmen:** to take away in the sense of depriving a person of the free use or enjoyment of something. The object cannot be a concrete object. *Nehmen* is used in the same sense, but expresses the idea less absolutely.

Jemandem die Aussicht, alle Gelegenheit, den Atem, die Sprache, den Appetit, den Schlaf, benehmen.

(d) **Einnehmen:** to capture, to take food or drink (on official instructions, e.g. on the label of a medicine bottle), to take a seat, to adopt an attitude (with *Haltung, Standpunkt,* and the like). The addition of *ein* expresses the idea of thoroughness and importance.

Die Festung wurde eingenommen (*genommen* possible).
Diese Medizin muß dreimal täglich eingenommen werden (*nehmen* is the ordinary human term).
Der König nahm seinen Platz ein.
Er hat eine unverständliche Haltung eingenommen.

(e) **Entnehmen.** The only common uses[1] are figurative. (i) To infer, (ii) to take information and the like from a source, to borrow it.

Ich habe aus Ihren Worten entnommen, daß Sie jetzt anders denken.
Ich habe alle diese Tatsachen einem Nachschlagewerk entnommen.

(f) **Festnehmen:** to apprehend, to arrest formally.

Der Dieb wurde festgenommen.

(g) **Hinnehmen:** to take something unpleasant passively, to accept it. See article on 'accept'. It should be distinguished from a closely related use of 'take': to have something inflicted on one, to suffer, without

[1] *Entnehmen* is sometimes used in the sense of 'to take' goods from a dealer.

adopting any attitude towards it (e.g. Berlin took terrible punishment from allied air-attacks).

Wir können eine solche Niederlage nicht ohne weiteres hinnehmen.
Er nahm das von uns hin (without demur).

(h) **Übernehmen:** to take over, primarily from someone else, but also in the more general sense of 'to assume'.

Können Sie jetzt die Aufsicht übernehmen?
Sie müssen die Verantwortung, Verpflichtungen, übernehmen (or: *auf sich nehmen*).

III. Convey to a destination.
The simple verb *nehmen* cannot be used in this sense.

(a) **Bringen,** the most general term, 'means to take to a destination and then leave'. It is accordingly not used in the sense of 'take' a person to a place of entertainment and remain there with him or her. It corresponds to this sense of 'take' because, unlike the English 'bring', it does not necessarily suggest that the destination is the place where the speaker is when he uses the word 'bring'.[1]

Ich werde ihn an den Bahnhof bringen.
Sie brachte die Kinder von England nach Amerika.
Das Schiff brachte die Flüchtlinge in ihre neue Heimat.
Ich brachte ihm die Bücher, um die er gebeten hatte.
Bringen Sie ihm bitte diesen Brief so schnell wie möglich.

(b) **Mitbringen,** to bring, to take, with one, in the literal sense can suggest a friendly attitude of mind, and is used typically of taking a gift to a person. *Bringen* does not imply a gift.

Sie brachten ihr ein Geschenk mit.
Willst du mir ein paar Flaschen Wein aus der Stadt mitbringen? (not necessarily a gift).

(c) **Mitnehmen:** take with one on foot or in a vehicle, suggests a friendly relationship and can mean: to give a person a 'lift' to his destination, to take out or with one for entertainment.

Kann ich Sie in meinem Wagen mitnehmen?
Wir haben ihn auf unseren Ausflug mitgenommen.
Er nahm sie ins Theater mit.
Sie nimmt die Kinder immer mit, wenn sie ausgeht.

(d) **Führen** suggests a leader in the sense that he knows more than those he leads about what he shows them or that he is officially acting as host

[1] *Bringen* is a much wider term than 'bring'.

or guide. In this sense it can refer to entertainment. It is also applied to the relation between author and reader.

Er führte uns durch das Museum (*bringen* would suggest a destination, to reach which it was necessary to pass through the museum).
Der Botschafter führte den ausländischen Gast in eine Aufführung von 'Figaros Hochzeit'.
Die Handlung der 'Penthesilea' führt uns auf den Kampfplatz vor Troja.
Thomas Mann führt uns im 'Zauberberg' durch die ganze europäische Welt der Vorkriegszeit.

(e) **Tragen,** to carry, i.e. in the hand or on some other part of the body, is frequently used for carrying things a short distance, e.g. about the house when weight or manner is implied. English generally uses 'take' if no idea of weight or manner is conveyed (e.g. take this tray into the next room; carry...carefully...).[1] *Tragen* can refer to the weight a vehicle is capable of supporting, but unlike 'carry' is not used in the sense of transporting goods by vehicle. It can, however, be used of a ship or an aeroplane with reference to the carrying of people.

Wir müssen den Tisch in das andere Zimmer hinübertragen.
Tragen Sie bitte die Teller sorgfältig ins Eßzimmer hinüber.
Der Portier hat Ihr Gepäck in Ihr Zimmer getragen.
Er trug den Brief auf die Post, sein Geld auf die Bank.
Das Flugzeug trug ihn schnell nach Amerika.

(f) **Befördern:** to transport goods in an organized way, by a firm, the railways, and the like.[2]

Die Eisenbahn wird diese Güter befördern.

IV. Some extended meanings of 'take' not rendered by *nehmen* or its compounds. The aim of the following list is to point out these meanings rather than to discuss exhaustively their German equivalents. The German terms given are merely the commonest of a number of possible translations.

(a) To interpret in a certain way: *auffassen* (see 'sense'). *Nehmen* is used in a closely related sense, but means to take more passively, also emotionally.

Wie soll ich diese Bemerkung auffassen?
Er faßte die Bemerkung anders auf.

[1] See also 'move'.
[2] *Befördern* also means 'to promote' a person to a higher position. In earlier German it was sometimes used in the sense of 'to further', 'to advance', i.e. of *fördern.*

(b) Not to be able to take a thing with equanimity: *vertragen* (see 'bear').
Er verträgt keinen Spaß, wenig Wein.

(c) To derive an emotional experience from: *finden.*
Er findet Freude, Vergnügen, an Ihrem Hiersein.

(d) To conceive an emotional attitude towards: *fassen.*
Diese Familie hat eine Neigung zu ihm gefaßt.

(e) To require: *erfordern* (see 'demand') is the most general term with an impersonal subject. *In Anspruch nehmen* (see 'claim'), for which *nehmen* alone is occasionally used, means: to draw heavily on time or energy. *Dauern* (see 'last'), used impersonally, is applied to time. *Brauchen* is used with a personal subject.

Der Plan würde viel Zeit, Geld, Energie, erfordern.
Die Reise hat viel Zeit, Energie, in Anspruch genommen.
Es dauerte nicht sehr lange, bis ich das Buch fand.
Ich brauchte nur zwei Stunden für die Fahrt.

TASTE 1. **Schmecken** suggests sensitiveness to flavour. It can mean (*a*) to perceive the taste of a thing; (*b*) to test the taste of a thing. The first meaning is sometimes rendered by using *schmecken* intransitively.[1]

While *schmecken* in sense (*b*) suggests a connoisseur (compare *Feinschmecker*), **abschmecken** can be used of anyone and means 'to test during the process of cooking whether the ingredients and quantities are correct'. It does not suggest the testing of subtle flavours.

(a) *Ich schmeckte den Knoblauch im Salat* (*heraus*).
Man kann nichts schmecken, wenn man eine Erkältung hat.

(b) *Schmecken Sie diesen kostbaren Wein.*
Eine gute Köchin muß abschmecken können.
Schmecken Sie jetzt die Suppe ab.

2. **Kosten** only means 'to test the taste of' a thing. In conversation it is apt to sound pretentious or genteel and is better replaced by *probieren* or *versuchen* (see 'try out', 'test').

Sie müssen diesen Käse kosten, probieren.

[1] Of the verbs treated in this article only *schmecken* can be used intransitively in the sense of 'taste'. *Der Wein schmeckt süß, sauer.* Followed by the dative of the person *schmecken* can be turned by 'like', 'enjoy'. *Der Wein, das Gemüse, hat mir geschmeckt. Lassen Sie es sich gut schmecken* (enjoy it).

3. Both *schmecken* and *kosten* are used figuratively. *Schmecken* suggests greater sensitiveness, but *kosten* is more common, particularly in conversation. Both may be ironical.

Er hat das Glück, die Freude, gekostet.

'*Wer die anderen Tage geschmeckt hat, die bösen, die mit den Gichtanfällen...*' (H. Hesse, *Der Steppenwolf*).

4. In the sense of 'to eat or to drink a small quantity of' *essen* or *trinken* must be used.

Ich habe seit 3 Tagen nichts gegessen (tasted food).

TEACH 1. **Lehren**[1] draws attention to the teacher and to the subject rather than to methods of instruction. It is used of imparting knowledge, skills, behaviour, and attitudes of mind, admitting with the latter both a personal and impersonal subject. With reference to knowledge it suggests an authority in the subject as teacher, and is accordingly used regularly of a university teacher, but rarely of a school teacher or private coach. In reference to skills (e.g. swimming, singing) it is applied to a superior (e.g. *mein Vater lehrte mich reiten*) when no question of systematic lessons arises. When ascribed to a teacher other than of the kinds mentioned, it sounds pretentious. Its use with the dative is gaining ground in popular speech.

It cannot be used in the passive with a personal subject.

Er lehrt an der technischen Hochschule.
Er lehrt Geschichte in Wien.
Er lehrte mich schwimmen.
Er, die Erfahrung, lehrte mich die Dinge anders sehen.
Die Geduld kann nicht gelehrt werden.

2. **Unterrichten** (and *Unterricht geben, nehmen*) refers to methods of instruction, with regard to both knowledge and skills, and therefore suggests a school teacher or a paid private coach.

Er unterrichtet Geschichte an einem Gymnasium.
Er unterrichtet mich in Geschichte.
Er hat mir Schwimmunterricht gegeben.
Sie nimmt Gesangunterricht (in a small way, *Gesangstunden* refers to something more ambitious).

[1] *Belehren* also concentrates attention on the teacher as a superior and means (*a*) to correct an error (with personal object); (*b*) to preach at, of someone given to correcting faults in others. *Er belehrte uns über die wahre Sachlage* (which we had mistaken). *Sie lassen sich nicht belehren. Er will immer belehren.* English has no exact equivalent.

3. **Beibringen** is the most modest of the three terms. It means: to get a thing into a person's head, to make him see; to train a person or an animal in a skill. It is therefore used of casual instruction or help.

Er hat mir Deutsch, Tanzen, beigebracht.
Hast du dem Hund diesen Trick beigebracht?

TEASE **Necken** is an intimate and affectionate term, and can easily suggest affectionate physical contact. For this reason it is not normally used in conversation. For the latter purpose **aufziehen** is the commonest term. **Hänseln** is not quite as strong. **Veräppeln** is a slang term for *aufziehen.*

Er neckt sie sehr gern.
'Uns aber neckten von fern und lockten
Freundliche Stimmen. . . .' (Mörike, *Peregrina.*)
Seine Gutgläubigkeit gab uns manche Gelegenheit, ihn aufzuziehen.
Den haben wir heute schrecklich aufgezogen, veräppelt.

TEMPT,[1] ENTICE, ALLURE 1. **Versuchen** is strong and always serious, but not necessarily in a bad sense. Except in a few fixed phrases, it is used in the sense of 'tempt' only in the passive voice. It is not a common term.

Das Schicksal, die Vorsehung, versuchen.
Bei dem schönen Wetter fühlte ich mich stark versucht, meine Arbeit zu vernachlässigen und auszugehen.
Ich bin versucht, Ihr Angebot anzunehmen.

2. **In Versuchung kommen, bringen** are used more freely in conversation and ordinary prose than *versuchen.* They cannot be used with *Schicksal, Vorsehung* and the like.

Jedesmal, wenn ich hier bin, komme ich in Versuchung, nicht mehr wegzugehen.

3. **Locken** and **verlocken** both mean 'entice' and 'allure', and because of the restricted range of application of the above verbs are often used to translate 'tempt'. Both suggest a strong appeal, but *verlocken,* unlike *locken,* is applied to something conceived as bad. *Locken,* on the other hand, unlike *verlocken,* can mean 'to entice' a person to a place. *Verlocken* differs again from *locken* in that it can be followed by an infinitive. 'Tempting' used adjectivally is *verlockend.*

Die Speise, Ihr Angebot, lockt mich sehr.
Wir haben den Feind in eine Falle gelockt.

[1] See also *reizen* under 'charm'.

TEMPT

Das schöne Wetter lockte uns hinaus.
Das schöne Wetter verlockte uns auszugehen.
Ich war verlockt, seinen Ratschlägen zu folgen.
Die Qualität des Weines verlockte mich, zu viel davon zu trinken.
Der Posten ist sehr verlockend.

4. **Große Lust haben** may be used of trivial things, particularly with reference to oneself and in the present tense. The addition of *große* to *Lust haben* suggests hesitation, which may, however, be merely polite or deferential.[1]

Ich habe große Lust, ein zweites Stück Torte zu essen, aber ich muß darauf verzichten.

THANK 1. **Danken** is the general term in the sense of 'to express gratitude' to a person for something. **Sich bedanken** (*bei jdm.*) is a formal expression of thanks, either spoken or written. It is not used, however, in the first person of the present tense, i.e. in addressing the person to whom thanks are due.

Ich danke Ihnen sehr für Ihre Hilfe.
Ich bedankte mich und ging weg.
Ich möchte mich für das Paket bedanken.

2. 'Have to thank' in the sense of 'owe'[2] is translated both by **danken** and **verdanken**. The distinction is that *danken* merely expresses a consequence, while *verdanken* denotes also the intention. Further, *danken* mostly indicates an unfavourable consequence, which is sometimes expressed ironically.

Meine Stellung habe ich ihm, seinen Bemühungen für mich, zu verdanken.
Dieses Buch verdankt seine Entstehung einer Anregung meines alten Lehrers.
Sein unstetes Leben dankt er den gespannten Verhältnissen des Elternhauses.
'*...wenn man merkt wie sehr Kleists Zeitgemäßheit seiner Abnormität selbst zu danken ist*' (F. Gundolf, *Heinrich von Kleist*).

THEN 1. **Dann** has all the meanings of 'then' except 'at that time', i.e. in the past. The latter meaning can only be translated by **damals**.

Dann ging er weg.
Dann müssen Sie sich fragen, ob es viel Zweck hat.

[1] *Ich habe keine Lust dazu*: it does not tempt me.
[2] 'To owe' money and the like is *schulden, schuldig sein.*

Was soll ich dann tun?[1] (that being so, under those circumstances).
Wenn er mir die nötigen Versicherungen gibt, dann kann er es haben (on that condition).
Dann wollen Sie es mir verbieten (as is to be inferred).
Damals war er sehr arm (at that time).
Der damalige Sekretär schrieb den Brief.

2. Neither *dann* nor *damals* can be preceded by a preposition. In some cases other adverbs are possible.

Seither, seitdem (since then); *bis dahin* (till then).

THEREFORE, HENCE, ON THAT ACCOUNT, SO, THUS[2] 1. **Daher**, i.e. from there, is the most objective of the German terms and introduces a statement of the effect of the cause given in the preceding clause. Its reference to cause and effect is seen clearly in the phrase *daher kommt es, daß...*, in which *daher* could not be replaced by any of the other terms. It should only be used in objective statements.

Es hat vier Monate lang nicht geregnet, daher verdorrt das Gras, muß das Wasser rationiert werden.
Das Obst war schlecht, daher konnte man es nicht essen.

2. **Darum** is emphatic and less objective than *daher*. It introduces a statement of an action or an attitude and follows a statement of the motives for this. 'That is why' is a common English equivalent.

Er hat uns früher sehr schlecht behandelt, darum wollen wir heute nichts mit ihm zu tun haben (this is the reason and no other).
Er war sehr unzuverlässig, darum habe ich ihn entlassen.

3. **Deshalb** indicates only in a vague way that one thing is the result of another. It means no more than: in consideration of what precedes, on that account, that being so. Because of its vagueness it can be used instead of the above terms, but without their precise reference. It must, however, be preceded by a clause setting out the circumstances taken into account.

Er hat nicht die nötigen Kenntnisse, deshalb können wir ihn nicht anstellen.
Die Reise ist sehr anstrengend, ich möchte deshalb lieber zu Hause bleiben.

4. **Also** indicates nothing more than that there is a connection between two things. It concentrates attention more on the result than on the

[1] *Denn* in a question in combination with *wer, was, wie,* corresponds to 'ever'. *Was soll ich denn tun?*
[2] 'So' is to 'this' as 'thus' is to 'that'.

reason, and can even be used in reference to a reason that is implied and not stated. In this it corresponds to 'so'.[1]

Er kommt also nicht (so he's not coming).
Er hat nicht angerufen, also wissen wir nicht, ob er zurück ist.

THICK 1. **Dick** refers primarily to the third dimension, i.e. between opposite surfaces.[2] **Dicht** means 'close in texture, dense'.[3] The normal objective term for 'thick' as applied to words such as *Dunkel, Nebel* is *dicht. Dick,* applied to these words, has an emotional connotation (e.g. *er tappte im dicksten Dunkel*).

Ein dicker Baumstamm, ein dickes Buch, eine dicke Mauer, dicke Lippen, dicker Schlamm.
Ein dichter Wald, dichter Nebel, ein dichter Bart, dichte Augenbrauen.
Diese Gegend ist dicht bevölkert.
Dicke Wolken (refers to their shape); *dichte Wolken* (density).
Ein dicker Nebel zog herauf (subjectively felt as vast and impenetrable).

2. *Dick* is also applied (*a*) to liquids which tend to become solids; (*b*) in the sense of 'in large numbers'; (*c*) in the sense of 'intimate' (a slang use).

Dicke Suppe, Milch (sour milk).
Die Leichen lagen dick auf der Erde (contrast third example in 1).
Sie sind dick befreundet, dick miteinander.

THIN, LEAN 1. Of living beings.

Mager: having little fat, i.e. lean.[4] **Dünn:** having little thickness, i.e. between opposite surfaces. *Dünn* is therefore applied to the figure and to extremities.

Er ist sehr mager (lean, thin).
Seine Wangen sind sehr mager.
Er hat dünne Beine, Arme, eine dünne Haut.

[1] German *so* renders other meanings of English 'so', but not that discussed here.

[2] (*a*) *Dick* is therefore the normal term for 'fat' in reference to the size of persons (e.g. *Sie sind in den letzten Monaten etwas dicker geworden*). *Fett* is applied to persons in reference to layers of fat, particularly when they are felt as repulsive (e.g. *ein fetter Mann*). It is the regular term when the substance 'fat' is meant (e.g. *fette Kost*). (*b*) *Dick* also means 'swollen' with reference to a part of the body (e.g. *eine dicke Backe*).

[3] *Dicht* also means 'tightly closed so that nothing can penetrate', particularly of containers (e.g. *wasserdicht*: waterproof).

[4] *Mager* corresponds to 'lean' in most uses (e.g. *die mageren Jahre*). *Feist* is 'obese', *hager* the opposite, 'gaunt'. *Schlank* means both 'slim' (suggesting little of a thing) and 'slender' (suggesting gracefulness and good proportions) in reference to the human body. 'Slim' has, particularly in figurative use, something of its German cognate *schlimm,* therefore 'meagre, insufficient' (e.g. his chances are slim).

2. Other uses of **dünn**.

(a) Having little thickness, of things (the opposite of *dick*).

Dünnes Papier, ein dünner Faden, eine dünne Scheibe Brot, ein dünner Baumstamm.

(b) Having little density, sparse (the opposite of *dicht*).

Ein dünner Wald, Bart, Nebel.
Diese Gegend ist sehr dünn bevölkert.

(c) Unsubstantial, weak, particularly of liquids, sounds, and mental products. Applied to the last of these it is somewhat popular.

Dünne Suppe, dünnes Bier, dünnes Blut, eine dünne Stimme.
Ein dünnes Argument, eine dünne Entschuldigung.
Ihr Aufsatz war sehr dünn.

3. **Dürftig** means 'lacking what is regarded as sufficient', either as a statement of fact or a judgment of value. It draws attention to the state or condition, i.e. thin, poor, paltry, shabby, needy. It does not emphasize the need for any specific thing.[1]

Der Aufsatz ist sehr dürftig.
Ein dürftiges Argument.

THING 1. (a) **Ding**[2] is applied to all concrete objects except those defined under *Sache*.

Ein Stuhl ist ein Ding.
Was ist das Ding da drüben?
Wie nennen Sie dieses Ding?

(b) In a figurative sense it is little used in the singular, mostly only in fixed phrases, in which, however, *Sache* could also be used.

Das ist ein ander Ding.
Es ist ein komisches Ding um seine Hüte.

(c) It is used freely in the plural in a figurative application. Its serious, sober tone contrasts with that of *Sachen*.

Er hat manche Dinge getan (gesagt, gedacht, verlangt), die ich ihm nie zugetraut hätte.

[1] This latter sense is rendered by *bedürftig*, i.e. in need of (e.g. *ruhebedürftig*). See 'need'. *Notdürftig* means 'sufficient at a pinch, barely sufficient' (e.g. *das Zimmer war nur notdürftig möbliert*). *Kümmerlich* as a synonym of *dürftig* differs from it in suggesting a subjective attitude, therefore 'miserable' (e.g. *eine kümmerliche Predigt, ein kümmerliches Geschöpf*).

[2] *Dings*, neuter, is used colloquially like 'thingumajig'. Plural: *Dinger*.

Er hat mir wichtige Dinge mitzuteilen.
Das sind Dinge, die nur mich angehen.
Solche Dinge dürfen nicht wieder vorkommen.
Die Dinge wachsen ihm über den Kopf.
Wie die Dinge nun einmal liegen (things being what they are).

(d) It is applied to persons in an affectionate or derogatory sense.

Sie ist ein niedliches, kleines, ein dummes, Ding.[1]

2. (a) **Sache**[2] is applied to concrete objects which are things of immediate concern, personal belongings, particularly clothes, or small things (e.g. implements) used for a specific purpose. *Ding* is impossible in the sense of personal belongings.

Ich packte meine Sachen zusammen und ging fort.
Nehmen Sie bitte Ihre Sachen weg.
Wollen Sie Ihre Sachen ablegen?
Das sind die Sachen, die sie brauchen, um ihre Schuhe zu reparieren.

(b) In figurative use, singular and plural, *Sache* corresponds to 'affair', 'business', 'matter', as well as to 'thing'.[3] In the plural it is more offhand than *Dinge*, and vaguer in the sense that the speaker has a less serious attitude to, and a less clear idea of, what he refers to. It translates 'thing' in the singular in a statement which makes a judgment about a thing.

Die Sache geht Sie, nicht mich an.
Seine Sachen gehen nicht gut.
Die Sache ist schlimm.
Es ist eine gefährliche Sache, ihm zu widersprechen.
Es ist Ihre Sache, die Berichte zu überprüfen.
Er hat dumme Sachen gemacht.[4]
Verrat ist eine häßliche Sache (a judgment).

3. In the sense of 'something done, to be done, said, thought', 'an act, achievement, happening, fact', 'the proper thing' (see *S.O.D.* 'Thing', 1, 4, 5), German often uses (*a*) the neuter adjective or (*b*) an indefinite pronoun. When 'thing' is qualified numerically the forms in *lei* may be

[1] *Ein kleines Ding von Mädchen*: a slip of a girl.

[2] The primary meaning of *Sache* is *Streit*, particularly at law (e.g. *Sachwalter*). It also means 'cause', often with the addition of *gut* (e.g. *für die gute Sache kämpfen*). Also 'point' in such phrases as: *die Sache ist die, daß . . .*; *bei der Sache bleiben*; *zur Sache!*; *von der Sache abweichen.*

[3] *Angelegenheit* is the weightiest term for 'affair, matter', etc. It means a 'matter of concern'.

[4] See 'do' for *Ding* and *Sache* combined with *tun* and *machen* respectively.

used and *Dinge* omitted (*zweierlei, dreierlei, mancherlei,* etc.). *Eins* = one thing.

Das Wichtigste ist auszuhalten, bis Hilfe kommt.
Das Beste wäre, ihm Ihre Pläne mitzuteilen.
Was Sie sagten, war sehr unfreundlich (that was not a kind thing to say).
Gut, daß Sie es mir sagten (a good thing).
Es ist gerade das, was ich brauche.
Es ist etwas Ernstes geschehen (a grave thing).
Er sagte gestern etwas sehr Ulkiges.
Wissen und Handeln sind zweierlei (two different things).
Eins möchte ich klar machen.

THINK 1. To have an opinion, mostly with a following 'that' clause. **Denken** is only used to indicate surprise that an opinion one has held has proved erroneous or when one seeks confirmation of an opinion about which one entertains doubts. In the sense of 'believe', whether the grounds for belief are sufficient or insufficient, **glauben** must be used.

Ich glaubte, Sie hätten schon bezahlt.
Ich dachte, Sie hätten schon bezahlt.
Ich glaubte, Sie wollten gehen.
Ich dachte, Sie wollen gehen.
Wer hätte das gedacht?

2. 'To think of' in the sense of 'to direct one's thoughts towards', 'to call to mind',[1] must be distinguished from 'to think of, about' in the sense of 'reflect, ponder over'. The former is **denken an,** the latter **nachdenken über.**[2]

Ich habe garnicht daran gedacht.[3]
Ich habe garnicht darüber nachgedacht.
Sie müssen an Ihre Pflicht denken.
Sie müssen über den Begriff der Pflicht nachdenken.

3. 'To form or have an idea of (a thing, action, or circumstance, real or imaginary) in one's mind; to imagine, conceive, fancy, picture' (*S.O.D.*, 1, 4). The sense is not 'to hold an opinion' (see 1), but 'to represent a thing to one's mind'. **Sich denken** must be used.[4]

Ich kann mir nicht denken, was Sie meinen.

[1] For the close synonym *bedenken* see 'consider'.
[2] *Nachdenken* suggests prolonged thought, which need not be the case with *sich überlegen* (see 'consider').
[3] *Einfallen*, to occur, is much used in the sense of 'to think involuntarily of something'.
[4] For the close synonym *sich vorstellen* see 'imagine'.

THINK

Ich kann mir nicht denken, wie ich ihn für den Plan gewinnen soll.
Ich kann mir nicht denken, daß Sie es ernst meinen.
Wenn ich mir denke, daß er mich belog, werde ich wütend.
Denken Sie sich bloß, er ist freigesprochen worden.

4. To have an opinion with regard to the value of a person or thing.

Halten must be used with the indefinite pronouns *was, viel, nichts, allerhand,* and the like. With words which have a more concrete content (e.g. well, badly) **denken** is used.

Was halten Sie von ihm, von dem Plan?
Ich denke nur Gutes von ihm.

5. 'To conceive or entertain the notion of doing something; to intend, mean' (*S.O.D.*, II, 4). **Denken** is the usual term in the present tense and with a following 'that' clause, **glauben** is used to indicate a firmer intention than is expressed by *denken* (compare 1).

Ich denke, morgen wegzugehen.
Ich dachte, ich würde hier warten.
Ich denke, ich werde nach Hause gehen (said tentatively).
Ich glaube, ich werde nach Hause gehen.

6. *Denken* cannot be used impersonally in the passive voice to translate 'it is thought (that...)' (German = *man denkt*). On the other hand it can be used passively with a thing as subject. Example: *Das Ding wird als belebt gedacht* (thought of, conceived).

THOUGHT 1. **Gedanke** is a mental image formed in the process of thinking, the content of thinking, a notion.[1]

Ein Gedanke fiel mir plötzlich ein.
Der Gedanke an deinen Abschied beschäftigt mich sehr.
Sein einziger Gedanke ist, Geld zu verdienen.
Er hat viele fruchtbare Gedanken im Kopf.
Es ist ein beruhigender Gedanke, daß so viel guter Wille in den Menschen steckt.

2. **Denken** must be used for 'thought' in the sense of the 'activity of thinking' or a 'way of thinking'.

Das Denken ist frei.
Im Denken und im Handeln ist er gleich unberechenbar (in thought and in action).
Hegels Denken hat Marx beeinflußt.
Das Denken des Mittelalters war teleologisch, das der Neuzeit ist kausal.

[1] *Gedanke* is, unlike 'thought', sometimes used in the sense of 'conception'. *Der Staatsgedanke in Hebbels 'Agnes Bernauer'.*

3. **Nachdenken**, i.e. reflection, must be used when the activity of thinking is meant as distinct from its content. See 'think'.

Angestrengtes Nachdenken tut not.
Er war in Nachdenken versunken.

4. **Gedankengut** refers to a body of thought of a specific age, movement, or the like.

Das romantische Gedankengut.
Das griechische Gedankengut des 5ten Jahrhunderts v. Ch.

5. To have no thought, i.e. intention, of....

Ich dachte nicht daran, Sie zu beleidigen.

THOUGHTFUL, LOST IN THOUGHT 1. **Gedankenvoll** means not 'thoughtful', but 'lost in thought', i.e. absorbed in thoughts, musings, which take one away from the present. It is mostly used to describe facial expression, hence as an adjective qualifying nouns such as *Blick* and as an adverb. Direct application to a person as in the following example from Hermann Hesse's *Der Steppenwolf* is rare. '*...vielleicht auch waren sie vereinsamte und entgleiste Burschen wie ich, stille gedankenvolle Säufer über bankrotten Idealen, Steppenwölfe und arme Teufel auch sie.*'

Er hatte einen gedankenvollen Blick.
Er saß gedankenvoll da.

2. In the sense of 'giving thought to a matter', i.e. as a contrast to 'rash, unthinking', the following terms, which are approximations to 'thoughtful', may be used.[1]

Überlegt suggests an examination of all sides of a matter with a view to action. **Nachdenklich** suggests caution and particularly the presence of doubts. **Besonnen** refers to a temper of mind, which is level-headed, balanced, but not necessarily on an exclusively practical or prosaic level.[2]

Das ist ein wohl überlegter Plan.
Er handelt überlegt.
Er ist ein nachdenklicher Mensch.
Er hat einen nachdenklichen Gesichtsausdruck.
Es stimmte mich nachdenklich.
Er ist ein besonnener Mensch, Künstler.

3. For the sense of 'giving signs of original thought' (*P.O.D.*), as applied to persons and their writings, German has no exact term. 'A thoughtful

[1] See 'to consider'.
[2] Further: *bedächtig*, which adds to the idea of circumspection that of slowness. *Er sprach sehr bedächtig.*

student' could be paraphrased by *ein Student, der voller Gedanken (Ideen) steckt.* A thoughtful essay: *ein gedankenreicher Aufsatz* (an abundance of ideas with a touch of brilliance).

4. In the sense of 'considerate' **rücksichtsvoll** may be used, i.e. taking care not to hurt, inconvenience, people. In the more positive sense of 'going out of one's way to do things for people', i.e. when omission would not cause hurt, inconvenience, or the like, **aufmerksam,** i.e. attentive, can be used.

Er ist immer sehr rücksichtsvoll.
Ein aufmerksamer Freund, Gatte.
Es war sehr aufmerksam von ihm, mir diese Zeitungsnotiz zu schicken.

THOUGHTLESS, WITH ONE'S MIND A BLANK 1. **Gedankenlos** generally means 'with one's mind a blank' and is mostly used as an adverb. It can also mean 'unthinking', as a mild criticism of one's own behaviour towards others. It is not as strong as 'inconsiderate', the implication being: I did not mean it.

Ich saß stundenlang gedankenlos da.
Ich habe es gedankenlos hingesagt.
Es war gedankenlos von mir, das gesagt zu haben.

2. In the sense of 'not reflecting sufficiently' **unüberlegt** and **unbesonnen** (for explanation see 'thoughtful'), further, **unbedacht** may be used. The latter is as a stricture the weakest term and simply means 'without thinking'.[1]

Ich war unbedacht genug, ihm meine Pläne mitzuteilen.
Ich habe meinen Besuch unbedachterweise abgesagt.

3. German has no exact equivalent for the sense of 'inconsiderate'. **Rücksicht nehmen** in the negative may sometimes be used.[2] See also 1.

Warum nimmst du so wenig Rücksicht auf die Eltern?

THREATEN 1. **Bedrohen** suggests the immediacy of violent action, not the uttering of a threat with regard to future action. It cannot

[1] *Leichtsinnig*, light-minded, means either 'not sufficiently serious', 'frivolous in thought', or 'exposing unthinkingly to danger'. In the latter use it approximates closely to 'thoughtless'. Examples: *eine leichtsinnige Haltung* (frivolous); *es ist sehr leichtsinnig von Ihnen, so lange in der Kälte zu sitzen. Leichtfertig* suggests irresponsibility (e.g. *ein leichtfertiger Schritt*).

[2] *Rücksichtslos* means 'ruthless', not 'inconsiderate'.

therefore be followed by an infinitive or be used adjectivally in the present participle.

Der Feind bedroht die Stadt.
Er bedrohte mich mit einem Hammer.
Ich fühle mich bedroht.

2. **Drohen** suggests weaker or more remote action, often nothing more than an attitude. This action need not be physical violence, and can even take the form of a reprimand. An infinitive can follow or, in its place, a phrase with *mit* indicating what is threatened. The present participle is used regularly as an adjective.

Er drohte mir mit der Faust, dem Hammer.
Der Staat drohte ihnen mit Beschlagnahme ihrer Güter.
Er drohte, ihn anzuzeigen.
Ein Sturm droht.
Er gab uns einen drohenden Blick.

TOTTER, SWAY, ROCK, STAGGER, REEL, LURCH, WOBBLE

1. **Schwanken** suggests a wide swing from side to side and is mostly applied to tall and slender objects.[1]

Der Zweig, der Mast, schwankt heftig im Winde.
Als er aufstand, schwankte er und schlug dann hin.
Der Boden schwankte unter uns (heaved violently in one direction and then in another).

2. **Wanken** suggests an inner instability[2] rather than a wide range of movement and is applied mostly to broad-based objects.

Das Gebäude, der Boden, wankt.
Die Knie wankten mir.
Das Reich wankt.

3. **Taumeln** suggests disorderly movement, inability to keep a regular course, a headlong pitching in some direction. It approximates most closely to 'lurch' and 'reel'.

Er taumelte ein paar Schritte und sackte dann zusammen.
Er taumelte in die offene Tür hinein.

4. **Torkeln** suggests an unsteady walk, without actual falling, and is commonly applied to a drunk, i.e. to stagger.

Der Betrunkene torkelte über die Straße.

[1] In figurative use it means 'to vacillate'. *Er schwankt sehr in dieser Angelegenheit.*
[2] In figurative use it means 'to falter' in a decision. *Er wankt in seinem Entschluß.* The addition of *in seinem Entschluß* is necessary.

5. **Wackeln** is mostly applied to objects which are loosely attached to another object and so often rattle when in movement.

Das Schild mit der Nummer ist so locker am Wagen angebracht, daß es wackelt (wobbles).
Das Bett wackelt.

6. **Schaukeln** always suggests a rhythmic movement from side to side,[1] i.e. not irregularity. Only in this sense does it translate 'rock'.[2]

Der Kahn schaukelte auf den Wellen (but not of the rocking of a ship).

TOUCH 1. **Berühren** means in its literal sense 'to touch lightly'[3] with a part of the body, mostly the fingers, or with an extension of these (e.g. a stick). It cannot indicate forceful contact, pressure, or the laying hold of a thing with the whole hand. It is used in the negative imperative only with such objects as suggest danger to the person or to the object itself because it is precious or fragile. In the same way it is applied to things which touch, either while in movement or when lying alongside each other.

Figuratively, it is used of: (*a*) food and drink in the literal sense of contact with the lips, the application to food growing out of the literal sense of touching with the fingers; (*b*) touching a place on a journey; (*c*) brief reference to a subject.[4]

Er berührte bloß den Hahn, und das Gewehr ging los.
Er berührt schon das Ufer (of a swimmer).
Er berührte ihn leicht mit dem Schwert.
In diesem Teich kann ich den Boden berühren.
Können Sie die Zehen mit den Händen berühren?
Sie berühren eine wunde Stelle.
Berühren Sie diese Blumen nicht.
Die zwei Häuser berühren sich.
Seine Lippen berührten den vergifteten Wein.
Auf der Reise berührten wir Heidelberg.
Ich habe dieses Thema berührt.

2. **Anrühren,** which is mostly used negatively or with a virtual negative, expresses an attitude of mind, one of aversion, to the object. It may, but need not, imply contact in the literal sense.

Alkoholische Getränke, süße Speisen, rührt er nie an.

[1] Therefore also 'to swing'.
[2] Also in transitive use. *Die Mutter schaukelt das Kind.*
[3] For lightness of contact *berühren* is comparable with the French *effleurer.*
[4] For another sense of *berühren* see 'affect'.

Er hat seine Suppe nicht angerührt.
Das Geld werde ich nicht anrühren, wenn es in dieser Weise verdient worden ist.

3. **Anfassen:** to make contact with a thing with the hand, particularly with reference to whether it is safe to do so or not. It is the normal term to render the negative imperative.[1]

Wenn Sie den Hund anfassen, wird er beißen.
Fassen Sie den Teller nicht an, er ist heiß.

4. **Betasten:** to touch in order to ascertain the feel, the nature, quality of a thing; to finger. See 'feel'.

Er betastete die Wunde, um ihre Empfindlichkeit festzustellen.

5. **Rühren.**

(a) With a direct object: to touch emotionally.[2]

Ihr Schicksal hat mich tief gerührt.
Eine rührende Geschichte.

(b) With *an* and the accusative case: to interfere with. Actual contact is implied.

Rühren Sie nicht an meine Papiere.

6. Examples of more specific terms used in the literal sense of 'touch'.

Ich klopfte ihm auf die Schulter.
Drücken Sie den Knopf (press).
Die Decke ist so niedrig, daß er daran stößt, wenn er aufrecht steht (knocks against it; *berührt* would suggest that he touches it with his fingers).

7. Examples of specific terms used in the figurative sense of 'touch'.

Er fängt an, das Geld, das er gespart hat, anzugreifen (make a hole in).
Es ist ein Werk, das die Phantasie nicht anspricht (does not appeal to the imagination).
Was Sie sagen, reicht nicht bis in den Kern des Problems.

TRUST (verb) 1. **Trauen** expresses a generalization about the character of a person or a thing, i.e. an absolute judgment that he or it can be trusted without reference to any particular action. Since it indicates a judgment, not faith, its use with *Gott* as object would amount to blasphemy.

[1] See footnote to 'seize' (p. 302, n. 1).
[2] See footnote to *bewegen* under 'move' (p. 233, n. 1).

It must be used also in the sense of regarding a thing (but not a person) as reliable on a particular occasion.

Ich traue ihm (nicht) (a judgment about his (un-)trustworthiness in general).
Ich würde ihm nicht über den Weg trauen.
Ich weiß nicht, wieweit ich ihm überhaupt trauen kann.
Wenn Sie ihm nicht trauen, wäre es doch besser, alle Beziehungen zu ihm abzubrechen.
Ich traue deiner Freundschaft nicht.
Ich traue seinem Talent nicht.
Ich traue seinem Wort nicht.
Ich traue dem Wetter nicht.
Ich traue den Berichten, dem Frieden, nicht.
Dem können Sie ruhig mit dem Auto trauen.[1]

2. **Vertrauen:** to trust a person or some quality he has or some action he performs (but not a thing) with reference to what it is expected the object will or will not do in a specific matter. This specific reference gives it an emotional connotation.

(a) Followed by the dative it means that the subject has confidence that the object will refrain from any action that may harm him, i.e. it has a negative colouring.

Ich vertraue ihm, daß er mich nicht verraten wird.
Ich vertraue seinem gesunden Menschenverstand.
Ich vertraue der Rechtsprechung dieses Landes (*trauen* also is possible).

(b) Followed by *auf* with the accusative *vertrauen* means that the subject has confidence that the object will do something, i.e. it has a positive colouring.[2]

Ich vertraue auf ihn, daß er Schritte für mich bei der zuständigen Stelle unternehmen wird.
Ich vertraue auf seinen gesunden Menschenverstand.
Er vertraut auf Gott.
Ich vertraue auf deine Freundschaft.
Ich vertraue auf sein Talent, daß er sich aus dieser Schwierigkeit ziehen wird.
Ich vertraue auf sein Wort.

[1] *Dem können Sie das Auto ruhig anvertrauen* (entrust). The sense is wider than that of 'trust', i.e. he will look after it for you, not steal it, and the like.

[2] Only *vertrauen auf* can be followed by a *daß* clause (i.e. not *vertrauen* alone or *trauen*). It translates 'trust' followed by a 'that' clause or by the accusative and the infinitive (but not the reflexive accusative). *Ich vertraue darauf, daß er die Erlaubnis für mich erlangen wird* (trust him to..., trust that he...).

3. **Zutrauen:** to think capable of bad as well as good. It can thus be used ironically.

Sie können es ihm zutrauen, Sie im Stich zu lassen (or: *daß er Sie...*).

4. 'Trust' followed by the reflexive accusative and the infinitive: **sich getrauen.**

Er getraute sich nicht, das Thema zu berühren.

5. In the sense of 'hope', e.g. at the end of a letter: **hoffen.**

TRUST (noun), **CONFIDENCE, FAITH**[1] 1. **Zutrauen** is more intimate and personal than **Vertrauen.**[2] Germans often use the latter, however, to express both shades of meaning. They are followed by *zu* and *in*, the former being more intimate than the second.

Ich hatte kein Vertrauen zu ihm (*in* impossible).
Wir haben unser Vertrauen zu unseren Führern (*in unsere Führer*) *verloren* (*Zutrauen* impossible).
Ich habe kein Vertrauen in deine diplomatischen Fähigkeiten (*Zutrauen* and *zu* impossible).
Ich habe kein Zutrauen mehr zu ihm.

2. **Zuversicht**[3] expresses a high degree of confidence that things will happen as one wants them. It denotes confidence in a person only as a secondary idea, and then only in the phrase *Zuversicht setzen auf.*

Meine Zuversicht, daß der Sieg unser sein würde, war unerschütterlich.

TRY (OUT), TEST, PROVE[4] 'Test' and 'try (out)' are at times practically synonymous, particularly with personal qualities (e.g. to test, try out, someone's courage), but in discriminating use, 'test' suggests an accurate, often a scientific, method, frequently preceding the use for which the thing is intended. It also suggests a more precise result. 'Try (out)' means 'to put a thing to the use for which it is intended and to observe it'. The process is stressed more than the result.

[1] 'Faith' in the religious sense of 'belief' is *Glaube.*

[2] *Zutraulich* = confiding, trusting in an intimate way (e.g. *ein zutrauliches Kind*). *Vertraulich* = confidential. *Vertraut* = 'familiar' in the sense of 'well-known'.

[3] *Zuversichtlich* (confident) is only correctly applied to a person in an emphatic context (e.g. in the imperative, with *sehr*) (*Sei zuversichtlich*; *er ist sehr zuversichtlich*). But: *eine zuversichtliche Stimmung.* I am confident that... = *Ich glaube zuversichtlich, bin voller Zuversicht, erwarte mit Zuversicht, daß....* *Getrost* (used only as an adverb) = 'confidently' in the sense of 'with nothing to worry about', rather because of the absence of evils than because of the presence of positive good. It is cognate with *Trost.*

[4] For the sense 'to give a logical proof of' a thing see footnote to 'show' (p. 324, n. 1).

TRY (OUT)

1. **Versuchen** and **probieren,** which are close synonyms, mean 'to put a thing to the use for which it is intended'. *Versuchen* emphasizes effort, and can, though it need not, suggest a systematic procedure, while *probieren* always denotes an empirical, non-expert, often casual approach. Both can be applied to food and drink.[1]

Wollen Sie nicht etwas von dieser Platte versuchen?
Probieren Sie diesen Wein!
Versuchen, probieren, Sie diesen Federhalter.
Nun werde ich noch diese Schraube probieren (e.g. a layman using it as a last resort).
Ich habe alle Mittel versucht, aber nichts hat geholfen.

2. **Prüfen** means 'to submit before use to a test which will yield exact knowledge'. It therefore corresponds closely to 'test'.[2]

Der Kandidat, die Tragfähigkeit des Flugzeugs, ist sorgfältig geprüft worden.
Der Arzt hat sein Herz geprüft.
Ich habe seine Zuverlässigkeit geprüft.

3. **Erproben:** to prove the value of a thing by experiment. This can mean (*a*) to put to the test, particularly with reference to the future; (*b*) but more often 'to prove' the mettle, the work, of a person or thing. The past participle used adjectivally has only the latter sense. Reflexive use is not possible. The object is not normally a person.

Diese Arznei muß erst mal erprobt werden.
Wir haben seinen Mut erprobt.
Ein erprobtes Mittel, ein erprobter Freund, ein erprobter Wein.

4. **Bewähren** is now used only reflexively or adjectivally in the past participle. It means that the worth of a thing has been proved through the lapse of time, often despite doubts. It does not mean 'to subject to a test', the results of which are unknown.

Dieses System, diese Methode, hat sich bewährt.
Ein bewährter Freund, ein (alt)bewährtes Mittel.

TURN 1. The verbs *wenden, kehren, drehen* translate 'turn' in its literal sense of bringing into another position, to which is sometimes added that of facing another direction. Only to a very limited extent does *wenden* render the numerous figurative uses of 'turn', while *kehren* and *drehen* do so still less.

[1] See also 'taste'.
[2] *Überprüfen* means 'to check' in the sense of 'to run over a thing quickly' to make sure that it is in order. *Die Bremse überprüfen. Nachsehen* is used similarly.

(a) **Wenden** is a more dignified term than the others and normally implies consciousness of the action performed. It can mean 'to turn partly or completely (round)'. The distinction between the weak and the strong verb is in general that *wandte* emphasizes the result, the new direction, while *wendete* draws attention to the operation of turning in its various stages. From this dominant tendency follow others which are more or less clearly recognizable: (*a*) that *wandte* tends to be sudden, quick, *wendete* slow; (*b*) that while both can mean 'right round' *wandte* only has this meaning in certain contexts, a partial turn being expressed by *wendete*. In any given case one or all of these tendencies may be operative. Further distinctions are that only *wendete* can be used intransitively, and that *wandte* when used reflexively is normally followed by a phrase denoting or suggesting the new direction (e.g. *um*). In reflexive use the distinction is often obliterated, the form *wandte* being the commoner.[1]

Er wendete, wandte, den Kopf.
Er wandte das Gesicht von dem Richter (*ab*).
Er wandte den Blick nach oben.
Er wendete den Wagen, den Stuhl, den Schrank, das Bett, den Anzug (an operation in stages, *wandte* being impossible).
Er wandte die Matratze (*um*) (turned over).
Er wandte die Waffe gegen sich selbst.
Ich wandte mich um (suddenly).
Ich wendete mich um (more slowly).
Ich wandte mich nach ihm um (*wendete* impossible because the new direction is stressed by *nach ihm*).
Er wandte sich seinem Sohne zu.
Der Botschafter wandte sich zur Linken.
Er wandte sich zum Gehen.
Der Wagen, das Flugzeug, der Schwimmer, wendete.
Der Wagen, das Flugzeug, der Schwimmer, wandte sich in eine neue Richtung.

(b) **Kehren** generally means 'to make face the opposite direction', but sometimes denotes merely a partial turn. Often it suggests that the broad side is turned. It can also imply speed, force, or hostility.[2]

[1] In compounds (e.g. *verwenden*) both forms are sometimes used, one being more common with one noun, the other with another (e.g. *er verwandte das Geld für sich, hier wird nur gutes Fett verwendet*). But in general the distinction is the same as in the literal use.

[2] In figurative use it sometimes suggests vigour or violence (e.g. *das Haus von unterst zu oberst kehren*). *Umkehren*: to retrace one's steps, e.g. because one has gone the wrong way: *sich umkehren*: to turn round and stay where one is.

Sie kehrte ihm den Rücken.
Kehrt! (about turn!—a military command).
Er kehrte die Waffe gegen sich selbst (more forceful than *wandte*).

(c) **Drehen** means (*a*) to make turn, spin round an axis,[1] (*b*) to bring into any new position, except that of upside down. In the second sense it does not suggest any special care or skill, and is the most common rendering of 'turn' when the latter implies the dragging or pulling of a thing round. It is the normal colloquial term when reflexive or when a thing is the object. Sometimes *umdrehen* is required.

Er drehte den Schlüssel um.
Das Wasser dreht das Rad.
Sie drehte sich um, um ihn nicht ansehen zu müssen.
Er dreht sich viel im Schlaf (um).
Dreh' dich um.
Er glaubt, daß die Welt sich um ihn dreht.

2. **Biegen:** to turn in a new direction when the person or thing is in motion and then proceeds in the new direction, i.e. does not merely face it. It is followed characteristically by a preposition.

Wir bogen in die zweite Querstraße.
Biegen Sie rechts ab, ein.

3. For 'turn into' in the sense of 'change into' see 'change'. The verbs treated above are not used in this sense. Note: *etwas in sein Gegenteil verkehren.*

UNDERSTAND 1. **Verstehen** is the general term and refers to clear ideas or knowledge. **Begreifen,** in accordance with the literal meaning of *greifen*, suggests an effort to grasp, to encompass, to bring within one's powers of understanding. It raises the question whether the object is thinkable, conceivable for the mind of the subject, but says nothing about clarity of ideas. It thus corresponds more closely to 'comprehend' than 'understand', and like the former has a more limited range of application than *verstehen.* Kleist constantly uses it negatively to refer to what is unreasonable or monstrous. '*Das Unbegreifliche*' is a dominant motive in each of his works.

Kinder begreifen sehr gut, daß sie ihren Eltern gehorchen müssen.
Ich kann nicht begreifen, warum er eine Frau heiratet, die so viel älter ist als er.

[1] The idea of spinning, twisting is preserved in figurative use. *Es dreht sich mir alles im Kopf herum.* Note: *Er hat die Geschichte gedreht*: worked it by tricks. *Verdreht*: twisted.

Können Sie begreifen, warum er sich so seltsam benimmt?
'*Er begriff nicht, warum er dem Tode, den seine jammervolle Seele suchte, entflohen sei*' (Kleist, *Das Erdbeben in Chili*).

Meanings of *verstehen* which correspond clearly to those of 'understand' are: to perceive the meaning of (words, person, or language, etc.); to perceive the significance or explanation or cause or nature of; to interpret as meaning; to express uncertainty or surprise or indignation; to introduce a warning or threat.[1,2] See *P.O.D.*

Ich verstehe nicht, was Sie sagen.
Verstehen Sie mich?
Er versteht Deutsch.
Ich verstehe nicht, warum er kam.
Ich verstehe seine Schwierigkeiten.
Ich kann ihn, sein Benehmen, nicht verstehen.
Darunter verstehe ich, daß Sie zu einem Kompromiß bereit sind.
Soll ich verstehen, daß Sie sich weigern?
Verstehen Sie mich, das muß aufhören!

2. **Sich verstehen auf** combines the meaning of 'understand intellectually' and 'be expert in doing, in dealing with'. Similarly **verstehen** followed by the infinitive means 'to understand how to deal with a thing'.

Er versteht sich auf Pferde, die politische Taktik.
Er versteht es, aus seinen Studenten das Beste herauszuholen.

3. Sense: implied, not stated. This sense frequently approaches that of 'implicitly agreed'. **Sich verstehen** with an impersonal subject means: it is a matter of course.

Es versteht sich, daß wir die Beute teilen.
Das versteht sich.

4. Meanings of 'understand' which can be translated by *verstehen* only in special cases. The senses: to have knowledge of, to know or learn, by information received; to take or accept as a positive fact, without positive knowledge or certainty, to believe. See *S.O.D.* 4 (*b*) and (*c*). **Zu verstehen geben** is used in the same way as 'to give to understand', often with an implied warning. Otherwise such expressions as *erfahren* (to learn), *sich sagen lassen* (after enquiry), *entnehmen aus* (to infer from), must be used.

[1] *Verstehen*, not *hören*, is used in the sense of 'to catch' what a person says. *Was haben Sie gesagt? Ich habe nicht verstanden.*

[2] *Kapieren* is much used colloquially in the sense of 'to understand the meaning or significance of' a thing. *Ich kapierte nicht, worauf er hinaus wollte.*

UNDERSTAND

Man hat mir zu verstehen gegeben, daß die Löhne in diesem Betrieb erhöht werden sollen.
Ich habe mir sagen lassen, daß alle Bankkontos gesperrt werden sollen.
Ich habe erfahren, daß Ihr Gesuch abgelehnt worden ist.
Niemand hätte das aus meinen Worten entnehmen können.

5. In the sense of 'supply mentally something not expressly stated' (mostly a grammatical term), German has to use such expressions as *hinzudenken, ergänzen* (see 'complete').

Das Fürwort muß man hinzudenken, muß ergänzt werden.

UNDERSTANDING 1. **Verstand:** the faculty of, capacity for, understanding.

Der Verstand ist ein unschätzbares Gut.
Er ist ein Mann von Verstand.
Das geht über meinen Verstand.

2. **Verständnis:** the act or process of understanding in a specific matter. It often approaches sympathy.

Ihr Verständnis der Lage geht nicht sehr weit.
Er hörte meinen Vorschlag mit Verständnis an.
Er hat wenig Verständnis für unsere Schwierigkeiten.

3. **Einverständnis:** an agreement between people. It suggests a process of reflection followed by agreement. It is not interchangeable with *Verständigung.*

Er hat sein Einverständnis erklärt.
Es besteht ein Einverständnis zwischen ihnen.
Er hat im Einverständnis mit mir gehandelt.

4. **Verständigung** suggests a formulated agreement, either written or spoken, after the clearing away of obstacles by discussion.

Sie haben endlich eine Verständigung erzielt.
Es war keine Verständigung zwischen ihnen möglich.

UNFORTUNATE, UNHAPPY 1. Applied directly to persons.

(a) **Unglücklich** thus used, whether attributively or predicatively, can only mean 'unhappy', i.e. depressed in feeling.[1]

Er ist ein sehr unglücklicher Mensch.
Er ist sehr unglücklich.

[1] *Unglückselig* means 'very unhappy', 'wretched'. *Ein unglückseliges Geschöpf.*

(b) 'Unfortunate' (and 'unlucky'), applied directly to persons, can be translated as follows. (i) Attributively, only by some such phrase as *vom Unglück verfolgt*, i.e. dogged by misfortune. (ii) Predicatively, by **Unglück haben** (i.e. ill-luck).

Ein vom Unglück verfolgter Mensch.
Er hat viel Unglück gehabt.

2. The impersonal phrase 'it is unfortunate that...' can only be translated by **es ist ein Unglück, daß....**[1]

Es ist ein Unglück, daß Sie so lange gewartet haben.

3. In other uses 'unfortunate' and 'unhappy' approach each other more closely in meaning, and both are translated by *unglücklich*.

Er hat eine unglückliche Tendenz, aus einem Extrem ins andere zu fallen.
Seine unglückliche Veranlagung.
Ein unglückliches Zusammentreffen.

4. **Unselig** approaches 'unfortunate' in meaning as under 3, but is stronger, i.e. as though the misfortune were the working out of a curse.

Ein unseliges Laster.
Eine unselige Begegnung.
Der unselige Krieg zwischen den europäischen Völkern.

5. **Bedauerlich,** regrettable, must be used in formal expressions of regret.

Ihr bedauerlicher Unfall.
Es ist meine bedauerliche Pflicht, Ihnen den Tod Ihres Sohnes mitzuteilen zu müssen (or: *traurige Pflicht*).

URGE, INCENTIVE, IMPULSE[2] 1. **Trieb** is an innate disposition towards a thing and is therefore thought of as permanent. It is therefore a close synonym of *Instinkt*[3] (e.g. *der Selbsterhaltungstrieb*).

Er kann seine Triebe nicht zügeln.

[1] The same difficulties and distinctions arise in the translation of 'fortunate' and 'happy' in the predicative position. *Er hat Glück gehabt*; *es ist ein Glück, daß...* (fortunate; lucky). *Er ist sehr glücklich* (happy). In the attributive position, however, *glücklich*, while it primarily means 'happy', often suggests the meaning of 'fortunate'. *Er ist ein glücklicher Mensch.*

[2] The *Fremdwort 'Impuls'* suggests suddenness and capriciousness more clearly than any of the native German terms. When these aspects are not emphasized, *Regung* (a stirring of feeling) and *Antrieb* may be used.

[3] *Trieb* is a wider term than *Instinkt*. As a psychological term it is translated and introduced into English by American psychologists as 'drive'.

'*Selbst die scheinbar einzige Ausnahme, die Hermannsschlacht, ist keine Ausgeburt ursprünglichen Haßes...sondern ebenfalls jenes rasenden Ausdruckstriebs — nur traf hier allerdings dieser Trieb mit dem Affekt zusammen...*' (F. Gundolf, *Heinrich von Kleist*).

2. **Antrieb** denotes the stimulus, the inciting cause of an urge or impulse as well as the latter itself, and is therefore thought of as functioning at a particular moment. It is frequently, though not necessarily, followed by a phrase with *zu* denoting the action in which the impulse issues. Its closest English equivalent is 'incentive'.[1,2]

Die Habsucht ist ein sehr starker Antrieb zum Handeln.
Er fühlt keinen Antrieb, sein Geschäft zu erweitern.
'*Gewiß ist der Wille zum Ausdruck ein Grundantrieb jedes Künstlers, der etwas zu sagen hat*' (F. Gundolf, *Heinrich von Kleist*).
'*Bei allen echten Dichtern kommen die Versbewegungen und Versinhalte aus demselben Antrieb...sie verhalten sich zueinander wie die Lebenskraft und der Leib eines Menschen*' (F. Gundolf, *Heinrich von Kleist*).

3. **Drang** is a particularly strong, almost irresistible urge, which is not innate, but dominates one at the moment. The plural is rare.[3]

Er fühlte einen unwiderstehlichen Drang zu morden.
Der Drang, den er fühlte, alles stehen und liegen zu lassen, war außerordentlich heftig.

USE (verb) 1. **Benutzen** points to a definite, specific purpose for which a person or thing is used, these being regarded as nothing but means to this end. It should not be used in the sense of 'use up', even if a purpose is stated.

Er benutzte ein Beil, um ins Haus einzudringen.
Er benutzte ein unbewohntes Zimmer zum Aufbewahren seiner Bücher.
Das ist ein viel benutzter Weg.
Er benutzt Worte, nur um sich daran zu berauschen.
Er benutzt das Wörterbuch, um einen Artikel zu übersetzen.
Er benutzte mich zu seinen Zwecken.
Die Kinder dürfen dieses Zimmer zum Spielen benutzen (the purpose is known before the room is found).

[1] In the phrase *aus eigenem Antrieb* the meaning approximates closely to 'initiative', which in general can only be translated by the *Fremdwort 'Initiative'*.

[2] Synonyms are: *Anreiz*, a sensuous stimulus or incentive to something pleasant (*Antrieb* is not limited to what is pleasant); *Ansporn*, a spur to action. For *anstiften* (=to incite) see footnote to 'found' (p. 145, n. 1).

[3] *Drang* also means 'pressure' in a figurative sense.

2. **Gebrauchen:** to find, to see, some use for. When a purpose is present, it is not necessarily represented as a specific purpose. The treatment of, or the effect on, the person or thing used is rather emphasized. With substances the sense approaches that of *verbrauchen* (use up).

Können Sie diese alte Jacke gebrauchen?
Wieviel Butter würden Sie eventuell gebrauchen, wenn Sie Kuchen backen?
Die Kinder dürfen dieses Zimmer zum Spielen gebrauchen.
Ich gebrauche ein neues Heilmittel gegen Schnupfen (stresses the act of using rather than the purpose).
Sie könnten den Ausdruck hier gebrauchen.
Ich gebrauche noch das Wörterbuch.
Rilke gebraucht ausgefallene Reime.
Das ist ein viel gebrauchter Weg.
Sie gebrauchen mich zu schlechten Zwecken.
Ich kann soviel Geld nicht gebrauchen.

3. **Verbrauchen:** to use up, consume. It must be used to translate 'use' when the idea of consumption is stressed.

Wieviel Butter verbrauchen Sie, wenn Sie Kuchen backen?
Ich werde wahrscheinlich 1000 *Mark auf dieser Reise verbrauchen.*

4. **Ausnützen,** to exploit, should only be used to translate 'use' when the idea of exploitation is stressed, or 'to make full use of' limited facilities, i.e. in a good sense.[1]

Er nützt mich nur aus (*nur* stresses the idea).
Wir müssen den Raum stärker ausnützen.

5. **Anwenden**[2] suggests care, skill, discrimination of means to an end. It is the normal equivalent of 'apply' in this sense.

Er wandte all seine Überzeugungskraft an, aber umsonst.

VAIN (IN) 1. **Umsonst** indicates merely that a result has not been achieved.[3]

[1] *Verwenden*: to turn to account, to utilize for some purpose. *Nur gutes Fett wird verwendet. Sie können dieses Eisen zur Herstellung von Betten verwenden. Er hat viel Zeit und Fleiß darauf verwendet.*

[2] *Nutzen* and *nützen*, used transitively, mean 'to turn to account in some way'. They are also common in the intransitive sense of 'to be of use', particularly with a following dative (e.g. *wenn Ihnen das Buch etwas nützt, behalten Sie es*). The forms with the *Umlaut* are more frequent in Northern, those without the *Umlaut* in Southern, German—contrary to what one would expect.

[3] The idea of 'for nothing' occurs also in the meaning of 'without payment'. *Sie können das Buch umsonst haben. Sie müssen umsonst arbeiten. Unentgeltlich* means that payment is not asked for, i.e. free of charge.

Ich habe mich umsonst bemüht.
Ich habe ihn umsonst darauf aufmerksam gemacht.
Die Mühe war umsonst.

2. **Vergeblich** suggests in addition the effort expended. Of the three terms treated it alone can be used as an attributive adjective.

Ich habe mich vergeblich bemüht.
Ich habe ihn vergeblich darauf aufmerksam gemacht.
Vergebliche Mühe.

3. **Vergebens** adds to the idea of effort that of a lament that the effort has been fruitless. It is accordingly used in emotional and elevated style.

Ich habe mich vergebens bemüht.
Ich habe ihn vergebens darauf aufmerksam gemacht.
Die Mühe war vergebens.

VIEW,[1] SIGHT 1. **Blick** means in the first place 'the act of seeing' (look, glance), and in this sense translates 'sight'. It also means 'thing seen', i.e. 'view' whether big or small. In this sense it cannot be followed by the genitive.

Auf den ersten Blick gefiel es mir garnicht (at first sight).
Von hier haben wir einen Blick auf das Meer, über den Hafen.
Der Blick von hier aus ist sehr schön.

2. **Anblick:** 'view', 'sight', only in the sense of 'thing seen'. It can be followed by the genitive. It suggests (*a*) the act of coming into view of a thing; (*b*) an emotional reaction on the part of the beholder.

Beim ersten Anblick des Meeres (at the first sight of...).
Der Anblick des Meeres erregt ihn sehr.
Der verstümmelte Körper bot einen schaurigen Anblick.
Der Anblick des Unfalls war grauenhaft.

3. **Aussicht:** a wide or distant view, a vista, prospect, panorama in which one thinks of all the individual objects seen.[2]

Die Aussicht aus dem Fenster ist überwältigend.
Das ist eine der schönsten Aussichten, die die Küste zu bieten hat.

4. **Ansicht:** a partial view of a thing from a side, an angle, as represented by a painting or a photograph. Apart from this use it occurs in

[1] See also 'opinion'.
[2] *Ausblick* is a sudden vista seen when emerging from a narrow passage or defile. *Aussicht* suggests no such emergence.

this sense only in a few fixed expressions such as *zur Ansicht ausliegen* (to be on view).

Ansichtskarten.
Diese Ansicht von der Kirche ist sehr schön.
Dieses Buch bringt viele Alpenansichten.

5. **Sicht:** 'sight', 'view' in the sense of 'visibility'. It occurs mostly in fixed phrases (e.g. *in Sicht kommen, außer Sicht sein, auf lange Sicht*).

6. **Sehkraft** must be used in the sense of 'power of sight'. But: he has good sight = *er hat gute Augen.*

Seine Sehkraft ist geschwächt.

VIOLENT 1. **Heftig** is used of emotions which are eruptive, impulsive, uncontrolled or emphatically expressed.[1] It is applied in the same sense to physical phenomena. It excludes the idea of violent external actions.

Sie schluchzte heftig.
Sie wechselten heftige Worte miteinander.
Er brach in heftigen Zorn aus.
Er stieß auf heftigen Widerstand.
Er hat heftige Kopfschmerzen.
Der Wind blies heftig.
Ein heftiger Ausbruch des Vesuvs.

2. **Gewaltsam**[2,3] is used of violent actions.

Ein gewaltsamer Tod (from without, not an illness).
Ein gewaltsamer Umsturz.
Eine gewaltsame Lösung des Problems.
Er wurde gewaltsam aus dem Saal entfernt.

3. **Gewalttätig** is applied to persons who are given to violence, and to their acts. It suggests crime.

Ein gewalttätiger Mensch.

4. A violent clash in an aesthetic sense: **schroff.**

Ein schroffer Gegensatz (e.g. of colours).

[1] In this sense it also translates 'vehement'.

[2] *Gewaltig*: enormous, tremendous (not 'violent'). *Ein gewaltiger Saal, eine gewaltige Leidenschaft.*

[3] For *Gewalt* in the sense of (*a*) violence, (*b*) legitimate force, coercion, see under 'power'.

WAIT, AWAIT[1] 1. **Warten** is the general term.

Warten Sie! Ich komme gleich.
Ich habe stundenlang auf Sie gewartet.
Ich wartete eine Stunde auf seine Ankunft.

2. **Abwarten:** to wait in patience, to wait and see, to bide one's time.

Ich werde lieber abwarten (wait and see).
Warten Sie ruhig seine Ankunft ab, bevor Sie handeln.
Ich wartete seine Antwort ab, um mich danach zu richten.

3. **Erwarten:** to wait impatiently. In ordinary prose it only occurs in this sense in the negative or virtual negative, and mostly with *können.* In elevated diction it is used in other combinations.

Ich kann den Sommer, die Ferien, kaum erwarten.

WAKE (UP), WAKEN, AWAKE, AWAKEN[2] 1. Transitive.

(a) **Wecken** is the action of waking a person. It is the normal term for 'wake' or 'waken' unless the state of full wakefulness is emphasized, in which case **aufwecken**[3] is used. The distinction between these two verbs is observed more strictly than that between 'wake' and 'wake up'.

Wecken Sie mich bitte um 7 Uhr.
Der Lärm hat mich aufgeweckt.

(b) **Erwecken** is only used figuratively in the sense of 'call into life'.

Es gelang mir, ein reges Interesse für Musik bei ihm zu erwecken.

2. Intransitive.[4]

Erwachen, which in the literal sense is confined to literature, **wach werden** being a more common term, is the process of waking up, but does not necessarily indicate full wakefulness. In the latter case **aufwachen,** which does not exclude the process, is used (i.e. wake up). *Erwachen* is also used figuratively.[5]

Sie erwachte langsam (*wurde langsam wach*).
Ich wachte auf und sprang sofort aus dem Bett.
Hoffnungen erwachten in meiner Brust.

[1] *Auf etwas harren* is 'to wait persistently for something'. It is confined to literature. *Beharren* is 'to persist' in a state and represents the persistence as active, as an expression of will. *Er beharrt auf seiner Meinung. Verharren* means 'to remain' in a state, and stresses the persistence of the state, not the activity or will of the person. *Er verharrt im Amt, im Laster.* [2] See Fowler's article on these verbs in *Modern English Usage.*

[3] *Aufgeweckt* as an adjective means 'wideawake, alert'. *Ein aufgeweckter Junge.*

[4] *Wachen* means 'to be, keep awake'; 'to watch'. *Ich wachte die ganze Nacht hindurch.*

[5] *Auferwecken* and *auferwachen* mean 'to awaken from dead'. Compare *auferstehen,* 'to arise from the dead'.

WALL **Mauer** is an outside wall which encloses a space such as a town or a prison, and therefore of strong brick, concrete, or the like. Its purpose is to prevent free entry or egress. **Wand** is the wall of a building. Both are used figuratively, *Mauer* as something that cannot be penetrated, *Wand* as something that separates. The two are often so close as to be interchangeable.

Die Stadt, das Gefängnis, hat dicke Mauern.
In den meisten deutschen Städten stehen nur noch die Wände der Häuser, das Innere ist ausgebrannt.
Er schlug einen Nagel in die Wand (ein).
Die Wände dieser Hütte bestehen nur aus Stroh.
Es ist eine Mauer, eine Wand, zwischen uns.

WANT **A.** The sense of 'want' treated in this article is that defined by the *S.O.D.* as 'to desire, wish for', i.e. not 'lack' or 'need'. But 'want' in the sense of 'desire' can be weak or strong. When strong, it implies the power or authority, and sometimes the intention, to enforce one's will. Used positively, it then denotes a demand, a command, an intention, insistence, used negatively, a prohibition or a refusal. Examples of the weaker use are:

'I want this hat, please' (a request).
'Do you want sugar in your tea?'
'I really want you to stay here.'
'I did not want them to go out that day.'

Examples of the stronger use are:

'I want that money, give it to me.'
'I want that done immediately.'
'I don't want any nonsense.'

B, 1. **Wollen** has a still wider range of meaning than 'want'.[1] It translates 'want' in the sense of 'desire' in its strong, and in most of its weak uses. It also corresponds to 'will' as an auxiliary verb ('won't' as well as 'will not', in the negative), and to the verb 'to will'. The difficulty in considering *wollen* as a rendering of 'want' arises from the fact that *wollen* has the strong, peremptory sense more often than 'want'.[2] This applies particularly to the first person singular, present tense, less to the

[1] It does not mean 'lack', and means 'need', 'require' only when a thing is the subject. *Solche Dinge wollen* (=*müssen*) *geübt werden.*

[2] However, *durchaus* or *unbedingt* or a similar word is often added to *wollen* to give it the stronger sense (e.g. *wenn er durchaus will*, i.e. insists). *Wollen* in this sense must, on the other hand, often be translated into English by some term other than 'want'.

third person, hardly at all to the second person, more in the positive than in the negative, and not in the interrogative. Therefore, when 'I want' expresses a request, it should not be translated by *ich will*, which tends to mean 'I demand' or 'I insist' with reference to objects or the performing of actions which can be demanded or to actions which one insists on performing oneself. Thus *Ich will ein Zimmer für die Nacht haben* means 'I demand, I insist on...'. *Ich will hier bleiben* means 'I intend, mean to, insist on'. On the other hand, *Ich will deine Freundschaft* means 'I want' since friendship is not a thing that can be demanded. Similarly: *Das will ich mehr als alles andere in der Welt*; *ich will nur meine Ruhe.*

The negative *ich will nicht* is used more freely, in the sense of 'won't', 'forbid' (with a clause) and on the other hand 'do not want'. In the latter sense it implies a shorter rejection than *möchte nicht* (see **C**).

(a) Examples of the stronger use where *wollen* and 'want' correspond are:

Ich will den Revolver haben, gib ihn her.
Ich will keinen Unfug.
Ich will nicht, daß davon gesprochen wird (a prohibition).
Er will, daß die Arbeit schnell erledigt wird.

(b) Examples of the weaker use where *wollen* and 'want' correspond are:

Ich wollte diesen Hut haben.
Wir wollen den Frieden.
Wollen Sie Zucker in Ihren Tee?
Wollen Sie Tee oder Kaffee?
Er wollte das Haus niederreißen lassen.
Wollen Sie, daß ich noch länger hier bleibe?
Ich wollte das Konzert hören, kam aber nicht dazu.
Ich wollte nicht bleiben, aber ich mußte.

2. The above examples show that sometimes *wollen* and sometimes *haben wollen* is used to translate 'want'. With a following dependent infinitive or clause *wollen* alone is used. The difficulty arises with a noun or pronoun object. Here it is necessary to distinguish the desire to possess (e.g. I want that hat) and the desire to see a thing exist or an action performed (e.g. Hitler wanted war).

(a) **Haben wollen** is normally used with reference to the desire to possess an object or a non-tangible thing; also to render 'want' used elliptically in the sense of 'want to have, to see' with reference to a thing or a person and accompanied by an adverb of place (e.g. I want you here).

Ich wollte eine Tasse Tee haben.
Er wollte ein Haus in der Nähe des Bahnhofs haben.

Wollen Sie das Auto für die Ferien haben?
Er will sein Portemonnaie haben.
Er will seine Ruhe haben.
Er wollte Anerkennung haben.
Ich wollte das Haus hier haben.
Sie will ihre Kinder immer um sich haben.

(b) **Wollen** is used in the sense of 'to desire to see' the existence of a thing, or the performance of an action; also with pronouns which do not refer to specific nouns denoting objects, in the sense of 'desire to possess' and 'desire to see exist'; furthermore, with persons in the sense of 'to possess sexually'.[1]

It is often used, furthermore, negatively and interrogatively for the desire to possess an object or a non-tangible thing, where, positively, *haben wollen* is normal.

Wir wollen nur dein Glück.
Er will den Frieden, den Krieg.
Sie wollen ein geeintes Europa.
Was wollen Sie?
Sie können alles haben, was Sie wollen.
Das haben wir nicht gewollt.
Sie wollen immer, was sie nicht bekommen können.
Er will alles umsonst.
Ich will kein Geld von Ihnen.
Ich will keine Anerkennung.
Wollen Sie Tee oder Kaffee?

C. **Mögen,** to like, is used in the imperfect subjunctive (*möchte*) for 'want' in the sense of 'should, would, like', in cases where *wollen* would be too peremptory or absolute, i.e. for the first person singular, present tense (and to a lesser extent the third person) of 'want'. *Haben* is added or omitted in the same way as with *wollen*.

Ich möchte diesen Hut haben.
Ich möchte Sie nicht beleidigen.
Ich möchte, daß er hier bleibt.
Er möchte nicht, daß wir kommen.

WARM **Wärmen,** is the most general term and can be used of the warming of persons and things with the exception of food and drink. **Erwärmen** emphasizes that the object is cold before warmth is applied;

[1] 'Want' is also used with persons in two special senses: (*a*) to want to see, speak to (*wollen Sie ihn sprechen?*); (*b*) to seek (*von der Polizei gesucht*).

and suggests a lesser degree of warmth than *wärmen*, i.e. to take the chill off. It is also used figuratively in reference to feelings. **Warm machen** is the common term in respect to anything which should be warm, e.g. food and drink.

Ich habe mich, meine Hände, das Zimmer, die Teller, gewärmt.
Der Ofen wärmt gut.
Die Sonne hat mich durch und durch gewärmt.
Die Sonne hat die Ziegelsteine gewärmt.
Er hat sich die Hände am Ofen erwärmt.
Die Sonne hat die Erde wieder erwärmt.
Ich kann mich für die Idee nicht erwärmen (warm to the idea).
'*Ein Lächeln, das jedes Herz erwärmte...*' (Heine, *Das Buch Le Grand*).
Er hat mir das Wasser warm gemacht.
Machen Sie das Essen warm.

WARN 1. **Warnen.**

Warnen can only be used in the sense of 'inform' when the information explicitly refers to a danger or a threat, i.e. when the latter are not left to be inferred.

When a negative order is given by an infinitive following *warnen*, *nicht* should be omitted, although it is sometimes inserted in popular speech. The absence of *nicht* does not, however, necessarily mean that 'not' is used in the English equivalent. Thus: *ich warne Sie, vorsichtig zu sein*; *den Mund zu halten*, means 'I warn you to be careful, to keep quiet', not 'not to be careful, not to keep quiet'. When the infinitive itself indicates an abstention from activity, the form is positive, but the sense negative, both in English and German.

Die Truppen wurden gewarnt, daß der Feind heranrücke.
Er warnte die Polizei, daß Diebe in der Nachbarschaft tätig seien.
Wir haben ihn vor der Möglichkeit eines Unfalls gewarnt.
Man hat uns davor gewarnt, daß dieser Weg gefährlich sei.
Er wurde gewarnt, daß er ausziehen müsse, wenn er die Miete nicht rechtzeitig bezahle.
Wir wurden gewarnt, unangenehme Änderungen zu erwarten.
Ich habe ihn oft genug (davor) gewarnt, das zu tun (not to do).
Ich habe ihn davor gewarnt zu zahlen.

2. **Verwarnen** is used only of a warning in the form of a threat given by a superior officer. *Er ist verwarnt worden.*

3. Other terms must be used when neither danger nor a threat is explicitly mentioned. Those in common use are:

(a) **Mahnen:** to remind someone emphatically of an obligation that he is bound to fulfil, particularly of a debt that he is expected to discharge.[1]

Er wurde gemahnt, daß er bis zum 5. März zahlen müsse.

(b) **Vorbereiten,** to prepare (see article on 'prepare'), i.e. to draw one's attention to something about to happen; **anweisen,** to instruct (see article on 'order'); **benachrichtigen,** to inform, must at times be used.

Wir wurden auf große Änderungen vorbereitet.
Die Truppen wurden angewiesen, sich bereit zu halten.
Ich benachrichtigte ihn, daß er bis zum 5. März ausziehen müsse.

WASTE[2] 1. *Verschwenden, vergeuden* and *vertun*[3] all mean 'to use more of a thing than is necessary', often recklessly. They do not mean 'to leave a thing unused'. None of them is possible in official exhortations to be sparing even with small amounts. The first two are used figuratively as well as literally.

(a) **Verschwenden,** i.e. *verschwinden machen,* a factitive verb, means 'to use lavishly, to squander'. Since 'lavish' implies no objective standard of measurement, the amount used in excess of what is necessary may, but need not, be great. In reference to small quantities, it should, however, only be used in emotional contexts, e.g. in the imperative or in exclamations.

Er hat sein Vermögen innerhalb von sechs Monaten verschwendet.
Verschwende keine Elektrizität.
Du verschwendest aber viel Mehl!
Er verschwendet seine Zeit mit unfruchtbaren Experimenten.
Er verschwendet seine Kräfte an unbegabte Studenten.

(b) **Vergeuden** (in M.H.G. in the simple form without *ver,* 'to be loud, to boast') is stronger than *verschwenden* in its implication of greater senselessness and unprofitableness, though not necessarily with regard to the extent of the waste.

Er vergeudet sein ganzes Geld.
Vergeude kein Wasser bei der Trockenheit!

[1] *Vermahnen,* like *verwarnen,* in present-day German implies a warning in the form of a threat. *Ermahnen* expresses an exhortation rather than a formal reminder. Its subject can only be personal, while that of *mahnen* can be a thing. *Sein Zustand mahnt zur Vorsicht. Gemahnen*: to put someone in mind of a thing.

[2] 'Waste' is cognate with G. *wüst,* L. *vastare,* F. *gâter.*

[3] There are numerous synonyms compounded with *ver,* which mostly indicate specific ways of squandering: *verprassen, verspielen, verschleudern* (to sell rashly at a ridiculously low price). *Verzetteln* means 'to fritter away' goods, time, energy, and the like. *Durchbringen* is 'to get through money in riotous living'.

(c) **Vertun** refers only to money or goods and means 'to consume completely and without benefit'. It carries no secondary implications. Only the compound tenses are used.

Er hat sein ganzes Geld vertan.

2. In an official exhortation *sparsam sein, umgehen mit...* would be used.

Sei sparsam mit dem Kaffee! (geh'...um!).

3. German lacks a general term in the sense of 'not to use' with the implication of 'throw away' or 'allow to perish'. The following examples use specific terms which require no explanation.

Lassen Sie den Wein doch nicht stehen! (can also mean simply: don't take it away).

Es ist eine Sünde, Lebensmittel umkommen zu lassen, Brot wegzuwerfen.

WAY, MANNER, METHOD, MEANS The two main senses of 'way' treated here are those defined by the *S.O.D.* as follows: (*a*) 'Manner in which something is done or takes place; method of performing an action or operation'; (*b*) 'a course of action; a device, expedient, method, or means by which some end may be attained'. Each of these senses can imply the other, one, however, normally being emphasized. Thus: 'I discussed with them the way I had got letters through to the occupied territories' (manner); 'I am looking for a way to get letters...' (means). German uses different words for these two senses. In a few cases, however, the words for 'manner' (*Art, Art und Weise*) tend to emphasize the sense of 'means'. These border-line cases are discussed in this article.

A few other clearly defined and less clearly defined uses of 'way', which present difficulty in translation, are dealt with briefly.

A. MANNER, METHOD.

1. **Art** and **Art und Weise** contrasted with *so, wie.*

Neither *Art* nor *Art und Weise* is normally used to refer to trivial everyday acts. When so used, they tend to be emphatic. While it is possible to say *das ist die beste Art, abzuwaschen,* the normal statement is *so wäscht man am besten ab* (thus, in this way). Similarly *zeigen Sie mir die richtige Art, den Baum zu stutzen* and *zeigen Sie mir, wie man den Baum am besten stutzt.* In both these examples *Art* is possible because it suggests a method. When the idea of method is not present, or only in a rudimentary way, *wie* is preferred. *Ich sagte ihm, wie ich seine Adresse entdeckte* (the way I..., 'way' being used so universally that it can refer to something accidental).

When 'way' is accompanied by an adjective, German uses an adverb with *so* or *wie*. *Am besten schneiden Sie Blumen so* (that's the best way...). *Ich erklärte ihm, wie man Blumen am besten schneidet.* Further examples:

Beachten Sie, wie er den Ball anschlägt (*Art* would indicate a style).
Man tötet eine Schlange so: man tritt beiseite und schlägt ihr mit einem Stock auf den Kopf (the way to kill a snake is to...).
Hören Sie, wie sein Herz pocht (listen to the way...).
Es herrscht Besorgnis darüber, wie Unruhen überall ausbrechen (there is alarm at the way...).

2. **Weise** refers strictly to action, i.e. to the manner of doing, or happening. Unlike *Art* it cannot refer to what a person or a thing is, i.e. to its nature. For further explanation of its meaning see *Art und Weise*, with which in present-day use its meaning is identical, but by which it has been supplanted in most formal combinations.

Weise is now practically restricted to its use with *auf* and *in* (see **8** (a)).

It is followed by an infinitive only when the idea contained in the phrase thus formed can also be expressed as a compound noun (*seine Weise, die Dinge zu betrachten = seine Betrachtungsweise*).

It is sometimes found in combination with the possessive adjective, but with a rather old-fashioned flavour (see Grimm's Dictionary: *das ist doch sonst seine Weise nicht*).

It is not pluralized except in compounds. With words such as *viel, all, verschieden, zweierlei, vielerlei, mannigfach, mehrfach* it is used in the singular with a plural sense (*in verschiedener Weise* = in various ways).

3. **Art.**

(a) The primary meaning of *Art*[1] is 'kind', 'species', that of 'way' being a development from this meaning. The closeness of meaning in the English terms is seen in such phrases as 'a kind (style) of life', 'a way of life'.[2] Sometimes German prefers to follow *Art* by the genitive of the noun instead of the infinitive or a *wie* clause (the latter, however, not being impossible). Thus: *die Art des Möbelarrangements* (the way the furniture is arranged); *eine neue Art der Krebsbehandlung* (a new way of treating cancer); *einige Arten des bildlichen Sprachgebrauchs, die die Anschaulichkeit der Darstellung erhöhen* (a few ways in which the figurative use of language heightens the vividness of presentation).

[1] Kluge (*Etymologisches Wörterbuch der deutschen Sprache*) connects *Art* with Latin *ars* (art), which is, however, not a universally accepted view.

[2] In older English 'kind' was sometimes used in the sense of 'way' (see *S.O.D.* and *A Shakespeare Glossary* by C. T. Onions). Note also 'manner' in the sense of 'kind' in the phrase 'what manner of man' (see *S.O.D.* under 'manner').

To sum up: *Art* denotes a clearly recognizable type in its general characteristics.

Das ist eine bequeme Art zu reisen.

Es gibt verschiedene Arten, Brühe für ein Schwein zu machen (*S.O.D.*).

(b) *Art* refers to the result of an action, its effect, to a whole. The result of an action may be the production of a thing. *Die Art, wie das Schiff gebaut ist, macht es unbrauchbar für gewisse Manöver* refers to the nature of the ship, not to the process of building it (see *Art und Weise*).

Die Art, wie das Heer organisiert ist, trägt den neuesten Methoden der Kriegsführung Rechnung (the finished product).

Die Art, wie er unterrichtet, zeigt ihn von Pestalozzi beeinflußt (the type, character of his instruction).

(c) The effect of an action can be style, which is a common implication of *Art*. In the same way it denotes a person's manner of doing or being, his behaviour considered as an effect.

Die Art, wie Toscanini Beethovens fünfte Symphonie dirigiert, ist grundverschieden von der Furtwänglers.

Die Art seines Klavierspiels (*wie er Klavier spielt; seine Art, Klavier zu spielen*) *stempelt ihn zum Schüler Schnabels.*

Die ganze Art, wie der Staatsanwalt den Prozess führte, war höchst eindrucksvoll.

Die Art seines Benehmens zeugt von guter Herkunft.

Ich mag die Art nicht, wie er antwortete (*lachte, seine Kollegen behandelte*).

(d) From this reference to a whole follows a tendency of *Art* to denote a short act, i.e. one which is seen more or less in one moment of attention as a whole. This is clear in a movement of the body (*die Art, wie er den Arm hebt*). But it can also refer to other types of acts. *Die geschickte Art, wie er mit X fertig wurde...* implies a momentary device.

(e) In the plural *Arten* needs to be preceded by some defining adjective such as *verschieden, möglich, vorhanden* in cases where 'ways' is not preceded by any such defining word. *Zählen Sie die verschiedenen Arten der Krebsbehandlung auf.*

(f) Whereas 'way' can mean 'the right way', *richtig* must be added to *Art* (and *Art und Weise*) to render this sense. *Das ist die richtige Art, Wein zu trinken* (that's the way...).

4. (a) **Art und Weise** is used to refer to the sum of the details of an action, both those intimately and those loosely connected with it. It suggests the course of the action, a procedure, a technical process, and

the like. Since it does not refer to the general characteristics of the whole, it cannot be qualified by adjectives which indicate only these (e.g. *neu, ungewöhnlich*).

Strictly speaking the phrase should mean the sum of the general plus the sum of the particular characteristics (details).[1] In present-day use it has lost the sense of *Art*, retaining only that of *Weise*, and is used in those formal combinations where *Weise* alone is impossible. It can denote an individual and even arbitrary and capricious way, while in reference to style or behaviour it is often derogatory.

Die Art und Weise, wie das Schiff gebaut wurde, spricht viel für die Organisation der Arbeit.
Die Art und Weise, wie das Heer organisiert wurde, war ein Wunder.
Die Art und Weise, wie er unterrichtet, ist mustergültig.
Die Art und Weise, wie der Staatsanwalt den Prozeß führte, war sehr geschickt.
Die Art und Weise seines Klavierspiels paßt ins Kino (derogatory).
Die Art und Weise seines Benehmens war hanebüchen.
Die Art und Weise, wie er sich an seine Aufgabe machte, war verkehrt.
Er tadelte scharf (*lobte*) *die Art und Weise, wie wir die Verhandlungen führten.*
Er sprach ein paar Worte über die Art und Weise, wie er Briefe nach den vom Feinde besetzten Gebieten durchgebracht hatte.
Er beschrieb die Art und Weise, wie die verbotenen Waren eingeschmuggelt wurden.
Die Art und Weise, wie das Auto dahinsaust, zeigt, daß es nicht mehr in fester Hand ist.

(b) It follows from the fundamental meaning of *Art und Weise* (the sum of the details) that the action to which it refers tends to be an extended one (contrast *Art*).

Die geschickte (*gerechte*) *Art und Weise, wie er X behandelte....*

(c) *Art und Weise* cannot be pluralized.

5. **Manier** tends to be familiar in tone. It can be friendly, but is frequently derogatory or ironical. It is characteristically used with colloquialisms. As a synonym of *Stil* it can suggest a mannerism,[2] but compare the title of E. T. A. Hoffmann's work: *Fantasiestücke in Callots Manier.*

[1] See Sanders-Wülfing, *Handwörterbuch der Deutschen Sprache*: '...*Art und Weise, wo Weise die Art näher bestimmt, weil Weise genau genommen, sich auf die zufälligen, besonderen Eigenschaften bezieht, wie Art auf die wesentlichen, inneren, der Gesamtheit gleicherweise gemeinsamen....*'

[2] The plural *Manieren* means 'manners' and can be used in a good or bad sense.

Das ist die richtige Manier, Wein zu trinken (said to a friend, whereas *Art* is more objective and distant).

Er hat eine tölpelhafte Manier, Brot zu schneiden.

Das ist eine nette Manier, Geschäftchen zu machen (but: *eine nette Art, Geschäfte...*).

Die einzige, beste, Manier, den Kerl loszuwerden, ist, ihm Grobheiten zu sagen.

Die unnatürliche Manier dieses Menschen geht einem auf die Nerven.

6. **Methode** translates 'method' and also 'way' when the latter clearly denotes a scientific process or strongly suggests a systematic procedure.

Es gibt eine neue Methode, Krebs zu behandeln (also: *eine neue Art der Krebsbehandlung*, i.e. kind of...).

Er hat eine neue Methode erfunden, alte Kleider zu entglänzen.

Er hat verschiedene Methoden ausprobiert, seine Studenten für lyrische Dichtung zu interessieren.

Ärzte haben jetzt schmerzlose Methoden, Zähne auszuziehen.

Wir haben eine Methode ausgedacht, Briefe nach den besetzten Gebieten durchzubringen.

Keine der Methoden, die sie angewandt haben, um die Moral der Truppen aufrechtzuerhalten, hat Erfolg gehabt.

7. **Haltung** (see 'attitude') is often used in the sense of a manner towards someone else.

Seine Haltung mir gegenüber wurde plötzlich anders.

8. **IN A WAY, MANNER, FASHION**[1] (a) *Auf, in* before *Weise.*

(i) *Auf* concentrates attention on the manner in which the action expressed by the verb is performed or takes place. The manner of the action is apprehended with the senses in its concrete reality and is felt as vivid, direct, immediate, individual, unique, as though one were pointing to it. An appeal to the eye is frequently suggested. In addition to this objective vividness *auf* can indicate an emotional participation on the part of the speaker (commiseration is expressed by its use in the sentence: *er starb auf dieselbe Weise wie sein Bruder*).

The verb with which such a phrase is associated is normally, though not necessarily, a verb of external action. If it denotes an inner attitude of mind, this is by the use of *auf*, so to speak, externalized, made palpable to the senses. Such uses should be left to the accomplished writer (see example below from Thomas Mann's *Lotte in Weimar*).

[1] Where 'in this way' does not describe the manner of an action, but merely emphasizes the fact of its being performed, only *so* is possible in German. 'I cannot let you cut an old friend in this way' (*S.O.D.*) = *Ich kann es nicht zulassen, daß Sie einen alten Freund so schneiden.*

Führen Sie den Prozess auf diese Weise (followed by a detailed description).

Auf diese Weise brachte er die Gesellschaft wieder in heitere Laune (following a full description of the way).

Er drohte ihm mit einem Revolver und hinderte ihn auf diese Weise, ins Haus zu treten.

Wir erfreuten uns auf diese Weise der neugewonnenen Freiheit (the way has been described in detail).

Dazu war er auf keine Weise zu bewegen (we think of the possible ways individually).

'*Madame Mozart konnte oder wollte von der Richtung, die sein leicht bewegliches Gefühl hier mehr und mehr nahm, auf keine Weise ablenken*' (Mörike, *Mozart auf der Reise nach Prag*).

'*...den entnervenden, sich täglich erneuernden Kampf zwischen seinem... Willen und dieser wachsenden Müdigkeit...die das Produkt auf keine Weise, durch kein Anzeichen des Versagens und der Laßheit verraten durfte*' (Thomas Mann, *Der Tod in Venedig*).

'*Und er...schürte und nährte sie (die Flamme seiner Liebe) auf alle Weise, weil er treu sein wollte*' (Thomas Mann, *Tonio Kröger*).

Ich habe es auf alle mögliche Weise versucht.

Das Abenteuer konnte nur auf zweierlei Weise enden: entweder würde er unerhörte Macht gewinnen, oder er würde das Land dem Untergang nahebringen.

Er hat sich auf seltsame Weise benommen (we visualize the way).

Er ist auf jämmerliche Weise umgekommen.

Die Gefangenen wurden auf barbarische Weise umgebracht.

'*Können Sie einen vernünftigen Gedanken fassen, Kröger,...wenn es Ihnen auf eine unanständige Weise im Blute kribbelt und eine Menge von unzugehörigen Sensationen Sie beunruhigt*' (Thomas Mann, *Tonio Kröger*).

'*Er spricht wirklich ganz so, wie Ingrid es nachgemacht hat: nasal und auf besondere Weise gedehnt, aber offenbar ohne jede Affektation...*' (Thomas Mann, *Unordnung und frühes Leid*).

'*...daß Kestner ihm (Goethe) auf eine Weise vertraute, die ihm nicht grade zur Ehre gereichte*' (Thomas Mann, *Lotte in Weimar*) (a daring use of *auf*, normal practice requiring *in*).

(ii) The use of *in* with *Weise* makes the reference to the manner of the action expressed by the verb less vivid, dynamic, and individual than *auf*, in other words, more remote. In place of the visualization and sensuous appeal suggested by *auf*, *in* indicates an intellectual awareness of the manner of the action. This may take the form of a mere report of or reference to the manner (*in solcher Weise verlor er sein Vermögen* gives a colourless reference to the manner, whereas *auf solche Weise* would evoke it). It may be a judgment (*er hat sich in gradezu schändlicher Weise benommen*, where not an image of a disgraceful act is suggested, but a moral judgment that the way is disgraceful). In contrast to the individual, unique way denoted by *auf*, *in* refers to the normal, well-established way (*in dieser Weise kam er nach England* gives a mere reference to some usual way such as ship, aeroplane, whereas *auf diese Weise* would conjure up a complete picture of some strange way in its individual features).

In combinations where attention is focused less on the manner in its sensuous reality than on some association gathered to it, *in* is normally used, *auf* being exceptional, emphatic and generally denoting emotional participation. Examples of such combinations where the association is stressed more than the manner of the action are *Weise* followed by a result clause (often in the form of a relative clause) or in comparison (*er sprach in solcher Weise, daß uns allen die Galle überlief*; *er sprach in einer Weise, die uns alle empörte*; *er spricht in derselben Weise wie sein Bruder*). Another association may be that of content, sense (*in dieser Weise läßt sich der Roman befriedigend auslegen*, where the reference is to content, *auf*, which would refer to the act of interpreting, being absurd; *er sprach in folgender Weise*, a sentence which would be followed by an account of the contents of what is said, while *auf* would look forward to a description of the manner; *Sie können das Wort nicht in dieser Weise gebrauchen*, i.e. sense).

Since *in* does not evoke an image of a particular way, its use in such phrases as *in keiner Weise*, *in solcher Weise*, *in jeder Weise* often gives *Weise* the meaning of 'respect' (see **D**). These phrases are practically equivalent to 'altogether', 'in no wise', 'not at all', 'thus'.

Nur wenn man das Radio in dieser Weise gebraucht (e.g. for educational purposes, where *Weise* refers not to the manner of handling it, but to an idea associated with its use).

Die Kunst des Dichters kommt hier in einer Weise zur Geltung wie sonst selten.

Handeln Sie in solcher Weise, daß Ihr Gewissen rein bleibt.

Hier tritt der Philosoph des Sozialismus hervor, aber in ganz anderer Weise als im 'Kapital'.

'*Wir wagten es nicht, dem alten Mann in derselben Weise mitzuspielen wie den anderen. . . . bewegten wir uns mit solcher Geschwindigkeit und in so mannigfacher Weise, daß er sich durchaus keine deutliche Vorstellung von uns hätte bilden können*' (Ricarda Huch, *Teufeleien*).

Er ist imstande, den Vorlesungen in jeder Weise zu folgen.

Dazu war er in keiner Weise zu bewegen (not at all, *keineswegs*).
Er äußerte sich in einer Weise, wie sie für eine solche Haltung typisch ist.
Er handelte in der ihm eigenen Weise (in his usual way).
'*Aber andererseits kann er auch in der Weise die Contenance verlieren, daß er selbst in das unangenehmste Ausplaudern gerät und sein Intimstes nach außen kehrt*' (Thomas Mann, *Buddenbrooks*).
Man hat ihm in der übelsten Weise mitgespielt (*auf* would make one see the manner).
Sein Zorn wuchs in unerträglicher Weise (from the point of view of the sufferer, *auf* from that of the onlooker).
Er redete in unzusammenhängender Weise.
'*. . . indem er in etwas unerzogener Weise den Damen den Rücken zuwandte*' (Thomas Mann, *Tristan*). (*Auf* would produce a purely visual effect and sacrifice the detachment at which Mann is here aiming.)
'*Er verbeugte sich und begann dann, offenbar ein wenig verlegen, zu essen, indem er Messer und Gabel mit seinen großen, weißen und schön geformten Händen, die aus sehr engen Ärmeln hervorsahen, in ziemlich affektierter Weise bewegte*' (Thomas Mann, *Tristan*). (*Auf* would unduly emphasize the movements of the hands.)

(b) *Art* preceded by *auf* and *in*.

(i) *Art* distinguished from *Weise*.

Sie ist schön auf südländische Art (she is a southern type of beauty; *Weise* being impossible, because it must refer to the manner of doing something, whereas only *Art* can express what one is).
Auf diese Art werden wir alles verlieren (a method mentioned as a type). *Auf diese Weise* would be preceded or followed by a description of the details of the action.

(ii) *Auf* and *in* distinguished. *In seiner* (*ihrer*, etc.) *Art* means 'in his (her) species, class, category', while *auf seine* (*ihre*, etc.) *Art* means 'in his (her) individual way'. *Diese Katze ist in ihrer Art ganz nett* (nice for a cat, *auf* suggesting nice in an individual way, unlike other cats).

B. MEANS TO AN END.

As was pointed out in the general introduction to 'way' the senses of 'manner' and 'means' are often both present, though one or the other is the primary sense. With certain verbs such as 'find', 'invent', 'seek', 'apply', the idea of 'means' is stressed. In such cases *Art* and *Art und Weise*, which primarily refer to 'manner', are impossible. *Mittel, Weg, Mittel und Wege* must be used or another construction resorted to. With verbs such as 'have', 'know' either sense of 'way' may predominate.

Contrast 'he has a way of making you feel uncomfortable' (manner), with 'he has a way to bring him to his senses' (means). Similarly 'I know the way his confidence was won' and 'I know a way to win his confidence'. German normally uses different words for these senses.

1. *Art* as 'means'. *Art* makes a statement about the manner in which an action has been performed or has taken place. If it suggests a plan or advice how to achieve a purpose, this is subordinate to the primary meaning. In the sentence *ich tadelte seine Art, ein Vermögen zu machen,* what is stressed is his manner or method in making money. In *das ist eine einfache Art, reich zu werden, Art* denotes manner, but combines with it a suggestion of a means to an end. The important point is that the sentence merely points out objectively this existing 'way', without regarding it first and foremost as an instrument to achieve a purpose. This combination (*Art* and the verb *sein*), which expresses purpose in a secondary sense, is not uncommon. Similarly: *das ist die beste Art, eine Stellung zu bekommen*; *die beste Art, Lebensmittel zu bekommen, wenn sie knapp sind, ist, morgens um 9 Uhr im Laden zu sein.*

In other combinations (e.g. with *kennen* or *wissen*) *Art* is found, but less commonly, other words being preferred. Thus, while it is possible to say *ich weiß eine sichere Art, das Geld, das Sie im Augenblick nicht brauchen, anzulegen,* it would be more common to turn the sentence as follows: *ich weiß, wie Sie Geld...sicher anlegen können.*

It will be observed that the infinitive or *wie* clause may be taken as indicating a result, intended or not intended, as much as a purpose. Thus *das ist die beste Art, sich unbeliebt zu machen* clearly expresses a not intended result. *Art,* thus used, is most common and natural when it refers to behaviour.

If the phrase which denotes the purpose or the result (the infinitive phrase or the *wie* clause) is omitted, *Art* is impossible. Thus, while the following is admissible: *die sicherste Art, das Buch zu bekommen, wäre, es in Amerika zu bestellen,* the omission of *das Buch zu bekommen* would make it necessary to substitute *der sicherste Weg* or *das Sicherste* (the safest thing to do) *wäre...*'.

2. **Mittel, Mittel und Wege** translate the English 'means' and 'ways and means' and also 'way' when the latter is considered primarily as an instrument to achieve an end.

Ich habe ein wirksames Mittel in der Hand, ihn zur Vernunft zu bringen.
Sie wandten ein bekanntes Mittel an, ihn zum Reden zu bringen.
Er hat ein neues Mittel erfunden, Malaria zu heilen.
Ich suchte Mittel und Wege, meine Ansichten in weiteren Kreisen bekannt zu machen.

3. **Weg** can be used in this sense provided that something of the physical image contained in its literal sense is preserved. The verb, adjective, preposition combined with *Weg* should therefore be compatible with this image. Hence it is found in such combinations as: *einen Weg finden, suchen, kennen, beschreiten*; *ein Weg, der...führt*; *der Weg zu...*, *auf einem Wege*. It should not, however, be used with verbs like *haben, verstehen*. Because of this condition the process indicated by *Weg* tends, though not necessarily, to be lengthy. A loose use, without retention of the image, sometimes occurs.

A following infinitive, but not a *wie* clause is possible.

Ich habe einen Weg ausfindig gemacht, Briefe nach den vom Feinde besetzten Gebieten durchzubringen.

Daß sie diesen Weg eingeschlagen haben, die Finanzen in Ordnung zu bringen, macht sie gradezu zu Revolutionären.

Ich sehe mich nach einem Weg um, der mir aus dieser Sackgasse heraushilft.

Ich sehe einen Weg, der uns vielleicht eine Stufe weiterbringt.

Er hat auf neue Wege zum Verständnis der Kunst hingewiesen.

Ich weiß (kenne) einen sicheren Weg, Geld zu verdienen.

Er ist auf indirektem Wege an die Schwierigkeit herangegangen.

C. **Möglichkeit** translates 'way' in the sense of 'possible way', i.e. in contexts which define the number of ways in which a thing can be done (or thought, conceived). It is thus common with numerals and words such as *kein, einzig, viel, verschieden*. The emphasis is on the fact of possibility rather than on the content of the way.

Gibt es denn keine Möglichkeit für ihn, seinen Lebensunterhalt hier zu verdienen?

Die einzige Möglichkeit, ihn für Ihre Pläne zu gewinnen, wäre, ihn zum Partner zu machen.

Ich sehe (wüßte) keine Möglichkeit, ihm weiter zu helfen.

Es bestehen unendlich viele Möglichkeiten, Waffen hier einzuschmuggeln.

Es gibt zwei Möglichkeiten, diese Stelle zu deuten.

D. RESPECT, ASPECT, FEATURE.

Weise (in the singular) can be used in such expressions as: *in jeder, keiner, mancher, keinerlei, mancherlei, vielerlei, zweifacher, dreifacher*, etc., *Weise. Hinsicht* is also used in the singular in this sense.

Er kann dem Vortrag in jeder Weise (Hinsicht) folgen.

Sie haben in zweifacher Weise (Hinsicht) recht.

E. EXTENT, RATE.

When 'way' has these meanings, *Umfang, Ausmaß, Tempo* must be used. *Es besteht Besorgnis über den Umfang (das Ausmaß, das Tempo) des*

Geburtenrückganges (the way the birthrate is falling). *Das Tempo, in dem der Baum in den letzten Monaten gewachsen ist, ist erstaunlich* (the way the tree has grown).

F. POSITION.

Die Stellung, in der (colloquially: *wie*) *er im Bett liegt, muß sehr unbequem sein* (or: *es muß sehr unbequem sein, wie...*) (the way he lies...).

G. 'Way' does not denote 'manner' or 'means' but emphasizes the fact itself. Here only a noun or verbal noun or *wie* is possible.

Das Wellige der Landschaft macht sie idyllisch (the way the landscape undulates...).

Das Flickern der Lichter verleiht dem Hafen einen Zauber (the way the lights twinkle...).

Ihr Lächeln gewinnt alle Herzen (the way she smiles...).

Der Haß gegen den Besiegten zeigt sich darin, wie die Soldaten nicht zögern, Vorübergehende vom Bürgersteig zu stoßen (in the way the soldiers...).

WEAKEN **Schwächen** is 'to make weak', i.e. lacking sufficient strength. **Abschwächen** is 'to make a thing (not a person) weaker than it was before', but not in such a way that it completely lacks strength. It is mostly used in the sense of 'to tone down' the intensity of an effect. Hence, it is the only possible term with *Wort*.

Die Strapazen haben mich sehr geschwächt.

Eine solche Politik muß die Regierung schwächen.

Der Gebrauch von 'gern' schwächt 'möchte' ab.

Diese Szene hat die Spannung, die Wirkung, des Stücks (ab)geschwächt (*abschwächen* could be deliberate).

Er muß manchmal seine impulsiven Äußerungen abschwächen.

WEIGH **1. Wiegen** is used both transitively in the literal sense of 'to ascertain the weight of 'a person or thing by any means, and intransitively in the literal sense of 'to be of a specified weight'. Figuratively, it means 'to have influence'.

Er wiegt das Gemüse sehr genau.

Wieviel wiegen Sie?

Das Buch wiegt 3 Pfund.

Solche Gründe wiegen nicht schwer bei mir.

2. Wägen is used in the literal sense only in poetry and in exalted prose. *Wog* and *gewogen* have replaced *wägte* and *gewägt* in ordinary prose. Figuratively, it is used in ordinary prose in the sense of 'to estimate the effect, values, of' a thing only with a few nouns (e.g. *seine Worte, Handlungen, wägen*; see Duden). **Abwägen** means 'to balance' one thing carefully against another. **Erwägen** means 'to consider all aspects of a matter' (see 'consider'), but does not emphasize the balancing of two things against each other.

Sie müssen das Für und das Wider, die Argumente, gegen einander abwägen.
Ich habe meine Chancen noch nicht erwogen.

WHILE 'While' must always be translated in ordinary prose by **während**, except when it expresses a condition, i.e. when it is equivalent to 'as long as'. In the latter case it must be translated by **solange**.[1]

Während ich die Straße hinunterging, marschierten Soldaten vorbei.
Diese Politik wird Sie retten, während die andere bestimmt zum Untergang führen wird (whereas).
Sie können nicht herein, solange Sie keinen Paß haben.

WISH Case treated: 'wish' followed by a dependent clause.

1. **Wollte** and **wünschte** (both imperfect subjunctive) have a narrower range of application than 'wish'. The distinction between them is as follows. *Wollte* is strongly emotional, often expressing feelings that are near breaking point, and represents fulfilment as remote, if not altogether impossible. *Wünschte* is less emotional and more detached, sometimes, as in a rebuke, to the point of superiority. Fulfilment is conceived as less remote than with *wollte*.

Ich wollte bloß, er würde mit dem Geschwätz aufhören.
Ich wollte, ich hätte ihn frühzeitig genug gewarnt.
Ich wünschte, Sie würden das nicht tun.
Ich wünschte, ich hätte ein Auto.

2. In conversation, when it is not desired to express the above shades of meaning, 'wish' can best be rendered by an exclamation with *wenn*, etc.

Wenn das Feuer bloß brennen würde!
Hätte ich ihm das nur rechtzeitig gesagt!

WOMAN **Weib** emphasizes the sexual side of 'woman', and should be used where 'woman' is conceived or presented exclusively in this way

[1] In present-day German *indem* does not mean 'while'. It indicates manner, means, and can be translated by (*a*) 'by' as an approximate synonym of *dadurch, daß*, (*b*) 'in that' or (*c*) the present participle without preposition. *Indem er ins Zimmer trat, sagte er...* ('entering', not 'while entering', which would separate the two actions in all except time). *Indem* now rarely occurs where the subjects of the two clauses do not refer to the same person. It associates the two actions very closely.

(e.g. in Wedekind's plays). It is also used to denote an ugly old woman without special reference to sex, and when preceded by an appropriate adjective approximates to 'hag'. The plural is only used pejoratively. **Frau,** while it refers to sex, does so less emphatically and less exclusively. It can denote all the qualities of a woman and is thus the most general term. The adjectives which can be combined or not combined with the two words are the best illustration of their meaning. Thus *ein schönes Weib* refers only to a beautiful body, *eine schöne Frau* includes this, but can suggest other qualities as well. *Gebildet* can be applied to *Frau* only. In compounds *Frau* is the normal term to denote the social, intellectual activities, and the like, of woman (e.g. *Frauenverein*). *Weib* is sometimes used disparagingly (e.g. *Weiberklatsch*).

Frauenzimmer,[1] which has gone through several changes of meaning, is now pejorative, and refers particularly to stupidity or silliness (e.g. *ein blödes Frauenzimmer*).

WONDER 1. **Sich wundern:** to be astonished, not to be able to understand. It is followed by *über*, the infinitive, or a clause (e.g. *daß*). It is stronger, more emotional than the impersonal *es wundert mich.*[2]

Ich wundere mich, daß Sie sich so etwas gefallen lassen.
Ich wundere mich, Sie hier zu finden.
Ich wunderte mich über seine Kenntnisse.

2. **Verwundern** is used in the same sense as *wundern*, but normally only in the passive with *sein*, and in the phrase *es ist nicht zu verwundern.*[3]

Es ist nicht zu verwundern, daß er durchgefallen ist (not to be wondered at).
Darüber war ich äußerst verwundert.

3. *Wissen mögen* suggests curiosity, a desire to know; *gespannt sein, wie* (etc.) intense interest or curiosity; *sich fragen* deliberation or doubt.

Ich möchte wissen, wie er das fertig gebracht hat.
Ich bin gespannt, was er sagen wird.
Ich frage mich, ob es möglich ist.

[1] Both *Weibsbild* and *Mannsbild* refer to sex, but the former is more vulgar than the latter.

[2] *Es wundert mich* is the closest equivalent of 'to be surprised' (e.g. *es wundert mich, daß der Kerl noch nicht eingesperrt ist*). *Überraschen* suggests suddenness and unpreparedness much more forcibly than 'surprise' does.

[3] But note the reflexive use in the following passage from E. T. A. Hoffmann's *Klein Zaches:* '*Der Professor Mosch Terpin war sonst ein aufgeklärter, welterfahrener Mann, der dem weisen Spruch Nil admirari gemäß sich seit vielen, vielen Jahren über nichts in der Welt zu verwundern pflegte.*' This is a rare use and only appropriate in ironical style.

4. **Vielleicht** is used in a polite request or question.

Könnten Sie mir vielleicht sagen, wie man am schnellsten zum Bahnhof kommt?

WORK **Arbeit** is primarily 'labour, activity'; **Werk** primarily 'result of labour', 'finished product'. *Arbeit* can also be used in the sense of the finished product, but in reference to more humble things, particularly school-boys' and students' essays, a piece of work. *Werk* is used in the sense of 'activity' only in a few fixed phrases meaning 'to set to work' (e.g. *zu Werke, ans Werk, gehen*).

Die Arbeit war sehr anstrengend.
Er hat sein Arbeitspensum noch nicht erledigt.
'Faust' gehört zu den größten Werken der Weltliteratur.
Laut einem Bericht des früheren Botschafters U. von Hassel sagte Hitler einmal zu Frank, er möchte mit seinem Teufelswerk in Polen fortfahren.

LIST OF WORDS TREATED

WORDS FOR WHICH PAGE REFERENCES ARE NOT GIVEN ARE THOSE WHICH HEAD THE ARTICLE CONCERNED

(*The part of speech is indicated where necessary* (*n.* = *noun*, *v.* = *verb*, *a.* = *adjective*). *An asterisk is attached to words treated only briefly, whether in footnotes or incidentally in the main article.*)

abbreviate 322
abridge 322
accept
accident
account (on that) 361
accuse
acknowledge 286
acrid* 314
act (*n.*)
action 3
add
admit 80
adopt* 1
adroit* 71
adulterate 126
affect
again
agree
all
allow 154
allure 359
alter 65
angry
annihilate 96
announce
annoyed 19
answer (*v.*)
anxiety (cause) 146
anxious
apparently
appeal (*n.*) 68
appear
appearance
appoint
appreciate
approach (*v.*)
appropriate* (*a.*) 346
approve* 154
arrange
arrangement* 17, 32
ashamed 319
ask
assemble 148
associate* 171, 172
attitude
attract
austere* 314
authority* 266
avid* 23
avoid
await 384
awake 384

bad
barefaced 319
bashful* 320
bear
bearing* 45
beat
befitting* 347
before
begrudge* 155
behave
behaviour 45
belief
belong
bend
bequeath* 169
bequest 169
better* (*v.*) 166
bind* 172
blame (*v.*)
blend 231
blind (*v.*)
block (*v.*)
body
boil 86
borrow 196
bother (*v.*)
bow (*v.*) 47
boy
brain
break
bright* 223, 71
broad
burn
burst* 53
bury
busy

calculate
call
care (*n.*)
careful 60
carry on* 104, 268
catch
cause 100, 146, 204, 364
cautious 60
censure 48
change (*v.*)
charm (*n.*)

LIST OF WORDS TREATED

cheat (*v.*) 92
check* 301, 337, 374
cheek
cheerful 223
choice (*n.*)
choose
chop* 91
civilization* 107
claim (*v.*)
clever
climb
close* (*v.*) 50, 201
close* (*a.*) 239
clothe 105
collect 148
collide* 342
combine* 172, 173
comfortable
commensurate* 347
common
complain
complete (*v.*) 134
complete (*a.*)
concede 80
concept 162
conception 162, 248
concern* (*v.*) 13, 51
conclude* 201, 202
condition 335
conduct 45
confess
confidence 373
confident 373
connect* 172, 173
connection 291
consider
consolidate
constant
continue
cook
corner
corpse
costly
cost(s)
cosy 73
course
cover
crafty* 72
cramped* 239
crash* (*v.*) 125
cross (*v.*)
culture* 107
curse
curtail 90, 322
custom 156
cut

damage (*v.*)
dare
date
dazzle 49
dear 87
decay* (*v.*) 125
deceive
decide
decline 290
deed 3
degree 120
delicate 327
delude 92
demand (*n.*)
demand (*v.*)
deny
depress 270
desire* (*n.*) 23
destroy
deter* 271
determine 93
dexterous* 71
different
difficult
dip* 100
disappear
disaster 2
disclose 295
disgrace 319
disgraceful 319
disguise* 105
dive
divulge 295
do
doubt (*v.*)
drag 277
draw 277
dress (*v.*)
drink
drunk

eager 23
earnest* 307
educate
education* 107
embitter
employ* 29
end (*v.*) 134
end (in the) (*adv.*) 189
engage 28
enjoy
ensue 140
enter
entice 359
entire 77
entirely 281
equip* 275
error 231
escape
estate 169
estimate
evaluate
even (*adv.*)
event
eventual 189
evil (*a.*) 38
exact* (*a.*) 318
exchange 65
excite

exercise (*v.*) 268
expand* 335
expense(s) 87
expensive 87
experience (*n. and v.*)
express
extend* 335
extent
extinguish
extol 268

fact (in)* 116
fail
faith* 373
fall
falsify
far* 55
fat* 362
fate
fear (*v.*)
feed
feel
few
fight
fill
finally 189
find
finish
fire
first (at first)
fit (*v.*) 346
fitting* 347
flat
float
follow
food
fool
force (*n.*) 262
forge 126
fortunate* 379
found
freeze
friend* 146
friendly
frighten
full
funny
furnish* 275, 276

gather
gay 223
general 75
gentle 327
genuine 284
get (1)
get (2) 204
give
glad
glide* 327
go
grant
grave (*a.*) 307
greet
grievous 98, 316
grow (up)* 107
guard (*n.*)
guide* (*v.*) 171

habit
hang
harsh* 315
hasten 162
have 204
head
hear
heart
hearty
heat (*v.*)
heavy* 316, 317
heighten 282
hence 361
hide
hinder* 274, 275
hit 342
hold* 176, 177, 188
however
hurry

idea
ignominy* 319
illuminate
imagination* 164
imagine
imply* 220
improve
impulse 379
incentive 379
incident 117
incline 47
increase
indeed* 116
individual* 213, 306, 326
information* 185
inhabitant
inherit
inheritance
initiative* 380
inspect* 82
insult* (*n.*) 319
interested (in)
interpret
introduce
introduction* 171
invest 105

job 261
join
joyful 152
judge (*v.*)

keep
kill
kind (*n.*)
kind (*a.*)
kindly 183

knock* 53, 342
know
knowledge

lack
last (*v.*)
last (at last)
lazy
lead* 171
lean 362
learn
least (at)
leave
legacy 169
lend
lessen 287
let 204
level* 259
lift 282
like* 24, 215
limit
listen
live
lively
lock
longer (no)
look (at)
look after* 51
loose
lot* (*n.*) 126
lower* 327
lurch 369

maintain 174
make
man
manner 390
marry
may
meal* 143
mean (*v.*)
means 390
measure (*n.*) 120
meet
mend* 164
merry
method 390
might (*v.*) 214
mild 327
mind
mingle 231
miserable* 363
miss
mistake (*n.*)
mix
morals* 157
more (no) 202
move
much
murder

name (*v.*) 59
narrow
nature
nasty* 43
necessary
necessity 241
need
negate 95
nevertheless 160
noise 330
nominate 28
note* 243
notice (*v.*)
nourishment 142
now
number
nutrition 142

object (*v.*)
objection 245
obliterate* 96
obtain* 149, 150
obvious* 344
occur
offer (*v.*)
only (*adv.*)
open (*v.*)
opinion
oppress 270
order (*v.*)
ordinary* 156, 76
other
owe* 360

painful
pale
pallid 253
passage* 255
path 341
pay
people
perfect (*a.*) 77
performance* 170
permanent 84
persistent* 84
person* 213
place (*n.*)
poky* 239
popular
position (1) 257
position (2) 259
position (3) 261
possibly
power
practise
praise
precious 87
prepare
preserve 174
press
prevent
proclaim 21
proportion 291
propriety* 157
prosecute* 141

protect
protest (*n.*) 245
prove 373
provide
public (*n.*)
pull
punish
pursue 140
put

quality
quick* 71
quite

raise
ratio 291
ready* 134, 270
real
really
reason* 225
reasonable 225
receive
recently
reckon 58
recognize
reduce
reel 369
refer
refuse
regard* (*v.*) 83
rejoin 22
relation(ship)
remainder* 293
remark* (*v.*) 243
remember* 82
repeat
reply 22
report 21
represent* 170
request* 34, 28
require* 34, 47
resolve (*v.*) 93
responsibility
rest (*n.*)
rest (*v.*)
restrict 198
retort 22
reveal
road 341
rock 369
roll
room
run
ruthless* 368

safe
same (all the) 160
satisfy
scale 120
seal
seat* 256
secret (*a.*)
secure 297
see
see to* 51
seem 25
seethe 86
seize
select 70
selection 70
self-assured 303
self-conscious
self-possessed* 303
selfish
send
sense
sensible* 225
sensitive* 128
sentimental* 318
separate(ly)
serious
servant
serve
service (*v.*)
sever* 90
severe
shake
shame (*n. and v.*)
shameful 319
shameless 319
share (*n. and v.*)
shoot
shorten
show
shrewd* 71, 72
shut 50, 201, 248
sight 382
sign
silence
silent* 325
silly* 325
simple
single
sink
situation 257, 259, 261
skilful 71
slender* 362
slide* 327
slim* 362
slip
sluggish 190
sly* 72
small* 287
smart* 71
so 361
soft
some
sore* 128, 328
sort 181
sound (*n.*)
space 296
spare
species 181
spend
spit

spot* 255
spread
sprightly 223
squeeze 270
stagger 369
state
stern 314
stick* (*v.*) 280
stoop 47
stop
strange
street
strength 262
strengthen
stretch* 335
strict 314
strike
study* 190
sue* 2
suffer
suggest
suit
suitable* 346
summon 59
supply 276, 348
support
sure 297
surprised* 402
suspect 348
suspicion
suspicious 348
swallow
sway 369
swear 90
swindle* 92

take
taste
teach
tear* (*v.*) 277
tease
tempt
tender 327
test 373
thank
then
therefore
thick
thin
thing
think
thought
thought (lost in) 367
thoughtful
thoughtless
thrash 44
threaten
thus 361
tight* 239
totter
touch
touchy* 128, 318
transform 65
traverse* 89
trouble* 51
true 284
trust (*n.*)
trust (*v.*)
try (out)
tug* (*v.*) 277
turn
type 181

understand
understanding (*n.*)
unfortunate
unhappy 378
unify* 173
unite 173
unveil* 295
urge (*n.*)
urge (*v.*) 270
use (*v.*)
usual* 156
vacillate 369
vain (in)
view (*n.*) (1)
view (*n.*) (2) 248
vigil* (*n.*) 156
violent
vulgar 76, 156

wait
wake
waken 384
walk* 153
wall
want
warm (*v.*)
warn
waste (*v.*)
watch* 384
way
weaken
weigh
while
whole 18
wicked 38
wide 54
willing* 270
win* 151
wipe out* 96
wish (*v.*)
wobble 369
woman
wonder (*v.*)
work (*n.*)
worry (cause) 146
wrathful 19
writhe* 296

yet 160

zealous 23

GERMAN WORD LIST

abbrechen, 53, 339
abfahren, 196
abfinden (sich), 1
abfüttern, 128
abhalten, 271, 337
abholen, 149, 221
abkürzen, 323
ablehnen, 290
ableugnen, 96
abmachen, 34
abnehmen, 353
Abneigung, 246
Abrede (in...stellen), 96
abreisen, 196
abschlagen, 290
abschließen, 201
abschmecken, 357
abschwächen, 400
absehen, 301
absprechen, 96
abstürzen, 125
abwägen, 81, 401
abwarten, 384
abweisen, 290
acht (geben, nehmen), 62
achten (auf), 61
addieren, 10
ahnen (lassen), 346
Ahnung, 163, 348
Akt, 6
Aktion, 7
akzeptieren, 1
albern, 325
all, 18 f.
alle, 136
alleinstehend, 326
allerhand, 181
allerlei, 181
allgemein, 75, 257
alltäglich, 75
also, 361
amüsieren (sich), 109
anbieten, 246 f.
Anblick, 382
anbrennen, 56
andauern, 187
ander(s), 97, 252, 294
ändern, 14, 65, 66
andeuten, 345
anerkennen, 286
anfahren, 343
anfangen (mit), 100
anfassen, 371
Anforderung, 94
anfragen, 35
anfühlen (sich), 129
angehen (um), 32
angehören, 47
Angelegenheit, 364
angemessen, 347
angenehm, 74
Angewohnheit, 157
angreifen, 14, 371
Angst, 127, 146
ängstigen, 146
ängstlich, 25
anhalten, 188, 337, 339
anhören, 200
anklagen, 2
ankleiden (sich), 105
ankündigen, 21
Anlage, 264
anmelden, 21
anmutig, 69
Annahme, 46
annehmen, 1, 354
anordnen, 251
anpassen, 347

anpreisen, 268
anregen, 118, 345
anrufen, 59
anrühren, 370
ansammeln, 149
anschaffen, 150
Anschauung, 250
Anschein, 27
anscheinend, 25
anschicken (sich), 269
anschießen, 322
anschließen (sich), 171
anschuldigen, 2
ansehen, 202 f.
Ansicht, 16, 83, 249, 382
anspielen, 289
Ansporn, 380
ansprechen, 371
Anspruch (in...nehmen), 71, 357
Anstalten (treffen), 34
anstellen, 29, 100
Anstellung, 261
anstiften, 145, 380
Anteil, 320
antreffen, 221
Antrieb, 380
antun, 103
antworten, 22
anweisen, 251, 389
anwenden, 381
Anzahl, 245
Anzeichen, 324
anzeigen, 22
anziehen, 36
anziehen (sich), 105
Arbeit, 403
arg, 41, 316
ärgerlich, 20
ärgern (sich), 20
Argwohn, 348
argwöhnen, 349
argwöhnisch, 349
arrangieren, 33
Art, 181, 390 f., 397 f.
Art und Weise, 392 f.
auch nur, 117
aufbewahren, 178
auferlegen, 252
auffallen, 36, 242
auffangen, 62
auffassen, 356
Auffassung, 250
Auffassungsgabe, 229
auffordern, 251
aufführen (sich), 45
aufgebracht, 20
aufhalten, 179, 337
aufhalten (sich), 338
aufhängen, 158
aufheben, 178
aufhören, 339
aufkommen (für), 276
auflaufen, 343
auflösen, 339
aufmachen, 248
aufmerksam, 36, 368
aufnehmen, 1, 285, 354
aufpassen, 61
aufrechterhalten, 176
aufregen, 118
aufsagen, 292
aufschlagen, 53, 248
aufschließen, 248
aufstellen, 28
auftun, 248
aufwachen, 384
aufwachsen, 107
aufwecken, 384
aufziehen, 107, 283, 359
aus- (*finish*), 135
ausbessern, 164
ausbleiben, 122
Ausblick, 382
ausbrechen, 113

ausbreiten, 334
ausdehnen, 335
Ausdehnung, 121
ausdrücken, 119 f.
ausfallen, 122
ausfragen, 35
Ausführung, 5, 9
Ausgabe(n), 88
ausgerechnet, 58
ausgleiten, 327
auskennen (sich), 185
auskommen, 189
auslegen, 170
ausleihen, 197
auslöschen, 121
ausmachen, 34
Ausmaß, 121, 399
ausnützen, 381
ausruhen (sich), 294
ausrüsten, 275
ausrutschen, 327
ausschlagen, 290
Aussehen, 27
Äußeres, 27
äußern, 120
Aussicht, 382
aussprechen, 120
ausstatten, 275
ausströmen, 115
aussuchen (sich), 70
austilgen, 96
ausüben, 268
Auswahl, 70
auswählen, 70
auswechseln, 67
auswirken (sich), 14

Backe, 69
balgen (sich), 131
beängstigen, 147
beantworten, 22
bearbeiten, 34
beargwöhnen, 349
bedacht, 24
bedächtig, 367
bedanken (sich), 360
Bedarf, 94, 242
bedauerlich, 379
bedecken, 88
bedenken, 82, 365
bedeuten, 219
Bedeutung, 219, 304
bedienen, 313
Bediente(r), 313
bedrängen, 270 f.
bedrohen, 368
bedrücken, 271
Bedürfnis, 242
beeilen (sich), 162
beenden, 136
beendigen, 136
beerdigen, 56
befangen, 303
befassen (sich), 82
befehlen, 251
befestigen, 84
befinden, 133
befolgen, 141
befördern, 356
befragen, 35
befreien (sich), 114
befremdet, 146
befriedigen, 299
Befugnis, 267
befürchten, 126
Begebenheit, 117
begegnen, 220, 222
begehren, 23
Begierde, 23
begierig, 23
begleiten, 301
begraben, 56
begreifen, 376
begrenzen, 198

begrenzt, 240
Begriff, 163
begründen, 144
begrüßen, 155
behaglich, 73
behalten, 174, 177
beharren, 384
behaupten, 71
behindern, 274
behutsam, 61
beibringen, 359
beichten, 80
beisetzen, 56
beitreten, 171
bekannt, 184
bekannt (machen), (geben), 21, 171
Bekannte(r), 146
bekennen, 81
beklagen (sich), 76
bekleiden, 105
bekommen, 18, 149, 347
bekümmern, 51
belassen, 195
belebt, 57
belehren, 358
beleuchten, 164
belieben, 70
beliebt, 256
beloben, 268
belügen, 93
bemächtigen (sich), 302
bemerken, 243
bemüht (sein), 24
benachrichtigen, 389
Benehmen, 45
benehmen, 45, 354
benennen, 60
benutzen, 380
beordern, 252
bequem, 73
berauscht, 107
berechtigt (sein), 267
bereit, 18, 270
bereiten, 151, 269
bereitwillig, 270
berichten, 22
berücksichtigen, 83
berufen, 30, 59
beruhen, 295
berühren, 12, 370
besagen, 220
beschädigen, 91
beschaffen, 150
Beschaffenheit, 241
beschäftigt (sein), 57
beschämen, 320
Bescheid (wissen), 185
beschlagnahmen, 302
beschließen, 93, 202
beschränken, 198
beschränkt, 240
beschuldigen, 2
beschützen, 275
beschweren (sich), 76
beschwerlich, 253
besetzen, 133, 302
besiegeln, 299
besinnen (sich), 82
besonder(s), 306
besonnen, 367
besorgen, 33, 103, 151
bessern, 164 f.
beständig, 84
bestärken, 341
bestätigen, 287
bestatten, 56
bestellen, 28, 252, 261
bestimmen, 94
bestrafen, 278
bestreiten, 95, 132
betasten, 371
Betracht (in...kommen), 83
betrachten, 82
Betragen, 45

betreffen, 12 f.
betreiben, 179
betreten, 111
betrügen, 92
betrunken, 107
beugen, 48
beurteilen, 174, 249
Bevölkerung, 168
bevor, 45
bewahren, 174, 178
bewähren (sich), 374
bewegen, 15, 233, 371
bewegen (sich), 233
Bewegung, 233
bewerten, 116
bewilligen, 154
Bewohner, 168
bewußt, 184
bezahlen, 254
bezaubern, 69
bezeigen, 324
beziehen (sich), 289
Beziehung, 291
bezweifeln, 105
biegen, 47, 376
bieten, 247
bilden, 107
billigen, 154
binden, 172
bitten, 34
blaß, 253
bleiben, 191, 192, 338
bleich, 253
blenden, 50
Blick, 382
blind machen, 49
bloß, 262
borgen, 197
böse, 20, 43
Brand, 138
Brauch, 157
brauchen, 357
brechen, 52, 54
breit, 54
breiten, 334 f.
brennen, 24, 55, 138
bringen, 211, 284, 344, 355
Bube, 51
bücken, 48
Bursche, 51

daher, 361
damals, 360
daneben, 230
danken, 360
dann, 360
darstellen, 170
Darstellung, 170
darum, 361
Datum, 92
dauern, 187, 357
davonkommen, 115
decken, 88
dehnen, 335
delikat, 328
dementieren, 96
Denkart, 229
denken, 365 f.
denken (sich), 365
denn, 361
dennoch, 161
deshalb, 361
deuten, 170, 345
dicht, 362
dick, 362
dienen, 313
Dienst, 313
Dienstbote, 313
Ding, 363
doch, 161
dolmetschen, 170
Drang, 380
drängen, 270
drängen (sich), 132

drehen, 376
dringen, 112, 270
drohen, 369
drücken, 270
dulden, 343
dumm, 144
dünn, 362
durchaus, 282
durchfallen, 122
dürfen, 92, 218
dürftig, 363

echt, 284
Ecke, 87
ehe, 45
eifrig, 23
eigen, 305
Eigenschaft, 266, 280
eigentlich, 285
eilen, 162
eilig, 162
ein- (*enter*), 112
ein- (*insert*), 11
ein- (*single*), 326
einberufen, 60
einbilden (sich), 164
Einbildung, 164
einbringen, 171
eindringen, 112
einfach, 325 f.
einfallen, 365
einfältig, 325
einfangen, 64
einführen, 170
Einführung, 171
eingeben, 344
eingestehen, 81
einhalten, 179, 339
einheizen, 159
einholen, 63
einig, 16 f.
einig(e), 329
einigen (sich), 17
einkehren, 338
einkleiden, 106
einleiten, 171
Einleitung, 171
einleuchten, 301
einnehmen, 354
einräumen, 155
einrichten, 33, 34
einrichten (sich), 33
einsammeln, 149
einscharren, 57
einschnappen, 65
einschränken, 198, 287, 323
einschreiten, 9
einsehen, 300
einsetzen, 29
einstellen, 340
einstellen (sich), 35
Einstellung, 35
eintreten, 111, 171
einüben, 268
einverstanden (sein), 16 f.
Einverständnis, 378
Einwand, 245
einwenden, 245 f.
Einwendung, 245
einwilligen, 17
einwirken, 14
Einwohner, 168
Einzel-, 326
einzeln, 305, 306, 326
einzig, 326
Empfang (in...nehmen), 285
empfangen, 221, 285
empfinden, 128, 133
empfindlich, 318, 328
empört, 20
Ende (am), 190
Ende (machen), 136, 339
endgültig, 190
endlich, 189

eng, 239
ent- (*escape*), 113 f.
entdecken, 295
entfallen, 321
entgegenkommen, 222
entgegnen, 22
enthaupten, 158
enthüllen, 295
entlehnen, 197
entleihen, 197
entnehmen, 354
entreißen, 302
entscheiden, 93
entschleiern, 295
entschließen (sich), 93
entschwinden, 100
entsenden, 304
entsinnen (sich), 82
entsprechen, 222
er- (*choose*), 70
Erachten, 249
Erbe, 169
erben, 168
erbieten (sich), 247
erbitten (sich), 34
erbittern, 108
erbleichen, 253
erblinden, 50
Erbschaft, 169
Ereignis, 117
ererben, 168
erfahren, 119, 222
Erfahrung, 119
erfassen, 303
erfolgen, 142
erfordern, 94, 357
erfreuen, 109
erfüllen, 132, 222
ergänzen, 137
ergreifen, 301 f.
erhalten, 174, 175 f., 178, 285
erhängen, 158
erheben, 282 f.
erhitzen, 159
erhöhen, 167, 283 f.
erinnern, 345
erinnern (sich), 82
erkennen, 184, 286, 300
Erkenntnis, 185
erklimmen, 73
erleben, 119, 184
Erlebnis, 119
erledigen, 103
erleiden, 344
erlernen, 190
erleuchten, 164
Ermächtigung, 267
ermahnen, 389
Ermahnung, 312
ermangeln, 124, 186
ermäßigen, 289
ermorden, 180, 239
ernähren, 127
Ernährung, 144
ernennen, 28
ernst, 307 f.
ernsthaft, 309 f.
ernstlich, 284, 310, 311
eröffnen, 248, 295
erproben, 374
erregen, 36, 118
erreichen, 63
Erscheinen, 28
erscheinen, 26, 345
Erscheinung, 27 f.
erschießen, 322
erschließen, 248
erschüttern, 318
ersparen, 332
erst, 138, 247
erstrecken (sich), 335
ersuchen, 34
ertappen, 63
ertragen, 44

erwägen, 81, 401
Erwägung (in...ziehen), 82
erwärmen, 387
erwarten, 221, 384
erwecken, 384
erweisen, 324
erweitern, 335
erwidern, 22
erwischen, 63
erzeigen, 324
erziehen, 107
Essen, 143
essen, 127, 358
etwas, 329
eventuell, 262
extra, 307

Fähigkeit, 265
fahren, 153, 196, 343
fallen, 125, 181
fällen, 91
fälschen, 126
fangen, 62
fassen, 302, 343, 357
faul, 190
fechten, 131
fehlen, 186
Fehler, 231
Fehlgriff, 231
fehlschlagen, 122
feist, 362
fern, 55
fertig, 80, 134, 135
fest, 315
festhalten, 179
festigen, 84
festnehmen, 354
fett, 362
Feuer, 137
finden, 133, 222, 286, 301, 357
flach, 139
Fleck, 255
fliehen, 114
fluchen, 90
flüchten, 115
folgen, 140
fordern, 94
Forderung, 94
fortfahren, 86
fortsetzen, 85
Frage (in...kommen), 83
fragen, 35
fragen (sich), 402
Frau, 402
Frauenzimmer, 402
fremd, 340
Freude (machen), 109
freudig, 152, 223
freuen (sich), 109, 152
Freund, 146
freundlich, 146, 183
freundschaftlich, 146
frieren, 145
froh, 152
fröhlich, 152, 223
fügen, 172
fühlen, 128
fühlen (sich), 129
führen, 171, 179, 355
füllen, 132 f.
Furcht, 146
fürchten, 126, 127
für sich, 306
Fuß (zu...gehen), 153
füttern, 128

ganz, 19, 281
gänzlich, 79, 318
Garde, 156
Gasse, 341
geben, 151, 278
gebieten, 251
Gebrauch, 157
gebrauchen, 381

gebräuchlich, 75, 156
Gedanke, 163, 366
Gedanken, 226
Gedankengut, 367
gedankenlos, 368
gedankenvoll, 367
geeignet, 346
Gefahr, 298
gefallen, 109
Gefühl, 305
gegen (sein), 246
geheim, 299
gehen, 89, 110, 153, 154, 196
Gehirn, 52
gehören, 47
Geist, 224 f.
geistig, 225
geistreich, 72
gelind(e), 329
gelingen (nicht), 123
gelten (lassen), 2
gemahnen, 389
gemein, 75
gemeinsam, 76
Gemüt, 228
gemütlich, 74
genau, 318
genehmigen, 154
genieren (sich), 303
genießen, 108
genügen, 299
geraten, 153
Geräusch, 331
gering, 287
gern (möchten), 24
Geschehnis, 118
gescheit, 72
Geschick, 126
geschickt, 71
gesondert, 306
gespannt (sein), 23, 25
gestatten, 155
Geste, 3
gestehen, 80
Getränk, 106
getrauen (sich), 373
getrennt, 306
getrost, 373
gewählt, 71
gewähren, 154
Gewalt, 263, 266, 383
gewaltig, 383
gewaltsam, 383
gewalttätig, 383
gewandt, 72
Gewicht, 264
gewinnen, 151
gewissermaßen, 120
Gewohnheit, 156
gewöhnlich, 76, 156
glatt, 75
Glaube, 46, 373
glauben, 365 f.
gleiten, 327
gliedern (sich), 125
Glück, 379
glücklich, 379
gönnen, 155
Grad, 121
grenzen, 173
gründen, 144
gründlich, 318
grüßen, 155
gut, 74, 183, 298
Gutachten, 249
gutheißen, 154
gutherzig, 183
gütig, 183

haben, 177, 179
haben (wollen), 386
hager, 362
halten, 176 f., 179, 188, 337, 366
halten (an-, auf-, *etc.*), 337

halten (für), 83
Haltung, 35, 45, 258, 394
Handeln, 8
Handlung, 3 f.
hängen, 158, 280
hängen (bleiben), 63
hänseln, 359
harsch, 315
hart, 315
hastig, 162
hauen, 91
hauen (sich), 131, 342
häufig, 75
Haupt, 158
Hausangestellte(r), 313
heben, 282 f.
heftig, 383
heimlich, 299
heiraten, 213
heiß (machen), 159
heißen, 60, 220, 251
heiter, 223
heitzen, 159
hell, 223
henken, 158
herabsetzen, 288
heranreichen, 32
herantreten, 32
heraushören, 65
hereinkommen, 111
hergeben, 152
hernehmen, 151
herunterbringen, 289
Herz-, 159
herzhaft, 159
herzlich, 159
Hetze, 57
hindern, 271 f.
hinein- (*add*), 11
hinein- (*enter*), 110
hingeben (sich), 152
hingezogen (sein), 36
hinnehmen, 1, 354
hinrichten, 158
Hinsicht, 399
hinterlassen, 194
Hinterlassenschaft, 169
hinterlistig, 72
hinzu- (*add*), 10 f.
Hirn, 52
holen, 151
holen (sich), 64, 151
hören, 199 f.
hören (von), 158
hüten (sich), 62

Idee, 162 f.
immerhin, 161
Impuls, 379
indem, 401
Individuum, 306
innehalten, 339
interessieren (sich), 170
interpretieren, 170
irgend, 262
Irrtum, 231

Jammer, 319
jeder, 19
jedoch, 160
jetzt, 244
Junge, 52

kämpfen, 130
Kapazität, 265
kapieren, 377
kaputt, 54
kehren, 375
kennen, 183
kennen (lernen), 222
Kenntnis(se), 185
klagen, 76
Klang, 330
kleiden (sich), 105

klettern, 73
klingeln, 331
klopfen, 342
klug, 72
Knabe, 51
knapp, 239
kochen, 86
komfortabel, 74
komisch, 148
kommen, 153
können, 184, 217 f.
Konzeption, 163
Kopf, 158, 226
Körper, 51
Kost, 143
kostbar, 87
Kosten, 87
kosten, 357
köstlich, 87
kostspielig, 87
Kraft, 263, 265
kräftigen, 342
kreuzen, 89
kriegen, 150
Kultur, 107
kümmerlich, 363
kümmern, 51
kündigen, 21
kürzen, 287, 322
kürzlich, 286

Lage, 258, 260
länger (nicht), 202
Lärm, 331
lassen, 177, 192 f., 195 f., 205–10, 251, 339
lassen (sich), 206
Lauf (im), 88
laufen, 296
lauschen, 200
Laut, 330
läuten, 331
leben, 200
lebendig, 201
Lebensmittel, 142
lebhaft, 201
ledig, 326
legen, 279, 334
lehren, 358
Leib (*and cpds.*), 51
Leiche, 51, 87
Leichnam, 87
leicht, 75
leichtsinnig, 368
leiden, 343
leihen, 196
leise, 328
leiten, 171
lenken, 171
lernen, 190
letzt, 189
letzter Zeit (in), 286
leugnen, 95
Leute, 254
liebenswürdig, 183
liefern, 276
liegen (an), 24, 259
listig, 72
loben, 268
locken, 359
locker, 203
los, 204
löschen, 121
lose, 204
loslassen, 195
Lust (haben), 360
lustig, 223

machen, 151, 210, 279
Macht, 262
mager, 362
mahnen, 389
manche, 330
Mangel, 231

mangeln, 186
Manier, 393
Mann, 213
Maß, 120
Maßnahme, 9
Mauer, 385
mehr (nicht), 202
mehren, 167
meiden, 37
meinen, 219
Meinung, 46, 83, 248
melden, 21
mengen, 232
Mensch(en), 213, 254
merken, 242
Methode, 394
mild, 328
mindern, 288
mindestens, 191
mischen, 231
Mißgriff, 231
mißlingen, 123
mißtrauen, 350
mißtrauisch, 349
mitbringen, 355
Mitleidenschaft, 14
mitmachen, 172
mitnehmen, 355
Mittel, 398
mögen, 24, 214 f., 387
möglicherweise, 262
Möglichkeit, 399
morden, 239
mühsam, 253
mühselig, 253
munter, 224

Nachdenken, 367
nachdenken, 81, 365
nachdenklich, 367
nachfolgen, 141
Nachfrage, 94
nachkommen, 142, 222
Nachlaß, 169
Nachricht (bekommen), 159
nachsehen, 301
nachsuchen, 34
nahe gehen, 15
nahe (kommen), 32
nahelegen, 344
nahen, 31
näher (kommen), 31
nähern (sich), 31 f.
nähren, 127
Nahrung, 142
Nahrungsmittel, 142
Narr, 144
Natur, 240
necken, 359
nehmen, 1, 351 f., 357
neigen, 48
nennen, 60
Nerven, 20
neugierig, 23
neulich, 286
nicht einmal, 116
noch, 16
noch ein, 252
nochmal, 16
Not, 241
notdürftig, 363
nötig, 241
notwendig, 241
Notwendigkeit, 241
Nummer, 245
nun, 244
nunmehr, 244
nur, 247, 262

offenbaren, 295
Öffentlichkeit, 277
öffnen, 248
ordinär, 76
ordnen, 32

Ort, 255

packen, 302
passen, 346
passend, 346
peinlich, 353
penibel, 253
Person, 213
Personal, 313
Pfad, 341
pflegen, 158
Phantasie, 164
Plan, 32
planen, 33
platt, 139
Platz, 256, 261, 296
platzen, 53
pochen, 342
populär, 257
Portion, 321
Position, 257, 259
Posten, 155, 261
preisen, 268
pressen, 270
probieren, 374
prüfen, 82, 374
prügeln, 44, 342
Publikum, 277

Qualität, 280
quetschen, 271

ranken (sich), 73
rasten, 295
Raum, 296
rechnen, 58
Recht, 267
recht, 18, 282
recht (geben), 16
regen, 235
Regung, 379
reichen, 188, 335
Reine (ins...bringen), 33
reisen, 196
reißen, 53, 278
reißen (sich), 131
Reiz, 69
reizen, 69, 359
reizend, 69
rennen, 296
repartieren, 321
Rest, 293
retten (sich), 114
richten, 173
richtig, 282
rinnen, 115, 296
rollen, 296
rücken, 237
Rücksicht, 83, 368
rücksichtsvoll, 368
rufen (*and cpds.*), 59
ruhen, 294
rühmen, 269
rühren, 233, 234, 371
rütteln, 318

Sache, 364
sacht, 328
sammeln, 148
sammeln (sich), 148
sanft, 327
sauer, 315
schade, 319
schaden, 15, 91
schädigen, 91
schaffen, 100, 238
Schall, 330
Scham, 319
schämen (sich), 320
Schamgefühl, 318
schamlos, 320
Schande, 319
schändlich, 320
scharf, 316

GERMAN WORD LIST

Scharm, 69
schätzen, 30, 115
schauen, 202
schaukeln, 370
Schein, 26
scheinbar, 25
scheinen, 25
scheitern, 122
schenken, 151, 332
schicken, 303 f.
schicklich, 347
Schicksal, 126
schieben, 238
schießen, 321
schlagen, 342
schlagen (sich), 131
schlank, 362
schlau, 72
schlecht, 38
schleppen, 277
schlicht, 325
schließen, 201, 345
schließlich, 189
schlimm, 39, 307, 316
schlingen, 350
schlucken, 350
schlüpfen, 327
Schluß (machen), 339
Schluß (zum), 189
Schmach, 319
schmal, 239
schmecken, 109, 357
schmerzhaft, 252
schmerzlich, 253
schmieren, 334
schneiden, 90
schonen, 331 f.
Schritt, 9
schroff, 383
schulden, 360
schuld sein, 49
schütteln, 318
schützen, 275
schwächen, 400
schwanken, 369
schweben, 140
Schweigen, 325
schwer, 98, 312, 315, 316
schwerfällig, 316
schwierig, 98
schwimmen, 140
schwinden, 99
schwören, 90
Seele, 229
sehen, 203, 299 f.
Sehkraft, 383
sehr, 238
selbst, 116
selbstbewußt, 303
seltsam, 340
senden, 303
senken, 327
seriös, 307
setzen, 279
sicher, 297 f.
Sicherheit, 298
sichern, 297
Sicht, 383
sieden, 86
sinken, 326
Sinn, 31, 226, 304 f.
Sitte, 157
Situation, 260
sogar, 116
solange, 401
sonder, 306
sonderbar, 340
sonst, 293
Sorge, 146
sorgen, 62, 276
sorgfältig, 60
sorgsam, 61
Sorte, 182
spalten, 91

sparen, 332
sparsam, 333, 390
speien, 333
Speise, 143
speisen, 127
sperren, 50
Spesen, 88
sprechen, 289, 301
springen, 53, 100
spucken, 333
spüren, 64, 128, 244
Stand, 259, 336
ständig, 84
Standort, 259
stark, 317
Stärke, 264
stärken, 341
Stätte, 256
stecken, 280
stecken (bleiben), 64, 280
stehen, 259, 260, 338, 347
Stehen (zum...bringen), 338
steigern, 167
Stelle, 255, 259, 261
stellen, 276, 279
stellen (sich), 35
Stellung, 258, 261, 400
Stellungnahme, 36
stet, 85
stetig, 85
stiften, 145
Stillschweigen, 325
stoppen, 337
stoßen, 172, 173, 342, 371
strafen, 278
Straße, 341
streichen, 334
Streit, 364
streiten, 132
streng, 314
streuen, 335
studieren, 190
stürzen, 125
stützen, 347
stutzig, 349
suggerieren, 344
suggestiv, 345

tadellos, 77
tadeln, 49
tasten, 128
Tat, 5
tauchen, 100
taumeln, 369
tauschen, 67 f.
täuschen, 93
täuschen (sich), 231
Teil, 320
teilen, 321
Tempo, 399
Termin, 92
teuer, 87
Tod (finden), 181
Ton, 331
Tor, 144
torkeln, 369
töten, 179, 181
totschlagen, 180
träge, 190
tragen, 44, 356
Trank, 106
trauen, 214, 371 f.
treffen, 12, 64, 221, 342
treiben, 139
trennen, 306
treten (*and cpds.*), 110 f.
Trieb, 379
trinken, 107, 358
trotzdem, 161
trügen, 92
Trunk, 106
tüchtig, 315
Tun, 7
tun, 57, 100, 278, 280

tunken, 100
Typ(us), 182

übel, 43
übelnehmen, 49
üben, 268
übereilen, 162
übereinstimmen, 16 f.
übergeben, 289
übergreifen, 334
überlassen, 194
überlegen (sich), 81
überlegt, 367
übernehmen, 1, 355
überqueren, 89
überraschen, 63, 402
überschreiten, 90
überstürzen, 162
übertragen, 29
überzeugen, 299
Uberzeugung, 46
üblich, 75, 156
übrig, 293
übriglassen, 195
umbringen, 180
Umfang, 121, 399
umknicken, 53
umkommen, 180
umsonst, 381
umwandeln, 68
unabhängig, 305
unbesonnen, 368
unentgeltlich, 381
unerzogen, 107
Unfall, 2
ungehalten, 20
Unglück, 2, 379
unglücklich, 378
Unheil, 2
Unkosten, 87
unselig, 379
unterbrechen, 339
unterhalten, 176, 178
unterlassen, 124
unternehmen, 9
unterrichten, 358
unterstellen, 346
unterstützen, 347
unüberlegt, 368
unverheiratet, 326
unvermindert, 288
unverschämt, 320
unwillig, 20
urteilen, 173

verabreden, 17, 34
verängstigen, 147
veranlassen, 210
veranstalten, 33
verantwortlich, 49
Verantwortlichkeit, 292
Verantwortung, 292
veräppeln, 359
verärgern, 20
verbergen, 160
verbessern, 165
verbeugen, 48
verbieten, 339
verbinden, 172
Verbindung, 292
verbitten, 108
verbitten (sich), 245
verblenden, 50
verbrauchen, 135, 381
verbreiten, 335
verbrennen, 55
verbringen, 333
Verdacht, 348 f.
verdächtig, 348
verdächtigen, 349
verdanken, 360
Verdienst, 314
verdrießen, 19
vereinbaren, 17

vereinigen, 173
verfallen, 125
verfälschen, 126
verfangen, 65
verfehlen, 124, 230
verfluchen, 90
verfolgen, 141
vergebens, 382
vergeblich, 382
vergeuden, 389
vergönnen, 155
vergraben, 57
Verhalten, 35, 46, 261
verhalten (sich), 35, 46
Verhältnis, 31, 291, 336
Verhängnis, 126
verharren, 384
verhauen, 131
verhehlen, 160
verheiraten, 214
verhindern, 271 f.
verkehren, 232
verklagen, 2
verkleiden, 105
verkleinern, 288
verknüpfen, 173
verköstigen, 128
verkünden, 21
verkürzen, 322
verlangen, 23, 34
verlassen, 191
Verlauf, 88
verlegen, 236
verleihen, 197
verleugnen, 96
verlocken, 359
Vermächtnis, 169
vermählen (sich), 214
vermahnen, 389
vermehren, 167
vermeiden, 37
vermengen, 232
vermindern, 287
vermischen, 232
vermissen, 229
vermitteln, 33
Vermögen, 264
vermuten, 350
vernachlässigen, 124
verneigen (sich), 48
verneinen, 95
vernichten, 96
verordnen, 252
verpassen, 124, 229
verpflanzen, 236
verpflegen, 128
Verpflegung, 143
Verpflichtungen, 293
verprügeln, 44
verringern, 287
verrücken, 237
verrückt, 144
versagen, 122, 290
versammeln, 148
versäumen, 124, 229
verschaffen, 150
verschärfen, 316
verschieben, 237
verschieden, 97, 305
verschleppen, 277
verschließen, 202
verschlingen, 351
verschlucken, 350
verschonen, 332
verschwenden, 389
verschwinden, 99
Versehen, 231
versehen, 275
versenken, 327
versetzen, 22, 236
versichern, 297
versiegeln, 299
versinken, 326
versorgen, 276

versperren, 50
Verstand, 225, 305, 378
verständigen (sich), 18
Verständigung, 378
Verständnis, 31, 378
verstärken, 341
verstatten, 155
verstecken, 159
verstehen, 65, 300, 376 f.
verstehen (sich), 377
verstellen, 237
versuchen, 359, 374
Versuchung, 359
verteilen, 335
vertilgen, 96
vertragen, 44, 357
vertragen (sich), 18
Vertrauen, 46
vertrauen, 372
vertun, 390
verursachen, 205
vervollständigen, 137
verwahren, 178
verwahren (sich), 245
verwandeln, 68
verwarnen, 388
verweigern, 290
verweisen, 289
verwenden, 375, 381
verwickelt (sein), 232
verwundern, 402
verwünschen, 90
viel, 238
Volk, 255, 277
volkstümlich, 257
voll, 133, 137, 147
vollenden, 136
vollendet, 77
vollends, 79
völlig, 79
vollkommen, 77
Vollmacht, 267
vollständig, 78
vorbei-, 230
vorbereiten, 269, 389
vorbereiten (sich), 269
Vorfall, 118
Vorgang, 117
Vorgehen, 8
vorhalten, 188
Vorkehrungen (treffen), 33
vorkommen, 246
vorkommen (sich), 129
vorschlagen, 28, 344
vorschreiben, 252
vorsichtig, 61 f.
vorstellen, 170
vorstellen (sich), 164, 365
Vorstellung, 163, 170
Vorwurf, 49
vorziehen, 71
Vorzug, 280

Wache, 156
wachen, 156, 384
wachsen, 107
Wächter, 156
wackeln, 370
wagen, 92
wägen, 400
Wahl, 70
wählen, 70
wahr, 284
wahren, 174
währen, 187
während, 401
wahrhaft, 284
wälzen, 296
Wand, 385
wandeln (sich), 68
Wange, 69
wanken, 369
warm (machen), 388
wärmen, 387

warnen, 388
warten, 384
Wärter, 156
wechseln, 66
wecken, 384
Weg, 341, 399
weg sein, 196
Weib, 401
weich, 327
weigern (sich), 290
Weise, 390 f., 394 f., 399
-weise, 262
weisen, 324
weit, 55
weiter, 252
weiter-, 86
weiterführen, 85
weitergeben, 289
weitersagen, 292
wenden, 375
wenig(e), 129 f.
wenigstens, 191
Werk, 403
werten, 116
Wesen, 240
widmen, 152
wieder, 15
wiederholen, 292
wiederum, 15
wiegen, 400
willig, 270
Winkel, 87
wirken, 13
wirklich, 284
Wirkung, 266
Wissen, 185
wissen, 183
wissen (mögen), 402
wohnen, 200
wollen, 270, 290, 385 f.
wollte, 401
Wucht, 264
wunderlich, 340
wundern (sich), 402
Wunsch, 23
wünschte, 401
würdigen, 30

Zahl, 245
zahlen, 254
zanken, 132
zart, 328
zärtlich, 328
Zauber, 69
zaubern, 69
Zeichen, 324
zeigen, 324
Zeitpunkt, 92
zerbrechen, 53
zerfallen, 125
zerreißen, 53, 278
zerren, 278
zerstören, 96
ziehen, 238, 277
ziemlich, 282
Zivilisation, 107
Zorn, 19
zubereiten, 269
zubringen, 333
zudecken, 89
zu Ende, 135
zuerst, 138
Zufall, 2
zugeben, 80
zugestehen, 81
zuhören, 200
zuletzt, 189
zumachen, 201
zumindest, 191
zunächst, 139
zunehmen, 168
zunichte machen, 97
zupfen, 278
zurecht machen, 33

zurückhalten, 339
zurücklassen, 193
zusammen- (*join*), 173
Zusammenhang, 291
zusammenlegen, 173
zusammenrechnen, 10
zusammenstoßen, 342
zusammenstreichen, 323
zusammentreffen, 221
zusehen, 301
Zustand, 336
zusteigen, 172
Zutrauen, 373
zutrauen, 373
zutraulich, 373
Zuversicht, 373
zuweisen, 29
zweifeln, 105
zweit, 252
zwingen, 211
Zwischenfall, 118